lobal Knowledge Network Certification Press

1999 MCSD CERTIFICATION REQUIREMENTS

CORE EXAMS (3 REQUIRED)

SOLUTION ARCHITECTURE (REQUIRED):

Exam 70-100: Analyzing Requirements and Defining Solution Architectures

DESKTOP APPLICATIONS DEVELOPMENT (1 REQUIRED):

Exam 70-016*: Designing and Implementing Desktop Applications with Microsoft® Visual C++® 6.0

Exam 70-176*: Designing and Implementing Desktop Applications with Microsoft® Visual Basic® 6.0

(Designing and Implementing Desktop Applications with Microsoft Visual FoxPro available in 1999.)

(Designing and Implementing Desktop Applications with Microsoft Visual J++ available in 1999.)

DISTRIBUTED APPLICATIONS DEVELOPMENT (1 REQUIRED):

Exam 70-015*: Designing and Implementing Distributed Applications with Microsoft® Visual C++® 6.0

Exam 70-175*: Designing and Implementing Distributed Applications with Microsoft® Visual Basic® 6.0

(Designing and Implementing Distributed Applications with Microsoft Visual FoxPro available in 1999.)

(Designing and Implementing Distributed Applications with Microsoft Visual J++ available in 1999.)

ELECTIVE EXAMS (1 REQUIRED):

Exam 70-015*: Designing and Implementing Distributed Applications with Microsoft® Visual C++® 6.0

Exam 70-016*: Designing and Implementing Desktop Applications with Microsoft® Visual C++® 6.0

Exam 70-029: Designing and Implementing Databases with Microsoft® SQL Server™ 7.0

Exam 70-024: Developing Applications with C++ Using the Microsoft® Foundation Class Library

Exam 70-025: Implementing OLE in Microsoft® Foundation Class Applications

Exam 70-055: Designing and Implementing Web Sites with Microsoft® FrontPage® 98

Exam 70-057: Designing and Implementing Commerce Solutions with Microsoft® Site Server 3.0, Commerce Edition

Exam 70-175*: Designing and Implementing Distributed Applications

Exam 70-176*: Designing and Implementing Desktop Applications

Exam 70-069: Application Development with Microsoft® Access for Developer's Toolkit

Exam 70-091: Designing and Implementing Solutions with Microsoft Visual Basic® for Applications

Exam 70-152: Designing and Implementing Web Solutions with Microsoft® Visual InterDev™ 6.0

★ Core exams that can also be used as elective exams can only be counted once toward a certification.

For complete information on MCSD Certification, visit **www.microsoft.com** and click on Training and Certification.

MCSD Visual Basic 6
Desktop Applications
Study Guide

(Exam 70-176)

Syngress Media, Inc.

Osborne/McGraw-Hill

Berkeley   New York   St. Louis   San Francisco   Auckland   Bogotá   Hamburg   London   Madrid   Mexico City
Milan   Montreal   New Delhi   Panama City   Paris   São Paulo   Singapore   Sydney   Tokyo   Toronto

Osborne/McGraw-Hill
2600 Tenth Street
Berkeley, California 94710
U.S.A.

For information on translations or book distributors outside the U.S.A., or to arrange bulk purchase discounts for sales promotions, premiums, or fund-raisers, please contact Osborne/**McGraw-Hill** at the above address.

MCSD Visual Basic 6 Desktop Applications Study Guide (Exam 70-176)

234567890 DOC DOC 90198765432109

ISBN 0-07-211930-6

Publisher	**Copy Editors**	**Illustrators**
Brandon A. Nordin	Kathleen Faughnan	Brian Wells
	Laura Poole	Beth Young
Editor-in-Chief		
Scott Rogers	**Proofreader**	**Series Design**
	Linda Medoff	Roberta Steele
Acquisitions Editor		
Gareth Hancock	**Indexer**	**Cover Design**
	Valerie Robbins	Regan Honda
Project editor		
Betsy Manini	**Computer Designers**	**Editorial Management**
	Mickey Galicia	Syngress Media, Inc.
Editorial Assistant	Ann Sellers	
Debbie Escobedo		
Technical Editor		
Michael Knowles		
Julie U. Davis		

FOREWORD

From Global Knowledge Network

At Global Knowledge Network we strive to support the multiplicity of learning styles required by our students to achieve success as technical professionals. In this series of books, it is our intention to offer the reader a valuable tool for successful completion of the MCSD Certification Exam.

As the world's largest IT training company, Global Knowledge Network is uniquely positioned to offer these books. The expertise gained each year from providing instructor-led training to hundreds of thousands of students worldwide has been captured in book form to enhance your learning experience. We hope that the quality of these books demonstrates our commitment to your lifelong learning success. Whether you choose to learn through the written word, computer-based training, Web delivery, or instructor-led training, Global Knowledge Network is committed to providing you the very best in each of those categories. For those of you who know Global Knowledge Network, or those of you who have just found us for the first time, our goal is to be your lifelong competency partner.

Thank you for the opportunity to serve you. We look forward to serving your needs again in the future.

Warmest regards,

Duncan Anderson
President and Chief Operating Officer, Global Knowledge Network

January 12, 1998

Dear Osborne/McGraw-Hill Customer:

Microsoft is pleased to inform you that Osborne/McGraw-Hill is a participant in the Microsoft® Independent Courseware Vendor (ICV) program. Microsoft ICVs design, develop, and market self-paced courseware, books, and other products that support Microsoft software and the Microsoft Certified Professional (MCP) program.

To be accepted into the Microsoft ICV program, an ICV must meet set criteria. In addition, Microsoft reviews and approves each ICV training product before permission is granted to use the Microsoft Certified Professional Approved Study Guide logo on that product. This logo assures the consumer that the product has passed the following Microsoft standards:

- The course contains accurate product information.
- The course includes labs and activities during which the student can apply knowledge and skills learned from the course.
- The course teaches skills that help prepare the student to take corresponding MCP exams.

Microsoft ICVs continually develop and release new MCP Approved Study Guides. To prepare for a particular Microsoft certification exam, a student may choose one or more single, self-paced training courses or a series of training courses.

You will be pleased with the quality and effectiveness of the MCP Approved Study Guides available from Osborne/McGraw-Hill.

Sincerely,

Becky Kirsininkas

Becky Kirsininkas
ICV Program Manager
Microsoft Training & Certification

words, go back to the previous section and follow the steps to prepare for an exam composed of knowledge-based questions.

The second step is to familiarize yourself with the format of the questions you are likely to see on the exam. You can do this by answering the questions in this study guide, by using Microsoft assessment tests, or by using practice tests. The day of your test is not the time to be surprised by the convoluted construction of Microsoft exam questions.

For example, one of Microsoft's favorite formats of late takes the following form:

Scenario: You have an application with . . .

Primary Objective: You want to . . .

Secondary Objective: You also want to . . .

Proposed Solution: Do this . . .

What does the proposed solution accomplish?

A. Satisfies the primary and the secondary objective

B. Satisfies the primary but not the secondary objective

C. Satisfies the secondary but not the primary objective

D. Satisfies neither the primary nor the secondary objective

This kind of question, with some variation, is seen on many Microsoft certification examinations.

At best, these performance-based scenario questions really do test certification candidates at a higher cognitive level than knowledge-based questions. At worst, these questions can test your reading comprehension and test-taking ability rather than your ability to use Microsoft products. Be sure to get in the habit of reading the question carefully to determine what is being asked.

The third step in preparing for Microsoft scenario questions is to adopt the following attitude: Multiple-choice questions aren't really performance based. It is all a cruel lie. These scenario questions are just knowledge-based questions with a little story wrapped around them.

To answer a scenario question, you have to sift through the story to the underlying facts of the situation and apply your knowledge to determine the correct answer. This may sound silly at first, but the process we go through in solving real-life problems is quite similar. The key concept is that every scenario question (and every real-life problem) has a fact at its center, and if we can identify that fact, we can answer the question.

Simulations

Simulation questions really do measure your ability to perform job tasks. You *must* be able to perform the specified tasks. There are two ways to prepare for simulation questions:

■ Get experience with the actual software. If you have the resources, this is a great way to prepare for simulation questions.

■ Use official Microsoft practice tests. Practice tests are available that provide practice with the same simulation engine used on Microsoft certification exams. This approach has the added advantage of grading your efforts.

Signing Up

Signing up to take a Microsoft certification examination is easy. Sylvan operators in each country can schedule tests at any testing center. There are, however, a few things you should know:

■ If you call Sylvan during a busy time period, get a cup of coffee first, because you may be in for a long wait. Sylvan does an excellent job, but everyone in the world seems to want to sign up for a test on Monday morning.

■ You will need your Social Security number or some other unique identifier to sign up for a Sylvan test, so have it at hand.

■ Pay for your test by credit card if at all possible. This makes things easier, and you can even schedule tests for the same day you call, if space is available at your local testing center.

The Global Knowledge Network Advantage

Global Knowledge Network has a global delivery system for its products and services. The company has 28 subsidiaries, and offers its programs through a total of 60+ locations. No other vendor can provide consistent services across a geographic area this large. Global Knowledge Network is the largest independent information technology education provider, offering programs on a variety of platforms. This enables our multi-platform and multi-national customers to obtain all of their programs from a single vendor. The company has developed the unique CompetusTM Framework software tool and methodology which can quickly reconfigure courseware to the proficiency level of a student on an interactive basis. Combined with self-paced and on-line programs, this technology can reduce the time required for training by prescribing content in only the deficient skills areas. The company has fully automated every aspect of the education process, from registration and follow-up, to "just-in-time" production of courseware. Global Knowledge Network, through its Enterprise Services Consultancy, can customize programs and products to suit the needs of an individual customer.

Global Knowledge Network Classroom Education Programs

The backbone of our delivery options is classroom-based education. Our modern, well-equipped facilities staffed with the finest instructors offer programs in a wide variety of information technology topics, many of which lead to professional certifications.

Custom Learning Solutions

This delivery option has been created for companies and governments that value customized learning solutions. For them, our consultancy-based approach of developing targeted education solutions is most effective at helping them meet specific objectives.

Self-Paced and Multimedia Products

This delivery option offers self-paced program titles in interactive CD-ROM, videotape and audio tape programs. In addition, we offer custom development of interactive multimedia courseware to customers and partners. Call us at 1 (888) 427-4228.

Electronic Delivery of Training

Our network-based training service delivers efficient competency-based, interactive training via the World Wide Web and organizational intranets. This leading-edge delivery option provides a custom learning path and "just-in-time" training for maximum convenience to students.

ARG

American Research Group (ARG), a wholly-owned subsidiary of Global Knowledge Network, one of the largest worldwide training partners of Cisco Systems, offers a wide range of internetworking, LAN/WAN, Bay Networks, FORE Systems, IBM, and UNIX courses. ARG offers hands on network training in both instructor-led classes and self-paced PC-based training.

Global Knowledge Network Courses Available

Network Fundamentals
- Understanding Computer Networks
- Telecommunications Fundamentals I
- Telecommunications Fundamentals II
- Understanding Networking Fundamentals
- Implementing Computer Telephony Integration
- Introduction to Voice Over IP
- Introduction to Wide Area Networking
- Cabling Voice and Data Networks
- Introduction to LAN/WAN protocols
- Virtual Private Networks
- ATM Essentials

Network Security & Management
- Troubleshooting TCP/IP Networks
- Network Management
- Network Troubleshooting
- IP Address Management
- Network Security Administration
- Web Security
- Implementing UNIX Security
- Managing Cisco Network Security
- Windows NT 4.0 Security

IT Professional Skills
- Project Management for IT Professionals
- Advanced Project Management for IT Professionals
- Survival Skills for the New IT Manager
- Making IT Teams Work

LAN/WAN Internetworking
- Frame Relay Internetworking
- Implementing T1/T3 Services
- Understanding Digital Subscriber Line (xDSL)
- Internetworking with Routers and Switches
- Advanced Routing and Switching
- Multi-Layer Switching and Wire-Speed Routing
- Internetworking with TCP/IP
- ATM Internetworking
- OSPF Design and Configuration
- Border Gateway Protocol (BGP) Configuration

Authorized Vendor Training
Cisco Systems
- Introduction to Cisco Router Configuration
- Advanced Cisco Router Configuration
- Installation and Maintenance of Cisco Routers
- Cisco Internetwork Troubleshooting
- Cisco Internetwork Design
- Cisco Routers and LAN Switches
- Catalyst 5000 Series Configuration
- Cisco LAN Switch Configuration
- Managing Cisco Switched Internetworks
- Configuring, Monitoring, and Troubleshooting Dial-Up Services
- Cisco AS5200 Installation and Configuration
- Cisco Campus ATM Solutions

Bay Networks
- Bay Networks Accelerated Router Configuration
- Bay Networks Advanced IP Routing
- Bay Networks Hub Connectivity
- Bay Networks Accelar 1xxx Installation and Basic Configuration
- Bay Networks Centillion Switching

FORE Systems
- FORE ATM Enterprise Core Products
- FORE ATM Enterprise Edge Products
- FORE ATM Theory
- FORE LAN Certification

Operating Systems & Programming
Microsoft
- Introduction to Windows NT
- Microsoft Networking Essentials
- Windows NT 4.0 Workstation
- Windows NT 4.0 Server
- Advanced Windows NT 4.0 Server
- Windows NT Networking with TCP/IP
- Introduction to Microsoft Web Tools
- Windows NT Troubleshooting
- Windows Registry Configuration

UNIX
- UNIX Level I
- UNIX Level II
- Essentials of UNIX and NT Integration

Programming
- Introduction to JavaScript
- Java Programming
- PERL Programming
- Advanced PERL with CGI for the Web

Web Site Management & Development
- Building a Web Site
- Web Site Management and Performance
- Web Development Fundamentals

High Speed Networking
- Essentials of Wide Area Networking
- Integrating ISDN
- Fiber Optic Network Design
- Fiber Optic Network Installation
- Migrating to High Performance Ethernet

DIGITAL UNIX
- UNIX Utilities and Commands
- DIGITAL UNIX v4.0 System Administration
- DIGITAL UNIX v4.0 (TCP/IP) Network Management
- AdvFS, LSM, and RAID Configuration and Management
- DIGITAL UNIX TruCluster Software Configuration and Management
- UNIX Shell Programming Featuring Kornshell
- DIGITAL UNIX v4.0 Security Management
- DIGITAL UNIX v4.0 Performance Management
- DIGITAL UNIX v4.0 Intervals Overview

DIGITAL OpenVMS
- OpenVMS Skills for Users
- OpenVMS System and Network Node Management I
- OpenVMS System and Network Node Management II
- OpenVMS System and Network Node Management III
- OpenVMS System and Network Node Operations
- OpenVMS for Programmers
- OpenVMS System Troubleshooting for Systems Managers
- Configuring and Managing Complex VMScluster Systems
- Utilizing OpenVMS Features from C
- OpenVMS Performance Management
- Managing DEC TCP/IP Services for OpenVMS
- Programming in C

Hardware Courses
- AlphaServer 1000/1000A Installation, Configuration and Maintenance
- AlphaServer 2100 Server Maintenance
- AlphaServer 4100, Troubleshooting Techniques and Problem Solving

ABOUT THE CONTRIBUTORS

Syngress Media creates books and software for Information Technology professionals seeking skill enhancement and career advancement. Its products are designed to comply with vendor and industry standard course curricula, and are optimized for certification exam preparation. You can contact Syngress via the Web at http://www.syngress.com.

Michael Cross is an MCSE, MCPS, and MCP + Internet computer programmer and network support specialist. He works as an instructor at private colleges, teaching courses in hardware, software, programming, and networking. He is the owner of KnightWare, a company that provides consulting, programming, network support, Web page design, computer training, and various other services. In his spare time, he has been a freelance writer for several years, in genres of fiction and nonfiction. He currently lives in London, Ontario.

John Fuex is an MCP and an MCSD, and works as a programmer for InfoEdge Technology, Inc. (http://www.nfo.com) in Austin, Texas, where he writes custom litigation support applications and consults on the use of technology in law offices. His development work centers primarily on document management and imaging systems written in Visual Basic and Access. Prior to his position at InfoEdge technology he worked as a database analyst and LAN administrator at Tracor Aerospace, Inc., where he wrote and maintained contract management systems in Microsoft Access. John has also done database consulting and training as an independent consultant. In 1998, he finished the WinArch track to become an MCSD. His formal education was in Computer Science at the University of Texas, and in Computer Information Systems at Austin Community College. His current pet projects are Active Server Pages, Visual C++, and SQL Server. John lives in Webberville, Texas, with his wife Athene and son Julian (resident webmaster and football star for the Elgin Wildcats). When he has some free time, he is an avid basketball fanatic and confirmed number one fan of the Houston Rockets. John can be contacted via e-mail at jfuex@nfo.com.

Mike Martone is an MCSD, MCSE, MCP+Internet, and LCNAD. He is a senior software engineer and consultant for Berish & Associates (http://www.berish.com), a Cleveland-based Microsoft Certified Solutions Provider—Partner Level. In 1995, Mike became one of the first thousand MCSDs, and is certified in VB 3, 4, and 5. Since graduating from Bowling Green State University with degrees in Computer Science and Psychology, he has specialized in developing Visual Basic, Internet, and Office applications for corporations and government institutions. In a previous life, Mike worked as a software developer in the court of Caesar Augustus, where he attempted to fix the Year Zero bug, caused by the inability of early Roman computers to handle positive numbers. Mike lives in Lakewood, Ohio, and can be reached at martone@berish.com.

Wade Sorenson is an MCSD and specializes in Visual Basic application development. Wade currently lives in Savage, Minnesota, and works for Strategic Technologies Incorporated as a software developer and project manager. He has also worked as a developer for Cargill and Andersen Consulting. Wade received his undergraduate degree in Computer Science from the University of North Dakota, and is currently enrolled in the M.B.A. program at the University of Minnesota Carlson School of Management. He enjoys travelling, and has studied in both Norway and the former Soviet Union.

Steve Jones is an MCSD, and is a programmer/analyst for Cincinnati State Technical and Community College. Steve was born in Scottdale, Pennsylvania and moved to Cincinnati in 1993 to work on a Masters of Divinity at the Cincinnati Bible Seminary, having finished a B.S. in Civil Engineering at the University of Pittsburgh. While attending school, Steve did programming work for both institutions. Steve works primarily with MS SQL Server, as well as VB and Interdev applications for SQL Server.

Technical Reviewers

Michael Knowles (MCSE+I, MCSD, MCT) is an instructor with rare breadth and depth in Microsoft Technologies. He has passed 22 Microsoft Certified Exams. His work history includes supporting and administering Windows NT, Windows 95, UNIX, and Macintosh in a variety of networking environments. Michael has programming experience in Visual Basic, VBA,C/C++, Pascal, Delphi, HTML, Java, and PERL.

Julie U. Davis (MCP) has been working as a developer of client/server systems for over three years. Julie does most of her work with Visual Basic front ends running on a Windows NT or Windows 95 platform, with SQL Server or Access backends. She has a B.S. degree in Data Processing Management. She is currently working as a computer consultant creating a VB/SQL Server data-mining tool. She also does technical reviews and/or small projects for small businesses.

From the Classroom Contributor

Michael Lane Thomas (MCSE+I, MCSD, MCT, MCSS, A+) is a consultant, trainer, developer, and all-around technology slave who has spent eight years in the fields of computers and training. Michael has written for many computer trade publishers and magazines, including Microsoft Certification Professional Magazine. Michael has also served as guest speaker at assorted users groups, and at the 1998 MCP TechMentor Conference. Having earned his MCSE+I by passing the IEAK exam in beta, Michael has the distinction of being tied as the first MCSE+I recipient in the world.

Additionally, Michael is one of the top 20 Microsoft certified computer professionals in the world, having passed approximately 25 Microsoft certification exams, holding seven Microsoft certification titles, and being certified to teach 28 Microsoft Official Curriculum courses. Michael graduated from the University of Kansas with two bachelor's degrees in mathematics. He is currently working on an M.S. in Engineering Management at the University of Kansas. Occasionally known by his online name of Shiar, Michael can be reached at mlthomas@winning-edge.com, but only if his beautiful wife of three years, Jennifer, gives permission.

ACKNOWLEDGMENTS

e would like to thank the following people:

- Richard Kristof of Global Knowledge Network for championing the series and providing us access to some great people and information. And to Patrick Von Schlag, Robin Yunker, David Mantica, Stacey Cannon, and Kevin Murray for all their cooperation.

- All the incredibly hard-working folks at Osborne/McGraw-Hill: Brandon Nordin, Scott Rogers, and Gareth Hancock for their help in launching a great series and being solid team players. In addition, Betsy Manini, Steve Emry, Anne Ellingsen, and Bernadette Jurich for their help in fine-tuning the book.

- Becky Kirsininkas and Karen Cronin at Microsoft, Corp. for being patient and diligent in answering all our questions.

CONTENTS

market needs. In June 1998, Microsoft revamped the MCSD program, providing new requirements and tests required to achieve this status. However, they did not discontinue the existing path, which leaves developers with the challenge of determining which to pursue.

Original and New MCSD Tracks Compared

The primary difference between the two tracks concerns the emphasis on architecture. The new track reduces the number of generalized architecture tests, but requires at least one test that covers distributed application development. A test-by-test comparison of the exams required is presented in the table below:

Test	Original Track Requirements	New Track Requirements
1	Core: Microsoft Windows Architecture 1 (70-160).	Core: Analyzing Requirements and Defining Solutions Architectures (70-100).
2	Core: Microsoft Windows Architecture 2 (70-161).	Core: Desktop Application Development (in C++ 6, VB 6, FoxPro, or J++).
3	Elective: One elective from the table below.	Core: Distributed Application Development (in C++ 6, VB 6, FoxPro, or J++).
4	Elective: One elective from the following table	Elective: One elective from the following table

*Tests 3 and 4 must cover different Microsoft products. For example, you cannot use Programming with Microsoft Visual Basic 4.0 for Test 3 and Developing Applications with Microsoft Visual Basic 5.0 for Test 4.

†Although the test choices for Test 2 and Test 3 are available as electives, the same test cannot be used to fill both a core and an elective test requirement.

Note that the Microsoft Windows Architecture exams were introduced to replace the original Windows Operating System and Services Architecture exams used for MCSD certification. Microsoft has already retired these, so they are excluded from the preceding list.

Tests Available for MCSD Certification

As of this writing, there are 27 exams that can be used to achieve the MCSD certification (although some of these will be retired soon). These tests are listed below, sorted by the subjects they cover:

Subject	Test Number	Full Test Name	Original	New
Architecture	70-160*	Microsoft Windows Architecture I	C	
Architecture	70-161*	Microsoft Windows Architecture II	C	
Architecture	70-100	Analyzing Requirements and Defining Solution Architectures		C
Visual Basic	70-065*	Programming with Microsoft Visual Basic 4.0	E	E
Visual Basic	70-165	Developing Applications with Microsoft Visual Basic 5.0	E	E
Visual Basic	70-176	Designing and Implementing Desktop Applications with Microsoft Visual Basic 6.0	E	C, E
Visual Basic	70-175	Designing and Implementing Distributed Applications with Microsoft Visual Basic 6.0	E	C, E
FoxPro	70-054*	Programming in Microsoft Visual FoxPro 3.0 for Windows	E	
FoxPro	(none)	Designing and Implementing Desktop Applications with Microsoft Visual FoxPro	E	C
FoxPro	(none)	Designing and Implementing Distributed Applications with Microsoft Visual FoxPro	E	C
C++	70-024	Developing Applications with C++ Using the Microsoft Foundation Class Library	E	E
C++	70-025	Implementing OLE in Microsoft Foundation Class Applications	E	E
C++	70-016	Designing and Implementing Desktop Applications with Microsoft Visual C++ 6.0	E	C, E
C++	70-015	Designing and Implementing Distributed Applications with Microsoft Visual C++ 6.0	E	C, E
J++	(none)	Designing and Implementing Desktop Applications with Microsoft Visual J++	E	C

Subject	Test Number	Full Test Name	Original	New
J++	(none)	Designing and Implementing Distributed Applications with Microsoft Visual J++	E	C
Access	70-051*	Microsoft Access 2.0 for Windows-Application Development	E	
Access	70-069	Microsoft Access for Windows 95 and the Microsoft Access Developer's Toolkit	E	E
Access	(none)	Designing and Implementing Database Design on Microsoft Access	E	E
Office	70-052*	Developing Applications with Microsoft Excel 5.0 Using Visual Basic for Applications	E	
Office	70-091	Designing and Implementing Solutions with Microsoft Office 2000 and Microsoft Visual Basic for Applications	E	E
SQL Server	70-021*	Microsoft SQL Server 4.2 Database Implementation	E	E
SQL Server	70-027	Implementing a Database Design on Microsoft SQL Server 6.5	E	E
SQL Server	70-029	Designing and Implementing Databases with Microsoft SQL Server 7.0	E	E
Internet	70-055	Designing and Implementing Web Sites with Microsoft FrontPage 98	E	E
Internet	70-152	Designing and Implementing Web Solutions with Microsoft Visual InterDev 6.0	E	E
Internet	70-057	Designing and Implementing Commerce Solutions with Microsoft Site Server 3.0, Commerce Edition	E	E

An "E" means that a test can be used as an elective, while a "C" means that a test can be used as a core requirement. "Original" refers to the Original MCSD track, while "New" refers to the New MCSD track.

Exams with no number are not scheduled to be available until 1999.

Test numbers with an asterisk are scheduled to be retired by Microsoft. (Note that after Microsoft retires an exam, it usually remains valid for certification status, but only for a limited time.)

Note that this test list is adapted from the content available at http://www.microsoft.com/mcp/certstep/mcsd.htm. This content frequently changes, so it would be wise to check this site before finalizing your study plans.

Choosing a Track

So which track should you choose? Good question! Although Microsoft is obviously providing more support for the New track, there are legitimate reasons for considering both options.

Advantages of the Original Track

- *You may already be partway there.* If you already have, or are close to obtaining, the Windows Architecture 1 or 2, you should pursue the Original track. These tests are of no value in the New track. Similarly, if you have already passed an exam such as Access 2 or FoxPro 3, that is a valid elective for the Original track but not for the New track (though of course, these exams will be retired soon).

- *You cover more architecture.* The system architecture exams are excellent overviews of client/server development. The Original track consists of two architecture tests, but the New track only has one.

- *You don't have to use the most recent versions of the tools.* If your current job responsibilities make it unlikely that you will be working with the newest versions of C++, Visual Basic, FoxPro, or J++, you should pursue the Original track. The New track requires that you pass two tests on one of these four environments, and it seems very unlikely that these tests will be adapted to support prior versions. In other words, if you are an expert in VB version 5 but won't have an opportunity to significantly use VB version 6 for at least a year, it will be very difficult for you to use the New track.

- *You can start now.* As of this writing, some of the tests used for the New track (Desktop and Distribution for FoxPro and J++, for example) are scheduled to be available in 1999, and haven't even been released in beta yet.

Advantages of the New Track

■ *Your credentials will last longer.* The Architecture 1 and 2 exams required for the original track will be retired more quickly than any of the New track core exams. However, this may not be as much of a disadvantage as it may originally seem. After all, all of the exams you take will be retired within a few years. The certification process is designed not just to determine which developers have achieved a base level of competency, but to identify which developers are doing the best job of keeping their skills current.

■ *You can become more of a specialist in your chosen tool.* Arguably, because the New track offers more exams for each product, the Original track encourages product breadth while the New track encourages depth. Therefore, if you're selling yourself as a specialist, the New track may be an advantage. (Specialists often can have higher salaries, though sometimes generalists have more continuous employment.)

■ *You'll be more closely aligned with Microsoft's strategies.* If you are just beginning to consider certification and haven't already invested time pursuing the Original track, you should probably pursue the New track. The changes made by Microsoft are a product of their research into the needs of the marketplace, and it couldn't hurt for you to leverage their investment. In addition, if Microsoft revises the MCSD requirements again, the transition would probably be easiest for those who used the New track.

■ *You'll be "New and Improved!"* Works for laundry detergent . . .

Of course, the best choice may be not to choose at all, at least not yet. As the tables in this chapter have shown, many of the exams are equally applicable to both tracks. For example, the Designing and Implementing Desktop Applications with Microsoft Visual Basic 6.0 exam counts not only as a core requirement for the New track, but also as an elective for either track. You do not need to declare to Microsoft which track you are pursuing, so you can delay that decision until after you have passed your first test.

And with this book at your side, you're well on your way to doing just that.

The CD-ROM Resource

This book comes with a CD-ROM that contains test preparation software and provides you with another method for studying for the exam. You will find more information on the testing software in Appendix C.

How to Take a Microsoft Certification Examination

Good News and Bad News

If you are new to Microsoft certification, we have some good news and some bad news. The good news, of course, is that Microsoft certification is one of the most valuable credentials you can earn. It sets you apart from the crowd and marks you as a valuable asset to your employer. You will gain the respect of your peers, and Microsoft certification can have a wonderful effect on your income.

The bad news is that Microsoft certification tests are not easy. You may think you will read through some study material, memorize a few facts, and pass the Microsoft examinations. After all, these certification exams are just computer-based, multiple-choice tests, so they must be easy. If you believe this, you are wrong. Unlike many "multiple guess" tests you have been exposed to in school, the questions on Microsoft certification examinations go beyond simple factual knowledge.

The purpose of this introduction is to teach you how to take a Microsoft certification examination. To be successful, you need to know something about the purpose and structure of these tests. We will also look at the latest innovations in Microsoft testing. Using simulations and adaptive testing, Microsoft is enhancing both the validity and security of the certification process. These factors have some important effects on how you should prepare for an exam, as well as your approach to each question during the test.

We will begin by looking at the purpose, focus, and structure of Microsoft certification tests, and examine the effect these factors have on the kinds of questions you will face on your certification exams. We will define the structure of examination questions, and investigate some common formats. Next, we will present a strategy for answering these questions.

Finally, we will give some specific guidelines on what you should do on the day of your test.

Why Vendor Certification?

The Microsoft Certified Professional program, like the certification programs from Lotus, Novell, Oracle, and other software vendors, is maintained for the ultimate purpose of increasing the corporation's profits. A successful vendor certification program accomplishes this goal by helping to create a pool of experts in a company's software, and by "branding" these experts so that companies using the software can identify them.

We know that vendor certification has become increasingly popular in the last few years because it helps employers find qualified workers, and because it helps software vendors like Microsoft sell their products. But why should you be interested in vendor certification rather than a more traditional approach like a college or professional degree in computer science? A college education is a broadening and enriching experience, but a degree in computer science does not prepare students for most jobs in the IT industry.

A common truism in our business states, "If you are out of the IT industry for three years and want to return, you have to start over." The problem, of course, is *timeliness;* if a first-year student learns about a specific computer program, it probably will no longer be in wide use when he or she graduates. Although some colleges are trying to integrate Microsoft certification into their curriculum, the problem is not really a flaw in higher education, but a characteristic of the IT industry. Computer software is changing so rapidly that a four-year college just can't keep up.

A marked characteristic of the Microsoft certification program is an emphasis on performing specific job tasks rather than merely gathering knowledge. It may come as a shock, but most potential employers do not care how much you know about the theory of operating systems, testing, or software design. As one IT manager put it, "I don't really care what my employees know about the theory of our network. We don't need someone to sit at a desk and think about it. We need people who can actually do something to make it work better."

You should not think that this attitude is some kind of anti-intellectual revolt against book learning. Knowledge is a necessary prerequisite, but it is not enough. More than one company has hired a computer science graduate as a network administrator only to learn that the new employee has no idea how to add users, assign permissions, or perform the other everyday tasks necessary to maintain a network. This brings us to the second major characteristic of Microsoft certification that affects the questions you must be prepared to answer. In addition to timeliness, Microsoft certification is also job task–oriented.

The timeliness of Microsoft's certification program is obvious, and is inherent in the fact that you will be tested on current versions of software in wide use today. The job task orientation of Microsoft certification is almost as obvious, but testing real-world job skills using a computer-based test is not easy.

Computerized Testing

Considering the popularity of Microsoft certification, and the fact that certification candidates are spread around the world, the only practical way to administer tests for the certification program is through Sylvan Prometric testing centers. Sylvan Prometric provides proctored testing services for Microsoft, Oracle, Novell, Lotus, and the A+ computer technician certification. Although the IT industry accounts for much of Sylvan's revenue, the company provides services for a number of other businesses and organizations, such as FAA preflight pilot tests. In fact, most companies that need secure test delivery over a wide geographic area use the services of Sylvan Prometric. In addition to delivery, Sylvan Prometric also scores the tests and provides statistical feedback on the performance of each test question to the companies and organizations that use their services.

Typically, several hundred questions are developed for a new Microsoft certification examination. The questions are first reviewed by a number of subject matter experts for technical accuracy, and then are presented in a beta test. The beta test may last for several hours, due to the large number of questions. After a few weeks, Microsoft certification uses the statistical feedback from Sylvan to check the performance of the beta questions.

Questions are discarded if most test takers get them right (too easy) or wrong (too difficult), and a number of other statistical measures are taken of each question. Although the scope of our discussion precludes a rigorous treatment of question analysis, you should be aware that Microsoft and other vendors spend a great deal of time and effort making sure their examination questions are valid. In addition to the obvious desire for quality, the fairness of a vendor's certification program must be legally defensible.

The questions that survive statistical analysis form the pool of questions for the final certification examination.

Test Structure

The kind of test we are most familiar with is known as a *form* test. For Microsoft certification, a form usually consists of 50–70 questions and takes 60–90 minutes to complete. If there are 240 questions in the final pool for an examination, then four forms can be created. Thus, candidates who retake the test probably will not see the same questions.

Other variations are possible. From the same pool of 240 questions, *five* forms can be created, each containing 40 unique questions (200 questions) and 20 questions selected at random from the remaining 40.

The questions in a Microsoft form test are equally weighted. This means they all count the same when the test is scored. An interesting and useful characteristic of a form test is that you can mark a question you have doubts about as you take the test. Assuming you have time left when you finish all the questions, you can return and spend more time on the questions you have marked as doubtful.

Microsoft may soon implement *adaptive* testing. To use this interactive technique, a form test is first created and administered to several thousand certification candidates. The statistics generated are used to assign a weight, or difficulty level, for each question. For example, the questions in a form might be divided into levels one through five, with level-one questions being the easiest and level-five questions the hardest.

When an adaptive test begins, the candidate is first given a level-three question. If it is answered correctly, a question from the next higher level is presented, and an incorrect response results in a question from the next lower level. When 15–20 questions have been answered in this manner, the scoring algorithm is able to predict, with a high degree of statistical certainty, whether the candidate would pass or fail if all the questions in the form were answered. When the required degree of certainty is attained, the test ends and the candidate receives a pass/fail grade.

Adaptive testing has some definite advantages for everyone involved in the certification process. Adaptive tests allow Sylvan Prometric to deliver more tests with the same resources, as certification candidates often are in and out in 30 minutes or less. For Microsoft, adaptive testing means that fewer test questions are exposed to each candidate, and this can enhance the security, and therefore the validity, of certification tests.

One possible problem you may have with adaptive testing is that you are not allowed to mark and revisit questions. Since the adaptive algorithm is interactive, and all questions but the first are selected on the basis of your response to the previous question, it is not possible to skip a particular question or change an answer.

Question Types

Computerized test questions can be presented in a number of ways. Some of the possible formats are used on Microsoft certification examinations, and some are not.

True/False

We are all familiar with true/false questions, but because of the inherent 50 percent chance of guessing the correct answer, you will not see questions of this type on Microsoft certification exams.

Multiple Choice

The majority of Microsoft certification questions are in the multiple-choice format, with either a single correct answer or multiple correct answers. One interesting variation on multiple-choice questions with multiple correct answers is whether or not the candidate is told how many answers are correct.

Example:

Which two of the following controls can be used on a MDI form? (Choose two.)

or

Which of the following controls can be used on a MDI form? (Choose all that apply.)

You may see both variations on Microsoft certification examinations, but the trend seems to be toward the first type, where candidates are told explicitly how many answers are correct. Questions of the "choose all that apply" variety are more difficult, and can be merely confusing.

Graphical Questions

One or more graphical elements are sometimes used as exhibits to help present or clarify an exam question. These elements may take the form of a database diagram, flowcharts, or screen shots from the software on which you are being tested. It is often easier to present the concepts required for a complex performance-based scenario with a graphic than with words.

Test questions known as *hotspots* actually incorporate graphics as part of the answer. These questions ask the certification candidate to click on a location or graphical element to answer the question. As an example, you might be shown the diagram of a three-tiered application and asked to click on a tier described by the question. The answer is correct if the candidate clicks within the hotspot that defines the correct location.

Free-Response Questions

Another kind of question you sometimes see on Microsoft certification examinations requires a *free-response* or type-in answer. An example of this type of question might present a complex code sample including loops and error trapping and ask the candidate to calculate and enter the final value of a variable.

Knowledge-Based and Performance-Based Questions

Microsoft certification develops a blueprint for each Microsoft certification examination with input from subject matter experts. This blueprint defines the content areas and objectives for each test, and each test question is created to test a specific objective. The basic information from the examination blueprint can be found on Microsoft's Web site in the Exam Prep Guide for each test.

Psychometricians (psychologists who specialize in designing and analyzing tests) categorize test questions as knowledge based or performance based. As the names imply, knowledge based questions are designed to test knowledge, while performance-based questions are designed to test performance.

Some objectives demand a knowledge-based question. For example, objectives that use verbs like *list* and *identify* tend to test only what you know, not what you can do.

Example:

Objective: Identify the ADO Cursor Types that support read and write operations.

Which two of the following ADO Cursor Types support write access? (Choose two.)

A. adOpenStatic

B. adOpenDynamic

C. adOpenForwardOnly

D. adOpenKeyset

Correct answers: B and D

Other objectives use action verbs like *connect, configure,* and *troubleshoot* to define job tasks. These objectives can often be tested with either a knowledge-based question or a performance-based question.

Example:

Objective: Connect to a data source appropriately using ADO Cursor Type properties.

Knowledge-based question:

What is the correct Cursor Type to allow users to view new records created by other users?

A. adOpenStatic

B. adOpenDynamic

C. adOpenForwardOnly

D. adOpenKeyset

Correct answer: B

Performance-based question:

Your company supports several travel agents using a common data store, and each agent needs to be able to see the reservations taken by all the other agents. What is the best application development strategy to allow users to be able to see records modified and created by other users?

A. Use an adOpenKeyset Cursor Type to create the record set, and keep the same Recordset object open continuously.

B. Use an adOpenDynamic Cursor Type to create the record set, and keep the same Recordset object open continuously.

C. Use an adOpenStatic Cursor Type to create the record set, but destroy and create the Recordset object after every data update.

D. Use an adOpenForwardOnly Cursor Type create the record set, but destroy and create the Recordset object after every data update.

Correct answer: B

Even in this simple example, the superiority of the performance-based question is obvious. Whereas the knowledge-based question asks for a single fact, the performance-based question presents a real-life situation and requires that you make a decision based on this scenario. Thus, performance-based questions give more bang (validity) for the test author's buck (individual question).

Testing Job Performance

We have said that Microsoft certification focuses on timeliness and the ability to perform job tasks. We have also introduced the concept of performance-based questions, but even performance-based, multiple-choice questions do not really measure performance. Another strategy is needed to test job skills.

Given unlimited resources, it is not difficult to test job skills. In an ideal world, Microsoft would fly MCP candidates to Redmond, place them in a controlled environment with a team of experts, and ask them to design, author, debug, and revise a Windows application. In a few days at most, the experts could reach a valid decision as to whether each candidate should or should not be granted MCSD status. Needless to say, this is not likely to happen.

Closer to reality, another way to test performance is by using the actual software, and creating a testing program to present tasks and automatically grade a candidate's performance when the tasks are completed. This *cooperative* approach would be practical in some testing situations, but the same test that is presented to MCP candidates in Boston must also be available in Bahrain and Botswana. Many Sylvan Prometric testing locations around the world cannot run 32-bit applications, much less provide the complex networked solutions required by cooperative testing applications.

The most workable solution for measuring performance in today's testing environment is a *simulation* program. When the program is launched during a test, the candidate sees a simulation of the actual software that looks, and behaves, just like the real thing. When the testing software presents a task, the simulation program is launched and the candidate performs the required task. The testing software then grades the candidate's performance on the required task and moves to the next question. In this way, a 16-bit simulation program can mimic the look and feel of 32-bit operating systems, a complicated network, or even the entire Internet.

Microsoft has introduced simulation questions on the certification examination for Internet Information Server version 4. Simulation questions provide many advantages over other testing methodologies, and simulations are expected to become increasingly important in the Microsoft Certification Program. For example, studies have shown that there is a very high correlation between the ability to perform simulated tasks on a computer-based test and the ability to perform the actual job tasks. Thus, simulations enhance the validity of the certification process.

Another truly wonderful benefit of simulations is in the area of test security. It is just not possible to cheat on a simulation question. In fact, you will be told exactly what tasks you are expected to perform on the test.

How can a certification candidate cheat? By learning to perform the tasks? What a concept!

Study Strategies

There are appropriate ways to study for the different types of questions you will see on a Microsoft certification examination.

Knowledge-Based Questions

Knowledge-based questions require that you memorize facts. There are hundreds of facts inherent in every content area of every Microsoft certification examination. There are several keys to memorizing facts:

- *Repetition.* The more times your brain is exposed to a fact, the more likely you are to remember it.

- *Association.* Connecting facts within a logical framework makes them easier to remember.

- *Motor Association.* It is often easier to remember something if you write it down or perform some other physical act, like clicking a practice test answer.

We have said that the emphasis of Microsoft certification is job performance, and that there are very few knowledge-based questions on Microsoft certification exams. Why should you waste a lot of time learning filenames, property values, and other minutiae? Read on.

Performance-Based Questions

Most of the questions you will face on a Microsoft certification exam are performance-based scenario questions. We have discussed the superiority of these questions over simple knowledge-based questions, but you should remember that the job task orientation of Microsoft certification extends the knowledge you need to pass the exams; it does *not* replace this knowledge. Therefore, the first step in preparing for scenario questions is to absorb as many facts relating to the exam content areas as you can. In other

I

Essentials of Microsoft Visual Basic

CERTIFICATION OBJECTIVES

This chapter will familiarize you with the essentials of Microsoft Visual Basic 6.0 (VB). You will be introduced to the VB environment and all the tools available to assist you in developing applications. You will also create two sample applications, one of which you will be guided through, and one which will involve minimal help from the book. You will then be introduced to the debugging and error-handling processes used in VB. Finally, you will compile your sample application so that it creates an EXE file, allowing it to run on other computers.

Understanding Microsoft Visual Basic-Based Development

Visual Basic contains many tools to assist in the development of your applications. These tools allow you to see exactly how your program will look when it is completed. This capability provides the VB user a tremendous advantage over nongraphic programming languages that do not allow you to see how your program will look until you are finished.

First of all, let's take a look at what the VB interface looks like by examining Figure 1-1. Though at first it may look somewhat intimidating, it's really not that complicated. We will examine the tools that comprise the interface, and see how they can help you create applications.

The menu bar provides the user with most of the commands that control the VB environment. This menu bar operates according to Windows-based standards, and the commands can be accessed by using either the mouse or keyboard.

The toolbar is located directly below the menu bar and is a collection of buttons that provide shortcuts for executing commands and for controlling the VB programming environment.

The Project window contains three buttons. The first button allows you to view the code in the project. The second button allows you to view the objects in the project. The third button toggles the folders in the Project window. When the toggle folder button is highlighted, the folders are expanded, showing the contents of each folder.

CERTIFICATION OBJECTIVE 1.02

Creating an Application

Now that you've been introduced to the VB environment, it's time to see how to use the visual environment to create an application. Of course, any project demands some sort of planning and VB is no different. Once you have decided what you wish to develop, you will need to plan how you would like it to appear. When you have passed the planning stage, it's time to start working. For this example, we will create an application that converts values in kilograms to values in pounds. Basically, there are three steps in creating an application. The first step is to create the user interface, which includes placing the objects and setting their properties. The second step is to write the code for the program. The third step, if necessary, is to do the debugging. Let's get started!

Creating the User Interface

When you launch VB, the New Project dialog box, shown in Figure 1-4, appears.

This screen gives you many different options as to what you want to create. For our purposes, choose the Standard EXE icon.

Though not necessary, it is a good idea to save the project as soon as you begin. For our purposes, we will call the program *kilo*. When you click the

FIGURE 1-4

The New Project
Dialog Box

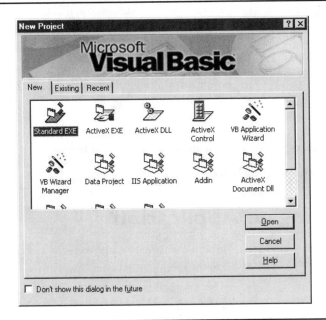

Save icon on the toolbar or access it through the menu bar, you will be prompted with two screens. Figure 1-5 shows the first of the dialog boxes that will ask how you want to save the file.

Notice that the dialog box is titled Save File As and the Save as Type is listed as Form Files (*.frm). The first dialog box is asking how you wish to save the form. Save the form under the name *kilo*. When you save your form you also save its objects and code in a file.

The second dialog box, shown in Figure 1-6, then asks you how you want to save the project. Your project components (listed in the Project window) are saved in a separate file from your form.

Notice that now the title of the dialog box is Save Project As and the type of file is Project Files (*.vbp). Save the project as *Kilo*.

Save File As dialog box

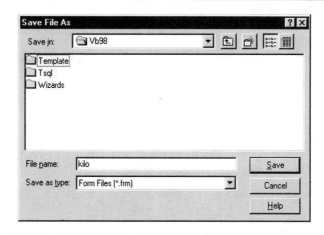

Next, we will give the project a name by highlighting Project1 in the Project window and changing the name property to Kilo (see Figure 1-7).

Save Project As dialog box

FIGURE 1-7

Naming the project

The Project window should now resemble the illustration below, showing the new project and form names.

First, a word about naming your objects. It is a good idea to devise a consistent method of naming your objects. For example, if it's a form, begin the name with the three letters *frm;* if it's a label, begin the name with *lbl,* a text box, begin with the three letters *txt,* if a command button, *cmd,* and so on. The current standard for naming objects is called the Hungarian naming convention. For more information on this convention, see Appendix D. It is a good idea to become familiar with this naming convention because the exam uses this method for naming all its objects. Ultimately, this may save you some confusion, especially when you begin to develop more sophisticated applications.

FIGURE 1-12

Properties of the
Calculate button using the
ampersand character

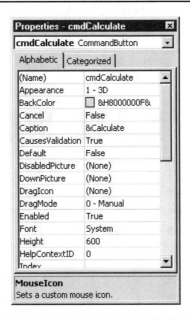

Notice the change in the next illustration, showing the Calculate button
with the "C" now underlined.

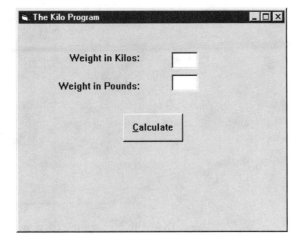

This is called an *access key* and allows the button to be activated by pressing the ALT-C keystroke combination. This can be a helpful tool to utilize while creating applications.

Now create the Exit button and set its properties to those shown in the following table.

Property	Input
(Name):	cmdExit
Caption:	E&xit
Font:	System, Bold, 10
Height:	600
Left:	2280
Top:	2600
Width:	1335

You are now finished creating the user interface and the form should resemble the finished form in the following illustration.

Now that you have some experience in working with an object's properties, here are some more properties you can use to enhance your applications.

QUESTIONS AND ANSWERS

What are the TabStop and TabIndex properties for?	TabStop and TabIndex allow you to change the order in which the TAB key will proceed through the objects on your form. When the object is highlighted, it is known as *having the focus*. When the TabStop is set to True and the TabIndex is set to 0 (zero), that object will have the focus when the application begins. If you change a TabIndex for a particular object, VB will automatically renumber the tab stops of the other objects. There will likely be a question about this on the test.
What if I want to use some code from another form that I want to remain hidden from the user during runtime?	The form has a property called Visible that, when set to False, makes the form invisible to users during runtime (runtime itself will be explained later). This can be useful when you have a form that contains some code that is referenced in another form. When code is referenced in a form, that form is loaded. However, by having the Visible property set to False, the code may be used without the form being seen.
Can the user resize the form during runtime?	Your form has two different properties, called MaxButton and MinButton, that allow you to determine whether you wish for the users to minimize or maximize the form during runtime. By changing the settings of these two properties to False (see Figure 1-13), you can remove the Maximize and Minimize buttons from the form. However, the user will still be able to resize the form.

The finished form without the Minimize and Maximize buttons will then look like this illustration:

FIGURE 1-13

Minimize and Maximize
buttons set to False

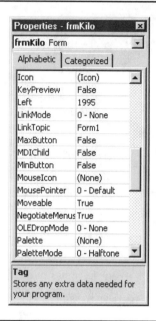

Writing the Code for the Kilo Program

Now that you have created the user interface, the next step in developing your application is to write the code. In this case, the only code that is necessary will be for the two command buttons. Double-click the Calculate button. The Code window should appear (Figure 1-14).

Now it is time to enter the code for the Calculate button (Figure 1-15).

Notice that there is a line in green that begins with an apostrophe. VB ignores anything that follows an apostrophe. These are known as *comments*. Though not necessary, it is a good idea to insert comments into your code. This may assist you down the road in the debugging process and also make it easier for others who may need to work with your code. Everyone writes code a little differently, and comments will help bridge the gap of individual differences.

FIGURE 1-14

The Code window for the
command buttons

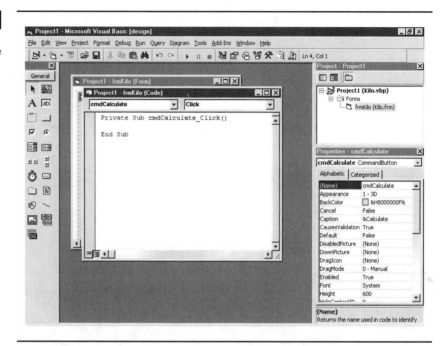

FIGURE 1-15

Entering the code for the
Calculate button

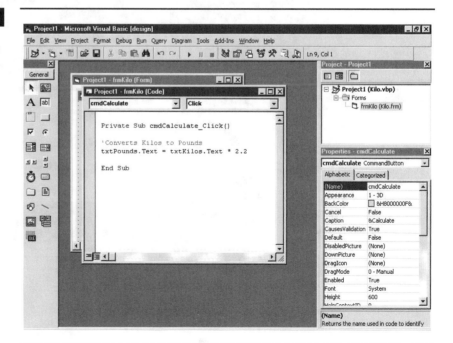

Next, consider the code for the Calculate command button. We've basically told VB to get a value for the txtPounds text box by retrieving the value entered in the txtKilos text box and multiplying this value by 2.2.

For the Exit command button, simply enter **End**. This will allow the user to terminate the program by clicking this button (Figure 1-16).

We have finished the second step in the development process, so it's time to see if the program actually works. Click the Run icon in the toolbar or select Run from the menu bar. Now enter a numerical value of 5 in the txtKilos text box and click the Calculate button. If the program returns a value of 11, then congratulations, it works! You have created

Entering the code for the Exit button

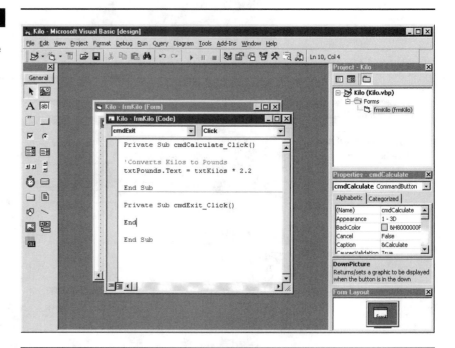

your first VB application. See the following illustration showing the Kilo program in action.

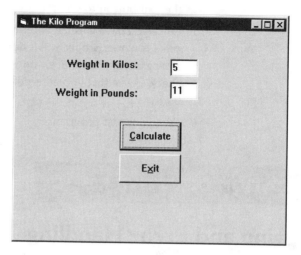

Now that we have created an application together, it's time for you to try one on your own.

Creating a Simple Application

You will now create an application that will display the text you type into a text box. This project will consist of two labels, two text boxes, and two command buttons.

1. First, open a new project and save it.

2. Now, create the form on which these objects will reside.

3. Next, create and place each of the objects on the form. Give one command button the name "Display Text" and give the other one the name "Exit."

4. Finally, write the code for the command buttons. You will need to enter code that will display the text "My first application." This means you will need to enter code that will reference the text box and state what you want the text of the text box to be. For

example, you might use txtTextBox1.Text = txtTextBox2.Text. (TextBox2 will be the box you will enter text into.) Enter code for the Exit button to end the program.

5. Once you have finished entering the code, execute the program to see if it works properly. If it does, congratulations, you have created a program almost entirely on your own. If it doesn't run correctly, check to see that you entered the code correctly for the command button.

6. Save your test program.

CERTIFICATION OBJECTIVE 1.03

Debugging and Error Handling

Suppose your application did not work for some reason. What would you do then? This is where the troubleshooting or debugging process begins. VB contains many tools to help you determine what is causing your program to work improperly. Some of the tools used to aid in the debugging are breaks, watches, the Err object, and the Debug object.

A *break* stops the execution of a program while it's running and places the program in *Break mode*. The statement being executed while Break mode is entered will be displayed with a bullet to the left of that line. Break mode allows you to examine, debug, reset, step through, or continue execution of the application. You may enter Break mode:

■ by encountering a breakpoint during program execution

■ by pressing CTRL-BREAK during program execution

■ by clicking the Break button on the Debugging toolbar (it looks like the "Pause" button on a cassette recorder)

■ by encountering a Stop statement during program execution

■ by pressing the F9 key on a line of code

■ by adding a Break When True watch expression (which will stop execution when the watch is True)

■ by adding a Break When Changed watch expression (which stops the execution of the program when the value of the watch changes).

A *watch* allows you to monitor the values of variables, properties, and expressions at runtime. These watch expressions appear in the Watch window, which lets you observe their values. As mentioned above, you may also use watch expressions to switch the application into Break mode whenever the expression's value changes or equals a specified value. For example, you may use a watch expression to put the application in Break mode when a loop counter reaches a specific value, or you may want the application to enter Break mode whenever a flag in a procedure changes value. *Watch variables* allow you to change the display format of variables in the Watch window or the Quick Watch dialog box using formatting symbols. Watches can only be added during design time or while the program is in Break mode. You may add a watch by clicking on the Debug window and selecting Add Watch; by clicking on the View menu, choosing Watch Window, then right-clicking in the Watch window; or by right-clicking on a line of code and selecting Add Watch. Watches, watch expressions, and watch variables are sure to be found on the certification exam.

VB also utilizes something called the Err object. It contains data that your application needs to know in order to respond properly to errors. The Err object has six properties (Number, Description, Source, HelpFile, HelpContext, and LastDLLError) and two methods associated with it (Clear and Raise). Number returns the error number of common VB errors and Description returns a description for that error number. Source contains information as to where the error occurred. HelpFile contains a fully qualified path to a help file (if no help file is specified, no help will be displayed). HelpContext is a string containing a HelpContext ID associated with the error that occurred. LastDLLError contains the result code of the last external call made to the Windows API or another DLL. Clear is used to clear the contents of the Err object. Raise is used to deliberately cause a runtime error.

The Debug object is only available during the development process, not at runtime. It has two methods, Print and Assert. Debug.Print is used to send output to the Immediate window without breaking the execution of the application. Any references to the Debug object are stripped from the code when an EXE file is created.

Finally, the Debugging toolbar is a great help in isolating problems. It allows you to start the program; enter Break mode; end the program; toggle breakpoints; step into; over or out; view the Locals, Immediate, and Watch windows; use quick watch; and call stack.

We have already discussed Break mode. The break button appears on the toolbar in the form of a button that looks like the "Pause" button on a cassette recorder.

- *Toggle breakpoint* sets or removes a breakpoint at the current line. You can only use breakpoints on lines containing executable code. It will not operate on lines like comments, declaration statements, or blank lines.

- *Step Into* executes the statement at the current execution point. If that statement is a call to a procedure, the next statement displayed is the first statement in the procedure being called.

- *Step Over* executes the procedure as a unit, and then steps to the next statement in the current procedure. This displays the next statement in the procedure regardless of whether the current statement is a call to another procedure. This is available in Break mode only.

- *Step Out* executes the remaining lines of a function in which the current execution point lies. The next statement displayed is the statement following the procedure call. All of the code is executed between the current and the final execution points. Available in Break mode only.

- The *Locals window* automatically displays all of the declared variables in the current procedure and their values. This window is automatically updated whenever there is a change from Run to Break mode or you navigate in the stack display. It also allows you to change the value of a variable.

- The *Immediate window* displays information resulting from debugging statements in your code (such as Debug.Print) or from commands typed directly into the window. It also allows you to call other procedures within the current procedure.

- The *Watch window* displays the current watch expressions. If watch expressions are defined in the project this window will appear automatically. It also allows you to add a watch on any variable or expression, change the value while the code is suspended, or view the properties of objects at runtime.

- The *call stack* button displays the Call Stack dialog box, which lists the procedures called in the application that have started but are not completed. The Call Stack dialog box will display a number beside each program listed with the highest number indicating the currently executing program.

The Call Stack dialog box, shown in the following illustration, is available only in Break mode.

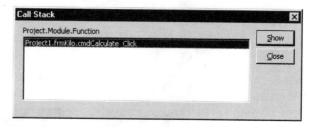

Debugging

There are three types of errors that you may encounter. The first error is a syntax error. This could be a misspelled word or simply an error in the format of the code. An example of a syntax error is illustrated in Figure 1-17.

Notice that the code for the Calculate button contains a reference to txtPound where it should be txtPounds.Text. Now when the program is run, there is no output to the txtPounds text box.

The next error you may encounter is a runtime error. This is an error that occurs during the execution of the program and causes the program to halt. Now if we change the code for the Calculate button to read txtKilo.Text instead of txtKilos.Text and run the program, we will encounter a runtime error. You will notice there is very little difference between the runtime error and the syntax error. Basically, what

FIGURE 1-17

An example of a syntax error

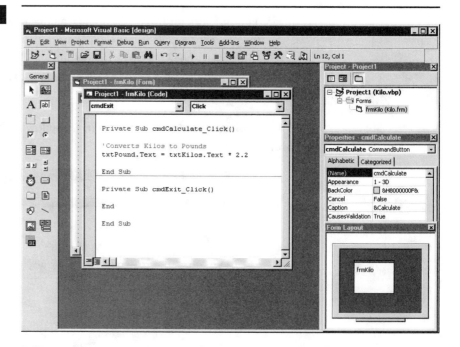

distinguishes the two is that a runtime error is an error in syntax that causes the program to stop unexpectedly, as in the following illustration.

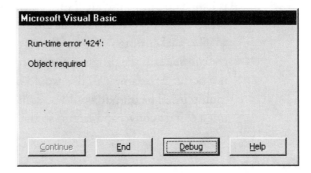

If you click the Debug button, the screen shown in Figure 1-18 will appear.

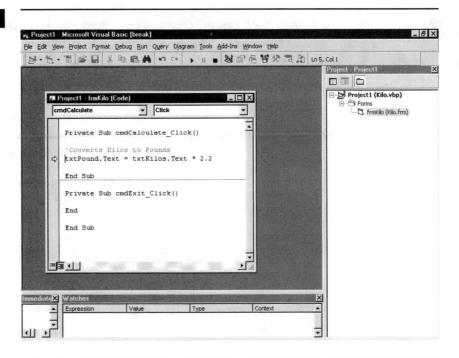

Notice that the offending line is highlighted and there is an arrow next to that line. That arrow is called a *watch*. A watch allows you to examine what is happening in your code. Notice also the Watch window at the bottom of the screen. This gives you some clue as to what is causing the error.

The final error that will be discussed is a logic error. This is where the code is fine and the program runs correctly, but the desired outcome does not occur. An example of this would be if we divided by 2.2 rather than multiplied. The output would be consistent with what was coded, though not a correct conversion factor, so the actual response would be wrong.

Error Handling

Error handling is where you anticipate certain problems with your code and build in safeguards to keep your application from crashing. You may also program your application to return an error code to give you a better idea of what is happening.

QUESTIONS AND ANSWERS

How does a watch statement help in the debugging process?	A watch allows you to view the code as it is executed, and by viewing the Watch window you can get some input on what is creating the error.
How do I add a watch statement?	You can add a watch by performing a right-click at the beginning of the line in which you wish to add the watch. You may also add a watch by clicking the Debug item on the menu bar and selecting Add Watch, which will launch the window seen in Figure 1-19. You then choose the procedure (in this case cmdCalculate_Click), the module (frmKilo), and the Project.
How do I add a breakpoint to my code?	You may add a breakpoint by clicking the gray area to the left of the line you wish to contain a breakpoint and clicking the left mouse button, or by clicking the Toggle Breakpoint button on the Debugging toolbar.

Adding a watch to
your application

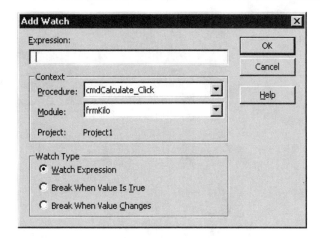

The Kilo program will still operate if you enter a zero or any negative number in the txtKilos text box. However, if you had written a program and needed the user to input a positive number greater than zero, you could write code that would not proceed unless a valid number was entered. If that number was not entered you could have VB return an error that would alert the user to try again. Next enter the code shown in Figure 1-20 for the cmdCalculate button.

If your user tries to enter a zero, the program will ask the user for another number, as shown in Kilo message box illustration below.

In this way, you can head off potential errors or even force the user to input the desired data.

FIGURE 1-20

Adding code for a
message box

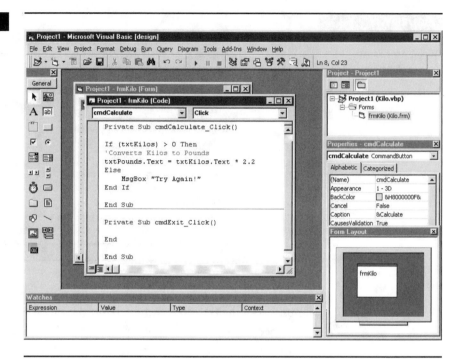

CERTIFICATION OBJECTIVE 1.04

Compiling an EXE File

Once you have finished with your program and wish to produce it in a form
usable on any computer, you need to compile it into an EXE file. To do so,
click File on the menu bar and select Make kilo.exe (see Figure 1-21).

FIGURE 1-21

Making an EXE file

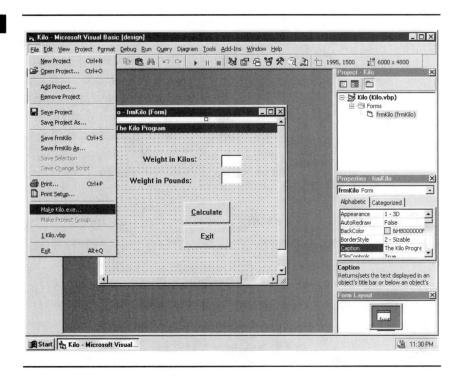

You will then be prompted to give your project a name (shown in the following illustration). For our purposes, let's just name your EXE file Kilo.

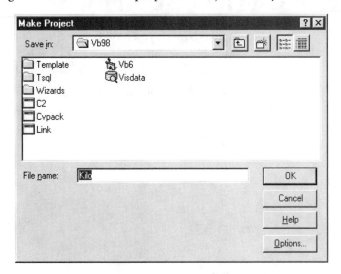

You now have a file that will run on any computer. However, in order to use it, you first must ensure that the msvbm60.dll file is in your Windows system directory. This file contains all the necessary information that allows your project to be contained in a much smaller EXE file. The msvbm60.dll, at 1.376MB, is rather large, but this file allows the EXE files to be so small. If you have already installed VB on your computer, this file should already exist. It is only an issue if you wish to distribute the application to others. Previous versions of VB have their own versions, of this DLL. For example, VB 5.0 applications need the msvbm50.dll file in the Windows system directory.

EXERCISE 1-2

Creating a Simple Application

You will now create an EXE file for the application that you created in the first exercise.

1. First, open the project.

2. Click on the File menu and select Make *projectname.exe*.

3. Give the file a name.

4. You now have created an EXE file that will run on any computer that has the necessary VB DLL files.

CERTIFICATION SUMMARY

In this chapter, you have become familiar with the VB programming environment and even learned to create a simple program. You have learned some of the basics in creating objects and manipulating the properties of these objects. You have also briefly worked with some of the inherent debugging and error handling procedures of VB. This chapter will give you a basis to create more advanced applications with VB.

TWO-MINUTE DRILL

❑ The menu bar provides the user with most of the commands that control the VB environment.

❑ The toolbar is located directly below the menu bar and is a collection of buttons that provide shortcuts for executing commands and for controlling the VB programming environment.

❑ The toolbox contains various *controls* that are used to construct an application, including command buttons, text boxes, labels, and combo boxes.

❑ The project container window contains the Form window. The Form window is the area on which objects are placed during design time.

❑ The Properties window allows you to change the property settings of objects on your form, including font size, background color, or name.

❑ The Project window allows you to see the name of the project (the default name is Project# for unnamed projects), any forms with the same naming convention, and the files contained in the project.

❑ It is a good idea to save a project as soon as it is started. When the Save icon on the toolbar is clicked, or when Save is accessed through the menu bar, you will be prompted with the Save File As dialog box, and the Save Project As dialog box.

❑ The Hungarian naming convention is the current standard for naming objects and is used on the exam.

❑ Objects are created on a form by clicking the desired control on the toolbox, moving the mouse over the form, and drawing the boxes for the desired controls.

❑ Access keys on command buttons are enabled by including the ampersand character (&) in the caption. An Access key enables a command button to be activated by pressing ALT and the first letter of the caption (underlined when an access key is enabled).

❑ The Code window for an object on a form is accessed by double-clicking on the object.

❑ Comments are added to VB code by including an apostrophe (') before the comment. They can assist in the debugging process and make it easier for others to work with your code.

❏ VB contains many debugging tools, including breaks, watches, the Err object, and the Debug object.

❏ A *break* stops the execution of a program while it's running and places the program in *Break mode*. Break mode allows you to examine, debug, reset, step through, or continue execution of the application.

❏ A *watch* allows you to monitor the values of variables, properties, and expressions at runtime.

❏ The *Watch window* displays the current watch expressions and allows you to add a watch on a variable or expression, change the value while the code is suspended, or view the properties of objects at runtime.

❏ *Watch variables* allow you to change the display format of variables in the Watch window or in the Quick Watch dialog box, using formatting symbols.

❏ The Err object contains data an application needs in order to respond properly to errors. The Err object has six properties (Number, Description, Source, HelpFile, HelpContext, and LastDLLError), and two methods (Clear, Raise) associated with it.

❏ The Debug object is only available during the development process and has two methods (Print and Assert) associated with it.

❏ There are three types of errors: syntax errors, runtime errors, and logic errors.

    ❏ A syntax error results from an error in the format of the code (for example a misspelled word).

    ❏ A runtime error occurs during the execution of a program and causes the program to stop unexpectedly.

    ❏ A logic error occurs when the program runs correctly, but the desired output outcome does not occur.

❏ Error handling is anticipating certain problems with your code, and building safeguards in the code to keep the application from crashing.

SELF TEST

The following Self Test questions will help you measure your understanding of the material presented in this chapter. Read all the choices carefully, as there may be more than one correct answer. Choose all correct answers for each question.

1. You have a form that contains some code you want to use in your project, but you want the form to remain invisible during the execution of the program. How can you do this? (Choose all that apply.)

    A. By setting the Hide property of the form to True

    B. By using the Hide method on the form

    C. By setting the Visible property of the form to False

    D. By using the Unload method on the form

2. How does the Immediate window help you debug your projects ? (Choose all that apply.) It allows you to:

    A. Call other procedures from within the current procedure.

    B. Display all the visible variables from the procedure currently being executed.

    C. Display the name of all procedures being executed preceded by the name of the object to which it belongs.

    D. Type in any valid line of code.

3. Which of the following is true of the Err object? (Choose all that apply.)

    A. It can display the location where an error occurred.

    B. It can contain the fully qualified path to a help file.

    C. It can display the value of a variable.

    D. It can produce an error number.

4. Your form has four command buttons from top to bottom. How can you ensure that the top command button receives the focus when the form loads?

    A. By entering code in the GotFocus event of the top button

    B. By setting the TabStop property of the top button to True

    C. By setting the TabIndex property of the top button to 0

    D. By setting the TabIndex property of the top button to 1

5. What does the Description property of the Err object do? (Choose all that apply.)

    A. Returns the number and description of an error

    B. Returns the description of an error

    C. Describes the error that just occurred

    D. Defaults to an "Application defined or object-defined error"

6. Which of the following contexts are available in the Add Watch window? (Choose all that apply.)

    A. Class

    B. Module

    C. Procedure

    D. Project

7. You want to view the properties of an object variable in Break mode. What is the best tool to use? (Choose all that apply.)

    A. The Call Stack window

    B. The Immediate window

    C. The Locals window

    D. The Watch window

8. The Locals window allows you to do which of the following tasks? (Choose all that apply.)

    A. View variables adding new variables

    B. Change the value of variables

    C. Remove variables

    D. Add variables

9. When can you add a watch expression?

    A. At design time

    B. In Break mode

    C. At runtime

    D. At design time or while in Break mode

10. What does the Number property of the Err object do?

    A. Returns a message box displaying an error number

    B. Stores the number of the last error that occurred

    C. Displays the value of the variable that caused the error

    D. Returns the HelpContextID associated with the error that occurred

11. What function does the TabStop property on a command button perform?

    A. It determines whether the button can get the focus.

    B. If set to False, it disables the TabIndex property.

    C. It determines the order in which the button will receive the focus.

    D. It determines if the access key sequence can be used.

12. You want to specify a path to a Help file that can be displayed when a particular error occurs. Which of the following will return the path to the Help file?

    A. Err.Help

    B. Err.HelpContext

    C. Err.HelpFile

    D. Err.Number

13. You have not specified a help file. A command button contained on the form receives the focus. What will occur if you press the F1 key?

A. No help will be displayed. The standard Help topic for command buttons will be displayed.

B. The standard Help topic for buttons will be displayed.

C. The standard Help topic for forms will be displayed.

D. An error message stating that no help file is specified will be displayed.

14. Which debugging window(s) displays the values for all visible variables from within the procedure currently being executed?

A. The Call Stack window

B. The Immediate window

C. The Locals window

D. The Watch window

15. How can you print the object name associated with the last VB error to the Immediate window?

A. Debug.Print Err.Number

B. Debug.Print Err.Source

C. Debug.Print Err.Description

D. Debug.Print Error.LastDLLError

16. How do you enter Break mode while running an application? (Choose all that apply.)

A. Click Break on the Debug toolbar

B. Use a watch expression

C. Use a breakpoint

D. Press F9 on a line of code

17. How would you create an access key sequence for a command button?

A. Insert an ampersand (&) before the letter to be used as the access key in the Name property of the command button.

B. Insert an ampersand (&) after the letter to be used as the access key in the Name property of the command button.

C. Insert an ampersand (&) before the letter to be used as the access key in the Caption property of the command button.

D. Insert an ampersand (&) after the letter chosen as the access key in the Caption property of the command button.

18. Which is **not** a property of the Err object? (Choose all that apply.)

A. Clear

B. Description

C. Raise

D. Source

19. Which window will allow you to halt the execution of your code when a variable changes?

A. The Call Stack window

B. The Immediate window

C. The Locals window

D. The Watch window

20. How do you add a watch expression? (Choose all that apply.)

    A. Click the Debug menu, then choose Add Watch to access the Add Watch dialog box.

    B. Right-click a line of code and select Add Watch.

    C. Click the View menu, select the Immediate window, then right-click in the Immediate window.

    D. Click the View menu, select the Watch window, then right-click in the Watch window.

MICROSOFT CERTIFIED SOLUTION DEVELOPER

2

Establishing the Development Environment

CERTIFICATION OBJECTIVES

T he first step to using any program is installing and configuring it. You certainly wouldn't get too far without doing that! Fortunately, Visual Basic is a relatively straightforward program to set up, thanks to those lovely wizards. Once it is installed, it is highly configurable to suit your needs and personal preferences.

In addition to the installation methods and configuration, this chapter will also cover Microsoft's Visual SourceSafe. While the Microsoft exam doesn't deal with this very much, you are expected to know about implementing source code version control, which is what SourceSafe is all about.

So grab a cup of coffee, sit back, and prepare to step through all the options that Microsoft gives you—before you code a single thing!

CERTIFICATION OBJECTIVE 2.01

Establish the Environment for Source Code Version Control

Any programmer who's worked on a big project can testify to the necessity of version control. Sometimes changes are made that don't work or changes that need to be made aren't, and the need for tracking and sometimes returning to a previous version becomes apparent. In addition, large projects often mean large groups of files that can be difficult to manage. For this purpose, Visual SourceSafe (VSS) comes to the rescue.

VSS keeps a record of changes made to your source code. Changes to source code are saved to a database, and can then be edited and restored as you need it. Visual Basic 6.0 (VB) has the built-in capability to create projects from, add projects to, and invoke VSS. This is all done from the SourceSafe submenu on the Tools menu.

Also in the SourceSafe submenu, you can configure how VB will interact with VSS. Opening "Options" from this submenu, you can configure the options shown in the following illustration. For each of these options, you have three choices: Yes, No, and Ask. Setting these options will determine whether VB will open and save files to the VSS database, or if it should ask you each time you attempt to open or save a file. The final option in this dialog box determines whether deleted forms from your VB project should also be deleted from the VSS database.

The user of VSS must have a valid user account. Accounts are created with SourceSafe's Admin utility. If a user does not have a valid account, he or she won't be able to access the database. Instead, the user will receive a message stating that the user in question isn't found.

Using VB with VSS is almost transparent and is easy to use. Most of the work for SourceSafe is done by the VSS Administrator. A programmer's interaction with a VSS database is mainly limited to a logon screen. When saving to the database, the VB programmer will be asked to provide his or her username, password, and the database he or she wishes to save to (or open projects from, if that is the case).

exam
Watch

In the exam, you may encounter a question in which a user is unable to access the VSS database. Remember that the VSS Administrator must set up a valid account for the user before he or she can use SourceSafe.

Install and Configure Visual Basic for Developing Desktop Applications

If Microsoft were to change its motto, it would probably be to something like "All roads lead to Rome." Microsoft has always had the habit of giving users more than one way of doing things. The installation of Visual Basic 6.0 is no different.

Visual Basic 6.0 is available as a stand-alone program, or it can be installed as part of the Visual Studio 6.0 suite of products. VB is the same program in either installation, but the methods of installation are slightly different. In this chapter, we will cover how to install VB both as part of Visual Studio and as a stand-alone program.

Before performing the installation, make sure that the computer on which you're installing VB meets the system requirements. There's no better way of wasting money and time than not having hardware that's powerful enough to run the software. The system requirements for VB are listed in Table 2-1.

Many installation questions revolve around system requirements not being met. This is not only the case on the VB 6.0 exam, but other Microsoft exams as well. Make sure you know the system requirements for VB.

Installing Visual Basic 6.0

The installation of VB 6 is a simple process. When you start the setup program, a wizard will step you through each phase of the installation process. It is rare to experience problems during the installation.

	Component	Requirements
TABLE 2-1 System Requirements for Visual Basic 6.0	Operating system	Microsoft Windows 95, Microsoft Windows 98, or Microsoft Windows NT Workstation 4.0 (Service Pack 3 recommended) or later
	Processor	486DX/66 MHz or higher processor. It should be noted that a Pentium or higher processor is recommended. Any Alpha processor running Microsoft Windows NT Workstation.
	Memory	16MB of RAM for Windows 95 or Windows 98. 32MB of RAM is required for Windows NT Workstation.
	Display	VGA or higher resolution
	Other devices	CD-ROM drive (to install the software) and a mouse or other suitable pointing device
	Disk space	Standard Edition: typical installation 48MB, full installation 80MB. Professional Edition: typical installation 48MB, full installation 80MB. Enterprise Edition: typical installation 128MB, full installation 147MB.

Installing Visual Basic 6 Through Visual Studio

As you know, the first step of starting the installation process is starting the setup program from your installation CD-ROM. Once this is done, you'll be met with the typical opening screen that welcomes you and tells you that you'll be walked through the setup of Visual Studio. Clicking Next, you are then faced with the End User License Agreement. If you want to continue, click the "I accept the agreement" option button, then choose Next. If you do not accept the terms of the agreement, you cannot continue with the installation. All other command buttons will become disabled except the Exit button.

After accepting the agreement, you will be given the option of uninstalling previous installations of Visual Basic and other programs that come with the Visual Studio suite (see Figure 2-1). While the Uninstall screen proclaims that it wants to remove Visual Studio 97, stand-alone versions of these programs will also appear checked off. In other words, if you've never owned Visual Studio 97 and have a copy of Visual Basic 5 on your system, Visual Basic will appear checked. If you wish to keep your previous version of Visual Basic, simply uncheck the box beside the program's name.

The next step is finally deciding what kind of installation you'd like to perform. You have three options here: Custom, Products, or Server Applications (see Figure 2-2). This may be a little different from some of the options given by other suites. Visual Studio, offers different options for servers, workstations, and stand-alone computers. The Server Applications installation skips over workstation programs and will install server tools. The Products installation will install programs used on workstations and stand-alone computers, such as the Visual Basic program. The Custom

FIGURE 2-1

During the installation process, you are given the option to remove previous versions of Visual Basic and other programs

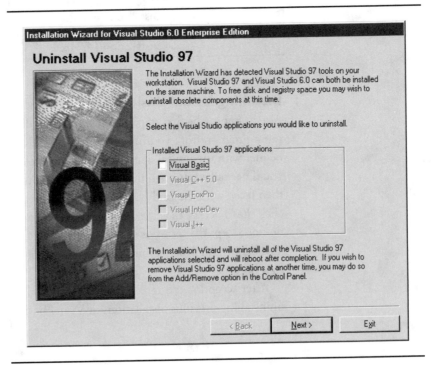

FIGURE 2-2

Visual Studio 6 offers three kinds of setup options

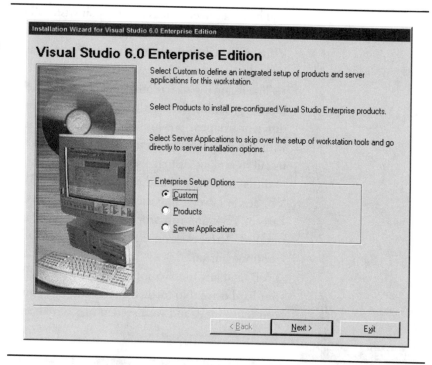

installation allows the installation of server and workstation/stand-alone products. For stand-alone computers, choose either Products or Custom.

Following this, you will get a screen telling you that Visual Studio Setup is starting, followed by a screen welcoming you to the setup program. Clicking the Continue button will get you on your way. You are then required to verify your name and company name, which it will enter for you from information it obtains from the system. If this information is incorrect, this is your only chance to change it. You are also required to enter the CD key that comes with your installation package. You will not be able to continue without a valid CD key.

After verifying and inputting this information, click Next and you'll see a Product ID screen. This is the same information that will appear in the About screen in VB's Help menu. The Product ID is occasionally requested by Microsoft when you call their support number. It is a good idea to write this number down. It will do you little to no good that it appears in the About screen in Help if you're unable to load Visual Basic!

The next screen will ask you if you wish to install other client products, such as InstallShield. This version of InstallShield is designed for use with Visual C++. Click the Install button if you're also installing Visual C++, or Next if you're not.

The following screen offers you a choice of changing the installation directory, exiting the installation, or customizing the installation. This is different from the previous option screen because this customization deals with choosing what programs you want to install. If the current directory to install to is okay, just click the Custom button. You'll be faced with a listing of different programs and tools (see Figure 2-3). If you just want to install VB, deselect everything except Microsoft Visual Basic 6.0 and Data Access. Parts of VB won't run properly without the Data Access components installed. After selecting the components you wish to install, click the Continue button.

VB (and any other components you selected) will now be installed onto your hard drive. No further interaction is required until after all files have been transferred, and your system files have been updated. Once this is

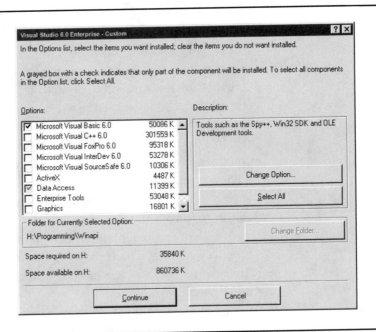

FIGURE 2-3

To install just Visual Basic 6.0 through Visual Studio, select Microsoft Visual Basic 6.0 and Data Access

done, a screen giving you the option to either exit setup or restart your computer appears. Clicking the Restart Windows button will reboot the computer; on loading Windows, your system files will finish being updated. Upon entering Windows, you can start VB and begin programming.

Installing Visual Basic 6.0 as a Stand-Alone Program

One of the most important aspects of installing a program occurs before you even purchase it. As I mentioned earlier in this chapter, make sure your system has the minimum requirements to run VB. The minimum requirements are listed in Table 2-1.

In addition, make sure you've purchased the version of VB that suits your needs. As with many of Microsoft's development programs and suites (such as Visual Studio 6.0), VB comes in several flavors. These are Standard, Professional, and Enterprise. With each flavor comes different tools. The basic components needed to create programs come in the Standard package. Extra tools and files are added to the Standard package in Professional, and the Enterprise version carries tools that allow you to create robust network and stand-alone applications.

Once you've decided on the package you need and determined that your system will support VB, you're ready to install it. After starting the setup program from the installation CD-ROM, you'll be greeted with a Welcome screen. After clicking Next, a screen appears that outlines the End User License Agreement, outlining your agreement in using the product. There are two choices here: one that accepts the agreement, and another that declines it. To continue with the installation, you must accept the agreement.

Continuing with the installation, you will be faced with a screen that requires information about you and proof that you are performing a legal installation. Two of the three fields here, Name and Company, will be filled in already from information obtained from the Windows Registry. If this information is incorrect, this will be your only chance to change it. The third field asks for a CD key. This is the registration number that appears on the package containing the installation CD-ROM. Its use is to determine that you are making a valid installation, rather than installing pirate software. After confirming and inputting the necessary information, click Next.

The dialog box that follows is a Product ID screen. This contains an identification number that has been made up from the CD key you entered and information coded into the setup program. It is wise to write this number down. While this serial number can be viewed after your installation is complete (select Help | About Microsoft Visual Basic), that won't do you any good if VB isn't installed properly or won't start at all. It is also a good idea to keep this number in a safe place.

The remaining screens involve choosing the type of installation you wish to perform, and where you want the files to be installed. If you don't want VB to be installed onto the default C: drive and directory, you'll have the opportunity to change the default settings. However, if Setup detects that not enough room is available on the drive you've chosen, you will be given another chance to choose a different target directory. The types of installation are Typical, Full and Custom. Typical installation will install the main components required to run VB on your system. Full installation will fully install VB and all of its components and documentation from the CD-ROM to your hard drive. Custom installation allows you to adjust the installation to suit your needs. If you choose Custom, you will also have to choose which components of Visual Basic you want to install. For most installations, Full is all that is required.

Following this, files will be transferred from the installation CD-ROM to your hard disk. This can be a long process, depending on the components or type of installation you've chosen, and the speed of the system. Information about VB will be displayed throughout the installation at this point. Also, a bar will display the progress of the installation. If, for some reason, this bar freezes and no hard disk activity occurs for some time, you may need to reboot your computer. Depending on when the problem occurred, VB installation may automatically continue from the point of failure, or you may be forced to run Setup again.

When all of the files have been successfully transferred, you will be informed that Windows will need to be restarted and asked whether you want to reboot the computer. Choose Yes, and your computer will restart, and the Windows system files will be updated. When Windows reloads, a

submenu named "Microsoft Visual Basic 6.0" will appear on the Start |
Programs menu. This is where you can start VB and begin programming.

Installing Visual Basic 6.0

1. From the installation disk, start the setup program.

2. You will be met with an initial welcome screen. Click Next to continue.

3. Accept the End User License Agreement. Click Next to continue to an information screen.

4. The information screen will already have your name and company name information filled in. It acquires this information from Windows. If the information is incorrect, change it. Enter your CD key, which is located on the back of the Visual Basic installation CD-ROM cover. Click Next.

5. The next screen is a Product ID screen. This includes an ID number that should be written down.

6. Follow the remaining screens, choosing the type of installation you want to perform. If you choose Custom, you will also have to choose the components of VB you wish to install.

7. When prompted, reboot the computer. Your system files will be updated when Windows reloads.

8. After installation, VB will be available from the Start | Programs menu.

Configuring Visual Basic 6.0

Visual Basic is a highly configurable development program. To configure
VB, click Tools | Options. This will bring up a dialog box that has the
following tabs: Editor, Editor Format, General, Docking, Environment,
and Advanced. Clicking on the different tabs will bring up various options
that you can change to best suit your needs.

Before accessing the Options dialog box, it is important to realize that
you must have a project open. It doesn't matter if this is a current project or
a new project. If you don't have a project open, Options will be disabled
(grayed out) in the Tools menu.

Editor

The Editor tab allows you to configure the Code and Project windows. The Project window enables you to navigate through the forms and modules that make up the application you're working on. This window also allows you to switch between viewing the design of a form (the buttons, fields, and other items that will appear as the user sees them), and viewing the code for that form. Viewing the code brings up the Code window. This is where you do your actual programming (that is, write your code). The top section of this tab controls settings that deal with code, while the lower section controls window settings (see Figure 2-4).

In the Code Settings section, there are a number of different options. The first of these is the Auto Syntax Check, which helps you prevent syntax errors in your code. VB will verify if the correct syntax has been used if this option is checked.

Below this is the Require Variable Declaration option. If this is checked, "Option Explicit" will be added to any new modules, making it a requirement that explicit variable declarations are used. When Option

FIGURE 2-4

The Editor tab of the Options dialog box

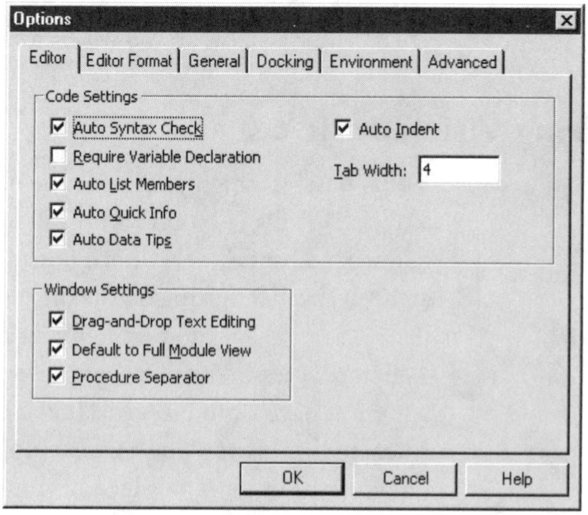

Explicit is added to the General Declaration section of your code, only explicit variables are allowed.

For those not familiar with variables—explicit or otherwise—it is important that you understand them. A variable is used to temporarily hold values during a program's execution, almost like putting something in a box until it is needed. When variables are used, a section of memory is held for any data we assign to the variable. You can then manipulate data in the variable as you would any other value.

The first step in using variables is choosing a name. As with everything in programming, there are rules to naming variables:

- They must begin with a letter.
- They can't contain a period or type-declaration character.
- They can't be more than 255 characters.
- They must be unique within the same scope—the range in which the variable is referenced. In other words, you can't have two variables named "MinWage" in the same procedure, form, and so on.

It is also a wise idea to give the variable a name that's meaningful. In the MinWage example you can guess that it refers to the minimum wage pay rate. One of the worst habits you can pick up is giving a variable a meaningless name. Imagine if you named a variable used for minimum wage "Bob" or "MyVariable." It might make sense now, but it won't be of any use to you six months from now, when you've forgotten what it is.

Once you've chosen a name, you're ready to use the variable in your program. The common (and best) method of doing this is to "declare" the variable by using the Dim keyword:

```
Dim MinWage As Integer
```

What you are doing when declaring a variable is telling your program that at one point in the program a variable called MinWage will be used to hold a value. The As Integer keyword tells the program that the type of value will be an integer. You could also specify any of the data types in Table 2-2 to be used in the variable.

Data Type	**Description**
Boolean	Can accept values of "True" or "False" Storage space: 2 bytes
Byte	Numbers ranging in value from 0 to 255 Storage space: 1 byte
Currency	−922,337,203,685,477.5808 to 922,337,203,685,477.5807 Storage space: 8 bytes
Date	Represents dates ranging from 1 January 100 to 31 December 9999 Storage space: 8 bytes
Double	−1.79769313486232E308 to − 4.94065645841247E-324 for negative values and from 4.94065645841247E-324 to 1.79769313486232E308 for positive values Storage space: 8 bytes
Integer	−32,768 to 32,767 Storage space: 2 bytes
Long	−2,147,483,648 to 2,147,483,647 Storage space: 4 bytes
Object	Used to refer to objects. By using the Set statement, a variable declared as an Object can then have any object reference assigned to it. Storage space: 4 bytes
Single	−3.402823E38 to −1.401298E-45 for negative values and from 1.401298E-45 to 3.402823E38 for positive values Storage space: 4 bytes
String	Codes in the ASCII character set (the first 128 characters on a keyboard), and special characters (such as accents, international symbols, etc.) making up the remaining 128
Variant	Default data type. This is used when no data type has been specified, and takes up 16 bytes of storage space. It represents numeric values ranging from 1.79769313486215E308 to − 4.94066E-324 for negative values and from 4.94066E-324 to 1.79769313486235E308 for positive values.

TABLE 2-2

Variable Data Types and Descriptions

Visual Basic doesn't force you to explicitly declare a variable before using it. You could just put a variable in your code, as in the following examples:

```
MinWage=6.85
Minwage=6.65
```

Using this method creates implicit variables. However, while these appear to be the same variable with two values being assigned to it, notice that one variable is called MinWage, while the other is called Minwage. Visual Basic will create two variables because of this possible spelling error. This is a major problem with implicitly declaring variables.

This is where "Option Explicit" comes in handy. By typing this at the top of a module, every variable must be explicitly declared before it can be used. This will keep you from making such mistakes.

Continuing with the other options on the Editor tab, Auto List Members is an option that makes it easier to program. When typing code in the Code window, a box will appear that completes a statement from where you point the cursor. Auto Quick Info determines whether information about functions and function parameters will be shown. Auto Data Tips will display a variable's value where you place the cursor.

When typing code, it is always a good idea to use tabs. This is done by pressing the TAB key on your keyboard to indent certain lines of code. While this is by no means a requirement of programming, it is good practice. Look at the two examples of code, and you'll quickly see how indenting makes code easier to read:

```
If x > y Then
Msgbox "X is greater than Y"
Else
Msgbox "Y is greater or equal to X"
End If
```

```
    If x > y Then
        Msgbox "X is greater than Y"
    Else
        Msgbox "Y is greater or equal to X"
    End If
```

However, continually tabbing can quickly become monotonous. If the Auto Indent option is set, when you tab the first line of your code, all of the following lines of code will subsequently be indented. The width of the tabbing is determined by the value in the Tab Width property. This is a numerical value; and while its default is four spaces, you can set it anywhere from one to 32 spaces.

The Window Settings section contains three different options: Drag-and-Drop Text Editing, Default to Full Module View, and Procedure Separator. Drag-and-Drop Text Editing lets you drag and drop code from the Code window into the Immediate and Watch windows. When Default to Full Module View is checked, you can look at procedures in the Code window as a scrollable list of subprocedures. If this option is unchecked, the Code window will display one subprocedure at a time. The Procedure Separator property determines whether separator bars that appear between subprocedures will appear in the Code window. If this box is unchecked, no separation bars will appear before or after procedures.

Editor Format

The Editor Format tab allows you to configure the appearance of your code in the Code window (see Figure 2-5). Through this tab, you can set how each text style appears.

FIGURE 2-5

The Editor Format tab of the Options dialog box

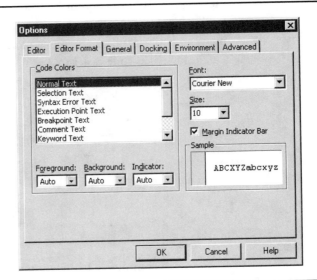

The Code Colors section contains a list of various text styles. These include comments, keywords, and so on. After selecting a text style from this list, you can set the foreground, background, and indicator colors. The foreground is the text that is typed; background is the background color of the Code window. The margin indicator is the left and right margin of the Code window. To the right of this, you can configure the font and font size. Remember that changes to text styles here don't reflect text that will appear in your program. They only affect the appearance of code in the Code window. Before saving any of these changes (by clicking the OK button), you can view what the changes will look like in the Sample window.

General

The General tab allows you to configure settings for your Visual Basic project. Error handling and compiling settings are found on this tab. There are three main sections on this tab: Form Grid Settings, Error Trapping, and Compile (see Figure 2-6).

The Form Grid Settings allow you to configure the appearance of the form grid in Design mode. This section contains a number of options.

FIGURE 2-6

The General tab of the Options dialog box

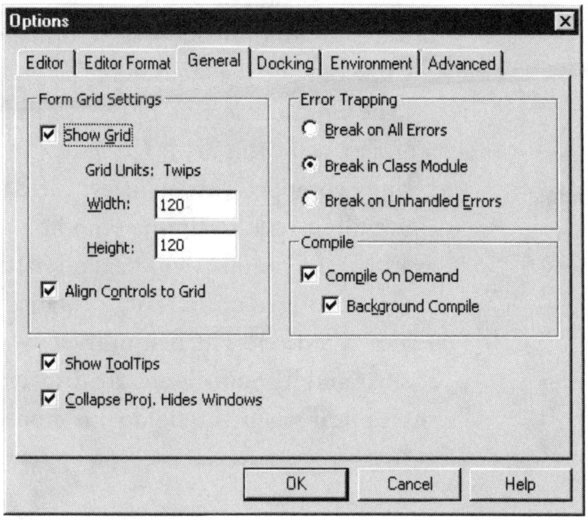

Show Grid specifies whether the grid appears on your form. Grid Units sets the units of measurement used in the grid. The default unit of measurement is twips. (For more information on twips, see the Exam Watch that follows). This option is separated into two parts: width and height. Below this is the Align Controls to Grid. Enabling this option will automatically align a control's outer edges to the grid lines.

You probably won't encounter much regarding twips on your exam, but it's interesting to know what one is. A twip is a unit of measurement that's screen independent. This allows the placement and proportion of items to appear the same on every display. How small is a twip? Very small . . . there are about 1,440 twips to an inch or 567 twips to a centimeter.

The Error Trapping section determines how Visual Basic will handle errors (which is covered more in depth in Chapter 3). Break on All Errors will cause the project to enter Break mode when an error is encountered. If you have incorporated an error handler in your code, it doesn't matter. This option will cause a break to occur regardless. Break in Class Module, the default setting, will only enter Break mode when an unhandled error is produced in a class module. This option will cause VB to enter Break mode at the end of the code that produced the error. Break on Unhandled Errors will make Break mode occur when an error is trapped and no error handler is found. If an unhandled error is in a class module, the break will occur on the line of code that caused the error.

The Compile section of the General tab has settings that determine how a project will compile. If Compile On Demand is checked, the project must be fully compiled before it starts. If Background Compile is checked, idle time will be used to finish compiling a project. This property is only available if Compile On Demand has also been selected.

The final two options on this tab are Show ToolTips and Collapse Proj. Hides Windows. The first of these two determines if ToolTips for the toolbar and Toolbox items are displayed. ToolTips are those little labels that appear when you hold your mouse over an object for a length of time.

The second option sets whether a window is hidden when your project is collapsed in Project Explorer.

Docking

If you use a laptop computer, you may get the wrong impression when you first see the Docking tab in the Options dialog box (see Figure 2-7). This tab has nothing to do with docking stations. What this deals with is how windows in VB interact with one another. Docking occurs when one window can attach itself to other windows. If an option here isn't selected, you will be able to move a window on the desktop, and leave it there. In such a case, one window won't connect itself to another.

There is only one section to the Docking tab, and it offers a list of windows that you can make dockable. Checking the check box beside an item will make that window dockable, while unchecking it will disable a window's ability to attach to other windows.

FIGURE 2-7

The Docking tab of the Options dialog box

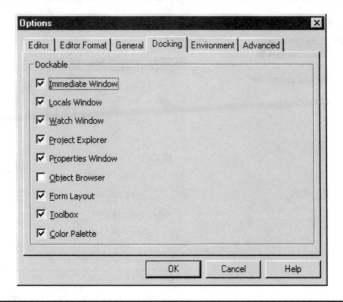

Environment

As its name suggests, the Environment tab allows you to configure your Visual Basic development environment (see Figure 2-8). One of the features on this tab is the When Visual Basic Starts section. Here you can specify whether VB will create a new project when it starts, or if it will prompt you for what kind of project you'd like to open or create.

In this dialog box, you can also configure how VB will react when you start (by pressing F5, for example) a program you've created. You can have it automatically save changes to your project, prompt you to save changes, or not save changes at all.

Templates can also be configured through the Environment tab. You can specify which templates to show and the directory in which you want to save templates. Various kinds of templates are listed. To not show them, simply deselect the check box beside the template type that you don't want shown. If you wish to change the directory in which your templates are stored, you must know the path—no browse feature is available here.

FIGURE 2-8

The Environment tab of the Options dialog box

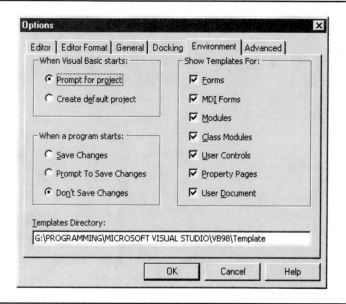

Advanced

The Advanced tab determines settings for various features of your current Visual Basic project. As you can see in Figure 2-9, there are four configuration options for this tab:

- Background Project Load
- Notify when changing shared project items
- SDI Development Environment
- External HTML Editor you wish to use

The Background Project Load affects how fast control is returned when a project is loaded. It determines if code is loaded in the background, an option that returns control to the developer faster. By default, this option is checked.

Notify when changing shared project items allows you to be notified when you change and try to save a project item that is shared. When items are shared by two or more projects, each project has a copy of that item. Because of this, this option will ask if you wish to synchronize all copies of an item before the project is saved.

The SDI Development Environment allows you to configure VB's Integrated Development Environment (IDE). You can use a Single Document Interface (SDI) environment or a Multiple Document Interface (MDI) environment. When the SDI Development Environment is checked, windows can be moved anywhere on the screen, and will remain on top of other applications (when VB is the current application). In other words, you can see your other open applications (or the Windows Desktop) looming in the background. MDIs contain child windows, which are contained in a single parent window. The differences become obvious when you look at Figure 2-10 and Figure 2-11. The SDI Development Environment option allows you to choose between these two styles. Changing this option will only become apparent after you restart VB.

The final setting on the Advanced tab allows you to configure which program you would like to use as your default external HTML editor. If unaltered, VB will use the Windows Notepad program for your HTML editor.

FIGURE 2-10

How VB appears with the SDI Development Environment option unchecked

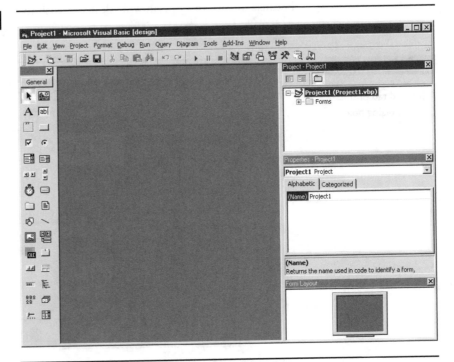

FIGURE 2-11

How VB appears with
the SDI Development
Environment option
checked

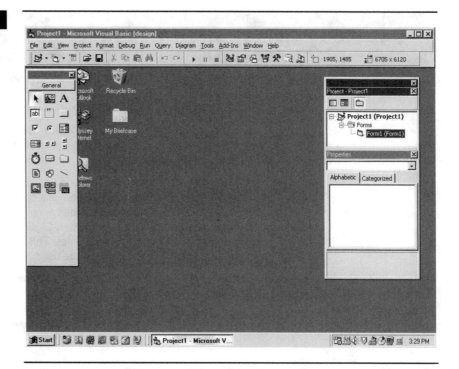

EXERCISE 2-2

Configuring Visual Basic 6.0

1. Select Tools | Options.

2. The Editor tab should be shown. If it isn't, click it. From here, click the check box for Require Variable Declaration so that a check mark appears beside it. This will automatically add Option Explicit to each new module, forcing you to use explicit variables rather than implicit variables.

3. Click the General tab. In the Error Trapping section, select Break on All Errors. This will cause VB to enter Break mode whenever an error is encountered.

4. Click the Environment tab. Under When a Program Starts, choose Prompt to Save Changes. This will cause VB to ask you if you want to save your project when you attempt to run it.

5. Click the OK button to implement the changes you've made.

QUESTIONS AND ANSWERS

I want to install Visual Basic 6.0 on my system, but I don't want any other programs installed.	Install either the stand-alone version of Visual Basic, or during setup of Visual Studio 6.0, choose Visual Basic 6.0 and Data Access.
We've just installed a new hard disk and I moved my templates to a new directory on the new hard disk. Now when I attempt to use a template, VB can't find them.	In the Options dialog box, click the Environment tab and input the path of the new template directory.
I'm tired of writing "Option Explicit" at the top of every module.	From the Options dialog box, click the Editor tab and choose Require Variable Declaration. This will insert "Option Explicit" at the top of each of your new modules. This means that explicit variables must be used in these modules.
I'm worried about making changes to my source code and finding that the old source code worked better.	Implement source code version control with VSS.

CERTIFICATION SUMMARY

VSS allows for source code version control. The ability to create projects from, add projects to, and run VSS is integrated into VB. Source code files are saved to a database. This allows you to restore previous versions of source code if needed.

In addition to the different flavors of VB (Standard, Professional, and Enterprise), you can install this development program through stand-alone installation or through the setup of Visual Studio 6.0.

While the installation process is different between Visual Studio and stand-alone setups, configuration is identical. VB is a highly configurable development program. You can set how code will appear, how compiling will occur, how projects appear, and much more. Configuring VB is a simple matter of pointing and clicking the options you wish to set.

✓ TWO-MINUTE DRILL

❑ VB is a relatively straightforward program to set up and is highly configurable once installed.

❑ Visual Basic 6.0 is available as a stand-alone program, or it can be installed as part of the Visual Studio 6.0 suite of products.

❑ Upon starting the setup program, a wizard steps you through each phase of the VB6 installation process.

❑ Visual Studio offers different options for installation on servers, workstations, and stand-alone computers.

❑ The Enterprise Setup screen allows you to change the installation directory, exit the installation, or customize the installation by choosing the programs to install.

❑ The stand-alone version of VB comes in Standard, Professional, and Enterprise flavors.

❑ VB is configured by clicking Tools | Options. You must have a project open in order to access the Options dialog box.

❑ The Options dialog box includes the Editor, Editor Format, General, Docking, Environment, and Advanced tabs.

❑ The Editor tab allows you to configure the Code and Project windows.

❑ The Project window enables you to navigate through the forms and modules of an application and allows you to switch between viewing the design and viewing the code for a form.

❑ The Code Settings section contains the Auto Syntax Check and Require Variable Declaration options.

❑ When the Require Variable Declaration option is selected, "Option Explicit" is added to any new module, requiring you to use explicit variable declarations.

❑ A variable is used to temporarily hold values during a program's execution.

❑ Variable names must begin with a letter, cannot contain a period or type-declaration character, cannot be more than 255 characters long, and must be unique within the same scope (within the range of the module in which the variable is referenced).

❑ The best method for using a variable is to declare the variable using the Dim keyword.

❑ The Editor Format tab allows you to configure the appearance of your code in the Code window.

❑ The General tab allows you to configure Visual Basic project settings for error handling and compiling, and includes the Form Grid Settings, Error Trapping, and Compile sections.

❑ The Form Grid Settings section allows you to configure the appearance of the form grid in Design mode and includes the Show Grid, Grid Units, and Align Controls to Grid options.

❑ The Error Trapping section is used to set how Visual Basic will handle errors and includes the Break on All Errors, Break in Class Module, and Break on Unhandled Errors options.

❑ The Compile section is used to set how a project will compile and includes the Compile On Demand and Background Compile options.

❑ The Docking tab in the Options dialog box is used to set how windows in VB will interact with one another and contains a list of windows that you can make dockable.

❑ The Environment tab in the Options dialog box allows you to configure your VB development environment and includes the following options: When Visual Basic starts (Prompt for project , Create default project), When a program starts (Save changes, Prompt to Save Changes, Don't Save Changes), Show Templates For (list of template options).

❑ The Advanced tab in the Options dialog box determines settings for Background Project Load, Notify when changing shared project items, SDI Development Environment, and External HTML Editor.

❑ The Background Project Load option affects how fast control is returned to the developer when a project is loaded.

❑ The Notify when changing shared project items option allows you to be notified when you change and try to save a project item that is shared.

❑ The SDI Development Environment option allows you to configure VB's Integrated Development Environment (IDE) and includes the Single Document Interface (SDI) environment or Multiple Document Interface (MDI) environment settings.

SELF TEST

The following Self-Test questions will help you measure your understanding of the material presented in this chapter. Read all the choices carefully, as there may be more than one correct answer. Choose all correct answers for each question.

1. During installation of VB, you decide that you don't agree with the End User License Agreement. Choosing the option that you don't agree, what will happen?

   A. You can click the Next button and continue.

   B. VB will be installed as a limited evaluation copy.

   C. You must either accept or exit the installation process.

   D. None of the above.

2. You install VB through Visual Studio and find that parts of VB aren't running correctly. What is the reason for this?

   A. You didn't select Microsoft Visual Basic 6.0 during the installation.

   B. You failed to install Visual InterDev.

   C. You failed to install the Data Access components.

   D. You didn't select Win32 SDK during the installation.

3. You are tired of typing "Option Explicit" in every new module you add to projects.

What can you configure so that this is automatically added to your modules?

   A. Require Variable Declaration in the Editor tab of the Options dialog box.

   B. Require Variable Declaration in the Editor Format tab of the Options dialog box.

   C. Require Option Explicit Declaration in the Editor tab of the Options dialog box.

   D. Require Option Explicit Declaration in the Editor Format tab of the Options dialog box.

4. You want to configure windows in VB so that one window can attach to another. Which tab in the Options dialog box will you use to make this configuration?

   A. Environment

   B. Docking

   C. General

   D. Advanced

5. Which of the following menus will give you access to Options, where you configure VB?

   A. File

   B. Project

   C. View

   D. Tools

6. You want VB to check your syntax as you enter code. Which property will you check to enable this?

   A. Auto Correct

   B. Auto Syntax Check

   C. Syntax Check

   D. Auto Syntax

7. If implicit variables are not allowed in a module's code, what must appear in the General Declaration section of the Options dialog box?

   A. Explicit Declaration

   B. Explicit Only

   C. Option Explicit

   D. Explicit Only

8. What must you enable for VB to complete a statement of code as you type it?

   A. Auto List Members

   B. Auto Quick Info

   C. Auto List Tips

   D. Auto Statement

9. What tab of the Options dialog box allows you to configure indentation in your code?

   A. Editor

   B. Editor Format

   C. General

   D. None of the above

10. You want windows in VB to attach to one another when one window is placed over another. Which tab in the Options dialog box will you use to achieve this?

    A. General

    B. Editor

    C. Advanced

    D. Docking

11. You want to configure VB to save changes you've made to your project each time you run a program you create. Which tab in the Options dialog box allows you to configure VB to do this?

    A. General

    B. Environment

    C. Advanced

    D. Compile

12. You have decided to move your templates directory to another location on your hard drive. Which tab in the Options dialog box allows you to configure VB to do this?

    A. General

    B. Environment

    C. Advanced

    D. Properties

13. While surfing the Internet, you found a program that you want to use as your default HTML editor. Which tab in the Options dialog box will allow you to specify this new program as your default HTML editor?

    A. General

    B. Environment

    C. Advanced

    D. ActiveX

14. During installation of VB, you reach the screen that requires you to input several pieces of information. Which of the following pieces of information is required by the VB installation? (Choose all that apply.)

    A. Name
    B. Company
    C. CD key
    D. Version ID

15. As an experienced user, you decide that you don't want ToolTips to be displayed in VB. Which tab in the Options dialog box will you choose to disable ToolTips?

    A. General
    B. Help
    C. Environment
    D. Advanced

16. You want to speed up the time it takes for control to be returned to you when a project loads. What will you configure for this to happen?

    A. Background Project Load from the Advanced tab of the Options dialog box
    B. Background Project Load from the Environment tab of the Options dialog box
    C. Load Project in Background from the Environment tab of the Options dialog box

    D. Load Project in Background from the Advanced tab of the Options dialog box

17. When installing VB through Visual Studio 6.0, you are given different setup options for installing Visual Studio. Which option will install workstation or stand-alone components (such as Visual Basic 6.0 and Data Access)? (Choose all that apply.)

    A. Custom
    B. Workstation
    C. Products
    D. Server applications

18. When installing VB through Visual Studio 6.0, you are faced with a screen that says "Uninstall Visual Studio 97." You don't have Visual Studio 97, but you do have a stand-alone copy of Visual Basic 5.0. What will happen if you don't touch any of the checked programs listed and click the Next button?

    A. Nothing. The Uninstall only affects copies of Visual Studio 97.
    B. Visual Basic 5.0 will be uninstalled.
    C. Visual Basic 6.0 will overwrite the previous version.
    D. Visual Basic 5.0 will be moved to a different directory.

19. You change the code colors for comment text (in the Editor Format tab of the

Options dialog box) to red. You create a new form, and in the comment property for a label, you write some text. What will happen when you run the program?

A. Text in the label will appear in red.

B. Text on the form will appear in red.

C. Nothing. You can't enter text during Design mode into a label.

D. Nothing. Only comments in your code will be affected.

20. When attempting to create a new project with VSS, you find you are unable to perform this action. A message appears stating that the user isn't found. What is most likely the problem?

A. VSS isn't installed on your system.

B. The database is invalid.

C. You need to have an account created with the Admin tool.

D. You need to create an account through VSS's Options.

21. When connecting to the VSS database, you are required to provide three pieces of information. Of the following choices, what information must you provide to save to the VSS database? (Choose all that apply.)

A. Name

B. Password

C. Database

D. User ID

22. What is the largest tab space you can set for your code in the Editor Format tab of Options?

A. 4 spaces

B. 32 spaces

C. 64 spaces

D. 256 spaces

23. Compile on Demand is an option available from the General tab in the Options dialog box. What will enabling this feature do?

A. Allow you to press F5 to compile a program.

B. Compile the program without saving the project.

C. The project must be fully compiled before it starts.

D. The project will start before it's fully compiled.

24. You have VB installed on a laptop and want to configure it to interact with a docking station. Which tab in the Options dialog box will you choose to perform this action?

A. General

B. Advanced

C. Docking

D. None of the above

25. During installation of VB, you reach the screen that requires you to input several pieces of information. Assuming your

computer has the proper information about you, you must input something into one of these fields. You are not allowed to continue unless you enter this particular piece of information. What is it?

A. Name

B. Company

C. CD key

D. Version ID

26. You want VB to create a new project each time it starts. Which tab in the Options dialog box will allow you to configure this?

A. General

B. Advanced

C. Environment

D. Startup

27. What error trapping method will cause Break mode to occur whenever any error is encountered?

A. Break

B. Break on All Errors

C. Break in Class Module

D. Break on Unhandled Errors

28. What is the default measurement of grid units on a VB form?

A. Pixels

B. Points

C. Millimeters

D. Twips

29. You want to change the font and color of certain text styles that appear in the Code window. Which tab in the Options dialog box would you use to configure its appearance?

A. Editor

B. Editor Format

C. General

D. Styles

30. Where must Option Explicit appear in your code if implicit variables are *not* to be allowed?

A. General

B. General Options

C. General Declaration

D. Option Declaration

31. You attempt to install VB on a 386DX/33 computer with 16MB of memory, and a CD-ROM drive. The operating system used on the computer is Windows 95. Unfortunately, you find that VB won't run. Why?

A. VB requires 32MB of RAM.

B. VB requires Windows 98 to be running.

C. VB requires a 486DX/66 or higher processor.

D. The computer doesn't meet all of the requirements.

32. You attempt to install VB on a Pentium computer with 16MB of memory, SVGA

display, CD-ROM drive, and Windows NT Workstation 4.0 as its operating system. Unfortunately, you find that VB won't run. Why?

A. VB requires 32MB of memory.

B. VB won't run on a Windows NT workstation.

C. VB can't use SVGA display.

D. VB requires a floppy drive to be installed.

33. You attempt to access the Options dialog box from the Tools menu. When you click the Tools menu, Options is grayed out and can't be accessed. Why?

A. Insufficient memory.

B. There isn't a project currently opened.

C. Options isn't in the Tools menu, it's in the View menu.

D. The user doesn't have proper permissions set through the VSS Admin tool.

34. Which of the following are valid names for variables?

A. 1st Option

B. This.Is.A.Valid.Variable.Name

C. ThisIsAValidVariableNameToUseInA Project

D. None of the Above

35. You are finding it distracting that you can see applications and the Windows Desktop behind VB's development environment. What would you do to change VB's appearance so that other applications and the Desktop aren't appearing behind VB?

A. Check the SDI Development Environment check box on the Advanced tab in the Options dialog box.

B. Uncheck the SDI Development Environment check box on the Advanced tab in the Options dialog box.

C. Check the SDI Development Environment check box on the Environment tab in the Options dialog box.

D. Uncheck the SDI Development Environment check box on the Environment tab in the Options dialog box.

36. You attempt to install VB Enterprise Edition on the following computer: a Pentium with 16MB of memory, SVGA display, CD-ROM drive, 80MB of free hard drive space, and running Windows 98 as its operating system. Unfortunately, you find that VB won't install. Why?

A. VB Enterprise requires more RAM than the system currently has.

B. VB Enterprise requires more hard drive space than the system currently has.

C. VB Enterprise won't run on Windows 98 without Service Pack 3.

D. VB Enterprise requires a minimum Pentium II processor.

37. Which of the following operating systems can run VB? (Choose all that apply.)

   A. Microsoft Windows 95

   B. Microsoft Windows 98

   C. Microsoft Windows NT Workstation 4.0

   D. Microsoft Windows 3.11

38. Which keyword is used to declare a variable?

   A. Dimension

   B. Declare

   C. Void Main ( )

   D. Dim

39. You want to change the color of certain text that appears in the Code window.

Which of the following would you change?

   A. Text

   B. Foreground

   C. Background

   D. Indicator

40. You call Microsoft for support help and you are asked for the Product ID or serial number of your VB installation. In what two places were you able to obtain this number? (Choose all that apply.)

   A. From the Product ID screen during setup

   B. From the box that VB came in

   C. From Help | About Microsoft Visual Basic

   D. From the README file VB setup places in the root directory

MICROSOFT CERTIFIED SOLUTION DEVELOPER

3

Creating
User Services

CERTIFICATION OBJECTIVES

T his chapter covers a number of nontrivial items that Microsoft definitely wants you to know. In other words, be prepared to see them on the exam!

First up, we'll be covering a number of important aspects of programming. These include navigational design, creating input forms and dialog boxes, validating input, and more. We'll also be going through Microsoft's version of COM: ActiveX. The final coverage this chapter will deal with is making a more robust application by providing help and error handling.

While this chapter covers a substantial amount of material, it's important to keep in mind that Visual Basic 6.0 provides numerous tools that assist in making the work easy. VB remains the most user-friendly and easy-to-use development program on the market. As we work through this chapter, these facts quickly become apparent!

CERTIFICATION OBJECTIVE 3.01

Implementing Navigational Design

If you can't get around in a program, it probably shouldn't have been written. That's exactly how important navigation in a program is. The way you implement navigation in your VB program is with menus and controls. In this chapter, we'll cover adding both of these to your fledgling applications.

The way to implement menus on forms is with the Menu Editor. This tool allows you to add, view, and delete a list of menu items for a particular form. Because menus, like other controls, belong to individual forms, this allows you to create different menus for each of your forms. This means that you will have to specify each form's menu interface separately.

To start the Menu Editor, you must have an open form and be in Design time. If you're viewing code, Menu Editor won't start. After confirming that you're in the right mode, you can start the Menu Editor in one of three ways:

- Selecting Tools | Menu Editor
- Pressing CTRL-E
- Clicking the Menu icon on the toolbar

After launching the Menu Editor, you'll see a screen similar to that shown in Figure 3-1. The big difference between the figure and what you'll see on your screen is that yours won't have any menu items . . . yet!

The top half of the Menu Editor dialog box displays properties of a menu item selected from the scrolling list on its bottom half. Notice that the structure of the menu system is hierarchical—similar to the structure of directories and subdirectories in Windows Explorer. In the middle of the Menu Editor are buttons that allow you to add, delete, and modify your menu system.

FIGURE 3-1

The Menu Editor
dialog box

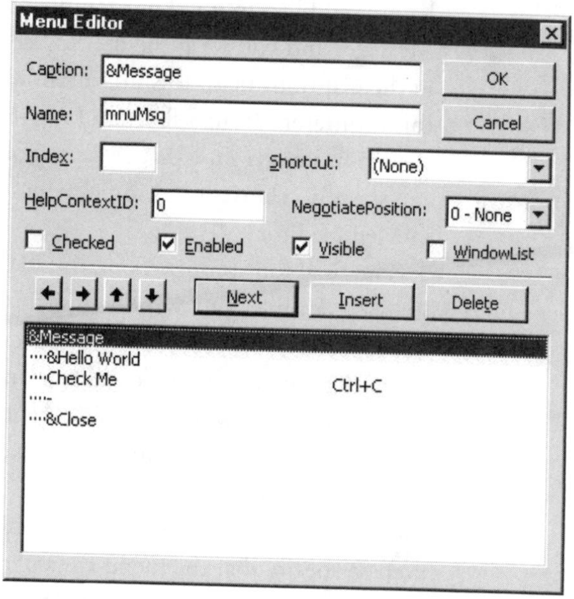

Captions and Names and Indices . . . Oh My!

Like everything else, items in your menu system must have names. The standard prefix (called Hungarian notation) for a menu item is "mnu." The logic behind this is that when you're looking through your code, you'll automatically be able to see that the code is for a menu item.

Each menu item must have a different name, or you must use the Index field. When more than one menu item has the same name, each item becomes an element of an array, and thereby needs an index number. Imagine that you named three menu items "mnuItem," and you call mnuItem in your code. Which mnuItem are you referring to? By adding an index number, you can have mnuItem(0), mnuItem(1), and so forth. Each element of the array can be accessed by its index number, which can be set to 0 or 1 to start the array. The largest number the Index property can be set to is 32,767, giving you a total of 32,768 elements to work with!

Captions are what a user sees on the menu. If you'd like the user to press the ALT key to access a menu item, just put an ampersand (&) before the letter you'd like to use. For example, if you have a menu item called Messages and you want the user to use ALT-M to access it, type **&Messages** in the Captions field. It is important to remember that an access key like this is different from a shortcut key—an access key is only available when the menu item is showing, while a shortcut key can be used anytime. You can specify a shortcut key for a menu item with the Shortcut drop-down list in Menu Editor.

The final four properties that we'll discuss at this point are Checked, Enabled, Visible, and WindowList. If the Checked check box is enabled in Menu Editor, a check mark will appear beside the menu item. If this box is unchecked, no check mark will appear. The Enabled property determines whether the item will respond to events. If it is unchecked, the menu item will be grayed out by default in your application. The Visible property is fairly straightforward, as it determines whether your item will appear on the list. If it is unchecked, the menu item won't appear. Finally, WindowList is used to specify that the menu control contains a list of open Multiple Document Interface (MDI) child forms in an MDI application. MDI child forms are windows that appear within your main application (such as multiple spreadsheets open in Excel). When WindowList is checked, any MDI child forms will be displayed under this menu control. Together, each of the properties here will determine the appearance of your menu or menu item.

EXERCISE 3-1

Creating a Menu Interface

1. Select Tools | Menu Editor.

2. Type **mnuMsg** in the Name field, and **&Message** in the Caption field. Click the Next button.

3. Click the right arrow button to indent this menu item. This will make this entry appear as an item in the menu you just created.

4. Type **mnuHello** in the Name field, and **&Hello World** in the Caption field. Click the Next button.

5. Type **mnuCheck** in the Name field, and **Check &Me** in the Caption field. Select Ctrl-C from the Shortcut combo box to be able to invoke this item at any time. Click Next.

6. Type **mnuSep** in the Name field, and a hyphen (-) in the Caption field. This will create a separator bar between your entries when the menu displays. Note that while each bar appears the same on a menu, it still requires a distinctive name. Click Next.

7. Type **mnuClose** in the Name field, and **&Close** in the Caption field. Click the OK button and you're ready to view your menu.

Adding Code to a Menu Interface

After finishing Exercise 3-1, you notice that while you have a nice interface, it doesn't do anything. Don't worry. Throughout this chapter we'll use the form and menu created in the preceding exercise and add code to it. By the end of this chapter, it will be a functioning (though not particularly functional) application.

In Design mode, you can view and select items on your menu interface. By clicking on a menu item, you'll bring up the Code window for that particular item. This will enable you to program what will happen when a user clicks that particular item.

While each item has its own methods and properties, it only has one event procedure—Click. In other words, when the program is running, the code will only execute when you click that menu item (or programmatically call the click code, which simulates a user clicking the menu item). No other event can execute the code.

Adding Code to a Menu Item

1. Using the form in Exercise 3-1, click the "Hello World" menu item. The Code window appears. Type the following:

   MsgBox "Hello World"

2. Close the Code window.

3. Click the "Close" menu item on your form. The Code window will again come up. This time type

   Unload Me

4. Close the Code window.

5. Press the F5 key on your keyboard to run your application. Check the two menu items.

In the preceding exercise, you'll note that for the Close menu item we didn't specify the name of the form that we wanted to close. Instead, we used the Me keyword. This keyword acts as an implicitly declared variable, allowing us to unload the form without referring to its name. Because it was the only form in our program, when it closed, our program was completely shut down.

Dynamically Modifying the Appearance of a Menu

The easiest way to modify the appearance of a menu is by toggling its property values. Rather than adding or deleting menu items programmatically from your interface, you can simply change the Visible property. Another example is having a check appear beside a menu item to show whether an option is selected or not during runtime. Such appearances can easily be manipulated by adding code to your program that will change a menu item's properties.

EXERCISE 3-3 ### Dynamically Modifying the Appearance of a Menu

1. Using the form in Exercise 3-2, click the Check Me menu item under Message. This will bring up the Code window.

2. Type in the following code:

   ```
   mnuCheck.Checked = True
   ```

3. Press the F5 key to run your program. Click the Check Me menu item under Message, then select the Message menu again. The Check Me menu item now appears with a check mark beside it.

Each of the properties for Checked, Visible, WindowList, and Enabled can be toggled by using the code *Object.Property*=True or *Object.Property*=False. You can also change the caption that will appear in your menu. To do so, go into the Code window and type *Object.Caption*="**New Name**". By altering the properties of a menu, you can dynamically modify the menu's appearance.

Adding Pop-Up Menus to an Application

Often, applications will also have menus that pop up when a user right-clicks the screen. You might think that this is a highly evolved bit of coding, but it's actually one of the simplest, handiest bits of code you'll come across.

In the MouseDown event of a Form or Control, type the following code:

```
If Button = vbRightButton Then
    Me.PopupMenu mnuMsg
End If
```

What this snippet of code will do is look at whether the user clicked his or her right mouse button. If so, the menu named mnuMsg (which we just created) will appear. While the Me keyword was used, it can easily be replaced with the name of the Form or Control.

Creating an Application That Adds or Deletes Menus at Runtime

By creating a menu control array, you can dynamically add menu items to or delete them from your program. You can think of an array as an expanding file folder to which you add elements (which are like files). Because we can add and delete elements in an array, it is possible to add items to and remove them from our menu interface.

Before we dynamically add menu items, we'll create a control (for our own use) to see our results. In Menu Editor, create a new menu. Select the last item in your current menu and click Next. Click the left arrow button to create a new menu. Name your new menu "mnuNew", with the caption "New Menu." Click Next, and then click the right arrow button to create a menu item. Add the following menu items:

Name	Caption	Index
MnuAdd	Add	—
MnuRemove	Remove	—
MnuArray	—	0

exam
Ⓦatch

Remember that to create a separator bar, you should use a hyphen in the caption.

In the following exercise, we will add items to our menu by adding elements to our menu control array. We created our array by inputting a **0** into the Index of mnuArray (the separator bar). In the end, we'll be able to click Add to add a menu item, and Remove to remove a menu item.

EXERCISE 3-4

Adding and Removing Menus at Runtime

1. First, we'll create a variable that will allow us to manipulate the index number of our array. In the Code window, go to the general declaration section of your code. This is done by selecting General and Declarations from the list box in the Code window. Choose (General) from the Object list box (at the top left of the Code

window), and Declarations from the Procedure list box (at the top right of the Code window). Type in the following:

```
Option Explicit
Dim IntCount
```

2. While in the Code window, go to the Form Load section of your code. Choose Form from the Object list box and Load from the Procedure list box. We will now create a variable that we can manipulate. Since the last element in the mnuArray array is 0, we can set our variable to 0. In the Form_Load procedure, type the following:

```
IntCount=0
```

3. Next, go to the mnuAdd_Click section. In this section, type the following code:

```
intCount = intCount + 1
Load mnuArray(intCount)
mnuArray(intCount).Caption = "Array " & mnuCount
mnuArray(intCount).Enabled = True
```

4. What the first line of this code does is increment our counter by one. This adds one element to our array. We then tell our program to load the menu item, so that we can use it. The third line gives our new menu a caption (with the counter number added to make it distinct). The fourth line of code enables the menu so that we can use it.

5. Our final step (in coding) is to set up our program to remove any items that we add. The procedure is similar to the code we used in step 3. In the mnuRemove section of the code, type the following:

```
Unload mnuArray(intCount)
intCount = intCount - 1
```

6. Close the Code window and press the F5 key to run your program. Notice that each time you click Add, a new menu item appears below the separator bar. Notice that each time you click Remove, the last added menu item is removed.

Adding Controls to Forms

Adding controls to your forms is one of the easiest things to do in VB. Older programmers know the difficulties of programming each and every control from scratch; but with VB, you're a double-click (or a simple drag of the mouse) away from adding controls. It's as simple as that.

VB comes with a toolbar that has icons depicting common controls (see Figure 3-2). These include buttons, text boxes, labels, and much more. By double-clicking on one of these icons, a control will automatically be placed on your active form. You can also single-click on a toolbar icon, then drag your mouse across the form—thereby drawing a control to the size you want.

After adding a control to your form, you can click it to display handles that will allow you to resize your control. Doing so enables you to adjust the control to a size that matches other controls on your form. You can also

FIGURE 3-2

The left side of this picture shows the toolbar containing icons of different controls

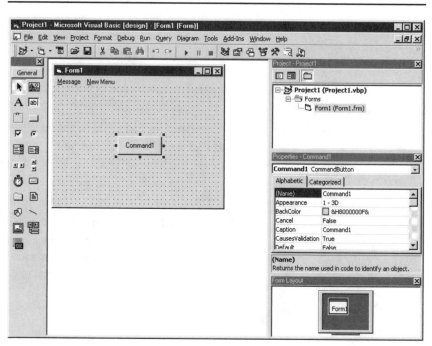

move the control anywhere on your form, allowing you to create a structure with better function and visual appearance.

Remember to limit the amount of controls you add to a form. Not only will this increase the performance of your application, but it will make the application easier to use. Having too many controls on one form can make an application confusing for a user.

Setting Properties for Command Buttons, Text Boxes, and Labels

Clicking a control you've added to your form brings up the properties for that control in the Properties window (see Figure 3-3). If the Properties window isn't already open, you can view it by selecting View | Properties Window or by pressing F4. In viewing the Properties window, you'll notice that many of the properties for each of the controls are similar to one another. Through this window, you can alter the name, color, and other aspects of each control.

FIGURE 3-3

The Properties window allows you to change the properties of a control or form

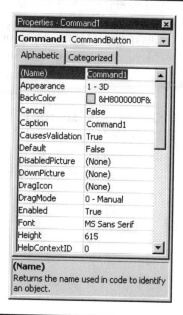

If there are no other properties that you change on a control, you should change the Caption and Name properties. While VB gives each control a default name, it is not very descriptive. For example, the first command button you place on a form is given the Name and Caption of Command1. Any additional buttons will be Command2, Command3, and so on. Imagine a user's confusion as to what tasks each of these controls perform! Also imagine your own confusion when writing code for each of these controls. It would be much easier to view cmdExit with the caption Exit to know what that button does. It is always important to give meaningful names and captions to controls in good programming. For a full listing of naming conventions, see Appendix D Conventions of this book.

As you click each of the properties for a control or form in the Properties window, you'll notice that the text at the bottom of the window changes. This text provides help, describing what each property does.

It is also important to note the methods offered for changing each of the properties. Here are some examples. When clicking a form, you bring up that form's properties. You can click the Name property and type in **frmForm**. However, when you click the Picture property, a button with an ellipsis appears. Clicking this button brings up a window that allows you to browse your hard disk for a graphic, which will appear on your form. Clicking the Appearance property displays a list box that allows you to choose whether you want objects to appear as flat or with a 3D effect. In these different ways, you can alter the appearance of the form.

Command Buttons

Command buttons are the most common control in an application (see the illustration that follows). Clicking a command button will run the code associated with that event. In looking through the events associated with a command button (by checking the Event combo box of the Code window), you'll see that there isn't a double-click event for this control. The default event for a command button is Click. For a full listing of the standard namings of controls and variables, refer to the object reference at the end of this book.

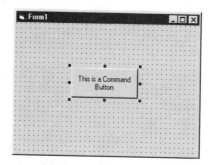

Of the properties associated with command buttons, the Name property is most commonly changed in Design time, while the Caption and Enabled properties are most commonly manipulated at runtime. The Hungarian prefix for command button names is "cmd." The caption is what appears to the user on the button face, while the Enabled property determines whether the user can use this object. The Enabled property has a Boolean value (true or false), and can be changed at Design time through the Properties window, or during runtime with code.

Text Boxes

Text boxes are another of the most common controls found in programs (see the illustration that follows). It is commonly used to obtain input from users and is often useful for returning information. By default, information can only be written and returned to a single line. However, the MultiLine property allows for text to be written to multiple lines. If MultiLine is set to true, word-wrapping will be performed and will break text into paragraphs when hard returns are used. If the MultiLine property is changed to do this, you should also change the ScrollBars property during Design time. The default value for this property is None, but you can set this to Vertical, Horizontal, or Both, allowing users to scroll down and across long pieces of text.

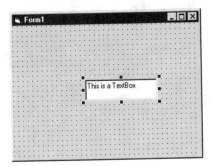

As with other controls, the first thing you'll change in the Properties window for this control is the Name. The Hungarian prefix for this control is txt.

The default property for this control is Text. This is what appears in the text box. You can not only set this property in Design time, but also during runtime. Whatever appears in this property is the contents of the text box and can be read and edited (by default) during runtime.

Labels

The Label control displays text to a user and can't be directly changed by the user. The most common use for labels is to provide information to the user about what other controls are for, and what information to place in such things as text boxes (see the illustration that follows). Now, doesn't that make labels sound unimportant? Not at all. Providing information is the cornerstone of any application. Whether it's a game or a database program, the user must know what's expected from them and what's going on. Labels are often used to provide that information.

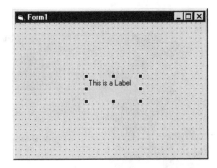

The Label control is depicted in VB's toolbox with a capital A. As with any control, the first property to change is the Name. The Hungarian prefix for labels is lbl. The Caption property allows you to change the text displayed in the label. This property can be changed during Design time, or during runtime programmatically.

Assigning Code to a Control to Respond to an Event

As mentioned throughout this chapter, controls respond to events. For example, when you click a command button, code executes. When the Text property of a text box alters, the Change event is triggered. Each control has different events that can cause code to be executed.

Assigning code to a control is a simple process. We've already done a similar process when we created menus, and assigning code to respond to an event in a control isn't really any different. You assign code to a control through the Code window. Accessing the Code window can be done by either clicking the View Code button of the Project window or by double-clicking the control. Double-clicking a control will bring up the Code window with the default event for that control. After that, it's just a simple matter of typing.

If you wish to navigate through the Code window and assign code to a different event, the right list box at the top of the Code window provides a list of events associated with that control (see Figure 3-4). Selecting an event

Assigning code to a
control's event is done
through the Code window

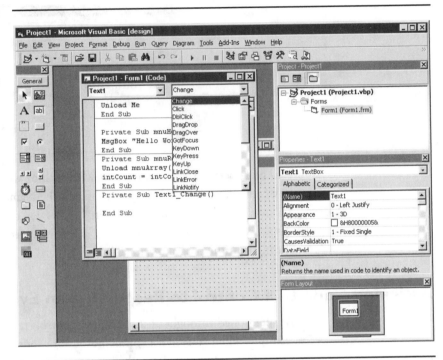

from the list provided will take you to the subprocedure associated with that
event. Also, if you wish to assign code to a different control on that form (or
the form itself), the left list box at the top of the Code window allows you
to switch to other sections of code associated with controls. Navigation is
always as simple as a mouse click.

Creating Data Input Forms and Dialog Boxes

Creating data input forms and dialog boxes is done by combining the
various controls we've covered and a few controls we'll cover next. To create
a standard data input form, simply add the number of text boxes required

and some method of accepting the data entered (such as with a command button). After doing so, users can enter text into the text box. Clicking the command button, for example an OK button, will execute code that will manipulate, save, and so on, the information in the text box.

As an example, let's say you wanted to create a small application that determines how much you would pay in taxes for a product purchased in Ontario, Canada. For this, you would need a means to accept input and let the user know that the input should be in Canadian dollars. The user would also have to perform an action so that the answer would be given when he or she is finished inputting data. The following exercise steps you through creating such an application.

EXERCISE 3-5

Creating a Data Input Form

1. On a form, create a label that asks "Input amount in Cdn. Funds:". Beside this, create a text box. Name the text box in the Properties window **txtAmount**. In the Text property, erase everything so that the text box appears blank.

2. Create a label below your first label that has the caption "What you will pay in taxes:". Create a label below the text box, and name it **lblAnswer**. Erase the current caption so it appears blank.

3. Create a command button and name it **cmdOK**. In the Caption property, type **OK**.

4. Double-click the command button. This will bring up the Code window. Type in the following code:

```
Dim x As Currency
x = txtAmount.Text
lblAnswer.Caption = "$" & x * 0.15
```

5. Run the application and make sure it works. After you input a number and run the code, an amount (with a dollar sign in front of it) should appear in the label.

Creating dialog boxes is also a matter of adding controls and code to a VB form. An example of a dialog box is a file dialog box. Most of the work involved in creating a file dialog box is simply putting the controls on the form. For such a dialog box, you need a DirListBox, a FileListBox, and a DriveListBox. After placing these controls on the form, you must make each control aware of the others. To do this, double-click each of the following controls and add the following code:

Control	Code
DirListBox	File1.Path=Dir1.Path
DriveListBox	Dir1.Path=Drive1.Drive

Remember that (as with other examples) the code will only work if the names are correct. If you have named your objects differently than appears in the code, then you must change the examples of code to suit these objects.

Upon adding this code, you'll be able to change from one directory to another by clicking what appears in each control. While this small application does very little, it does illustrate how easy it is to create a dialog box.

Displaying and Manipulating Data by Using Custom Controls

Sometimes the general controls in the toolbar just aren't enough. That's when you use custom controls. Custom controls are stored in OCX files and contain controls that allow you to do all sorts of things. A few of the more popular ones are listed below. It is, however, important to remember that when you use a custom control in your project, you will have to include the OCX file with the distribution of that product. Failing to do so will cause the control not to appear on the form, as the code for that control is contained in the OCX file.

You can add custom controls to your project by selecting Project | Components. A dialog box appears showing a list of available components that you can add to your project. The ones we will cover are part of Microsoft Windows Common Controls 6.0 (MSCOMCTR.OCX). By selecting the check box beside this item and clicking OK, the controls will appear in the toolbar.

For each of these controls, you can click the related icon and draw the control onto your form. Right-clicking the control and choosing Properties will bring up special property pages. You can also bring up the Property pages from the regular Properties window by clicking the Custom item. In these Property pages, you can alter various aspects of the control.

ListView

This control allows you to display items in one of four views: large icons (standard), small icons, list, or report. When configured and run, ListView looks like the right pane in Windows Explorer. The view style and other properties can be configured either programatically or through the control's property page.

The General tab of the property page allows you to set which view is used to display items in the list. You can also sort items, configure how they will appear in the list, and set whether labels for items use single or multiple lines.

ImageList

The ImageList control acts as a repository for image files. These files can be bitmaps, GIFs, JPEGs, icons, or cursors. Instead of storing such images throughout your application, it allows you to store the files in one or more ImageLists, which can be used to provide images to other controls.

When you place an ImageList on a form, it appears as a box containing a number of squares. This will not be visible when you run the application. Instead, images can be called from the ImageList. Before this is done, you must put images into the ImageList through its properties page.

Images are added to the ImageList through the Images tab (see Figure 3-5). Clicking the Insert Picture button allows you to add images. Each new image will have a new index number (incremented by one). If you want to remove a picture, click the Remove Picture button. Each of the images following that image will have its index renumbered. It is important to remember that the image index is renumbered. If you removed image 2 from the ImageList, image 3 would now have the index number of 2. This could cause problems if you were calling on image 3 (or higher) in your code!

FIGURE 3-5

The Images tab of the ImageList Properties page

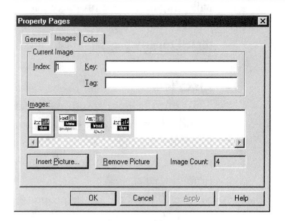

Toolbar

The Toolbar control is just what it sounds like. It allows you to put a toolbar with buttons on your form (see Figure 3-6). It is configurable, so you can add as many or as few buttons as you wish. Bringing up the property page for this control, you can add new buttons and alter the caption, ToolTip text, and so forth. Code can be associated with the button through the Code window, allowing code to be executed when a button on the toolbar is clicked.

FIGURE 3-6

A form with the Toolbar control (as seen during runtime)

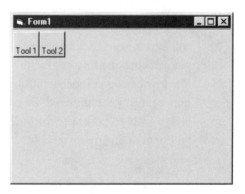

Status Bar

This control is a standardized way of providing status information to a user (see Figure 3-7). From its property page you can change settings that alter its behavior and appearance. Of the different tabs available from this page, the most important one is the Panels tab.

A status bar is made up of different panels that display different information. This information can exist in the form of text, date, time, the current status of a key, and so on. Because each panel displays different information, each must be configured and/or programmed to display the information. Such changes are made through the Panels tab of the StatusBar property page (see Figure 3-8).

Adding and deleting panels from the status bar can be done with the Insert Panel and Remove Panel buttons. You can navigate from one panel's options to another's by clicking on the arrow buttons beside the index number. The index reflects which panel's options you are viewing.

The Text property allows you to enter text that can appear in your status bar. It will only appear if the Style property (explained later) is set to sbrText.

The ToolTipText property allows you to display text that will appear when the user puts his or her mouse over the panel. This text should be descriptive, to show the user what that panel does.

FIGURE 3-7

A form with the StatusBar control (as seen during runtime)

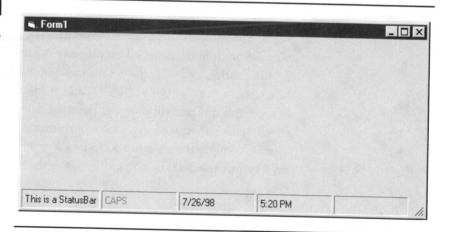

FIGURE 3-8

The Panels tab of the
StatusBar property page

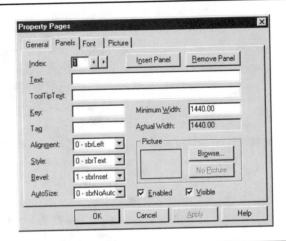

The Key property allows you to identify a particular panel in your code. It is text that allows you to name a panel, and should, therefore, be different from other panels.

The Alignment and Bevel properties affect the appearance of a panel. Bevel allows you to change the appearance of the border surrounding a panel. There are three options for this property: sbrNoBevel, sbrInset, and sbrRaised. The Alignment property determines the alignment of the contents of a panel. With this property, you can set a panel's contents to be justified left, justified right, or centered.

The Style property determines the contents of a panel: sbrText assigns information from the panel's Text property to appear in the panel; sbrCaps, sbrNum, sbrIns, and sbrScrl will set a panel to display the toggle status of the CAPS LOCK, NUM LOCK, INSERT, and SCROLL LOCK keys, respectively; sbrTime and sbrDate will show the time and date in a panel, respectively. The sbrKana option is often a source of confusion. It is only useful on Japanese computers that have a Kana lock key. For those truly curious, you'll be interested to know that this toggles the display into Kanji mode.

There are many custom controls available for purchase through third-party companies. There are also a number of Freeware controls for use on the Internet. While Visual Basic allows you to create your own custom controls, it is well worth your time investigating whether or not what you need already exists. Buying or using such controls may save you time and money in the long run.

Creating an Application That Adds and Deletes Controls at Runtime

Adding and deleting controls at runtime can be done effectively with a control array. To create an array of controls, you must start by creating one control in Design time. In the Properties window, you must then select the Index property for this control and input a value (0 or 1). After doing this, you can then add and delete controls at runtime.

Another name for this is a "controls collection." While you must create at least one control in Design time, you can create more than one for your controls collection. One method for creating multiple controls in Design time is adding controls to the form and giving them the same name. In the Index property for each of these controls, you increment the value by one. Another method is creating one control, then copying and pasting the same control as many times as you want onto your form. Because it is the same control, VB will automatically assign index values. It is important to remember that you can't delete controls from the array that were created in Design time. Only controls created at runtime can be removed from the array.

Adding controls during runtime is done with the Load statement and by incrementing the index associated with the controls. For example, to add a control named txtMyBox to an array with one existing control that has the value 0, you would type the code

```
Load txtMyBox(1)
```

You could also increment the value by using a variable for the index, which we saw in the section, "Creating an Application That Adds or Deletes Menus at Runtime."

To remove controls from a control collection, the Unload statement would be used. To remove the text box we added in the previous example, you would use the following code:

```
Unload txtMyBox(1)
```

Using the Controls Collection to Manipulate Controls at Runtime

There is very little difference between manipulating controls in a control collection and manipulating individual controls at runtime. For a single control, you specify the name of the control in your code, the property you wish to change, and the value you're changing it to. For example, to change the text in a text box named txtMyBox, you might type

```
txtMyBox.Text="This is my text"
```

There is one major difference between this and manipulating a control that's a member of a controls collection—the index. Remember that each member of a controls collection has the same name, but different indices. As such, to change the third text box's text in a collection, the code would read

```
txtMyBox(2).Text="This is my text"
```

In the previous example, it is assumed that the first text box had an index of 0, the second had the value of 1, and the third index was 2. While this example shows only one value of a text box, you could have changed the properties of any control in a similar manner. The major difference is to specify the index of the control you wish to alter.

Using the Forms Collection to Manipulate Forms at Runtime

Forms collection refers to all forms that currently exist in memory. Remember that a collection is a special group of objects. Collections also have a Count property that you can use to count the number of elements that are part of the collection. You can also use looping to go through each form currently in memory. An example of how to do this is shown in the following code:

```
Dim frmForm as Form
For Each frmForm in Forms
        frmForm.Show
Next frmForm
```

In the preceding code, a variable named frmForm is declared. The next snippet of code loops through each form in memory and shows it on the screen.

CERTIFICATION OBJECTIVE 3.03

Writing Code That Validates User Input

Mistakes happen and people are unpredictable. It is always a good idea to prepare for those mistakes and implement code that verifies that a user put in the information that the user was expecting. For example, imagine someone typing in his or her name in a field that required a numerical value. When the application attempts to calculate that value, errors will occur. For situations like this, it's important to validate the data a user has input.

Creating an Application That Verifies Data Entered by a User at the Field Level

The key to validating the information contained in a field (such as a text box you provided for user input on your form) is analyzing the field's contents. This is easily done with an If…Then statement. This will look at the data entered by a user, determine if it's valid, and then perform (or not perform) some sort of action.

EXERCISE 3-6

Verifying Data Entered at the Field Level

1. Create a label with the caption **Enter a number between 1 and 10**.

2. Create a text box beside the label, and name it **txtInput**.

3. Create a command button, name it **cmdOK**, and give it the caption **OK**.

4. Double-click your new OK button and add the following code:

```
If txtInput.Text < 1 Or txtInput.Text > 10 Then
    MsgBox "Number must be between 1 and 10"
End If
```

5. Press the F5 key to run the program. Enter different values below 1 and above 10, as well as valid numbers.

Another method of validating user input is through keystroke events. There are three such events that can be used. Each event occurs in the following order: KeyDown, KeyPress, and KeyUp.

The KeyPress event occurs if the key that's pressed represents an ASCII character. As this suggests, KeyPress has a single parameter of KeyASCII, which is an integer that reflects an ASCII value. Most keys have such a value. For a listing of character values, review the two ASCII Character Set charts in VB's help documentation.

The following example of code can be placed in the KeyPress procedure of any text box. When the user presses a key, it takes the ASCII value of the key pressed and (in the next line) automatically changes to lowercase. In this way, you can ensure that all input is in lowercase (such as when asking the user to input the URL of a Web site).

```
Char = Chr(KeyAscii)
KeyAscii = Asc(LCase(Char))
```

In addition to the KeyPress event, there are also the KeyDown and KeyUp events. KeyDown occurs when the user presses a key, and KeyUp occurs when the user releases a key. In other words, when the key goes down, KeyDown occurs. When the key is released, and goes back up, KeyUp occurs. By separating a keystroke into these events, the programmer is given greater flexibility in programming what happens during certain keystrokes.

KeyDown and KeyUp events don't look at the same information as the KeyPress event. While KeyPress looks at the KeyASCII parameter, KeyDown and KeyUp look at the KeyCode. The KeyCode is a collection of constants that reflect certain keys. These constants include such things as navigation and function keys that aren't recognized by the KeyPress event. KeyCode allows KeyDown and KeyUp to detect keystrokes that the KeyPress event wouldn't be able to detect.

KeyCodes start with the prefix vbKey. There are numerous constants, and all can be viewed by referring to KeyCode constants in VB's help documentation. By using these constants in your programming, you can control what happens when certain keys are pressed and released. In the following example, if the user presses the F5 key (or releases it, depending on whether the code is put in KeyDown or KeyUp), a message box is displayed:

```
If KeyCode = vbKeyF5 Then
    MsgBox "You pressed F5"
End If
```

By using these different events, you will be better able to control what happens when certain keys are pressed. This will enable you to control what the user can and can't do with input and certain keystrokes (such as function keys, navigation keys, and so on). In doing so, the end result will be a more robust program.

Creating an Application That Verifies Data Entered by a User at the Form Level

You can also verify data input at the form level. This is done by inserting code into the General section. To use a version of our previous exercise, let's change the code in the command button to

```
intDept = txtInput.Text
checkInt
```

This will invoke a procedure that we'll set up at form level.

First, in the General Declarations section, declare a variable named intDept. This is done by typing

```
Dim intDept as Integer
```

After creating this variable, create the following procedure in the General section:

```
Private Sub checkInt()
If intDept <> 10 Then
     MsgBox "This program is only for members of Dept. 10"
End If
End Sub
```

Now, when information not equal to 10 is placed in the field and the OK button is clicked, a form-level procedure will be executed. It will check whether the number is equal to 10, then provide a message box stating that the user must be from Dept. 10. In this procedure, we have verified at the form level whether the input was valid.

Creating an Application That Enables or Disables Controls Based on Input in Fields

Different events can cause controls to be enabled or disabled. An example you've already experienced was when you installed VB in Chapter 2. If you refused to accept Microsoft's agreement for using the product, the Back and Next buttons were disabled. This action left you with the choices of accepting the agreement or exiting the installation program. This choice was made by toggling the properties of the command buttons.

Enabling Controls Based on Field Input

By adding code to the Change event of a field, you alter the Enabled property of a control. Let's say we wanted a user to input his or her name before he or she could progress to the next screen. By analyzing the input of the field, the program could determine if the field was blank or not, then enable the Next button. This can be done with an If…Then statement.

```
If txtInput.Text <> "" Then
    cmdNext.Enabled=True
End If
```

The first line of this code analyzes the contents of the text box and determines if it's not equal to being empty. If it isn't empty, it changes the command button's Enabled property to True.

Disabling Controls Based on Field Input

Similarly, we can disable controls by analyzing input. This is done by changing a control's Enabled property to False.

```
If txtInput.Text <> "" Then
    cmdNext.Enabled=False
End if
```

We can also use an If...Then...Else and combine these two code snippets. Have the code look at the field's contents and, if we want it to have information in it, enable a command button. If it were empty, it would be disabled.

```
If txtInput.Text <> "" Then
    cmdNext.Enabled=True
Else
cmdNext.Enabled=False
End If
```

CERTIFICATION OBJECTIVE 3.04

Writing Code That Processes Data Entered on a Form

As we have seen in this chapter, code can be added to a form that will process data entered into any field on that form. In addition to this, code can be added to different events associated with the form object. Code will then execute when certain events are triggered, such as the form loading or unloading.

Adding Code to the Appropriate Form Event

An important part of writing code to a form is knowing under which events one should write it. The Form object has a number of different events associated with it. While some events seem remarkably similar, their importance lies in what they do and the order they do it in.

Initialize

When an instance of a form is created, the Initialize event is triggered. This event will run before the Load event actually runs. Initialize occurs when an instance of a form is created by your application.

Terminate

Terminate is the flip side of Initialize. It is the last event triggered in a form. The Terminate event occurs when all variables in a form have been set to nothing. It occurs immediately after the Unload event.

Load

When a form loads into memory, the Load event is triggered. It is the traditional place to set form-level variables, properties, and other startup code.

Unload

The Unload event is the common place to put "cleanup" code. Code placed in this event generally closes any forms that are still open, cleans up any variables, and clears memory space that has been used by the application.

QueryUnload

The QueryUnload event takes place immediately before the Unload event. This event is used for code that prompts the user to save changes or give the user the option to cancel the Unload. An example of a QueryUnload event is when you exit from Microsoft Word and you are asked if you would like to save changes to an open document. Clicking Cancel will stop the Unload (closing of document and shutting down Word) from occurring. Microsoft put the code that enables you to have these options in the QueryUnload event.

Activate

The Activate event doesn't occur when the form loads, but when it becomes visible with the Visible or Show property. When a form becomes the active window, the Activate event is triggered. The way to visibly tell if the form is the active window is that the title bar will appear highlighted and the window will appear on top of the Desktop screen.

Deactivate

This event occurs when the form is no longer the active window. It does not occur when a form is unloaded. This event is triggered when a user switches from one window to another. The form is then no longer the active window, and the form's Deactivate event triggers.

It's All About Timing

To help you understand the relative timing of these Form events, Table 3-1 has been provided. Because questions may appear on your VB exam that deal with the order these events occur, it is advisable to review them before going into your exam. Table 3-1 shows the order of a form loaded and then unloaded from memory, and explains when the event occurs.

TABLE 3-1	When a form is loaded into memory	
Events That Occur When a Form is Loaded and Unloaded from Memory	**Event**	**Occurs**
	Initialize	Occurs when an instance of a form is created.
	Load	Occurs when a form is loaded into memory.
	GotFocus	Occurs when there are no enabled or visible controls on the form. This is the case when implementing splash screens in your application.

TABLE 3-1

Events That Occur When a Form Is Loaded and Unloaded from Memory (*continued*)

When a form becomes the active form	
Event	**Occurs**
Activate	Occurs when the form becomes the active window or when it becomes visible with the Show or Visible property.
GotFocus	Occurs when there are no enabled or visible controls on a form.
When another form becomes the active form	
Event	**Occurs**
LostFocus	Occurs when there are no enabled or visible controls on a form.
Deactivate	Occurs when the user switches from one form or window to another.
When a form is unloaded from memory	
Event	**Occurs**
QueryUnload	Used to prompt user to save changes or cancel the Unload event.
Unload	Occurs when a form is Unloaded from memory.
Terminate	Occurs when all variables in a form have been set to nothing.

CERTIFICATION OBJECTIVE 3.05

Adding an ActiveX Control to the Toolbox

Adding ActiveX controls to the Toolbox is as easy as adding any other custom control. It is done through Components on the Project menu. When you scroll through the list, various ActiveX controls are available. Clicking the check box will select the control, which can then be installed in the Toolbox. Once an ActiveX component is added, it will (or should) act like any other control in VB.

EXERCISE 3-7

Adding ActiveX Controls to the Toolbox

1. Select Project | Components.

2. Scroll through the list of components until you see RealAudio ActiveX Control Library. If this component isn't available on your machine, choose another ActiveX component from the list. Check the check box to the left of this item.

3. Click OK, and the control will appear in the Toolbox.

CERTIFICATION OBJECTIVE 3.06

Using Data Binding to Display and Manipulate Data from a Data Source

Data binding occurs when you bind a data source, such as the Data controls, with a data consumer, such as the DBCombo box or a text box. When this is done, information contained in the data source can be displayed in the data consumer. You can also manipulate the data displayed through the data consumer.

The traditional way of data binding in VB is to add a data source and data consumers to your form, then set the properties that bind the data during Design time.

EXERCISE 3-8

Binding Data During Design Time, and Manipulating Data

1. Add the Data control to your form. Leave the Data control's name as Data1.

2. In the Properties window, set the Connect field to Access. This will allow the Data control to connect to a Microsoft Access database.

3. Select the DatabaseName field, then click the button that appears with an ellipsis. Browse your hard disk and select the database you wish to use. In this case, we will use the Nwind.MDB database found in your VB directory.

4. Select the RecordSource field. From the combo box that appears, select the table or query you wish to use. In this case, we will use the Employees database.

5. Add a text box to your form. Leave the text box's name as Text1.

6. Click the text box, so it is selected and its properties appear in the Properties window. In the Properties window, select the DataSource field and choose the name of the Data control you wish to use. In this case, only one option (Data1) appears.

7. From the DataField field, select the field of data you want to appear in your text box. In this case, choose Lastname.

8. Run the program by pressing F5. As you click on the right and left arrows of the Data control, the text box reveals the various entries, which it accesses through the Data control.

9. In the text box, change the name of one of the entries. Click the right-arrow button on the Data control to move to the next entry. Your change is automatically saved to the database. Click the left-arrow button to return to your previous entry. Notice your name has been saved to the database and now appears as a permanent entry.

VB 6 also allows you to set the DataSource during runtime. This is a new ability for programmers that wasn't permitted in previous versions. Doing so is straightforward, and similar to setting the value of any other property during runtime. By using the following example of code, you can set the DataSource, DataField, and table or query you wish to use with your program.

```
Text1.DataMember="Employees"
Text1.DataField="LastName"
Set Text1.DataSource=Data1
```

Instantiating and Invoking a **COM** Component

The term COM stands for component object model. COM is a standard that defines how different objects communicate with each other and how separate components can manipulate each other. In short, it allows different objects to interact. Not only does it allow you to use reusable components, but it enables you to use objects that are exposed by existing programs (such as Microsoft Office). An exposed object, in its most basic definition, is something (such as a text box in another program) that our program can "see," and thereby manipulate. Exposing objects will be covered in more detail in Chapter 9.

Both ActiveX technology and OLE (object linking and embedding) are based on the COM specification. OLE is an obsolete form of the COM. It has been replaced by ActiveX components, which have increased functionality over COM's predecessor, OLE.

exam
ⓦatch

ActiveX has replaced OLE, but you may still see some references to OLE in the exam. Also, some older features of ActiveX still use the term OLE in their names. An example of this is the OLE container control. Don't allow this to confuse you.

ActiveX components were referred to as *OLE servers in* Visual Basic 5 and older versions. Because the term *server* has a completely different meaning in networking terms, this often leads to some confusion. "Doesn't this mean that the server component has to be on a server, and the client portion on a workstation?" was a common question that popped up. Not at all. ActiveX components expose objects to your application. The ActiveX component your application is using could be on the same hard drive, or accessed on a computer halfway around the world!

ActiveX components have an object structure that is visible to the ActiveX client application. Objects that are visible to other programs are known as *exposed objects*. However, for an object to be exposed, it must be listed in the Windows Registry.

Creating a Visual Basic Client Application That Uses a COM Component

The first step in creating a VB client application that uses ActiveX components is to set a reference to the server for your application. This can be done by clicking Project | References. You will see a listing of libraries that have been registered with the Registry. The next step is using the ActiveX component name and classes.

If you don't know the objects available in a library, pressing F2 will bring up the Object Manager. This will display all objects in your current project, VB, and any objects exposed to it through the library you selected from References.

Once the references have been set, you can begin using the ActiveX components in your code. The first step is to create and instantiate object variables for the ActiveX component classes. This is done with regular object declarations, and the CreateObject and GetObject functions or the As New keyword.

You can declare an ActiveX component as a new object with the following declaration:

```
Dim variable As New Object
```

If you were going to use Microsoft Excel as an ActiveX component, this would be written as

```
Dim objXL As New Excel.Application
```

You can also use the Set keyword to return a reference to an ActiveX component by returning its value to a variable. This is done with CreateObject and GetObject. Using the previous example, the syntax would be

```
Set objXL = GetObject ("Excel.Application")
```

or

```
Set objXL = CreateObject ("Excel Application")
```

Why the different possibilities? Because many applications (that is, ActiveX components) don't support the As New keyword. Because of that, you may have to use CreateObject or GetObject.

Once you've declared the variable, you can begin to evoke an exposed object in your code. The syntax for this is

```
Servername.classname.procedure
```

Therefore, if you had made a reference to Microsoft Access 8.0 and wanted it to close down, you would type into your code

```
Access.Application.Quit
```

In this example, if Microsoft Access were currently open, the application would shut down.

Creating a Visual Basic Application That Handles Events from a COM Component

Handling events associated with ActiveX components is done with the WithEvents keyword. An example of this would be declaring an instance of a Module in Microsoft Access. In the form's General Declaration section, you would type

```
Private WithEvents AccRep As Access.Report
```

After typing this in, you can check the Object section of your Code window (the left combo box), and see that it is now listed as an object of the form. You'll also see that the right combo box lists all events associated with that object. You can now handle events of the ActiveX component as if it were an object you created as part of your own application.

CERTIFICATION OBJECTIVE 3.08

Creating Call-Back Procedures to Enable Asynchronous Processing

Without asynchronous processing (explained in the next paragraph), a client will make a method call to an ActiveX component and then wait for the ActiveX component to return the call. This processing is known as *synchronous*. With asynchronous processing, the client application is freed to execute other code while it waits for the COM component to finish what it is doing. As you can see, using asynchronous processing makes for a much more robust program.

Asynchronous processing goes through several steps to complete a task. The first is when the client makes a method call. This starts the task, but does not instantly return the result. The client is then able to perform other tasks as the COM component works on its task of returning a result to the client. Since some time may pass before a result is returned, the ActiveX component must provide notification when a result is ready.

As you can see, asynchronous notifications are important to asynchronous processing. Without them, you would be quietly minding your own business, working on something else, and never knowing that a result has been achieved! These notifications must exist for the client to know that a result has been returned. Providing notifications can be done with events or with call-back methods.

The easiest way to provide notification is by raising an event. Implementing this method can be broken down into two parts, with the first part being the responsibility of the ActiveX component's author. The second part falls on the shoulders of you, the developer.

The COM component's author must first define the tasks and notifications to be performed and provide externally creatable classes that will manage notifications. These classes must be provided with methods that you can later call on. These methods will initiate the various tasks of the component and provide a way to request notifications. Events handled by clients must also be declared so that these clients can receive notification. Code is then written that starts tasks and watches for things that the component will find meaningful. Finally, code is written to raise the event when a task is complete or when something meaningful has occurred. When this is all done, the author's job is finished, and the client developer's job begins.

The developer who uses this COM component starts by creating a WithEvents variable that contains a reference to the object that provides notification. Event procedures associated with this variable will contain code to handle notification events. Code must also be written that makes a request of the COM component and calls the methods that perform the required tasks.

As you can see, implementing asynchronous processing has two parts to it: you start at the component side and finish on the side of the client application. When both sides write their code and follow procedures correctly, asynchronous processing can be achieved.

Implementing Online User Assistance in a Desktop Application

One of the most important things you can offer a user is online help. User assistance can exist in the form of help files, WhatsThisHelp, Messages, and HTML documents, among other options. By implementing online user assistance, users will find the program more functional and robust. I can't stress enough how important this is.

Setting Appropriate Properties to Enable User Assistance in a Desktop Application

Help files contain organized information and are displayed when the user presses F1, selects a Help feature from the Help menu, or performs another action that invokes Help. Standard help files are stored in a binary format and are compiled with a special compiler. To display this information in your application, you must set certain properties in your application to invoke the help files.

Help can be added to your project at Design time or runtime. Adding help at Design time is done through the Project Properties, and the Properties window of each control and form. After adding help files to your project at Design time, you can change these properties programmatically so their values alter at runtime. In doing so, you can control which help file your project uses.

Help File

Applications can only use one help file at a time. You can associate a help file with your application in Design time by designating the path and filename of a help file. This is done by selecting Project Properties from the Project menu, then inputting the location of the file in the Help File Name field on the General tab. However, since your application can only point to one such file at a time, you may want to change to a different file during runtime.

Assigning a help file during runtime is done programmatically. By using the following example of code, you can change which help file is associated with the program:

```
App.Helpfile= "C:\Win98\Helpfile.hlp"
```

HelpContextID

The HelpContextID property is used to provide context-sensitive help in an application. You can configure the HelpContextID for an object through the HelpContextID property in the Properties window, or programmatically. By using the following example of code, you can set the value of this property during runtime:

```
Object.HelpContextID=number
```

By default, the HelpContextID is set to zero. This means that no help is associated with that object. In such a case, help for the container or parent object (such as the form) will be displayed.

A problem that commonly occurs with HelpContextID is when an invalid number is associated with an object. In other words, you set the HelpContextID to a number that can't be found. Say you meant to type **10** as the HelpContextID, but through a slip of the finger, typed **100**. That context number doesn't exist in Help, and the F1 key will be ignored when pressed.

exam
Ⓦatch

When the HelpContextID is set to zero, no help is associated with that object. In such a case, help for the parent object is displayed. When an invalid number is used (that is, a nonzero), the F1 key will be ignored.

WhatsThisHelp

WhatsThisHelp provides a pop-up screen for context-sensitive help in an application. The value of this property is Boolean, and it is set through the form's WhatsThisHelp in the Property window. By default, it is set to False. Setting it to True enables What's This-style help. However, while the ability to display this type of help is turned on through the form's properties, you must set an ID number for each object on that form. The ID number associates a particular object with a help topic and has a numerical value. You can set the WhatsThisHelpID through an object's Property window.

Creating HTML Help for an Application

While experienced programmers are familiar with standard help files (that have the HLP extension), they may be surprised that VB allows help files to be created using HTML. HTML stands for the hypertext markup language, and is most commonly used in creating Web pages. Unlike standard HLP files, HTML help is compiled through a special program and has the extension CHM.

While HTML files can be created using any HTML editor (such as Notepad, FrontPage, Dreamweaver, and so on), such documents must be compiled into a CHM file. A product that enables programs to create such help files is the HTML Help Workshop. With this program, you can create new HTML files, import existing HTML files, and compile them into a format that can be used for help. The program is relatively simple, but requires the user to either have existing HTML documents, or knowledge of HTML.

After being compiled, CHM files can be set as the application's help file in the same manner as associating HLP files. VB supports both formats.

Implementing Messages from a Server Component to a User Interface

When dealing with ActiveX components, it's very important to provide some sort of help for users. If extended help is to be used with a component, you must first create a help file with help topics for each item and context ID numbers for each topic. You then configure your project—through the General tab of Project Properties to use this help file. After this is done, it's just a matter of setting the help file topic to items in your project.

After pressing F2 to bring up the Object Browser, you must select your project from the Projects/Libraries list box at the top left of the browser. You then select the class from the Classes list, located at the top right of the browser. Right-click the member to which you want to assign help to display a pop-up menu. Choose Properties, and you will see a Member Options dialog box into which you will enter the context ID in the Help Context ID field. When this is done, extended help will be available to your component.

Implementing Error Handling for the User Interface in Desktop Applications

Imagine how displeased you'd be if you were working on a document in a word processor, and the thing crashed on you without warning. Imagine how relieved you'd be if the program gave you a chance to save the work before it exits from the error. This is an example of error handling. When a bad thing happens in the program, the error handler in that program deals with the problem.

As you can tell from this example, error handling is an important part of a robust application. It also saves you from lynch mobs of angry users.

Identifying and Trapping Runtime Errors

Runtime errors occur, as you might guess, only during runtime of an application. They occur in situations such as when there is an attempt to open a file that doesn't exist or when a user forgets to insert a floppy disk.

While they can't be completely avoided, they can be *trapped.* Trapping runtime errors involves writing code to catch the errors when they occur. This allows the program a chance of correcting, or offering a chance to correct, the error. It can, for example, prompt the user to save data before exiting, or skip over the offending code.

Writing an error-handling routine involves checking the error, handling the error in some way, and exiting the error handler. The On Error statement enables error trapping and redirects the program to code that will deal with the error. The error trap will stay enabled until the error-handling procedure ends or until the trap is disabled. By placing On Error in your code, followed by the GoTo statement and the name of your error handler, you can redirect the error to your error-handling routine as the following code illustrates.

```
On Error GoTo ErrHandler
```

The error is checked with the Err object. This object allows the routine to view an error number and allows the routine to then deal with the problem. This object has three very important properties:

- Number, which is an integer indicating the error that occurred.
- Description, which provides a description of the error.
- Source, which is the name of the object that contains or caused the error.

The Err object also has two important methods to help you with error handling: Clear (which resets the Err.Number to 0), and Raise (which causes an error that you can use to test your code). Together, the properties and methods of the Err object are invaluable to error handling.

Once you have dealt with the error, you must provide a way to exit the routine. You can use the Resume statement to return to the statement that caused the error. Resume Next can be used to return to the statement following the code that caused the error. You can also return to a specific line by typing **Resume** followed by the line number. If no resume statement is used, the procedure exits.

Now that we've covered the elements required for an error handler, let's look at an example of an error handler.

```
        On Error GoTo ErrHandler
Exit Sub
ErrHandler:
    If Err.Number=10 Then
        MsgBox "My Error Statement to User is Here"
        Resume Next
    Else
        MsgBox "Some other error has occurred"
        Resume
    End If
```

In both the real world and the Microsoft exam, there will be moments where you will need to know how to turn off error handling. An error handler is immediately disabled as soon as it exits a procedure. However, you can also disable error handling with the following code:

```
On Error GoTo 0
```

This will disable error handling, even if the procedure has a line numbered as 0.

Error handling does not necessarily need to be a separate procedure that is called when errors are encountered. It can also be implemented in a procedure. When this is done, you need to add code that keeps the error handler from always running. Remember that code will run from line to line until the procedure ends. Because there is occasional need to end or exit a procedure, the Exit statements are used.

Exit Sub or Exit Function is used to keep the error handler from running if no error occurs. Exit Function is used when the error handler is contained in a function (which is a procedure that returns a value). The error handler comes between the Exit Sub and End Sub statements to separate it from the procedure's normal flow. The following code illustrates its use:

```
Sub MyProcedure()
    On Error GoTo ErrorHandler
        . . .
    Exit Sub
ErrorHandler:
        . . .
    Resume Next
End Sub
```

Handling Inline Errors

While you can redirect and branch to errors, you can also set up error handling right after the place where they occur. This method is especially handy in areas where an error is likely or suspected. By typing code such as the following,

```
On Error Resume Next
```

the error is immediately dealt with. There is no need to redirect it to a separate error handler because the error is handled where it occurs.

QUESTIONS AND ANSWERS

I want to add menus to my program, but don't want to go through the hassle of creating them at runtime.	Use the Menu Editor that comes with VB. Menu Editor allows you to create custom menus in Design time for your application.
I want to spice up my help files, and provide help that people will find easy to navigate.	Use HTML help files with your application. HTML provides more powerful features to your help files, while offering them in a format that is familiar. HTML is the same language used to create Web pages, so users will find it easy to navigate through the help file.

CERTIFICATION SUMMARY

Navigation in an application is achieved by adding menus and controls to a form. Menus can be created by using the Menu Editor tool, while various controls are available on the toolbar. Also, you can add custom controls to your application. To do this, you must first add them to the toolbar by installing them from the Components item on the Project menu.

One of the primary objectives of programming is the manipulation of data. This is done by entering code through VB's Code window. Entering code can alter the properties of controls, verify information provided by user input, and manipulate data that has been entered. The Code window is where actual programming takes place.

An important aspect of creating applications is providing help. This is done in numerous ways. One method is through setting properties of controls. Online help is also available if you create help files. These can be the traditional HLP files or HTML help files.

Another important part of programming is error handling—trapping errors and controlling how errors are dealt with. How a program handles errors is an indication of how well a program functions.

 TWO-MINUTE DRILL

❑ Menus are implemented on forms using the Menu Editor, which can only be accessed in Design time. Menus belong to individual forms. Each form's menu interface must be separately specified.

❑ A menu item has only the Click event procedure. During runtime, a menu item's code will execute only when that menu item is clicked.

❑ The easiest way to modify the appearance of a menu is to toggle its property values.

❑ Menu items can be added to or deleted dynamically from a user interface by creating a menu control array.

❑ Controls can be added to forms in Design time by double-clicking (or dragging and dropping) control icons from the control icons toolbar.

❑ Command buttons are the most common controls in an application. Clicking a command runs the code associated with the command button's event. The default event procedure for a command button is Click.

❑ The Enabled property for a command button determines whether the user can use the object. This property has a Boolean (True or False) value, and can be changed in Design time or during runtime.

❑ Text boxes are most often used to obtain input from users and to return information. By default, information in a text box can only be written and returned to a single line. The MultiLine property for the Textbox control allows text to be written to multiple lines. The default property for the Textbox control is Text. This property can be set in both Design time and runtime.

❑ Custom controls, including ActiveX controls, are added to a project in Design time by selecting Project | Components. Code for custom controls is stored in OCX files. When custom controls are used, the OCX files must be included with the distribution of the project.

❑ Controls can be added or deleted at runtime with a control array or with a controls collection. Controls are added during runtime with the Load statement and are removed at runtime with the Unload statement. To manipulate a control at runtime by using a controls collection you must specify the index number for the control that you wish to alter in the collection.

❑ To validate user-input data contained in a field, use an If...Then statement to analyze the field's contents. User input data can also be validated through three keystroke events: KeyDown, KeyPress, and KeyUp.

❑ Command button controls can be enabled or disabled based on field inputs, by toggling the command button's properties.

❑ The Form object has seven different events associated with it. They are Initialize, Terminate, Load, Unload, QueryUnload, Activate, and Deactivate.

❑ Data binding occurs when a data source is bound with a data consumer to allow information contained in the data source to be displayed and manipulated through the data consumer.

❑ The Component Object Model (COM) is a standard that allows different objects to interact by defining how they communicate with (or manipulate) each other. The COM standard allows you to use exposed objects. An exposed object is an object that a program can "see" and manipulate. For an object to be exposed, it must be listed in the Windows Registry

❑ Both ActiveX technology and OLE (object linking and embedding) are based on the COM specification. OLE is an obsolete form of the COM specification, and has been replaced by ActiveX components.

❑ Asynchronous processing enables a client application to execute other code while it waits for a COM component to return a result. A COM component must provide notification to the client application when a result is ready. This is done with events or with call-back methods. The easiest way to provide notification is by raising an event.

❑ Help files contain organized information and are displayed when the user presses F1, selects a Help feature from the Help menu, or performs another action that invokes Help. Help can be added to a project at Design time through the Project Properties window, and through the Properties window for each control and form in the project. Help properties can be changed programmatically so that their values alter at runtime.

❑ Applications can only use one help file at a time. A help file can be associated with an application in Design time by designating its path and filename on the General tab of Project Properties in the Project menu, or it can be assigned programmatically during runtime.

❑ The HelpContextID property is used to provide context-sensitive help in an application. The HelpContextID for an object can be configured through the HelpContextID property in the Properties window at Design time, or can be altered programatically at runtime.

❑ A common problem with HelpContextID happens when an invalid HelpContextID number is associated with an object. If the HelpContextID for an object is set to zero, no help is associated with that object and help for the parent object is displayed instead. When an invalid nonzero number is used for the HelpContextID, help will not be displayed.

❑ WhatsThisHelp provides a pop-up screen with context-sensitive help in an application's forms. It is enabled by setting the WhatsThisHelp from its default (False) to True in the form's Property window. Use of WhatsThisHelp also requires that an ID number (numerical value) be set for every object on the form through its Property window.

❑ HTML help files can be created using any HTML editor, but must be compiled into .CHM files using a special program.

❑ Help messages may be implemented from server components to the user interface by creating a help file with help topics for each item, providing a context ID number for each topic, and configuring the project to use the help file.

❑ When runtime errors occur, they may be trapped by an error-handling routine. Writing an error-handling routine involves checking the error, handling the error in some way, and exiting the error handler.

❑ The On Error statement enables error trapping and redirects the program to the routine that will handle the error.

❑ An Err object allows a routine to view an error number and then deal with the problem. It has three important properties: Number (an integer indicating the error that occurred), Description (a description of the error), and Source (the name of the object that contains or caused the error). An Err object also has two important methods to assist with error handling: Clear (which resets the Err.Number to 0) and Raise (which causes an error that can be used to test the code).

❑ A Resume statement can be used to exit the error handler and return to the statement that caused the error.

❑ Error handling can also be implemented within a procedure rather than as a separate procedure. The Exit statements, Exit Sub or Exit Function, are used to keep the error handler from running if no error occurs.

SELF TEST

The following Self-Test questions will help you measure your understanding of the material presented in this chapter. Read all the choices carefully, as there may be more than one correct answer. Choose all correct answers for each question.

1. You want a menu item to appear grayed out on a menu. Which property of that menu item will you uncheck in Menu Editor?

    A. Checked

    B. Visible

    C. Appear

    D. Enabled

2. What event procedures does a menu item have? (Choose all that apply.)

    A. KeyDown

    B. KeyPress

    C. Click

    D. MouseUp

3. You want information to appear in your status bar, and you enter text in the Text property of a panel. When you run the form, you find that no text appears in the status bar. Why?

    A. The Text property is used to enter text in ToolTips.

    B. The text won't appear unless the Text check box is checked.

   C. The text won't appear unless the Style property is set to sbrText.

   D. The text won't appear unless the Text property is set to sbrText.

4. Which property determines the contents of a status bar panel?

    A. Contents

    B. Style

    C. The type of panel selected

    D. SbrContents

5. What is the minimum number of controls you must create in Design time to start a control array?

    A. One.

    B. Two or more.

    C. As few or as many as you like and the form allows.

    D. None. You can fully create controls collections at runtime.

6. You create five controls during Design time as a controls collection. During runtime, you add five more controls, then try to execute code that will delete six of them. You find you are unable to perform the action. Why?

    A. You can't delete controls during runtime.

    B. You can't delete the controls created during Design time.

C. You can't have this many controls in a collection.

D. None of the above.

7. At one time, how many help files can be associated with an application?

A. One

B. One for each control

C. As many as you choose to associate with the application

D. None of the above

8. Which of the following file extensions denote files that can be used as help files for applications created in VB? (Choose all that apply.)

A. HTM

B. HTML

C. HLP

D. CHM

9. Your application creates an instance of a form. What is the first event that will be triggered in the form?

A. Load

B. GotFocus

C. Instance

D. Initialize

10. Which of the following is Hungarian notation for a menu?

A. Menu

B. Men

C. mnu

D. MN

11. You are ready to run your program to see if it works. Which key on your keyboard will start the program?

A. F2

B. F3

C. F4

D. F5

12. Which of the following methods will enable you to start the Menu Editor? (Choose all that apply.)

A. Selecting Menu Editor from the Tools menu

B. Pressing CTRL-E

C. Clicking the Menu icon from the Toolbar

D. Pressing the F5 key on your keyboard

13. Which of the following keys would you press to bring up the Object Manager in VB?

A. F2

B. F3

C. F4

D. F5

14. You want users of your program to press ALT and the underlined letter on your menu to access that particular menu or menu item. In Menu Editor, what will you place before the letter you want to use for an access key?

A. Underscore

B. Ampersand

C. SHIFT

D. ALT

15. Which of the following snippets of code will unload a form named frmForm from memory?

    A. Unload Form

    B. Unload This

    C. Unload Me

    D. Unload

16. Which of the following serves as an example of declaring an ActiveX component?

    A. Dim *variable* As New *Object*

    B. Declare *variable* As New *Object*

    C. *component* As New *Object*

    D. *component* As New *Servername*

17. You want the text in a text box named txtMyText to read My Text. In which property will you place this string?

    A. Caption

    B. Text

    C. String

    D. None of the above

18. Which property in a text box will allow a string to appear like a paragraph, word-wrapped on different lines?

    A. WordWrap

    B. MultiLine

    C. SingleLine

    D. TextWrap

19. Which of the following best describes an ImageList?

A. Provides a list of images available on the hard disk

B. Provides the extensions of images available to load

C. Acts as a central repository for image files

D. None of the above

20. Which is the traditional place in a form to set form-level variables, properties, and other startup code?

    A. Initiate

    B. Load

    C. QueryLoad

    D. Instigate

21. In which form event would you put cleanup code?

    A. Load

    B. Unload

    C. Terminate

    D. QueryUnload

22. Which property allows you to provide context-sensitive help for your application?

    A. Help Context

    B. HelpContext

    C. HelpContextID

    D. Help

23. What object is used to check errors?

    A. Error.

    B. Err.

C. Enum.

D. There is no object that can check for errors.

24. Which event does *not* occur when a form unloads from memory?

A. Unload

B. QueryUnload

C. Terminate

D. Deactivate

25. Which form event occurs because of the Show or Visible property?

A. Activate

B. Terminate

C. Load

D. Peek

26. Which method will reset an error number to zero?

A. Clear

B. Reset

C. Null

D. None

27. What keyword handles events associated with ActiveX components?

A. ActiveX

B. OLE

C. COM

D. WithEvents

28. When dealing with ActiveX components, which of the following processing forms will release the client program, process the

work, and then notify the client that it has returned a result?

A. Asynchronous

B. Synchronous

C. Multiprocessed

D. Processed

29. What is the difference between an access key and a shortcut key?

A. A shortcut key can only be used while a menu item is showing, but an access key can be used at any time.

B. An access key can only be used while a menu item is showing, but a shortcut key can be used at any time.

C. There is no difference. Both can be used at any time.

D. There is no difference. They are synonymous.

30. Which of the following are properties of the Err object? (Choose all that apply.)

A. Description

B. HelpContextID

C. Number

D. Source

31. Which of the following are based on COM? (Choose all that apply.)

A. ActiveX

B. OLE

C. Thunking

D. HTML Help

32. You want to enable What'sThis help in your application. What are the two values associated with the What'sThis help in the Properties window of an object?

   A. Yes/No

   B. On/Off

   C. True/False

   D. Help/Me

33. A user forgets to insert a floppy disk into the drive when she saves. An error results from this. What kind of error has occurred?

   A. Runtime

   B. Design time

   C. Syntax

   D. Logic

34. You have decided to use HTML help in your application. Using FrontPage, you create a number of HTML documents that you plan to use for help. When you attempt to implement the HTM and HTML files, you find that VB won't accept them. Why?

   A. VB doesn't use HTML help.

   B. The files must have either the extension HTM or HTML. You cannot use both.

   C. You must use the default HTML editor. You can't use FrontPage to create the files because of this.

   D. The HTML files must be compiled before they can be used as help files.

35. Which of the following will cause a program to return to a statement that caused an error?

   A. Resume.

   B. Return.

   C. Resume Next.

   D. None. It would be pointless to return to a statement causing an error.

36. Which method of the Err object will cause an error to occur?

   A. Create

   B. Error

   C. Raise

   D. Lower

37. You want the text in a label named lblMyLabel to read My Text. In which property will you place this string?

   A. Caption

   B. Text

   C. Label

   D. None of the above

38. Which is the last event to occur when a form is closed?

   A. Terminate

   B. Unload

   C. QueryUnload

   D. TerminateLoad

39. Which of the following keys would you press to bring up the Properties window in VB?

A. F2

B. F3

C. F4

D. F5

40. What will the following snippet of code do when attached to a control named cmdButton?

```
Me.PopupMenu mnuMsg
```

A. It will have the same result as if you clicked the menu mnuMsg.

B. It will display the contents of the menu mnuMsg as a pop-up menu when the user right-clicks over the command button.

C. Nothing. The code is gibberish.

D. Nothing. The Me keyword is reserved for forms.

4

Using Visual Data Access Tools

This chapter discusses the technologies that Visual Basic provides to connect applications to data sources, and the terms Microsoft uses for these data access strategies. You will create data-enabled forms using the Data Environment Designer, the Data Form Wizard, and the ADO DataControl. You will also learn about some of the additional data tools provided in VB, including the Data Report Designer and the Query Builder.

CERTIFICATION OBJECTIVE 4.01

Universal Data Access

In Chapter 3, you learned that Microsoft provides tools for database integration. When you are working with a simple, local database (for example, a table in an Access database residing on your own hard disk), integrating an application with data can be quite simple.

However, things are rarely so straightforward in the real world. Your application may need to use data from the user's hard disk, from a separate relational database residing on your network, or from the Internet. You may even need to use a data store that is not traditionally considered a database, such as Excel or Outlook.

The challenge for developers is getting the data they need in a manner that is simple, reliable, and consistent. Microsoft's answer is Universal Data Access (UDA).

Microsoft defines UDA as their "strategy for providing high-performance access to all types of information (including relational and nonrelational data) across an organization from the desktop to the enterprise." For more information, see http://microsoft.com/data/.

UDA is a strategy, not a technology. (You're not going to drop a UDA control onto your form.) Microsoft defines UDA as the union of the following four technologies:

- ADO (ActiveX Data Objects)
- ODBC (Open Database Connectivity)
- OLE DB
- RDS (Remote Data Service)

ADO 2

ActiveX Data Objects are the direct, everyday interface between the VB developer and the data. An ActiveX Data Object behaves like any other object—you invoke its methods, you reference its properties, and you monitor its events.

A sample Access database for the fictional company Northwind has been provided with your copy of VB. The following VB code segment demonstrates how easy it is to use ADO to get any needed data from this Access database.

```
Dim myConnection As ADODB.Connection
Dim myRecordSet As New ADODB.Recordset

Set myConnection = New ADODB.Connection
myConnection.Provider = "Microsoft.Jet.OLEDB.3.51"
myConnection.Open "C:\Program Files\Microsoft Visual Studio" & _
"\VB98\NWIND.MDB", , "admin", ""            , "admin", ""
    myRecordSet.Open "SELECT * FROM Employees", myConnection
    txtName.Text = myRecordSet.Fields("LastName")

myRecordSet.Close
myConnection.Close
```

These nine lines are all that is required to use the ADO to read the LastName field from the first record in the Employees table and display the content in a text field txtName. All of the information contained in the database can be found in the Connection object myConnection and the Recordset object myRecordset.

ADO is a successor to and a superset of two previous object models: DAO (Data Access Objects) and RDO (Remote Data Objects). If you are maintaining previously authored applications in VB, it is possible to continue using these older technologies, but Microsoft recommends using ADO for new development.

ODBC 3

ODBC is a protocol for using SQL-based relational databases. After you install the appropriate ODBC driver for a particular database, it becomes possible to access the content in the database without having to know whether that particular database is implemented.

It is a common misperception that ODBC can only be used with sophisticated databases, such as Oracle or SQL Server. However, you can use ODBC to connect to any database if the appropriate driver exists. In addition to shipping drivers for Oracle and SQL Server with VB, Microsoft also ships ODBC drivers for Access, FoxPro, dBase, and even plain text. (This means you can use the power of SQL statements to run complicated queries on a simple text file, without importing it into a real database.)

The makers of any version of any database product, if they write the needed driver correctly, can allow every VB developer in the world to use their product without having to learn a new interface. So why would anybody want to use anything else? Here are three reasons:

- ODBC can be limited. Because ODBC defines a common interface for all database products, it tends to enforce the lowest common denominator of product functionality. Because the ODBC interface predates the database design, the newest features are sometimes inaccessible.

- ODBC can be slow. With a rigid interface, it is more difficult to tweak an application to optimize it for a destination platform. Each database vendor offers ways to optimize use of its own database, but ODBC doesn't always support these features.

- ODBC can be difficult to use. Although its complexity is often abstracted away from a VB programmer, the low-level native ODBC API is complex to use and difficult to master.

For these reasons and others, Microsoft predicts that ODBC will eventually be eclipsed by OLE DB, which is discussed in the next section.

OLE DB

Many developers are using OLE DB every day, and they don't even know it!

An application communicates with ODBC primarily by passing it text strings (usually SQL statements). By contrast, OLE DB uses a more granular object model. This is part of Microsoft's larger strategy of breaking down data sources to provide smaller and more flexible components of functionality. (This approach isn't accepted across the industry yet. Though Microsoft intends to expose all SQL Server functionality through OLE DB, this probably won't be an option for some third-party databases for at least a couple of years.)

There are some advantages to this approach to exposing database functionality:

- As applications become more decentralized, it may become easier for applications to distribute database processing across multiple servers and tiers.

- It is easier for database vendors to support OLE DB than ODBC, because more of the processing occurs within their own product.

- Because OLE DB is more of a specification than a technology, it should be able to accommodate a wider variety of future functionality than ODBC.

VB developers do not have direct access to OLE DB through a supplied control, but it is indirectly available, either through ADO or by using an available API.

If you do DCOM development in the future, you will become much more familiar with the details of OLE DB. However, because so much of its complexity is hidden from the VB developer, you can use it effectively without being familiar with all of its intricate workings. (If you do want to learn more about it, check out http://www.microsoft.com/oledb/.)

RDS 1.5

Of the four UDA components discussed, the only two that are directly accessible through the Toolbox controls are ADO and RDS. RDS is most useful for three-tiered applications—especially Web-based, three-tiered applications.

Three-tier architecture describes the distribution of application processing across the following three tiers:

- **Client tier (for example, a user's machine)**
- **Middle tier (such as Microsoft Transaction Server or an ActiveX DLL)**
- **Data source tier (such as an SQL Server)**

When developing networked applications, reducing bandwidth is always a priority. If you are designing an Internet application, and one of your Web pages contains controls bound to a data source, you wouldn't want your application to contact the data source tier across the network every time the user scrolls from record to record. RDS allows this information to be cached, either at the middle tier or at the client tier. This minimizes use of bandwidth, and thus speeds up execution.

RDS operates "on top" of ADO to negotiate the relationship with the data provider. While ADO works with a "live" connection to the data, RDO works with data that is disconnected and cached, either at the client or the middle tier.

You don't have to worry about distributing RDS to your users, as long as they are using Internet Explorer 4 or higher. (When users install Internet Explorer 4 on their machines, they also install the RDS client automatically.)

FROM THE CLASSROOM

Microsoft Universal Data Access Strategy

Microsoft has presented developers with a cohesive strategy for accessing information throughout the enterprise, from the desktop to enterprise server environments. Microsoft's universal data access uses OLE DB as its low-level data access interface. For developers weaned on OBDC, OLE DB provides access to relational and nonrelational data. Contrary to competing forms of universal storage, OLE DB allows user access to data where it resides, avoiding the need to move the data into a single storage source.

OLE DB providers form the basis for simultaneous access to heterogeneous data sources. OLE DB provides for accessing VSAM, AS/400, and IBM AIX, and more are under development. Microsoft's next version of SQL Server, version 7, will leverage OLE DB as its native data access interface.

Keep in mind that Microsoft ADO is the high-level data access interface built on top of OLE DB providers. RDO is an object model used for accessing relational data via OBDC.

DAO is an object model for accessing local or SQL data via the Jet engine. All future development should focus on using ADO on top of OLE DB.

ADO is currently shipping version 2. ADO 2 provides numerous new features, including persistent record sets, distributed transactions, and tighter integration with Visual Studio tools like the Data Environment Designer in VB.

The Data Environment Designer provides a highly programmable Design time environment for creating runtime programmatic data access. Data Environment objects can also leverage drag-and-drop operations to automate creation of data-bound controls.

For the exam, be sure to be familiar with the uses of the Data Environment, Data Form Wizard, Data Report Designer, and the ADO object model.

—*Michael Lane Thomas,*
MCSE+I, MCSD, MCT, A+

Connecting to a Data Source

If you have developed database applications in other environments, then you have probably experienced some frustration in working with your data sources. It can take pages and pages of code to read in all the required data, present it to the user for modification, and save it back into the data store.

VB provides a compelling alternative. In a few simple steps, you can take the controls you are familiar with (TextBox, CheckBox, and so on) and enable them to read from, and write to, the database. (This is the same approach described briefly in Chapter 3.)

In order to make this change, we must first connect to a data source. There are two ways of creating this connection:

- Using a DataControl on the form (common in VB version 5 and earlier)
- Using the Data Environment Designer (new in VB version 6)

Although the Data Environment Designer is more powerful, it takes a few extra steps to set up. Therefore, we will first examine the process of connecting to a Data Source using an ADO DataControl, and address the Data Environment Designer later in this chapter.

Bound Controls

When a control is connected to a data source, it is considered bound. Though in a previous code example we used code to manually populate the txtName control with the contents of the LastName field, we could have saved time by using Bound mode instead. This means that we would have instructed the TextBox control to automatically load the contents of the field into the text box, and then automatically save the user's changes back into the database when completed.

In its simplest form, using Bound mode requires only three steps:

1. Drag an ADO DataControl and a text box onto the form.

2. In the DataControl, identify the appropriate database and record source.

3. In the text box, identify the appropriate DataControl and field.

In this section, we will perform the first two steps. (We will perform step 3 in the section "Getting Data from a Connection.")

Before proceeding, we want to make a copy of the Northwind database, so that we may safely mutilate our own copy to our hearts' content. The location of this database may vary, but it probably will be in a path similar to C:\PROGRAM FILES\MICROSOFT VISUAL STUDIO\VB98\ NWIND.MDB. If it is in another path, use the Windows FIND command to learn its location; if it isn't on your machine, it is available from the VB installation CD-ROM.

Our goal in this exercise will be to create a simple VB program that links to the Northwind database. At the end of the exercise, you will be able to see how many records are in the Employees table, but you won't be able to see the records themselves.

EXERCISE 4-1

Creating a Program to View Data in the Northwind Database

1. Create a new directory on your hard disk: **C:\VBDEMO**. (If you choose to use a different path, make sure you use that directory for all future references where appropriate.)

2. Create a new VB application and save the project and form into your new directory. (You can accept the default project and filenames provided. In a real application, you would want to name your forms and controls according to your internal naming standards; but for the exercises in this chapter, we will be accepting the defaults in most cases.)

3. Copy the original NWIND.MDB into your new VBDEMO directory and rename it NWINDTEST.MDB.

4. Drag an ADO DataControl onto your form. Note that the default name is AdoDC1. (If you do not have this control available in your Toolbox, add Microsoft ADO Data Control 6.0 (OLEDB) from the Components menu. Do not confuse this control with the intrinsic Data control. The ToolTip over the control should be Adodc, not Data.)

5. Right-click the ADO DataControl and select ADODC Properties. From the General tab, click the Build button. On the Provider tab, select Microsoft Jet 3.51 OLE DB Provider; and from the Connection tab, enter **C:\VBDEMO\NWINDTEST.MDB**. (Together, this should populate the ConnectionString property.)

6. On the RecordSource tab, select the Command Type: 2 - adCmdTable and select the table Employees. (Note that VB provides you with a list of all the tables.) Click OK to return to the form.

7. Under the MoveComplete event of AdoDc1, add the following line of code:

```
AdoDc1.Caption = AdoDc1.Recordset.AbsolutePosition
```

8. Under the Load event of AdoDc1, add the following line of code:

```
AdoDc1.Recordset.MoveLast
```

9. Run the program. Note that the number 9 appears on the caption of the ADO DataControl. (During runtime, the AbsolutePosition property describes the ordinal position of the current record within the record set.)

10. Click the Move Last button (the rightmost button) on the ADO DataControl. Note that the number 9 should now appear on the caption.

11. Exit the application. Save all the files in the project, because the next exercise will build on this one.

If you're the kind of user who likes to click every button to see what you can break (you know who you are!), you've probably clicked the other buttons and seen how they provide navigation among the eight employee records.

on the **job**

Some databases (such as FoxPro) require you to connect to a directory. Unlike an Access database, which stores all the tables and indexes entirely contained in a single file, a FoxPro database is made up of a different file for each table and index in the database. Therefore, when selecting the location of the FoxPro database, instead of selecting a file, you will be selecting the directory where all of the resources reside.

Data Properties for Data Controls

Previously, we observed how to set the needed DataControl properties to connect to a data source. The three most important properties to support this process are ConnectionString, CommandType, and RecordSource.

ConnectionString

This property defines the location of the data source. Unfortunately, the contents used for this property vary greatly. When you use VB to populate this property, you are provided three options as shown in Figure 4-1.

Here are the options in ascending order of complexity.

- **ODBC Data Source Name**   The simplest option is to point to a previously created DSN on the local machine. Of course, this doesn't eliminate the work needed to create the connection; it just means it is created through the ODBC Control Panel instead. For example: DSN = Nwind.

- **Connection String**   The information stored in a DSN is just a concatenated list of needed parameters. Instead of pointing to a DSN to reference these parameters, it is possible simply to list the properties themselves. For example: ODBC;DSN=PubsSQLDB; UID=sa;PWD=Fnord, or Provider=Microsoft.Jet.OLEDB.3.51; Persist Security Info=False;Data Source=C:\VBDEMO\ NWINDTEST.MDB.

- **Data Link File**   Instead of specifying a DSN, or all the parameters required for a DSN, it is possible to point to a data-link file (extension UDL) that contains the needed parameters. In this way, it bears some similarities to a File DSN, but the contents of the file are not stored in a human-readable form. Also, the information in the UDL file is oriented more toward using OLE DB. For example: FILE NAME=C:\PROGRAM FILES\COMMON FILES\SYSTEM \OLE DB\DATA LINKS\MYDATALINK.UDL.

Three options to set the
ConnectionString property

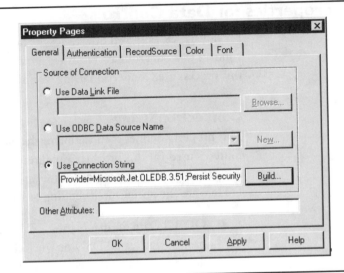

CommandType

The default for this property is 8 - adUnknown, but you will probably want
to change it to 1 - adCmdText (retrieve content using an SQL Statement),
2 - adCmdTable (retrieve an entire table), or 4 - adCmdStoredProc (retrieve
content as defined in a stored procedure). Note that stored procedures are
often more efficient than defining a query with adCmdText because, with
stored procedures, the database can preprocess the procedure, and execution
can be faster. However, you do need additional access rights on the database
to create new stored procedures.

RecordSource

Depending on the contents of CommandType, the RecordSource property
will be used to store the name of the stored procedure or table in the
database (for example, "Employees") or the SQL required for creating the
record set (for example, "select * from Employees").

It is necessary to set the properties ConnectionString, CommandType,
and RecordSource for every instance of the ADO DataControl used, but
the defaults for the other properties will frequently be acceptable. (More
information about these other properties is provided later in this chapter.)

Getting Data from a Connection

After completing the steps in Exercise 4-1, you can navigate back and forth among the employee records, but you can't actually see any of the underlying content. Many of the controls included with VB can be bound, and many third-party controls have this capability as well. (To determine if a control can be bound, see if it has a Data section when the properties are categorized.)

In Exercise 4-1, we used the ADO DataControl to connect to the Employee table of the Northwind database. In Exercise 4-2, we will illustrate how easy it is to bind controls to this DataControl by setting the DataSource and DataField properties.

EXERCISE 4-2

Binding Text Boxes to the Employee Table

1. Confirm that Exercise 4-1 has been completed successfully.

2. Drag three text boxes onto the form (the default names should be Text1, Text2, and Text3).

3. For all three newly created text boxes, set the property DataSource to point to the control we created in the previous section, AdoDc1. (You can select this value from the drop-down list.)

4. On the control Text1, set the DataField property to LastName.

5. On the control Text2, set the DataField property to FirstName.

6. On the control Text3, set the DataField property to BirthDate.

7. Add three labels next to the three text boxes, and set their captions to Last Name, First Name, and Birth Date, respectively.

8. On the control AdoDc1, set the EOFAction property to 2 - adDoAddNew. (This allows the user to create a new record without a code.)

9. Run the application. The screen should resemble the following illustration.

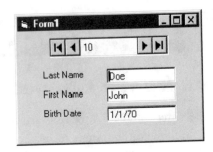

10. Scroll through the records and observe the values updating in the text boxes.

11. Scroll to the last record by clicking the rightmost button. The value of the LastName should be Dodsworth.

12. Scroll to the next record (second button from the right). All three fields should go blank.

13. In the three text fields, enter the following three values, in order: Last Name—**Doe**, First Name—**John**, Birth Date—**1/1/1999**. Scroll to the previous record (second button from the left). An alert should appear: "Birth Date can't be in the future." (This validation is programmed in the database itself, but VB is able to present this database error message directly to the user.)

14. Click OK, and replace the date with **1/1/1970**. Scroll to the previous record again. (The reason we are scrolling is because the validation occurs when you exit a record. This is the default behavior, but it can be changed.) This new data should be accepted into the table. If you scroll back and forth, you will now see your new content displayed just like the other records.

15. Scroll back to your new record, and replace the date with the text string **Not a date**. Scroll to the previous record. The application should report that it cannot accept this text data into a date field. (Low-level data type validation is performed by the database, and then reported back to VB.)

16. Exit the application. Save all the files in the project so they can be used for the next exercise.

As the preceding exercise should make clear, it is possible to create a simple application with very little work, if you are willing to accept the default behavior provided by VB and the underlying database.

Data Properties for Bound Controls

In this chapter, we have observed how to set properties to enable controls to bind to a data source. The four properties most frequently involved are DataSource, DataField, DataMember, and DataForm.

- **DataSource**   This can point either to a DataControl or a Data Environment. All of the Data Environments and all of the DataControls on the current form will appear in this property list, but not the DataControls on other forms.

- **DataField**   This determines which field from the DataSource or DataMember will be bound to the control.

- **DataMember**   When using the Data Environment Designer, this property defines the DECommand within that designer. When using a Data Control, this property is not used.

- **DataFormat**   This determines how to display the content of the field. (It is often not necessary to set this field.)

When using a DataControl it is necessary to set DataSource and DataField. When using the Data Environment Designer it is necessary to set DataSource, DataField, and DataMember.

In the examples in this section, we have bound controls to the DataControl at Design time. However, when using VB version 6, it is also possible to bind a control to a data source at runtime. (For example, we could have two separate connections, and a text box could switch back and forth, depending on user preferences.) Note that this was not an option in previous versions of VB.

Using Other Data-Bound Controls

You are not limited to the TextBox control when binding to a data source. A majority of the Microsoft intrinsic controls, and several nonintrinsic controls, support data binding. Some of these controls, and the issues involved in using them, are discussed in this section.

Note that this is not a comprehensive list of the available controls by any means. This section only covers the controls that support binding for the controls that are intrinsic to VB 6, and a few of the more common nonintrinsic data-bound controls. In order to observe these nonintrinsic controls, you must have the corresponding items enabled from the Components dialog box (as shown in Figure 4-2). Many third-party controls also support data binding. For details on their operation, consult the documentation supplied by the vendor.

TextBox and Label

In this chapter, we have already demonstrated the techniques required to bind a text box to a DataControl. Binding a Label control uses an identical process, except that it is the Caption property, not the Text property, that automatically binds to the field. (Note that as a rule, the property binding to the Database field is the same as the default property for that control.)

Although labels are, by their nature, not editable from the user interface, it is still possible to use them to update a database. If a Label control is

---

FIGURE 4-2

The Components dialog box—adding nonintrinsic controls

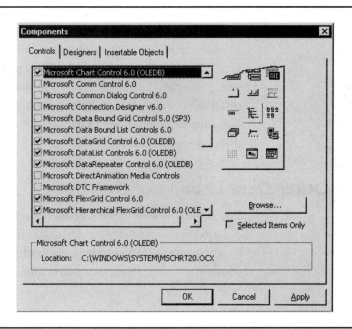

bound, and if the Caption property is modified programmatically, the new Caption value can be saved into the database.

CheckBox

Remember that the check box doesn't have two states, it has three: checked, unchecked, and grayed. You can usually bind a check box to your database's equivalent of a Boolean field, but the precise behavior may vary slightly from database to database. If you find that your results are unsatisfactory, consider using a combo box with Yes/No options bound to a text field or, alternatively, leaving the CheckBox control unbound and manipulating it with code instead.

PictureBox, Image, OLE

These controls allow you to view Binary Large Objects that are stored in a database. The PictureBox and Image controls can only be used with standard VB graphic types (BMP, ICO, WMF, GIF, or JPG). By contrast, the OLE control can be used with a much wider variety of graphic and document formats.

ComboBox, DataCombo, ListBox, and DataList

Distinguishing among these four controls is a cause of endless confusion, both in real-world development and on the exam. We will focus our discussion on the distinction between the ComboBox and the DataCombo, but you can apply the same principles to ListBox and DataList. (For an explanation of the distinction between the ComboBox and ListBox controls, refer to Chapter 3.)

A combo box binds to a DataControl exactly like a text box does, and with the same results: the Value field reads from and writes to the field specified in DataField and DataSource. The developer is still responsible for populating the List field manually to provide the options available for the Value field.

All that is added in DataCombo (and DataList) is the automated population of these lists. A separate DataControl needs to be created and referenced in the RowSource property of the DataCombo control, and the field to load needs to be referenced in the BoundColumn property. This can be disorienting, but Table 4-1 should clarify the issue.

TABLE 4-1		Field Populated	DataControl Name	DataControl Field
Fields Used in DataCombo and DataList	**Bound Field**	Value	DataSource	DataField
	Picklist Values	List	RowSource	BoundColumn

Note that it is conceivable that the DataSource and RowSource could refer to the same control, if you wanted a list to provide the values already entered in that field. However, in a majority of cases, the RowSource will be pointing to an entirely different table or query.

Value, DataField, and DataSource apply to most data-bound controls, but List, BoundColumn, and RowSource apply only to the population of the lists in the DataCombo and DataList controls.

DataGrid

A DataGrid is a very powerful way to create a lot of functionality very quickly. This control provides a direct exposure to all of the data defined by the DataControl in a spreadsheet format. Although the compact format sometimes can be disorienting to an end user, data grids are popular for presenting data for navigational or summary purposes.

Although a data grid has a DataSource property, unlike the controls listed earlier, it has no DataField property (or, more precisely, there are several DataField properties that are assigned to the specific columns inside the grid).

If you go back to the form created in Exercise 4-1, you can bind a new grid with the following steps:

1. Drag a DataGrid control onto the form (if it is not available in the Toolbox, add it from the Components dialog box).

2. While the grid is selected, press F4 (Properties) and change DataSource to AdoDc1. (If you select Properties from the right-click contextual menu, you will instead see the tabbed Property box.)

3. Right-click the DataGrid, and select Retrieve Fields. (When you retrieve fields, you copy the definition of each column currently defined in the record set into a corresponding column in the grid. These become the defaults for each column, but it is easy to override these definitions.)

4. Run the application. You should see a grid containing all the records and fields in the Employee table.

Though the appearance may look a little clumsy, these grids are easy to customize. If you stop the application and right-click in the data grid to investigate the properties available, you will see how easy it is to change the appearance of the grid—for example, making certain columns wider, locked, or invisible. Here are some of the more frequently used properties:

- **At the grid level** Caption, AllowAddNew, AllowDelete, ColumnHeaders, BorderStyle

- **At the split level** AllowRowSizing, RecordSelectors, MarqueeStyle, ScrollBars, AllowFocus (Splits are columns grouped together.)

- **At the column level** Caption, DataField, DataFormat, Alignment, Width, WrapText, Locked, Button

The full feature set of the data grid exceeds the scope of our discussion here, but you may want to browse through the various tabs of the DataGrid control to familiarize yourself with the options available before taking the certification exam. (If you like the functionality available in the data grid, you may want to investigate purchasing True DataGrid, manufactured by Apex, at www.apexsc.com/. The grid provided for free within VB is a simplified version of Apex's commercial product.)

We will observe an example of a form with a data grid on it, in the section of this chapter called "Creating Data-Bound Forms Using the Data Form Wizard."

MSHFlexGrid

The MSHFlexGrid control allows the user to visually sort, format, and combine summary and detail database content. There are two major differences between the MSHFlexGrid and the DataGrid:

- The data grid is read/write, and the MSHFlexGrid is read-only.

- While the data grid presents all data in a simple static matrix, the MSHFlexGrid can respond to user interaction to alter its presentation.

DataRepeater

The DataRepeater control allows multiple iterations of another control to be displayed in the space defined by the DataRepeater control. The control to be repeated should be populated into the RepeatedControlName property (for example, with MSCAL.Calendar.7 or with RICHTEXT.RichTextCtrl.1). This control is new in VB 6.

Chart

Although the more common use for this control is to programmatically populate it with data points, it is possible to bind this control and present the retrieved record set as a graph.

CERTIFICATION OBJECTIVE 4.04

Organizing Data

Microsoft provides a variety of tools in VB to view and manipulate your connections to your data sources. We will discuss three of them in this section:

- Data Environment Designer
- Data View Window
- Query Builder

Using the Data Environment Designer to View the Structure of a Database

In Exercises 4-1 and 4-2 we used a DataControl, but for the remainder of this chapter, we will use a new feature in VB 6 called the Data Environment Designer.

Using Data Environment Designer has many advantages over using form-based DataControls:

■ It segregates the complexity of database operations from your form code.

■ It enables a drag-and-drop interface with forms and DataReports.

■ It integrates with other Visual Studio tools.

■ It facilitates distribution of database connections across applications and among developers.

■ It permits more control over the formatting of the bound fields .

■ It allows multiple forms to access data in the same way.

The Data Environment Designer allows you to create and manipulate the following objects:

■ **DataEnvironment**   This is the highest-level object in the designer, but it really is only used to group the other content; it isn't used for programming.

■ **DEConnection**   This determines which database will be used, how the database will be accessed, and with what permissions.

■ **DECommand**   This is the actual definition of the data accessed within the DEConnection. It can refer to a table, an SQL statement, or a stored procedure.

Converting an Application from DataControls to DECommands

Because the Data Environment Designer didn't exist before VB version 6, you are likely to encounter DataControls if you are working on legacy applications. If you have to provide support for these existing applications, you can continue to use DataControls; but to take advantage of the newest Microsoft technologies, you will have to convert your application to support the Data Environment Designer. In Exercise 4-3 we will perform this conversion on the project built in Exercises 4-1 and 4-2.

EXERCISE 4-3

Converting from DataControls to Data Environment Designer Controls

1. Open the existing application, run it, and scroll back and forth to confirm that everything is still functioning. Stop the application. Delete the existing DataControl.

2. Select Project | More ActiveX Designers | Data Environment. Observe the DataEnvironment1 window that appears.

3. On the Provider tab, select Microsoft Jet 3.51 OLE DB Provider. Right-click Connection1 and select Properties to bring up the Data Link Properties window. (In some configurations, this window may come up automatically when creating a Data Environment.)

4. On the Connection tab, select the path to the database. (It should be in the VBDEMO directory.) Click Test Connection and confirm that your test connection succeeded. (The other options on the Connection and Advanced tabs are used for more sophisticated database operations.) Click OK.

5. Click the Add Command button. Right-click the newly created Command node (Command1) and select Properties. (Again, this window may automatically be displayed on creation of a new command.)

6. Set Database Object to Table and Object Name to Employees. Click OK.

7. Return to Form1. For each of the bound controls, change the DataSource to DataEnvironment1, and DataMember to Command1.

8. Run the application. The first record (Nancy Davolio) should appear on the form, but notice that there is no longer a navigation device on the form itself)

Your application is now connected to your database through the Data Environment Designer.

DEC Features

If you return to the Data Environment Controller you created, you will observe many more features available. Among other things, you will be able to:

- Define the access rights available for each DEConnection. The access rights are as follows: Read, ReadWrite, Share, Deny None, Share Deny Read, Share Deny Write, Share Exclusive, and Write. The default behavior is Share Deny None.

- Create DECommands under the DEConnection; these allow more detailed actions to be stored and distributed. The tabs containing the properties that can be modified are General, Parameters, Relation, Grouping, Aggregates, and Advanced. (The Grouping tab is shown in Figure 4-3.) You can also add child DECommands that nest under the existing DECommands.

- Change the default control mapping used to represent the DECommand field when dropped onto a form, under Options. (The default for all fields is a text box, except for the following two: Boolean is a check box, and a Caption is a label.)

FIGURE 4-3

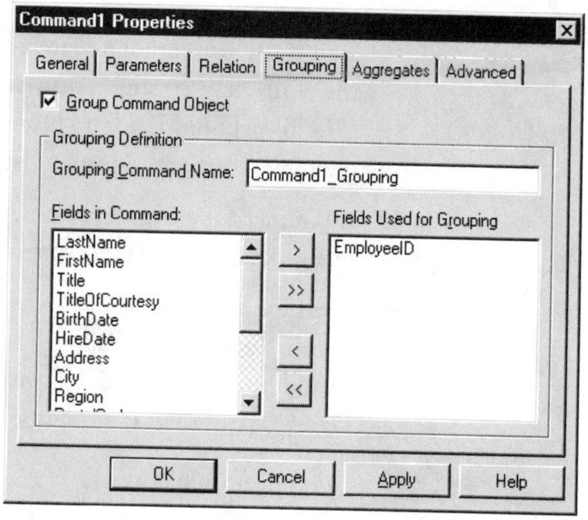

Setting properties for a DECommand on the Grouping tab

- Arrange the content by DEConnections, or by Objects. (Their relationship is hierarchical, but not permanent. Using the General tab of the Property dialog box, you can assign an existing DECommand to a new DEConnection.)

- Write VB code for the associated events at the DataEnvironment, DEConnection, or DECommand level.

The properties associated with the DEConnections and the DECommands will be discussed in the section of this chapter titled "Creating Data-Bound Forms Using the Data Environment Designer."

ADODC vs. DEC

If the Data Environment Designer offers all this, why would anybody ever use the ADODC control? Good question.

Data Environment Connections will eventually replace stand-alone DataControls. When Microsoft introduces a technology that is somewhat redundant to another Microsoft technology, support for the old technology usually withers and dies within a couple of years. (If you doubt me, go have a chat with a crusty old Excel Macro programmer.)

That said, there are some legitimate reasons for continuing to use DataControls, at least for a while:

- The configuration of a DataControl is slightly quicker than the equivalent configuration of a Data Environment Designer DEConnection. If you're building a very small application, you may save some development time.

- If you need a navigation mechanism on your form anyway, there's one built into the DataControl.

- Even for developing new forms, you may be able to find a lot of code that has been developed using DAO and RDO DataControls, and it would be slightly easier to convert that code to support an ADO DataControl than it would be to support DECommands.

■ Because Microsoft has years of experience supporting DataControls, while the Data Environment Designer is a new feature, it is possible that these DataControls may provide more consistent behavior, at least until the third Microsoft service release of VB 6.

UserConnection Designer

The UserConnection designer (available from Project | Add Microsoft UserConnection) is a simpler version of the Data Environment Designer, intended for developers who are still supporting RDO applications. Because Microsoft recommends using ADO for new development, it is unlikely that this designer would be used frequently, except for legacy applications. It is not on Microsoft's exam outline and is only mentioned here to put it in proper context.

Using the Data View Window to View the Structure of a Database

At first blush, it can be hard to tell the difference between the Data Environment Designer and the Data View window, both of which are new in VB 6. They both appear to be hierarchical lists of the tables and fields available to your application.

The primary distinction is that the Data Environment Designer interacts much more closely with your application, while the Data View Window interacts more directly with the databases. From the Data Environment Designer, you can drag fields onto a form; but from the Data View window, you can view the structure of the underlying tables using the Database Designer. It is also possible to drag items from the Data View window to the Data Environment Designer, but not vice versa.

on the
◊ o b

You can drag from the Data View window to a DataEnvironment Designer, and you can drag from a DataEnvironment Designer to a form or DataReport; but you cannot drag from the Data View window to a form or DataReport.

The Data View window provides an excellent summary of your data resources. In addition to allowing the user to view DEConnections from multiple DataEnvironments, it also allows drag-and-drop access to the DataEnvironment connectors.

Perhaps more valuable, however, is the integration of the Data View window with the Microsoft Visual Database Tools—the Database Designer and the Query Designer. (The Query Designer is discussed in the section "Creating Database Queries Using Query Builder," later in this chapter.)

The Database Designer provides a visual representation of relationships among the tables by creating database diagrams. Unfortunately, these diagrams cannot be used with every database provider. For example, they work with SQL Server databases, but they do not work with Access databases. Similarly, you can create new tables and views from the VB interface when using SQL Server databases, but not with Access databases. (Because our Northwind Access database will not support database diagrams, the screen shots from this section are from the Pubs database that comes with SQL Server.)

A Data View window illustrating this contrast is presented in the following illustration.

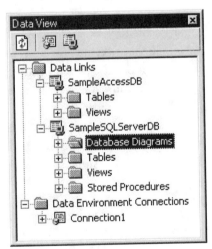

After creating a new Data Link to the Pubs database (right-click Data Links and then choose Add a Data Link), right-click Database Diagrams, and select New Diagram. This presents an empty, white screen. However, if you drag the Authors, Titles, and TitleAuthor tables from the Data View onto the white screen, you will not only see the fields available for these tables, but also the relationships among these tables.

on the **Job**

If you have worked with Access, you may be accustomed to seeing database diagrams that visually represent relationships at the field level. Unfortunately, the diagrams available in VB only represent relationships at the table level. However, you can right-click the link itself to observe which fields are being mapped.

The default behavior is to present the names of the columns only. However, if you right-click within the table in the database diagram, you can choose among these display options: Column Properties, Column Names, Keys, Name Only, and Custom. The properties shown by Custom are selected in Modify Custom View. An example of Column Properties is presented in Figure 4-4. Note that in many cases, the properties of the tables and relationships can be modified as well as displayed.

FIGURE 4-4

Database diagram, with Column Properties for the TitleAuthor table

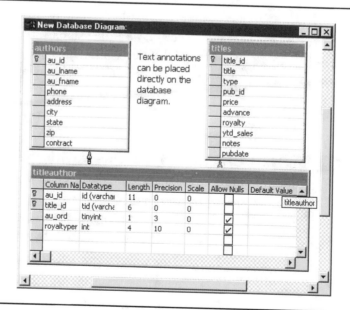

The remaining options available from the Diagram menu are primarily associated with formatting. The diagram in Figure 4-4 includes an example of a text annotation, which can be added by selecting New Text Annotation from the Diagram menu. Other options include

- Displaying labels to identify the relationships
- Viewing and recalculating the page breaks
- Resizing or arranging the tables on the diagram

Creating Database Queries Using Query Builder

If you've worked with other database applications in the past, you've probably worked with SQL statements. It probably wasn't too hard to hand-code simple SQL statements, like the following:

```
Select EmployeeID, Salary from Salaries where Salary < 50000
```

However, it can be difficult to manually construct correct grammar for SQL queries that span multiple tables with complex filtering. Fortunately, Microsoft has provided a visual tool to generate grammatically correct SQL statements automatically from simple parameters defined by the developer. In Exercise 4-4, we are going to use the Query Builder to create the SQL to filter all of the orders taken by employees who live in London. To do this, we will relate the Orders and Employees table using the Set Table Join button, and then apply the appropriate filter on the City field in the Employees table.

EXERCISE 4-4

Creating a New Query with the Query Builder

1. From the Add Ins menu, select Visual Data Manager.

2. From File, select Open Database | Access and browse to the NWINDTEST.MDB database. (Observe that you now can see the available tables in the Database window.)

3. From the Utility menu, select Query Builder.

4. From the table list on the left, select the tables Employees and Orders.

5. Click the table Set Table Joins.

6. From the Join Tables dialog box, highlight the Employees and Orders tables; then select the EmployeeID field in both of the field lists (as shown in the following illustration). Click Add Join to Query, and then Close. Underneath the Set Table Joins button should now appear the relationship Employees.EmployeeID=Orders.EmployeeID.

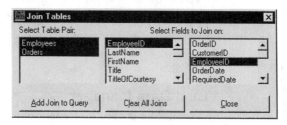

7. In Fields To Show, select the following fields: Employees.EmployeeID, Employees.LastName, Employees.FirstName, Employees.City, Orders.EmployeeID, and Orders.OrderDate.

8. In the three fields at the top of the screen, set Field Name to Employees.City, leave the Operator as =, and set Value to London. Note that in this instance, a list is available if you click List Possible Values after specifying your Field Name.

9. Click And Into Criteria. The following string should now appear in Criteria: Employees.City = 'London'.

10. Set Order By to Employees.FirstName. Your screen should now look like the following illustration.

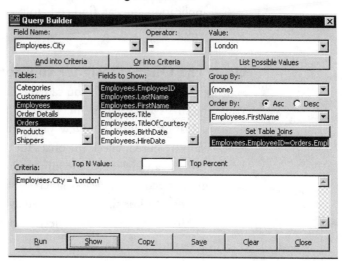

11. Click Run. When asked, confirm that it is not a pass-through query. The name appearing in the first record should be Anne Dodsworth.

12. Click Show. Note that the SQL statement that produced the result appears in a message box.

To use the queries built by this screen, click the Copy button to bring the SQL into the Clipboard. Then the SQL statement is available for use anywhere else in your application (for example, as the RecordSource for a DataControl).

Visual Data Manager

Query Builder is one component of the Visual Data Manager add-in, which is illustrated in Figure 4-5. The Visual Data Manager is not as new as the Database Designer, but it still has the following advantages over its rival:

- You can view and edit the actual data underlying the data source.

- You can use its form builder to automatically create forms based on an underlying database. This is a distinct tool from the Form Wizard, but in some ways it is more flexible.

- The entire Data View tool described earlier is itself programmed in VB, and Microsoft has provided the source code. If you're the kind of developer who learns more from sample applications than from formal documentation, you'll like the fact that in this application you can find code to perform almost every kind of data manipulation imaginable.

Using the Query Designer to Create SQL Statements

Starting with Visual Basic 6, you can also build queries by creating a New View from the Data View menu. To do so, simply drag the desired tables from the Data View into the New View window, create any additional relationships required, check the boxes for the fields you want, specify any needed criteria, and select Run from the Query menu to confirm that the query runs correctly. The resulting screen should resemble Figure 4-6.

The VB test outline mentions the Query Builder, but not the Query Designer. However, even if the Query Designer doesn't appear on your test,

FIGURE 4-5

Using the Visual Data Manager to view table structure

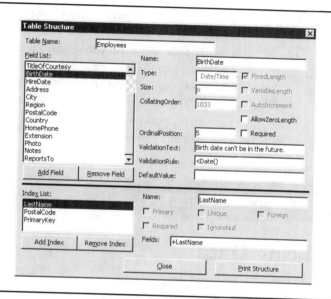

it is still valuable to know what functionality it provides. The Query Designer is a tool intended to create new views to be saved back into the database, but there is no reason you cannot use it to create grammatically correct SQL statements. Just select the SQL statements created, and then copy and paste to where you need them.

FIGURE 4-6

Using the Query Designer to generate SQL

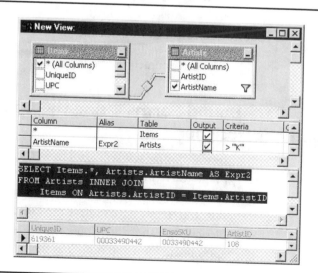

Because the Query Designer view is executing on the server side—depending on what database you are using—the grammar may be slightly different from the grammar used by ADO, RDO, or DAO. Common pitfalls include single versus double quotes, differing characters to indicate wildcards, and different interpretations of the UNIQUE statement. If you use this approach to generate SQL for your code, make sure that you test that the SQL works correctly in your current context.

CERTIFICATION OBJECTIVE 4.05

Presenting Data

Once you have determined and established access to your data sources, it is time to create the connection onto the form. In this section we will be discussing the following approaches to creating the needed forms:

■ Drag-and-drop using the Data Environment Designer

■ Automated form generation using the Data Form Wizard

■ Direct programming using the ADO DataControl

In addition, we will be discussing the Data Report Designer, which allows simple reports to be created and integrated with the Data Environment Designer quickly and easily.

Creating Data-Bound Forms Using the Data Environment Designer

Instead of dragging a control from the Toolbox and then setting its properties to bind to a DECommand, it is possible to automatically drag controls directly from a Data Environment Designer onto the form. To do this, you simply have to have the DECommand in the Data Environment Designer expanded to expose the fields, and then drag the field onto the appropriate form and drop it at the desired location.

This seems very impressive, and it is a nice addition to the development environment; but it is easier to understand what is happening if you realize that VB is simply performing the following three steps that you have already learned:

- Place a Label control on the form and set the Caption property to the field name.

- Place a TextBox control on the form.

- Set the DataField, DataMember, and DataSource properties of the text box to point to the Data Environment Designer.

The bound control is usually a text box, but Boolean and Caption fields have other defaults (CheckBox and Label, respectively). You can change these settings under Options from the corresponding Data Environment.

When using this technique, remember that you have no DataControl on the form, and so you will need to develop your own navigation interface.

Data Environment Designer Properties

Although you can implement a "quick and dirty" application by keeping the property defaults, an understanding of all the properties associated with DEConnection and DECommand is vital for developing more complex applications. Let's examine these properties. (Where applicable, sample values are listed in parentheses.)

DEConnection Properties

The following five properties are grouped under Connection:

- **Attributes**   Determines whether a new transaction is automatically started after the previous transaction is committed or rolled back.

- **CommandTimeout (30)**   The number of seconds to wait for a command to execute before generating an error.

- **ConnectionSource (Provider=...)**   Determines the source for the DEConnection (a connection string, a DSN, or data-link file).

- **ConnectionTimeout (15)** The number of seconds to wait to create a connection before generating an error.

- **CursorLocation (2 - adUseServer)** Determines where the responsibility is for remembering the current record position: with the client application or with the database. Client-side cursors are well suited for smaller ResultSets—they reduce client traffic—while database cursors can improve performance for larger result sets. The default leaves it to ADO to determine which to use.

The following four properties are grouped under Design Authentication:

- **DesignPassword** Password stored during development

- **DesignPromptBehavior (2 - adPromptComplete)** Determines when (and if) user must log on during Design time

- **DesignSaveAuthentication (False)** Determines whether user identification is retained during development

- **DesignUserName** Username stored during development

The following four properties are grouped under Run Authentication:

- **RunPassword** Password used during execution

- **RunPromptBehavior (2 - adPromptComplete)** Determines when (and if) user must log on during execution

- **RunSaveAuthentication (False)** Determines whether user identification is retained during execution

- **RunUserName** Username used during execution

DECommand Properties

The following three properties are grouped under Command:

- **CommandText (Customers)** Name of table, stored procedure, or SQL statement to execute

- **CommandType (2 - adCmdTable)** Determines what the CommandText is requesting (SQL, Table, Stored Procedure, or Unknown)

- **ConnectionName (Connection1)**   Specifies the name of the parent DEConnection

The following nine properties are grouped under Advanced:

- **CacheSize (100)**   Determines how many records are stored in memory at a time.

- **CallSyntax**   Identifies the structure of the CommandText parameter.

- **CommandTimeout (30)**   The number of seconds to wait for a command to execute before generating an error.

- **CursorLocation (3 - adUseClient)**   Determines where the responsibility is for remembering the current record position: with the client application or with the database. Client-side cursors are well suited for smaller ResultSets—they reduce client traffic—while database cursors can improve performance for larger result sets. The default leaves it to ADO to determine which to use.

- **CursorType (3 - adOpenStatic)**   Determines the type of cursor used. See the following section, "Cursor Type Details."

- **GrandTotalName**   Defines name used for record set when aggregated.

- **LockType (1 - adLockReadOnly)**   Determines when the database locks the record content to ensure that other users don't edit the same content—either when users first try to edit the record (2 - Pessimistic) or when they try to save it back to the database (3 - Optimistic and 4 - LockBatchOptimistic).

- **MaxRecords (0)**   Indicates whether there is a maximum number of records to return.

- **Prepared (False)**   Determines whether a command should be precompiled before executing (slows down first execution, speeds up subsequent use).

The makers of the test frequently include questions for which one or more of the answer options are properties or values that don't exist. Even if it isn't possible to memorize all of the terms, try at least to familiarize yourself with them so it is easier to tell when the test authors are pulling your leg.

Cursor Type Details

There are four cursor types. They are, in descending order of flexibility:

- adOpenDynamic
- adOpenKeyset
- adOpenStatic
- adOpenForwardOnly

A dynamic record set allows the user to see all updates made by other users. A keyset record set will be able to see changes to records that existed when the record set was generated, but will not be able to see new records that have been created since then. A static record set is a read-only copy of the record set; forward-only is like static, except the cursor can only move in one direction. These cursor types are compared in Table 4-2.

	Name	Read/Write	Advantages	Disadvantages
TABLE 4-2 Recordset Comparison	Dynamic	R/W	Reflects new and deleted records	Consumes more resources
	Keyset (previously Dynaset)	R/W	Reflects updated records	Does not reflect added or deleted records
	Static (previously Snapshot)	R	Faster performance	Consumes more resources
	Forward-only Snapshots	R	Fastest performance	Cannot move backward

ODBC and Connection Strings

When you use a connection string, you are essentially concatenating multiple parameters required by the database into a single property, separated by semicolons. For example:

```
ODBC;DRIVER=SQL Server;UID=sa;DATABASE=MyDatabase;SERVER=SqlServer65
```

A DSN is very similar to a connection string, storing the same parameters but in a different place—either in the Registry or in a stand-alone file.

There are three types of DSN connections: User, System, and File. These are segregated on the first three tabs on the ODBC Data Source Administrator dialog box, illustrated in Figure 4-7. All three of these DSNs allow similar access to database resources, but they are primarily distinguished by their scope.

- User DSN enables access for the user who is currently logged on.
- System DSN enables access for the users of that computer, and local system services.
- File DSN enables access for any application that can navigate to the current path.

The attributes for the File DSN are stored in a simple text file, so it provides an excellent resource to understand what is going on behind the scenes. (The User and System DSNs are stored in the Registry, so they're a little harder to observe.) If you have created a File DSN, then you can open this DSN as a text file. The DSNs are frequently stored in the directory C:\WINDOWS\ODBC\DATA SOURCES\; but if you have trouble finding this directory on your machine, use the Window Find feature and search on the filename of your File DSN. If you open up your File DSN with Notepad, the content should resemble the following:

```
[ODBC]
DRIVER=SQL Server
UID=sa
DATABASE=MyDatabase
WSID=MARTOMI
APP=Microsoft (R) Developer Studio
SERVER=SqlServer65
```

What this should emphasize is that the DSN doesn't contain mysterious information—just the parameters required to connect to the database.

When you use a connection string, you can either point to a DSN or pass additional parameters in the connection string that identifies the information that would normally be in the DSN. This is called using a DSN-less connection.

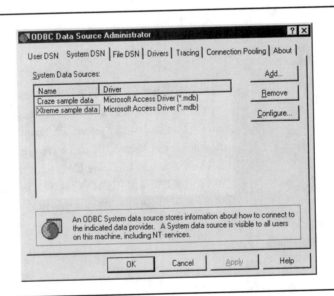

FIGURE 4-7

The System DSN tab of ODBC Data Source Administrator dialog box

Creating Data-Bound Forms Using the Data Form Wizard

The Data Form Wizard has been around for the last several versions of VB; but even though it isn't cutting edge, there are still times where it may be the best choice for form development. Because it creates forms using a one-time wizard, you cannot use this interface to make changes after the initial creation. However, it still may be useful in the following circumstances:

- When you need a "quick and dirty" interface for an application that is needed temporarily

- When you want to see examples of the code to support basic data manipulation

- When you want to develop your own custom forms and you're willing to do your own coding and layout manually, but you want to work from a template to save time

There are several ways to initiate this wizard:

- From Project | Add Form, select VB Data Form Wizard.

- From the Add-In Manager, select VB Data Form Wizard and check Loaded/Unloaded. Now the option Data Form Wizard should be available from the Add-Ins menu.

- From the Visual Data Manager, select Utility | Data Form Designer. This is not exactly the same wizard referenced by the previous two options, but the forms it creates are quite similar.

In Exercise 4-5, we will use the Data Form Wizard to create a data form containing the fields for the Employee record.

EXERCISE 4-5

Using the Data Form Wizard

1. From the Project menu, select Add Form, and then choose VB Data Form Wizard.

2. From the screen labeled Introduction, click Next. Ignore the profile setting. Although we will not be using profiles in this exercise, know that a Wizard Profile (extension RWP) allows you to create many forms with similar appearance and function.

3. From the screen labeled Database Type, select Access (the default). Click Next.

4. From the screen labeled Database, browse to the file C:\VBDEMO\NWINDTEST.MDB. Click Next.

5. From the screen labeled Form, select Master/Detail. Name the form frmEmployee. Select the binding type ADO Data Control. Click Next.

6. From the screen labeled Master Record Source, select Employees as the record source. Copy EmployeeID, LastName, FirstName, BirthDate, HireDate, and City to the left pane. Make EmployeeID the column to sort by. Click Next.

7. From the screen labeled Detail Record Source, select Orders as the record source. Copy OrderID, EmployeeID, OrderDate, RequiredDate, ShippedDate, and ShipName from the left pane to the right pane. Make OrderID the column to sort by. Click Next.

8. From the screen labeled Record Source Relation, select EmployeeID in both the Master and Detail columns. Click Next.

9. From the screen labeled Control Selection, accept all the defaults. Click Next.

10. From the screen labeled Finished, leave the profile name as (None). Click Finish.

11. Under the Project menu, select Project 1 Properties and change the Startup Object to frmEmployee. Click OK.

12. Run the application. Using the DataControl at the bottom of the form, scroll to employee #4 (Margaret Peacock). The lowest number OrderID for Margaret Peacock should be 10250. (The form should resemble the following illustration.)

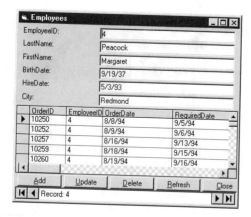

Using the Data Form Wizard, in just a few minutes you can construct a multitable relational interface. But more important, you now have an example that you can extend and customize to meet your specific needs.

Creating Data-Bound Forms Using the ADO DataControl

The approaches to development are somewhat different when using the ADO DataControl. For example, you can't drag bound fields directly onto the form, and you can't refer to the same DataControl from multiple forms.

However, the actual properties associated with the ADO DataControl are remarkably similar to those that are used when developing with the Data Environment Designer. The biggest difference, of course, is that the properties associated with both the DEConnection and the DECommand are rolled up into a single object.

ADO DataControl Properties vs. DEConnection/DECommand Properties

Table 4-3 lists the properties associated with ADO Data Control. As should be clear, most of them map quite closely to the DECommand or DEConnection; though in some cases, the mapping is approximate.

TABLE 4-3

Design Time Properties
for ADO DataControl
and DEConnection/
DECommand

ADO DataControl Properties	DEConnection or DECommand Properties
BOFAction	No exact equivalent
CacheSize	CacheSize
CommandTimeout	CommandTimeout
CommandType	CommandType
ConnectionString	ConnectionSource
ConnectionTimeout	ConnectionTimeout
CursorLocation	CursorLocation
CursorType	CursorType
EOFAction	No exact equivalent
LockType	LockType
MaxRecords	MaxRecords
Mode	No exact equivalent
Password	DesignPassword, RunPassword
RecordSource	CommandText
UserName	DesignUserName, RunUserName

The following properties map less definitively to the Data Environment Designer controls.

- **BOFAction**   Determines the behavior when the user tries to move the current location before the first record in the record set. The options are to reject the user's attempts to reposition, or to accept the attempt but trigger the reposition event on the invalid record.

- **EOFAction**   Is similar to BOFAction, but it applies to attempts to move past the end of the record set. There is a third option for EOFAction, that, instead of generating an error, allows the user to automatically create a new record and begin to populate it.

- **Mode**   Determines whether or not the user has rights to modify data.

✓ TWO-MINUTE DRILL

❑ Universal Data Access (UDA) provides high-performance access to all types of information (including relational and nonrelational data) across an organization from the desktop to the enterprise.

❑ UDA is the union of the following four technologies: ADO (ActiveX Data Objects), ODBC (Open Database Connectivity), OLE DB, and RDS (Remote Data Service).

❑ An ActiveX Data Object behaves like any other object. You invoke its methods, you reference its properties, and you monitor its events.

❑ ODBC is a protocol for using SQL-based relational databases.

❑ VB developers do not have direct access to OLE DB through a supplied control, but it is indirectly available either through ADO or by using an available API.

❑ RDS is most useful for three-tiered applications—especially Web-based three-tiered applications.

❑ Three-tier architecture describes the distribution of application processing across the following three tiers:

    ❑ Client tier (for example, a user's machine)

    ❑ Middle tier (such as Microsoft Transaction Server or an ActiveX DLL)

    ❑ Data source tier (such as an SQL Server)

❑ There are two ways to connect to a data source:

    ❑ Using a DataControl on the form (common in VB version 5 and earlier)

    ❑ Using the Data Environment Designer (new in VB version 6)

❑ When a control is connected to a data source, it is considered bound.

❑ The three most important Data Properties for Data Controls are ConnectionString, CommandType, and RecordSource.

❑ Many of the controls included with VB can be bound, and many third-party controls have this capability as well.

❑ The four most frequently involved Data Properties for Bound Controls are DataSource, DataField, DataMember, and DataForm.

❑ A majority of the Microsoft intrinsic controls, and several nonintrinsic controls, support data binding.

❑ Value, DataField, and DataSource apply to most data-bound controls, but List, BoundColumn, and RowSource apply only to the population of the lists in the DataCombo and DataList controls.

❑ Using Data Environment Designer has many advantages over using form-based DataControls.

❑ The Data Environment Designer interacts much more closely with your application, while the Data View Window interacts more directly with the databases.

❑ Microsoft has provided the visual tool Query Builder to generate grammatically correct SQL statements automatically from simple parameters defined by the developer.

❑ Data Report Designer allows simple reports to be created and integrated with the Data Environment Designer quickly and easily.

❑ It is possible to automatically drag controls directly from a Data Environment Designer onto the form.

❑ Although you can implement a "quick and dirty" application by keeping the property defaults, an understanding of all the properties associated with DEConnection and DECommand is vital for developing more complex applications.

❑ The Data Form; Wizard has been around for the last several versions of VB; but even though it isn't cutting edge, there are still times where it may be the best choice for form development.

❑ The approach to development is somewhat different when using the ADO DataControl. For example, you can't drag bound fields directly onto the form, and you can't refer to the same DataControl from multiple forms.

SELF TEST

The following questions will help you measure your understanding of the material presented in this chapter. Read all the choices carefully, as there may be more than one correct answer. Choose all correct answers for each question.

1. Which of the following are components of Microsoft's Universal Data Access? (Choose all that apply.)

    A. ADO

    B. ODBC

    C. ODBE DB

    D. OLE DB

    E. RDOC

    F. RDS

2. Which of the following ODBC drivers are supplied with VB version 6?

    A. Access

    B. FoxPro

    C. ISAM

    D. Oracle

    E. SQL Server

    F. Text files

3. Which of the following is **not** an advantage of OLE DB?

    A. It is easier to decentralize database processing.

    B. It is relatively easy for VB programmers to program using the OLE DB object model.

    C. Its implementation architecture is more open than ODBC.

    D. Unlike ODBC, OLE DB allows the developer to pass SQL statements to the database.

4. Which of the following are controls included with VB version 6? (Choose all that apply.)

    A. ADO Data Control 6 (OLEDB)

    B. ODBC Control 6

    C. OLEDB Data Control 6 (ADO)

    D. RemoteData Control 6

    E. Universal Data Access Control 5

5. Which of the following would be least likely to be used with a VB application that used a database that resided on the user's own hard disk?

    A. ADO

    B. ODBC

    C. OLE DB

    D. RDS

6. Which of the following properties would contain a 3 when the user was on the third record in the record set?

    A. AbsolutePosition

    B. Bookmark

    C. CursorLocation

    D. Index

7. What are the three options available from the ADO Data Control General Property Page to populate the ConnectionString property? (Choose all that apply.)

A. Use Connection String

B. Use Data Link File

C. Use Database Link File

D. Use ODBC Data Source Name

E. Use RecordSource Name

8. What is an advantage of using adCmdStoredProc instead of adCmdText?

    A. Stored procedures support SQL, while this is not an option when using adCmdText.

    B. Stored procedures are supported by more database vendors than is the use of adCmdText.

    C. Using a stored procedure allows the command to be precompiled by the database and facilitates faster execution.

    D. You don't need as many database access rights to use stored procedures as you would need when using adCmdText.

9. Of the following options, which one best describes the ADO DataControl properties that always have to be set to access a data store?

    A. ConnectionString

    B. ConnectionString and RecordSource

    C. ConnectionString, RecordSource, and CommandType

    D. ConnectionString, RecordSource, CommandType, and Mode

10. You have two forms in your project. On Form 1 you have two data controls, on Form 2 you have one more, and you have three data environments. You add a text box to Form 1 and select the list for the DataSource property. How many items are available from the list?

    A. None

    B. One

    C. Two

    D. Five

11. For most controls (TextBox, CheckBox, and so on) what properties, at a minimum, must be set to bind a field?

    A. DataSource

    B. DataSource and DataField

    C. DataSource, DataField, and DataMember

    D. DataSource, DataField, DataMember, and DataFormat

12. When can you bind a DataControl to data sources?

    A. Runtime only

    B. Design time only

    C. Runtime or Design time

13. In general, which control property contains the value that is bound to the field?

    A. The Bound property

    B. The Data property

    C. The Value property

    D. The default property for the control

14. Which of the following data-bound controls can never update content to the database? (Choose all that apply.)

A. Chart

B. DataGrid

C. DataList

D. Label

E. MSHFlexGrid

F. TextBox

15. You have two combo boxes on a form—one ComboBox and one DataCombo. Of the following options, which properties are available for the DataCombo that are not available for the ComboBox?

A. DataField and BoundColumn

B. DataSource and DataField

C. DataSource and RowSource

D. RowSource and BoundColumn

16. Which of the following properties can be set for a single column in a DataGrid? (Choose all that apply.)

A. AllowRowSizing

B. Caption

C. ColumnHeaders

D. DataField

E. Format Type

17. Select the best definition of what functionality the DataRepeater allows.

A. It allows itself to be presented several times within the space defined by another control.

B. It allows multiple instances of another control to be displayed within the space defined by the DataRepeater control.

C. It allows the user to repeat the content available in a data source across a wide variety of different controls.

D. It allows the user to visually sort, format, and combine summary and detail database content.

18. What objects are available from within the Data Environment Designer? (Choose all that apply.)

A. DataControl

B. DataEnvironment

C. DataView

D. DECommand

E. DEConnection

F. DEControl

19. Which of the following are not access permissions available from the Advanced tab of the Data Links Property dialog box? (Choose all that apply.)

A. Exclusive

B. None

C. Read

D. ReadWrite

E. Share Deny None

F. Share Deny Read

G. Share Deny ReadWrite

H. Share Deny Write

I. Share Exclusive

J. Write

20. Which of the following are tabs that exist under the Command Properties dialog box? (Choose all that apply.)

A. Aggregates
B. DesignPassword
C. General
D. Parameters
E. Public
F. Relation

21. Which of the following have a text box as the default field type mapping in the Data Environment Designer? (Choose all that apply.)

A. Binary
B. Boolean
C. Caption
D. Integer
E. Variant

22. Which of the following are groupings offered in the Data Environment Designer? (Choose all that apply.)

A. Arrange by Commands
B. Arrange by Connections
C. Arrange by Data Environments
D. Arrange by Objects

23. Drag-and-drop operation is supported from the Data Environment Designer to which of the following? (Choose all that apply.)

A. Data Report
B. Data View Window
C. Form
D. Visual Data Manager

24. Which of the following actions can you perform from the Database Designer accessible through Data View?

A. Edit the structure of an Access database.
B. Edit the structure of a SQL Server database.
C. Edit the data in an Access database.
D. Edit the data in a SQL Server database.

25. What option do you choose from Query Builder to define which fields should link between two tables?

A. The Foreign Key button
B. The Relate Tables button
C. The Set Table Joins button
D. The Tables button

26. How do you get the SQL created by the Query Builder into an application?

A. Use the Copy button to bring the SQL into the Clipboard, and then paste the SQL in the appropriate location in your application.
B. Use the Create button to generate a form and all the needed bound controls to bind to the SQL statement.
C. Use the Export button to automatically create a DataControl that uses the query as its record source.
D. Use the SQL button to save the content to the SQL Designer.

27. Which DEConnection property determines if the record location is maintained on the server or on the user's machine?

A. CurrentLocation
B. CursorLocation
C. IndexLocation
D. PositionLocation

28. What setting for the DECommand property LockType will automatically lock the row as soon as the user attempts to edit it?

    A. Optimistic

    B. Pessimistic

    C. Safe

    D. Unprotected

29. Which of the following record set types could reflect changes made by other users, assuming other users have created no new records since the record set was created? (Choose all that apply.)

    A. Dynamic

    B. ForwardOnly

    C. Keyset

    D. Static

30. Which of the following record set types usually provides the fastest performance?

    A. Dynamic

    B. Forward-only

    C. Keyset

    D. Static

31. Which of the following terms refers to a DSN that is enabled for the users on a machine, and for all system services on that machine?

    A. Global DSN

    B. System DSN

    C. Universal DSN

    D. User DSN

32. Where can you configure VB to add the command Data Form Wizard to the VB menu?

    A. Add-in Manager

    B. Components

    C. Options

    D. Properties

    E. References

33. Which of the following best describes what a Wizard Profile (RWP) allows you to do?

    A. Add new form layouts to the Data Form Wizard.

    B. Create many forms with similar appearance and function.

    C. Export all the properties of a form to a text file, to enable reuse in other Interdev components.

    D. Re-edit an existing form with the Data Form Wizard.

34. Which of the following Form Layouts does the Data Form Wizard offer? (Choose all that apply.)

    A. DataRepeater

    B. Grid (Datasheet)

    C. Master/Detail

    D. Detail/Master

    E. MS Chart

    F. MS HFlexGrid

    G. Pivot Table

    H. Single Record

35. Which is **not** an advantage to using the ADO Data Control instead of the Data Environment Manager?

    A. A navigation device is built into the Data Control.

    B. Developing with the ADO Data Control is very similar to developing with the DAO and RDO Data Controls from previous versions of VB.

C. It is easy to use the same data control on multiple forms.

D. You need to set fewer properties with the ADO DataControl than you would with the Data Environment Manager.

36. The ADO Data Control contains most of the properties also associated with what other two objects?

A. Data and ADODC

B. DataField and DataSource

C. DataView and Data Environment

D. DEConnection and DECommand

37. Without writing code, which of the following tasks can be performed by clicking the buttons on the ADO Data Connection control?

A. Create a new record.

B. Delete the current record.

C. Move to the first or last record.

D. Move to the previous or next record.

38. Which of the following Data Form Controls can be bound to a DataField in the Detail Section?

A. RptFunction

B. RptImage

C. RptLabel

D. RptPicture

E. RptTextBox

39. Which of the following can be created with the Data Report Designer?

A. A field that displays an image from a database

B. A graph that links to the data

C. A summary field that sums up the contents of a single field

D. A summary field that sums up the contents of two fields

40. Into which areas on a Data Form can you legally drag fields from a Data Environment Designer?

A. Page Header—gray bar

B. Page Header—body

C. Detail—gray bar

D. Detail—body

E. Report Footer —gray bar

F. Report Footer—body

MICROSOFT CERTIFIED SOLUTION DEVELOPER

5

Using Class Modules

One of the biggest mistakes that programmers make is thinking that they can create an application by just jumping into Visual Basic and coding away. This is far from reality. Imagine how reliable a car would be if the auto makers allow people on the line to slap together cars, giving no real thought about design. It's the same with programming. A good chunk of the work you do on any program should be spent on designing the program and thinking about how to best make the program work for your user.

Beyond design issues, this chapter covers—as its title says—class modules. These allow you to create your own components, data sources and consumers, which you can add to your VB project. In doing so, you're getting into the meaty part of programming.

Finally, we'll expand on some of the things you learned in Chapter 4, by delving into how to access data from databases. This discussion includes using data consumers, and also using the Recordset object to add, delete, and modify records.

CERTIFICATION OBJECTIVE 5.01

Designing an Application

Before any controls are added to a form, and before any code is written, an application must be designed. This doesn't simply mean choosing the background color or font sizes and styles. It involves deciding and planning the architecture of your application.

In the old days (and today, with bad programming), creating an application was a matter of building one monolithic program. The preferred method these days, however, is breaking your application up into components.

exam
⚠ atch

Microsoft's new MCSD path doesn't include the two Windows Architecture exams. Because these two exams will be retired in 2000, there is a stronger emphasis on design in other Microsoft exams, such as that for Visual Basic 6.0. The material covered in the Windows System Architecture exams still exists, but it is now spread over the Desktop, Distributed, and Analyzing Requirements exams.

When I mentioned components, you probably guessed that this has something to do with ActiveX. If you did, you're right—but there's more to it than that. As we saw in Chapter 3, ActiveX components allow us to split an application so that parts are spread across a network or a computer. We can also use things such as stored procedures, class modules, and so on, to break our application into manageable pieces. In doing so, programmers are able to focus on what they do best, and parts of the application are reusable and accessible to other programs. Using this method of design, you are able to split application design into two main tasks: creating reusable components (ActiveX, stored procedures, and so forth), and integrating those components into your application.

Designing an application in this manner is a matter of organizing or separating an application's requirements, deciding what each component is to do, and deciding what each component requires. This is a conceptual process, and there are a number of conceptual models available to help you with application design. The one that Microsoft recommends is the three-tiered "services model." As its name suggests, the services model organizes your application's requirements into specific services. Typically, such requirements fall into one of the three tiers or categories: user services, business services (and other middle-tier services), and data services.

The top tier of this model is user services. You can associate this category with the user interface, which presents the data to the end user. In other words, this is the compiled program that allows the user to actually view and manipulate data. While it is usually the executable program that the user starts at his or her workstation, it can also be a separate component. For example, if you needed to display financial data, you might use an ActiveX control that can display data in a grid.

The middle tier covers a number of services. For example, one such service might be off-loading graphic-intensive processing to a server, rather than using a workstation's CPU. However, this tier is associated primarily with business services, which applies business rules to tasks that a program performs. An example of this in action is a sales program. The user inputs an order into the program, which then checks the customer's credit limit before adding the order to the customer's account. Here, there is a "business rule" of a customer needing to have enough available credit before new items can be added to his or her account. If there isn't enough credit, the item can't be purchased. You've probably experienced such a program when you tried to charge something on a maxed-out credit card. When such rules are applied to a program, they are done so at the middle tier.

Another example of business services might involve the markup on a product. When a company sells a product, they add to the cost of the product (mark it up) so they make some profit on selling the item. In such cases, there must be a component of the program that looks at how much the company paid for the item, adds the markup, and then produces the selling price. With this business rule, the program is adding a percentage to the original amount. However, the percentage added often changes due to the law of supply and demand. This means the programmer will probably have to change this percentage fairly regularly. Because business rules like this change more often than the actual tasks (in this case, the task of accepting input of an item and returning a price), business tasks are prime candidates for being components of a program. By having such rules incorporated into components, the entire program doesn't need to be changed—just a component of that application.

The final and bottom tier of this model is data services. What this tier does is define, maintain, access, and update data. When business services make a request for data, data services manages and satisfies the request. The ability to manage and satisfy the request can be implemented as part of the database management system (DBMS) or as components.

While the previous discussion explains the levels of the design model, it doesn't explain the stages of the design process. Now that we've gone through how a program can be split into components and what each service is and does, we need to go through the steps of developing such an application. The design process is made up of four stages: conceptual design, logical design, physical design, and deployment.

Conceptual design is the process of identifying an application's requirements. In other words, what is the thing supposed to do? This sounds simple in theory. However, in real life, it can be one of the most frustrating design stages. This stage involves interviewing business owners, managers, and end users to find out what they require from the application.

Unfortunately, you will find that many times the people you interview will forget to mention certain things that they consider essential.

on the
job

It is common for new programmers to neglect design and jump straight into coding. They talk with a manager or owner of a company, and then create the program on the fly. The problem with this is that many problems can be worked out through the design process, which saves you time and frustration in the long run. Also, outline in your contract what you originally agreed upon—that way you can charge for such things as adding spreadsheet functionality to a database.

Logical design is a process that's made up of five activities. Like the other stages of design, each of these parts of logical design are refined and revised as later stages are being worked on. It is not a process that is completed in a single pass.

The first part of logical design is identifying business objects and services. Business objects are abstract representations of real-world things or concepts (such as orders, customers, and so on). Something should be considered a business object if one or both of these things are true:

- It is something (or someone) the system is required to know about. This could be a customer, record number, or other piece of data.

- It is something (or someone) the system gets information from or provides information to. In an example of a travel agency booking program, this could be a reservation agent.

Once the business objects and services are identified, interfaces need to be defined. An interface in this case is simply a statement of preconditions and conventions (syntax, and input and output parameters) needed to call the service. It outlines what is needed to call on that particular component.

Business objects often call on services in other business objects. When this occurs, it is called "business object dependencies." One business object depends on the services of another business object. An example of this would be an order depending on the existence of a customer in a database. Such dependencies need to be identified at this stage. When this is done, validating, refining, and revising the logical design is all that is left.

Validation of the logical design requires a comparison of logical design to the requirements in the original conceptual view. This means assuring that the work done in the logical design stage matches what was originally outlined in the conceptual design. If the requirements are not met, the logical design is invalid and needs to be reworked.

While designing an application isn't completed in a single pass, the logical design stage is no different, and it goes through multiple iterations. Revision and refining the logical design requires problems to be hammered out and the design improved upon. This is the final activity of logical design.

The final two stages of designing an application are physical design and deployment. The physical design takes the business objects and services identified in the logical design and maps them to software components. Once these components have been established, the deployment stage comes into effect. It is here that decisions are made as to how components are or aren't distributed across the network.

It is important to stress that these stages aren't usually completed in a single pass. In most cases, each stage may need to be refined, and revisions will need to be made. Each time, improvements are made upon the previous incarnation. This is a normal occurrence in the four stages.

CERTIFICATION OBJECTIVE 5.02

Assessing the Potential Impact of the Logical Design

No amount of planning and design is complete without considering the impact it will have on your application, your computer system, and (more often than not) a network. While testing after the application is complete is an important part of development, it is equally important to consider what the program will do before coding has even begun. Imagine spending 80 hours coding a project, only to find that it runs too slowly or could have been improved by spending an hour or two considering your initial design!

Basically, the rule of thumb here is trying to get it right the first time. It is easier to improve an application in design than it is after coding. While you'll never get it perfect, there are a number of proven tips and tricks that allow you to improve the performance, maintainability, extensibility, and availability of your application.

on the Job

While there are no hard and fast rules regarding how much time should be spent on planning, there are some estimates on the time that should be spent on each phase of an application's life cycle. On average, you should spend 25% in analysis, 38% in design, 13% coding, 19% testing, and 7% in integration. Again, these are estimates, not laws. There will be times when more or less time is spent in various phases.

Performance

The life of a programmer would be incredibly easier if every user had fast processors, speedy networks, and unlimited hard disk space. At the very least, it would be nice if every user had the same system that the programmer uses to create an application. Unfortunately, this is pure fantasy. Amazingly enough, many programmers do forget that many (if not most) users don't have as good a computer system as the developer has. When the programmer does not take this into consideration, many users of an application wind up being hampered by processor, network, and/or disk space limitations.

As we'll see in Chapter 11, there are ways to optimize your VB application at the end of the development cycle. However, performance really comes into effect during the design stage.

One way you can improve the design of your application is with variables. By putting some thought into the data types you'll use for variables, you can increase the speed of an application and lower the amount of memory required by your application. Different data types use different amounts of memory. A variant uses more than an integer, for example. Also, you can use data types that provide a larger range of numbers than you could possibly need. In the case of a variable used to store a person's age, you would want to use an integer rather than a long.

Performance increases when consideration is given to the data types used in an application.

Because variables have to be looked up each time they're used, constants should be used where they can. Constants are resolved when an application is compiled. By using a constant for something like minimum wage, the application doesn't have to look up what the value of minimum wage is. The value is always the same, so the program's performance increases.

If a number of modules are loaded at startup, the result is a significant slowing of the startup time of an application. Modules should only be loaded on an "as needed" basis. If there are a number of modules that must be loaded at startup, it may be an idea to incorporate a splash screen in your application. You've seen splash screens when you've started VB (it's the form that first starts; it has no controls, and no min or max button). Splash screens let the user know that the application is actually starting, and mask the amount of time it takes to load the program. Such ways of improving the apparent speed of an application are covered in Chapter 11.

Forms are a tricky matter with performance. If all forms are loaded at startup, the application will run faster as it switches from one form to another. However, if your application uses a lot of forms, loading them all can gobble up memory. A rule of thumb is determining which forms will be used commonly during the design stage, and then having the commonly used forms loaded into memory when the application starts. Forms used less often (such as one used for configuring preferences, or "About This Program" forms) should not be loaded at startup.

Reducing the number of controls on a form and carefully choosing what should appear on a form can also improve performance. More controls on a form means more memory will be used by an application. Brevity is the key here. The second part of this issue is choosing what should appear on the screen, and what should be accessed by clicking a "More Information" or "Advanced" command button. An example of this might be a personnel application that allows you to move through information on each employee in a company. While it would be nice to have a picture of each employee appear on the screen, graphics are a well-known memory gobbler. It might also be nice to have everything known about a person appear on the screen at once, but this makes for a slow application. You can increase performance dramatically by designing the application with a command button that

By selecting Project | Add
Class Module, a class
module is added to your
project, and the module's
Code window appears

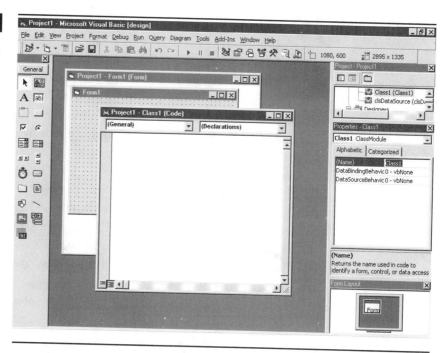

Creating a Class Module

1. Select Project | Add Class Module.

2. From the dialog box that appears, select Class Module.

3. When the class module is created, a Code window for it will appear. In the Properties window, change the Name property to a meaningful, original name.

CERTIFICATION OBJECTIVE 5.04

Using a Class Module

A class module is different from a standard module. In a standard module, there is only one copy of the module's data at any given time. Class modules have one copy of data for each instance of the class, meaning that there is a copy of the data for each object created from the class. The data is handled differently in each type of module.

The second difference between a standard and class module is its scope. A standard module's data exists for the life of the program, while data in a class module exists only for the lifetime of the object. Data in a standard module is always there when the program runs, while the class module's data is created when the object is created and removed when the object is removed.

The third and final difference between these two modules deals with Public variables. When you declare variables as Public in class modules, they are only accessible when object variables contain a reference to an instance of a class. This is different from variables declared as Public in standard modules. In standard modules, Public variables are visible from anywhere in a project.

Class modules can be used to create custom object variable types. While VB comes with a wide variety of built-in controls—like text boxes, combo boxes, command buttons, and so forth—you can use class modules to create your own objects. Like these built-in controls, you can add properties, methods, and events to your own objects.

The big reason to use class modules is that—unless you're creating ActiveX controls or documents—each custom object you create must have a class module behind it. You can think of class modules as the engine that gives your custom object power—no class module, and your custom object won't run.

Creating Instances of Classes or Objects

Creating an instance of a class is done with the Dim keyword . It is important to remember that you can have multiple instances of a class. Another term for an instance of a class is "object." While a class is a template for an object, an object is an instance of a class. In the following example, the objects Test1 and Test2 are objects of type Class1:

```
Dim Test1 As New Class1
Dim Test2 As New Class1
```

The other way to create an object is with the CreateObject function. This creates an instance of a server component, which your application can then call upon. The syntax for creating an object in this manner is

```
Server.CreateObject
```

As we'll see later, there are differences between using these two methods of creating objects.

COM Object-Creation Services

VB always uses COM object-creation services when objects are created from classes provided by other components. There is no difference between using the New operator, declaring a variable As New, and CreateObject when you are creating externally provided objects. This is not to say that there are not differences between these methods of creating objects.

The New operator and variables declared As New create objects that are part of your project. When New or As New are used, VB uses a private implementation of COM. However, when the object is provided by another component, it uses COM object creation services. It uses private object creation when a class is part of your project, and COM creation services when the object is provided externally by another component.

CreateObject always uses COM object creation services. It doesn't matter if the objects created are externally provided or part of your project. As far as the CreateObject function is concerned, no differences exist between an object provided externally or internally.

CERTIFICATION OBJECTIVE 5.05

Designing and Adding Component Properties, Methods, and Events

Creating components is great, but useless if they have no properties, methods, or events. It would be like buying a car that didn't have an engine, wheels, or gas tank; in short, you're not going to get very far without them.

When you create a new class module, it has two events associated with it: Initialize and Terminate. The Initialize event occurs when an instance of a class is created, before any properties are set. It is used to initialize any data used by the class and can be used to load forms used by the class. The Terminate event occurs when the object variable is set to nothing or goes out of scope. The way calling code destroys an object is with the syntax

```
Set Object = Nothing
```

The Terminate event is used to save information, unload forms, and handle any other tasks required to be done when the class ends. As you've probably assumed, Initialize is the first event that occurs between the two, and Terminate comes last.

Events are handled in class modules much the same as they are in built-in objects. By referring to Chapter 3, you can see that the Initialize and Terminate events in a form are identical to what occurs when dealing with these same events in a class. By adding code to such events, you can manipulate how your class module will act, just as you would manipulate the actions of a form.

Adding an event is first done by declaring it in the class module's General Declarations section. To do this, use the following syntax:

```
Public Event Eventname (argument list)
```

In this, *Eventname* is the name you've chosen to call the event, and *argument list* is a list of arguments declared by name and type. The argument list is similar to a list of parameters that you'd use in a regular procedure. If you were going to use an event called LoginName, with an argument of the current user's username, you might declare the following event in the General Declarations section of your class:

```
Public Event LoginName (UserName as String)
```

The code that raises the event, as we'll see in the next code sample, would then pass the value to the argument UserName.

To cause an event to run, you use the RaiseEvent keyword. Assigning a value to a variable then using the RaiseEvent keyword to call the event and pass the variable's value does this. To use our previous example, the LoginName event we created would be raised with the following code:

```
StrName="My Name"
RaiseEvent LoginName (strName)
```

Once a class is created, you can create methods. The methods you create are called in the same manner that you call methods in a standard VB class. Adding methods is done by creating Public procedures in the class module. You can create either subprocedures or functions. Once these procedures are added, other parts of your application, or ActiveX controllers, can call the procedures as methods of the object class. These procedures will appear in the Object Browser, which you can view to see what objects and methods are available for a class.

In addition to creating methods, you can create properties. Custom properties are implemented either as Public variables of the class, or by using the procedures Property Let, Property Set, and Property Get.

Public variables in a class become the properties of the object. Declaring Public variables is done the same way as declaring them in standard modules and forms. If you were going to add a property called UserName to the class, you would add the following code to your class module's General Declarations section:

```
Public UserName as String
```

Once you declare the Public variable, it becomes a property of the object. When the object has been instantiated, your calling code can manipulate the properties. You can then assign and manipulate values and get the values returned to your program. To expand on our previous UserName example, the following code assigns the value "Michael" to the UserName property of an object called Object1:

```
Object1.UserName = "Michael"
```

After doing this, we can create a message box that will display the UserName property of our Object:

```
MsgBox Object1.UserName
```

The other way to create properties is by using property procedures. These allow you to execute a procedure when a value is changed or read, have a property constrained to a small set of values, or expose properties that are read only. Property procedures are created in two parts: one part assigns values to the property, while the other returns its value.

Property Set and Property Let both assign values to a property. The difference between them is that Property Set is used when we are setting the value of an object property. If the property is a reference to an object, Property Set is always used. Property Let, on the other hand, is used for nonobjects like variables.

You can assign object references to an object variable by using the Property Set command. In the following syntax, Property Set is used to set x as a New Class object:

```
Dim x as Class1
Set x = New Class1
```

At this point, you've seen the Property Let statement used without even realizing it. In the early days of VB, you assigned a value to a variable by using the following syntax:

```
Let x=5
```

While the Let statement is still supported in VB, the common way to assign a value to a variable is with the following syntax:

```
x=5
```

You no longer need to explicitly use Let because the Let statement is always called, except in cases where a Set statement is used. VB will call the property procedure that goes with the type of assignment being used—Let for variables and Set for object properties.

There may be times when both Property Let and Property Set would be used. This is done in cases where you set a property that is a reference to an object, and then use Property Let to assign values to its properties, as shown in the following example:

```
Private Amnt As Integer
Dim x As Class1
Set x =New Class1
x.Amnt=13
```

In this example, we create a class module, setting x as a new Class1 object. We also have a property (Amnt) that has an integer value. By using Property Let, the value of 13 is assigned to the Amnt.

Property Get, as its name suggests, executes when the calling code reads the property. Since Property Set and Property Let write to the property, you can create read-only properties by using Property Get without a matching Property Set or Property Let.

To fully understand property procedures, let's work through the following example of code:

```
Private gstrUser As String

Public Property Let UserName (strInput As String)
    gstrUser=Lcase(strInput)
End Property
Public Property Get UserName () As String
    UserName = gstrUser
End Property
```

In the first line, we declare gstrUser as a String (a group of characters not longer than 255 characters in length). We then create our first property procedure. Notice that both the Property Let and Property Get procedures have the same name. You are able to do this because Property Let is writing to the property, while Property Get reads the property. They are not duplicates of one another; they perform different tasks. In the example, Property Let takes the value that our user has input and assigns the value to the variable gstrUser. In the example, Property Let is also converting the characters to lowercase. In the next procedure, Property Get UserName is reading the value of gstrUser and returning it. While Property Let assigns a value of UserName, Property Get is reading and returning the value.

EXERCISE 5-2

Using Class Modules

1. Start a new VB Standard ....EXE project.

2. Select Project | Add Class Module.

3. In the class module's General Declarations section, declare a Public variable called strUser as a string. This is done with the following code:

```
Public strDate As Variant
```

4. In your class module, create a public procedure that will return the the number of days until the millennium. Use the code as follows:

```
Public Function NewMil()
NewMil = "The Millennium is in " & DateDiff("d", Now, strDate) & " days!"
End Function
```

5. Now add a command button to your form, and add the following code. Since some people consider the new millennium to start in 2000, while others consider it to be in 2001, we will create a separate class instance (that is, object) for each. Each object will then return a string that will print the result on your form:

```
Dim Date1 As New Class1
Dim Date2 As New Class1

Date1.strDate = "January 1, 2000"
Date2.strDate = "January 1, 2001"
Print Date1.NewMil
Print Date2.NewMil
```

6. Run your program, click the command button, and test your program.

CERTIFICATION OBJECTIVE 5.06

Designing Visual Basic Components to Access Data from a Database

One of the truly exceptional uses for VB is creating database applications. VB provides a number of controls that specifically deal with creating programs of this type. As we saw in Chapter 4, the Data control allows you

object as an ADO Recordset object, you could use the following code in the General Declarations section of the module:

```
Private rs as ADODB.Recordset
```

After you've declared a Recordset object and used GetDataMember to specify the source of data you'll be using, you're ready to create a new instance of the Recordset object. This is done in the Initialize event of class with the following code:

```
Set rs = New ADODB.Recordset
```

In doing this, a new instance of the Recordset object we've called rs is created.

Following this, you would add code to the Initialize event that would add any necessary properties to your record set. Adding properties to a record set is done in the same manner as adding properties to components. The difference is that when dealing with ADO, you can use a shorthand method to append Field objects. A Field object represents a column of data, which has the same data type. The Fields collection is made up of Field objects and allows you to append Field objects that can be used to show, delete, and manipulate data. The following is an example of adding two different Field objects to the Fields collection:

```
With rs
.Fields.Append "YesNoField", adBoolean
.Fields.Append "MyField", adBSTR
End With
```

In this example, we have added one field that accepts Boolean data, and a second that accepts data of the string type. We can later populate the fields by either assigning information to the field, or having it read the data from a variable. In the next example, the MyField field is assigned a value:

```
Dim x As String
x="Michael"
With rs
        .AddNew
        .Fields.Item("MyField") = x
        .Update
End With
```

In the first and second lines of this example, the variable x is declared as a string, and then assigned the value Michael. The next section of code adds a new field to the Fields collection, assigned the value of *x*, and then updates the record set. In doing this, we have populated the record set with a single record.

Having stepped through how to create a data-bound class object, there is an easier way to create data source class modules. From the Project menu, select Add Class Module and then choose Data Source. This will create a class module that is preconfigured to work as a data source, as illustrated in Figure 5-3. The DataSource class module has its DataSourceBehavior set to vbDataSource and includes a number of comments to help you create a data source class. Not all of the work is done for you, but it does make your work easier.

One of the best ways to learn something is by doing it. In the next exercise, we'll create a DataSource class module. The data source will be

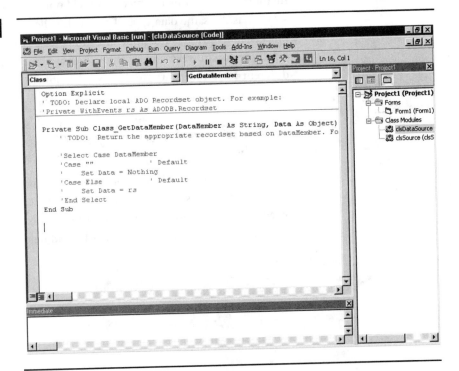

FIGURE 5-3

The DataSource class module

used through all remaining exercises in this chapter. After creating the following exercise, you must create a data consumer to view the results.

Creating a Data Source

1. Open a new Project. Select File | New Project | Standard EXE.

2. Select Project | Add Class Module | Class Module.

3. Rename the Class to "clsSource," and set the DataSourceBehavior property to vbDataSource.

4. Select Project | References. From the list that appears, select Microsoft ActiveX Data Objects 2.0 Library. Click OK to continue.

5. In the class module's General Declarations section, insert the following code:

```
Option Explicit
Private rs As ADODB.Recordset
```

6. In the Class object's GetMemberData event, assign the variable rs to the Data object:

```
Set Data = rs
Dim strPath, strFile As String
Dim count As Integer

strPath = "C:\"
strFile = Dir(strPath, vbDirectory)
```

7. The following code must be placed into the class Initialize event. In this procedure, we must first declare several variables that we'll use shortly, and assign values to these variables.

```
count = 0
```

8. Before using the rs object as a record set, we must create an instance of it and set its properties. An instance of the rs object is created with the Set keyword. Since we're setting more than one property, a With statement can be used to set multiple properties. Place the following code in the class Initialize event of your class module.

```
Set rs = New ADODB.Recordset
    With rs
        .Fields.Append "intRecord", adInteger
        .Fields.Append "strDir", adBSTR
        .Open
    End With
```

9. A database is useless without data. As such, we must populate the record set with data. In this exercise, data will be collected when the class initializes. Because of this, we'll add code that will loop through our hard disk, reading the folders and directories on the disk. Place the following code in the class Initialize event:

```
Do While strFile <> ""
    If strFile <> "." And strFile <> ".." Then
        If (GetAttr(strPath & strFile) And vbDirectory) = vbDirectory Then
        count = count + 1
            With rs
                .AddNew
                .Fields.Item("intRecord") = count
                .Fields.Item("strDir") = strFile
                .Update
            End With
        End If
    End If
    strFile = Dir
Loop
```

10. At the bottom of the Class Initialize procedure, place code that will set the record set to the first record in the record set:

```
rs.MoveFirst
```

Creating a Data Consumer

The first step in creating a data consumer is adding a class module to your project. The property you change to make the class a data consumer is DataBindingBehavior. By changing this property, you're setting whether the class is a data consumer and how it will be bound to the data source. You have three options to choose from: vbNone, vbSimpleBound, and vbComplexBound. If DataBindingBehavior is set to vbNone, you won't be able to set binding to a data source—which means the class won't be a data consumer. If you set the property to vbSimpleBound, the consumer can bind to single fields. If the property is set to vbComplexBound, binding to a rowset can occur.

To actually bind the data in the data source to the consumer, you use the Binding Collection. This is an object that allows you to bind a consumer to the DataSource supplied by the Binding Collection. In other words, the Binding Collection works as a link between the consumer and source, allowing information from the source to be passed to the consumer. Using the Binding Collection allows you to bind data during runtime.

Using the Binding Collection is relatively painless. To add an object to it, you must first create a new instance of the BindingCollection object. After this, the Add method is used, as shown in the following example:

```
Set objBinder = New BindingCollection
objBinder.Add objConsumer, "Name", "strDir"
```

In the first line, a new instance of the BindingCollection object is created and called objBinder. We then add an object to objBinder using the Add method. In this case, the Name property of a consumer called objConsumer was bound to a data source field called strDir. Any data in the strDir field will now appear in the consumer's Name property.

EXERCISE 5-4

Creating a Data Consumer

1. Using the project from Exercise 5-3, add a new class module.

2. Change the name of the class module to clsConsumer, and the DataBindingBehavior property of the module to vbSimpleBound.

3. Select Project | References | Add a reference to Microsoft Data Binding Collection. Click OK to continue.

4. In the General Declarations section of clsConsumer, declare a Private variable called NewDir as a String data type:

   ```
   Private NewDir As String
   ```

5. Add a Get and a Let procedure to clsConsumer. This will allow us to retrieve a record and then display it.

```
Public Property Get Name() As String
DirName = NewDir
End Property
Public Property Let Name(strDir As String)
NewDir = strDir
Debug.Print NewDir
End Property
```

6. We must now create an instance of clsConsumer, the Binding Collection, and the data source. We then add clsConsumer to the Binding Collection. The Name property of clsConsumer will be bound to the strDir field of the data source. To do this, we add the following code to the Load event of our Form:

```
Set objSource = New clsSource
Set objBindingCollection = New BindingCollection
Set objConsumer = New clsConsumer
Set objBindingCollection.DataSource = objSource
objBindingCollection.Add objConsumer, "Name", "strDir"
```

7. If you ran the program now, you would be able to view one record in the Immediate window. To view other records in the clsSource class module, we must add code that will allow us to navigate through the different records in the data source. To do this, add the following procedure:

```
Public Sub Move()
rs.MoveNext
    If rs.EOF = True Then
    rs.MoveFirst
    End If
End Sub
```

8. Add a command button to your Form. Name it "cmdNext," give it the caption "Next," and then add the following code to the Click event:

```
objSource.Move
```

This will allow you to toggle through the different records in your data source.

9. Press F5 to run your program. As you click the Next button, different records will appear in the Immediate window.

CERTIFICATION SUMMARY

There are four stages in designing an application. They are conceptual design, logical design, physical design, and deployment. Conceptual design identifies an application's requirements. Logical design involves taking this information, and is where a system actually evolves. Physical design maps the business objects and services established in logical design and maps them to software components. Deployment determines how components are distributed across a network.

Class modules are used to create objects. When these objects are created, you can then create methods, properties, and events. To create a class module, you use the Add Class Module item from the Project menu. Once this is done, code can be added to the module through the class's Code window. By changing the DataBindingBehavior or DataSourceBehavior properties, you can change a class module to act as either a data consumer or data source, respectively.

QUESTIONS AND ANSWERS

I want to create a data source, but I'm missing the Data Source Class Module template. How can I configure a class module as a data source from scratch?	Set the class module's DataSourceBehavior property to vbDataSource. This will add an event to the class called GetMemberData. The Data Source Class Module already has this configured, and has some comments to help you create a data source. Aside from that, there is no difference between a standard class module and the Data Source one that comes with VB.
What actually binds a data source to a data consumer?	The Binding Collection acts as a link between fields in the data source and the data consumer. This allows data to be passed to the consumer by binding one to the other.
I've added code to edit my record set, but I keep getting a runtime error.	Check to see that the record set's Update method follows the Edit method in the code. Update must be executed after Edit, or a runtime error will occur.

TWO-MINUTE DRILL

❑ Application design consists of two main tasks: creating reusable components, and integrating the components into the application.

❑ Microsoft recommends the three-tiered "services model" for application design: user services, business and other middle-tier services, and data services.

❑ The design process is made up of four stages: conceptual design, logical design, physical design, and deployment.

  ❑ Conceptual design is the process of identifying an application's requirements.

  ❑ Logical design is made up of five activities: identifying business objects and services; defining user interfaces; identifying business object dependencies; validating the logical design against the requirements of the conceptual design; and, finally, refining and revising the logical design to eliminate problems and improve the design.

  ❑ Physical design takes the business objects and services identified in the logical design and maps them to software components.

  ❑ In deployment, decisions are made as to how the software components are to be distributed.

❑ Classes are templates that are used to create objects. Using class modules, you can write code to specify methods, properties, and events for custom objects that you create in the module. Adding a class module to a project is done through the Project menu in VB.

❑ A class module is different from a standard module in three ways: Class modules have one copy of the data for each object created from the class and the data is handled differently for each type of module. A class module's data exists only for the life of the object. Finally, a Public variable in a class module is only accessible when the object's variable contains a reference to an instance of the class.

❑ A class module has two events associated with it: Initialize and Terminate. By adding code to events, you can manipulate how a class module will act. Adding an event is done by declaring the event in the class module's General Declarations sections. To cause an event to run, you use the RaiseEvent keyword.

❑ Data sources are classes that provide data from external databases. The data is then "consumed" or used by other objects. Unlike the Data control object, classes can act as data sources for any type of data. They can be data sources for ADOs, OLE (Object Linking and Embedding) providers, and ODBC (Open Database Connectivity) sources. To have a class act as a data source for an object, you must make a reference to an object library.

❑ To create a data consumer you add a class module to the project and change the DataBindingBehavior property to make the class a data consumer and determine how it will be bound to the data source.

❑ There are three binding options: vbNone, vbSimpleBound, and vbComplexBound.

❑ The Binding Collection is used to bind data in a data source to a data consumer and works as a link between the consumer and source. To add an object to the Binding Collection, you create a new instance of the BindingCollection object and use the Add method.

SELF TEST

The following Self-Test questions will help you measure your understanding of the material presented in this chapter. Read all the choices carefully, as there may be more than one correct answer. Choose all correct answers for each question.

1. Which of the following services represents the application's user interface?

    A. User services

    B. Business services

    C. Middle-tier services

    D. Data services

2. Which stage of design involves identifying an application's requirements?

    A. Conceptual

    B. Logical

    C. Physical

    D. Deployment

3. Which stage of design determines how components are distributed across a network?

    A. Conceptual

    B. Logical

    C. Physical

    D. Deployment

4. Why is it important to change the name of a class to a name that isn't in use?

    A. So that when the class calls on itself, it doesn't fall into an endless loop.

    B. If the name is already in use, the class module won't be able to initiate itself.

    C. If the name is already in use, controller code won't be able to instantiate objects.

    D. It doesn't matter if the name is already in use.

5. Validation is a necessary part of designing an application. Which of the following best describes what validation is in the design process?

    A. Validation is a comparison of deployment to the requirements of the logical design.

    B. Validation is a comparison of the physical design to the requirements of deployment.

    C. Validation is a comparison of logical design to the requirements in the original conceptual view.

    D. Validation is the concept of verifying that all variables meet the requirements of the logical design.

6. In a class module, how many copies of the module's data can exist at any one time?

    A. One

    B. Two

    C. A copy for each object created

    D. A copy for each instance of a standard module

7. How long is the lifetime of data in a standard module?

   A. The life of the object

   B. The life of the program

   C. The life of the programmer

   D. None of the above

8. What is the syntax used to destroy an object?

   A. Set Object = Nothing

   B. Get Object = Nothing

   C. Let Object = Nothing

   D. Set Object = 0

9. You use the following code in your application. When you test it, it appears that nothing happens in the current record in the record set (which you've called rs). Why?

   ```
   Sub cmdDelete_Click()
   rs.Delete
   End Sub
   ```

   A. The method of the record set should read rs.Del.

   B. There should be a MoveNext method executed after the Delete method.

   C. There should be a Next method executed after the Delete method.

   D. There is no reason why it shouldn't move to the next record.

10. Julie records a sale into an application. The application then adds the necessary taxes, checks the customer's credit rating, and determines whether the sale can be added to the customer's account. Which tier of the services model do the rules of to this procedure apply?

    A. User services

    B. Business services

    C. Data services

    D. Graduated services

11. Which design stage takes business objects and services and maps them to software components?

    A. Conceptual

    B. Logical

    C. Physical

    D. Deployment

12. How is a class module added to a VB project?

    A. Select Format | Add Class Module.

    B. Select Project | Add Class Module.

    C. Select Project | Add Class Module, then choose Class Module from the dialog box that appears.

    D. Select Tools | Add Class Module, then choose Class Module from the dialog box that appears.

13. In a standard module, how many copies of the module's data is there at any given time?

    A. One

    B. Two

    C. A copy for each object created

    D. A copy for each instance of a class module

14. In a class module, what is the lifetime of the module's data?

    A. The life of the object

    B. The life of the program

    C. The life of the programmer

    D. None of the above

15. What is wrong with the following code?

    ```
    Sub cmdEdit_Click
    rs.Update
    rs("strName")=txtName.Text
    rs.Edit
    End Sub
    ```

    A. The property of txtName should be Caption.

    B. The Edit method has to be implemented as part of an If...Then statement.

    C. The Edit method must come after the Update method.

    D. The Update method must come after the Edit method.

16. You want to add code to move three records ahead in the record set. Which of the following will do this?

    A. Recordset.Move -3

    B. Recordset.Move +3

    C. Recordset.Move 3

    D. Recordset.Move =3

17. You want to add a new record to the record set. Which of the following examples of code would add a record to a record set named rs?

    A. rs.AddNew

    B. rs.New

    C. rs.Add

    D. rs.New +1

18. Both the EOF and BOF of a record set are set to True. How many records are there in the record set?

    A. One

    B. Two

    C. Unknown

    D. None

19. Which of the following would you set to create a Data Source class module?

    A. DataSourceBehavior

    B. DataBindingBehavior

    C. vbSimpleBound

    D. Both DataSourceBehavior and DataBindingBehavior

20. When you create a standard class module, what two events does the Class object initially have? (Choose all that apply.)

    A. Initialize

    B. Terminate

    C. GetDataMember

    D. Load

21. What actually binds a data source to a data consumer?

    A. Class module

    B. DataBinding property of class module

    C. Binding Collection

    D. DataBondage argument

22. You want to cause an event to run programmatically. Which keyword will you use to make this happen?

   A. CallEvent

   B. RaiseEvent

   C. RunEvent

   D. Event

23. Which of the following always uses COM creation services?

   A. Property Let

   B. Property Get

   C. Dim

   D. CreateObject

24. When can data be bound to a control or consumer, when using the Binding Collection and a class module?

   A. Runtime

   B. Design time

   C. Anytime

   D. Never

25. Which of the following is used to set the source of the data to be used for a class module?

   A. Initialize

   B. Terminate

   C. Load

   D. GetDataMember

26. The record set can refer to how many records at one time as the current record?

   A. One

   B. Two

   C. Three

   D. Unlimited

27. A class module can be used as a data source for which of the following types of data? (Choose all that apply.)

   A. ADO (ActiveX Data Objects)

   B. OLE (Object Linking and Embedding) providers

   C. ODBC (Open Database Connectivity)

   D. None of the above

28. When you modify the DataBindingBehavior of a class module, what options are available to you? (Choose all that apply.)

   A. vbDataSource

   B. vbNone

   C. vbSimpleBound

   D. vbComplexBound

29. When you modify the DataSourceBehavior of a class module, what new event will be added to the Class object?

   A. GetData

   B. DataMember

   C. GetDataMember

   D. Load

30. Which of the following would you set to create a data consumer class module?

   A. DataSourceBehavior

   B. DataBindingBehavior

   C. VbDataSource

   D. Both DataSourceBehavior and DataBindingBehavior

MICROSOFT CERTIFIED SOLUTION DEVELOPER

6

Using COM Components

Earlier in this book, you learned how to use classes to encapsulate code into objects for reuse in an application. ActiveX COM components extend this model to allow code to be compiled into objects that can be reused between applications. This chapter will provide you with a basic understanding of ActiveX components, the different types of ActiveX components, and the steps necessary to create a Visual Basic client application that uses the services provided by an OLE server.

CERTIFICATION OBJECTIVE 6.01

Introduction to ActiveX Components and the Component Object Model

The idea that software components should be reusable within an application and between applications is fundamental in *object-oriented programming* (OOP). However, without a standard way to make objects talk to one another, it can be difficult or impossible for a developer to use components from other developers or from different development languages. Microsoft's solution to this problem was the introduction of the *component object model* (COM), a binary standard that defines the way software components should expose their functionality. By standardizing the communication method through a set of standard *interfaces*, COM allows developers to focus on the core task of what the application does, instead of how to make the various parts of an application communicate with each other. In VB, the compiler handles most of the technical details of implementing and calling COM interfaces for you, giving you the freedom to deal with COM components at a fairly high level of abstraction.

In VB, the principal COM object you use is the ActiveX component. ActiveX is a type of COM object built on Microsoft's object linking and embedding (OLE) technology. It is important to remember, however, that ActiveX components are COM components, but not all COM components are ActiveX components.

Microsoft loves COM, and they want you to know it. They have been known to sprinkle questions throughout the MCSD track exams on COM. For the VB exam, you probably only need to know what COM is and that ActiveX is based on it. However, if your track to the MCSD title goes through the dreaded Windows architecture exams, make sure you are familiar with the iUnknown, iDispatch, and iAdviseSink interfaces of COM components.

Benefits of COM

Because COM is just a standardized approach to OOP, its benefits closely mirror those commonly associated with OOP, such as the encapsulation and reuse of code. However, because COM is a standardized object model, some additional advantages are realized.

Interoperability

Because COM is a binary standard, components that conform to this specification are language independent. This means that software components can be written in any programming language and, as long as they adhere to the basic rules of COM, they will work in any other programming environment that supports COM components. The important point here for the VB programmer is that VB can use COM components without modifications to the client application, regardless of who wrote them, how they were written, and in what programming language they were written. Conversely, components written in VB will work in any COM-compliant client. This cross-language compatibility has led to a large number of components being available for use in your VB applications. Later in this chapter, I will demonstrate how to make these components work for you in your applications.

Versioning

The rules of COM are very specific regarding how the interface to that object can change between versions. Don't confuse the term *interface* here with a user interface like a form or control. When speaking the COM language, *interface* refers to a programmatic interface. That is, the properties and methods used to access the functionality of a software component. COM versioning rules can be summed up in the following statement: When creating a new version of an existing COM component, you can add interfaces, but you cannot remove or modify existing interfaces.

When creating a new version of an existing COM component, you can add interfaces, but you cannot remove or modify existing interfaces.

This rule is crucial when you consider the fact that COM is based on the principle of reuse between multiple applications. In order to ensure that applications using a particular component do not break when newer versions of that component are installed on the system, newer versions must be able to support all of the functionality of previous versions of the component. This rule does not preclude newer versions of the component from improving previously released features, as long as they are exposed in a way that would not break compatibility with clients that were built using older versions of the component. The beauty of this system is that by updating one component you can improve the functionality it provides in all of the applications that use it without updating any of the client applications themselves. Also, you can feel safe in the comfort that the rules of COM ensure that current applications using the older version of the component will not stop working when the component is updated.

Standardization

One way to make users feel more comfortable with a new application and to lessen their training burden is to write software that allows them to apply the skills that they have already learned to your applications. By reusing standard user interface components such as ActiveX controls, programs can be written that look and operate in ways that users are probably familiar with from using other applications or the Windows operating system itself.

To illustrate this point, consider scroll bars. Most applications have them, and they work the same way in each of those applications because the same software component is used to incorporate them in each application. It is easy for developers to take this skill for granted, but learning to use a scroll bar can be a major accomplishment for a novice Windows user. When this same novice user starts to learn a new application that also uses the scroll bar control, they immediately are familiar with this paradigm and have a head start on learning the application. Also, the more exposure a user has to scroll bar controls, the better they are able to use them in all of the applications that use them

Abstraction

When using nonstandardized component models, the developer of the client application must deal with each component separately regarding how to talk to that component from the client application. With a standardized model such as COM, the developer need not worry about making the components work inside their programs and can focus more on the tasks required in building an application.

Clients and Servers

When describing the interactions between components, there are two roles. These are the roles of the client and the server. These two terms get recycled quite a bit in technospeak and can have slightly different meanings when describing different technologies. Here I will describe these terms as they apply to components.

Client

The *client* is the application or component that calls the properties and/or methods of a component object. The client acts as a consumer of the functionality provided by the server. A standard EXE type application in VB can only act as a client and never as a server.

Server

The *server* is the component that provides services to the client through calls to its methods and properties. ActiveX servers are also commonly referred to as OLE servers (from the fact that ActiveX is built on OLE) or OLE automation servers (*OLE automation* is another term for the interaction between ActiveX components). Two examples of OLE servers are ActiveX controls and ActiveX code components.

It is important to understand that because a component can be built from other components, an OLE server can take on the client role with respect to one component and the server role with respect to another. Take, for example, the application outlined in Figure 6-1. The ActiveX control illustrated in the middle of the diagram acts as both an OLE server to the standard EXE client application and as client to both the ActiveX DLL and ActiveX EXE components. The ActiveX DLL could also be used as a client if it made use of another ActiveX DLL component to implement its functionality.

FIGURE 6-1

In this diagram, each component acts as server with respect to the components on its left, and client to components on its right. Note that the ActiveX control acts both as client and server with respect to different components

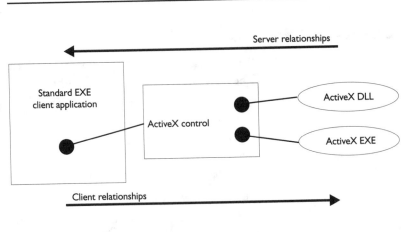

Types of ActiveX Components Available in Visual Basic

VB can be used to create three basic types of ActiveX components: ActiveX controls, ActiveX code components (DLL/EXE), and ActiveX documents (DLL/EXE). These types of components are described in more detail here.

ActiveX Controls

ActiveX controls are software components built around a visual element called a UserControl. (For more information on UserControl objects, refer to Chapter 9, "Building ActiveX Controls" in this guide.) When ActiveX controls are added to a VB project, they appear as new controls in the VB Toolbox. ActiveX controls are compiled into files with the OCX extension, which stands for OLE Control. (The X in OCX is just there to round out the extension to three characters.) ActiveX controls run in the memory area allocated to the client's process (In-Process).

ActiveX Code Components

ActiveX code components are libraries of classes that can be used by the client application to create objects. These components come in two flavors:

- DLL files, which run in the memory space of the client's process (In-Process).

- EXE files that run in their own process (Out-of-Process). These types of code components are commonly referred to as application servers, or automation server applications.

For more information on the differences between these types of servers, see "In-Process vs. Out-of-Process Servers" in Chapter 7. For the purposes of this discussion, the important difference is that In-Process components run more quickly because they do not have to access memory across process boundaries.

ActiveX Documents

ActiveX documents are components that are compiled so that they can be used inside OLE containers such as Microsoft Word or Microsoft Internet Explorer. The most common use for this type of component is for use in applications intended to run as Web pages in Internet Explorer. ActiveX documents can also be compiled as both in-process (DLL) and Out-of-Process (EXE) components. This type of ActiveX component will be discussed in more detail in Chapter 7, "Building COM Components."

Although ActiveX documents can be created in VB, they cannot be used in VB clients in the same way as ActiveX controls or ActiveX components. They must be embedded inside a Web browser control or other control that is designed to host these types of components.

CERTIFICATION OBJECTIVE 6.03

Using ActiveX Controls in a Client Application

Since Microsoft added the ability to create ActiveX controls to Visual Basic version 5, literally thousands of reusable controls have been created that do everything from displaying CAD drawings to browsing the Web. ActiveX controls allow you to skip a lot of the mundane programming tasks like adding text-editing functionality to your application by simply dropping a precompiled component into your application and using its functionality as if it were built into VB. The steps to add an ActiveX control to your project and use it are as follows:

1. Select Components… from the Project menu. This will bring up the Components dialog box, shown in the following illustration, which lists all of the ActiveX controls to the VB Toolbox registered on your system. For information on registering components, see the section titled "Registering and Unregistering Components" later in this chapter.

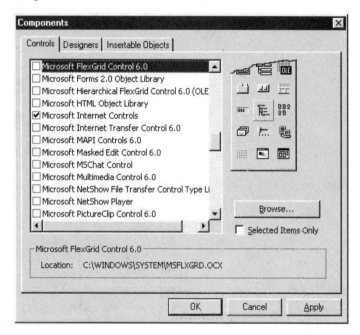

2. In the Components dialog box, select the ActiveX controls you want to add to your project. If the control you want to add is not listed, you can search for it by pressing the Browse… button and browsing to the correct OCX file.

3. After you press the OK or Apply button, the control will be added to your project. You can verify this by looking at the Toolbox. To open the Toolbox, select View | Toolbox. You should see at least one item in the Toolbox for each ActiveX component you selected, as shown in the following illustration. Because OCX files can contain multiple controls, you may see more than one control added to the Toolbox for each OCX you selected in the previous step.

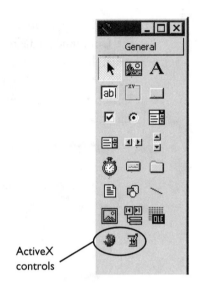

ActiveX
controls

4. To use the new control once you have added it to the project, simply select the control's icon in the Toolbox and add it to your form as you would any of VB's built-in controls.

5. To set the properties for the control once you have placed it on the form, open the property sheet as you would for any of VB's standard controls. Some ActiveX controls include custom property sheets that provide more visual methods for setting particular properties of a control. To access these custom property sheets, right-click the instance of the control on your form and select the Properties... item on the pop-up menu. If the control does not support a custom property sheet, you will see the standard VB property sheet. Otherwise, you will get the customized version that may look similar to the following illustration, showing the RichTextBox control and property sheet. Keep in mind, however, that although most of these custom property sheets are created from a template, they are very customizable and can look very different from one ActiveX control to another. In fact, they can even have other ActiveX controls on them.

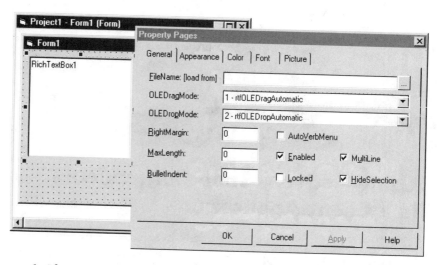

6. If necessary, you can add logic to the events raised by the ActiveX control. Again, this works exactly like you are used to with standard VB controls. The following illustration demonstrates this by adding code to the KeyPress event of the Rich Text Editor control, so that VB will click each time a key is pressed, simulating a typewriter.

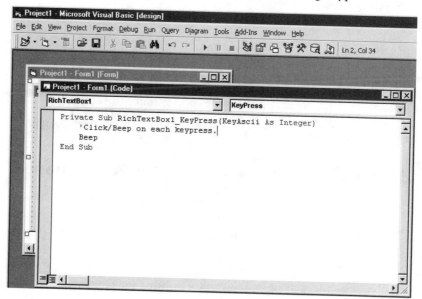

7. When creating an installer for your application, don't forget to add the controls to the installation package and register them on the target machine.

Using ActiveX Code Components in a Client Application

The exact procedures required to use an ActiveX code component in your application can vary somewhat based on the type of component you are using and your application's requirements for performance and features. At a top level, however, the steps required for using these components are

1. Add the component to the VB project to make its classes available in your client.

2. Declare a variable to hold a reference to the object.

3. Create an instance of the object from one of the component's classes.

4. Call the methods and properties of the object using the object reference variable.

5. Write code to trap events raised by the object.

6. Release the reference to the object when you have finished with it.

Creating a Reference to an ActiveX Component

Before you can use the classes in a component, you must first tell VB which components you will be using in your project. Here is how you accomplish this:

1. Select Project | References.... This will bring up the References dialog box listing the type libraries for the ActiveX code components registered on your machine. For information on registering

Late Binding Method

So far, I have presented the late binding method as a last resort approach when early binding is impossible because a component has not provided a type library. There actually is one benefit to using the late binding method to declare object references. The benefit is that a variable declared this way is not limited to referring to a specific type of object. This flexibility gives you the freedom to decide at runtime what type of object will be referenced with the variable. This also gives you the ability to reuse object variables to refer to different objects throughout the program, but this is generally considered a bad programming practice and is not recommended.

When using late binding, object variables are not declared with a specific class name. Instead, the variables are declared as type Object as shown in the following example:

```
Dim AdoRS as object
```

Declaring an object variable using the variant, form, or control type also forces VB to use late binding, so be careful to avoid accidentally invoking the late binding methods by using these nonspecific declarations. To ensure that the faster early binding method is used in situations in which you must declare an object to reference a form or control, refer to the specific type of form or control to create the reference, as shown below:

```
'*** Declarations that force late binding
Dim c as control
Dim f as form

'*** Early Binding alternatives
Dim c as CheckBox
Dim f as Myform
```

Because late binding does not allow VB to know what properties and methods are available to an object ahead of time, the compiler will not pick up on misspelled or incorrect property or method names in your code. When using late binding, be especially careful to check that the properties and methods you invoke actually exist in the class and are spelled correctly.

The New keyword is not available with late-bound objects; therefore, you cannot use it to create new instances of objects declared with the Object type. To provide a way to create a new instance of these objects, use the CreateObject method, as described next.

Using the CreateObject Function to Create a New Instance of an Object

The CreateObject function is provided to create a new instance of an externally creatable object from an ActiveX code component and return a reference to that object. When I refer to an object as externally creatable, I mean that it is a top-level object exposed by a component in such a way that the client can create it directly, as opposed to a dependent object, which is created by the component itself and passed back to the client through property references or method calls.

The CreateObject function is only used to create a new instance of an object that is not already running. If you want a reference to an object that already exists in memory, use the GetObject function described later in this section. The syntax for the CreateObject function is

```
Set objectvar = CreateObject("appname.classname",[servername])
```

QUESTIONS AND ANSWERS

I want to optimize my code for speed with an ActiveX DLL component that supplies a type library.	The type library allows you to use the faster early binding methods.
I need to use the same variable to reference several different forms within its lifetime.	Use late binding. Each form is created from its own class definition at runtime and is thus a separate type of object. The only way to reuse an object reference for different forms is to use the late bound Form or Object types.
I am using an ActiveX EXE component without a type library and want to optimize speed.	You have no choice here but to use late binding. The speed part of the equation will have to be worked in elsewhere.

This example demonstrates how to use the GetObject function to both start a new instance of Excel and return a reference to an existing instance of Excel.

```
'*** GetObject Examples

'*** Declare the object variable
Dim x1 as Object
Dim x2 as Object

'*** Reference existing excel object or create new one
Set x1 = GetObject("","Excel.Application")

'*** Get another reference to the Excel Application.
'*** This would normally cause an error if Excel was not open
'*** but we know it is open because the last call opened it.
set x2 = GetObject(,"Excel.Application")

'*** Reference Excel Spreadsheet named Budget.xls
Set x1 = GetObject("c:\spreadsheets\budget.xls")

'*** Display Number of Worksheets in Budget.xls
Msgbox x1.Worksheets.Count

'*** Release Object References (Decrementing Usage Counter)
Set x1 = Nothing
Set x2 = Nothing
```

Handling Events Generated by Components

When we added an ActiveX control to the form, VB automatically added the event handler stubs to the development environment of the form and passed the events raised by the control to the client application. ActiveX code components can do this as well, but only if they are declared in the Declarations section of the module using the WithEvents keyword. This keyword cannot be used unless the variable is declared using early binding techniques. Here is an example using the WithEvents keyword with the Access Data Objects component. Note the event handler stubs are available in the VB IDE after declaring the AdoRS variable in Figure 6-3.

```
'Declarations Section
'--------------------
'
'*** Create an Object Reference variable such
'*** that events are generated in Visual Basic
'*** from the object.
Dim WithEvents AdoRS as ADODB.Recordset
```

Releasing the Object

The last step in using a component is to release the resources associated with the component's objects when you have finished using them. Although the

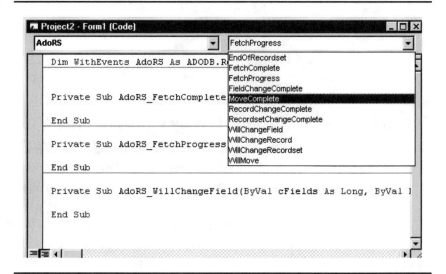

FIGURE 6-3

By using the WithEvents keyword to declare the ADO Recordset object, the events are added to the VB IDE

objects will be released when the variable goes out of scope, it is a better idea to explicitly release the object by setting it to the constant Nothing. This is especially true if, after you have finished with an object, there is more code that will need to execute before the variable referencing the object goes out of scope. Here is an example of releasing an object reference:

```
Set AdoRS = Nothing
```

A word of warning: because variables that reference objects are only pointers to the objects themselves, it is possible to set two variables that point to the same object. Because of this, COM uses reference counting to determine how many variables are still pointing to an object in memory. The object itself cannot be destroyed until the reference counter hits zero. The following code segment demonstrates this behavior.

```
Dim AdoRS as ADODB.Recordset
Dim AdoRS2 as ADODB.Recordset

'*** Object is created and reference counter is set to 1
Set AdoRS = NEW ADODB.Recordset

'*** ADORS2 now points to the same object as ADORS
'*** and Reference count is incremented to 2
Set ADORS2 = ADORS

'*** Frees the memory associated with pointing
'*** to the object and decrements the reference counter to 1
'*** Object is not destroyed because ADORS2 still references it!
Set ADORS = Nothing

'*** Frees the memory associated with pointing
'*** to the object and decrements the reference counter to 0
'*** Object is now destroyed since no variables reference it.
Set ADORS2 = Nothing
```

Managing Components

It won't be long before your development machine is brimming with ActiveX controls and components. With just a basic installation of VB, you will find that you have dozens of these components preinstalled on your system. Add to this the fact that you can download, purchase, and (using the techniques in Chapter 7) even create them yourself. This propagation of components on your machine can quickly make it a hassle to keep up with all of them, much less know how to use them all. Microsoft has given us the Visual Component Manager and the Object Browser to tame this mess.

The Visual Component Manager

Microsoft has been pushing the idea for some time that we should all be developing in components. With the introduction of the Visual Component Manager in VB version 6, Microsoft has finally given you a tool for keeping track of all these components you are creating and/or installing on your development machines. The Visual Component Manager (shown in Figure 6-4) was added to tackle the problem of managing a large number of separate components in an application. It provides a way to find the needed components when the time comes to reuse them in your applications.

Built on the Microsoft Repository technology, the Visual Component Manager allows you to publish components to a repository-based catalog, where they can easily be located, inspected, retrieved, and reused.

Publishing Components

Publishing a component to the Visual Component Manager stores it along with some basic fielded information and keywords into a Microsoft Repository database. The database can be stored locally in a Jet database, or

FIGURE 6-4   The Visual Component Manager is one of the new features in VB 6

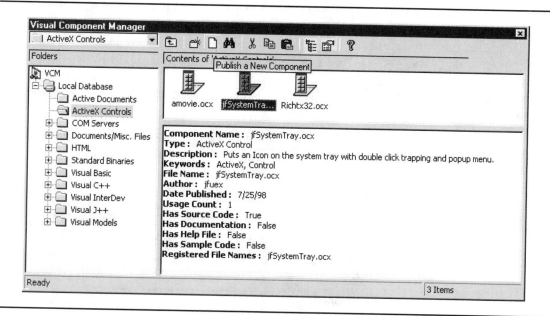

on the server in a Microsoft SQL Server database. The components can be searched and retrieved for use in other projects by any developer with access to the Repository database. The steps for publishing a component to the Repository are outlined here:

1. Open the Visual Component Manager by selecting View | Visual Component Manager.

2. Open the Local Database folder and select the subfolder that applies to the component you are adding to the repository.

3. Press the Publish a New Component button (it appears as a dog-eared sheet of paper on the Component Manager tool bar) to bring up the Visual Component Manager Publish Wizard.

4. Select the primary component file and follow the wizard prompts to catalog the component.

Finding Components

Using the Visual Component Manager, you can search for a particular component by name, type, description, keywords, or annotations. With full text search capability, you can find a component even if you don't know its exact name. To search for a component, follow these steps:

1. Open the Visual Component Manager by selecting View | Visual Component Manager.

2. Click the Find button (it appears as binoculars on the Component Manager tool bar) to bring up the Find Items in the Visual Component Manager dialog box, as shown in the following illustration, in order to locate a specific component, follow these steps.

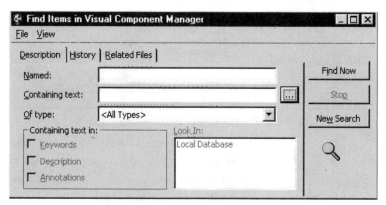

3. Fill in your search criteria and click the Find Now button.

Reusing Components

Once you have found the component that you want to use in your project, you can register it on your machine and add it to the project by simply clicking Add to my Project on the component's shortcut menu in Visual Component Manager. If a component has multiple files associated with it, they are added to the project along with the primary component file. For components stored in the Repository, you can use this process instead of using the Components and References dialog boxes for adding ActiveX controls or components to a VB Project.

The Object Browser

The Object Browser dialog box can be used as a quick reference for the type libraries that have been added to your project. It provides a searchable listing of class descriptions, including constants, properties, and methods associated with each type library. For each property or method, the calling conventions appear in the lower section of the dialog box when selected and, if the author of the component was thoughtful enough to provide it, each member item will have a short description of what its purpose is. This tool will save you a lot of trips to the reference manuals, and it is a lot easier to use than online help files. In Figure 6-5, I used the Object Browser to search for and find the purpose of the Filename property of the Rich Text control.

FIGURE 6-5

The Object Browser is displayed either by selecting View | Object Browser or by pressing the F2 shortcut key

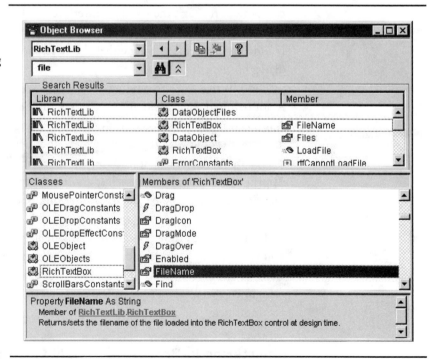

Registering and Unregistering Components

Before a component can be used in your application, it will need to be registered in the Windows Registry. Registering a component refers to the process of making entries into the Registry that specify where a COM component is and indexing it by a unique identifier. When an ActiveX component is compiled, it is assigned a ClassId that is represented as a GUID (globally unique identifier), which is stored as a 128-bit number that is guaranteed to be unique across time and space. What this means is that no matter how many components humans can create, we can be assured that each one of them has a unique number identifying it. The ClassID is used by the client application to request a particular object from COM, which looks the number up in the system Registry and uses the path stored there to find and create the component. Effectively, all the client application knows about the component is its ClassID. The rest of the information on that component is obtained by talking directly to the component through the standard interfaces outlined by COM. The ClassID is made available to the project when a reference to its type library is added to the project using either the References or Components dialog boxes.

For calls that use late binding, as you may recall, a type library reference is not required. In this situation, VB uses another Registry entry called an AppID. An AppID is stored in the Registry using the same human readable name that is used with the CreateObject and GetObject calls; for example, Excel.Application is the AppID for the Excel Application root object. This AppID entry in the Registry is just another layer of indirection that allows the client to look up the ClassID of the component by referencing a more friendly name.

There are two primary methods available in VB to register a component. You have already seen that this can be done automatically by the Visual Component Manager, but it can also be done manually. The type of component (In-Process/Out-of-Process) determines how this will be accomplished.

Registering In-Process (DLL/OCX) Components

In-process components are registered using the REGSVR32.EXE file that is located in the \WINDOWS\SYSTEM directory. In truth, all ActiveX components must provide an interface by which they can register and unregister themselves. The only thing the REGSVR32.EXE utility does is call that interface of the component.

To register ActiveX components Component.DLL and Control.OCX, the syntax is

```
REGSVR32 Component.DLL
REGSVR32 Control.OCX
```

To unregister the same components, the syntax is:

```
REGSVR32 /u Component.DLL
REGSVR32 /u Control.OCX
```

Registering Out-of-Process (EXE) Components

Registering EXE-type ActiveX components is even simpler. All you need to do is run the EXE file and the component will register itself automatically. When registering these components, you will normally only be notified if the component fails to register. That is, if you receive no message, it means that it registered normally.

exam
Watch

Once you have registered a component in Windows, the location to which it is registered follows the file when you move it around your hard disk. I have seen questions about whether this feature exists on more than one of the MCSD exams. One "gotcha" regarding this feature is that when you delete components, they can remain registered in the Recycle Bin directory. This can lead to confusing bugs in VB; so be sure, when deleting registered components, to delete them completely from the system or unregister them.

In Exercise 6-1, I will demonstrate how you can use ActiveX controls to add powerful functionality with very little effort to a VB application. This exercise demonstrates how to use the Rich Text Box and Common Dialog controls to create a simple text editor similar to Notepad that comes with Windows.

EXERCISE 6-1

Using ActiveX Controls

1. Open VB and create a new standard EXE-type project.

2. Bring up the Components dialog box by selecting Project | Components....

3. Select the Microsoft Rich Textbox Control 6.0 control.

4. Select the Microsoft Common Dialog Control 6.0 control.

5. Close the Components dialog box by pressing the OK button.

6. If the Toolbox is not visible, open it with the select View | Toolbox. At this point, you should see a new item in the Toolbox for each of the ActiveX controls you selected in the Components dialog box. If they do not appear as shown, you may need to enlarge the Toolbox pane.

7. Add a Rich Text Box control and Common Dialog control to your form by clicking them in the Toolbox and drawing them onto your form. Don't worry about sizing them or where you put them. Just drop them anywhere on the form.

8. Use the Menu Editor to create a file menu by adding the following items.

Item	Name
File	mnuFile
Open	mnuFileOpen
Save	mnuFileSave
Exit	mnuFileExit

9. Add the following code to the Click events of the newly created menu items:

```
Private Sub mnuFileExit_Click()
    'Unload the main form closing the application
    Unload Me
End Sub

Private Sub mnuFileOpen_Click()

    '*** Set properties of common Dialog control
    CommonDialog1.DialogTitle = "Open Text"
    CommonDialog1.CancelError = False

    '*** Display the open dialog box
    CommonDialog1.ShowOpen
```

```
            If CommonDialog1.FileName <> vbNullString Then
                RichTextBox1.FileName = CommonDialog1.FileName
            End If
        End Sub

        Private Sub mnuFileSave_Click()

            '*** Set properties of common Dialog control
            CommonDialog1.DialogTitle = "Save Text"
            CommonDialog1.CancelError = False

            '*** Display the Save dialog box
            CommonDialog1.ShowSave

            '*** If a filename was selected, save the file
            If CommonDialog1.FileName <> vbNullString Then
                RichTextBox1.SaveFile CommonDialog1.FileName
            End If
        End Sub
```

10. Add the following code to the Resize event of the form to make the Rich Text box stretch and shrink to hug the edges of the form.

```
Private Sub Form_Resize()
    On Error Resume Next
    'Size the Rich Textbox to use the whole form
    RichTextBox1.Left = 0
    RichTextBox1.Top = 0
    RichTextBox1.Width = ScaleWidth
    RichTextBox1.Height = ScaleHeight
End Sub
```

11. Using the property sheet of the form set the caption of the form to "MyTextEditor".

12. Compile and run the application.

That's it! If you compile and run your application, you will have a basic text editor, shown in Figure 6-6. It works a lot like Notepad, and even has some features that Notepad does not. For example, you will find that unlike Notepad, this application will open and save RTF documents and accept items dragged and dropped onto the text window. The best part is that you didn't have to deal with the complexities of making a scrollable window,

FIGURE 6-6

The MyTextEditor App

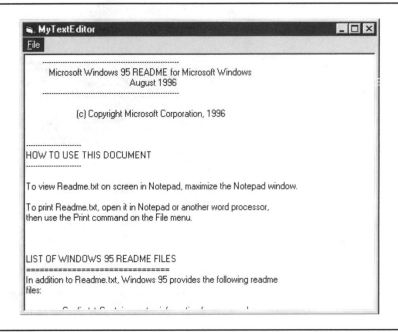

parsing RTF files, or designing a dialog box to select filenames for saving and loading files. You were left to deal with how the text editor and common dialog box elements work within the framework of your application.

In Exercise 6-2, we will take the MyTextEditor application we created in Exercise 6-1 and extend it using the Outlook ActiveX code component. You will need to have completed the previous exercise and have Microsoft Outlook (any version) installed on your system to perform this exercise. As you may know, there are just around a zillion text editors available today. In order to add some zip to our application, let's specialize this text editor so that it can be used to write letters to your mother.

EXERCISE 6-2

Using ActiveX Code Components

1. Open the MyTextEditor application from the previous exercise.

2. Bring up the Select Project | References....

3. Add a reference to the Outlook component by selecting Microsoft Outlook 8.0 Object Library and click the OK button to close the dialog box.

4. Open the main text editor form of your application and add the following menu item under the File menu.

Item	Name
Send To Mom	mnuFileSendToMom

5. Add the following code to the Click event of the new menu item:

```
Private Sub mnuFileSendToMom_Click()
'*** Declare variable to hold the reference to Outlook and Mail Item
'*** Note: These Declarations use early binding.
  Dim olApp As Outlook.Application
  Dim olMail As Outlook.MailItem

'*** Create a new instance of the Application object
'*** Note: This is an externally creatable object.
  Set olApp = New Outlook.Application

'*** Create a new mail Item Object by calling the CreateItem method
'*** of the Outlook Application object.
'*** Note: This is a dependant object.
  Set olMessage = olApp.CreateItem(olMailItem)

'*** Set the properties of the Mail Item object
'*** Insert Mom's E-mail Address here.
  olMail.To = "mother@florida.com"
  olMail.Subject = "Another Letter"
  olMail.Body = RichTextBox1.Text

'*** Send the Message using the Send Method of the Mail Item object.
  olMail.Send

'*** Release the object's references (decrementing reference counters)
  Set olMail = Nothing
  Set olApp = Nothing
End Sub
```

6. Compile and run the application.

Leveraging COM

Microsoft's solution to interoperability of binary components written in multiple languages, including VB, is known as the component object model (COM). This document- or component-centric focus is taking over the development universe. COM was designed to address four basic problems with component-based systems.

- *Interoperability* deals with the basic ability of components written by separate vendors to work together efficiently.

- *Versioning* is a concern addressing the ability to update individual components without disturbing the functionality of independent components.

- *Language independence* references the concerns of calling functions across components written in different languages.

- *Transport remoting* involves communication between components independent of the process, or even the computer on which the component process is running.

Visual Basic 6 can be used to create COM-based DLLs that encapsulate business services, addressing the middle layer in Microsoft's Solution Framework for *n*-tier application development. VB can create COM components as executable files (EXEs) or DLLs. Integration with Microsoft Transaction Server requires COM components be written as DLLs.

DLLs are In-Process, sharing the same memory space as the container application. EXEs are Out-of-Process components, using their own separate memory space from the container application. COM, or ActiveX, DLLs running In-Process are faster, but risk failing the entire host process on failure. COM, or ActiveX, EXEs are slower, but limit failures to the EXE process only. COM EXEs, written with the VB ActiveX application project, require a process known as marshalling, which entails processing the packaging and sending of COM interface parameters across process boundaries.

COM components entail the creation of VB class modules. A class module serves as a template for creating COM objects at runtime by creating instances of a class. COM components may involve more than one class.

Class modules involve only two built-in events, Initialize and Terminate. Methods are added to a class, and hence to any objects created at runtime via instantiation of the class, by adding public sub and function procedures.

Using COM objects requires registration on a system. Registration may be accomplished by a setup program, compiling a DLL in VB, or using REGSVR32.ESE with the appropriate command-line parameters. Adding a COM component to MTS will result in automatic registration of the component on the server on which MTS is running.

For the exam, remember the differences between In-Process and Out-of-Process, how to export a method from a class module, registration methods, and testing procedures for debugging COM DLLs.

— By Michael Lane Thomas,
MCSE+I, MCSD, MCT, A+

CERTIFICATION SUMMARY

ActiveX components are COM-based components built on Microsoft's OLE technology. When using ActiveX components, the component that is providing functionality is called the server or OLE server and the application or component that is using the services of another component is called the client. An OLE server can run either In-Process (OCX, DLL) or Out-of-Process (EXE) applications. In-Process servers run faster than Out-of Process servers. This is because the client does not have to make calls across process boundaries to access the methods and properties of the component. Components must be registered on the system they are used on to allow the client application to look up the component by its globally unique identifier (GUID) in the Windows Registry.

To use an ActiveX control, follow these steps:

Add a reference to the project using the Components dialog box

Add the control to your form from the Toolbox

Add code to the event handlers for the control.

Add code to use the properties and methods exposed by the control.

You can use the Object Browser as a quick reference to the functionality that the control supports.

To use an ActiveX code component, follow these steps:

Add a reference to the project using the References dialog box or the Visual Component Manager.

Declare a variable to hold a pointer to the object.

Use the WithEvents keyword if you want to trap the events raised by the object.

Use early binding whenever possible for faster performance. If the component does not provide a type library, you will have to use the late binding method.

Create an instance, or instantiate, the object.

Call the properties and methods of the object. You can use the Object Browser as a quick reference to the functionality that the component supports.

Release the object by setting it to the constant Nothing.

✓ TWO-MINUTE DRILL

- ❏ ActiveX components are COM components based on Microsoft's OLE technology.

- ❏ OLE clients are consumers of the services offered by a component.

- ❏ OLE servers are providers of services to OLE clients.

- ❏ A type library is a dictionary of classes in a component and the interfaces that those classes expose.

- ❏ In-Process servers are loaded into the process space and share memory with the client application. Consequently, they are able to exchange information with the client more quickly than Out-Of-Process servers.

- ❏ Early binding allows VB to use the fastest method for accessing the properties and methods of an object.

- ❏ Externally creatable objects are top-level objects exposed by a component to the client.

- ❏ Dependent objects are created by using the methods exposed by externally creatable objects.

- ❏ The Object Browser is used to quickly look up information on classes exposed by components, but cannot be used with components that do not expose type libraries.

- ❏ The Visual Component Manager is used to catalog components using Microsoft's Repository technology for easy retrieval for use in other projects.

- ❏ The Visual Component Manager can store its data either in Microsoft Access (Jet) databases or Microsoft SQL Server databases.

- ❏ Registering a control adds an entry to the Windows Registry that allows a client to look up the component by its ClassId. This ClassId can be looked up using the AppId entry in the Registry, which is also created in the registration process.

SELF TEST

The following Self Test questions will help you measure your understanding of the material presented in this chapter. Read all the choices carefully, as there may be more than one correct answer. Choose all correct answers for each question.

1. Which of the following project types *cannot* act as an OLE server?

    A. ActiveX DLL

    B. ActiveX EXE

    C. Standard Exe

    D. ActiveX control

2. Both Applications A and B use version 1.1 of FOO.DLL (an ActiveX component). An upgrade to Application B is installed that upgrades FOO.DLL to version 1.2. Which of the following is true?

    A. Both Applications A and B work normally.

    B. Application B works, but Application A throws a protection fault whenever the methods of FOO are called.

    C. Neither Application A nor Application B work.

    D. All of the functionality in A and B work, but Application A throws a protection fault whenever it references properties or methods where the interface has changed.

3. Which of the following is **not** a benefit of early binding?

    A. The variable used can reference any type of object.

    B. In the development environment, you can use the VB's IntelliSense technology to automatically see a list of properties and methods of the object.

    C. Object references are resolved more quickly.

    D. The New keyword can be used to define the object variable and assign a reference to a new object in the same statement.

    E. You can trap events triggered by the object.

4. What is the proper command-1 line syntax to register an ActiveX component called FOO.DLL manually?

    A. Register /U FOO.DLL

    B. REGSVR32 FOO.DLL

    C. REGSVR FOO.DLL

    D. REGSVR32 /U FOO.DLL

    E. RunDll FOO.DLL

5. If a component does not provide a type library it cannot

    A. be used with VB.

    B. be referenced using the New keyword.

   C. expose a property with the String type.

   D. be added to the project in the References dialog box.

   E. Both B and D.

   F. Both B and C.

6. When using the New keyword to declare an object variable, when is the object created?

   A. Immediately, when the variable is declared.

   B. When the object is first referenced.

   C. When the Object reference is created using the Set keyword.

   D. It is unpredictable.

7. In what types of files can you find type libraries?

   A. DLL and EXE only

   B. COM, EXE, and DLL

   C. OCX, TLB, and OLB

   D. OCX, EXE, DLL, TLB, and OLB

   E. DLL and OCX only

8. Which of the following declarations will allow VB to use the faster early binding method when accessing properties and methods?

   A. Dim X as New control

   B. Dim X as New Form

   C. Dim X as Object

   D. Dim X as New stdFont

9. Which of the following creates a new instance of an Excel Application object?

   A. CreateObject("Excel.Application")

   B. CreateObject("Excel","Application")

   C. GetObject("Excel.Application")

   D. GetObject("","Excel.Application")

   E. Both A and D

   F. None of the above

10. What must be done to allow events to be passed to a VB component that provides a type library?

   A. This cannot be done with components with type libraries.

   B. Declare the variable in the Declarations section using the WithEvents keyword.

   C. Declare the variable in the procedure definition using the WithEvents keyword.

   D. Check the Raise Events checkbox in the References dialog box.

11. Which of the following can you *not* accomplish in the Object Browser dialog box?

   A. Determine the proper syntax for calling a method of an object.

   B. Look up the constants used with a particular property of an object.

   C. Register component objects.

   D. Search for a member name to make sure there are no ambiguous references in your project.

12. What is the preferred method for clearing up ambiguous references?

    A. Set the priority of the components so the type library of the ambiguous reference is higher on the list.

    B. Compile a version-compatible revision of the component with the member property or method renamed.

    C. Use the type library or component name in the reference.

    D. Explicitly reference the complete path to the component file.

13. Which of the following sets the object variable O to a dependent object rather than an externally creatable object?

    A. `Set O = AppObject.AddItem("KeyName")`

    B. `Set O = CreateObject("Excel.Application")`

    C. `Set O = GetObject(,"MyApp.AppObject")`

    D. `Set O = GetObject("","MyApp.AppObject")`

14. Which of the following commands should be used to manually register the component COMP.EXE?

    A. COMP.EXE

    B. REGSVR COMP.EXE

    C. REGSVR32 COMP.EXE

    D. REGSVR32 COMP.EXE /U

15. When registering an ActiveX DLL, what is responsible for actually registering the component?

    A. The REGSVR32.EXE utility

    B. The component itself

C. The client application

D. The developer using Regedit

16. How does a client application internally refer to COM components that are referenced using early binding?

    A. Using the ComponentName.ClassName

    B. Using a globally unique identifier (GUID)

    C. Using the path to the component's DLL or EXE file

17. Where is the path to a component's DLL or EXE file stored?

    A. In the VB FRM file.

    B. In the VB VBP file.

    C. In the Registry.

    D. Inside the component itself.

    E. In the VB VBG file.

18. When is an object destroyed?

    A. When the reference count is set to 0

    B. When a variable referencing it is set to Nothing

    C. When a variable referencing it goes out of scope

    D. When the DestroyObject method is applied to it

    E. When you call the object's Terminate Event

19. Which of the following is *not* an advantage of using COM components?

    A. Versioning

B. Execution speed

C. Encapsulation

D. Reusability

E. Interoperability

20. Application A contains ActiveX control B. ActiveX control B in turn, uses the functionality provided by ActiveX control C. What roles do each of these components play?

A. A = Server, B = Client, C = Client

B. A = Client, B = Client, C = Server

C. A = Client, B = Server to A and Client to C, C = Server

D. A = Server, B = Client to A and Server to C, C = Client

21. How do you add an ActiveX DLL type code component to a project?

A. The Components dialog box.

B. The References dialog box.

C. Declare an object reference to it.

D. Use the CreateObject function.

MICROSOFT CERTIFIED SOLUTION DEVELOPER

7

Building COM Components

I n Chapter 5, you learned to create classes as templates for objects to be reused within your application. It is important that you feel comfortable with these procedures before continuing with this chapter, because COM components are simply classes compiled into external objects that can be reused between applications. In this chapter, I am going to expand on the topic of building classes and discuss how to compile them into ActiveX COM components. For this reason, if you feel a little shaky on classes, please review Chapter 5 before attempting to work through this chapter.

Introduction to Building COM Components

Planning is the key to building a COM component that is easy to use in a client application and is able to retain compatibility through multiple versions of the component. Keep in mind that the idea behind COM is reusability. If you design a component with an interface that is confusing or limiting, you (or the developer using the component) may be stuck working with this interface over and over. Worse yet, because of COM versioning rules, you may not be able to fix or update the interface to the component in a very graceful way, if you want the component to remain compatible with clients using previous versions.

Creating COM Components

Creating the actual component in most cases is not very different from creating classes as described in Chapter 5. I am assuming that you are already familiar with this process, and I will focus on the issues that come up when building classes that are going to be compiled as external components. Let's start by talking about the types of ActiveX components you can create in Visual Basic.

ActiveX Component Project Types

As soon as you start a new project in VB, you are prompted to select a project type with the dialog box pictured in the following illustration (note the ActiveX component project types). In this chapter I will be talking about the ActiveX project types, with the exception of ActiveX controls, which are complicated enough to get their own chapter. (See Chapter 9.)

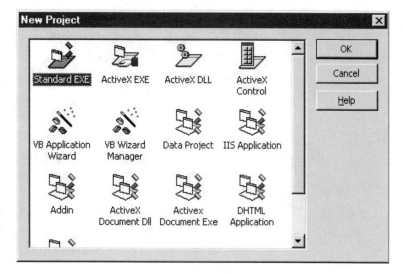

When selecting a component type to build, you need to answer two main questions:

- Where will the component be used? Will it be used on a form, from code, or possibly inside an OLE container application like Internet Explorer?

- What are the performance, stability, and feature requirements for this component?

The answer to the first question will tell you what major category of control you will need to use: ActiveX control, ActiveX code component, or ActiveX document. The second question will determine whether the DLL or EXE subtype is more in line with the functional requirements of the component you are designing.

Types of ActiveX Components

There are five types of ActiveX components shown in the New Project dialog box. They can be categorized into three major types:

- **ActiveX Controls** If you want a component that provides a user interface element that can be dropped into an application or Web page, an ActiveX control would be the most logical choice.

- **ActiveX Code Components** For components that run behind the scenes through calls to its methods and properties instead of user interaction with a visual element, an ActiveX code component is much more appropriate. ActiveX code components come in two subtypes, DLL and EXE.

- **ActiveX Documents** Choose this type of component when you need a component that can run in an OLE client application such as Internet Explorer or Word. They were originally developed to run inside the Microsoft Binder application, which didn't take off. Now they are used mostly in Internet Explorer, in intranet environments. Unlike ActiveX Controls that also can be used in Internet Explorer, an ActiveX document is not embedded in a Web page, but appears as the entire Web page, as shown in Figure 7-1. The advantage of using an ActiveX document instead of HTML for a Web page is that it is much easier to lay out a VB form than HTML. You get most of the functionality of VB behind your page, most of which HTML cannot support. The disadvantage of using ActiveX documents as Web pages is that they only work in Internet Explorer, and they can be much slower to load than the equivalent HTML page. ActiveX documents also come in DLL and EXE subtypes.

In-Process Components (DLL) vs. Out-of-Process Components (EXE)

For ActiveX code components and ActiveX documents, you can create the component as either a DLL or an EXE file. The primary distinction between these component subtypes is how they are loaded into memory

FIGURE 7-1

An example of an ActiveX document loaded in Internet Explorer

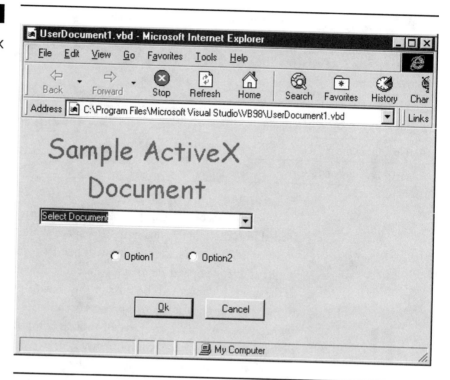

when used by a client (see Table 7-1). DLL components are created in the client application's process space (in-process) and EXE-type components are created in their own process space (out-of-process). ActiveX controls don't give you a choice in this matter; they can only be compiled as in-process OCX files.

When I talk about a process, I am referring to an area in memory that is allocated by the operating system to a particular application. In the Windows implementation of multitasking, each application is compartmentalized into processes. Effectively, each process serves as a virtual computer created for a particular application. In this model, each application can act as if it has the entire machine to itself. Behind the scenes, Windows intercepts all of the requests for memory, hardware devices, and processor time from each process, prioritizes them, and passes them on to the actual hardware.

TABLE 7-1	How Component Types Are Loaded into Memory	
Component Type	**In-Process**	**Out-of-Process**
ActiveX Control	✓	
ActiveX DLL Code Component	✓	
ActiveX EXE Code Component		✓
ActiveX Document DLL	✓	
ActiveX Document EXE		✓

When I talk about a component running in-process, I mean that it is loaded into the same virtual computer space as the client that is using it. By contrast, an out-of-process component gets its own virtual computer and might as well be operating on a separate machine (and sometimes is) as far as the client is concerned. Because of this, out-of-process servers must talk to the client application across process boundaries using a process called *marshalling*. For this reason, out-of-process components are sometimes referred to as *cross-process* components.

Now that you understand some of the underlying technical details of where a component runs and what it means to run in one process or another, why should you care? You should care because there are costs and benefits to both models that can make a real difference in the ways your component can be used, and how it performs. Here are the key points:

- **Speed** Winner by a landslide: in-process. When an application has to make calls across process boundaries, a marshalling process must occur. Marshalling is where Windows translates the communication between applications and/or components talking across process boundaries. As with any conversation that has to go through a translator, these conversations can move very slowly. In-process components don't need to take this extra step and can be called from the client as if they were part of the client itself. Although it might seem like almost all of the following items favor out-of-process components, this speed advantage is huge and should weigh heavily in your decisions.

- **Stability** Winner: out-of-process. If you are writing an application that requires the utmost in robustness, sometimes an out-of-process server is a better choice if the component is doing some dangerous stuff that might make it prone to crash. When code in a process causes a serious enough error (read as GPF), Windows has the option of dumping the entire process and everything in it. This means that if the component is running in the same process space as the client and makes a fatal mistake, the client will go down with the ship. On the other hand, a client is fairly insulated from a component in another process bombing, and if error handling is set up properly, the client can usually just re-create another instance of the object and recover gracefully.

- **Distributed computing** Winner: out-of-process. Because an out-of-process component runs in a separate process, and the communication between the client and component is brokered by Windows, only Windows needs to know where the component is actually running. Through *remote procedure calls* (RPCs) and *distributed COM* (DCOM), Windows can access the process of a component running on another machine and represent it to the client as if it were running locally. This gives a distinct advantage to components that have their own processes to run on a separate machine transparently. This is very useful in building multitier applications.

- **Bitness** Winner: out-of-process. For each process that is created for an application or component, Windows can simulate either a 16- or 32-bit machine, depending on the *bitness* of the code that is going to be executed on it. Each process can be either 16- or 32-bit, but never both. Following this logic, a 32-bit component (the only kind VB version 6 creates) cannot be loaded in the same process as a 16-bit client. If you want your component to work with 16-bit clients, you must use an out-of-process component.

- **Asynchronous execution** Winner: out-of-process. Out-of-process servers can be used to allow code to run asynchronously. See the section "Asynchronous Processing in Visual Basic," later in this chapter, for information on how to implement this feature.

While the EXE/DLL decision is commonly based on whether the in-process or out-of-process loading method is more appropriate, there is a situation in which you would want to select the EXE component type when using ActiveX code components. This is when you want the component to act as an *application server*. An application server is a component with a dual identity. It can be run like any standard EXE-type application, but can also be used by a client as an OLE server. DLL-type components cannot be used in this fashion.

exam
ⓦatch

Be sure you know which types of components are created in-process and which are created out-of-process. The VB exams always have questions about this in one form or another.

There are some sample scenarios to illustrate the process of selecting an ActiveX Project Type in the following Question and Answer box.

QUESTIONS AND ANSWERS

I want a component that will run inside of Microsoft Word.	ActiveX documents are the logical choice when your component is going to run inside an OLE container application.
I am developing a component to display a graph of mathematical functions for use in VB clients.	An ActiveX control is the best choice when you want interface-centric functionality that can be used as a tool to drop onto a form.
I need an application that can run stand-alone, but also exposes objects programmatically to VB and C++ clients.	ActiveX EXE code components are the only types of components that can be designed to run as application servers.
I want to encapsulate advanced math functions into a component. There will be a lot of information passed between the component and the client, and speed is essential.	ActiveX DLL Code Components run in-process and, therefore, can pass data back and forth to the application much more quickly than out-of-process components.
I am creating a component that will be used in an Active Server Page Script. The component is bound to be crash prone, and I don't want it to bring down my Web server with it.	ActiveX EXE components run in another process that can be terminated by the operating system, if necessary, without affecting the client.

Instancing

The Instancing property is used to designate classes as available to the client (public) or for internal use only (private). For public classes, the Instancing property is also used to control how objects are created when requested by a client. The instancing options for a class are set on the property sheet when the class is selected in the Project Explorer window, as shown in Figure 7-2.

Not all instancing options are available to all of the ActiveX component project types. Table 7-2 shows the instancing options available for each project type.

Private Instancing

The private instancing option is used to designate a class for internal use in the component only. These classes are not made available to the client.

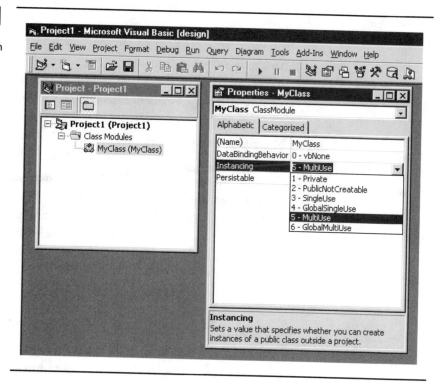

TABLE 7-2	The Instancing Options Available Vary Depending on the Type of Project		
Instancing Setting	**ActiveX Control**	**ActiveX DLL**	**ActiveX EXE**
Private	✓	✓	✓
PublicNotCreatable	✓	✓	✓
MultiUse	✓	✓	✓
GlobalMultiUse	✓	✓	✓
SingleUse			✓
GlobalSingleUse			✓

PublicNotCreatable Instancing

Classes defined this way cannot be created from the client application, but can be used by the client if they are created from within the component and then passed to the client. Objects created from this type of class are called *dependent objects*. A common way to give references to these types of objects back to the client is to provide an externally creatable collection class that exposes an Add method, which creates a new instance of the dependent object and returns a reference to the object to the client.

MultiUse Instancing

This setting is used for externally creatable classes. Externally creatable classes are classes that can be created from outside the component using the CreateObject method or the New keyword. The "multi" in MultiUse refers to the fact that a single instance of your component can create multiple instances of classes defined with this instancing option. This type of instancing makes much more efficient use of memory than the SingleUse method, because it only needs one instance of the component for all of the objects created from its classes.

SingleUse Instancing

This setting also allows for the creation of externally creatable classes. The only difference between this option and MultiUse is that each instance of

QUESTIONS AND ANSWERS

While working on a new version, I need to make interface changes that will break backward compatibility.	Use the No Compatibility option. Remember to change the filename of your component so that the incompatible version won't overwrite earlier versions on the users' hard disks.
I am compiling the first version of my component. Consequently, I do not have previous versions of the component to maintain compatibility with.	Use Project Compatibility. However, as soon as you have compiled the component, go back and set the compatibility option. That way, you won't mistakenly compile an incompatible version of the component the next time you update it.
I am updating a component and I want the new version of the component to work seamlessly with the other clients using an older version of the same component already on the users' machines.	Use Binary Compatibility.

Making Your Component User Friendly

In this section, I will describe several ways to make components that make life simpler for developers using your component in their client applications. In most cases, that developer using your component will be you! Remember that this code is supposed to be reusable. It is worth spending a little time now, to save yourself a lot of time later.

Custom Enumerated Types

Enumerated types allow you to use plain text identifiers in place of numbers or complicated parameters in your component. The following code how to set up the properties in your component to use the IntelliSense technology when using the objects created from your classes. Notice how the list of acceptable values is displayed in the VB IDE when setting the PetType property, as shown in Figure 7-5.

```
Public Enum PetTypes
     Cat = 1
     Dog = 2
     Fish = 3
     Bird = 4
     Wumpus = 5
End Enum

Public Property Let PetType(NewPetType as PetTypes)
     mPetType = NewPetType
End Property
```

This does more than just save the user a few keystrokes when writing the client application. It also makes the code much more readable. As you can see from the following example, it is much more evident what is going on when the enumerated type is used:

```
'*** This will work but, but it requires you to look up
'*** animal number 5 to figure out what is happening in
'*** this line of code

MyPet.PetType = 5

'*** Using the enumerated type clears things up

MyPet.PetType = Wumpus
```

FIGURE 7-5

Using enumerated types is a good way to make your component easier to use

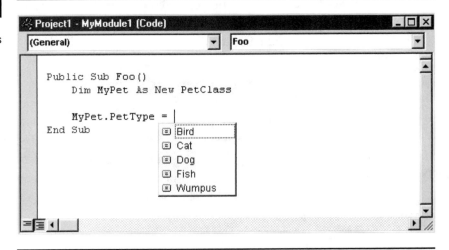

FROM THE CLASSROOM

Implementing COM with Visual Basic

Many COM component advantages occur through functionality contracts between the component author and consumer or developer. Known as interfaces, these contracts are groups of functions that encapsulate functionality into objects programmatically accessed through the interfaces that are implemented according to the COM standard.

Now this is all well and good, but what does this mean in layman's terms? Creating a COM component in VB begins by creating an abstract class. This class is used to define the interfaces of the COM components; it provides no actual implementation code of any kind. Additional classes created actually implement the defined interfaces, using the Implements keyword in your code. COM components can provide polymorphism by exposing different objects with a function of the same name, hiding the fact that the function may generate different behaviors. COM components may also involve

developing a hierarchy of objects within your component. Why would this be desired? A COM component might contain a single object that consists of so many interfaces and functions that dividing the complexity into separate, interdependent objects can significantly reduce the burden of using the component. This entails creating an object model for your component, which may be saved as a TLB or OLB file. The object model may also be saved internally within your ActiveX EXE or DLL compiled binary file.

Regarding the exam, make sure you are familiar with early and late binding, and how they would be implemented in a COM component. Be familiar with the purpose of iUnknown, QueryInterface, and iDispatch. Finally, be aware of the proper syntax for creating and manipulating objects defined within a COM component.

—By Michael Lane Thomas,
MCSE+I, MCSD, MCT, A+

Setting Interface Properties and Descriptions

You have already seen how the Procedure Attributes dialog box can be used to set the data-binding properties of a class. Now I will revisit this dialog box to show you how the top two-thirds of it can be instrumental in making your components easier to use. As you learned in Chapter 6, VB adds type library information to the DLL or EXE file when you compile an ActiveX component. What you may not know is that the Procedure Attributes dialog box (shown in Figure 7-6) allows you to customize the way the class is documented in that type library. This feature of VB allows you to compile documentation right into the component's EXE or DLL file.

The following options can be set for each member in the classes your component exposes.

- **Description** A short blurb is displayed in the bottom pane of the Object Browser dialog box, summarizing the use of the member

FIGURE 7-6

Entering a description in the Procedure Attributes dialog box adds a description to your property or method in the Object Browser dialog box

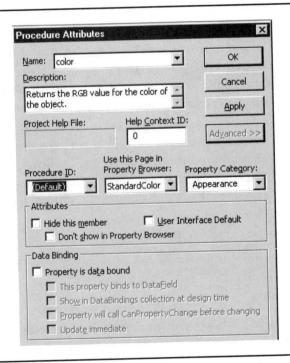

when the member is selected, as shown in the following illustration. This summary text is set in the Description field of the Procedure Attributes dialog box.

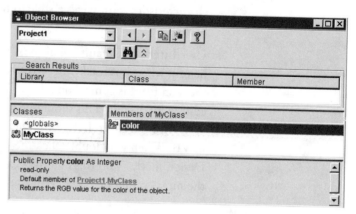

- **ProcedureID**   The ProcedureID field is used to choose a standard member ID for the selected property, event, or method. The member ID is used to identify a property, method, or event as a standard type that control hosts may know about. A property with this field set to Default becomes the default or value property of the class. A property specified this way is what is assumed when the member name is not explicitly specified. For example, if you define a person class and the name property is set as the default property, either of the following statements will retrieve the name value of the person object. (Note: Only one member of each class can be designated with the Default type ProcedureID.)

```
'*** Both of the following statements retrieve the name property
MyName = ObjPerson.Name
MyName = ObjPerson
```

- **Hide this member/Don't show in Property Browser**   These check boxes are used to hide properties in the IntelliSense lists and Object Browser. This is often done to remove the clutter of rarely used members that must be made public.

- **Use this Page in Property Browser** Use this option to enable custom Property Pages for members with complicated properties. A good example of this is Font properties, where multiple characteristics must be accessible to the developer using this property.

- **User Interface Default** This box, when checked, is especially helpful when it is used with ActiveX controls. When double-clicking the icon for this control on a form, VB will bring this method up for editing by default. This should be set to the method most commonly used with the control. An example of this is the Command button in VB. When you double-click the Command button on a form in Design mode, VB brings up the Click event subroutine, because it is the most commonly used event trapped by this control.

Creating an Enumerator for Your Collection Objects

There is a hidden feature of the ProcedureID field in the Procedure Attributes dialog box described above. You can set this property to allow a specifically designed property to act as a custom enumerator for collection type objects. Adding an enumerator to a collection object allows you to use VB's For Each...Next statements to iterate through the items in your collection. To enable this functionality, define a property of your class exactly as shown here:

```
Public Function NewEnum() As Iunknown
    Set NewEnum = mcolPeople.[_NewEnum]
End Function
```

After creating this property of the collection, open the Procedure Attributes dialog box and type -4 into the ProcedureID field on the Advanced tab. The last step is to select the Hide This Member option on the Procedure Attributes dialog box.

Enabling the For Each...Next functionality for your classes makes them work more like the built-in collection objects that the developers using your components will be used to.

on the **Job**

The For Each...Next construct also has the benefit of being somewhat faster in iterating through a collection than looping through a collection using a For...Next loop and using the index property of the collection to retrieve member objects.

Error Handling in Components

The preferred method for dealing with an error in a component is to correct the error silently and continue on normally. Of course, this is not always possible. When an error cannot be dealt with internally, a component should pass the error up the chain to the client using the Raise Method of the Err object. You can use enumerated types to assign meaningful names to the error codes your component uses, to make things a little easier on the developer using your component. Here is an example of error handling in a component:.

```
Public Enum WeaponType
    RIFLE= 1
    SPITWAD = 2
    MISSLE = 3
End Enum

Public Enum AnimalType
    WOMBAT = 1
    BABY_SEAL = 2
    ELEPHANT = 3
    TIGER = 4
End Enum

Public Enum SAFARI_ERROR_TYPE
    SAFARI_ERR_SUCCESS = 0
    SAFARI_ERR_INVALID_WEAPON = 1
    SAFARI_ERR_OUT_OF_AMMO = 2
Enum

Public Sub Hunt(Animal as AnimalType, Weapon as WeaponType)
    '*** Error Handling
    Dim ErrMsg as string
    If (Ammunition = 0) then
```

```
Select Case Weapon
   RIFLE: ErrMsg    = 'Out of Bullets.'
   SPITWAD: ErrMsg  = 'Out of spit.'
   MISSILE: ErrMsg  = 'Out of Missles.'
End Select

'*** Send the error up to the client
Err.Raise NUMBER:=SAFARI_ERR_OUT_OF_AMMO,, ErrMsg
Exit sub
End if
End Sub
```

on the job

In the previous code segment, I used the error values 0 through 3 for my component. In practice, it is probably not a good idea to use these values, as you tend to trample on error handling inside the client. It is recommended to add the VB constant vbObjectError to whatever error codes your component uses. This gives a good buffer for the error numbers used by VB and/or the client application.

A client application should only receive errors from the components it calls directly. You should not allow an error to be passed up the chain two levels. It is your component's responsibility to either deal with the error or translate the error message generated by the subcomponent into one that is meaningful in terms of your component. If the error in the subcomponent contains information that might be useful to the client in handling or debugging the error, it should be incorporated into the error generated by your component. Here is an example of this technique:

```
Public Function Calculate(ByRef V as Long)
    On Error Goto Error_Handler
    Dim VC as new Velocity.Calculator
    Dim Result as long

    Result = VC.GetVelocityCalculation(V)

    Exit Function

Error_Handler:
    Select Case Err.Number
      Case vbObjectError + 1000
          '*** Error 1000 means the velocity is negative
          '*** Get the absolute value and try again
```

```
        V = abs(V)
        Resume
    Case vbObjectError To (vbObjectError + 65536)
        '*** Unanticipated errors Velocity Component.
        Err.Raise ERR_VEL_UNK + vbObjectError,, _
                'Error Calculating Velocity'
        exit function
    End Select
End Function
```

CERTIFICATION OBJECTIVE 7.03

COM Tricks

This section presents some techniques available to you as a VB ActiveX component author. These items are clever tricks for improving performance and implementing difficult interactions between clients and servers. You might want to note that these techniques have been explicitly mentioned on the list of topics covered by the Visual Basic 6.0 Desktop Applications Exam.

Asynchronous Processing in Visual Basic

Normally, only one line of code in a VB program can be executing at a time. This behavior extends to COM objects as well. For example, when you call a method of a COM object, VB waits patiently for the method to finish executing before resuming on the next line of code in the client application. When a component is called in such a way that the component code must run its course before returning control to the client, the component code is said to be *blocking* or running synchronously. In most cases, this is exactly how you want your program to act. You generally want whatever that method was doing to finish before giving control back to the client, because it probably sets the stage for whatever comes after that call in the application. Blocking is caused by the fact that each process can only have one piece of code executing at one time.

When you run an in-process (DLL) component, it is loaded in the process space of the client. Thus, the component and the client must share the virtual machine created for the process, and only one piece of code between them can execute at one time. By using out-of-process components, you can get around this. As you'll recall, out-of-process components get their own virtual machine (process) to execute code on, so the component and the client can receive their own time slices and can effectively run asynchronously. This property of out-of-process components allows the client to make a call to the functionality in a component, and then go about its business while the component continues to process the request. The component will then notify the client when it has finished with the task, or when a certain state is reached. This asynchronous processing method can be accomplished by one of two methods: the call-back method and the event notification method. Both require some coding on both the client and server sides of the relationship. In this section, I will discuss how to take advantage of this benefit of out-of-process components.

Asynchronous Notifications Using Call-Back Methods

A call-back is just what its name implies. The application makes a call to a function or method, and goes about its business. When the external function has completed the task, it calls the application back by calling a function in the client designated to answer it. Although Windows programmers have done this for years, this technique is fairly new to VB.

On the application side of the component, you must do the following.

1. Create a new ActiveX EXE-type project.

2. Define an externally creatable class to manage each task or notification that will be handled by the component.

3. Create a type library containing the interface (or interfaces) that clients must implement in order to receive notifications. This interface must include all methods the component will call to notify the client. To create an interface, open a new ActiveX EXE or DLL project and add the properties and methods to a class module, but don't add any code to them. This class will serve as a template of the class that will be called back in the client application. Name the class with the interface name you want to assign to the component. The

Here is some sample code to call the component described in the preceding example:

```
Public WithEvents FileCopierObject as clsFileCopy

Public Sub DoFileCopy
    'Start File Copy process running asynchronously
    Set FileCopierObject = new clsFileCopy
    FileCopierObject.CopyFile(FileName,NewFileName)
End Sub

Public Sub FileCopierObject_FileCopyComplete()
    MsgBox "Notification: File Copy has been completed."
End Sub
```

Events cannot have named arguments, optional arguments, or ParamArray arguments. If you must use one of these constructs, you will have to use the call-back method.

Bundling Data to Improve Performance in Out-of-Process Components

As mentioned earlier in this chapter, making calls to properties and methods can be a fairly slow task when the client and component are not running in the same process. This was one of the factors that would push you away from the out-of-process or EXE-type components when opting for speed in your application. When designing an out-of-process component, you can minimize this performance sacrifice with the following technique.

A lot of the overhead required to make calls across process boundaries is not associated with passing the data, but with just opening a channel of communications between the two processes. With this in mind, we can minimize the damage by sending the same amount of data in fewer calls to the component's properties and methods. Take, for instance, the following example:

```
'*** Prepare for call to Purchase Ticket
objTicket.Smoking = True
objTicket.Class = TICKET_CLASS_COACH
objTicket.CreditCardNumber = PassengerCardNo$
objTicket.FrequentFlierNo = PassengerFreqFlierNo$
```

```
'*** Purchase the ticket
objTicket.PurchaseTicket
```

Although this method will certainly work, and is perfectly acceptable in terms of good programming practices, notice that the code initiates five calls to the properties and methods of the component. If the Airline component is in a separate process from the client executing the code, each of those calls is very costly. The following code executes the same functionality in a single call to the Ticket object:

```
'*** Purchase the ticket
objTicket.PurchaseTicket(Smoking:=True,
     Class:=TICKETCLASS_COACH,
     CreditCardNumber:=PassengerCardNo$,
     FrequentFlierNo:= PassengerFreqFlierNo$)
```

A side benefit of using this method is that the programmer using a component designed to use the second method can immediately see what information is necessary to execute PurchaseTicketMethod by looking at the method definition. This is one more example where forward-thinking design can make a big impact on the performance of a component.

CERTIFICATION OBJECTIVE 7.04

Designing an Object Model

The object model of a component is the blueprint for how clients will access the objects exposed by your component. The best implementation of an object model is also usually the simplest one. Navigating complex object models not only can be confusing, but also can take a lot of unnecessary time to de-reference all of the objects in the path of the object you are working with. This section offers some pointers on designing a good object model.

Root Objects

The name of the root object varies depending on the type of component. For example, application servers usually use the name Application for the root object, while in-process components usually use a name that is more indicative of the functionality of the component and which is very similar to the name of the type library.

The root object's function is twofold. Its first job is to pass out dependent objects (instanced as PublicNotCreatable) to the client application as they are requested through properties that are normally defined as collections. Because the root object is usually the gatekeeper for all of the objects lower down in the object model, you almost always want to instance it so that it is externally creatable—that is, use any of the options except Private or PublicNotCreatable. The second job a root object performs is to expose the properties and methods that affect the entire component. For example, if you wanted to allow the client to run the component in Silent mode and suppress all messages normally sent to the user by the component, you might implement a SilentMode property in the root object.

Getting References to Dependent Objects

The most common method by which root objects expose dependent objects to the client is an Add method. An Add method is exposed by root objects that expose collections of dependent objects. In the Add method, the client specifies the parameters for how the new instance of the object should be created. The root object will create the object, add it to a collection that is normally exposed through another property, and return a reference to that object. Here is an example of how this could be coded in a Book object that contains a Pages collection of Page objects:

```
'*** This code is contained in the Book Class

'****Local storage of property value
Private mPages as Pages

Public Property Get Pages as Pages
    Pages = mPages
End Property

'*** This code is exposed in the Pages class

'****Local storage of property value
Private mPagesCol as Collection

Public Function Add(PageNumber as integer, PageText as string ) as Page
    Dim NewPage as Page
```

```
     NewPage.PageNumber = PageNumber
     NewPage.PageText = PageText
     mPagesCol.Add NewPage
     Set Add = NewPage
End Function

'This is code in the client used to get a page object
Public Sub DoBookThing
     Dim MobyDick as New Book
     Dim NewPage as Page
     Set NewPage = MobyDick.Pages.Add(1,"Call me Ishmael…")
End Sub
```

Dealing with Circular References

Containment relationships, like the one shown in the preceding example, allow you to navigate through a hierarchy, from a high-level object to any of the objects it contains. Normally, these containment relationships flow down the chain, with each level containing the level below it. However, this model also allows for objects to be linked to objects higher in the chain. The most common form of circular reference is the parent property. A parent property is a property used to reference the parent object that contains it. In most cases, it is a good idea to avoid structures like this in VB, because they violate the rules of encapsulation and can cause problems by tearing down the object hierarchy when you have finished with it. I will use the Book component to illustrate this point. Say we have created a Book object that contains a Pages property, which references a Custom Pages Collection object, which in turn references Individual Page object. At some point in our program, after we have been using this object model in our library program, we destroy the object by setting the Book object to Nothing. Here is the sequence of events:

1. The Book object in the client is set to Nothing. The reference counter drops to zero for the Book object, and all of the local variables are released.

2. One of the local variables is the member variable that points to the Pages collection. When this variable is released, it lets the Pages object's reference counter hit zero. The Pages object is unloaded along with its local variables.

3. As each of the references in the Pages object to the individual pages is wiped out, their reference counters hit zero, and they are released until the entire object structure is unloaded from memory.

Now let's see what happens when we add a parent property to the Pages collection that points back to the Book object that contains it.

1. The Book object in the client is set to Nothing. The reference counter drops to one. (Remember, the Pages collection is still pointing at it.) The Book object remains in memory because it still has a reference pointing to it.

2. You now have no way to get back to the object hierarchy, because you no longer have a reference to any object in it from the client.

3. The objects remain in memory, inaccessible, until you shut down VB. The inevitable GPF occurs when one of those objects tries to reference memory in the process space that is now gone.

4. Oops!

If you must set up parent properties, the best way to avoid the problem I just outlined is by explicitly setting the parent property to Nothing before destroying the parent object. Here is an example:

```
'**** Clear the parental reference
Set MyBook.Pages.Parent = Nothing

'****Now it is safe to destroy the parent reference.
Set MyBook = Nothing
```

CERTIFICATION OBJECTIVE 7.05

Debugging COM Components

A component's external nature requires special techniques to debug the object. Here is some guidance on how to successfully test and debug an ActiveX component.

Debugging an In-Process Component

To debug an in-process component, you will need to create a client to test the component, because a component cannot run on its own. To set up a client to test your application, follow these steps.

1. With your component project open, select the Add Project item from the File menu and add a new standard EXE-type project to the development environment.

2. Make sure the new EXE project is selected in the Project Explorer window and add a reference to the component, using the References dialog box. (Note: VB sets up a temporary registration for the component when it is loaded into the current project. Any projects you add to this project group can use the component for testing purposes without the bother of registering the component first.)

3. Add code to the EXE project to instantiate each of the objects in your component and use their functionality.

4. Set breakpoints in either the client or component code as necessary; then run the project group by selecting Start With Full Compile from the Run menu. You will be able to step through code and stop on breakpoints in both the client and component, just as you would in a single, standard EXE project.

on the job   *In-process components will not unload while running in the development environment, even if all references to objects are released by the test project and all other component shutdown conditions are met. The only way to test DLL unloading behavior is with the compiled component.*

Debugging an Out-of-Process Component

Out-of-process means the component is running in a separate process from the client application. Therefore, you need to run your test program in a separate process. This means starting a separate instance of VB.

To test an out-of-process component, do the following.

1. Compile your component into an ActiveX EXE project. The executable is only used to allow the test project to keep its reference. It is not used for debugging the component.

2. If your component is an application server, set the Component mode in the Start Mode box on the Components tab of the Project Properties dialog box.

3. Start your component by selecting the Start option from the Run pull-down menu or by pressing CTRL-F5. Running your component makes VB switch the Registry entries for the component from the compiled version to a temporary reference to the one running in the VB IDE. This allows you to use breakpoints, watches, and all of the other debugging features of VB with your component.

4. Open a second copy of VB and start a new standard EXE-type project.

5. Add a reference to the ActiveX EXE project you are testing in the References dialog box. If it does not appear in the References dialog box, check that it is still running in the other copy of VB. If your project is running and you still don't see it in the References dialog box, make sure that the component has at least one externally creatable class in the project.

6. Create the test project that calls the methods and properties of each public class provided by the component you are testing.

7. If testing reveals that changes need to be made to the component—and there will be changes—make sure to recompile the component with the Project Compatibility or Binary Compatibility option selected after you make the changes and before you restart the test application.

Debugging an ActiveX Document Component

An ActiveX document component is yet another special case for debugging components. Because these projects run only in OLE container applications that support ActiveX documents like Word or Internet Explorer, they can

not normally be embedded in a VB client application. This means that you
will not be able to use either the in-process or out-of-process debugging
methods that I've just described on these components.

Don't be discouraged here—you can still use all the tools available in
VB, such as setting breakpoints, watching variables, and using debug
statements when debugging ActiveX documents; but you will need to use
the Internet as the test client. Set the project so that it starts in Internet
Explorer for debugging by selecting the Start Component radio button on
the Debugging tab of the Project Properties dialog box that is shown in
Figure 7-8.

At this point you should be able to debug the ActiveX document using
Internet Explorer as the test client. If you need to put an ActiveX document
in Break mode while it is running in Internet Explorer, press CTRL-BREAK.
Also, because the container that hosts the ActiveX document is using the
objects that the ActiveX document provides, Internet Explorer may throw a

---

FIGURE 7-8

If you have more than one
UserDocument in your
component, you can specify
which one you want to
debug on the Debugging
tab of the Project
Properties dialog box

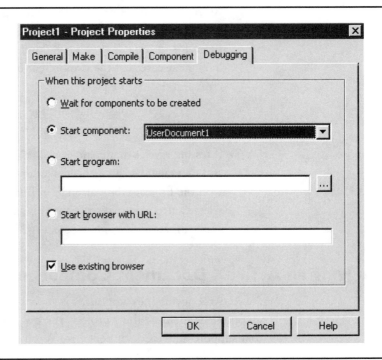

bunch of errors if you stop the project while the document is being displayed. To avoid this, close Internet Explorer before pressing the Stop button in VB.

Implementing Business Logic in COM Components

The modular nature of COM components, and the capability to use DCOM to seamlessly run components on separate machines, makes them a good choice for implementing multitiered applications. A multitiered application is simply an application that has its functionality broken out into components that are each tasked with a particular aspect of using the application. For example, the most common two-tier model is a server-side database. The database application is broken down into two pieces: the client piece, which presents the information to the user and collects information from the user; and the server piece, which receives requests from the client, executes them against its data, and returns the result to the client.

The main benefit in this type of client/server model is that the code executing against the data is run on a machine much closer to the data. Consequently, it can search the database more quickly, without the bottleneck of going over the wire to the network disk. Also, less network traffic is introduced, because only the answer is returned, not the entire database for parsing by the application running on the local machine. Yet another benefit of this approach is that, when you need to increase database performance, you only need to upgrade the server machine, rather than every workstation running the client.

This model worked so well that programmers kept finding ways to add levels (or tiers) to this structure. It is now very common to hear about a third tier in the mix, called a business logic or business services layer. The purpose of this layer is primarily to ensure that the data moving into the database has been checked and/or massaged to fit into the database, so that the business rules are enforced and data integrity is maintained. In this model, the business logic component acts as a translator of sorts for the data. By distributing the load over three components, we can split the processing onto yet a third machine, further improving performance in some cases. Although it is common for multitier architectures to split each tier onto a separate machine, this is not necessary. Many times, this is done to make a logical service more component based and easier to swap out should the need arise.

Creating Business Objects

Creating a middle layer is all about defining a good object model that resembles the data your application uses. The first step is to define the objects that your system will expose. These objects could represent employees, invoices, or orders, for example. At this stage, it is a good idea to put down the computer manuals, forget programming for a while, and think about your task in real-world terms. Answer the following questions about your data:

- **Objects**   What types of things do you need to keep track of?
- **Properties**   What will the client applications want to know about these things? What restrictions should be placed on changing the attributes of these things?
- **Methods**   What will the client applications want to do to or with these things?
- **Object model**   What is the relationship between the different types of things?

After answering these questions, an object model will begin to emerge. Fine-tune this model as you go, working through different scenarios with the objects you are defining. I would highly recommend modeling these structures on paper before attempting to code them. It is very easy to get started on the wrong track with object models to the point where you have invested too much time to go back and correct the model. I have said it before and I will say it again: Planning may seem time-consuming up front, but not planning is twice as time-consuming later in the application's life cycle.

Let's put these new skills to use and build an ActiveX document to function as a mortgage calculator that could be used on a Web page for a mortgage brokering company.

Creating an ActiveX Document

1. Open VB and select the ActiveX Document DLL project type. This will create a new project group containing a single UserDocument object. For the most part, you can treat these objects like forms.

2. Open the Project Properties dialog box and set the project name to Rcalc, and then close the dialog box to save the change.

3. Open the UserDocument1 object in Design mode and change its name property in the property sheet to udRateCalc.

4. Add the controls as shown in the following illustration to the UserDocument object, just as you would to a standard VB form. The TextBox control names are exactly as shown in the illustration. The command buttons should be named cmdCalculate and CmdGoHome.

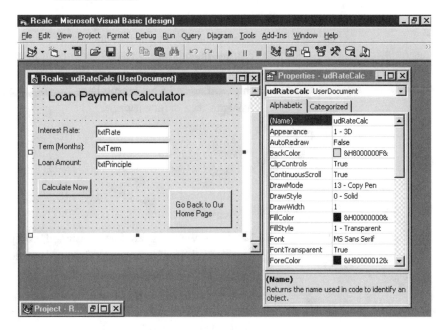

5. Add the following code to the Click event of the Calculate Now button:

```
Private Sub cmdCalculate_Click()
    Dim Payment As Currency
    Dim Term as double
    Dim MonthlyRate as double
    Dim Principle as Currency

    'Divide the Rate by 12 to get the monthly rate
    Let MonthlyRate = cDbl(txtRate/100)/ 12

    'Convert the Term and Principle values to Doubles for call to PMT
    Let Term = cDbl(txtTerm)
    Let Principle = cDbl(txtTerm)

    'Don't forget those seldom used VBA functions
    Let Payment = Pmt(MonthlyRate, Term, Principle)

    'Tell the user the damage
    MsgBox "Your monthly payment would be " & CCur(Abs(Payment))
End Sub
```

6. The UserDocument object, which is available in ActiveX document projects, exposes a Hyperlink property that allows you to force the container application to navigate to another document, replacing itself in the container. Add the following code to the Click event of the Go Back to Our Home Page button to allow the user to navigate to a different page.

```
Private Sub cmdGoHome_Click()

    'Send the user off to whatever website you designate
    UserDocument.Hyperlink.NavigateTo "http://www.microsoft.com"

End Sub
```

7. Now that we have our form designed, compile it using the Make option from the File menu. When prompted, the name of the compiled DLL will be RCALC.DLL.

8. Unlike compiling other project types, compiling an ActiveX document will produce several files. In this case, an RCALC.DLL and UDRATECALC.VBD file will be created. If we had added more

UserDocument objects to the project, there would be VBD (VB document) files for each UserDocument. The VBD file is the one that is opened from the OLE container application and links to the functionality of the ActiveDocument DLL or EXE.

9. Let's open our new VB document. A quick way to do this is to open Internet Explorer and then drag the VBD file onto it. You can also open the ActiveX document by typing the path or URL to it in the address bar, or even through a hyperlink on a Web page pointing to the VBD file. Open the VBD file in Internet Explorer using one of these methods.

10. Fill in values for the fields and click the Calculate button to see what the car payments would be on that new Ferrari.

11. Now click the Go Back to Our Home Page button to jump to Microsoft's Web site, and then look up dates for taking your next VB Exam.

CERTIFICATION SUMMARY

This chapter has covered a lot of material. I have discussed how to design your components to make the most efficient use of the resources on the client machine by selecting the proper component type, subtype, and instancing properties. You also should have picked up several new techniques to make the component more accessible to the developers using it. These include using a sound object model and taking advantage of the built-in features associated with VB class modules. Paying special attention to the issues of component and class will help you avoid making costly mistakes in your components, such as breaking compatibility or creating circular references that can be difficult to debug. Above all, planning is the key to developing good components.

✓ TWO-MINUTE DRILL

❑ DLL and OCX type components run in-process.

❑ EXE components run out-of-process.

❑ Out-of-process components can be used to enable asynchronous code execution.

❑ Blocking is the state in which a routine does not return control to the caller until it has completed executing.

❑ Parent properties are a common cause of problems when destroying object hierarchies because of circular references.

❑ Bundling multiple calls to an out-of-process component into a single call is a good way to speed up your application.

❑ Encapsulation requires that components do not let errors from subcomponents pass through to the client unless they have been translated into terms of the current component.

❑ Instancing allows the developer to define how objects from the component are created and who can create them.

SELF TEST

The following questions will help you measure your understanding of the material presented in this chapter. Read all the choices carefully, as there may be more than one correct answer. Choose all correct answers for each question.

1. Which of the following situations is not a good fit for an out-of-process component?

    A. The component will be run on a separate machine from the client using DCOM.

    B. The component needs to run very quickly and exchanges a lot of data with the client.

    C. The client needs to be able to call the component and not have to halt execution until the component is finished processing the tasks.

    D. The component must also act as a stand-alone application.

    E. The component must work in both 32- and 16-bit clients.

2. What types of projects cannot be compiled to run as out-of-process components?

    A. ActiveX documents

    B. ActiveX code components

    C. ActiveX controls

    D. None of the above

3. Which of the following instancing options is not available to ActiveX DLL components?

    A. Private

    B. PublicNotCreatable

    C. GlobalSingleUse

    D. MultiUse

    E. GlobalMultiUse

4. You are designing component A, which is used by component B. What should happen if an error occurs in component B?

    A. Components A and B should not trap the error, allowing it to propagate to the client for handling there.

    B. Component A should try to handle the error and, if it can't, pass it up to component B, which will try to handle the error. If it also can't deal with the error, it will translate the error message in terms of itself and pass it up to the client.

    C. Component B should in no situation pass an error up to component A.

5. A class has its instancing property set to MultiUse and the client requests two instances of the object provided by the class. Which of the following is true?

    A. MultiUse instancing does not allow a second instance to be created from the same component so an error is generated.

    B. Two instances of the component are created, one to handle each object instance.

C. A single instance of the component creates both objects for the client.

6. Which instancing option is used to create dependent objects?

   A. Multiuse

   B. PublicNotCreatable

   C. GlobalSingleUse

   D. Private

7. Which of the following versioning options can be used to make sure a component is compatible with earlier versions of the same component?

   A. Project compatibility

   B. No compatibility

   C. Version compatibility

   D. Binary compatibility

   E. All of the above

8. How can you set the description text for a member of a class to be shown in the Object Browser dialog box?

   A. Create a Description property in each class you want to document.

   B. Set the Description field in the Project Properties dialog box.

   C. Set the Description field in the Procedure Attributes dialog box.

   D. Add a specially formatted comment to the top of each method or property.

9. Which of the following components would need to use marshalling to talk to the client application?

   A. ActiveX controls

B. ActiveX document DLLs

C. ActiveX EXE code components

10. Which of the following is the best option for a component that will probably crash frequently?

    A. ActiveX EXE code component

    B. ActiveX DLL code component

    C. ActiveX document

    D. ActiveX server

11. Which of the following structures is a common cause of circular object references?

    A. Property containing a collection of another type of object in the component

    B. A HasChildren property

    C. A Parent property

    D. Too Many Root Nodes

12. When debugging an out-of-process component, why must you remember to compile the component after each change?

    A. Because the test project is using the compiled version of the component and must be updated

    B. To update the interface in the Registry so the client can access the new functionality of the component

    C. Both A and B

13. When creating a test project to debug an ActiveX EXE project, you don't see a listing in the References dialog box for the component. What could be the problem? (Choose all that apply.)

    A. The component is not in Run mode.

B. The component does not expose any publicly creatable classes.

C. The component needs to be registered using REGSVR32.

D. All of the above.

14. Which of the following instancing methods is a good choice for a Root object that is designed to be externally creatable?

A. Public Not Creatable

B. Private

C. MultiUse

15. Which of the following cannot host ActiveX documents?

A. Internet Explorer

B. Microsoft Word

C. Microsoft Binder

D. VB forms

16. Which of the following instancing options allows you to call the properties and methods of an object without first creating an instance of that object? (Choose all that apply.)

A. Private

B. GlobalMultiUse

C. SingleUse

D. GlobalSingleUse

17. What will happen when the following statement executes on the object named MyObject?

```
Dim V as variant
 V = MyObject
```

A. V will be assigned to the value of the default property if one has been defined.

B. V will now contain an object reference to an instance of MyObject.

C. V will be set to a long that is a handle to an instance of MyObject.

18. What is the term that describes methods that execute using synchronous processing?

A. Call-backs

B. Blocking

C. External component execution

D. MultiUse instancing

MICROSOFT CERTIFIED SOLUTION DEVELOPER

8

Using ActiveX Data Objects

CERTIFICATION OBJECTIVES

W ith the release of Visual Basic 6, a new, component-based data access standard has emerged from Microsoft. ActiveX Data Objects (ADO) and the underlying OLE DB interface have matured into a powerful technology designed to fulfill the vision of the Microsoft Universal Data Access initiative. The objective of Universal Data Access is to allow applications to access information from any location, regardless of where or how it is stored. Using ADO, you can easily access information from a variety of sources such as relational databases, mainframes, directory services, and Web-based content. As this technology continues to develop in the future, its open architecture will provide the capability to support many other nontraditional data sources.

In this chapter, we first discuss the architecture behind this new technology and examine each component in detail. Next, we'll cover the techniques necessary to use ADO in your VB programs. The final portion of this chapter describes several of the unique features available when using ADO.

CERTIFICATION OBJECTIVE 8.01

Overview of ActiveX Data Objects (ADO)

Microsoft ADO is a set of high-level objects that encapsulate the data access functionality of OLE DB. ADO is a provider-neutral object model designed for use in many languages, including VB, C++, Java, and VBScript. Regardless of the development language and the data platform, the ADO model provides a consistent set of objects and methods for data access. ADO supports nearly all of the functionality of previous data access methods such as Data Access Objects (DAO), Remote Data Objects (RDO), and Open Database Connectivity (ODBC). In addition to high-performance data access functionality, ADO provides the following benefits:

- Easier development using a simple object model.
- Reduction in network traffic and client memory requirements.
- Improved scalability and built-in support for resource pooling.

- Free-threaded objects for improved performance.

- Asynchronous operations, including event notification.

- Improved support for stored procedures and parameters.

- Support of multiple result sets and hierarchical record sets.

- Batch record updates and improved record set resynchronization.

- Support of client-side and server-side cursor locations.

- Support of local find, sort, and filter operations by record sets.

- Fabrication of record sets without a database connection.

- Saving of record sets to a physical file.

FROM THE CLASSROOM

ADO Accolades

Microsoft's newest champion of data access methods sports an ActiveX affiliation. Adding to Microsoft's alphabet soup of data access and management object libraries including DAO, RDO, OLE-DB, DMO, and ODBC, ActiveX Data Objects provide a slim and trim data access method designed for use in Active Server Pages; Visual Basic applications; and anywhere a developer could benefit from high speed, ease of use, low memory overhead, and a simplied object hierarchy.

What does ADO mean to the developer? With the release of ADO 2.0, a great deal of flexibility is provided to the developer. The combination of ADO/OLE-DB provider presents a high and low set of interfaces for data access. Furthering the functionality of ADO, Remote Data Service 1.5 has been combined with the ADO programming model to provide a simplified yet powerful and efficient method for pulling recordsets down to the client for reduced server overhead. With such a powerful model at their fingertips, it would seem obvious that familiarity with such a simplified data access method would be wise, prior to taking the exam.

Take a careful look at the ADO object model. It's simplified over predecessors, so it should not be a daunting task. Be familiar with the seven objects and four collections, including the proper syntax for establishing a collection and the minimum commands for doing so.

— *by Michael Lane Thomas,*
MCSE+I, MCSD, MCT, A+

Understanding Microsoft's Universal Data Access

It is very important that you are aware of the difference in the roles played by ADO and OLE DB. ADO is simply an application-level object interface that exposes the functionality of OLE DB system-level functions. In fact, you do not even need to use ADO to use OLE DB technology because nearly every feature of ADO could be accessed directly from OLE DB via system API calls. Although this would provide a slightly better data access performance, doing so is not recommended because it would increase the complexity of your application and lengthen your development time.

In the fall of 1996, Microsoft released the first versions of OLE DB, ADO, and the Advanced Data Connector. The Advanced Data Connector, a set of remote data access components, has since been replaced by Remote Data Services (RDS). RDS, in conjunction with the Remote Provider for ADO (sometimes referred to as ADO/R), provides the capability to access remote data in a distributed environment. Along with ODBC, these are the core components of the Microsoft Data Access Components (MDAC) package.

In July 1998, Microsoft released version 2 of the MDAC package. Included in this release are new and enhanced versions of all the components: OLE DB 2, ADO 2 (including an updated RDS), and ODBC 3.5. All of the components in this release have been highly optimized for speed and reliability for both desktop and distributed data access scenarios. Together, these technologies provide the tools necessary to realize and implement Universal Data Access.

At the heart of Universal Data Access lies OLE DB. OLE DB is an interface technology based on Microsoft's component object model (COM) architecture. The OLE DB specification model provides a standard definition of data access methods for data sources. For each supported data storage platform, there is a specific OLE DB provider that implements the standard data access methods defined in the OLE DB specification. See Figure 8-1 for more details about this architecture.

Currently, Microsoft is including three native OLE DB providers with the MDAC 2 package. These components provide native capabilities to Microsoft SQL Server, Microsoft Jet, and Oracle databases. A fourth OLE DB provider is also included in the MDAC 2 package, the OLE DB

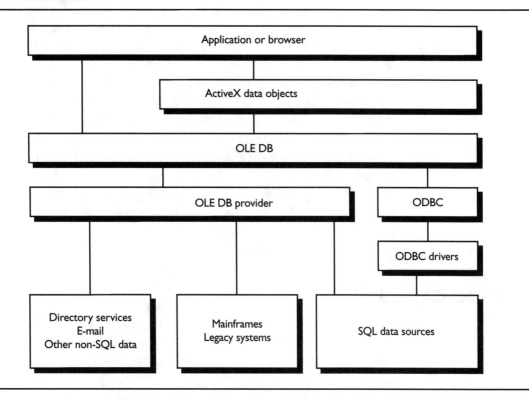

FIGURE 8-1   Data access architecture for ADO and OLE DB

provider for ODBC (sometimes referred to as Kagera). This provider acts as a translator for ODBC, and it allows OLE DB to access relational databases through their corresponding ODBC drivers.

The Benefits of the COM Architecture

Due to its open architecture based on COM, ADO is much more extensible than any of the other data access methods available today. COM provides several great advantages for ADO. COM interfaces are not restricted to only a baseline set of functions; each interface can provide additional functionality as needed. The use of COM and the distributed component object model (DCOM) allows ADO and OLE DB components to operate across multiple processes and even across multiple machines. This allows you to upsize the various data access components without affecting the actual program code. For example, a program originally configured to access a local Access database using a local ActiveX EXE could easily be upsized to use SQL Server through Microsoft Transaction Server. This location independence gives ADO a great amount of flexibility. It provides the capability to access data from any location, such as the local desktop, across a LAN or WAN, *n*-tiered client/server, mainframe, and data sources accessed across the Internet.

Another benefit derived from the COM architecture of OLE DB is that you can write your own OLE DB providers. Microsoft has released the MDAC Software Development Kit (SDK), which includes the OLE DB 2 specification. By using this specification, you can use VB 6 (or other COM-enabled development language) to write your very own OLE DB providers for any data source that you wish.

The ADO Object Model

For the most part, ADO now provides better performance than DAO and RDO. In addition to better performance, ADO provides a very compact object model with only seven objects (DAO has 17 objects and RDO has 10 objects). See Figure 8-2 for a diagram of the ADO object model. The primary objects in the ADO object model are the Connection, Recordset, and Command objects. The Connection object establishes a connection with a data source, the Command object executes commands, and the Recordset object manages result sets.

Both DAO and RDO use a hierarchical object model, which requires you to use the top-level object as the source for the lower-level objects. There is also a structured relationship between all ADO objects; however, you can create most ADO objects independent from other objects. For example, you can independently create a Command object and then execute the same Command object against several different Connection objects. This allows ADO objects to be very flexible and, ultimately, facilitates object reuse.

FIGURE 8-2   ADO objects and relationships

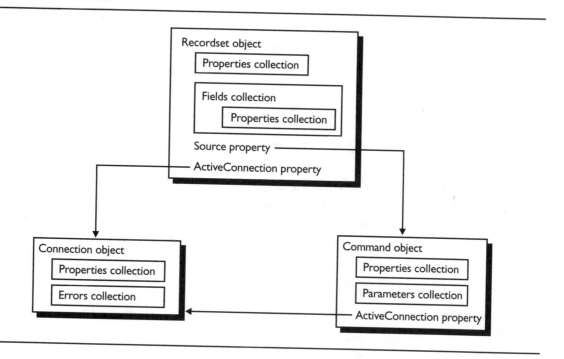

The Connection Object

The Connection object represents a session between your application and a data source. Using this object, you can configure various attributes before establishing the connection with the data source. You can also choose to use the client-side cursor library, which, depending on the OLE DB provider, may give support for special features such as batch updates.

You can open a connection asynchronously and use the State property to determine when the connection is completed. Once the connection is established, you can directly execute simple queries using the Execute method. The Execute method may also create a Recordset object. Connection objects manage transactions using the familiar BeginTrans, CommitTrans, and RollbackTrans methods; and Connection objects support different transaction isolation levels.

The Error Object

Connection objects contain an Errors collection, which is a collection of Error objects. You can use these objects to determine errors that have occurred at the OLE DB level. Errors that occur at the ADO object level *do not* produce Error objects; rather, they trigger the standard VB runtime error handler. With properties such as Description, Number, and Source, the Error object is very similar to the standard VB Err object. Two additional properties are available, SQLState and NativeError, which provide specific error details when using SQL data sources.

The Command Object

A Command object represents the definition for an instruction that you wish to run against a certain data source. Typically, this object is a SQL statement, query, or stored procedure name along with any parameters necessary to execute it. In the ADO model, Command objects are optional because some OLE DB providers may not include support for the ICommand COM interface.

If the command requires parameters, the parameter definitions are contained in the Parameters collection, a collection of Parameter objects. You can manually define the parameters for the command or you can use the Refresh method to force the OLE DB provider to create the Parameters collection. Using the OLE DB provider to refresh the Parameters collection may require the provider to execute several additional queries against the system catalog of the data source; so, for best performance, you should consider manually creating the Parameter objects.

Before you can execute a statement from a Command object, the Command object must be linked to a data source connection by setting the ActiveConnection property. By later changing the ActiveConnection property, you can link a Command object to a different Connection object. You can use the Execute method to execute the statement against the current data source connection. If it is a row-returning command, the Execute method will create a Recordset object.

The Parameter Object

Parameter objects represent the parameters and return values for stored procedures or parameterized queries. A Parameter object contains all the necessary details about a parameter, including the name, data type, value, and parameter direction (input, output, input/output, or return value). You can use the OLE DB provider to automatically refresh the entire Parameters collection or, for increased performance, you can create these objects manually. You must use the AppendChunk method when setting parameter values for long binary or character fields with more than 255 bytes.

The Recordset Object

The Recordset object is by far the most complex ADO object. This object represents a set of records returned from a data source. At any given time, however, the Recordset object refers to only a single record within the entire set. You can create Recordset objects from the Execute method of Command and Connection objects, or you can use the Open method of the Recordset object itself to create the contents of the object.

One of the most important properties of a record set is the CursorType property, which determines the behavior of the record set. This property must be set prior to opening the record set and the possible values include dynamic, keyset-driven, read-only, and forward-only cursors. The CursorType property determines if the record set is updateable and scrollable, and it determines how the record set handles records that have been concurrently created or modified by other users. You must use static cursor types when using a connection with client-side cursors.

Once you have created a Recordset object, you can navigate through the records using the familiar MoveFirst, MovePrevious, MoveNext, and MoveLast methods, as well as the BOF and EOF properties for location indicators. Using the Resync method, you can dynamically and nondestructively refresh a record set with the current values from the database. With record sets based on static or keyset-driven cursor types, you can use the BatchUpdate method to commit multiple updates to the database in one operation.

If you are using client-side cursors in your Connection object, you may be able to perform find, sort, and filter operations on the record set for additional data manipulation. Client-side cursors give you the capability to manually create record sets without database interaction and add records to it without using a data source, and you can save, or persist, a client-side record set to your hard drive for later use.

Be careful not to confuse the CursorType property with the CursorLocation property. The CursorType property only applies to Recordset objects and it determines the behavior of the record set. The CursorLocation property applies to both Connection and Recordset objects, and it determines where the record set cursor exists. By default, a record set will inherit the CursorLocation property from its Connection object; however, you can modify the CursorLocation property for the record set before opening it.

Field Object

Each Recordset object will have a Fields collection, composed of Field objects. Each Field object represents one column, or field, of data in the record set. In addition to the actual field value, you can retrieve and update additional properties for the field, such as Name, Type, Size, and Precision.

The Fields collection is the default collection of a Recordset object, so you can reference the individual fields in the following ways:

- Recordset.Fields("Last_Name")
- Recordset.Fields(1)
- Recordset("Last_Name")
- Recordset!Last_Name

The Property Object

In addition to the built-in properties that all ADO objects have, some objects have another set of dynamic properties as determined by the OLE DB provider. The Connection, Command, Recordset, and Field objects all contain a Properties collection, which is a collection of dynamic Property objects. A Property object contains Name, Type, Value, and Attributes properties. These are all read-only except for the Value property, which may be writable. To reference a Property object, you must use its name or ordinal index (for example, object.Properties("Name") or Object.Properties(0)) .

e x a m
ⓦ a t c h

The Properties collection contains only the special properties defined by the OLE DB provider. This collection does not contain any of the built-in properties that are associated with each object through the regular object.property notation.

Limitations of ADO and OLE DB

Currently, there are several limitations to this new technology. You may have noticed that the ADO object model does not have an equivalent object to the dbEngine or the rdoEngine. Without this type of top-level object, there is no way to create or manipulate the ODBC data sources on the local machine. Also, ADO 2 does not support parameterized queries for Microsoft Access databases, nor does it support the Access security model of users and groups. Microsoft has stated that this functionality will be included in future versions of ADO.

Adding ADO to Your Visual Basic Project

There are two different libraries supplied by ADO for use in your projects. To add either of these libraries, you must select Project | References from the VB IDE. In the list of libraries, you will find two libraries relating to ADO, the Microsoft ActiveX Data Objects 2.0 Library (ADODB) and the Microsoft ActiveX Data Object Recordset 2.0 Library (ADOR). The ADODB library contains the complete ADO object model and full ADO functionality; you will use this library for most of your full-scale applications. The ADOR library contains only the ADO Recordset object; this library is most useful for browser applications.

All of the examples in this chapter use the full ADODB library. You will also notice in the examples that the library name is included in the object declarations (for example, Dim rst as New ADODB.Recordset). This is a recommended precaution because many of the ADO objects have the same name as DAO objects.

ADO Threading Model

The ADO library is free-threaded; however, if you examine the Windows Registry, you will find the library listed as apartment threaded. Because not all OLE DB providers or ODBC drivers may be able to run free-threaded, ADO will normally run apartment threaded. You should run ADO as apartment threaded unless all of the OLE DB components that you are using are capable of running free-threaded.

QUESTIONS AND ANSWERS

How does ADO differ from OLE DB? Why not use OLE DB directly?	ADO is a high-level object model that simplifies the programming tasks involved with data access through OLE DB. Development time is decreased by using an abstract, high-level interface like ADO, rather than directly calling the low-level functions of OLE DB.
Why should I start using ADO for data access when I am already familiar with DAO or RDO?	For all practical purposes, ADO is a replacement for both DAO and RDO. While ADO 2 does not fully replace all the functionality of DAO and RDO, soon-to-be-released versions of ADO with enhanced functionality will provide the missing features. Also, ADO is faster, and it provides much more scalability and reliability than any other data access method.
What benefit is gained by specifying the cursor type for a record set (dynamic, keyset-driven, read-only, and forward-only cursors)?	Read-only and forward-only cursor types can provide increased performance in many situations because the amount of administrative processing overhead is reduced due to the limited functionality of the cursors themselves.

Handling Data Access Errors

When using ADO, you must deal with two main types of errors, application-level runtime exception errors and low-level provider errors. Application-level errors occurring within an ADO object initiate the regular VB runtime error-trapping routines. These ADO-specific errors trigger the On Error event and the error details appear in the VB Err object. These errors do *not* populate the Errors collection for a Connection object. For example, you would generate an application-level error if you attempted to execute a Command object without setting its ActiveConnection property to a valid Connection object.

Low-level provider errors are errors that occur below the ADO objects. These errors may occur in OLE DB or within a specific OLE DB provider. In addition to triggering the runtime error-trapping routine, these errors generate Error objects to populate the Errors collection for the associated Connection object. Usually when these low-level errors occur, the Errors collection is automatically cleared and repopulated with objects relating to the current error condition only.

In your program code, every time that you encounter a possible ADO error, you should check the Errors collection belonging to the current Connection object. If the Errors collection is not empty, then you should examine each Error object and take appropriate action to deal with the error. You should also note that unlike most other collections, the Errors collection is zero-based (the first item has an index of zero). The following code demonstrates how to loop through the Errors collection:

```
Dim cnn As New ADODB.Connection
Dim i as long
On Error GoTo Error_Handler

    'some error-causing operation on the cnn object.

    Exit Sub
```

```
Error_Handler:

    'Print out the VB Err Object
    Debug.Print Err.Number
    Debug.Print Err.Description
    Debug.Print Err.Source

    'Loop through the ADO Errors Collection
    For i = 0 To cnn.Errors.Count - 1
        Debug.Print cnn.Errors(i).Number
        Debug.Print cnn.Errors(i).Description
        Debug.Print cnn.Errors(i).Source
    Next I

End Sub
```

For a list of frequent OLE DB error codes, please consult article Q168354 in the Microsoft Knowledge Base.

(http://support.microsoft.com/support/kb/articles/q168/3/54.asp)

ADO Warning Messages

Some ADO operations will generate warning messages and place them in the Errors collection. A Recordset object can create warning messages when you set the Filter property, or when you call the Resync, UpdateBatch, or CancelBatch methods. A Connection object can also create warning messages when you call the Open method. These warning messages do *not* trigger the runtime error-trapping routine and they do *not* clear out the Errors collection before placing the warning message into the Errors collection. Before executing any of these operations, you should first call the Clear method on the Errors collection to clear out any previous errors. Then after completing the operation, you should check the Count property of the Errors collection to see if the operation returned any warning messages. If the Errors collection is not empty, you should examine each warning message and take appropriate action.

Connecting to a Data Source

In ADO, the Connection object establishes and maintains connections with data sources. The basic steps necessary to establish a connection are

1. Select which OLE DB provider you want to use.

2. Modify the characteristics of the Connection object (including the ConnectionString and CursorLocation properties).

3. Call the Open method of the Connection object to establish the connection.

The Provider and ConnectionString properties can be set as properties of the Connection object, or they can be included as parameters of the Open method.

Selecting an OLE DB Provider

By default, ADO will attempt to use the OLE DB provider for ODBC as the provider for new Connection objects. You can override this property by setting the Provider property of the Connection object to a different provider. For example, the following code demonstrates how to select the Microsoft Jet OLE DB Provider:

```
Dim cnn as New ADODB.Connection

    cnn.Provider = "Microsoft.Jet.OLEDB.3.51"
```

See Table 8-1 for a list of possible values for the Provider property. You can also specify the provider as part of the ConnectionString property as described in the following section of this chapter. In the preceding example, the complete ProgID for the provider was specified ("Microsoft.Jet.OLEDB.3.51"). You may use the shorter

TABLE 8-1	Connection Provider Property	Provider Name
OLE DB Providers	MSDASQL	(Default) Microsoft OLE DB Provider for ODBC
	SQLOLEDB	Microsoft SQL Server OLE DB Provider
	Microsoft.Jet.OLEDB.3.51	Microsoft Jet OLE DB Provider
	MSDAORA	Microsoft OLE DB Provider for Oracle
	MSIDXS	Microsoft Index Server OLE DB Provider
	ADSDSOObject	Microsoft Active Directory Service OLE DB Provider
	MSDataShape	Built-in provider for data shaping (only available with client-side cursors)
	MSPersist	Built-in provider for persistent record sets (record sets saved to files)

VersionIndependentProgID to specify the provider; however, for some providers it may be best to supply the complete ProgID to avoid potential version conflicts.

Building the ConnectionString Property

The ConnectionString property is a string value that contains connection-specific information relating to the target data source. There are four ADO-specific arguments, listed in Table 8-2, that the ADO Connection object supports and processes. ADO considers all other arguments to be provider-specific arguments and passes those arguments directly through to the selected OLE DB provider. The syntax for the ConnectionString argument list is based on the ODBC connection string format. For each argument, you must place an equal sign (=) after the keyword and a semicolon (;) must be used to separate each argument.

If you include a Provider argument in the ConnectionString, the value for that argument will override the current Provider property setting of the

TABLE 8-2	Argument Keyword	Description
ADO-Specific ConnectionString Arguments	Provider	The name of an OLE DB provider to use for this connection
	File Name	A file containing preset connection information
	Remote Provider	The name of a remote provider to use when opening a client-side connection with Remote Data Service
	Remote Server	The name of a remote server to use when opening a client-side connection with Remote Data Service

object. If you use the File Name argument to specify a file containing the connection details, you should not also set the Provider property because the file specification will cause the appropriate provider to be loaded.

Microsoft OLE DB Provider for ODBC

This is the default provider for ADO and it allows ADO to connect to any ODBC data source. This provider does not support any ConnectionString arguments; rather, it acts as a wrapper for ODBC and it passes all non-ADO arguments to the ODBC driver manager. The ODBC driver manager is then responsible for establishing the connection with the data source.

Similar to RDO, this provider allows you to connect to an ODBC data source with or without a predefined ODBC Data Source Name (DSN). In your ADO connection string, you can use any argument supported by the ODBC driver. For a list of common ODBC ConnectionString arguments, see Table 8-3. For example, to connect to a predefined DSN, your ConnectionString would look similar to this:

```
"Provider=MSDASQL;DSN=YourDSN;UID=sa;PWD=sa"
```

Alternatively, to create a DSN-less connection, your ConnectionString would look similar to this:

```
"Provider=MSDASQL;Driver={SQL Server};" _
  & "Server=YourServer;Database=YourDatabase;UID=sa;PWD=sa"
```

Argument Keyword	Description
DSN	The name of a predefined ODBC DSN entry
FileDSN	The name of a predefined ODBC File DSN entry
Database	The default database name
DBQ	The database qualifier or database name
DefaultDir	Default folder for desktop database drivers
Server	For non-DSN connections, the name of the database server
Driver	For non-DSN connections, the name of the ODBC driver to use for this connection (value must be enclosed in braces)
UID	User account ID
PWD	User password

For ODBC data sources, you can specify the user account and password in the ConnectionString property or you can specify this information as parameters for the Open method. If you provide this information in both places, the parameters for the Open method will override the settings in the ConnectionString.

The Connection object also provides a DefaultDatabase property that you can use to specify the default database for a connection. This can be set after you have opened the Connection, and it will override the Database setting in the ConnectionString. For certain databases, this property may need to be established to allow unqualified naming syntax (not having to specify the database or owner name) to access objects from the default database. Not all databases support this property, and setting it may return an error.

Microsoft SQL Server OLE DB Provider

This provider gives high-performance access to Microsoft SQL Server databases. It supports several additional ConnectionString arguments, listed in Table 8-4. These properties can be set as part of the ConnectionString,

Argument Keyword	Description
Data Source	The SQL Server name
Initial Catalog	The default database name
Integrated Security	Boolean value indicating whether Integrated Security should be used. If True, the OLE DB provider will rely on Windows NT Authentication for user authentication
Network Address	The network address for the SQL Server
Network Library	The name of a specific Net-Library DLL to use for this connection. The default value is taken from the SQL Server client configuration
Use Procedure for Prepare	Boolean value indicating whether commands should be prepared as temporary stored procedures
Auto Translate	Boolean value indicating whether the OLE DB provider should perform OEM to ANSI translation. Default is True
Packet Size	The network packet size. Valid range is 512 to 32767 and the default value is 4096
Application Name	String value indicating the client application name
Workstation ID	String value indicating the client workstation identity
User ID	User account ID
Password	User password

TABLE 8-4

Common ConnectionString Arguments for the SQL Server OLE DB Provider

or you can manipulate them through the Properties collection of the Connection object. In order to access these settings through the Properties collection, you must first set the Provider property of the Connection object to SQLOLEDB.

For SQL Server connections, you can specify the user account and password in three different locations: in the ConnectionString property, in the Properties collection of the Connection object, or as parameters for the Open method. If you provide this information as parameters for the Open method, the parameter values will override any User ID or Password settings in the ConnectionString or Properties collection. If you do not supply any parameters for the Open method, the ConnectionString arguments will override the settings in the Properties collection.

Microsoft OLE DB Provider for Microsoft Jet

Using this provider, you can access Microsoft Jet desktop database files. This provider supports several additional ConnectionString arguments, listed in Table 8-5. These properties can be set as part of the ConnectionString, or you can manipulate them through the Properties collection of the Connection object. In order to access these settings through the Properties collection, you must first set the Provider property of the Connection object to the Jet OLE DB Provider.

By default, this provider will open Jet databases in read/write mode. You must change the Mode property of the Connection object to adModeRead if you want to open a database for read-only access.

Selecting the Cursor Location

Before you open a connection, you can choose the location for the cursor engine. By default, ADO will use server-side cursors from the data source-provided cursor library. You can choose to use the local cursor library to create client-side cursors with added functionality. To use client-side cursors, you must set the CursorLocation property of the Connection object to adUseClient. To use server-side cursors, the CursorLocation property must have a value of adUseServer.

TABLE 8-5	Argument Keyword	Description
Common ConnectionString Arguments for the Jet OLE DB Provider	Data Source	The filename for the Jet database to open
	Jet OLEDB:System Database	The path and filename for the system workgroup database file
	Jet OLEDB:Registry Path	The Windows Registry key containing the Jet database engine configuration settings
	Jet OLEDB:Database Password	The database password

Opening a Connection

Once you have configured the Connection object, all you need to do in order to create the connection is to call the Open method. The syntax for the Open method is

```
Connection.Open ConnectionString, UserID, Password, OpenOptions
```

All of the parameters for the Open method are optional. If you supply the ConnectionString parameter, it will overwrite the ConnectionString property of the Connection object. The UserID and Password parameters will override any values specified in the ConnectionString property. If you set the OpenOptions parameter to adConnectAsync, the connection will be opened asynchronously. The following example illustrates three different techniques to open a connection to the same database:

```
'Example 1 uses the Provider property.
cnn1.Provider = "Microsoft.Jet.OLEDB.3.51"
cnn1.CursorLocation = adUseClient
cnn1.Open "C:\test.mdb", "admin", ""

'Example 2 specifies everything in the Open method.
cnn2.CursorLocation = adUseClient
cnn2.Open "Provider=Microsoft.Jet.OLEDB.3.51;Data Source=c:\test.mdb"

'Example 3 uses the default provider for ODBC (MSDASQL).
'This example also sets the ConnectionString before the Open Method.
cnn3.CursorLocation = adUseClient
cnn3.ConnectionString = "Driver={Microsoft Access Driver (*.mdb)};" _
    & "DBQ=c:\test.mdb;UID=admin;PWD=;"
cnn3.Open
```

Opening a Connection Asynchronously

There are many situations where the database connection may take a considerable amount of time to establish. For these situations, ADO provides the option of performing an asynchronous connection. This feature allows your program to continue executing while the connection is being established. This functionality is contained entirely within ADO and it is not dependent on the OLE DB provider, so this feature is available for all ADO data sources. Although you can establish data source connections using the ADO Recordset and Command objects, you can only establish data source connections asynchronously using the Connection object.

To execute an asynchronous connection, you must set the OpenOptions parameter of the Open method to adConnectAsync. Following the Open method, you can check the State property of the Connection object to find out the status of the asynchronous operation. Depending on the status of the operation, the value of the State property is a combination of the constants defined in Table 8-6. If an error has occurred during the asynchronous connection, subsequent checks of the State property may generate a trappable runtime error. The following code illustrates the use of the State property:

```
cnn.Open , , ,adConnectAsync

'Do a bit-wise comparison of the values
Do While (cnn.State AND adStateConnecting)
    Debug.Print "Connection is still in progress."
Loop
```

The Connection object also supports event notification for asynchronous operations. Therefore, if you are working inside a class module, you may be able to use the WithEvents option to establish programmatic event handlers that correspond to the events of the Connection object. You can establish two different event handlers for the asynchronous connection operation, obj_WillConnect and obj_ConnectComplete (where *obj* is the name of the Connection object). The obj_WillConnect event is triggered immediately before the object begins to connect and the obj_ConnectComplete event occurs after the operation has completed. You can examine the adStatus

TABLE 8-6	State Property Value	Description
	adStateClosed	The object is closed
Values for the State Property	adStateOpen	The object is open
	adStateConnecting	The object is in the process of connecting
	adStateExecuting	The object is executing a command
	adStateFetching	The object is fetching a record

parameter of the obj_ConnectComplete event to find out the outcome of the operation. For more information on these events, please consult the VB online documentation.

Stopping an Asynchronous Connection

If you wish to cancel an asynchronous connection operation before it has completed, all that you need to do is call the Cancel method on the Connection object:

```
cnn.Open , , ,adConnectAsync

'to cancel the asynchronous Open command
cnn.Cancel
```

Closing a Connection

When you are ready to close a connection with a data source, you need to call the Close method of the Connection object. This will terminate the connection, but it does not remove the Connection object from memory. After closing a Connection object, you can alter its properties and open it again. If you wish to completely remove the object from memory, you must set it equal to Nothing. For example:

```
'Close the connection
cnn.Close

'Remove the object from memory
Set cnn = Nothing
```

If you close a Connection object while there are open record sets associated with the connection, all of the open record sets will be closed and any pending changes will be canceled. If there is a transaction in progress when the connection is closed, a runtime error will occur. If a transaction is in progress and the Connection object falls out of scope, the transaction will be rolled back without an error. Any Command object that was linked to the closed Connection object will persist in memory; however, its ActiveConnection property will be set to Nothing. In addition, all provider-specific properties will be removed from the Properties collection of the newly orphaned Command object.

Retrieving Data from a Data Source

Once you have established a connection with a data source, you can use three different methods to create a record set containing data from that source. For simple commands, you can use the Execute method of the Connection object to create a record set. For more complex commands and commands that you want to use repeatedly, you should define the command using a Command object and then use the Execute method of the Command object to create a record set. You can also use the Open method of a Recordset object to retrieve data into the record set.

Connection Execute Method

You can use the Execute method of a Connection object to execute commands directly against the connection. This method is best suited for simple and infrequent commands that do not use any parameters. The syntax for this command is

```
Set Recordset = Connection.Execute (CommandText, RecordsAffected, Options)
```

The CommandText parameter is a string value that contains the statement that you wish to execute. This string may be a SQL statement, a stored procedure, a table name, or any other provider-supported command. The optional RecordsAffected parameter is a long value returned from the provider to indicate the number of rows affected by the execution of this command. The optional Options parameter is a long value that describes the command type; this allows the OLE DB provider to optimize the execution of this command. See Table 8-7 for a listing of the possible values for the Options parameter.

All Recordset objects created by this operation use a read-only, forward-scrolling cursor. If you wish to create a record set with a different

	Command Type	Description
TABLE 8-7 Command Type Values	adCmdText	Text command
	adCmdTable	Table name (provider creates an internal SQL query to return all rows in the table)
	adCmdTableDirect	Table name (provider returns all rows from the table)
	adCmdStoredProc	Stored procedure name
	adCmdUnknown	Unknown command type
	adExecuteNoRecords	Indicates the command or stored procedure does not return rows. If any rows are retrieved, they are discarded and not returned to the application. This can only be used in combination with the adCmdText or adCmdStoredProc command types.

cursor type, you must use the Open method of the Recordset object as detailed later in the "Recordset Open Method" section. If the command does not return any rows, you may omit the "Set Recordset =" portion of the statement.

The following listing shows several examples of the Execute method:

```
Dim cnn as New ADODB.Connection
Dim rst as New ADODB.Recordset
Dim lngDelRowCount as long

    'Open a connection to the Pubs database
    cnn.Open "Provider=sqloledb;Data Source=your_server;" _
        & "Initial Catalog=pubs;User ID=SA;Password=;"

    'Execute a row-returning SQL statement
    Set rst = cnn.Execute("SELECT * FROM Titles " & _
        "WHERE Type = 'psychology'", , adCmdText)

    'Execute a non-row-returning SQL Statement
    cnn.Execute "DELETE FROM Titles " & _
        "WHERE Type = 'psychology'", lngDelRowCount, adCmdText

    MsgBox lngDelRowCount & " record(s) were deleted."
```

Command Execute Method

You can also use the Command object to query a data source and retrieve a record set. In order to use the Command object, you must first define the object by setting several properties for it, including the CommandText and ActiveConnection properties. Once you have defined the object, you may call the Execute method to issue the command against a data source. Because this is a persistent object, once you have defined the command, you can execute it repeatedly without having to redefine the basic properties of it.

The CommandText property is a string value that indicates the main executable text for the command. In most situations, the CommandText property will be a SQL statement or stored procedure name. The ActiveConnection property links the command to a specific data source connection. You can set the ActiveConnection property to any valid Connection object or you can create an independent connection for this Command by setting the ActiveConnection property to a valid connection string.

Additional properties that you can set on a Command object include the CommandType property, the CommandTimeout property, and the Prepared property. The CommandType property is equivalent to the Options argument of the Connection Execute method and allows the OLE DB provider to optimize the execution of this command. Refer back to Table 8-7 for a listing of the possible values for the CommandType parameter. The CommandTimeout property can be set to indicate the number of seconds to wait before a timeout occurs. You can use the Prepared property to cause the provider to save a compiled, or prepared, version of the command, which can create faster execution of the command in the future. Refer to Table 8-8 for a summary of the Command object properties.

Command objects also have a Parameters collection, which is a collection of Parameter objects. For commands that use or require parameters, you can use this collection to create a detailed definition of the parameters.

	Property	Purpose
TABLE 8-8 Property Summary for a Command Object	CommandText	A string value containing the command to be executed.
	ActiveConnection	An object reference to the current connection object.
	CommandType	The type of command being executed (see Table 8-7).
	CommandTimeout	The number of seconds to wait before a timeout occurs.
	Prepared	A Boolean value. If True, the provider attempts to save a compiled version of the command to allow faster execution in the future.
	Name	A string value representing a programmatic moniker for the Command object. Can be used to call the command as a method of the Connection object.

Once you have set the properties for the Command object, you can call the Execute method to run the command against the current connection. The syntax for the Execute method is

```
Set Recordset = Command.Execute (RecordsAffected, Parameters, Options)
```

The optional RecordsAffected parameter is a long value returned from the provider to indicate the number of rows affected by the execution of this command. The Parameters argument is an optional variant array of parameter values for the command. You can use the Parameters argument if the command requires parameters and you have not defined the Parameters collection or if you want to override the values for some or all of the Parameter objects. The optional Options parameter is a long value that describes the command type and this allows the OLE DB provider to optimize the execution of this command. This parameter will override the value of the CommandType property. Refer back to Table 8-7 for a listing of the possible values for the Options parameter. If the command does not return any rows, you can omit the Set Recordset = portion of the function call.

The following code demonstrates how to use a Command object to create a record set:

```
Dim cnn as New ADODB.Connection
Dim cmd as New ADODB.Command
Dim rst as New ADODB.Recordset

    'Open a connection to the Pubs database
    cnn.Open "Provider=sqloledb;Data Source=your_server;" _
        & "Initial Catalog=pubs;User ID=SA;Password=;"

    'Execute a row-returning SQL statement
    cmd.CommandText = "SELECT * FROM Titles WHERE Type = 'psychology'"
    set cmd.ActiveConnection = cnn
    Set rst = cmd.Execute
```

Using Parameters with Commands

The ADO Command object provides support for parameters in two different ways. All Command objects have a Parameters collection, which you can use to define the parameters for the command. Alternatively, you can include a variant array of parameters as an argument for the Command Execute method.

The Parameters collection is a collection of Parameter objects. You can use ADO to populate this collection by calling the Refresh method of the Parameters collection. The Parameters Refresh method will require the ActiveConnection property to be set and it may provide poor system performance because it may need to query the database several times to gather the complete parameter specifications. For better performance, use the CreateParameter method to manually create the Parameter objects to fill this collection. You can use all types of parameters with Command objects (input, output, input/output, and return values). For input parameters, you simply need to set the Value property for the parameter before opening or executing the command. For output parameters and return values, you can check the Value property after completing the command to find out what values the command returned.

As part of the Command Execute method, you can also supply a variant array as the parameters for the command execution. If you have previously assigned values to the objects in the Parameters collection, any parameter values that are included in the Parameters argument will override the corresponding values in the Parameters collection. Also, you cannot use the Parameters argument to gain access to output parameters or return values.

The following code demonstrates several ways to use parameters with commands. This code uses a fictitious stored procedure in the pubs database called sp_AuthorSearchByName, which uses two input parameters, FirstName and LastName, and returns a record set containing the names of authors whose names match the parameters.

```
Dim cnn as New ADODB.Connection
Dim cmd1 as New ADODB.Command
Dim cmd2 as New ADODB.Command
Dim prm as New ADODB.Parameter
Dim rst1 as New ADODB.Recordset
Dim rst2 as New ADODB.Recordset

    cnn.Open "DSN=pubs;UID=sa;PWD="

    cmd1.ActiveConnection = cnn
    cmd1.CommandText = "sp_AuthorSearchByName"
    cmd1.CommandType = adCmdStoredProc
    'Use ADO to refresh the Parameters collection
    cmd1.Parameters.Refresh

    cmd2.CommandText = "sp_AuthorSearchByName"
    cmd2.CommandType = adCmdStoredProc

    'Manually create a parameter object and append it to the collection
    Set prm = cmd2.CreateParameter("FirstName",adVarChar, adParamInput, 25)
    cmd2.Parameters.Append prm

    'Or, create and append the parameter in one command
    cmd2.Parameters.Append cmd2.CreateParameter("LastName", _
        adVarChar, adParamInput, 25)

    'Use a variant array for the parameters
    Set rst1 = cmd1.Execute (,Array("Clark","Smith"))

    'Define the parameter object values
```

```
cmd2.Parameters("FirstName").Value = "Doris"
cmd2.Parameters("LastName").Value = "Jones"
set rst2 = cmd2.Execute
```

Commands as Connection Methods

Once you have associated a Command object with a Connection object, you can execute the Command object as if it were a built-in method of the Connection object. In order for this functionality to be available, you must first set the Name property of the Command object. This property then becomes the method name for the Connection object. The syntax for this operation is

```
Connection.CommandName Parameters, Recordset
```

The Parameters argument is an optional variant array of parameter values. The Recordset argument is an optional Recordset object that is only required for row-returning commands. You can also use this technique to execute stored procedures that are available to the Connection object and, if necessary, ADO will attempt to determine the parameter types. The following code demonstrates calling a Command object as a method of a Connection object:

```
Dim cnn as New ADODB.Connection
Dim cmd as New ADODB.Command
Dim rst as New ADODB.Recordset

    'Open a connection to the Pubs database
    cnn.Open "Provider=sqloledb;Data Source=your_server;" _
        & "Initial Catalog=pubs;User ID=SA;Password=;"

    cmd.CommandText = "SELECT * FROM Titles WHERE Type = 'psychology'"
    cmd.Name = "GetPsychologyTitles"
    set cmd.ActiveConnection = cnn

    'now call the command as a method
    cnn.GetPsychologyTitles ,rst
```

Recordset Open Method

Of all the methods that ADO provides for opening a record set, the Recordset object itself provides the most flexible method for creating record sets. By using the Recordset object, you have full control over the cursor type and record locking technique used by the record set, and the Recordset object provides the capability to independently create data source connections.

To use a Recordset object to open a record set, you must use the Open method. The syntax for the Open method is

```
Recordset.Open Source, ActiveConnection, CursorType, LockType, Options
```

The Source argument defines the text of the command. For this argument, you may provide a string variable containing the command text, or you can supply a Command object to use as the source. The ActiveConnection argument links the record set to a specific data source connection. You can set the ActiveConnection argument to any valid Connection object, or you can create an independent connection for this record set by setting the ActiveConnection parameter equal to a valid connection string.

The optional CursorType argument for the Open method is used to select the cursor type for the record set. See Table 8-9 for a list of the possible values for the CursorType argument. When using client-side cursors,

```
CursorLocation = adUseClient
```

you must use static-type cursors. Record sets based on client-side cursors may take longer to open because the operation must copy the entire result set from the server down to the client. Once you have opened a record set, you cannot change the CursorType property.

TABLE 8-9	CursorType Value	Description
CursorType Settings	adOpenForwardOnly	Open a forward-only cursor type (default)
	adOpenDynamic	Open a dynamic cursor
	adOpenKeyset	Open a keyset-driven cursor
	adOpenStatic	Open a static-type cursor

The LockType argument is an optional parameter that indicates the record locking, or concurrency, technique used by the record set. See Table 8-10 for a listing of the possible values for the LockType argument. When using client-side cursors, you cannot use the adLockPessimistic setting.

The final argument for the Open method is the Options parameter. This is an optional parameter that specifies the type of command being executed. Refer back to Table 8-7 for a list of possible values for this argument.

Several of the arguments supplied to the Open method can also be set as properties of the Recordset object (Source, CursorType, and LockType). For these settings, the values supplied in the Open method will override any previous property settings. In addition, if the source of the record set is a Command object and you set the ActiveConnection property in the Open method to any Connection object, you will generate a runtime error. In this scenario, the Command object must have its ActiveConnection property set to a valid connection before using the Recordset Open method.

The following code demonstrates the use of the Recordset Open method:

```
Dim cnn as New ADODB.Connection
Dim cmd as New ADODB.Command
Dim rst1 as New ADODB.Recordset
Dim rst2 as New ADODB.Recordset

    'Open a connection to the Pubs database
    cnn.Open "Provider=sqloledb;Data Source=your_server;" _
        & "Initial Catalog=pubs;User ID=SA;Password=;"

    'Define a command object
    cmd.CommandText = "SELECT * FROM Titles WHERE Type = 'psychology'"
     cmd.CommandTimeout = 30
     set cmd.ActiveConnection = cnn

    'Open rst1 based on the Command object
    rst1.Open cmd, , adOpenDynamic, adLockOptimistic, adCmdText

    'open rst2 based on a table
    rst2.Open "Titles", cnn, adOpenKeyset, adLockOptimistic, adCmdTable
```

TABLE 8-10	LockType Value	Description
Recordset LockType Settings	adLockReadOnly	The record set is read-only, and the data cannot be changed (default).
	adLockPessimistic	Individual records are locked while the user is in Edit mode for each record.
	adLockOptimistic	Individual records are locked only during the execution of the Update method for each record.
	adLockBatchOptimistic	Batches of updated records are locked only during execution of the UpdateBatch method.

Closing a Record Set

When you have finished using the record set, you can use the Close method to close it and free the system resources that were in use by the object. To completely remove the object from memory, you must set the Recordset object equal to Nothing.

QUESTIONS AND ANSWERS

There are three different ways to open a record set. Which method is the best?	The Recordset Open method provides the greatest amount of flexibility for opening record sets. The other two methods (Connection Execute and Command Execute) are best suited for executing commands that do not return any records.
Do I need to redefine a Command object if I change its ActiveConnection property?	No; one of the biggest benefits of using the Command object is that you can define it once and use it multiple times with different data sources.
Since server-side cursors are likely to provide faster performance, why would I ever want to use a client-side cursor?	Some operations can only be accomplished when working with a local copy of the data. These operations include batch updates, data shaping, record set fabrication, and record set persistence. For these features, it is necessary to have client-side cursor libraries available.

Sorting and Searching Data

Typically, when dealing with record sets from a data source in the past, the only method available to sort and search through the data was to use the ORDER BY and WHERE clauses of the SQL SELECT statement. ADO now provides several other methods that you can use to manipulate record sets.

Increase Performance with the Optimize Property

The ADO client-side cursor library provides the capability to dynamically create indexes on fields in local record sets. An index can dramatically improve performance when finding or sorting data in a local record set. Client-side Field objects include a dynamic property called Optimize; and if you set the Optimize property to True, an index will be created on the field. Once you have created an index, you can delete the index by setting the Optimize property to False. Because it is a dynamic property, you can only access this property through the Properties collection of the Field object.

Using the Find Method

You can use the Find method to locate a particular row within a record set. Using this method, you can quickly search through a record set without having to requery the data source. The syntax for the Find method is

```
Recordset.Find (Criteria, SkipRecords, SearchDirection, Start)
```

The Criteria argument is a string value that contains the search statement. The syntax for the Criteria argument is "*field operator value*" where *field* is one of the record set field names, *operator* is the comparison operator (=, <, >, or "like"), and *value* is the actual value being sought. When searching for dates, the target value must be enclosed by the # character (for example, "date_of_birth > #12/31/1997#"). When searching for string values the target value must be enclosed by single quotes (for example, "Name='Brooke'"). The "like" operator is used for string pattern matching and you may use * or _ wildcard characters in the string expression being sought where * will match any string of characters and _ will match any single character. Also, the Criteria argument can only be used to search for a single value (or string pattern) within a single field; it does not support multicolumn or multivalue searches.

You can optionally include the SkipRecords argument to specify an offset number of rows to use as the starting point for the search. The SkipRecords argument is a long value and it can be positive or negative. The offset direction is dependent on the direction of the search. For example, if the SkipRecords value is 1 and the search direction is forward, the Find method will start at the record immediately following the current record, and it will search through the end of the record set. If the SkipRecords value is 1 and the search direction is backward, the Find method will start at the record immediately preceding the current record and it will search back to the start of the record set. If you specify a bookmark location to use as the starting point for the search, the offset is calculated from the supplied bookmark location.

By default, the Find method will search forward through the record set; however, you can use the SearchDirection argument to specify the direction of the search. The values for the SearchDirection argument can be adSearchForward or adSearchBackward.

You can also use the Start argument to specify a bookmark location to use as the starting point for the Find method. Possible values for the Start argument include adBookmarkFirst (start at the first record) and adBookmarkLast (start at the last record).

If the Find operation is successful, it will set the record set position to the first record that satisfied the search criteria. If the operation did not find a record that met the search criteria, it will set the record set position to the end (EOF) or beginning (BOF) of the record set depending on the direction of the search. The following code illustrates the use of the Find method:

```
Dim cnn as New ADODB.Connection
Dim rst as New ADODB.Recordset
```

```
'Open a connection to the Pubs database using client-side cursors
cnn.CursorLocation = adUseClient
cnn.Open "Provider=sqloledb;Data Source=your_server;" _
    & "Initial Catalog=pubs;User ID=SA;Password=;"

'Open a recordset based on the Authors table
rst.Open "Authors", cnn, adOpenStatic, adLockOptimistic, adCmdTable

'To speed up the search, create an index on the last name field
rst.Fields("au_lname").Properties("Optimize") = true

'Find the first record with a last name that begins with S
rst.Find "au_lname like 'S*'"

if rst.EOF then
    msgbox "No authors were found with a last name starting with S."
end if
```

Dynamically Sorting Record Sets

After opening or creating a record set, you can dynamically sort the records by setting the Sort property of the record set. You can use this property to temporarily rearrange the records based on the values contained in one or more fields. The Sort property is a string value containing a comma-separated list of field names. The default sort order for each field is ascending; however, you can optionally include the ASCENDING or DESCENDING keywords after each field name to specify the sort order for the field.

After setting the Sort property, the record set will automatically reposition itself to the start of the record set. When using client-side record sets, ADO will automatically create a temporary index on the sorted fields. If you set the Sort property to an empty string, the records will be returned to their original sort order and any temporary indexes created will be deleted. The following code illustrates how to use the Sort property to sort a record set:

```
Dim cnn as New ADODB.Connection
Dim rst as New ADODB.Recordset
```

```
'Open a connection to the Pubs database using client-side cursors
cnn.CursorLocation = adUseClient
cnn.Open "Provider=sqloledb;Data Source=your_server;" _
    & "Initial Catalog=pubs;User ID=SA;Password=;"

'Open a recordset based on the Authors table
 rst.Open "Authors", cnn, adOpenStatic, adLockOptimistic, adCmdTable

'sort last name and first name in ascending order
rst.Sort = "au_lname, au_fname"

'sort last name in descending order and first name in ascending order
rst.Sort = "au_lname DESCENDING, au_fname"

'cancel the sorting to return the records to their original order
rst.Sort = ""
```

Dynamically Filtering a Record Set

ADO record sets also contain a Filter property that you can use to temporarily hide certain records from a record set. After setting the Filter property, you can later clear it and all of the original records will again be visible in the record set. The Filter property is a variant value that can contain several different types of values.

Filter Based on Criteria

You can set the Filter property to a string value containing multiple search clauses. These clauses are similar to criteria for the Find method where each clause must have the syntax of "*field operator value*". For the Filter property, the operator can include =, <, >, <=, >=, or "like" for string pattern matching. You must use single quotes to delimit string values and use # characters to delimit date values. The like operator supports the * and _ wildcards also. The Filter property can contain multiple clauses joined together using the AND or OR operators. For example:

```
'Find all authors where first name is Summer or Heather
rst.Filter = "au_fname = 'Summer' OR au_fname = 'Heather'"
```

You can also group clauses together using parentheses. However, there are some restrictions on the use of parentheses to group expressions together. Groups of clauses that are contained within parentheses can only be joined to other groups by the OR operator.

Filter Based on Bookmarks

You can also set the Filter property to a variant array of bookmark values. You can use this type of filter when you have a set of specific records that you want to be included in the filtered record set. Only the records referenced by the bookmarks in the array will be included in the filtered record set. For example,

```
Dim cnn as New ADODB.Connection
Dim rst as New ADODB.Recordset
Dim vaBookmark(2) as Variant

    'Open a connection to the Pubs database using client-side cursors
    cnn.CursorLocation = adUseClient
    cnn.Open "Provider=sqloledb;Data Source=your_server;" _
        & "Initial Catalog=pubs;User ID=SA;Password=;"

    'Open a recordset based on the Authors table
        rst.Open "Authors", cnn, adOpenStatic, adLockOptimistic, adCmdTable

    'Move to the second record
    rst.MoveNext

    'Add a bookmark for the second record
    vaBookmark(1) = rst.Bookmark

    'Add a bookmark for the last record using a bookmark enum value
    vaBookmark(2) = adBookmarkLast

    'Apply the bookmark array as the filter
    rst.Filter = vaBookmark

    'Only the second and last records remain from the original recordset.
```

Filter Based on Other Values

You can use several other special values for the Filter property. These filter types can help you when attempting to resolve batch update conflicts. See Table 8-11 for a list of these special values.

TABLE 8-11	Special Filter Value	Description
Special Filter Values	adFilterNone	Remove the current filter and show all records
	adFilterPendingRecords	Show only the records that have been modified locally but not yet updated on the server; only available for batch update mode
	adFilterAffectedRecords	Show only the records affected by the last Delete, UpdateBatch, CancelBatch, or Resync call
	adFilterFetchedRecords	Show only the records retrieved by the last call to the database
	adFilterConflictingRecords	Show only the records that failed during the last UpdateBatch call

Clearing the Filter

You can clear the filter by setting the Filter property to adFilterNone or to an empty string. After removing the filter, all of the original records will be visible in the record set.

CERTIFICATION OBJECTIVE 8.06

Updating Data

There are several methods that you can use to update records with ADO. From an ADO object perspective, the easiest way is to execute an action query (INSERT, UPDATE, or DELETE) to modify the records. Alternatively, using an ADO Recordset object you can change field values and then update the server with the new values. You can update individual records on the server using the Update method, or you can use the UpdateBatch method to commit multiple record updates at once. If your application requires transactional support, you can use the transaction methods provided by the ADO Connection object.

Modifying a Field Value

If you are using an updateable record set, you can modify the value of a field by setting the value of the field to a new value. Unlike previous data access methods, you do not need to issue an Edit command to place the record into Edit mode. In ADO, a record automatically enters Edit mode once you make changes to its value.

Update a Single Record

The Update method allows you to update the server with changes made to the current record of the record set. After modifying a record or adding a new record, all that you need to do is call the Update method to save the changes to the server. If you reposition the record set to a different record, ADO will automatically call the Update method to save the changes. If you want to discard your changes, you must call the CancelUpdate method.

As part of the Update method, you have the option of including a variant array of field names and a variant array of new values. This provides an additional way to update specific field values. If you do include these arguments, both arrays must contain the same number of elements.

The following code demonstrates the different ways to use the Update method:

```
Dim rst as New ADODB.Recordset
Dim vaField(2) as Variant
Dim vaValue(2) as Variant

    'Open a recordset based on the Authors table
    rst.Open "Authors", "DSN=pubs;UID=sa", adOpenKeyset, _
        adLockOptimistic, adCmdTableDirect

    'update several fields of the first record
    rst.Fields("au_lname") = "Smith"       'basic syntax
    rst("au_fname") = "Tammy"              'alternative syntax

    if msgbox ("Do you wish to update the name?", vbYesNo) = vbYes then
        rst.Update
    else
        rst.CancelUpdate
    end if
```

```
'move to a new record
rst.MoveNext

'Alternative syntax for the Update Method
vaField(1) = "au_lname"
vaField(2) = "au_fname"
vaValue(1) = "Westberg"
vaValue(2) = "Eric"
rst.Update vaField, vaValue
```

Update Multiple Records with UpdateBatch

ADO can also operate in a batch mode, in which multiple record changes are cached locally and then transmitted to the server as one combined batch. This can provide improved network performance by limiting the number of updates sent across the network. For this operation to be available, you must set the record set locking type to adLockBatchOptimistic. Many providers will also require that the cursor type be either keyset-driven or static for batch updates to work property.

You do not need to call the Update method after modifying records in batch mode. If you omit the Update method, ADO will automatically call it when the record set is repositioned. The Update method will place the record in the list of records that have pending changes. You must call the UpdateBatch method later to send a single update request to the server for the pending records. You can also call the CancelBatch method if you wish to cancel the changes for all the pending records. The following code demonstrates the UpdateBatch method:

```
Dim rst as New ADODB.Recordset

    'Open a recordset based on the Authors table
    rst.Open "Authors", "DSN=pubs;UID=sa", adOpenKeyset, _
        adLockBatchOptimistic, adCmdTableDirect

    'Change all the Authors' last names to Frost
    Do While (Not rst.EOF)
        rst!au_lname = "Frost"
        'rst.Update is optional here
        rst.MoveNext
    Loop
```

```
if MsgBox ("Click Yes to save the batch.", vbYesNo) = vbYes then
    rst.UpdateBatch
else
    rst.CancelBatch
end if
```

Adding and Deleting Records

To add a new record to a record set, you must use the AddNew method. If you call the AddNew method with no arguments, ADO will add a new blank record to the end of the record set. You can optionally supply a variant array of field names and a variant array of initial values. These will provide a way to initialize specific field values; if you include these arguments, they must both contain the same number of elements.

To save the new record into the record set, you can call the Update method or you can reposition the record set to automatically trigger the Update method. To cancel the addition of a new record, you must call the CancelUpdate method before repositioning the record set. Depending on the cursor type of the record set, you may not always be able to see newly added records. For these situations, you may need to call the Requery method of the record set to refresh the record set.

You can use the Delete method to remove records from a record set. This method can be used to delete either the current record, or all the records that satisfy the current Filter property of the record set. To delete the current record from a record set, all you need to do is call the Delete method with no parameters. If you wish to delete all the records that satisfy the Filter property, you must include adAffectGroup as the only parameter for the Delete method. When using the adAffectGroup parameter, the Filter property must be set to one of the special filter values defined back in Table 8-11.

In batch mode, ADO will cache record additions and deletions until you call the UpdateBatch or CancelBatch method. The following code demonstrates how to add and delete records using the Recordset object:

```
Dim rst as New ADODB.Recordset
Dim vaField(2) as Variant
Dim vaValue(2) as Variant
```

```
'Open a recordset based on the Authors table
rst.Open "Authors", "DSN=pubs;UID=sa", adOpenKeyset, _
    adLockOptimistic, adCmdTableDirect

rst.AddNew
rst!au_lname = "MacDonald"
rst!au_fname = "Jason"
rst.Update                      'Save the new record

'Add a record using variant arrays for initial values
vaField(1) = "au_lname"
vaField(2) = "au_fname"
vaValue(1) = "Sorenson"
vaValue(2) = "Darryl"
rst.AddNew vaField, vaValue

rst.MoveFirst                   'Reposition triggers Update method

'Remove the first record from the table
rst.Delete
```

EXERCISE 8-1

Manipulating an Access Database

You should not use any data-bound controls for the following exercise.

1. Create a new VB project and add the Microsoft ActiveX Data Objects 2.0 Library to the new project.

2. On the Load event for the Startup form, use a Connection object to establish a connection to the Northwinds Trader database (NWIND.MDB) using the OLE DB provider for Microsoft Access.

3. Also on the Load event, open an updateable record set based on the Categories table in the Northwinds Trader database.

4. Display the contents of the Categories table (Category Name and Description fields) in a list view control.

5. Create a button labeled "Delete" that gives the user the ability to delete from the database the category type that is currently selected in the list view.

6. Create a button labeled "Edit" that gives the user the ability to modify the values for the category type currently selected in the list view.

7. Create a button labeled "Add" that gives the user the ability to create a new category type.

8. On the form's Unload event, close the Recordset and Connection objects.

Using Transactions

You can use the ADO Connection object to manage transactions if the OLE DB provider supports transactions. To verify whether a provider supports transactions, you can check for a provider-defined property called Transaction DDL in the Properties collection of the Connection object.

There are three methods that you can use to manage transactions: BeginTrans, CommitTrans, and RollbackTrans. The BeginTrans method will return a long value indicating the nesting level of the new transaction, with one being the topmost transaction level. The other two methods have no arguments and do not return any values.

To begin a new transaction, all you need to do is call the BeginTrans method on a Connection object. From that point on, all changes made to data from that Connection will be contained within a single transaction and those changes will not be written to the database until the CommitTrans method is called. All of the changes can be undone simultaneously by calling the RollbackTrans method. If the provider supports nested transactions, you can begin a transaction within another transaction. Each of these nested transactions can be committed or rolled back independently of the outer transactions. The following code demonstrates how to use transactions with ADO:

```
Dim cnn as New ADODB.Connection
Dim lngCount as Long

    'Open a connection to the Pubs database
    cnn.Open "Provider=sqloledb;Data Source=your_server;" _
      & "Initial Catalog=pubs;User ID=SA;Password=;"

    'Begin the transaction
    cnn.BeginTrans
```

```
cnn.Execute "DELETE FROM Authors WHERE au_lname = 'Smith'", _
        lngCount, adCmdText

if msgbox (lngCount & " records will be deleted. " _
    & "Are you sure you wish to continue?", vbYesNo) = vbYes Then
      cnn.CommitTrans
else
      cnn.RollbackTrans
end if
```

CERTIFICATION OBJECTIVE 8.07

Using Disconnected Data

One of the key features of ADO and OLE DB is the support for remote data access and disconnected data manipulation. There are many situations in which it may not be possible to have a consistent open connection with a data source. For example, consider a Web-based browser application that may have only an intermittent connection with the data source. Or, consider an application for a traveling salesperson who needs to use a laptop continually during the day but can only connect up to the network once per day. These are situations where methods must be available to retrieve data to the local client, manipulate the data while offline, and later update the data source with the modified records. These situations also require the capability to determine whether the records have been changed by other users in the meantime, and provide the ability to resolve such conflicts. ADO provides methods for all of these operations.

Saving a Record Set to a File

ADO Recordset objects expose a Save method that you can call to save the record set, along with any pending changes, to a file. The syntax for this command is

```
Recordset.Save FileName, PersistFormat
```

The FileName argument is the complete path and filename indicating where to save the record set. You should only specify FileName on the first call to the Save method; and, if you include FileName on a subsequent call to the Save method, you will cause a runtime error. The only time that you should include FileName on a subsequent Save is if you need to change the filename. For any call to the Save method in which you include the FileName argument, if the file already exists, a runtime error will be generated.

You can use the optional PersistFormat argument to specify the format to use for the persistent file. Currently, ADO only supports one value for the PersistFormat argument, adPersistADTG. This value specifies the Advanced Data TableGram format, a proprietary data storage format from Microsoft.

Calling the Save method does not close the record set; both the record set and the persistent file will remain open until you call the Recordset Close method. Other applications will have read-only access to the persistent file while the record set is open in your application. If you call the Save method while the record set is in the process of completing an asynchronous operation, the Save function will execute after the asynchronous operation finishes.

To open a record set based on a persistent file later, you need to supply the filename as the source for the Recordset Open method. If the record set already has its ActiveConnection property assigned, you may also need to set the provider to MSPersist. The following code demonstrates how to save and reopen a record set using a persistent file resource:

```
Dim rst as New ADODB.Recordset

'Open a recordset based on the Authors table
rst.Open "Authors", "DSN=pubs;UID=sa", adOpenKeyset, _
    adLockOptimistic, adCmdTableDirect

'Save the recordset to a file
rst.Save "c:\SQLAuthorsTable", adPersistADTG

'Close the recordset and close the persistent file
rst.Close

'To re-open the recordset from the file
rst.Open "c:\SQLAuthorsTable", "Provider=MSPersist",,,adCommandFile
```

Record Set Fabrication

One of the most interesting features of ADO is the capability to create a record set without a data source. You can manually create a client-side record set, append fields to it, open it, and create and modify records within the record set without any database interaction whatsoever. This newly fabricated record set has all the functionality of a regular record set and it provides a powerful new tool for data storage and manipulation within your applications. The following code demonstrates how to create a record set without any database interaction.

```
Dim rst as new ADODB.Recordset

    rst.CursorLocation = adUseClient

    'Create the fields for the new recordset
    rst.Fields.Append "ID", adInteger
    rst.Fields.Append "Description", adVarChar, 50, adFldIsNullable
            rst.Fields.Append "Effective_Date", adDate

    'Open the recordset without any source
    rst.Open , , adOpenStatic, adLockBatchOptimistic

    'Now you have a fully functional recordset
    rst.AddNew
    rst!ID = 1
    rst!Description = "Initial Status"
    rst!Effective_Date = #1/1/1999#

    rst.AddNew
    rst!ID = 2
    rst!Description = "Second Status"
    rst!Effective_Date = #1/31/1999#

    rst.UpdateBatch

    rst.MoveLast
    MsgBox rst.RecordCount

    rst.Close
```

Synchronizing Record Sets with the Server

ADO provides the capability of determining whether other users have modified records on the server since the current record set was retrieved and updated. ADO provides this ability through a combination of the OriginalValue property, the UnderlyingValue property, and the Resync method.

The OriginalValue property is a property that belongs to Field objects. This property contains the original value of the field prior to any user modification. This value may not be consistent with the current value in the database if another user has made changes to the record.

The UnderlyingValue property is also a property of Field objects. This property contains the current database value for the field. If other users have made changes to the record since the current record set was retrieved, the UnderlyingValue property may be different from the OriginalValue property.

The Resync method is a Recordset method that you can use to refresh the fields in the current record set with the latest values from the database. This method is not the same as the Requery method, which refreshes the record set by re-executing the underlying command for the record set. The record set created by the Requery method will include new records, and it will not include deleted records or other records that no longer fit the selection criteria.

In contrast to the Requery method, the Resync method will only attempt to update the values for the records contained in the current record set. The syntax for the Resync method is

```
Recordset.Resync AffectedRecords, ResyncValues
```

You can limit the records that the Resync method will affect by setting the AffectedRecords argument to one of the values defined in Table 8-12.

The Resync method also gives you the option to completely refresh the field values (thus canceling any pending changes) or to only update the UnderlyingValue properties. To select the field update method, set the ResyncValues argument to one of the values defined in Table 8-13.

```
Do Until rst is Nothing
    Do While Not rst.EOF
        Debug.Print rst.Fields(0)
        rst.MoveNext
    Loop
    Set rst = rst.NextRecordset
Loop
```

Data Shaping with Hierarchical Record Sets

One of the most interesting new features of ADO 2 is the Hierarchical Cursor feature, which allows you to create record sets that contain child record sets embedded as fields within the parent records. You can also create multilevel record set hierarchies by nesting record sets within other child record sets. There is no specified maximum depth of record set nesting; however, if you have large parent record sets, you probably will notice severe performance degradation as you increase the number of embedded nesting levels.

To provide this "data shaping" functionality, ADO 2 includes a new Shape command language. The Shape commands are a part of the MSDataShape provider, which is only available when using the client-side cursor engine. These commands allow you to define a hierarchy based on record relations, parameters, or aggregate function groupings. The syntax used by the Shape language is relatively complicated and you should refer to the online help for more information about the Shape syntax. You can use the Data Environment Designer to assist you in creating Shape commands, and you can use the Microsoft Hierarchical Flexgrid Control to display the hierarchical record sets created by the Shape command.

By default, fields that contain child record sets will have a field name of "chapter" and the data type for the field will be adChapter. To work with the record set contained in a chapter field, you must set a Recordset object to the Value property of the chapter field. You can also set hierarchical record sets to always synchronize with changes made to the underlying child records on the data source. By setting the StayInSync property of the record set to True, the parent record set will always be updated when the underlying child record set, or chapter, is changed. If this property is

False, the parent record set will never be updated to reflect changes to the child record sets.

The following code demonstrates how to use data shaping:

```
Dim cnn as New ADODB.Connection
Dim rstAuthors as New ADODB.Recordset
Dim rstTitles as New ADODB.Recordset

    'Open a connection using the Shape Provider
    cnn.Provider = "MSDataShape"
    cnn.Open "Shape Provider=MSDASQL;DSN=pubs;UID=sa;PWD="

    'Open a hierarchical recordset
    rstAuthors.StayInSync = true
    rstAuthors.Open "SHAPE {SELECT * FROM authors} " _
             & "APPEND ({SELECT * FROM titleauthor} AS chapter" _
             & "RELATE au_id TO au_id)", cnn

do while not rstAuthors.EOF
    Debug.Print rstAuthors!au_lname & ", " & rstAuthors!au_fname

    'Assign a recordset to the child recordset
    Set rstTitles = rstAuthors!chapter

    'Loop through all the child records
    do while not rstTitles.EOF
        Debug.Print rstTitles!title_id
        rstTitles.MoveNext
    loop
    set rstTitles = Nothing

    'Move to the next parent record
    rstAuthors.MoveNext
loop
```

CERTIFICATION OBJECTIVE 8.09

Understanding Performance Considerations

You can also create multilevel record set hierarchies by nesting record sets within other child record sets. There is no specified maximum depth of record set nesting; however, if you have large parent record sets, you probably will notice severe performance degradation as you increase the number of embedded nesting levels. As with all client/server or distributed applications, it is always prudent to limit the amount of data that must flow across the network. The client should only request the data that it truly needs, and the server should attempt to do as much of the work as possible.

Beyond the physical limitations of the network and the basic architecture of the system, ADO provides several ways to optimize performance. When you execute ADO commands, you should always specify the command type. Otherwise, the OLE DB provider may need to make several additional requests to the server to determine what type of command you have issued. When you are executing commands that do not return any records, you should use the adExecuteNoRecords value as part of the command type.

You should also attempt to avoid using the Refresh method for the Parameters collection of Command objects. While it may be a great convenience to have the application automatically build the parameter list, it comes at relatively high cost, especially in distributed environments. Although the manual parameter definition may require a great deal of coding, it will offer improved performance because the OLE DB provider does not need to make additional calls to the server to retrieve the parameter definitions.

Another method to reduce network traffic is to use hierarchical record sets and stored procedures that return multiple result sets. This can result in less network traffic for both data requests and data retrievals. You should also use the UpdateBatch method to combine multiple record update requests into a single call.

Whenever possible, you should attempt to perform operations asynchronously. ADO makes it very simple to connect asynchronously and to execute asynchronous commands. It only makes sense that your programs should take advantage of this because it can increase the overall performance of your system and provide additional control for time-consuming events.

CERTIFICATION SUMMARY

ADO is a language-independent, application-level object interface to OLE DB, Microsoft's newest and most powerful data access paradigm. ADO is a lightweight interface designed to be flexible and powerful enough to handle any data access requirements. Using the OLE DB provider architecture, ADO supports connections to many different data sources.

ADO is made up of three main objects (Connection, Command, and Recordset), which can all be instantiated independently from one another. The Connection object establishes connections with data sources, manages transactions, and reports errors from the underlying OLE DB components. The Command object defines commands and parameters and can execute commands against Connection objects. The Recordset object provides methods to manage and manipulate result sets of information in both immediate and batch modes. Record sets can use server-side cursors for better performance, or they can use client-side cursors, which provide added functionality. ADO also supports the creation of dynamic record sets containing multiple result sets or hierarchical record sets.

ADO record sets provide several unique features that are designed to improve network performance and to aid in distributed and disconnected environments. Record sets provide methods to sort, filter, and search the contents of the record set without requiring a requery of the database. Record set fabrication allows you to create a record set without using a data source, and record set persistence allows you to save a record set to a file for later use. Record sets also provide additional methods to help identify and resolve conflicts that may arise due to batch or disconnected record updates.

For the latest information on Universal Data Access and ADO, please refer to the following Microsoft Web sites:

http://www.microsoft.com/data
http://www.microsoft.com/data/ado

A. Requery method

B. Refresh method

C. Resync method

D. Recreate method

36. If a record set contains multiple return sets, what method can be used to retrieve the next set of records?

A. NextSet

B. NextRecordset

C. MoveNextSet

D. MoveRecordset

37. What provider must be used, along with the client-side cursor library, to gain access to the Shape command language to create hierarchical record sets?

A. SQLOLEDB.

B. MSPersist.

C. MSDataShape.

D. Any OLE DB provider can be used.

38. When working with hierarchical record sets, what is the data type for fields that contain a child record set?

A. adChapter

B. adRecordset

C. adChildRecordset

D. adUnknown

39. Which method to populate the Parameters collection of a Command object will execute faster?

A. Use the Parameters Refresh method.

B. Manually create the parameter definitions.

C. Use the Execute method.

D. Use the Parameters Rebuild method.

40. What command type should you always specify for commands that do not return any records?

A. adCmdStoredProc

B. adCmdUnknown

C. adCmdText

D. AdExecuteNoRecords

MICROSOFT CERTIFIED SOLUTION DEVELOPER

9

Building ActiveX Controls

CERTIFICATION OBJECTIVES

A ctiveX controls are custom controls that you can create and add to an application or HTML document. Programmers of ActiveX controls often are called authors, while the programmers who use these controls often are called developers. ActiveX controls are compiled as OCX files. Developers add these controls to the Visual Basic development environment through the Components item under the Project menu. When added to a project, an icon for the control appears in the VB Toolbox. Once the control is added to the Toolbox, developers can use it in their applications.

The capability to create ActiveX controls first appeared in VB version 5, but as we'll see in this chapter, version 6 has a number of exciting new features for such controls. By creating ActiveX controls, you'll be creating controls that specifically suit your needs in developing applications.

CERTIFICATION OBJECTIVE 9.01

Creating an ActiveX Control

There are three ways to create an ActiveX control. The first, and most common, is to select New Project from the File menu and choose ActiveX control from the New Project dialog box that appears. When you do this, a form-like container called a UserControl appears, and a new node labeled User Controls appears in the Project window. The UserControl, explained in greater detail later in this chapter, is a container into which you add other objects to create your ActiveX control.

The second method is to change an existing project into an ActiveX control. This is done through Project Properties, which is accessed from the Project menu. By selecting the General tab, you'll see a list box named Project Type. Clicking the list box reveals the possible types of projects into which you can change the project. Selecting ActiveX Control converts the project into an ActiveX control project.

Finally, you can create an ActiveX control by adding a user control to a project. This is done by selecting Add User Control from the Project menu. This brings up a dialog box with the following choices, which are covered in this chapter:

- User Control
- ActiveX Control Interface Wizard
- Colorful Control
- Control Events
- MacButton

In addition to adding one of the above ActiveX controls to your project, you can click the Existing tab and search your hard disk for an existing ActiveX control.

The UserControl is similar to a form in a standard EXE project. It acts as a container that holds controls and features that you add to your ActiveX control. To add a control from the Toolbox to a UserControl, you first need to bring up the Form object so it is visible on the screen (by selecting the UserControl from the Project window and then clicking View Objects). It is then a matter of double-clicking a control on the Toolbox, or clicking a control from the Toolbox and drawing it on your UserControl. Also like forms, the UserControl has properties and events that you can manipulate, which are covered later.

The differences between a UserControl and a form really stand out. For example, you are able to refer to the UserControl itself in code. Unlike forms, you don't refer to the UserControl by its name in code. If you had a UserControl named UserControl1 or MyControl, you would always refer to it as UserControl, as in the following example:

```
UserControl.BackColor=vbBlue
```

If you wrote that code with the UserControl's name as Me, an error would result.

It is important to remember that, as with forms, you can't name your UserControl with the same name as your project. This is a more common occurrence with UserControls than with forms, as many people feel their project should reflect the name of the control. If you give your UserControl the same name as your project (or vice versa), an error results.

Colorful control is a UserControl that has a Shape object, color, and code already added, which affect its appearance. This control is useful if you want to create an ActiveX control with a bit of pizzazz.

The Events control is also a UserControl with code that's already been added. Much of this code writes to the Local window. Code within this UserControl displays such things as mouse movement and Click events in the Immediate window.

The MacButton control provides a control that changes color when clicked. This is useful as a foundation for a control, if you want the user to visually recognize that the click has been made. Special effects are generally well received by end users, so this is a useful UserControl to start with.

The ActiveX Control Interface Wizard starts a wizard that steps you through the process of adding properties, methods, and events to your control, as well as creating code for the interface. Contrary to its name, it does not help you with creating an interface for the control itself. Before using this wizard, you'll need to add elements of a user interface to a UserControl and add Property Pages (discussed later in the section called "Creating Property Pages").

When you add a UserControl to an existing project or create a new ActiveX control project, one of the properties you should change is the ToolBoxBitmap. This property allows you to select an image that will appear in the VB Toolbox when your control is added to a project. By selecting the ToolBoxBitmap property of a UserControl, a button with an ellipsis appears. Clicking this button brings up the Load Bitmap dialog box, which you use to browse your hard disk for a graphic file to use as an icon for the control in the Toolbox.

When you compile an ActiveX control project, it is compiled as a file with an OCX extension. Each custom control added to the project is saved as a file with the extension CTL. If you've created your ActiveX control as part of an existing project, like a standard EXE, the CTL file is included as part of your EXE or DLL project.

Creating an ActiveX Control

1. From the File menu, select New Project, then choose ActiveX Control from the dialog box.

2. In the Property window for the UserControl, change the Name property to Y2K.

3. Add four TextBox controls to the UserControl, and erase the value of each of their Text properties in the Property window. Arrange them in a vertical row, so they appear like the text boxes in Figure 9-1.

4. Add a label to the UserControl. Change the Caption property to **There are**. Place the caption above the text boxes, so it looks like the label in Figure 9-1. If you want, you can also change the font size (with the Font property) so it appears similar to that in the figure.

5. Add a label to the UserControl. Change the Caption property to **until the millennium!** Place the caption below the text boxes, so it appears like the label in Figure 9-1. Change the font size (with the Font property) if you want, so it appears similar to that in the figure.

FIGURE 9-1

Y2K control

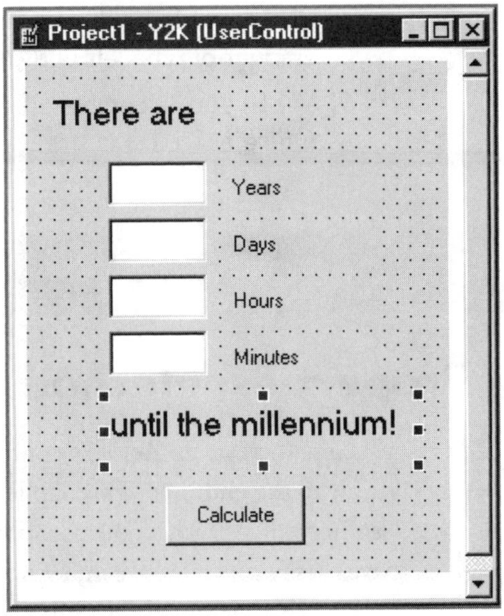

6. Add four labels to the UserControl. Change the Caption property for the labels to **Years**, **Days**, **Hours**, and **Minutes**. Place the labels so they look like the ones in Figure 9-1.

7. Add a CommandButton control to the UserControl. Change the Caption property to **Calculate**. Double-click the command button. This will bring the Click event up in the Code window. Add the following code:

```
Dim yearsleft, daysleft, hoursleft, minutesleft
    yearsleft = 2000 - (Year(Now) + 1)
    daysleft = Int(DateSerial(Year(Now) + 1, 1, 1) - Now)
    hoursleft = 24 - Hour(Now)
    minutesleft = 60 - Minute(Now)
    Text1.Text = yearsleft
    Text2.Text = daysleft
    Text3.Text = hoursleft
    Text4.Text = minutesleft
```

8. Press F5 to run the control. Since it hasn't been added to a project, a Project Properties debugging dialog box will appear. To continue, select Start Component and check Use Existing Browser. An HTML document will be created automatically, and the control will be displayed in your browser. Click the Calculate button to view the amount of time left until 2000.

9. When you've completed this exercise, save it. We will be using it for future exercises in this chapter.

CERTIFICATION OBJECTIVE 9.02

Exposing Properties, Methods, and Events

When you create an ActiveX control, the properties of the UserControl aren't visible to the end user. This applies not only to the UserControl itself, but also to controls such as the constituent controls added from the Toolbox. To have these properties become visible, you will have to *expose* them.

As mentioned earlier in this chapter, the ActiveX Control Interface Wizard can be used to automate the task of adding and deleting properties, methods, and events. However, to get the most out of the wizard, you will need to understand how to delegate or map properties. By understanding this, you will also be able to deal with situations that are too complex for the wizard to handle. In this section, we will deal with exposing properties, methods, and events manually, as well as how to use the ActiveX Control Interface Wizard.

Implementing methods in an ActiveX control is similar to implementing methods in other ActiveX components and class modules. You can create your own custom methods as Public procedures in the UserControl, then invoke the methods in code. After adding code to your Public procedure, you can add the ActiveX control to a form. Code within the form (or a control on the form) invokes the method, as you would invoke any other method of an object. For example, let's say you created a Public procedure called BoldAll to add to your UserControl. After adding the control to a form and naming it MyControl, you could then have code in the form invoke the method as follows:

```
MyControl.BoldAll
```

When adding a constituent control (that is, a control from VB's Toolbox) to a UserControl, the constituent control's methods are unavailable to any developer using your control. This is because the methods of a constituent control are Private. If you've authored a control, and want a developer to access the methods of a constituent control on your UserControl, you must create a "wrapper" for it, which delegates a method as Public. This is shown in the following example:

```
Public Sub TextHelp()
Text1.ShowWhatsThis
End Sub
```

While the ShowWhatsThis method for a TextBox control on our ActiveX control isn't available to the developer using our control, the Public procedure wrapping it allows access to the method.

Implementing custom events into a UserControl is also similar to creating custom events in class modules and other ActiveX components. This is done with the words Public Event, as seen in the following example:

```
Public Event MyNewEvent()
```

After creating this event, you can raise it with RaiseEvent, as seen here:

```
RaiseEvent MyNewEvent
```

Like methods, the events of a constituent control are unavailable to a developer using your control. As such, you need to implement *delegated events*, which act as wrappers for constituent controls. To do this, you first add a Public event to your UserControl, which is used to reflect the Private event of the constituent control. In the constituent control's event that you want made Public, you then raise the new custom event you just created. Raising the custom event allows the developer using this control to see that constituent control's event.

Creating an ActiveX Control That Exposes Properties

You can create custom properties for an ActiveX control with either Public variables or Property procedures. It is advised that you use Property procedures (that is, Property Let, Property Set, and Property Get) rather than Public variables. This is because, if more than one instance of your ActiveX control is used by a developer, problems could arise if the system accessed a property used in the two instances. If you use Property procedures, you could prevent such an occurrence.

Using Property procedures for ActiveX control properties is virtually identical to using Property procedures in class modules (which we covered in Chapter 5). The first step to implementing a property is to create a Private variable that will be used to store the property's value. Property Get is used to retrieve the value from this variable. Property Let and Property Set are used to store the property's value.

Property Let or Property Set procedures are used in a manner similar to Sub procedures. A parameter is used to accept a value, which is assigned as the new value of the property. This value is stored in the Private variable you set up to store the property value.

The Property Get procedure is used in a way similar to a function, in that it returns a value. Property Get is used to return the Private variable's value.

The major difference between using Property procedures and using public variables in ActiveX controls is the benefit of the PropertyChanged method with Property procedures. This method is used to notify VB that the property has been modified, and it is used to ensure that the WriteProperties event (explained in the next section) fires. By using PropertyChanged, Property procedures, and a Private variable, you are able to expose properties.

Using Control Events to Save and Load Persistent Properties

In using events to load and save persistent properties, the PropertyBag object is used. PropertyBag is just what it sounds like—an object of the UserControl that allows you to store property values. It allows the property values to persist, because the object itself persists, as instances of a control are created and destroyed.

exam
ⓦatch

Expect the PropertyBag object to make an appearance on questions dealing with ActiveX controls. It is fundamental to storing and retrieving persistent property values.

The PropertyBag object is used in the parameters of the WriteProperties and ReadProperties events. The WriteProperties event is used to save property values to the PropertyBag object, using the WriteProperty method. The ReadProperties event is used to load property values from the PropertyBag object using the ReadProperty method. In the following paragraphs, we will review each of these in greater depth.

When at least one property value has changed, the WriteProperties event occurs immediately before the UserControl's Terminate event. This allows a property value to be saved just before an instance of a UserControl is destroyed. To save a property value, the WriteProperty method of the PropertyBag object is used. This can be seen in the following example of code:

```
Private Sub UserControl_WriteProperties(PropBag As PropertyBag)
    Call PropBag.WriteProperty("BackColor", Text1.BackColor, &H80000005)
End Sub
```

In this example, an event parameter called PropBag is used as a PropertyBag object. The WriteProperty method of PropBag is then invoked to save the value of the BackColor property of a TextBox control called Text1.

As mentioned earlier, the PropertyChanged method is used to ensure that the system knows a property has been changed. If this method isn't used, it is possible the system will overlook a changed property value. By invoking this method, you make sure that the WriteProperties event is fired.

The ReadProperties event is used to load values of properties from the PropertyBag. The PropertyBag is a parameter of ReadProperties under the name of PropBag. Also similar to WriteProperties, the PropertyBag is used to invoke a method within the event. ReadProperty is a method of PropertyBag that has two arguments: the property's name (as a String value) and the value of the property.

The ReadProperties event occurs almost every time a control is instantiated. The only time the property doesn't occur when the control is instantiated is when a developer puts the control on a container (such as a form) from the Toolbox. This is because the properties haven't been initialized yet. When this happens, the InitProperties event occurs.

InitProperties is used to set the default values of the custom properties you create—constant values used to initialize values to default properties, when an instance of the control is created for the first time. In fact, the only time InitProperties fires is when a developer places your control on a container for the first time. This allows your suggested settings to be applied to the control, but it doesn't affect changes made by the developer once the control is used.

ActiveX Control Interface Wizard

The ActiveX Control Interface Wizard is used to define the properties, methods, and events of a user interface, and to create code for the members you define. This program automates much of the programming we've covered in this section.

To run the wizard, open an ActiveX control project to which you wish to apply the wizard's settings. From the Project menu, select Add User Control, and select ActiveX Control Interface Wizard from the dialog box that appears. This will start the wizard.

As in VB version 5, you can also load the ActiveX Control Interface Wizard into the Add-Ins menu by way of the Add-In Manager. To have the wizard appear as a menu item in your Add-Ins menu, click the Add-Ins menu and select Add-In Manager. The Add-In Manager will appear with a listing of available Add-Ins. Select VB 6 ActiveX Ctrl Interface Wizard from the list. To load the wizard into the menu, check the Loaded/Unloaded check box. To have the wizard automatically load when you start VB, check the Load on Startup check box. Click OK, and you can now start the wizard from your Add-Ins menu.

The first screen of the wizard explains what it is used for. If you don't want to see the introduction screen in the future, click the check box labeled Skip This Screen In The Future. Clicking Next will bring you to the Add Interface Members screen, shown in Figure 9-2. Here, you can select properties, methods, and events you'd like to use for your control. The left pane lists available members to add to the control, and the right pane lists all members that have been made Public in your UserControl. By clicking the arrow buttons between the panes, you are able to add and remove members from your control.

After selecting the members you want from your control, click Next to bring yourself to the Create Custom Interface Members screen. This screen allows you to add, edit, and delete events, properties, and methods to your control. By clicking the New button, you are greeted with the Add Custom Member dialog box. This dialog box allows you to enter a name for your member and select whether it is a property, method, or event. The screen that appears when clicking Edit is similar to this, allowing you to choose what kind of member it will be. You are not able actually to enter code for the member through this screen.

The next screen is Set Mapping, which allows you to map properties, events, and methods to specific constituent controls in your ActiveX control. For example, if you wanted to apply the BackColor property to a

Select Interface Members
screen of the ActiveX
Control Interface Wizard

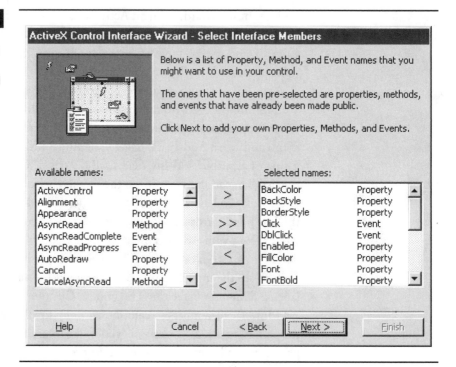

text box, you would first select BackColor from the left pane. In the Maps
To section, you would select your TextBox object from the Control list box
and the control's member (such as BackColor) from the Member list box.

Any members you don't map on this screen are dealt with when you
click Next. The Set Attributes screen allows you to set the attributes—data
type, default value, arguments, and read and write behavior—for any
members you didn't map in the previous screen. Members listed here have
default values already set for them, which will be applied if you don't
change them. After you've set these attributes, clicking Next brings you to
the final screen. Clicking Finish here or on the final screen will apply your
settings to the UserControl.

Testing a Control

Because developers will be using your ActiveX control in their applications, it is important to test the Design time behavior of your control in addition to its runtime behavior. This means seeing how the control behaves in VB's Design time environment when it is added to a form and coded. When you've finished testing its Design time behavior, it is important that you run the control, to see that it doesn't cause errors at runtime.

Testing and Debugging an ActiveX Control

The easiest way to test the Design time behavior of a control is to add a separate VB project to your ActiveX control project. In doing so, you can add your control to the test project and determine if its behavior is what you expected or desired. To create a test project for your control, select Add Project from the File menu, and then choose Standard EXE. This will create a project group.

When you have a project group, you can work on the design of a form and the control at the same time. However, when you have the ActiveX control's designer open, its icon in the Toolbox will be disabled and will appear grayed-out. This means you must close the designer if you want to add it to a form in your test project.

exam
ⓦatch

Microsoft loves to include questions that deal with things that go wrong. Remember that if your ActiveX control is grayed-out in the Toolbox, you most likely have the UserControl open in the background.

Once the control's icon becomes available in the Toolbox, you are able to add it to a form, just as you would any standard control. After adding it to a form, you can see if its features act properly in the Design time environment by using it as any developer would. You should add code to the form that manipulates its properties and events to see if these result in errors. Once you've confirmed that its Design time behavior is what you expected, you are then ready to see how the control performs at runtime.

Before running the project, you must specify which project you want to set as the startup project. This is the project that you want to start when Start is chosen from the Run menu. Right-clicking a project in the Project window and selecting Set as Start Up will set it as the startup project. If you want to see how your control runs by itself in a browser, set the ActiveX control project as the startup. If you want to see how code in a form interacts with the control and view it in a window, set the standard EXE project as the startup.

When debugging an ActiveX control, you should add Debug statements to the control's code to see if the values are what you expect them to be, and to ensure that code is acting as expected. For example, if you had a variable name intNum, you could add the following line of code to view what its value is at runtime:

```
Debug.Print intNum
```

When this line of code is reached, the value of intNum will be displayed in the Immediate window. You can also set watch variables and use other debugging tools in VB (as covered in Chapter 11) to test and debug your control.

Testing and Debugging an ActiveX Control

1. Open the project you created in Exercise 9-1.

2. From the File menu, select Add Project, and then choose Standard EXE.

3. Open your control's designer and double-click the command button, so the Code window appears. Below the code you added in Exercise 9-1, add the following code:

```
Debug.Print yearsleft
Debug.Print daysleft
Debug.Print hoursleft
Debug.Print minutesleft
```

4. Close the control's designer and open the form of your new standard EXE project. Double-click the Y2K icon in the Toolbox to add the control to your form. Resize the control and form, so the control is fully visible in the form.

5. In the Project window, select the standard EXE project. Right-click it and select Set as Start Up.

6. From the View menu, select Immediate Window. This will bring up the Immediate window, which you will use to view the values of your variables.

7. Press F5 to run your project. Notice that it starts in a window. Click the command button and view the values of your variables in the Immediate window.

8. Stop your project, and return to Design time. In the Project window, select the ActiveX control project as your startup project. Right-click the project and select Set as Start Up.

9. Press F5 to run your project. Notice that your Internet browser starts, displaying the control. Click the command button and view the values of your variables in the Immediate window.

CERTIFICATION OBJECTIVE 9.04

Creating Property Pages

If you're using VB, you're probably already somewhat familiar with the concept of Property Pages. They allow you to display properties through a screen that appears when the user right-clicks the control and chooses Properties. Rather than just displaying properties in the Properties window, the developer is able to use a more organized, and occasionally more advanced, grouping of properties.

The first step in creating a Property Page is to select Add Property Page from the Project menu. This will display a dialog box with two choices: you can select Property Page to add a blank Property Page to your project, or Property Page Wizard, which steps you through the process of creating a Property Page. In this section, we'll cover both options.

Creating and Enabling Property Pages for an ActiveX Control

Once you've decided which route you're going to use (that is, using the wizard or creating a Property Page manually), you must decide what properties you want to add to the page. Choosing Property Page places a blank Property Page in your project that looks like a UserControl or form. It is in this container that you can add the controls you want to use for accessing various properties.

When you create a Property Page, you should place complex properties on different pages or tabs. For example, on a Fonts tab, you could have Font Size, Font Name, and other related properties. As you go through the Properties window, you can spot such complex properties by the ellipsis button that appears when a certain property is selected.

While a Property Page appears similar to a form, it quickly becomes apparent that they are not the same. For example, one thing lacking is a Load event, while a number of events that aren't part of a form appear in the Property Page. These events are essential to programming with Property Pages.

The SelectionChanged event is used to check the values of properties and change them. This event fires when the Property Page is displayed, or when there is a change in the selected controls. A change in selected controls is a result of the SelectedControls collection. This is a collection of all controls that have been selected on the page. When you hold the CTRL key down while clicking controls, or lasso a number of controls by holding down the left mouse key and dragging over them, they become elements of the SelectedControls collection. The collection is zero-based, making its first element designated as shown in the following example:

```
SelectedControls(0)
```

The collection also has a Count property that allows you to tell how many controls are part of the collection. To refer to a property of one of the controls in the collection, you use the following syntax:

```
SelectedControls(Index).BackColor
```

The ApplyChanges Event is used to write information from a Property Page to the actual property of a selected control. This event occurs when the user clicks an Apply or OK button on the Property Page, or switches to another Property Page on the control. For the Apply button to work, however, the Changed property of the Property Page has to be set to True. The Changed property acts as a flag that enables the Property Page to determine if some property has indeed been changed.

After you've added code to the different events, you are ready to connect the Property Page to your control by double-clicking the UserDocument in the Project window. Doing this will bring up the properties for the UserDocument in the Properties window. In the Properties window, select the PropertyPages property, and then click the ellipsis button that appears. This will bring up the Connect Property Pages dialog box.

This dialog box contains a list of all Property Pages available in the current project. By clicking the check box beside the name of a Property Page, the pages are associated with your control. The arrows adjacent to the listing allow you to specify the order in which these pages will appear. In other words, when the developer chooses Properties, he or she sets the order of the tabs that appear.

Using the Property Page Wizard

The Property Page Wizard automates the task of creating a Property Page. Once this wizard is started, you are greeted with an introduction screen. To avoid seeing this in later sessions, click the Skip This Screen In The Future check box.

The Select the Property Pages screen is next in the wizard. This screen allows you to specify what Property Pages, which are already part of the project, you'd like to associate with your control. When you click a check box beside a Property Page name, it will be added to the group of pages for that control. If you would like to add a new page, click the Add button and type in a name for your new Property Page. The Rename button allows you to rename an existing Property Page.

The next screen is Add Properties, shown in Figure 9-3. The right-hand side of this screen has a number of tabbed pages, with each tab possessing the name of each Property Page added in the previous screen. Clicking these tabs allows you to switch from one Property Page to another. After selecting the Property Page you want to modify, you can add various properties from a pane on the left side of the screen. These are all Public properties that are part of your control. Arrows between this pane and the tabbed pages allow

The Add Properties
screen of the Property
Page Wizard

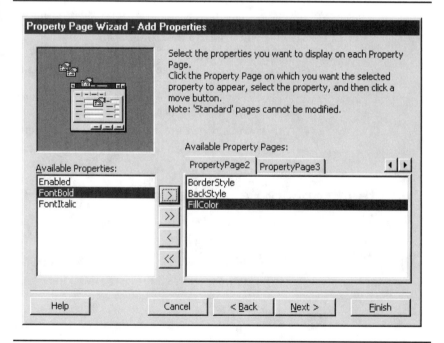

you to add and remove properties from the pages. When you've arranged the properties you want on each page, click Next to continue to the final page. After you click Finish, your Property Page(s) will be built and associated with your control.

Once you've created the page, you are ready to add any necessary code to its events and to test it. To view the Property Page, simply right-click your control and choose Properties. The Property Page will appear.

on the
job

The Property Page Wizard is a handy tool for creating Property Pages. It is often easiest to create Property Pages with this wizard and then edit or add code to the necessary events afterward. Many programmers turn up their noses at wizards because of their limited uses. It's true that many wizards take longer to use than it takes to create something manually. This is not the case with the Property Page Wizard, which creates and associates Property Pages faster than you could ever do it manually.

CERTIFICATION OBJECTIVE 9.05

Creating a Data-Bound Control

VB enables you to bind properties of your ActiveX control to a data source, thereby making data-aware controls. This means your control needs a DataSource and DataField property to indicate which control and which field to bind to, respectively. In creating a data-bound control, you can bind the properties, and display data from the data source.

Enabling the Data-Binding Capabilities of an ActiveX Control

To enable the data-binding capabilities of an ActiveX control, you must first open the Code window of your UserControl and move to the Property procedure to which you want to bind the data. This is done through the Procedure Attributes dialog box, which is accessed from the Tools menu. From this dialog box, confirm that the Property procedure that will reflect the data is displayed in the Name list box. If it isn't, expand the dialog box by selecting the correct Property procedure from the list box, and then clicking the Advanced button. The dialog box will look like the screen illustrated in Figure 9-4.

The Data Binding section of this dialog box is where you will enable the data-binding capabilities of the control. First, you must click the Property Is Data Bound check box to enable the settings below it. Checking the box labeled This Property Binds To DataField finishes your task.

Once the task is done, the DataField and DataSource properties will display in the Properties window whenever developers use your control. They are then able to set what field and source will be used to retrieve data from, and to save data to.

FIGURE 9-4

Procedure Attributes dialog box expanded

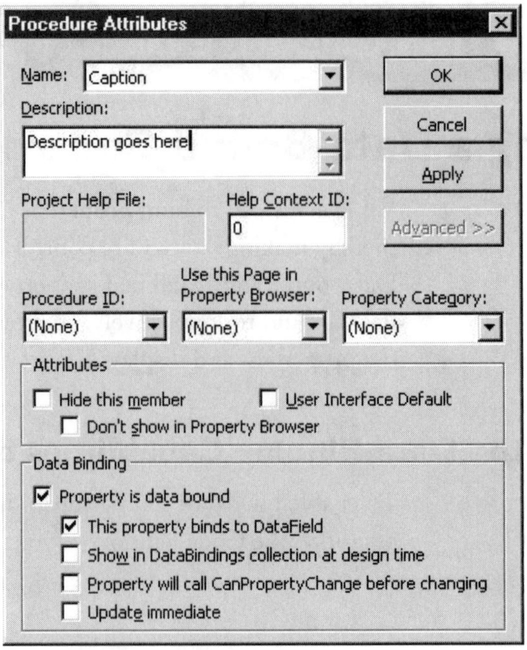

CERTIFICATION OBJECTIVE 9.06

Creating a Data Source Control

In Chapter 5 we learned how to create a data source from a class module. Creating a data source from a UserControl is essentially the same process. In many ways, you will find this section a review of what you learned in Chapter 5.

Like class modules, an ActiveX control can act as a data source for any type of data. This includes ActiveX Data Objects (ADO), OLE (object linking and embedding) providers, and ODBC (open database connectivity) sources. When you've created your data source, you are then able to have data consumers use it to display and manipulate data.

Creating an ActiveX Control That Is a Data Source

The first step in creating a data source is to make a reference to an object library. The object library you choose depends on the type of data you wish to use. If you were creating a data source for ADO, you would need to make a reference to Microsoft ActiveX Data Objects 2.0 Library by selecting References from the Project menu, and then selecting the library from the list that appears.

Once you've made the reference to an object library, you must change the DataSourceBehavior property of your UserControl, as shown in Figure 9-5. This property appears in the Property window and is used to set whether the UserControl will act as a data source. In this property, you have two choices: 0—vbNone and 1—vbDataSource.

By default, vbNone is selected for a UserControl, and signifies that the UserControl isn't set to be a data source. When the DataSourceBehavior is set to vbDataSource, it sets the control as a data source and adds a new procedure to the UserControl. If you checked through the events of your UserControl, you would see a new event called GetDataMember.

GetDataMember is an event that's used to set the source of data used by the control. It is here that you'll specify what record set is to be used. A

FIGURE 9-5

Properties window
showing how the
DataSourceBehavior
property is changed

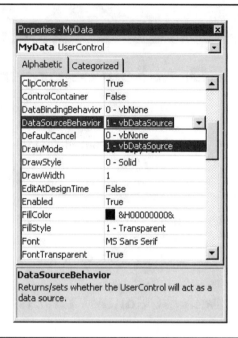

Recordset object contains a set of records from a database. Should you wish to provide an option of multiple data sources, you could use a Select Case statement in this procedure. The source name would be passed to the Select Case statement as a DataMember argument. In most cases, however, you'll use a single source of data that is set as shown in the following syntax:

```
Set Data = RecordsetName
```

or, as is more commonly done,

```
Set Data = rs
```

By using Set Data = rs, you are assigning the variable rs (which would be the record set) to Data, which is an argument of GetDataMember. For this example to work, however, the variable rs would be declared as a Recordset object, as shown below:

```
Private rs as ADODB.Recordset
```

The next step is to create a new instance of the Recordset object in the Initialize event of your UserControl. This is done with the following example of code, which creates a new instance of a record set called rs:

```
Set rs = New ADODB.Recordset
```

Having created your record set, you must then add any necessary properties to it. This is done the same way that properties are added to components; but since we're using ADO, we're able to use a shorthand method of appending Field objects. These are objects that represent columns of data that have the same data type. These Field objects are what make up the Fields collection, which you use to append Field objects that show, delete, and modify data. To append a field, use the following syntax:

```
Fields.Append "fieldname", data type
```

Using this example of code, we can create fields that are then populated with data, as shown here:

```
Dim intNum As Integer
intNum=1000
With rs
    .AddNew
    .Fields("MyNumber") = intNum
    .Update
End With
```

In this example, a variable called intNum is declared as an Integer and assigned the value of 1,000. We then add a new field to the Fields collection, which is assigned the value of intNum. The record set is then updated, populating it with our first record.

FROM THE CLASSROOM

The ActiveX Generation

What does a developer call a $300 million industry of third-party OLE or COM objects? The ActiveX Generation, of course! Visual Basic programmers who came into the fold with version 5 have grown up on a diet of ActiveX controls. Given their rapid rise in popularity—especially in Web-based development, where the developer can dictate the brand of browser used as a thin-client host container—ActiveX controls are one hot form of COM object. Now with the second edition of Visual Basic capable of authoring ActiveX controls, the ActiveX control industry is poised to explode.

In addition to the introduction of database application support in VB 3.0, and classes and OLE automation servers in VB 4.0, Visual Basic 5.0 brought the first introduction to ActiveX controls, continuing the march of Microsoft's first product into the universe of object-oriented development.

ActiveX controls start with a Visual Basic ActiveX Control project. This creates a default UserControl object, which provides the windowless canvas for adding user interface elements. ActiveX can leverage Property Pages and expose properties, methods, and/or events. In essence, ActiveX controls are miniapplications that can be embedded in a variety of host applications, including Internet Explorer; other ActiveX controls; and, of course, stand-alone applications.

Exam concerns should focus on the basic elements involved in creating ActiveX controls, syntax for embedding ActiveX controls in Web pages, registration of controls on a client system, syntax for using the Web Browser control, and syntax issues for exposing properties, methods, and events defined within an ActiveX control. Be aware of how to define read-only properties and digital signature issues.

—By Michael Lane Thomas,
MCSE+I, MCSD, MCT, A+

QUESTIONS AND ANSWERS

I want to change the icon that will appear in VB's Toolbox, representing my ActiveX control. How do I do that?	Use the ToolBoxBitmap control to specify what icon will represent your control in the Toolbox.
I've created a project group consisting of an ActiveX control project and a standard EXE. I want the form with my control to start when I press F5, but Internet Explorer keeps starting to display my control. Why?	You haven't set the standard EXE project as the startup project. To do this, right-click the project in the Project window and select Set as Start Up.
I want to add properties, methods, and events to my ActiveX control. What's the easiest way?	Use the ActiveX Control Interface Wizard. It will step you through the process of defining members for your control.
I want to create a Property Page. What's the easiest way?	Use the Property Page Wizard. It will step you through the process of creating a Property Page for your control.
What is the DataSourceBehavior property in a UserControl?	This is used to set whether the UserControl will act as a data source.

CERTIFICATION SUMMARY

ActiveX controls can be created in VB by creating a new project and choosing ActiveX control, adding a User Control to an existing project, or by changing an existing project to an ActiveX control project through Project Properties. When you have created an ActiveX control, you can then begin to add features and controls to it.

By implementing code into a UserControl, you are able to expose properties, methods, and events to other objects. This can be done by creating new Public members or by delegating members through wrapper code.

Because other developers may use your ActiveX controls, it is important to test them both in Design mode and at runtime. By creating a project group, you can add your control to a form and determine if it behaves as expected in Design mode. By using VB's debugging tools and DEBUG statements in your code, you can debug your control during runtime.

Property Pages provide an alternative way of displaying properties. Property Pages allow your control to have an interface for displaying related and detailed properties. These can be created either manually or by using the Property Page Wizard.

Creating a data-bound control is a relatively simple procedure. Creating a control that acts as a data source, on the other hand, is more involved and requires setting the DataSourceBehavior to vbDataSource, creating a record set, and populating it. If these procedures aren't followed correctly, your data source will fail to work.

TWO-MINUTE DRILL

- ❑ There are three ways to create an ActiveX control. The first is to select New Project from the File menu and choose ActiveX control from the New Project dialog box that appears. The second method is to change an existing project into an ActiveX control. The third method is to create an ActiveX control by adding a user control to a project.

- ❑ The UserControl is similar to a form in a standard EXE project. It acts as a container that holds controls and features you add to your ActiveX control.

- ❑ You can create custom properties for an ActiveX control with either Public variables or Property procedures. I advise you to use Property procedures (Property Let, Property Set, and Property Get) rather than Public variables.

- ❑ The PropertyBag object is used to load and save persistent properties. It allows property values to persist as instances of controls are created and destroyed, because the PropertyBag object itself persists.

- ❑ The ActiveX Control Interface Wizard is used to automate the task of defining the properties, methods, and events of a user interface, and to create code for the members you define. Using this program automates much of the programming.

- ❑ It is important to test the Design time behavior of your control by seeing how the control behaves in VB's Design time environment when it is added to a form and coded. When you've finished testing its Design time behavior, it is important that you run the control, to see that it doesn't cause errors at runtime.

- ❑ The easiest way to test the Design time behavior of a control is to add a separate VB project to your ActiveX control project. You can then add your control to the test project, and determine whether its behavior is what you desired.

❑ When you have the ActiveX control's designer open, its icon in the Toolbox will be disabled, and appear grayed-out. You must close the ActiveX control's designer if you want to add it to a form in your test project. Once the control's icon becomes available in the Toolbox, you can add it just as you would any standard control.

❑ Before running the project group, you must specify which project you want to set as the startup project. This is the project that you want to start when Start is chosen from the Run menu. Right-clicking a project in the Project window and selecting Set as Start Up will set it as the startup project.

❑ If you want to see how your control runs by itself in a browser, set the ActiveX control project as the startup. If you want to see how code in a form interacts with the control, and view it in a window, set the standard EXE project as the startup.

❑ Once you've decided to create a Property Page, you must decide what properties you want to add to the page. Choosing Property Page places a blank Property Page in your project that looks like a User Control or form. You add the controls you want to use for accessing various properties in this container.

❑ VB enables you to bind properties of your ActiveX control to a data source and make data-aware controls. Your controls then need a DataSource and DataField property to indicate which control and which field to bind to, respectively.

❑ To enable the data-binding capabilities of an ActiveX control, you must first open the Code window of your UserControl and move to the Property procedure to which you want to bind the data. This is done through the Procedure Attributes dialog box, which is accessed from the Tools menu.

❑ Like class modules, an ActiveX control can act as a data source for any type of data. When you've created your data source, you are able to have data consumers use it to display and manipulate data.

❑ GetDataMember is an event that's used to set the source of data used by the control. It is here that you'll specify what record set is to be used. A Recordset object contains a set of records from a database. Should you wish to provide an option of multiple data sources, you could use a Select Case statement.

SELF TEST

The following questions will help you measure your understanding of the material presented in this chapter. Read all the choices carefully, as there may be more than one correct answer. Choose all correct answers for each question.

1. Which of the following are valid ways to refer in code to a UserControl named UserControl1?

   A. UserControl

   B. Me

   C. UserControl1

   D. None of the above

2. Which of the following are valid ways of creating an ActiveX control? (Choose all that apply.)

   A. Select New Project from the File menu, and then choose ActiveX Control.

   B. Change the project type of a current project to ActiveX control in Project Properties.

   C. Click the ActiveX Control button from the VB toolbar.

   D. Select Components from the Project menu, and then select ActiveX Control.

   E. Select Add User Document from the Project menu, and select an ActiveX Control.

3. You have decided to use the ActiveX Control Interface Wizard to create a user interface for your ActiveX control. When you try to use this wizard, it refuses to create the interface. Why?

   A. You must start with an empty UserControl before starting the wizard.

   B. You must have a form added to your project before starting the wizard.

   C. The wizard isn't used to create user interfaces.

   D. The project must be saved before starting the wizard.

4. What are ActiveX control projects compiled as?

   A. DLL files

   B. EXE files

   C. CTL files

   D. OCX files

5. What property will determine the icon representing an ActiveX control, which will appear in the developer's VB Toolbox?

   A. Picture

   B. Image

   C. ToolBitmap

   D. ToolBoxBitmap

6. You want to test an ActiveX control's behavior in Design mode. How can you do this?

   A. Set the Debug property in Project Properties to Design mode.

   B. Compile the project into a CTL, and then start a new EXE project for testing.

D. From the Project menu, select Add User Control, and then select ActiveX Control.

31. You have created a custom event called GetNames. Which of the following examples of code will cause this event to fire?

   A. Raise GetNames

   B. RaiseEvent GetNames

   C. GetNames.RaiseEvent

   D. GetNames.Raise

32. What event is used to set the source of data used by a control?

   A. WriteProperties

   B. ReadProperties

   C. Initialize

   D. GetDataMember

33. You want to change the BackColor of the third element of the SelectedControls collection. Which is the correct code to use to access this element?

   A. SelectedControls(1).BackColor

   B. SelectedControls(2).BackColor

   C. SelectedControls(3).BackColor

   D. SelectedControls(4).BackColor

34. When does the InitProperties event occur?

   A. Any time a control is instantiated

   B. When a developer places a control on a form from the Toolbox

   C. Whenever the ReadProperties event is fired

   D. Whenever PropertyChange is invoked

35. What is wrong with the following example of code, which is used in a UserControl named MyUserControl?

```
MyUserControl.BackColor=vbRed
```

   A. There is no property called BackColor for a UserControl.

   B. You can't refer to a UserControl by its name in code.

   C. The Me keyword should have been used to refer to the UserControl.

   D. You must specify the color by its hexadecimal value.

36. You have created a project group to test your ActiveX control project. When you try to add the control to a form, you find the ActiveX control is grayed-out in the Toolbox. Why?

   A. You must close the form for the control to become available.

   B. You must close the ActiveX control's designer before the control becomes available.

   C. You need to initialize variable values before the control becomes available.

   D. You need to give the control a custom icon before it becomes available.

37. Which of the following can an ActiveX control act as a data source for?

   A. ADO

   B. OLE providers

   C. ODBC sources

   D. All of the above

38. You are using the Property Page Wizard. You have reached the Add Properties screen. What does this screen enable you to do?

    A. Add properties, methods, and events to your ActiveX control.

    B. Add properties, methods, and events to your PropertyPage object.

    C. Add properties to a Property Page, which will display when Properties is invoked from the contextual menu.

    D. Add custom properties to your ActiveX control.

39. You are creating a custom property for your ActiveX control. In this property you have created a Private variable, which will be used to store the property's value. What will you use to store the value of this variable? (Choose all that apply.)

    A. Property Get

    B. Property Let

    C. Property Set

    D. Property Net

40. Which of the following events is used to load property values from the PropertyBag object?

    A. WriteProperties

    B. GetDataMember

    C. ReadProperty

    D. ReadProperties

```
Debug.Print rstTitles!Title
rstTitles.Close
cnn.Close
```

To implement NT Authentication Mode, change strCnn to

```
strCnn = "Provider=sqloledb;server=pc6742;Initial _
  Catalog=pubs;Integrated Security=SSPI;"
```

In this example, I use ADO (ActiveX Data Objects) to connect to the SQL Server running on my system. The connection string, strCnn, provides the information ADO uses to find the data. The SQLOLEDB provider has a number of optional parameters beyond those the Connection object exposes. When we set Integrated Security to SSPI (Security Support Provider Interface), the authentication service for Microsoft NT Integrated Security, SQL server uses the trusted connection to obtain a username. If we choose SQL authentication, we provide a username and password with the User Id and Password parameters.

Implementing database security in VB applications is easy, just a matter of a parameter or two. With security, as with other aspects of programming, planning requires more attention and careful thought. SQL Server takes care of the permissions and authentication. VB presents the data to the user, who's unaware of the cooperation between desktop application, NT networking, and SQL Server just in verifying the user's right to view or change data.

On the test, you may come across scenarios like the following:

QUESTIONS AND ANSWERS

"A user connects through the Internet . . . "	Use Mixed mode, with SQL authentication.
"My application produces a read-only view."	Give the database users Select, but not Insert, Update, or Delete permissions.
"My application must give users access to a limited set of columns from several tables."	Create a view for those columns and assign Select permission to the view, but not the underlying tables.
"New users need access to the application every day."	Use NT Authentication mode and assign a domain group to one SQL login.

Using Cursors

Often in developing applications for Relational Database Management Systems (RDBMS), such as SQL Server, we find that query-type operations fall short of our design goals. In other words, we just can't get it done without looping through records one at a time. VB uses *cursors* to give us programmatic control over result sets. Once the application makes a connection to a database, it creates a Recordset object to process rows of data from a table, view, or query statement. This result set is a cursor. Cursors are not as efficient as ANSI SQL statements for operating on a database, so there are numerous options to consider to get the best performance.

Cursor Libraries

Cursors use resources, both memory space and processor time. By selecting a cursor library, you can choose to build your result set on the client or on the server. *Server-side cursors* use the resources of the server to create the cursor. The server sends only the cursor data to the client. With ADO, you set the CursorLocation property of the recordset to determine the cursor library. The following example creates a server-side cursor. The SQL server queries the titles table and returns to the client only those rows with the value "business" in the type column.

```
Set rstTitles = New ADODB.Recordset
rstTitles.CursorLocation = adUseServer
rstTitles.Open "SELECT * FROM titles WHERE type = _
'business'", cnn, adOpenStatic, adLockReadOnly
```

By changing the constant adUseServer to adUseClient, we turn the record set into a *client-side cursor*. This means that the server will send all the data needed to process the cursor to the client. In this case, all the rows from the titles table travel over the network to the client. The client then allocates space to hold the temporary data and perform the creation of the cursor, finally selecting titles with a type equal to "business."

SQL Server does support server-side cursors, but not all databases do, so client-side cursors will be necessary in some cases. Server-side cursors are more efficient when network traffic is a limiting factor, but the server must be up to handling the load. For large tables, client-side cursors may be next to impossible. But client-side cursors can provide extra features.

Cursor Types

Besides establishing where best to run a cursor, you can further improve efficiency by limiting its capabilities. Some uses don't demand as much flexibility as others. For instance, printing a report from cursor data doesn't require the level of sophistication of an update screen. Table 10-1 shows a list of the primary cursor types.

Static

Static cursors give you a snapshot of the data. Use a static cursor when you don't need to see changes to the underlying data and when you might need to move back and forth through the set. Static cursors can perform well because the server doesn't need to keep the data current. A good use for a static cursor would be a search screen, where the user enters a value that the cursor then uses to filter its rows, displaying the matching records.

Forward Only

Forward-only cursors also provide a data snapshot, but limit the record set to forward scrolling. Forward-only cursors are the best choice for reports or any other function that only requires one pass through the data. An identical loop through a static cursor would use more resources and could be noticeably slower. Forward-only cursors may seem very restrictive, but situations where they fit perfectly are in fact quite common.

TABLE 10-1		
Cursor Type	**ADO CursorType Constant**	**Result**
Static	adOpenStatic	An updateable copy of the data. Changes made to the original tables after the creation of the cursor do not appear.
Forward only	adOpenForwardOnly	The same as a static cursor, except that it only allows forward scrolling.
Dynamic	adOpenDynamic	The cursor will change to reflect inserts, updates, and deletes of the underlying data.
Keyset	adOpenKeyset	The cursor will change to reflect updates and deletes, but not inserts, into the underlying data.

Choose Cursor Types with Speed in Mind

Dynamic

Dynamic cursors use more resources than any other type, but they also give the most flexibility. Dynamic cursors receive updates to the data from the server whenever another application causes an insert, update, or delete. You can imagine that the overhead needed to maintain this link could be considerable. You might choose a dynamic cursor in cases where not having live data can result in conflicts, such as in an airline reservation system.

Keyset

Keyset cursors use a saved set of keys to maintain a link to the underlying data. So, if another application changes a column, that change will bubble through to the keyset cursor. Deletes also appear, but not new records. Keysets work well when you want accurate, but not necessarily the newest data, or if your application gets a lot of new entry.

Be able to select the most efficient cursor for a given scenario.

Locking

Before starting to use a cursor, you have to decide on a locking method, also called *concurrency*. The problem lies with two or more users trying to access the same data concurrently. Locking conflicts cause headaches for DBAs and frustration for users. Planning appropriate concurrency will help your cursors do their job smoothly. In this section, I'll present standard locking options that are supported by SQL Server, using ADO as the example access technology. Table 10-2 shows the available methods.

Read-Only Concurrency

Always use read-only concurrency when you know you don't need to edit the data that you request from the server. The server will put shared locks on the pages containing the records that the cursor needs. This will prevent other users from making exclusive locks, but not shared locks. SQL Server does not lock every row in the cursor, just those that the cursor requests at one time.

Optimistic and Batch Optimistic Concurrency

With optimistic concurrency, the server does not apply any locks to the data until the time of update. When an update occurs, an exclusive lock is made

TABLE 10-2

Choose the Right Locking Method to Reduce Conflicts

Concurrency	ADO LockType Constant	Result
Read Only	AdLockReadOnly	No exclusive locks are made. The result set does not accept edits.
Optimistic	AdLockOptimistic	The server applies an exclusive lock at the time of update.
Batch Optimistic	AdLockBatchOptimistic	Exclusive locks are requested when the batch updates are applied.
Pessimistic	AdLockPessimistic	The server requests exclusive locks at cursor creation.

and the change applied. The danger here is that after the cursor reads the records, another user will make a change that can then conflict with the update you want to make. For example, you make an optimistic lock on a customer's demographic record, then another user locks and updates that same record. When you begin to apply your changes, the update will fail. In this case, an error will be produced when the cursor attempts an exclusive lock. Set your locking to batch optimistic when you want to change multiple records in one swoop.

Pessimistic Concurrency

If your application *must* succeed in its data edits, then pessimistic concurrency is the necessary choice. Pessimistic locking poses the greatest danger of freezing your data. At cursor creation the server locks whatever set of rows it sends to the client. The whole cursor does not receive an exclusive lock, just those records that the cursor processes at one time. Other users cannot obtain either shared or exclusive locks on this data until the cursor moves off the block of records.

Implementing Cursors

Having planned so carefully, what do you do with the cursor once you've created it? I'll give a typical example that uses a cursor to fill a listbox. This example also brings together the concepts we've covered and illustrates them with a practical application. Figure 10-6 shows the output. Here's the only code contained in the program, attached to the click event of the command button:

```
Private Sub cmdFillList_Click()

Dim cnn As ADODB.Connection
Dim rstAuthors As ADODB.Recordset
Dim strCnn As String

    'Create Connection
    strCnn = "Provider=sqloledb;server=pc6742; _
    Initial Catalog=pubs;Integrated Security=SSPI;"
    Set cnn = New ADODB.Connection
    cnn.Open strCnn
```

```
'Create Recordset
Set rstAuthors = New ADODB.Recordset
rstAuthors.CursorLocation = adUseServer
rstAuthors.Open "SELECT * FROM Authors", cnn, _
adOpenForwardOnly, adLockReadOnly

'Fill Listbox
lstNames.Clear
rstAuthors.MoveFirst
While Not rstAuthors.BOF And Not rstAuthors.EOF
    lstNames.AddItem Trim(rstAuthors!au_fname) _
    & " " & Trim(rstAuthors!au_lname)
    rstAuthors.MoveNext
Wend

rstAuthors.Close
cnn.Close

End Sub
```

When the user clicks the button, the application initiates a connection to the pubs database on SQL Server, using a trusted connection. Then the code creates a new record set, called rstAuthors. This record set contains all the fields for all the rows in the authors table. I've made it a forward-scrolling cursor with read-only locking, using the resources on the server.

After the program clears the listbox, a loop moves through each record in the set, adding the first and last names of each author to the box. Note the

A cursor can be used to fill a list box programmatically

MoveFirst and MoveNext methods of the record set. These do exactly as their names indicate. There are a number of cursor movement methods:

- Move
- MoveFirst
- MoveLast
- MovePrevious
- MoveNext

The Move method accepts a signed parameter of type Long, which then moves the given number of records forward or back. The EOF (end of file) and BOF (beginning of file) properties work hand in hand with the move methods. Once MoveNext, for example, moves beyond the last record, the EOF property becomes true. Another MoveNext will produce an error. Because the example uses a forward-only cursor, only the Move and MoveNext methods will behave predictably.

By using read-only locks and a forward-scrolling cursor, the example minimizes the impact on the database. One possibility that I didn't account for is the size of the authors table. If I hadn't known that the authors table contained just a few rows, setting the MaxRecords property of the record set would prevent problems due to a very large table. Adding a WHERE clause to the SQL statement is a more efficient way to control record set size, if the design allows.

EXERCISE 10-1

Demonstrating a Dynamic Cursor

In this exercise, we'll modify the example from the previous section to demonstrate the difference between a dynamic and a static cursor. Between creating the record set and filling the list box, the program will pause and give us a chance to change the data on the authors table.

1. Create a new standard EXE in VB.
2. Put a listbox and a command button on the form, as shown in Figure 10-6.
3. To the click event of the button, add the code as it appears in the preceding section.

4. Before the Fill Listbox segment of the code add the following:

```
'Wait for Update
Msgbox 'Run update now'
```

5. Save your work and run the application. Click on Fill List.

6. When the message box appears, open SQL Query Analyzer and run the following query against the pubs database on your server:

```
UPDATE authors SET au_lname = 'Black' _
WHERE au_lname = 'White'
```

7. Return to your VB application and click OK in the message box.

8. Notice that the first author's name is still Johnson White.

9. Reset the data with this query:

```
UPDATE authors SET au_lname = 'White' _
WHERE au_lname = 'Black'
```

10. Change the open method for the record set to read as follows:

```
rstAuthors.Open "SELECT * FROM Authors", cnn, _
adOpenDynamic, adLockReadOnly
```

11. Repeat steps 5, 6, and 7. Notice that this time the author's name has changed.

CERTIFICATION OBJECTIVE 10.03

Enforcing Data Integrity

In my occasional consulting work, I've often had the pleasure of working with other people's data. The companies that call me usually do so because they're in a mess and need help. For various reasons, the data has become corrupted. Organizations that fail to put adequate planning and design into their business logic end up, over time, with aging and increasingly useless data. Applications can be replaced, but data is the lifeblood of a company. Once it gets tired, making it pure again takes a fearful amount of work. You can stop this drift before it starts by building solid validation and referential integrity rules.

Validation

Both VB and SQL Server have an array of tools to help with data validation. Your application validates data by checking it as it's entered. The tools range from simple to sophisticated. First, I'll discuss what can be done with VB to ensure data integrity, then I'll cover the powerful SQL Server methods.

Client-Side Validation

Client-side validation happens through the controls of a form. Controls provide validation because of their basic nature, by the use of their properties, and by using events that the user generates in entry. All of these controls, illustrated in Figure 10-7, can be used with validation logic:

- CheckBox
- OptionButton
- Masked Edit
- ListBox
- ComboBox
- TextBox

CHECKBOX   A CheckBox control forces the user to input a Boolean value. Unlike Jet databases, for instance, SQL Server doesn't have a Yes/No data type, though the bit data type works well. Depending on how you intend to store Boolean data, a checkbox can help limit input.

OPTIONBUTTON   The OptionButton control allows you to give the user a usually small set of fixed choices, which are written on the form as labels. Each option button has a true or false value, which you must then relate to your data through code.

MASKED EDIT   The Masked Edit control lets the developer limit input in a text box type control though the use of an input mask. The classic example of this is the telephone number. The mask requires that

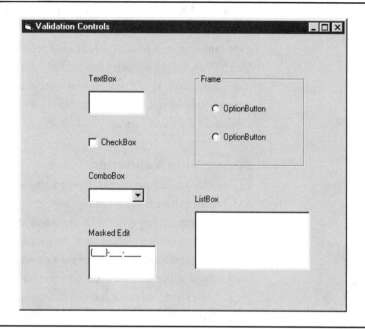

three digits be entered between parentheses, then three more, a dash, and the final four numbers. Input masks help you to establish standards among users. Not everyone enters a Social Security number, for instance, in the same way. Some people like to put dashes, others spaces, others just run the numbers together. Sorting or searching this kind of hodgepodge can become very ineffective. The Masked Edit control helps you unify these personal preference issues.

LISTBOX The ListBox control presents the user with an often numerous list of choices, with many, if not all, visible at one time. The ListBox control can be fully controlled by programming, and is a great way to limit choices and assure uniform, unambiguous input.

COMBOBOX The ComboBox control adds to the functionality of a list box by letting the user enter data. Sometimes appearance governs the choice between the two; but if you want the user to be able to type in new data, rather than choosing from a fixed list, the ComboBox is what you need.

TEXTBOX By themselves, text boxes do not do much for validation, but the KeyPress and Validate events give you total programmatic control over input. When focus shifts from a text box to another control with the CausesValidation property set to true, the Validate event fires, giving you a change to check the input by whatever standards you choose, and if necessary, hold the focus on the text box until the user meets your validation requirements.

Server-Side Validation

Client-side validation works, but server-side validation has real advantages. A database can be used by many applications, with many more programmers having a hand in development. Also, educated users can learn to access data through their own methods, such as forming links to user-level databases. Server-side validation rules reside with the data. No matter how someone connects to the data, the server can apply its validation logic. Server-side validation centralizes control over the integrity of the data. I'll present SQL Server's validation methods in some detail.

CONSTRAINTS SQL Server validates data primarily with *constraints*. Constraints give you tremendous flexibility in policing data input. SQL Server recognizes five types of ANSI standard constraints: CHECK, DEFAULT, UNIQUE, PRIMARY, FOREIGN KEY. PRIMARY and FOREIGN KEY constraints relate to referential integrity, which we'll discuss in the next section.

See Figure 10-8 for an example of a CHECK constraint. In this example, the constraint makes sure employees are at least one day old. You can see that a CHECK constraint evaluates a condition that includes the column name. All constraints are saved with the table structure and can be related to multiple columns. Also, each column can have more than one constraint.

DEFAULT constraints differ from defaults in that they apply only to one column of one table. The function, though, is the same. It's not a surprise that defaults supply a value for a column when the user inserts a new record without input for that column. The ANSI standards disallow the use of null, which many RDBMSs nevertheless permit. To avoid null fields, use a

up to you, the developer. SQL Server will never let your application violate referential integrity, but you need to make sure that a failure to insert, update, or delete doesn't introduce problems into a larger segment of logic.

Executing Statements on a Database

The Execute method of the ADO Connection object opens up a world of possibilities to you, the developer. With this one method you can

- Run stored procedures
- Perform action queries
- Return result sets
- Send commands to the database server

Microsoft has optimized SQL Server for running stored procedures and executing statements. As a programmer, you have the choice of performing logic on the client VB application or on the server. Executing statements on the server takes advantage of server resources and reduces network traffic. Let the server do database work whenever possible.

Let's start with an example. This procedure updates the authors table, changing a last name for one record, then prints the names in the authors table. Both operations use the Execute method:

```
Private Sub ExecutingStatements()

Dim cnn As ADODB.Connection
Dim rstAuthors As ADODB.Recordset
Dim strCnn As String
Dim sqlUpdate As String

'Create Connection
strCnn = "Provider=sqloledb;server=pc6742;Initial _
Catalog=pubs;Integrated Security=SSPI;"
Set cnn = New ADODB.Connection
cnn.Open strCnn
```

```
'Execute Update Statement
sqlUpdate = "UPDATE authors SET au_lname = 'Kornau' WHERE au_id = 3"
cnn.Execute sqlUpdate, , adCmdText

'Fill Recordset with stored procedure output
Set rstAuthors = cnn.Execute("AuthorList", , adCmdStoredProc)
'Print results
rstAuthors.MoveFirst
While Not rstAuthors.BOF And Not rstAuthors.EOF
    Debug.Print rstAuthors!au_fname, rstAuthors!au_lname
    rstAuthors.MoveNext
Wend
rstAuthors.Close
cnn.Close

End Sub
```

The Execute method takes three parameters. The first is a string variable containing an SQL statement or command text. In the above example, sqlUpdate contains the text of an UPDATE action query. Any valid SQL statement will work, including INSERT, UPDATE, and DELETE statements. If your goal is to return a result set from a SELECT statement, use the Open method of the Recordset object. I've omitted the second parameter, RecordsAffected, from both Executes, because it's not useful in this case. This parameter returns the number of records affected by a query or command. Those familiar with ISQL will immediately recognize this standard output from query statements. The third parameter takes a constant that tells SQL Server how to handle the command text. Table 10-3 lists the applicable constants.

In addition to running an action query, the example populates a record set with the results of a stored procedure. The stored procedure AuthorList is nothing more than a SELECT statement, but take a look at Figure 10-10, a more complicated stored procedure. Stored procedures accept parameters and can perform any task possible with Transact-SQL. Using the Execute method to run stored procedures gives your application the power to run resource-intensive operations without causing a drag on the client machine. Learning Transact-SQL may take some work, but it adds a lot of potential to your VB applications.

Constant	Use
AdCmdText	The string is a standard command, such as an action query.
AdCmdTable	ADO builds a query to return all rows from a table.
AdCmdTableDirect	SQL Server returns all rows from a table.
AdCmdStoredProc	The string contains the name of a stored procedure.
AdCmdUnknown	The application does not know the type of command.
AdExecuteAsync	The application continues execution without waiting for the command to complete. The ExecuteComplete signals completion.
AdFetchAsync	The application waits for the number of rows specified with the CacheSize property and then moves on while the command completes.

FIGURE 10-10

A VB application can call
SQL Server stored
procedures

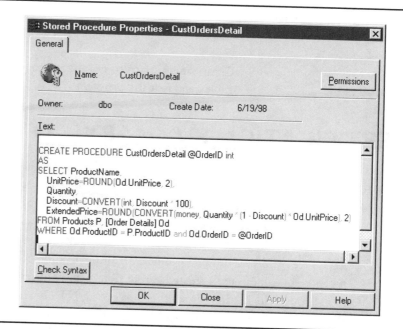

Executing INSERT Statements on the Server

Using SQL statements to do your inserts on a table will often be the most efficient method. In this exercise you'll send an INSERT statement to SQL Server to add a record to the authors table of the pubs database.

1. Create a new standard EXE.

2. Open the Code window for the form and begin a new procedure. Call it whatever you want.

3. Declare variables for the query string, connection, and connection string. Follow the example from this section, if it helps.

4. Create a connection to the pubs database on your SQL Server, and open it.

5. Set your query string equal to the following INSERT statement:

```
INSERT stores (stor_id, stor_name) VALUES (1111, _
  "The New Bookstore")
```

6. Use the Execute method of the Connection object to run your statement.

7. Optional: add code to verify the results of the operation and to handle errors.

8. Create an interface to call the procedure by a method of your choice and test the program.

CERTIFICATION SUMMARY

SQL Server uses permissions to enforce security on database objects. The DBA grants permissions to users and roles: select, update, insert, delete, execute, and DRI. Roles are groups of database users. Both users and roles are specific to the database. SQL Server uses logins for authentication. Logins are specific to the server and are mapped to database users. SQL Server can perform its own authentication of a username and password, or it can use a trusted connection to authenticate an NT domain username. A login can represent one user or an NT domain group. With ADO, the connection string either supplies a username and password, or instructs the provider to use a trusted connection.

Cursors let the application loop through a set of records, one row at a time. The cursor library determines if the cursor will run on the server or

A. When SQL Server is running on Windows 95.

B. When trusted connections are not available.

C. When connecting to a database from a Web site.

D. Mixed mode is not available in SQL Server 7.

8. Which parameter of the connection string for an ADO connection causes the server to use SQL authentication?

A. Provider

B. Server

C. Integrated Security

D. None of the above

9. Which parameter of the connection string for an ADO connection causes the server to use NT authentication?

A. Provider

B. Server

C. Integrated Security

D. None of the above

10. Which ADO object represents a query result set?

A. Recordset

B. Connection

C. Error

D. Resultset

11. Which cursor type will give the best overall performance for a report?

A. Static

B. Forward only

C. Dynamic

D. Keyset

12. Which cursor type uses the most resources?

A. Static

B. Forward only

C. Dynamic

D. Keyset

13. Which term is a synonym for *locking*?

A. Keyset

B. Pessimistic

C. Unlocking

D. Concurrency

14. When should you use pessimistic concurrency?

A. When the table is half empty

B. When the cursor is read only

C. When the updates made with the cursor must commit

D. When you need an exclusive lock

15. Which ADO record set property determines the cursor library?

A. CursorLibrary

B. CursorDLL

C. LockType

D. CursorLocation

16. Which method(s) can you use to move to the next record in a record set? (Choose all that apply.)

A. Move

B. MoveFirst

   C. MovePrevious

   D. MoveNext

17. Which cursor will run fastest?

   A. A forward-scrolling, read-only cursor

   B. A dynamic, pessimistic cursor

   C. A static, optimistic cursor

   D. A C++ cursor

18. Which control can help the user format a phone number?

   A. OptionButton

   B. ListBox

   C. TextBox

   D. Masked Edit19.

The user of your application must assign department codes to new courses. Which control will provide the best validation?

   A. CheckBox

   B. OptionButton

   C. ListBox

   D. Masked Edit

20. Which is the primary method of server-side validation?

   A. Constraints

   B. Rules

   C. Defaults

   D. Triggers

21. How does the DEFAULT constraint differ from a saved default?

   A. One DEFAULT constraint can be applied to multiple columns of one table.

   B. One DEFAULT constraint can only apply to one column of one table.

   C. One DEFAULT constraint can apply to multiple columns in multiple tables.

   D. They are the same thing.

22. Triggers are like

   A. Chiggers.

   B. The VB Change event.

   C. Rules.

   D. Primary keys.

23. Which example does **not** allow referential integrity?

   A. A products table with multiple products for each record in a suppliers table

   B. A students table that has one possible row for each row in a people table

   C. A books table that may or may not have a corresponding record in a publishers table

   D. A transcript table that has multiple rows for each row in a student table

24. The suppliers table has a one-to-many relationship with a products table. The SupplierID column is in both tables. Therefore,

   A. SupplierID is a primary key in suppliers and a primary key in products.

B. SupplierID is a primary key in suppliers and a foreign key in products.

C. SupplierID is a foreign key in suppliers and a primary key in products.

D. SupplierID is a foreign key in suppliers and a foreign key in products.

25. When is a FOREIGN KEY constraint created?

A. When the table is created

B. During performance tuning

C. Immediately after the table is created

D. Any time

26. Which type of query **cannot** result in a referential integrity violation?

A. Select

B. Insert

C. Update

D. Delete

27. Which collection of the ADO Connection object can be used to handle referential integrity errors?

A. Err

B. Er

C. Description

D. Errors

28. Which method of the ADO Connection object will allow you to run a stored procedure with a VB application?

A. Run.

B. Command.

C. Execute.

D. Stored procedures can only be run from SQL Server.

29. Why should you use the Execute method to populate a record set with the output from a complex stored procedure?

A. SQL Server is optimized to run stored procedures.

B. The Execute method is the only way to populate a record set.

C. Stored procedures use client resources.

D. To avoid concurrency problems.

30. Which constant is used with the Execute method to run a stored procedure?

A. AdCmdText

B. AdCmdTable

C. AdCmdUnknown

D. AdCmdStoredProc

31. Which event can you use with an asynchronous command?

A. The Asynchronous event

B. The CommandFinish event

C. The ExecuteComplete event

D. The Synchronize event

32. VB front ends can be used with which database(s)? (Choose all that apply.)

A. SQL Server

B. Oracle

C. Access

D. Unidata

33. Which database access technology should you use to connect a Web site to SQL Server?

A. RDO

B. DAO

C. SQL-DMO

D. ADO

34. Which are SQL Server 7 Authentication modes? (Choose all that apply.)

A. Standard

B. Mixed

C. Integrated

D. Separated

35. SQL Server

A. Never stores passwords.

B. Stores passwords for some users.

C. Stores passwords for all users.

D. Never stores passwords when running on Windows 98.

36. Which method opens an ADO database connection?

A. Connect

B. Query

C. Open

D. Execute

37. When should you use a cursor?

A. To loop through a result set one record at a time

B. To add one row to a table

C. To sum values in a table

D. For all database operations

38. Which type of change is not reflected in a keyset cursor?

A. Update

B. Insert

C. Delete

D. Select

39. Optimistic locking

A. Never applies shared locks.

B. Never applies exclusive locks.

C. Never applies any locks.

D. Can apply both shared and exclusive locks.

40. Validation can occur

A. On the client.

B. On the server.

C. On both the client and the server.

D. Neither on the client nor on the server.

In the first line of this code, we assign a bitmap called GRAPHIC.BMP to the Picture property of a picture box called picPicture. In the next line, we clear the Picture property by using LoadPicture(). This frees up memory that was previously used to store the graphic.

Picture boxes are useful for simulating groups of controls. As we just mentioned, large groups of controls eat up memory and slow performance. By using a picture to simulate a control set, you can decrease the amount of memory used.

Another way to decrease the overhead of graphics is by using an Image control. The Image control uses less memory than the PictureBox control. It should be used instead of picture boxes in cases where you're just using a graphic to respond to a Click event.

The AutoRedraw property of a form can also be used to increase performance. AutoRedraw sets the output of a graphic to either Graphics method or Persistent Graphic. Graphics method performs runtime drawing operations and is used for animation and simulations. Persistent Graphic is a method that stores output in memory and retains the graphic during screen events. An example of a screen event would be if you switched between applications in Windows, and hid and redisplayed a form. When AutoRedraw is set to False, Graphics method is used, while Persistent Graphic mode is used when AutoRedraw is set to True. If your application uses or generates complex graphics, it is better to use Graphics method (setting AutoRedraw to False), and handle the repainting of graphics yourself through code.

Up until this point, we've dealt with real ways of increasing performance. Other methods more closely resemble sleight of hand. There are a number of ways to make users *think* performance has increased, when in fact nothing has changed.

One way of masking the slow speed of an application is through the use of *splash screens*. As your application first starts to load, you might display a form with its MinButton, MaxButton, and ControlBox properties set to False. The contents of the form might include the application's name, your company name, and so forth. You've seen these types of screens when you load VB—a form appears telling you the program name as the application loads. This not only masks the time spent while a large application loads, but also reassures the user that something is happening. Without such visual feedback, the user might think that something was wrong and might try to start the application again.

Another way to let users know that an application hasn't locked up is by using progress indicators. The Professional and Enterprise editions of VB include the ProgressBar control in the Microsoft Windows Common Controls. After adding this control to a form, you can use DoEvents at points in your program to update the value of the progress bar. The point is to let the user know that the application is working. This technique is especially useful when doing such things as populating a large array or loading a particularly large database. If you decide not to use a progress bar, you should at least change the mouse icon to an hourglass.

Finally, although we've just discussed the problems of loading multiple forms into memory, you should load commonly used forms and keep them hidden. Hidden forms can be displayed more quickly than forms that must be loaded from disk. This doesn't mean you should load every form in an application—just the common ones a user will access most often. For example, you shouldn't hide things like About This Program or forms that supply configuration options. They aren't used often, and would eat up unnecessary memory.

EXERCISE 11-1

Optimizing a Program

1. From the Project menu, choose New Project, and then choose Standard EXE. Add a new form to the project. Under Project, choose Add Form, and then choose Form.

2. Under the Project menu, choose Components. Select Microsoft Windows Common Controls from the list, and check the check box beside it. Click OK.

3. Add a Timer control to Form1. In the Property window, change the Interval value to **2000**. The Interval value sets the number of milliseconds between events. After doing this, add the following code to the Timer's Timer event:

```
Unload Form1
```

4. In the Property window for Form1, change the MinButton, MaxButton, and ControlBox values to **False**. Change the BorderStyle to **0 – None**. In the Form1_Load event, add the following code:

```
Form2.Show
```

5. On Form2, add a progress bar and a command button. Change the Caption property of the command button to **Array**.

6. Now add the following code in the command button's Click event to create an array, populate the array with the value of the counter, and show the progress of this work in the progress bar:

```
Dim counter As Integer
Dim intNum(100) As Integer

For counter = 1 To 100
    intNum(counter) = counter * 5
    ProgressBar1.Value = counter
Next counter
ProgressBar1.Value = ProgressBar1.Min
```

7. Save the project so we can use it later. Press F5 and test your application.

CERTIFICATION OBJECTIVE 11.02

Selecting the Appropriate Compiler Options

Visual Basic allows you to control how your project is compiled into an executable. It also allows you to tweak your application, so it is optimized in a way that best suits your needs and the needs of your user. The options you can set are found under the Project menu, and can be accessed by selecting Project Properties.

The Make tab of the Project Properties dialog box allows you to add information to an executable. By adding code to your project, you can retrieve the property values of the application object. Other applications can also retrieve this information with API calls. Figure 11-1 illustrates the Make tab of the Project Properties dialog box.

The Make tab of the
Project Properties
dialog box

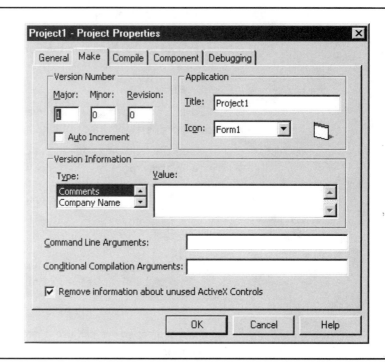

The first section of the Make tab allows you to set the version number of
your application. You can set Major, Minor, and Revision release numbers
from 0 to 9,999. Selecting the Auto Increment check box increases the
revision number by one, each time you compile your project with the Make
Project command on the File menu.

Additional version information can be placed in the Version Information
section. By scrolling through the Type list, you can choose different kinds
of information and then type the value for the particular type in the Value
area. The types of information that are available to you are Comments,
Company Name, File Description, Legal Copyright, Legal Trademarks, and
Product Name.

On occasion you may write applications that require the user to type an
executable name followed by required arguments. For example, you might
create a program called TIME.EXE that performs actions within a certain

amount of time. The user might start the application by using Run from the Windows Start menu, and typing the executable's name followed by the argument of how many minutes before the task starts. If the application should perform its activities in 60 minutes, for example, the user would type **TIME.EXE 60**.

In Design mode, however, you can only run an application by pressing F5 or by choosing Start from the Run menu. This doesn't give you the opportunity to add arguments. In cases where arguments are required, you can type them into the Command Line Arguments field. When you do, VB starts as if the application had been started from a command line with the arguments. Any arguments placed in the Command Line Arguments field won't be compiled with the project. This allows users to provide their own arguments when starting the executable, without conflicting with Command Line Arguments used in Design mode.

The Conditional Compilation Arguments field on the Make tab requires significant discussion, and will be covered in the next section of this chapter.

The Compile tab allows you to predetermine how your application compiles, and—depending on the method you choose—allows you to set a number of options for optimization. The two choices offered to you in the Professional and Enterprise editions of VB are Compile to P-Code and Compile to Native Code.

P-code is short form for *pseudo-code*, which is an intermediate step between high-level instructions (the code you write in VB) and low-level instructions (the native code your computer executes). When you compile your project, your VB code is converted, and elements of the code are compiled into compressed *tokens*. These tokens are placed into the compiled executable. Compressing the VB language code allows it to be executed faster than if it were in its original format. Programs compiled as p-code are generally smaller in size than native-code executables.

Compiling into native code skips over the intermediate step of p-code, and compiles the application into instructions used directly by the processor. This increases the speed of processing loops and mathematical calculations. When compiled, VB uses the same compiler engine that Microsoft uses for C++ development suites. Because the native code uses the same format that C executables are compiled in, you can use debugging tools for C language executables on VB executables.

There are numerous benefits to compiling in native code over p-code. Choosing to compile in native code offers you a number of options for optimization, which are illustrated in Figure 11-2. As we mentioned at the beginning of this chapter, optimization involves trade-offs, and they become apparent in the options on the Compile tab. You can choose to optimize for speed, size, or neither. You can't choose both size and speed. You can only set the compiler to favor one over the other when it compiles your project.

The other two general optimizations on this screen are Favor Pentium Pro and Create Symbolic Debug Info. Favor Pentium Pro causes your application to run faster on computers with Pentium Pro processors. If you select this option, your application will still run on computers with other processors, but it will run a bit slower. Create Symbolic Debug Info has the compiler create a debug file with the extension PDB. This file can be used by external debugging tools to debug the application as it runs.

FIGURE 11-2

The Compile tab of the Project Properties dialog box

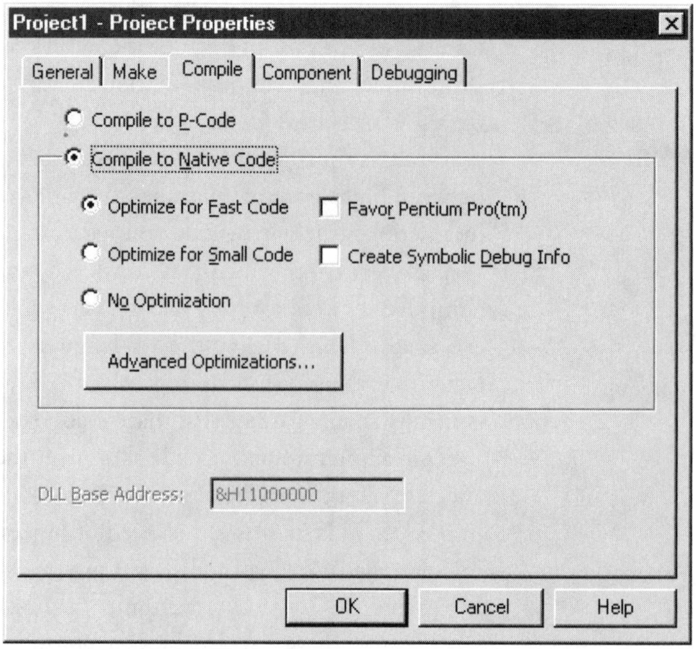

Also on this screen is the Advanced Optimizations button. By clicking this button, you bring up the dialog box shown in Figure 11-3. This dialog box has a number of options that allow you to increase the speed or reduce the size of your executable. However, they are set apart from the other optimization options for a reason. As the warning on the dialog box says, depending on how you've written your code, setting these options can cause serious problems.

exam

Watch

It is important to know the optimization options on the Project Properties tabs and the effect that each will have on compiling. Many questions on the exam deal with problems resulting from changing settings. Knowing the settings and their effects can lead you to the correct answers.

An *alias* is a name that refers to an area of memory that's already referred to by another name. The Assume No Aliasing check box tells the compiler that the application doesn't use aliasing. When you check this box, the

FIGURE 11-3

Advanced Optimizations

Advanced Optimizations

Warning: enabling the following optimizations may prevent correct execution of your program

☐ Assume No Aliasing

☐ Remove Array Bounds Checks

☐ Remove Integer Overflow Checks

☐ Remove Floating Point Error Checks

☐ Allow Unrounded Floating Point Operations

☐ Remove Safe Pentium(tm) FDIV Checks

[OK]   [Cancel]   [Help]

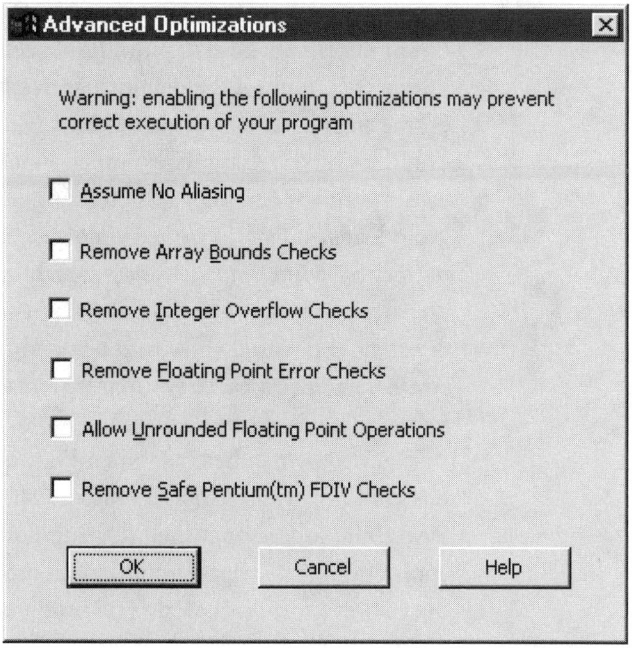

compiler can then optimize your code in ways that it wouldn't normally be able to, and performance will increase. However, if you have included any code in your project that passes arguments by reference (the default argument-passing style in VB), problems will result when the application is run.

In an array, there is a range of indices that can be accessed. For example, if you have an array of 100 indices, and you try to access index 101, an error message appears because VB adds code to your application that checks the array bounds. If you select Remove Array Bounds Check, the compiler doesn't add this code, and your application will run faster. However, if the program reads and writes outside of the array, it will be reading and writing to unrelated memory areas. Not only can this cause problems for your application, but it can affect other programs as well.

The next two options on the Advanced Optimizations screen are similar. Remove Integer Overflow Checks determines whether a value is within the range of Byte, Data, and Integer data types. Remove Floating Point Error Checks does the same thing, but with Single and Double data types. The compiler normally adds these checks to your application and generates a runtime error if the value is greater than or less than what the data type is meant to contain. Selecting this box speeds up calculations, but can produce unexpected results if the data type is overflowed. Selecting these options turns off the error checking, while deselecting them enables the error checks.

Checking the Allow Unrounded Floating Point Operations check box causes your application to use floating-point registers more effectively, and avoid loads and stores from memory. In addition, it increases the precision of floating-point comparisons—which sounds great, but can cause some unexpected errors. When the floating-point numbers are compared precisely, they can be found to be unequal when you expect them to be equal! This might cause your code to react unexpectedly, or might provide results that you deem incorrect.

You may remember that when Pentium chips first came, out there was a big stink shortly afterward about bad chips. In 1994, Intel admitted to a flaw in the processor. When floating-point algorithms were used in an application, and a certain combination of digits are divided by each other, the answer came up flawed. The problem seemed to affect only arithmetic division in math-intensive programs. Intel claimed this problem would crop up only once every 27,000 years, while IBM claimed it might occur once every 24 days. No matter which company you believe, owners of these Pentium chips have been able to replace the chips by contacting Intel. Unless your application uses math extensively, the Pentium problem shouldn't affect it.

Because the problem exists, your compiler adds code that will produce the correct answer, even if the processor running the application is flawed. After this code is added, your application's performance will probably decrease, as extra work needs to be performed by the code to check answers. When you consider the points in the preceding paragraph, it becomes apparent that it is fairly safe to enable the Remove Safe Pentium FDIV Checks option. Checking this option removes the added code and makes your application run faster. However, if your application is math intensive (such as a science or engineering program that does lots of calculations), you should leave this option unchecked.

on the **Job**

While the Advanced Optimizations options allow you to set numerous settings for optimizing a program, you should use them only if you've considered the implications of each setting. If you configure these settings and experience problems, try removing the settings before altering your code. The optimization settings in Advanced Optimizations may be causing your problem, and it's easier to test that (by clicking a check box) than to rewrite code.

CERTIFICATION OBJECTIVE 11.03

Using Conditional Compilation to Control an Application

There may be times when you don't want certain code to appear in certain compilations of your application. For example, you may have different versions of a program with different features, or applications that are distributed to different countries. Depending on the countries to which you're distributing your application, you may need to change the language or currency symbol. When you require certain code to be included or removed from an application, you can use *conditional compilation*.

Conditional compilation allows you to create one project that deals with all versions of your application. Compiler constants are created to indicate version information about code to be used, and compiler directives are used to specify what code is to be added to a project. You can differentiate compiler constants and directives in your code by preceding them with the pound sign (#).

Compiler constants allow you to specify which version of the application is to be used during compilation. You can almost think of a compiler constant as a title. You define the constant in your code with #CONST and give it a True or False value. When the compiler works through the code, it looks at whether the constant is True or False, and then compiles the code related to it. Examples of #CONST are

```
#CONST conEnglish=True
#CONST conSpanish=False
#CONST conEnglish=-1
#CONST conSpanish=0
```

The values of True and –1 are synonymous, as are False and zero. You can use either in your code when defining such constants.

Conditional directives outline what is to be added and ignored during compilation. If the value of the compiler constant evaluates to True, that section of code is compiled. Any constant evaluating to False is ignored. For example,

```
#If conStandardVersion Then
'Insert code specific to Standard version here
#ElseIf conProfessionalVersion Then
'Insert code specific to Professional version here
#Else
'Insert code for other versions here
#End If
```

The scope of compiler constants is Private, and cannot be made Global in your code. However, when you specify compiler constants in the Make tab of the Project Properties dialog box, they are global. Specifying constants on the Make tab is done in the Conditional Compilation Arguments field. In this field, you can enter assignment expressions, such as

```
conEnglish=-1
```

or

```
conEnglish=1;conSpanish=0
```

As you can see in the second line of the preceding code, you can enter multiple assignments by separating them with a semicolon.

It is important to remember that any compiler directives and constants you add to your project won't be compiled into the application. They are instructions for the compiler, and not part of the actual executable. As such, you needn't worry about the size of directives affecting performance.

EXERCISE 11-2

Conditionally Compiling an Application

1. Open the project from Exercise 11-1. In the General Declarations section of Form2, add the following code:

```
#Const conOne = False
#Const conTwo = False
```

2. In Form2's Load event, add the following code:

```
#If conOne Then
    MsgBox "First conditional option was used"
#ElseIf conTwo Then
    MsgBox "Second conditional option was used"
#Else
    MsgBox "Welcome!"
#End If
```

3. Run the program, and verify that a message box appears saying "Welcome!"

4. Change the value of conOne to **–1**, so it now says #CONST conOne=-1. Then run the program, and verify that a message box appears saying "First conditional option was used."

5. Change the value of conOne to **zero**, so it now says #CONST conOne=0. Change the value of conTwo to **True**, so it now says #CONST conTwo=True. Run the program, and verify that a message box appears saying "First conditional option was used."

Monitoring the Values of Expressions and Variables Using the Debug Window

The Debugging windows allow you to monitor what's happening to data in your code. You can see what the values of variables and expressions are, and you can determine whether logic errors are present. Logic errors occur when your code returns an unexpected result, such as subtracting sales tax rather than adding it. Though the code runs properly, the results are not what you wanted. By using the Debugging windows in VB, you can monitor the values of expressions and variables to uncover the problem.

The Debugging windows consist of three separate windows: the Immediate, Watch, and Locals windows. The Locals window allows you to monitor the value of any variables within the current procedure's scope. The Immediate window lets you type code that responds as if it were directly in your code. Through this window, you can also view the results of debugging statements in your code. The Watch window allows you to specify which expressions to watch and returns information about their values as your program runs. Together, they are essential tools for debugging your application.

Before going into each of these windows in depth, it is important that you understand the Debug toolbar. When working with any of these three windows, the Debug toolbar, shown in the following illustration, is used to step through statements of code and bring up the Locals, Watch, and Intermediate windows. To view the Debug toolbar, click View, select Toolbars, and then click Debug.

The Debug toolbar has a number of options that save you from having to constantly access the Debug, Run, and View menus. By using the Debug toolbar, you can start, stop, and pause execution, as well as use functions to step through code. The different buttons are listed in Table 11-1, and detail each of the toolbar's buttons from left to right.

Button	Other Methods to Access This Function	Description
Start/ Continue	F5, or click Start item on the Run menu	Starts an application. This button becomes the Continue button if the application is in Break mode.
Break	CTRL-BREAK, or click Break item on the Run menu	Temporarily stops execution of the program.
End	Click End item on the Run menu	Stops running the application, and returns the user from runtime to Design mode.
Toggle Breakpoint	F9, or click the Toggle Breakpoint item on the Debug menu	On the current line of your code, clicking this option sets up or removes a breakpoint. A breakpoint signals that execution should stop on that line.
Step Into	F8, or click the Step Into item on the Debug menu	Clicking this option executes your code one line at a time.
Step Over	SHIFT-F8, or click Step Over item on the Debug menu	Clicking this option executes code/ one line at a time; but when a call to another procedure is reached, that procedure is executed as one step before moving to the next line.
Step Out	CTRL-SHIFT-F8, or click Step Out on the Debug menu; only available in Break mode	Clicking this option executes code one line at a time. If the line is a call to another procedure, the next line to be displayed is the first line of the called procedure.

TABLE 11-1

Buttons on the Debug
Toolbar (*continued*)

Button	Other Methods to Access This Function	Description
Locals Window	Click Locals Window item on the View menu	Displays Locals window.
Immediate Window	CTRL-G, or click Immediate Window item on the View menu	Displays Immediate window.
Watch Window	Click Watch Window item on the View menu	Displays Watch window.
Quick Watch	SHIFT-F9, or click the Quick Watch item on the Debug menu	Displays Quick Watch dialog box. The value displayed is the current value of the expression you selected.
Call Stack	CTRL-L or click Call Stack item on the View menu; only available in Break mode	Displays Call Stack dialog box. This dialog box shows procedures called by the current procedure, but not yet completed.

The Watch window allows you to monitor the information dealing with watch expressions, which are expressions (variables, properties, and so on) that you've decided to watch during your application's execution. You can specify which expressions to monitor, and then view their values as the program runs.

As shown in the next illustration, the Watch window is made up of four columns. The Expression column shows the name of the expression being monitored. These expressions can be variables, arrays, properties, and so on. The Value column shows the current value of the expression, and the Type column shows the data type of the expression. Finally, the Context column shows the context of the current expression, such as what procedure the expression is associated with.

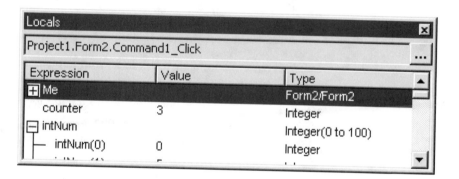

The Locals window (shown in the next illustration) gives the current value of all values declared in the current procedure when your application enters Break mode. You can specify where in the code you would like Break mode to occur by clicking on the desired part of code and then clicking the Toggle Breakpoint button on the Debug toolbar. When execution reaches this part of the code, it automatically enters Break mode. You can also click the Break button on the Debug toolbar, although this won't be a precise method of entering Break mode.

The Locals window is made up of three columns. The first column shows the name of the expression in the scope of the current procedure. All declared variables are shown here, as are object variables. The Me expression appears in the Locals window, showing the current form. The Value column shows the current value of an expression, and the Type column shows the expression's data type. If the expression is an object, the Type column displays what object it is.

As with the Watch window, any structured variables (such as arrays or object variables) have a plus sign (+) beside the expression's name. By clicking the plus sign, you can view additional information dealing with that expression. For example, if you had an array named intNum, you could view the values of each element in the array by clicking the plus sign. To collapse this expanded view of the expression, click the minus sign (−) that appears when the expression is expanded.

The Immediate window, shown in the following illustration, allows you to view the current value of an expression at runtime, and allows you to type code during runtime as you would during Design mode. If you wanted to test a line of code you'd just come up with, you could use the Immediate window. In addition, you can print the values of expressions in the Immediate window to see what their current values are.

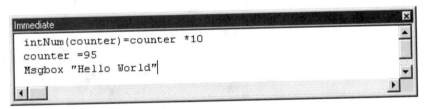

To use the Immediate window, your application must be in Break mode. Once in Break mode, you can type code into the Immediate window as if you were using the Code window in Design mode. Any code you type is immediately executed when you press ENTER. (This, of course, assumes that your cursor is on the line of code you want to execute when you press ENTER.)

Using the Immediate Window to Check or Change Values

The Print method allows you to view the values of variables in the Immediate window. There are two variations of the Print method, which are quite similar. With the first method, type the word **Print** followed by the variable of the value you want to view. The second method is a shorthand version of the Print method. By typing a question mark (?) followed by the variable name, you can view the current value. These methods are shown in the following examples:

```
Print intNum
? intNum
```

can be referenced anywhere in the application) or local (the variable can only be referenced within a limited area, such as a procedure). For example, if you declare a variable called intCount in a procedure, only code within that procedure can access and modify the value of intCount. When watching a variable, you need to be aware of its scope.

Depending on how a variable is declared, it can have procedure-level or module-level scope. Procedure-level scope means the variable is available only to code within the procedure in which it is defined. Module-level scope allows the variable to be declared as Private or Public. Private variables are available to the module that they appear in, while public variables are available to all modules.

When using variables that are out of scope (that is, not available to the currently running code), the Watch window shows the variable. The Value column shows <Out of Context>, meaning that the expression being monitored is out of scope. If the variable needs to be monitored at all times, you should define a different scope for it. For example, if the variable originally was declared at a procedure level, you should return to Design mode and declare it as Private or Public.

Using the Locals Window to Check or Change Values

The Locals window allows you to check and change the values of expressions in the current procedure. It also shows the Me variable, which is the current form. These values appear only when the application is in Break mode.

If you want to change the value of an expression through the Locals window, click the value of the expression in the Value column. You can then change the value. When you move the cursor off the expression again (by pressing ENTER, using navigation keys, pressing TAB, or clicking somewhere else), it retains its new value.

EXERCISE 11-5

Checking and Changing Values in the Locals Window

1. Open the project from Exercise 11-4. There should still be a breakpoint set in your code. Run the application, and click the Locals window button on the Debug toolbar so that the Locals window is displayed.

2. Click the command button on Form2. When your code reaches the breakpoint it will enter Break mode. Notice that the Me variable for the form object is shown, as are all other variables declared for this procedure.

3. In the Locals window, click on the plus sign (+) beside the intNum expression. Notice that all elements of the intNum array are displayed with their current values. Click the Debug toolbar's Step Into button several times and notice that the values change.

4. In the Locals window, click on the value (shown in the Values column) of the counter expression. Change the counter's value to **20**, and press ENTER.

5. Click the Step Into button on the Debug toolbar several times. Notice that the value of the counter has affected the program's execution. By looking through the intNum elements in the Locals window, you'll see that elements of the intNum array are now being filled from the twenty-first element on.

6. Stop your program. In the Code window, click the highlighted breakpoint you created in Exercise 11-1 (in the Click event of Form2's command button). On the Debug toolbar, click the Toggle Breakpoint button to remove the breakpoint.

7. Save your project for later exercises.

CERTIFICATION OBJECTIVE 11.05

Implementing Project Groups to Support the Development and Debugging Process

Until this point, you've been working with only one project at a time. VB allows you to work on multiple projects at once, called *project groups*. By working with project groups, you can increase your productivity by having several projects loaded at once to work on.

You can also use project groups to test your code in a test project, before adding it to the application you plan to distribute. One project can be used to test your code, while another is used as your "real" application. In this way, you don't need to worry about ruining a project by adding code that you're not sure will work.

To create a project group, you need to add a project to your current project. From the File menu, choose Add Project. You can then add a new project or an existing one. You can select from Standard EXEs, ActiveX EXEs, and so forth, just as you can when creating a new project.

When a project is added, you have created a project group. The Project window reflects this by displaying Project Group, followed by the Group name (that is, Group 1) in the title bar. You can move between projects in the group by double-clicking the forms or projects contained in the group.

Since multiple projects now exist as a group, you must designate one of these projects as the startup project. The startup project is the project that will start when you press F5 or use the Run menu's Start command. To set a specific project as the startup project, select the project in the Properties window, and then right-click to bring up the contextual menu. From this menu, select Set as Start Up. The startup project appears boldfaced, showing that this is the designated startup project. All other projects appear in normal text.

The Professional and Enterprise editions of VB can be used to create project groups for creating and debugging applications that use ActiveX components. By using project groups, you can create and debug groups that contain ActiveX dynamic-link library projects, ActiveX control projects, ActiveX EXEs, or standard EXE projects.

To change an existing project to any of these ActiveX projects, you must use the General tab of the Project Properties dialog box (which is accessed from the Project menu). On the General tab, use the Project Type list box. This list box allows you to determine what type of project the currently selected project will be. You can choose from Standard EXE, ActiveX EXE, ActiveX Control, or ActiveX DLL. This allows you to convert a project after it has been created with the Add Project menu item.

Debugging DLLs in Process

By using project groups, you can load in-process components with your standard executable application and run all the projects together. This allows you to step from the application's code into the in-process component's code. To do this, you must create a project group consisting of your standard executable, and whatever in-process components you want to include.

Once you've included your ActiveX DLL in a project group, you can go about debugging the DLL. The process of debugging ActiveX DLLs is the same as debugging most other in-process components.

The first step in debugging an ActiveX DLL is setting breakpoints and watch expressions, as shown in the preceding section of this chapter. After adding breakpoints and watch expressions in the class module and control code, you are ready to fully compile the project.

To debug an ActiveX DLL (or most other ActiveX components), you should fully compile the project because ActiveX components won't unload while the project is running in the development environment. You might have released all references to it and met all of the shutdown conditions, but the DLL will still remain in memory. Therefore, to test the unloading of a DLL, you must fully compile components.

The default behavior of VB 6 is to compile on demand. This means that some code isn't compiled until a client calls for it. As compiling errors often must be fixed in Design mode, this means you would have to return the entire program group to Design mode to fix an error.

To resolve compiling errors, you should fully compile your project or remove the Compile on Demand setting. To run the project after fully compiling it, start your project by choosing Start with Full Compile from the Run menu, or by pressing CTRL-F5. You can disable the Compile On Demand setting from the General tab of Options, which is accessed from the Tools menu. On the General tab, uncheck the Compile On Demand check box. When your program now runs, everything will be compiled before starting.

After running your debugging session, it is important to shut down your application properly. This means using the Close button on your application's main window to return to Design mode. The reason for this is that using the End button on the Debug toolbar will cause every project to close down. Your DLL will not receive Terminate events from the application, so you won't be able to effectively test how it shuts down. To test the shutdown behavior of a DLL effectively, you must always use the Close button.

Testing and Debugging a Control in Process

To debug and test a control in process, you should follow the procedures outlined in the section above. First, create a project group by adding your ActiveX controls to the initial project. You must then add the necessary breakpoints and watch expressions to your control, and you should fully compile the project before testing the code. Fully compiling the project will allow you to deal with compiling errors before dealing with problems (such as logic errors) that exist in the control itself. Once this is done, you're ready to deal with the issues that affect controls.

Debugging controls is not the same as debugging other objects. This is because parts of the code in your control have to execute while the form (on which the control instance is placed) is in Design mode. If the code can't run, you can't access such things as property procedures and resizing.

There are several areas of control code that you must consider when debugging a control. The first area includes the property procedures that are used to set your control's properties using the Properties window. The next area involves the code that saves and retrieves property values. When you load a form containing a control instance, run the project, or save it to disk, this code must run in Design mode. Finally, the Resize event must run in Design mode so that you have an appearance of the control on your form. If the control is user drawn, the Paint event must be run.

The way that you allow such code to run in Design mode is by closing the control's visual designer. This is done by clicking the visual designer's Close box, or by using CTRL-F4. Once the visual designer is closed, the icon representing the control appears in the Toolbox, so you can add instances of the control to your forms.

When the control's visual designer is open, all instances of the control are disabled. The icon for the control, which appears in the tool bar, is disabled and appears grayed out. A control whose visual designer is open is covered with cross-hatching.

Since your control is running when the visual designer is closed, breakpoints encountered in the control during Design mode will engage, as if the program as a whole were running. When this occurs, Break mode is entered. You can either click the Continue button on the Debug toolbar or press F5 to continue so that you avoid having to remove the breakpoint while using the control in Design mode.

CERTIFICATION OBJECTIVE 11.06

Deploying an Application

There are two ways to deploy a VB application: manually or with the Package and Deployment Wizard. The Package and Deployment Wizard is covered in the later sections of this chapter. In this section we will cover manual deployment.

Deploying an application manually takes a little more thinking than using the wizard, but it's not very difficult. Before packaging and deploying your application, you must first compile it. From the File menu, choose the Make command. This command is followed by the name of your project; so if your application were named Project1, the command would read: Make Project1.exe. A dialog box appears, allowing you to choose where the executable will be compiled. After you click the OK button, the project compiles and becomes an EXE file.

If your project is part of a project group, you must first select which project in the group you want to compile. In the Project window, select the project you want, and then select the Make command from the File menu. If you would like to compile the entire project group, select Make Project Group from the File menu. A dialog box appears. After you click the Build button, the group will be compiled.

Once the project is compiled, you're ready to copy the files onto the distribution media you intend to use. After that, it's just a matter of uploading it to the site. (If you're using other deployment methods, the procedures may be a little more involved.)

Using floppy disks requires that you put the files for your application in a certain order. You must put the SETUP.EXE and SETUP.1ST on the first disk, then all files that are listed in the Bootstrap section of the SETUP.1ST file. To view this file, you can use any text editor. Any other CAB files are then placed on additional disks.

To distribute your application to a network share, you must first ensure that you have the necessary permissions or rights (depending on the network operating system used) to access the share. You then use the command prompt of Windows Explorer to access the share and copy the setup files to the target directory.

Group button allows you to add groups to the Start menu. New Item opens a dialog box identical to the one that appears when you choose Properties for a menu item, and adds a new item to the menu. If you want to remove any groups or items, click the Remove button.

The next screen is Install Locations. It lists certain files (like your application's executable) for which you can modify the installation location. At the end of the listed files, there is a column called Install Location. Clicking an item in this column displays a drop-down list with a number of choices for installation. You can choose to install into the application path, the system path, or numerous other places.

Following this list, you will see the Shared Files screen. The wizard displays a list of files that can be shared by other applications. At the very least, the list will display the name of your application's executable. If you want a file in this list to be shared, select the check box beside the file's name.

The final screen allows you to specify the name of the script for this session. This script will contain the settings you choose for your session with the wizard. After naming it, you can later duplicate, rename, or delete the script by clicking the Manage Scripts button on the Package and Deployment Wizard's main screen. If you don't want to save the settings, simply accept the default name and click the Finish button. Clicking the Finish button starts the bundling of your application based on the settings you chose using the wizard.

Registering the COM Components in a Desktop Application

When you deploy an application, you must include all of the COM components you use in your application. ActiveX controls (OCX files) and ActiveX DLLs must be included with the package. They are listed under Included Files of the Package Wizard, and you should verify that all have been included.

If a user installs your application, and a COM component can't be found, the VB Runtime Library produces a "File not found" message. You should install all of your OCX files in the Windows\System directory. If an OCX doesn't have this path, change it in the Install Location column of the Install Locations screen.

If you are using COM components that are included with VB version 6, you won't need to worry about registering them with the Windows Registry. This is because these files are self registering. If you want to use an ActiveX component that you've created, you should create a dependency file so that the component can be added to the SETUP.1ST file and then registered upon installation.

Dependency files have the extension DEP and contain information about runtime requirements of an application or component, including such things as required files, where these files should be installed, and how they should be registered with the Registry. When you click the Package button in the Package and Deployment Wizard, the wizard scans for dependency information. It reads the information, builds a list of required files, and builds a list of installation information. Dependency files are read, and the information is added to a SETUP.1ST file that resides outside of a Standard Setup Package's SETUP.EXE file. Internet packages have this file written to an INF file stored in the CAB.

After clicking the Package button, the Package portion of the wizard starts. As mentioned earlier in this chapter, you can then choose to create a standard setup package or a dependency file. After selecting Dependency File and clicking the Next button, you are presented with the Package Folder screen, which allows you to specify where the package will be assembled. For further information on this screen, see the preceding section, "Creating a Setup Program for Desktop Application Installation." Click Next to reach the Included Files screen.

Included Files allows you to specify what files are to be included with the package. The list contains all dependent files that the wizard has determined are necessary from analyzing your project. Click the Add button to include any additional files you want. A dialog box appears that allows you to browse your hard disk. After specifying the files to add, click Next.

The next screen is important only if you are bundling the dependency file into a CAB file for dependency on the Internet. Here you can enter the name for the CAB file, a URL from which it can be retrieved, and the default file to execute when the file is downloaded. The file to execute can be either an executable or an INF file. If you are not packaging the dependency file for the Web, accept the defaults, and choose Next.

The screen after this is the Install Locations screen. This screen allows you to specify where files are to be installed. As mentioned in the preceding section, you can modify the location through the final column on this screen. The Install Location column allows you to change the installation location of a particular file via a drop-down list.

The final screen allows you to name a script for the dependency settings you specified. You can duplicate, rename, and delete the script by clicking the Modify Scripts button that is on the Package and Deployment Wizard's main screen.

Manipulating the Windows Registry

The GetSetting and SaveSetting functions allow you to read and write information to and from the Windows Registry, respectively. These are built-in VB procedures that access entries under the HKEY_CURRENT_USER\Software\VB and VBA Program Settings. You can use these functions to manipulate the Windows Registry programmatically.

GetSetting and SaveSetting both have the following arguments: appname, section, and key. The appname argument is the application's name, section is the name of the section where a key setting is found, and key is the name of the key to return. SaveSetting also has a fourth argument called value, which allows you to specify the contents to be stored in the Registry.

If you wanted to save settings to the Registry, you could do something like this:

```
SaveSetting app.exename, strUser, strID, txtUser.Text
```

In this example, the SaveSetting function takes the name of the currently running program and the values of the other variables and saves them to the Registry. To retrieve this information, you could use the following code:

```
txtRegInfo.Text=GetSetting (app.exename, strUser, strID)
```

Unlike most of the other material in this chapter, you use the GetSetting and SaveSetting functions in your code. By so doing, you can access and write to the Registry and manipulate data contained therein.

Allowing for Uninstall

While no programmer likes to admit it, there are times where users won't want to use your application anymore. Despite all your hard work, they'll want to cast your application by the wayside and uninstall it from their system. I know you'll read this with tears in your eyes, but it's important to know how to provide a user with the ability to uninstall your program.

Users can use the Add/Remove Programs applet in Control Panel. However, the Package and Deployment Wizard installs a program that works with Add/Remove Programs, so that the user can uninstall an application. While packaging your program, it adds a file called ST6UNST.EXE, which is the application-removal utility. The wizard installs this to the \WINDOWS or \WINNT directory.

Also, when the user installs your application, the file ST6UNST.LOG is created in the application directory. This file contains information on directories that were created during installation, Registry entries that were created and modified, and self-registered DLL, EXE, or OCX files. The log file has additional information on links and Start menu items that were created and the files that were installed (and their locations). The listing of files is comprehensive. It includes all files in the setup program, even ones that weren't installed because newer or identical files existed. It also specifies whether files are shared, and which existing shared files were replaced during setup.

ST6UNST.EXE reads the log file and determines all files that should be removed. When executed, it removes all files, directories, and other items logged in the ST6UNST.LOG. It allows users to fully remove your application from their systems.

CERTIFICATION OBJECTIVE 11.08

Planning and Implementing Floppy Disk- or Compact Disc-Based Deployment for a Desktop Application

In cases where you're selling your application, the most common methods of deployment will be compact discs (CD-ROM deployment) or floppy disks. The Package and Deployment Wizard allows you to deploy to such media easily. By following the wizard's onscreen instructions, you should have few problems.

on the job

It is important to offer both CD and floppy installations of your applications. CD deployment is better, as the user won't have to keep switching disks during the installation. However, remember that not everyone has a CD-ROM drive. Though an application may have to be split up over several floppies, it is wise to offer both installation methods. Not doing so might preclude a significant number of people from using your application.

Floppy Disk-Based Deployment of a Desktop Application

Floppy disk deployment requires that you package your application into multiple CAB files. As shown in Figure 11-7, the Cab Options screen allows you to choose whether to bundle your application in a large, single CAB file, or into multiple CAB files. You can select different CAB sizes that

FIGURE 11-7

Cab Options screen of the Package portion of the Package and Deployment Wizard

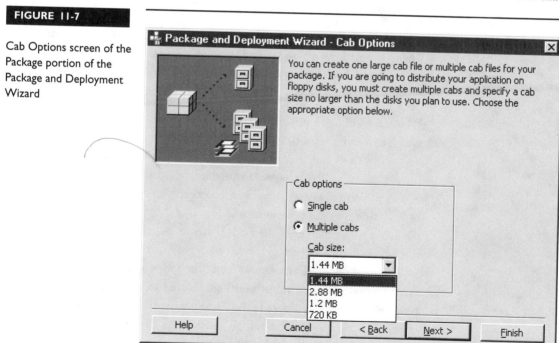

apply to your CAB files. These sizes range from 720KB to 2.88MB. The size you choose depends on the size of the blank disks you are using to distribute the application. You can't use disks of different sizes or choose to deploy to more than one size of disk. Whatever size you choose applies to all of the blank disks you use.

Once you have properly packaged your application, you're ready to deploy your application to floppy disks. After selecting the package you want to deploy, from the Select Package list box on the Package and Deployment Wizard's main screen, click the Deploy button. The wizard analyzes the project, and you see a screen that asks you which script you want to use. Select the package you want to deploy from the list box of scripts available, and then click the Next button.

The Deployment Method screen asks you what method you wish to use to deploy your application. On the list of available deployment methods, there should be an entry for floppy disks. If you didn't choose to package the application as multiple CABs, the floppy disks option won't appear. If it doesn't, you have to return to the Package Wizard and repackage the application as multiple CABs.

<table>
<tr><td>exam
ⓦatch</td><td>*Floppy disk deployment won't appear on the Deployment Method listing if you haven't packaged your application as multiple CAB files. If this is the case, you must return to the package portion and repackage the application as multiple CABs.*</td></tr>
</table>

After selecting floppy disks, click the Next button, and you'll be asked which drive you want to use. If you have a single floppy drive, only one drive appears in the drive box. Floppy disk deployment requires blank, formatted disks. If you have existing data on a disk, deployment will fail. In addition, you've probably experienced buying a box of formatted floppies, only to find that the occasional one (or all of them) haven't been formatted. To avoid problems, select the Format before copying check box. Then select the floppy drive to which you want to deploy, and click Next.

The final screen allows you to name the script used to save settings for your deployment session. As mentioned earlier in this chapter, you can rename, duplicate, or delete this script through the Manage Scripts portion of the Package and Deployment Wizard. Click the Finish button on this screen to begin transferring files to the floppy disks.

Packaging and Deploying an Application to Floppy Disk

1. Open the Package and Deployment Wizard. On the main screen, click the Browse button and open the project you saved in Exercise 11-5.

2. Click the Package button. Wait as the wizard analyzes your project. Accept the Standard Setup Package 1 script name default and click Next. On the Package Type screen, select Standard Setup Package and click Next.

3. Accept the default for the wizard to package the application in the project's folder. Click Next, and accept the confirmation message box that appears. A new folder named Package will be created in your project's folder.

4. Accept the files to be included with your package. Click the Next button, and you'll be brought to the Cab Options screen. On this screen, select Multiple cabs. The Cab Size list box will be enabled. Select the size of disks you are using from this list and click Next.

5. On the following screen, enter a title for your installation. Click Next. On the Start Menu Items screen, change the group name and application name using the Properties button. Select the group or item, click Properties, and enter a new name in the Name field. Click Next to continue.

6. Accept the defaults for the next few screens. Toggle through them, clicking Next. At the end, click Finish and your application will be packaged.

7. On the Package and Deployment Wizard's main screen, click Deploy. Because this is your first time using Deploy, only one package script will appear on the first screen. Click Next.

8. Select Floppy Disks from the Deployment Method screen, and click Next.

9. Select the floppy drive you want to use. Check the Format before copying check box, and then click Next. This brings you to the final screen. Click Finish, and your package will be deployed.

Compact Disc-Based Deployment of a Desktop Application

The CD-ROM deployment of a desktop application is very similar to folder deployment, which is discussed later in this chapter. In fact, you can use the folder deployment method for CD-ROM deployment. You would use the

Folder option, and then transfer the files afterward to CDs. In most cases, this is the option you will use in the real world, because you will rarely encounter a CD burner attached to every programmer's workstation.

A CD burner is also called a *writeable CD-ROM drive*. While normal CD-ROM drives only allow you to read from a CD, CD burners allow you to read from and write to CDs. To write your packaged application to a writeable CD, you must insert a blank CD into your CD burner. While the price of writeable CD-ROM drives is still quite high, it is dropping to a level that many people and smaller companies are able to afford.

Depending on the writeable CD-ROM drive you own, you may be able to deploy files with the settings you've chosen directly to a CD with the Package and Deployment Wizard. For such a deployment, you can use either a single or multiple CAB files, though a single CAB is more commonly used. The files are transferred to the CD in the same manner used for network folder deployment.

CERTIFICATION OBJECTIVE 11.09

Planning and Implementing Web-Based Deployment for a Desktop Application

The Internet is an effective way of deploying an application to users. Deploying a package via the Web requires you to have some sort of Internet access and necessary permissions to a directory on a Web site. Since you'll be deploying your application to a directory on an Internet server, you must ensure that you're able to post (upload or transfer files) to a particular directory. Check with your Internet Service Provider or ask your system administrator to determine if these permissions exist.

You can package your application as single or multiple CAB files, but single is often the better choice for Web deployment. Having too many files can often confuse novice users, and a single CAB file limits their choices as to what they need to download. After packaging your application, start the Deploy portion of the Package and Deployment Wizard.

On the Deployment Method screen of the Deploy Wizard, select Web Publishing and click Next. The Items To Deploy screen lists all of the files in your package (SETUP.EXE, SETUP.1ST, and CAB files). If you don't want to deploy certain files, deselect the check box beside the file's name. You will generally want to deploy all files listed. Click Next to move to the next screen.

You are given the option of selecting other files and folders to deploy. A tree is shown on this screen, displaying all files and directories in the directory containing your Package folder. Checking the check box beside a file or directory's name will include the file. This is useful if you are deploying a sample application, and want to include the code (that is, forms) for the application. It is also useful if you're deploying database applications and want to deploy a blank copy of the database. That way, if users experience problems, they can access a fresh database file.

Clicking the Next button brings you to the Web Publishing Site screen. This screen allows you to enter the URL (uniform resource locator, or Web site address) of the location where you want the application deployed. In the Destination URL combo box, you must enter a valid URL for a location to which you have the necessary permissions to upload. If you leave this blank, you won't be able to continue. In addition, you have two protocols to choose from in the Web publishing protocol list box: HTTP Post and FTP. Check with the Internet server's system administrator to determine the preferred protocol.

Click the Next button to reach the final screen. You can enter a name to save the settings for this session to a script, or just click Finish to complete the session. Your package will then be deployed to the Web site.

CERTIFICATION OBJECTIVE 11.10

Deploying an ActiveX Control

If your project contains an ActiveX control, you can deploy the project as an Internet package. This creates a CAB package that can be either downloaded from a Web site or posted to a Web server. Using the Package and Deployment Wizard to deploy an ActiveX control is significantly easier than deploying it manually.

From the main screen of the Package and Deployment Wizard, select the project you want to package from the Select Package list box, or click Browse to add your project to the list, and then click Package. Your project will be analyzed. If you have created previous Internet packages, you can select a script to use from the list box, or choose None to create a fresh installation package.

The next screen allows you to determine the type of package to create. Since the wizard has determined that this project contains an ActiveX control, it offers the choice of creating an Internet package. Select this package, and then move through the next two screens to determine where the package is to be bundled and what files are to be included.

Next, you encounter the File Source screen, which lists runtime CAB files that are linked to those on Microsoft's Web site or another location, such as the CAB file itself. Clicking on each of the files determines where the links reside. The Files Source section of this screen allows you to modify the source, so you can include the information in the CAB file, download it from Microsoft, or download it from another source. Depending on the file, you may be limited in the options available in the Files Source section. For example, the OCX file for the ActiveX control you created may only be able to include the information or download it from a site other than Microsoft's.

The next screen allows you to specify safety settings for your components. If certain components can't be determined as safe to initialize or script, they are listed here. Files listed here will have a value of No for initialization and scripting safety. To set your component as Safe for Scripting and Safe for Initialization, click each of the columns for these settings and change their values to Yes.

Clicking Next brings you to the final screen. You can rename an Internet package and save the settings for this session. Clicking Finish creates the package.

Clicking Deploy analyzes the project and brings up the first screen of the Deploy portion. The Package to Deploy list box lists a new script for your Internet package. Select this script and click Next.

The next screen allows you to specify whether to use a deployment method of Folder or Web Publishing. Select Web Publishing and click Next to have your packaged application published to a Web server. The remaining screens that appear are identical to those described in the preceding section.

FROM THE CLASSROOM

Optimization and Deployment

Throughout the countless development cycles, an ongoing process of optimization should be undertaken. Application optimization should focus on one area (or two at most) of the following application characteristics: calculation speed, display speed, perceived speed, memory size, or executable size. Advances in one area often contradict desired progress in other areas, forcing either a balancing act of optimization procedures or a distinct trade-off. It is very important for developers to properly recognize not only what to optimize, but where to optimize code for maximum return on development time.

Visual Basic also provides for conditional compilation directives for providing conditional logic during the compiling of an application executable. This greatly increases the flexibility of debugging and selective code inclusion during binary compiling.

In addition to application optimization, debugging plays a crucial role in application development. Be aware of the part the Watch, Locals, and Immediate windows play in the debugging process. Knowing what options are available in each is crucial to understanding application debugging. Also note how project

groups can assist in application development. Be prepared to describe the established methods for debugging DLLs, ActiveX controls, and using all the possible ways to invoke breakpoints for debugging standard executable projects.

After successfully wading through the mirage of development, optimization, and debugging cycles, application development remains. Be aware of the syntax for declaring conditional compilation directives, limitations on conditional compilation syntax structure, and how conditional compilation techniques can assist application debugging. For the exam, you should be able to explain the ramifications of choosing p-code versus native-code compilation, especially the effect of altering the Advanced Optimization choices available in Visual Basic.

To cover the bases, also be aware of the basics of application deployment methods, such as floppy disk-, compact disc-, and Web-based deployment, including the files generated.

—*By Michael Lane Thomas, MCSE+I, MCSD, MCT, A+*

CERTIFICATION OBJECTIVE 11.11

Planning and Implementing Network-Based Deployment for a Desktop Application

If you plan to deploy your application to a folder on a network, you must first ensure that you have the necessary permissions or rights (depending on whether your network is NetWare or NT) to do so. In addition, the people you're planning to have use your application must also have necessary permissions. If you or they do not, people won't be able to access the directory containing your application. Check with your network administrator to ensure that you and others can access the network directory.

After doing this, you are ready to use the Package and Deployment Wizard. After packaging your application as either a single- or multiple-CABs bundle, click the Deploy button to start the deployment portion of the wizard. The first screen displays a list box that allows you to select the package you want to deploy.

The screen that follows this is the Deployment Method screen (shown earlier in Figure 11-7). Select Folder from the list, and click Next to see the Folder screen, as shown in Figure 11-8. The Folder screen allows you to select a local or network folder for deployment. A Windows Explorer-style tree is displayed, allowing you to navigate through folders on your hard disk. If you want to deploy locally, you could select a folder from the tree. To create a new folder, you click the New Folder button, and then name the newly created folder.

Since we're deploying to the network, we'll use the Network button on this screen to display a dialog box that shows a tree of the network, similar to what you see when you use Network Neighborhood in Windows. By clicking through the listing, you can find the networked computer to which

FIGURE 11-8

The Folder screen of the
Package and Deployment
Wizard

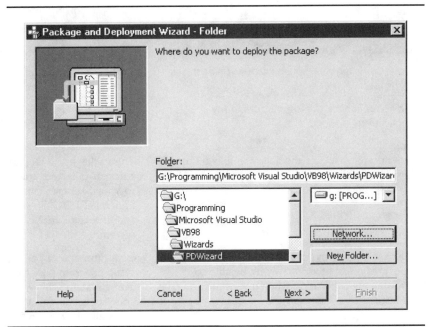

you wish to attach. You can then navigate to an existing folder or—
depending on your permissions—create a new folder for deployment.

Depending on the network you're on and how your computer is
configured, you may also be able to switch to the network drive using the
Drive box. You could then navigate through the tree of folders to find the
one you want to deploy to. (This would be the case if you were on a Novell
NetWare network and had drives mapped to your computer.)

Clicking the Next button brings you to the final screen. Here, you can
name the script that will contain the settings chosen in this session. Clicking
the Finish button initiates the deployment and transfers the files to the
network folder.

QUESTIONS AND ANSWERS

How can I optimize an application for both size and speed?	You can't. Optimization is a trade-off, and you can only optimize for speed or for size, not both.
How can I check for logic errors in my application?	Use the Debugging windows in VB. They will allow you to test your program and help you find and fix logic errors.
How do I give a user the ability to fully uninstall my application?	The Package and Deployment Wizard automatically adds the file called ST6UNST.EXE to your package. This file will read the ST6UNST.LOG file created during installation, and fully removes your application from the user's system.
If a user already has the ST6UNST.EXE installed, does this mean he or she won't be able to uninstall my application when my installation tries to install it?	Each time one of your applications is installed, the setup program puts the ST6UNST.EXE on the user's system. This won't affect an uninstall of your application, as the ST6UNST.EXE file reads uninstall information from the ST6UNST.LOG file that's created in the application directory.
I am using only controls that are included with VB 6.0. Do I need to create a dependency file for my package?	Generally, no. The Package and Deployment Wizard will analyze your project and include the files required for your application.

CERTIFICATION SUMMARY

Optimization allows you to improve the size or speed of an application. VB 6.0 allows you to configure a number of optimization options through the Project Properties dialog box tabs. In addition, there are advanced optimization options you can set, which should only be configured if you understand what effects they will have on your application.

VB's Debugging windows allow you to monitor what is happening to data as you step through execution. The Debugging windows consist of the Watch window, the Locals window, and the Immediate window. They are tools provided with VB to allow you to debug your application.

The Package and Deployment Wizard allows you to bundle an application into an installation package, and then to deploy it to a distribution site or media. By using the wizard, you are able to create professional installations quickly and easily. The wizard steps you through the process, allowing you to package and deploy an application by answering its questions.

 # TWO-MINUTE DRILL

- ❑ One of the easiest ways to increase performance is by using the correct data type. Another way is to cache properties in variables when you're using a loop.

- ❑ When you've finished with data, you should discard it from memory. However, removing the values of variables to reclaim space should be done only if the variables are going to be out of memory for some time.

- ❑ There are a number of ways to make users think performance has increased. One way is through the use of splash screens. Another way is by using progress indicators.

- ❑ VB allows you to control how your project is compiled into an executable. It also allows you to tweak your application to optimize it to best suit your needs and the needs of your user.

- ❑ P-code is short for pseudo-code, which is an intermediate step between high-level instructions and low-level instructions.

- ❑ When you compile your project, your VB code is converted, and elements of the code are compiled into compressed *tokens*. These tokens are placed into the compiled executable.

- ❑ Conditional compilation allows you to create one project that deals with all versions of your application. Compiler constants are created to indicate version information about code to be used, and compiler directives are used to specify what code is to be added to a project.

- ❑ The way you can differentiate compiler constants and directives from other code is by preceding them with the pound sign (#).

❑ The Debugging windows consist of three separate windows: the Immediate, Watch, and Locals windows. The Locals window allows you to monitor the value of any variables within the current procedure's scope. The Immediate window lets you type code that responds as if it were included directly in your code. The Watch window allows you to specify which expressions to watch and returns information about their values as your program runs.

❑ Setting a watch expression in Design mode is done through the Debug menu, by selecting Add Watch. Any expression that you've placed your cursor over in the Code window appears in the Expression text box of the Add Watch dialog box.

❑ The scope of a variable describes the extent to which other parts of the application are aware of an object or variable. A variable can have a procedure-level or a module-level scope, depending on how it is declared. Procedure-level variables are available only to code within that procedure. Module-level variables can be declared as Private or Public.

❑ VB allows you to work on multiple projects at once in project groups. You can use project groups to test code in a separate test project, before adding it to the application you plan to distribute.

❑ The Professional and Enterprise editions of VB can be used to create project groups for creating and debugging applications that use ActiveX components. Once you've included your ActiveX DLL in a project group, you can debug the DLL.

❑ After running a debugging session, it is important to shut down your application by using the Close button on your application's main window to return to Design mode.

❑ There are two ways to deploy a VB application: manually, or with the Package and Deployment Wizard.

❑ Using floppy disks requires that you put the files for your application in a certain order. You must put the SETUP.EXE and SETUP.IST on the first disk, then all files that are listed in the Bootstrap section of the SETUP.IST file.

❑ To distribute your application to a network share, you must first ensure that you have the necessary permissions or rights (depending on the network operating system used) to access the share. You then use the command prompt or Windows Explorer to access the share and copy the setup files to the target directory.

❑ The Package and Deployment Wizard includes two wizards and one dialog box. The Package Wizard allows you to package your program into CAB files or a self-extracting executable. The Deployment Wizard allows you to send your package to a distribution site or media, such as an Internet site, floppy disk, and so on. The Manage Scripts button opens a dialog box that allows you to rename, delete, or duplicate package and deployment scripts.

❑ When you deploy an application, you must include all of the COM components you use in your application. ActiveX controls (OCX files) and ActiveX DLLs have to be included with the package.

❑ The GetSetting and SaveSetting functions are built-in Visual Basic procedures that access entries under the HKEY_CURRENT_ USER\Software\VB and VBA Program Settings. They allow you to read and write information to and from the Windows Registry, respectively.

❑ The Package and Deployment Wizard adds a file called ST6UNST.EXE, the application-removal utility, to the \Windows or \WinNT directory.

❑ When the user installs your application, ST6UNST.LOG is created in the application directory. This file contains information on directories that were created during installation, Registry entries that were created and modified, and self-registered DLL, EXE, or OCX files.

❑ The most common methods of deploying an application are on compact disc or on floppy disks. Floppy disk deployment requires that you package your application into multiple CAB files.

❑ You can select different CAB sizes that will apply to your CAB files. These sizes range from 720KB to 2.88MB. You can't choose to deploy to more than one size of disk.

❑ CD-ROM deployment of a desktop application is very similar to folder deployment. You can use the folder deployment method for CD-ROM deployment. In most cases, this would be the option you would use in the real world.

❑ You can package your application as a single or multiple CAB files, but using a single CAB file is often the better choice for Web deployment. Having too many files can confuse novice users, and a single CAB file limits their choices as to what they need to download.

❑   If your project contains an ActiveX control, you can deploy the project as an Internet package. This creates a CAB package that can be either downloaded from a Web site or posted to a Web server.

❑   If you plan to deploy your application to a folder on a network, you must first ensure that you have the necessary permissions or rights to do so. In addition, users must also have the necessary permissions.

SELF TEST

The following questions will help you measure your understanding of the material presented in this chapter. Read all the choices carefully, as there may be more than one correct answer. Choose all correct answers for each question.

1. You have decided to increase performance of an application by using the correct data types for variables. One of your variables is used to store the current year. What data type would you use?

   A. Double

   B. Single

   C. String

   D. Integer

2. Which tab of the Project Properties dialog box allows you to set version information for an executable?

   A. General

   B. Make

   C. Compile

   D. Debugging

3. Which of the following will remove the value of a String variable to reclaim space?

   A. strName = Null

   B. End strName

   C. strName=""

   D. Reclaim strName

4. You have decided to compile to p-code and then set optimization settings for this to optimize for both speed and size. When you go to the Compile tab, you find you cannot accomplish this. Why?

   A. You can only optimize for either speed or size.

   B. P-code doesn't offer optimization settings for compiling.

   C. You need to make these settings on the Make tab.

   D. None of the above.

5. What will be the effect of the following conditional compilation code?

```
#CONST conEnglish=0
#CONST conFrench=-1
#CONST conSpanish=False
```

   A. conEnglish will be compiled.

   B. conFrench will be compiled.

   C. conSpanish will be compiled.

   D. All constants will be compiled.

6. You want to display the value of intNum in the Immediate window by including code directly in a procedure. Which of the following would be valid to use in your code to perform this action?

   A. ? intNum

   B. Print intNum

   C. Debug.Print intNum

   D. All of the above

7. You are deploying your application to floppy disks. Part way through the deployment, you find that one of the floppies isn't formatted. What can you do?

   A. Stop the packaging and return to the Package portion of the Package and Deployment Wizard. Check the Format before copying check box, and repackage your application.

   B. Stop the packaging and return to the Deploy portion of Package and Deployment Wizard. Check the Format before copying check box, and redeploy your package.

   C. Repackage and redeploy your application. All information will be lost when you stop deployment.

   D. Repackage your application on formatted floppy disks.

8. You want to remove a picture from memory, to reclaim the memory space. What will you do?

   A. Use the LoadPicture( ) function.

   B. Use the RemovePicture( ) function.

   C. Use LoadPicture to load a nonexistent graphic file.

   D. Use UnloadPicture( ) function.

9. You want to configure your form to use Graphics method rather than Persistent Graphics. What will you set to do this?

   A. AutoRedraw to False

   B. AutoRedraw to True

   C. AutoRedraw to Graphics

   D. AutoRedraw to Persistent

10. You have entered code to load all of the commonly used forms at application startup. What effect will this have on performance?

    A. It will give the appearance that performance has increased.

    B. It will give the appearance that performance has decreased.

    C. It will increase the size of the application.

    D. It will decrease the speed of the application.

11. You have decided to use the Web Publishing option in the Deploy portion of the Package and Deployment Wizard. What protocols are available for you to send your package to a Web site? (Choose all that apply.)

    A. HTTP Post

    B. HTTP Get

    C. FTP

    D. HTML Post

12. What Deployment method would you select to deploy your application to a network folder?

    A. Web Publishing

    B. Folder

    C. Network Folder

    D. NT Folder

13. What file contains a listing of files installed, directories created, and so on, when the application is installed, and what is it used for?

A. ST6UNST.LOG contains a list of installed files for ST6UNST.EXE to use if the application is uninstalled.

B. SETUP.LOG contains a record of how the installation went and what files are installed, for review by the user.

C. UNINSTALL.LOG contains a list of installed files for ST6UNST.EXE to use if the application is uninstalled.

D. INSTALL.LOG contains a list of installed files for Add/Remove Programs to use if the application is uninstalled.

14. You want to register a COM component. What is the easiest and best way to do this?

A. Use the Package and Deployment Wizard to create a dependency file.

B. Use the Package and Deployment Wizard to create a Registry file.

C. Using a text editor, manually edit the SETUP.1ST file.

D. Using a text editor, create a SETUP.1ST file.

15. You are debugging a DLL in process, but find that when you click the End button on the Debug toolbar, you are unable to test the shutdown behavior of the DLL. Why?

A. DLLs don't have a shutdown behavior.

B. The End button closes down every project, so you must close the application properly.

C. The code that determines the shutdown behavior has a bug in it.

D. The DLL can't be loaded in the design environment.

16. In the Watch window, the value of the variable intMyInt reads <Out of Context>. What does this mean?

A. intMyInt hasn't been declared.

B. intMyInt is out of scope.

C. intMyInt has a value of zero.

D. intMyInt has a null value.

17. During runtime, you notice the Quick Watch button on the Debug toolbar is inactive. Why?

A. There are no watch expressions currently set.

B. There are no variables in the current procedure.

C. The Quick Watch button becomes active in Break mode.

D. There are no breakpoints set in the project.

18. The variable intNum has a value of four (4). You type the following code in the Immediate window. What will be printed?

```
Print intNum * .25
```

A. 4

B. intNum * .25

C. 1

D. Error will result

19. You have a variable with a Boolean value of False that you want to monitor. You want the application to break when this value changes. Which of the following options would you set in the Add Watch dialog box? (Choose all that apply.)

    A. Watch expression

    B. Break when value is True

    C. Break when value changes

    D. Break when value is False

20. You want to fully resolve compiling errors before debugging a DLL in process. What can you do to resolve any compiling errors before doing this? (Choose all that apply.)

    A. From the Run menu, select Start with Full Compile.

    B. From the Run menu, select Start.

    C. In Options, uncheck Compile on Demand.

    D. Press F5.

21. You have decided to distribute an application to Web sites like http://www.microsoft.com. When you attempt to deploy the package, the deployment fails. Why?

    A. You selected single CAB rather than multiple CABs for packaging.

    B. You selected multiple CABs rather than single CAB for packaging.

    C. You don't have the necessary permissions to deploy to that site.

    D. You aren't able to deploy to Web sites with the Package and Deployment Wizard.

22. The application removal program is automatically added to your package by the Package and Deployment Wizard. When installed to a user's computer, where is this program found?

    A. The APPLICATION directory

    B. The SYSTEM directory

    C. The WINDOWS or WINNT directory

    D. A subdirectory in the APPLICATION directory

23. A user installs your application. Unfortunately, you forgot to include a COM component with the package. What will happen when the application can't find the COM component?

    A. The VB Runtime library will give a "File not found" message.

    B. The problem will cause the program to crash.

    C. The problem will be ignored.

    D. The problem will cause the installation to uninstall itself.

24. You want to manipulate information contained within the Registry. Which of the following functions would you use? (Choose all that apply.)

    A. GetSetting

    B. SaveSetting

C. GetKey

D. SaveKey

25. Which button will allow you to step through code one line at a time but, when it reaches a called procedure, will execute the called procedure as a single step and then move to the next line?

A. Step

B. Step Into

C. Step Over

D. Step Out

26. What does the Create Symbolic Debug Info option on the Compile tab of the Project Properties dialog box do?

A. Allows breakpoints to be set

B. Creates a file for use with the Package and Deployment Wizard

C. Logs debugging problems that occur during a debugging session

D. Creates a debug file for external debugging tools

27. Which of the following can you use to test code before adding it to your actual application? (Choose all that apply.)

A. Project groups

B. Immediate window

C. Locals window

D. Watch window

E. Code window

28. Which of the following would you use to save settings to the Registry?

A. PropertyGet

B. PropertyLet

C. SaveSettings

D. GetSettings

29. You want to change the value of an expression in the Locals window. How will you do this?

A. Right-click the value, and select Properties from the contextual menu.

B. Click the value in the Value column and enter the new value.

C. Click the expression and enter the new value.

D. Click the variable associated with the expression. A properties box will appear.

30. How can you create a project group?

A. From the File menu, select Make Project Group.

B. From the File menu, select Add Project.

C. From the File menu, select New Project.

D. From the Project menu, select Make Project Group.

31. Where can you rename, delete, and duplicate package and deployment scripts?

A. Manage Scripts in the Package and Deployment Wizard

B. Scripts in the Package and Deployment Wizard

C. The Scripts utility that comes with VB

D. The Package portion of the Package and Deployment Wizard

32. Which entries do GetSetting and SaveSetting allow you to access?

A. Anything in the Registry

B. Entries under HKEY_CURRENT_USER\Software\ VB and VBA Program Settings

C. Entries under HKEY_CONFIG\SOFTWARE\VB PROGRAM SETTINGS

D. Any currently open Key

33. During installation, the file called ST6UNST.LOG is created. Where is this file stored on the user's hard disk, and why?

A. The application directory, for use in uninstalling the application

B. The system directory, for use in uninstalling the application

C. The root directory, for logging the success or failure of installation

D. The system directory, for logging the success or failure of installation

34. You are using the Locals window and see that an expression called Me is displayed in it. You don't recall setting a watch expression for it. What does this expression represent?

A. This is an error.

B. This expression represents the Locals window.

C. This expression represents the current form.

D. This expression represents the current project.

35. An array called intArray is displayed in the Locals window. You want to view the elements of this array, and each of the values contained. What can you do to view this information?

A. Click the Plus sign beside the variable's name.

B. Click the Minus sign beside the variable's name.

C. Nothing. Each of the variables appears by default in the Locals window.

D. Nothing. The variable is shown in the Locals window, but elements of the array can't be shown.

36. Which file is included with your application to allow for the removal of your application from a user's computer?

A. SETUP.EXE

B. SETUP1.EXE

C. UNWISE.EXE

D. ST6UNST.EXE

E. Add/Remove Programs

37. You are packaging and deploying an application to floppy disk. You have a mix of different disks. Some are 1.44MB, others are 1.2MB. What must you do for packaging the application with different CAB sizes?

A. On the Cab Options screen, choose Mix from the Cab Size list box.

B. On the Cab Options screen, select 1.44MB and 1.2MB.

C. You can't package using a mixture of CAB sizes.

D. You can't package on 1.2MB disks.

38. You want to display the value of intNum in the Immediate window. Which of the following would be valid to use in the Immediate window to perform this action? (Choose all that apply.)

    A. ? intNum

    B. Print intNum

    C. Debug.Print intNum

    D. All of the above

39. Your application loads a large database that takes a considerable amount of time to load. Which of the following can you do to let the user know the application hasn't locked up when loading the database? (Choose all that apply.)

    A. Implement a splash screen.

    B. Implement a progress bar that shows that the database is loading.

C. Set AutoRedraw to False.

D. Optimize the application for size.

40. You have decided to compile to native code and then set optimization settings to optimize for both speed and size. When you attempt to go to the Compile tab, you find you cannot. Why?

    A. You can only optimize for speed *or* size. You can't optimize for both.

    B. Native code doesn't offer optimization settings for compiling.

    C. You need to make these settings on the Make tab.

    D. None of the above.

MICROSOFT CERTIFIED SOLUTION DEVELOPER

12

Building Internet Applications

CERTIFICATION OBJECTIVES

These days, everything's Internet. Every day, more people are gaining access to the World Wide Web. People have begun to use browsers such as Microsoft Internet Explorer and Netscape Navigator like common household items. Many network administrators recognize this phenomenon, and have incorporated Internet technology into local networks to create intranets.

One of the new features of Visual Basic 6.0 is the ability to create full-blown Internet applications. You can use the WebBrowser control to add the functionality of a browser to applications you create. In addition, you can use VB to create Dynamic HTML (DHTML) applications, IIS applications, and ActiveX documents. Not only can you enhance applications by incorporating the ability to access the Net, but you can create applications that run on Web servers.

CERTIFICATION OBJECTIVE 12.01

Using the WebBrowser Control

Ever think you could make a better browser than Microsoft or Netscape? Using the WebBrowser control (with a few other controls), you can add browsing capabilities to an application. Through this control, a user can view Web pages. By combining it with the functionality of other controls on a form, you can even create your own Web browser!

The WebBrowser control acts as a window that the user can activate at runtime to view Web pages. You add this control to your project by clicking Components from the Project menu, and selecting Microsoft Internet Controls from the list of available components. After you click OK, the icon for the WebBrowser control appears on the Toolbox.

After adding this control to a form, the first property you should change is the Visible property. Because the WebBrowser control displays visual elements inside of it, you should always set this control's Visible property to False in Design mode. Having the Visible property set to True may cause problems when the user starts the application, as the control may try to display other visual elements of the screen inside of it. By setting it to False, you can then have your code specify an HTML document to display. If you initialize the control and specify a default Web page to display, the user won't become confused by seeing meaningless garbage in the control.

The WebBrowser control is made up of numerous members for accessing the Internet. While this section covers many of the commonly used properties, methods and events you'll use, you should view VB's Help for a full listing and description of members associated with this control.

Among the members you will use most in your applications are those that deal with navigation. The Navigate method of the WebBrowser control is used to specify the Web page displayed in GoHome. GoHome is a method used to navigate to the Web page specified in the Internet Options dialog box in the Control Panel. Whatever URL has been set as the home page is what will display when GoHome is used. In the case of Navigate, you must specify a specific Web site immediately after invoking the method:

```
WebBrowser.Navigate "www.microsoft.com"
WebBrowser.Navigate mysite
WebBrowser.Navigate cboURL.Text
```

In the preceding examples, the Navigate method is used to display a Web page in the WebBrowser control. The first line specifies a Web site, by stating the URL in quotations. The next line uses a variable to specify a Web site, while the third obtains the URL through the Text property of another control (in this case, a combo box). Through these methods you specify what will be displayed in the WebBrowser control.

In addition to these navigation methods, there are also GoForward, GoBack, and Stop. When a user has browsed through several Web pages (by indicating different URLs to go to, or by clicking hyperlinks), the GoBack method allows the user to navigate back to a page that was displayed earlier. Likewise, after using GoBack, the GoForward property can be used to allow a user to navigate to the previously displayed page. If you think of navigation like using a book, GoBack allows you to flip to previous pages, and GoForward allows you to return to where you started. In cases where you don't want to download an entire page (if it is incredibly long, or you are experiencing problems), the Stop method allows you to stop the download.

By using these members with the proper controls, you can add the functionality of a Web browser to any application. A tool bar can be added to a form, and methods like GoBack, GoForward, and Stop can be associated with its buttons. You can add combo boxes to your form, and use the Navigate method to enable users to type in specific URLs to which they can travel. Should you wish to limit the control a user has to Web sites, you can implement a list box, command buttons, or other controls. While the WebBrowser control acts as the foundation, other controls provide full browser-type functionality.

on the job

The WebBrowser control leads to numerous possibilities for applications. It allows you to add browsing functionality to an application, while enabling you to control where the user can go via code. As such, you could have your application access only sites that are business related, and can't be used for more salacious purposes. In cases where you wish to limit a user's control of navigation, use list boxes or other controls that limit navigation abilities.

Using the WebBrowser Control

1. Start a new project by clicking New Project in the File menu, and then selecting Standard EXE.

2. From the Project menu, select Components. From the listing of available components that appears, select Microsoft Internet Controls and Microsoft Windows Common Controls 6.0, then click OK. The WebBrowser control icon appears in the Toolbox.

3. Add a WebBrowser control to the form. In the Properties window, change its Visible property to False.

4. Add a ToolBar control to the form. Right-click the newly added control, and click Properties. Click the Buttons tab. Click the Insert button to add each of these captions: Home, Back, Forward, and Stop. Exit the Properties Page when you have finished.

5. Double-click the ToolBar control, and add the following code:

```
If Button = "Home" Then
    WebBrowser1.GoHome
ElseIf Button = "Back" Then
    WebBrowser1.GoBack
ElseIf Button = "Forward" Then
    WebBrowser1.GoForward
ElseIf Button = "Stop" Then
    WebBrowser1.Stop
End If
```

6. In the Load event of the form, add the following code:

```
WebBrowser1.Visible=True
WebBrowser1.GoHome
```

7. Add a command button and a combo box to your form. Change the command button's caption to Go, and erase the contents of the combo box's Text property. In the Click event of the command button, add the following code:

```
WebBrowser1.Navigate Combo1.Text
```

8. In the NavigateComplete2 event of the WebBrowser control, add the following code:

```
Combo1.AddItem URL
Combo1.Text=URL
```

The preceding code is used to add the last URL navigated to the combo box. This creates a history list the user can navigate with.

9. Press the F5 key on your keyboard to run the program, and test it.

CERTIFICATION OBJECTIVE 12.02

Creating ActiveX Documents

ActiveX documents are similar to the forms that you use to create VB applications. You can add controls, manipulate properties, invoke methods, and add code to events in an ActiveX document just as you would a form. They can be packaged in either in-process or out-of-process components. ActiveX documents integrate into container applications, such as Internet

Explorer (version 3 or higher), Microsoft Binder, and VB (version 5 or higher). Such applications can open ActiveX documents and access its data files.

To create an ActiveX document, you must start a new ActiveX document project or convert an existing project into an ActiveX document. First, we'll discuss creating one from scratch, then we'll cover how to convert one of your standard EXE projects into an ActiveX document.

You create an ActiveX document by selecting New Project from the File menu, and then selecting ActiveX document DLL, or ActiveX document EXE. You should choose EXE if you want to create a project that doesn't require the user to use a container application exclusively to view data. This allows the project to run as a stand-alone application. In addition, choosing EXE causes each instance of your ActiveX document to be started in a separate address space. A major reason to use an ActiveX DLL is speed, because a DLL has faster performance.

Choosing either EXE or DLL creates an ActiveX document project that contains a UserDocument. The UserDocument is an object that acts as a foundation for your ActiveX document, and appears similar to a form in a standard EXE project. It looks like a form that doesn't have a title bar, control box, or min and max buttons. It is the UserDocument object that you'll use to add controls, hyperlinks, and other objects with which the user will interact.

Adding objects to the UserDocument is the same as when you add objects to a form. One difference between the UserDocument and a form is the extension used to identify each when they are saved. While a form is saved with the extension FRM, UserDocuments are saved with the extension DOB.

In addition to creating ActiveX documents from scratch, you can convert existing projects into ActiveX documents. You do this by using the ActiveX Document Migration Wizard, which resides in the Add-Ins menu of VB. Using this add-in converts forms in a current project into UserDocuments.

When you start the Migration Wizard, the first screen you see is a welcome screen. If you don't want to see this screen each time you start up the wizard, click the Skip this screen in the future check box. Clicking Next then brings you to a screen that lists all forms in the project that's currently open. Beside each form's name in the list is a check box. If you check one of these boxes, the corresponding form is converted into a UserDocument. You must check at least one form to continue.

Next to appear is the Options dialog box, shown in Figure 12-1. It is here that you can determine what happens when the forms are converted. Since UserDocuments and forms aren't identical—just similar—you'll have to rewrite some code after conversion takes place because some form events don't exist in UserDocuments. You will also have to make sure that converted procedures are compatible with any container application you use. By checking the Comment out invalid code? check box, any code found to be invalid for an ActiveX document will be commented out automatically. You can also check the Remove original forms after conversion option to clean up your project, and have the forms that were converted removed from the project.

The options available under Your Project Type is invalid determine what kind of ActiveX document will be created. Some new programmers find this

FIGURE 12-1

Options dialog box of the ActiveX Document Migration Wizard

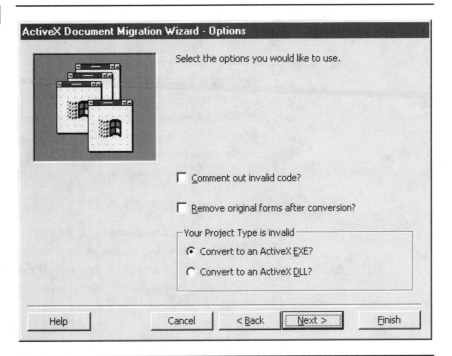

a little worrisome when they see this section, thinking that some problem has occurred and the project they're working with is invalid and can't be used. This is not the case. The options here determine how your current project will be converted, into either an ActiveX document EXE or ActiveX document DLL.

Click Next to reach the final screen. You have the option of viewing a report of your choices here, by clicking either the Yes or No option buttons. If you click the Finish button, your project is converted based on the settings you selected in this session. To save those settings for future use, click the check box labeled Save current settings as default.

Using Code Within an ActiveX Document to Interact with a Container Application

Because an ActiveX document resides in a container application, you will need to incorporate code that interacts with a container. When implementing code, you need to realize that ActiveX documents behave differently in different containers. To deal with the problems caused by some applications not recognizing things like hyperlinks, you need to use different code for different container applications.

The first step in incorporating different code for different containers is having your ActiveX document detect what type of container is being used. The Parent method of the UserDocument and the TypeName function can both be used to obtain information about the container application. UserDocument.Parent returns the name of the container. TypeName can be used to return the type of container, as illustrated in the following code:

```
TypeName(UserDocument.Parent)
```

In this line of code, TypeName takes an argument, which can be a variable or object and a property. It looks at the name passed to it and returns its data type as a string. For example, if the container used were Internet Explorer, UserDocument.Parent would return "Microsoft Internet Explorer." Using the TypeName function with this argument, TypeName would look at this argument and return "IWebBrowser2." This shows that the type of container is a Web browser.

By using an If...Then structure, you can conditionally control what code will be executed based on the type of container. In so doing, you can use TypeName and the Parent property of UserDocument to look at what container is used, then have certain code run based on the type of container or container name. This allows you to control what code is executed in certain container applications.

Even though an ActiveX document resides in a container application, it does have some control over its appearance in the container. By changing the properties of the UserDocument, you can control how a document is displayed, and how scroll bars will be used in the display.

The screen area used to display an ActiveX document in a container application is called a *viewport*. To determine the size of the viewport, you can use the ViewPortHeight, ViewPortWidth, ViewPortTop, and ViewPortLeft properties. The first two of these properties return the height and width of an area, respectively, in twips. A *twip* is a screen-independent unit of measurement that equates to 1/1440 of an inch. The ViewPortTop and ViewPortLeft return the y and x coordinates, respectively, of where the document appears in the viewport. For example, let's say you have a large document that you have to scroll across and down. As you scroll right, you are moving away from the left side of the document, and the value of ViewPortLeft increases. Likewise, as you scroll down from the top of the document, the value of ViewPortTop increases. In short, while ViewPortHeight and ViewPortWidth return the size of the viewport, ViewPortTop and ViewPortLeft return the position in which a document is displayed in the viewport.

Here is the syntax for each property:

```
UserDocument.ViewPortHeight
UserDocument.ViewPortWidth
UserDocument.ViewPortTop
UserDocument.ViewPortLeft
```

For each of these properties, the data type returned is Single. They are used to return only the current value.

To set the coordinates of the ViewPortLeft and ViewPortTop properties, you use the SetViewPort method. This allows you to configure the position at which the UserDocument will be visible in the viewport. The syntax for this method is

```
UserDocument.SetViewPort left,top
```

There are two required parameters to the SetViewPort method. *Left* is used to specify how far a document is scrolled from the left, while *top* determines how far down the document is scrolled in the viewport.

Through the ScrollBars property you can set whether scroll bars exist when your ActiveX document appears in the viewport. The ScrollBars property can be set through the Properties window, or programmatically using VB constants. In setting this property, you have four options, which are shown in Table 12-1. The default setting of the ScrollBar property is 3-Both or vbBoth.

exam
Ⓦatch

Unlike VB version 5, the default ScrollBar property setting for a UserDocument in VB version 6 is 3-Both (that is, vbBoth). This allows both vertical and horizontal scroll bars to appear.

If you've set your UserDocument to use scroll bars, the determining factors for them to appear are the MinHeight and MinWidth properties. These properties are used to return or set the minimum height and width of a viewport at which scroll bars appear. If scroll bars have been set, and the ViewPortHeight is less than the MinHeight, a vertical scroll bar appears. If the ViewPortWidth is less than the MinWidth, a horizontal scroll bar appears.

TABLE 12-1	**Property Value**	**Constant**
Settings for the UserDocument ScrollBar Property	0—None	VbSBNone
	1—Horizontal	VbHorizontal
	2—Vertical	VbVertical
	3—Both	VbBoth

The MinHeight and MinWidth properties aren't available in the Properties window, and only can be set programmatically. This is done with the following syntax:

```
UserDocument.MinHeight=value
UserDocument.MinWidth=value
```

MinHeight and MinWidth have a Single data type value, and must be set in your code. You cannot set either of these values in Design mode.

Navigating to Other ActiveX Documents

It is not unusual for a container application to contain a number of documents at the same time. It is important, therefore, to be able to navigate from one ActiveX document to another.

Hyperlinks can be used to navigate between ActiveX documents in Internet-aware containers. The Hyperlink object is a property of the UserDocument and has methods that allow you to jump from one document to another. The methods of the Hyperlink object that allow for navigation are NavigateTo, GoBack, and GoForward.

NavigateTo allows you to specify a document to jump to. This method has one required argument, which is the URL or local document that you want to navigate to. The following example shows the syntax used to invoke this method, and an example that links to Microsoft's Web site:

```
UserDocument.Hyperlink.NavigateTo URL
```

or

```
UserDocument.Hyperlink.NavigateTo "http://www.microsoft.com"
```

While this code takes you to a Web site, you can also use NavigateTo to jump to a specific local document. This is done with the following syntax:

```
UserDocument.Hyperlink.NavigateTo "file://c:\docs\mydoc.vbd"
```

In this example, the hyperlink jumps to a file called MYDOC.VBD, which is located in the path C:\docs.

Once you have gone to another document, you can return to the previous ActiveX document using the GoBack method. This method works only if you've moved from one document to another. Its syntax is

```
UserDocument.Hyperlink.GoBack
```

The GoBack method requires no arguments because you are navigating through previous documents or Web sites in the history list.

The GoForward method is a sister method to GoBack. When you've used GoBack, you are able to move forward in the history list, to return to the site or document you were viewing before GoBack was invoked. The GoForward method requires no arguments. Its syntax is

```
UserDocument.Hyperlink.GoForward
```

ActiveX Document Menus

When creating ActiveX documents, you can implement menus as you would any other VB application. As we discussed in Chapter 3, you can create menus using the Menu Editor. While the process of creating menus for an ActiveX document is identical to creating menus for other applications, some extra consideration is needed.

ActiveX documents reside within container applications. When an ActiveX document is loaded into the container, the document's menus merge with those of the container application. Because the two menu systems have to coexist, this can lead to problems. For example, when creating the ActiveX document's menu system, you should always use original and distinctive captions so that these menus don't conflict with the container's menus. In addition, you shouldn't create a Windows menu that switches from one document to another, or a menu (such as the File menu) that saves or prints data or closes the container application. Such menus are the responsibility of the container application and can create conflicts. By keeping these restrictions in mind, you can avoid problems when incorporating menu systems into ActiveX documents.

When creating menus with the Menu Editor, the NegotiatePosition property allows you to specify the position of an ActiveX document's menu item in relation to the container's menu. Your options for this property are None, Left, Middle, and Right.

Use the 0—None setting of NegotiatePosition if you don't want a menu item to merge with a container's menu system. If you set this value, the menu item doesn't appear in the container's menu system.

1—Left is a little misleading. Setting this value does not cause a menu to be placed in the leftmost position on the menu bar because that spot is reserved for the container's File menu. When you set a menu item's NegotiatePostition to left, the item will be placed as far to the left as possible without encroaching on the reserved spot. In other words, it will appear on the left side of the menu, usually next to the container's File menu.

Use the NegotiatePosition setting of 2—Middle when you have more than two menus, with one set as left and another as right. When a menu item is set to middle, the container places the item somewhere in the middle of the menu. You have no control over where in the middle the menu item will appear.

If a menu item has NegotiatePosition set to 3—Right, the menu appears on the right side of a container's menu system. The exception to this rule occurs when you have a Help menu that you want to merge with the container's Help menu. When this is the case, the ActiveX document's Help menu items will appear in the container's Help menu.

To merge two such Help menus, the ActiveX document's Help menu must have a caption of &Help or Help. After setting this, set NegotiatePosition to 3—Right. You then need to add your menu items under this menu. If you don't add any menu items to your Help menu, the menu will appear to the left of the container's Help menu. If you do add items, your Help menu will appear as a submenu item in the container's Help menu.

Creating Dynamic Hypertext Markup Language Applications

A new feature in VB version 6 is the ability to create DHTML applications. DHTML is an acronym for Dynamic Hypertext Markup Language, which is a set of additions to HTML, traditionally used for creating Web pages. DHTML allows Web page authors to dynamically change elements of an HTML document. Using DHTML you can add, delete, and modify what appears on a page.

DHTML applications combine DHTML with VB code, resulting in a browser-based application. The application responds to mouse movement, keyboard input, and other actions that are expected in VB programs. Through these actions, the application can respond by changing a Web page, adding text, retrieving data from a page to query a database, and so on.

A DHTML application is made up of HTML pages, VB code that handles events, and a project DLL that contains your code and is accessed at runtime. For the DHTML application to run, the browser or Web control accessing it must use the runtime DLL called MSVBVM60.DLL. A browser that meets the criteria is Internet Explorer 4.01 with Service Pack 1.

Many of the tasks a DHTML application can perform are the same as those that can be performed by CGI and other scripts. These are scripts residing on a server, which respond to an action and perform some task. Because the DHTML application resides on the user's computer, rather than on a server, processing is performed on the client side. Using methods such as CGI, an event (such as a mouse click) is transmitted to the server, processed, and the result is sent back. With DHTML, many events can be taken care of on the client side, while still enabling requests to be made of the server. This decreases the response time to user requests, because the server isn't processing everything.

To create a DHTML application, click VB's File menu and select New Project. When the New Project dialog box appears, select DHTML Application, and then click OK. A new DHTML Project appears in the Project window.

A DHTML project is an ActiveX DLL project that has references set to access the DHTML Page Designer. It also sets the Toolbox to the HTML tab that contains controls for creating an HTML page, shown in Figure 12-2. DHTML applications consist of one or more HTML documents, and you will use these tools to design the HTML documents that make up your application.

on the **job**

If a network administrator has upgraded you to VB version 6, be sure that your copy of Internet Explorer has also been upgraded to at least version 4.01 with Service Pack 1. To use the DHTML Page Designer, you must be using Internet Explorer 4.01 with Service Pack 1 or greater. If you are using an earlier version than this, an error message will result, and the DHTML Page Designer will fail to load. Upgrading Internet Explorer when installing VB is an easy oversight, but you can't create DHTML applications when older versions of IE reside on your system.

When viewing the contents of the Project window, you'll see that the project contains two folders: Modules and Designers. Double-clicking a

---

FIGURE 12-2

A DHTML application project, showing the DHTML Page Designer and HTML tools in the Toolbox

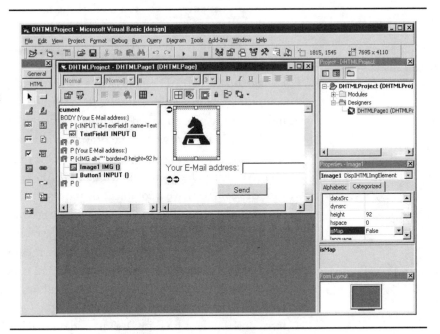

folder, or clicking the plus symbol (+) beside the folder, expands it to reveal its contents. The Modules folder contains a module in which you can write VB code. The Designers folder contains an HTML page. This is your foundation for creating an HTML document that, when double-clicked, opens the DHTML Page Designer, as was shown in Figure 12-2.

The DHTML Page Designer allows you to create HTML documents without previous knowledge of HTML. There is one designer for each HTML page in your project. To add pages to a project, select Add DHTML Page from the Project window.

The left pane of the designer is the Treeview pane. It contains a hierarchical representation of an HTML document's contents. All items in the HTML document—such as images, text, and buttons—are called elements. Once elements are added, they can be manipulated during runtime through code. Each element listed in the Treeview pane includes information on the type of control, the beginning of its content (for elements such as text), and (when available) an ID. IDs are used to identify an element in code, and appear boldfaced in the TextView pane. IDs can be added or changed through the Properties window.

The document is at the top level of the hierarchy in the Treeview pane. Double-clicking the document or clicking the plus symbol beside it expands the tree to show the BODY( ). Everything you add to your page will be contained within the body. This goes back to HTML coding, where a page is made up of a HEAD section and a BODY section. The HEAD is commonly used for information geared toward the browser, or information indicating the program used to create the document. The BODY is used for the data that appears within the browser window.

HTML authors may be interested to know that pages created with the DHTML Page Designer don't contain HEAD sections. The pages created with the designer have a comment denoting that it was created with this program, the object ID, and class ID. The pages you create with the designer use the BODY to contain information displayed in the browser window, and a closing </HTML> tag (which shows where the document ends).

The right pane of the designer is the Detail pane. This is a visual representation of the HTML page, and it allows you to add, delete, and modify elements of the page. You can use the Detail pane as you would a form in a standard EXE in Design mode. Double-clicking a control on the Toolbox adds a control to the pane. You can also click a control on the

Toolbox, then draw it in the Detail pane. Should you wish to modify any existing elements on the page, you merely click any added controls and resize or delete them like controls on a form.

Text can be added to the page by clicking within the pane and typing. The list box at the top left corner of the designer allows you to apply different styles to your text. These text styles correspond to the various styles of an HTML document, and are covered in Table 12-2. The HTML tags

TABLE 12-2

Styles for Text Offered in DHTML Page Designer

Style	HTML Tag (Opening Tag . . . Closing Tag)	Description
Heading 1	`<H1>...</H1>`	Very large text style commonly used for titles.
Heading 2	`<H2>...</H2>`	Text style that's slightly smaller than an H1 style. Commonly used for subheadings.
Heading 3	`<H3>...</H3>`	Text style that's slightly smaller than an H2 style. Commonly used for headings that appear below subheadings.
Heading 4	`<H4>...</H4>`	Text style that's similar to normal boldfaced text.
Heading 5	`<H5>...</H5>`	Text style that's smaller than normal boldfaced text.
Heading 6	`<H6>...</H6>`	Extremely small text style.
Normal	`<P>...</P>`	Normal text. Doesn't use tags. The `<P>` tag is used to denote a new paragraph. The `</P>` isn't actually used for anything and is ignored by the browser. `</P>` is only used for conformity with other tags.
Formatted	`<PRE>...</PRE>`	Used for preformatted text. Will display text as it was originally formatted.

TABLE 12-2

Styles for Text Offered in
DHTML Page Designer
(*continued*)

Style	HTML Tag (Opening Tag ... Closing Tag)	Description
Address	<Address>...</Address>	Italicized text used for addresses.
Numbered List	<OL>...</OL> <LI>...</LI>	Used to display numbered items as 1., 2., etc. The <OL> tag is used to show where the list begins, while <LI> is used to denote each individual list item. This type of list is also called an *ordered list.*
Bulleted List	<UL>...</UL> <LI>...</LI>	Used to display items in a list with bullets. The <UL> tag is used to show where the list begins, while <LI> is used to denote each individual item. This type of list is also called an *unordered list.*
Directory List	<DIR>...</DIR>	Used for displaying a directory of items.
Menu List	<MENU>...</MENU>	Used for displaying a menu of items.
Definition Term	<DL>...</DL> <DT>...</DT>	Used for terms that are going to be defined. The <DL> tag is used to show where the definition list begins, while <DT> is used to denote the term being defined.
Definition	<DL>...</DL> <DD>...</DD>	Used for definitions. Commonly used after defined terms. The <DL> tag is used to show where the definition list begins, while <DD> is used to denote the definition.

displayed here are what the designer will place in your page. A starting tag, such as <H1> denotes the beginning of a style, while an ending tag (</H1>) specifies where that style ends. While the designer shields you from having to know HTML, some tags are offered here for reference.

Beside the Style list box, you have controls that allow you to further manipulate text that appears in the page. The bold, italic, and underline buttons provide the same functionality as identical buttons that appear in the VB design environment. There is also a list box for setting font size, and another for specifying the font face. At the far right of the top tool bar, you can select whether text appears as left- or right-justified, or centered.

on the job

In general, you should avoid changing the font to nonstandard Windows fonts. If you select a custom font that appears on your computer, but may not appear on the end user's computer, the display will be unpredictable. This is because the user's computer attempts to use the closest font available. In some cases this can be extremely different from the font you chose, and hard to read. In one case, I used a comic book–style font, and it appeared in an extremely difficult-to-read script font on an end user's computer. To avoid this, only use the fonts that come with the Windows installation.

The tool bar below the one we just covered contains additional features for creating, opening, and saving pages. The button farthest to the left accesses the DHTML Page Designer Properties dialog box, shown in Figure 12-3. This allows you to specify whether a page you've created will be saved as part of the VB project, or as a separate, external file. If it is saved separately, you should give it a file extension of HTM or HTML. These are standard extensions used for HTML documents.

Choosing to save as a separate, external file also allows you to specify the path and filename of the document. It also enables the New and Open buttons. Clicking the New button allows you to save your current HTML page as an external file. This brings up a Create New dialog box, which enables you to specify the pathname and filename by browsing your hard disk. Using the New button saves you from having to memorize the correct pathname and filename of your page.

DHTML Page Properties
dialog box

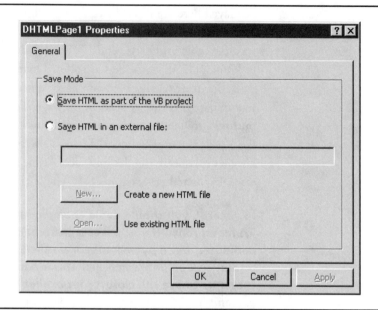

The Open button is used to open an existing HTML file in the page designer. You use this when you've already created your HTML page using a program that creates Web pages, like FrontPage. The ability to import such pages into the designer is useful in companies that have a Webmaster on staff who creates Web pages for the company, or when you wish to hire Web page authors to create your pages. By using the Open button, you can import these pages and then assign code to specific elements of the page.

exam
🐶*atch*

You are expected to know how to import pages as well as create pages using the designer. Remember that you aren't limited to creating pages with a designer, but can import them through DHTML Page Designer Properties.

Should you wish to use an external editor to modify your pages, you must first save your page in the designer as an external file. You can then click the Launch Editor button, located beside the DHTML Page Designer Properties button on the tool bar. This will launch the application specified in VB. By default, the editor used will be Notepad. To specify another editor, select Options from the Tools menu, and then select the Advanced tab. In the External HTML Editor field, specify the path and filename of the application you wish to use as your editor. This can be an application such as FrontPage, or any other program that allows you to create and edit Web pages.

The next two buttons on the designer allow for special formatting. The Wrap selection in <DIV>...</DIV> option allows you to group several tags together for processing. For example, you might want to group several paragraphs with different headers together, and then format them as a unit. The Wrap selection in <SPAN>...</SPAN> option applies HTML tags that allow you to select a portion of text for processing. This enables you to select a few words and format them differently from the rest of the text. After selecting the text you want in the Detail pane, you can click either of these two buttons, and the text will appear in the Treeview pane preceded by the word SPAN or DIV. When you click on the item in Treeview, the text will become highlighted, allowing you to format it as you wish.

The Link button allows you to make highlighted text into hyperlinks. After selecting the text you want to make into a link, click the button with a picture of the world and a chain. The text becomes underlined and changes to a different color. By right-clicking this text and choosing Properties, you can configure where the user will jump to when clicking the hyperlink.

The Property Page of a hyperlink, shown in Figure 12-4, allows you to configure what will happen when a user clicks the link.

FIGURE 12-4

Property Page of a hyperlink

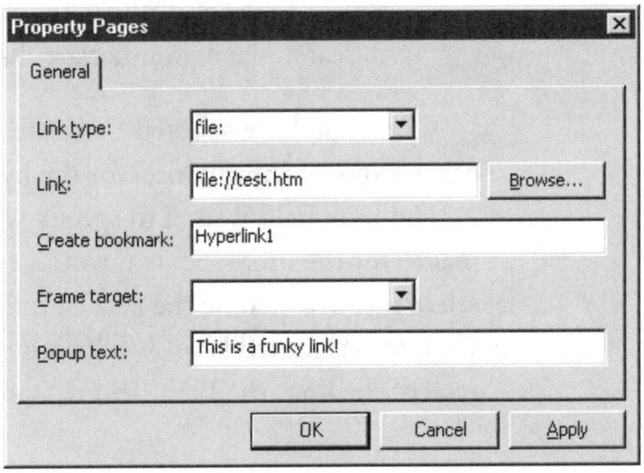

The Link type list box allows you to select the kind of link this will be. Your options are as follows:

- **(other)** Used for jumping to a bookmark on the current page.

- **file** Opens a file on your disk when clicked.

- **ftp** Connects to an FTP site, which is like a directory of files. When you click a filename that is hyperlinked to an FTP site, it sends the file to you using File Transfer Protocol.

- **gopher** Connects to a Gopher site, which is similar to an FTP site. They are outdated, but a number still exist on the Internet.

- **http** Connects to a Web page on the Internet, or on your network's intranet.

- **https** Connects to a secure Web site, using HTTP over Secure Socket Layer (SSL).

- **mailto** Used when creating hyperlinks for sending e-mail. The link would be your e-mail address. When users click this, their e-mail programs open new mail windows with the e-mail address already placed in the To field.

- **news** Used for linking to a news server. News servers provide files, stored messages, and other services.

- **telnet** This is another leftover from the old days of the Internet that allows access to remote computers.

- **wais** Links to a Wide-Area Information Service. WAIS allows users to search databases that are distributed across the Web.

When you have selected the correct link type, you are ready to specify the other required information for the hyperlink.

The Link field is used to specify what you want to link to. If you choose mailto for the link type, you would enter your e-mail address here. If you select file, it would be the path and filename, while http would require a URL to be entered here. While link type is used to specify the protocol and type of the link, the Link field narrows what it is you're linking to.

The final three fields are Create bookmark, Frame target, and Popup text. The first of these allows you to enter a name and create a bookmark. You can then create another link to jump to this bookmark. Frame target allows you to specify whether a linked file or site will appear in the current window or frame, or another browser or frame. Finally, Popup text is used to specify a small explanation of what this link does. When the user holds the mouse cursor over the link, the pop-up text appears in a small box next to the cursor.

After you've created or imported your pages, you can add code to controls and elements. Any element of a page can have code attached to it, as long as it has an ID. As mentioned previously, an ID is used to identify an element, and can be modified by selecting the element and changing the ID property in the Properties window. You can add code to an element just as you would a control in a standard EXE project. Selecting Code from the View menu, double-clicking a control, or right-clicking an element and selecting View Code will bring up the Code window. From there, you can add code to events.

In Exercise 12-2 we will create a DHTML application that converts temperature measurements in degrees Fahrenheit to degrees Celsius. It will add text to the page indicating whether a temperature is hot, cold, or nice.

EXERCISE 12-2

Creating a DHTML Application

1. From the File menu, select New Project, and then choose DHTML Application from the dialog box.

2. In the Project window, open the Designers folder, and select DHTMLPage1. Double-click it, or click the View Object button on the Project window, so that the DHTML Page Designer appears.

3. In the Detail pane of the designer, type **Fahrenheit:** and press ENTER twice. Type **Celsius:** and then press ENTER six times. Change the heading for this final line to Heading 1.

4. In the TreeView pane, expand the document and elements until you see an item that says H1. This is the final line in your Detail pane, and should be the bottom element in the hierarchy of the TreeView. Select this item. In the Properties window, change the ID to Temp.

5. Add a text field to the Detail pane, below the line that says Fahrenheit. Add another text field below the line that says Celsius. In the Properties window, erase the Value field for each of these text fields, so that no text appears in them.

6. Add a button below the Celsius text field. In the Properties window, change the Value property to Clear.

7. Select View Code from the Project window. Select TextField2 from the Object list box (the left one) and Onkeyup from the Event list box (the right one). Add the following code to convert Celsius to Fahrenheit:

```
TextField1.Value = (TextField2.Value * 9 / 5) + 32
```

8. Select TextField1 from the Object list box, and Onkeyup from the Event list box. Add the following code to convert Fahrenheit to Celsius:

```
TextField2.Value = (TextField1.Value - 32) * 5 / 9
```

9. Below this, enter the following code to add text that will tell us if a temperature we type is hot, cold, or nice.

```
If TextField1.Value >= 80 Then
    Temp.innerText = "Hot"
ElseIf TextField1.Value <= 60 Then
    Temp.innerText = "Cold"
Else
    Temp.innerText = "Nice!"
End If
```

If you feel comfortable enough, attempt to modify this code so it does the same for temperatures entered in the Celsius text field.

10. In the Onclick event of Button1, add the following code to clear the values created by our previous code:

```
TextField1.Value = ""
TextField2.Value = ""
Temp.innerText = ""
```

11. Press F5 and run your project. Internet Explorer 4.01 with Service Pack 1 should open, displaying your application. When you type a number in the Fahrenheit field, it is automatically converted and its Celsius equivalent appears in the Celsius text field. Depending on the temperature you enter in the Fahrenheit field, "Hot," "Cold," or "Nice!" appears on the page.

FROM THE CLASSROOM

Abundant Internet Applications

Few can argue that the nature of application development is stubble-deep in the momentum of paradigm shifting toward Internet applications. Fat is out, while thin is the "in" thing in development, assuming *thin* is a synonym for *Web based.*

VB has greatly expanded the options for Internet application development. Microsoft Internet Explorer introduced the WebBrowser control for exposing the encapsulation of HTML rendering and HTTP protocol functionality into one simplified programmable object. Through the Web browser control, the Internet Explorer and DHTML object models are exposed, yet VB goes far beyond these capabilities. VB version 6 introduced both DHTML applications and IIS applications.

DHTML application projects are actually just ActiveX DLL projects that automatically configure and set the proper project preferences, toolbox tab, and controls to allow access to the HTML page designer introduced with VB 6. DHTML applications therefore create an in-process component that extends the functionality of the client browser to accommodate and encapsulate the VB code necessary for the DHTML pages that make up the application.

IIS applications are also a special type of ActiveX DLL project that automatically include an instance of the brand-new ActiveX designer called a *WebClass object.* The WebClass object forms the base of an IIS application, utilizing multiple HTML templates and WebItems. An IIS application is deployed as a single CAB file by use of the Package and Deployment Wizard. This CAB file contains project DLLs, DSXs, DSRs, and all other associated project files.

For the exam, you should be familiar with the differences between IIS and DHTML applications, the type of files produced by the Package and Deployment Wizard, the common properties and methods of the WebBrowser control, and the basics of ActiveX documents. These include navigation issues and how they compare to other ActiveX components in terms of use, hosting requirements, and development.

—By Michael Lane Thomas, MCSE+I, MCSD, MCT, A+

Creating Microsoft Internet Information Server Applications

Internet Information Server (IIS) is a Web server for Internet or intranet uses. With VB, you can create applications that reside on IIS. These applications receive requests from browsers, run code associated with a request, and return a response to the browser. Like DHTML applications, IIS applications use HTML pages as a user interface. Unlike our previous topic, IIS applications use special objects called *WebClasses*.

When your IIS application runs, the WebClass processes data from the browser and returns a WebItem. A WebItem is an HMTL page or other data that is sent in response to the request. The procedures you create define how the WebClass will respond and what WebItems are sent.

When a browser accesses a WebClass, a logical instance of that WebClass is created for the browser. What this means is that there is an instance of a WebClass for each browser using a particular WebClass in your application. This one-on-one relationship lasts for the WebClass's lifetime.

Before creating an IIS application with VB, you must first ensure that a number of system requirements are met. In addition to having VB version 6 installed on your computer, you'll need a Web server that can run Active Server Pages. If your machine is NT Server 4 or higher, you can install Internet Information Server 3 or higher with Active Server Pages. If you're using NT Workstation 4, Windows 95, or higher versions of these operating systems, you'll need to install Peer Web Services 3 or higher, with Active Server Pages. You must also have Internet Explorer 4 for testing the application; you'll need to install Internet Explorer 4 or higher.

on the
job

To create IIS applications, you need Peer Web Services 3 or Internet Information Server 3 (or higher versions of these) on your development computer. If you don't have a Web server that runs Active Server Pages, you won't be able to create a new IIS application in Visual Basic 6.0. In addition, you'll need a browser like Internet Explorer 4 to run and debug your application. If you don't have these, let your network administrator know you need them installed.

The reason that these requirements are in place is due to the relationship between Active Server Pages and WebClasses. When you compile or debug your application, an Active Server Page with the extension ASP is created for each WebClass. The Web server reads the ASP file that hosts the WebClass and generates its runtime component. The relationship between ASP files, WebClasses, and WebItems is this: one Active Server Page file is associated with one WebClass, which can contain many WebItems. You can think of an ASP file as a doorway to your application. When a user types in a URL, it accesses the ASP file that runs the WebClasses, which return WebItems.

exam

Watch

Active Server Pages, WebClasses, WebItems, and their relationships are important. You should understand them before taking the exam. Even if you don't get a question that relates directly to them, you may be asked questions that indirectly require knowledge of these items and their relationships.

Once you've ensured that you meet the system requirements for creating an IIS application, you can use VB to create one. When you select New Project from the File menu, the New Project dialog box appears. Select IIS Application from the dialog box and click OK.

In the Project window, you'll see a hierarchy of your new project containing a folder called Designers. Expanding this folder displays a single WebClass. You can add WebClasses to your project by selecting Add WebClass from the Project menu. Each WebClass you add has its own designer, but will appear under the Designers folder in the Project window.

By selecting a WebClass from the Designers folder and clicking the View Object button on the Project window, the WebClass designer is displayed, as shown in Figure 12-5. The designer is similar to the one seen in the preceding section. When you create a new WebClass or use the empty WebClass in a new project, it will look different from what's shown here. A new or empty WebClass will contain an HTML Template WebItems folder and a Custom WebItems folder, to which you can add HTML documents and WebItems. Figure 12-5 shows a WebClass that has templates and WebItems added to it. The HTML documents and custom WebItems are what makes up a WebClass.

FIGURE 12-5

WebClass designer

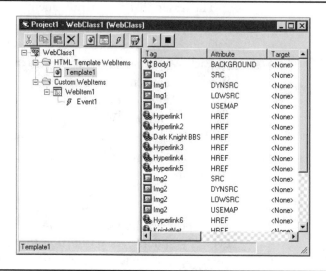

The left pane of the designer is the Treeview pane. It displays a hierarchical view of a WebClass. Within this pane, you can view WebItems and events of the WebClass. As shown by the two folders in Treeview, there are two kinds of WebItems. HTML Document Templates are HTML files returned to a browser in response to a request. Custom WebItems contain events, which consist of VB code that can be accessed at runtime. By using the Treeview pane, you can navigate through your WebClass to specific HTML files, custom WebItems, and events.

The right pane of the designer is the Detail pane. What you select in the Treeview pane determines what is displayed in the Detail pane. For example, selecting the HTML Document Templates or Custom WebItems folders, respectively, displays either all of the HTML files or all of the custom WebItems they contain. Selecting the WebClass itself displays these two folders, while selecting a custom WebItem displays the events of that item. The Detail pane is particularly useful when template files are selected.

When you select a template in HTML Document Templates, you can view the contents of an HTML file that can be used as an event. For example, in Figure 12-5, the template shows a number of hyperlinks. By double-clicking one of these hyperlinks, the Code window appears, allowing you to add code.

Four columns of information about an HTML file appear in the Detail pane. The first is the Tag column, which shows a graphical representation of the item and the information describing what that item is. The Attribute column shows the HTML attribute of the tag. An attribute is used in HTML to specify what an object is or does. For example, a hyperlink has an HREF attribute that defines where the browser will jump to when the link is clicked. The Target column indicates whether a particular element has been "connected" to an event. When this element is activated—for example, when a hyperlink is clicked—the event associated with it in the Target column is triggered. If the tag is "disconnected," and has no event associated with it, <None> appears in this column. Finally, the HTML context column shows the HTML code associated with the object.

The tool bar of the designer allows you to configure what will be part of the WebClass and to control Peer Web Services. The first four buttons on this tool bar allow you to cut, copy, paste, and delete items, respectively. This is useful if you have an event you'd like to duplicate and change, or if you no longer need a particular item in the WebClass.

The next button on this tool bar is Add HTML Template WebItem. When you click this button a dialog box opens that allows you to search your hard disk for an HTML file to add to the WebClass. The WebClass can then return this file in response to a browser request.

Add Custom WebItem adds a new custom WebItem to the Custom WebItems folder. When you've added a new custom WebItem, you can click the button beside this one on the tool bar to add events to the item. You add events to an existing WebItem by selecting the item in Treeview and clicking Add Custom Event on the tool bar.

The Edit HTML Template button allows you to launch an HTML editor and modify an HTML template in your WebClass. Which editor is launched is determined by what you've set in Options. To change the default editor, Notepad, select Options from the Tools menu. When the Options dialog box appears, select the Advanced tab, and enter the path and filename of the new editor in the External HTML Editor field. If you don't have the path and filename memorized (as few of us semi-sane programmers do), you can click the button beside this field to browse your hard disk. To edit the HTML file, you will need to know HTML or have configured VB to launch a graphic editor like FrontPage.

Finally, the last two buttons on the tool bar allow you to start and stop Peer Web Services. These two buttons look like the start and stop buttons on a VCR. If Peer Web Services is currently running, the Start button will be disabled, while Stop will be enabled. Conversely, if you've stopped Peer Web Services, the Stop button will be disabled and Start will be enabled. Shutting down Peer Web Services keeps users from accessing Web pages available on your computer over an intranet. These services should always be shut down when using the Internet from a stand-alone computer used for development.

When creating a WebClass, there are several properties you should always set. The first of these is StateManagement, which can be changed from the Properties window. StateManagement can be set to 1—wcNoState or 2—wcRetainInstance. When set to wcNoState, the WebClass is used for the duration of a browser request, then destroyed. When wcRetainInstance is used, the instance of a WebClass isn't destroyed until the ASP session times out, or the WebClass calls ReleaseInstance. How you set this property determines whether the WebClass stays alive between requests or is destroyed when a request is completed.

The Public property can also be set in the Properties window, and determines whether the WebClass can be shared by other applications. By default, this property is set to True. If it's set to False, your application won't be able to run, because other applications can't access it.

The final two properties you should set are Unattended Execution and Retained in Memory. These properties are set on the General tab of Project Properties, which is accessed from the Project menu. Unattended Execution can be enabled or disabled by a check box on this tab. When checked, instances of a DLL class in your project can be allocated on any thread; when unchecked, it forces all WebClass instances to be allocated on the same thread. If the Unattended Execution check box is unchecked, the Retained in Memory option is automatically disabled. Retained in Memory allows the runtime support state to be permanently loaded on a server's threads. If either of these check boxes is unchecked, the result is that the project runs more slowly.

IIS Application Events

Once you've properly set the properties for your project and WebClass, you are ready to apply code to events. WebClasses have three kinds of events associated with them: standard, custom, and template. These events are initiated when a user clicks an element in his or her browser.

A *standard event* occurs in templates and custom WebItems, and automatically appears in the Code window. These are predefined events, and only appear in the Code window's Procedure list box. There are three standard events associated with every WebItem: Respond, ProcessTag, and UserEvent. The Respond event is the default event of a WebItem when it is activated by a request. ProcessTag is used to replace the content of a tag with data specified in your code. Finally, the UserEvent is used to process the events of a WebClass that are created at runtime.

As previously mentioned, you can add code to elements of a template that appear in the designer. When you double-click an element appearing in the designer, a new event with this name is generated and appears beneath the template's name in the Treeview pane. These are known as *template events*. Template events are generated when VB parses the HTML document, and they appear in both the Code window (after an attribute is connected) and the designer.

As mentioned earlier, the Target column of the Design pane displays events associated with an element. This shows that a particular attribute is connected to an event. You can connect an attribute to an event by double-clicking the attribute and writing code for it when the Code window appears.

By clicking the Add Custom Event button on the tool bar, you can add a *custom event* to a WebClass. Custom events appear in the designer and in the Code window. You can double-click a new event in the Treeview pane and write code for it when the Code window appears. This feature allows you to add specialized event handling for a WebItem.

When a WebClass gets a request, it goes through events in a specific order. First, when a specific event is requested, an attempt is made to fire the event by matching the request with the specified WebItem and procedure. If this fails, and the request doesn't match any existing WebClass or event, the UserEvent for the HTML template is fired. If no event has been specified in a request, the Respond event for the template is fired by the WebClass. Finally, if no WebItem has been specified in a request, the Active Server Page for the application is launched, and the Start event for the WebClass is fired.

QUESTIONS AND ANSWERS

I can't view the ActiveX documents I created in Internet Explorer 2, VB 4, and some Microsoft Office applications. Why?	ActiveX documents are relatively new. Versions equal or higher than Internet Explorer 3, VB 5, and Microsoft Binder 1 applications are able to view ActiveX documents.
I want to add the functionality of a Web browser to my application. How can I do it?	Add the WebBrowser control to a form, then write controls that allow the user to navigate from one Web page to another.
I have a standard EXE project that I'd like to use as an ActiveX document. How can I convert it?	Open the standard EXE project you want to convert. Use the ActiveX Document Migration Wizard, and follow the instructions on each screen.
I've created a DHTML application, but it won't run in Internet Explorer. What's wrong?	Make sure that you are using Internet Explorer 4.01 with Service Pack 1. Any version lower than this will fail to display the DHTML application.
I tried to create an IIS application, but VB won't let me. Why?	You must be running Internet Information Server, or Peer Web Services 3 or higher must be installed. WebClasses won't be able to run without them.

CERTIFICATION SUMMARY

The WebBrowser control allows you to add the functionality of users being able to view Web sites through your application. Using its methods and properties, you can combine this control with other controls to make a full-fledged Web browser.

ActiveX documents allow you to create applications that are displayed in container applications like Internet Explorer. You can create ActiveX documents by selecting ActiveX document EXE or ActiveX document DLL when starting a new project. You can also use the ActiveX Document Migration Wizard to convert existing projects into ActiveX documents.

DHTML applications combine VB code with HTML to create dynamic Web pages. With DHMTL applications, you can provide the functionality of a VB program to a Web page.

While DHTML applications are processed on the client's browser, IIS applications reside on a Web server. Such a Web server must support Active Server Pages, as is the case with Peer Web Services 3 (or higher) and Internet Information Server 3 (or higher). The IIS application responds to user requests, processes the request on the server, and returns information to the browser.

TWO-MINUTE DRILL

❏ Visual Basic 6.0 has the ability to create full-blown Internet applications. You can use the WebBrowser control to add the functionality of a browser to applications you create.

❏ The WebBrowser control acts as a window through which the user can view Web pages at runtime. You add this control to your project by clicking Components from the Project menu, and selecting Microsoft Internet Controls from the list of available components.

❏ ActiveX documents are similar to the forms you use to create VB applications. You can add controls, manipulate properties, invoke methods, and add code to events in an ActiveX document just as you would a form. They can be packaged in either in-process or out-of-process components.

❏ You create an ActiveX document by selecting New Project from the File menu, and then selecting ActiveX document DLL or ActiveX document EXE. You should choose EXE if you want to create a project that doesn't require the user to exclusively use a container application to view data. This allows the project to run as a stand-alone application.

❏ Choosing either EXE or DLL creates an ActiveX document project that contains a UserDocument. The UserDocument is an object that acts as a foundation for your ActiveX document, and is similar to a form in a standard EXE project. It looks like a form that doesn't have a title bar, control box, or min and max buttons. You'll use the UserDocument object to add controls, hyperlinks, and other objects with which the user will interact.

❑ Because an ActiveX document resides in a container application, you will need to incorporate code that interacts with a container. When implementing code, you need to realize that ActiveX documents behave differently in different containers.

❑ Hyperlinks can be used to navigate between ActiveX documents in Internet-aware containers. The Hyperlink object is a property of the UserDocument, and has methods that allow you to jump from one document to another.

❑ When an ActiveX document is loaded into the container, the document's menus merge with those of the container application. Because the two menu systems have to coexist, this can lead to problems. When creating an ActiveX document's menu system, you should always use original and distinctive captions so that these menus don't conflict with the container's menus. In addition, you shouldn't create a Windows menu that switches from one document to another, or a menu that saves or prints data, or closes the container application.

❑ A new feature to VB 6 is the ability to create Dynamic Hypertext Markup Language (DHTML), which is a set of additions to HTML. DHTML allows Web page authors to dynamically change elements of an HTML document.

❑ DHTML applications combine DHTML with VB code, resulting in a browser-based application. The application responds to mouse movement, keyboard input, and other actions that are expected in VB programs.

❑ A DHTML application is made up of HTML pages, VB code that handles events, and a project DLL that contains your code and that is accessed at runtime. For the DHTML application to run, the browser or Web control accessing it must use the runtime DLL called MSVBVM60.DLL.

❑ DHTML applications can perform many of the same tasks as server-side CGI scripts that respond to an action and perform some task. Because DHTML applications reside on the user's computer, rather than on a server, processing is performed on the client side.

❑ With DHTML, many events can be taken care of on the client side, while still enabling requests to be made of the server.

❑ Internet Information Server (IIS) is a Web server that can be used for Internet or intranet uses. With VB, you can create applications that reside on IIS. These applications receive requests from browsers, run code associated with a request, and return a response to the browser.

❑ When your IIS application runs, the WebClass processes data from the browser and returns a WebItem. A WebItem is an HMTL page or other data that is sent in response to the request.

❑ In order to create an IIS application with VB, you must have a Web server that can run Active Server Pages. You should also have Internet Explorer 4 for testing the application.

❑ WebClasses have three kinds of events associated with them: standard, custom, and template.

❑ A standard event occurs in templates and custom WebItems, and automatically appears in the Code window. Standard events are predefined events and only appear in the Code window's Procedure list box. There are three standard events associated with every WebItem: Respond, ProcessTag, and UserEvent.

SELF TEST

The following questions will help you measure your understanding of the material presented in this chapter. Read all the choices carefully, as there may be more than one correct answer. Choose all correct answers for each question.

1. You have decided to add the functionality of a Web browser to a project's form. You notice this control's icon doesn't appear in your Toolbox. How will you add this control to the Toolbox so you can add it to your form?

   A. From the Project menu, select Components, and then select WebBrowser from the list.

   B. From the Project menu, select Components, and then select Internet Explorer Controls from the list.

   C. From the Project menu, select Components, and then select Microsoft Internet Controls from the list.

   D. Reinstall VB. This is a common control that appears in the Toolbox.

2. Which of the following lines of code will enable Microsoft's Web site to appear in the WebBrowser control?

   A. WebBrowser.Navigate www.microsoft.com

   B. WebBrowser.Navigate "www.microsoft.com"

   C. WebBrowser.GoHome www.microsoft.com

   D. WebBrowser.Navigate URL

3. You want to convert a standard EXE project into an ActiveX document. How will you do this?

   A. Change the FRM extension of all Forms to DOB.

   B. Use the ActiveX Control Interface Wizard.

   C. Use the ActiveX Document Migration Wizard.

   D. Use the ActiveX Document Conversion Wizard.

4. Which of the following are used to return the x and y coordinates for where a document appears in the viewport? (Choose all that apply.)

   A. ViewPortTop

   B. ViewPortHeight

   C. ViewPortWidth

   D. ViewPortLeft

5. You have set the ScrollBar property of a UserDocument to vbBoth. What will happen if the value of ViewPortHeight exceeds the MinHeight value?

   A. A horizontal scroll bar will appear.

   B. A vertical scroll bar will appear.

   C. Both horizontal and vertical scroll bars will appear.

   D. No scroll bars will appear.

6. Which of the following best defines what a viewport is?

   A. A control added to a UserDocument to view Web pages

   B. The screen area used to display an ActiveX document in a container application

   C. An ActiveX document displayed in a container application

   D. A container application used to display an ActiveX document

7. Which of the following examples of syntax would return the name of a container application?

   A. TypeName(UserDocument.Parent)

   B. UserDocument(TypeName.Parent)

   C. UserDocument.Parent

   D. Parent.TypeName

8. When can you set the value of the MinHeight and MinWidth properties?

   A. Design mode.

   B. Runtime.

   C. You can't set these properties. They are used to return a value.

   D. You can't set these properties. They are read-only.

9. You create a new UserDocument. What is the default value of its ScrollBar property?

   A. 0—None

   B. 1—Horizontal

   C. 2—Vertical

   D. 3—Both

10. Which of the following hyperlink methods will allow you to navigate from one ActiveX document to another?

    A. Navigate

    B. NavigateTo

    C. Back

    D. GoTo

11. Which of the following browsers can use a DHTML application created with VB 6?

    A. Internet Explorer 3

    B. Internet Explorer 4

    C. Internet Explorer 4.01 with Service Pack 1

    D. Peer Web Services 3

12. Which of the following browsers can use an IIS application created with VB version 6? (Choose all that apply.)

    A. Internet Explorer 3

    B. Internet Explorer 4

    C. Internet Explorer 4.01 with Service Pack 1

    D. Peer Web Services 3

13. You are using Menu Editor to create a menu for an ActiveX document. Which property allows you to specify where a document's menu will appear in relation to a container's menu?

    A. DocumentMenu

    B. NegotiatePosition

    C. MenuPosition

14. Three users access a WebClass with their browsers. How many instances of the WebClass will exist for these users?

    A. One logical instance of that WebClass will be created for each browser.

    B. One instance of that WebClass will exist at any given point.

    C. One instance will exist for the server and one for each browser.

    D. One logical instance of that WebClass and two of each WebItem will be created for each browser.

15. You have set the ScrollBar property of a UserDocument to vbBoth. What will happen if the value of ViewPortWidth is less than the MinWidth value?

    A. A horizontal scroll bar will appear.

    B. A vertical scroll bar will appear.

    C. Both horizontal and vertical scroll bars will appear.

    D. No scroll bars will appear.

16. Your IIS application is being used, and a request is made for a specific event in a WebClass. The request doesn't match any existing WebClass event. What will happen?

    A. The application will crash.

    B. The browser will freeze.

    C. The Respond event of the WebClass is fired.

    D. The UserEvent for the HTML template is fired.

    E. The Start event for the WebClass is fired.

17. Which of the following are standard events associated with every WebItem? (Choose all that apply.)

    A. Respond

    B. ProcessTag

    C. UserEvent

    D. Start

18. What does the acronym DHTML stand for?

    A. Don't Help Tourists Making Lunch

    B. Dynamic Hypertext Mock Language

    C. Dynamic Hypertext Transaction Markup Language

    D. Dynamic Hypertext Markup Language

19. You have decided to create an IIS Application with VB. What other system requirements must be present to create such an application? (Choose all that apply.)

    A. Internet Information Server 3 or higher with Active Server Pages

    B. Internet Explorer 3 with Active Server Pages

    C. A connection to a network

    D. Peer Web Services 3 or higher with Active Server Pages

20. A DHTML application is made up of which of the following? (Choose all that apply.)

    A. HTML pages

    B. WebClass

C. VB code

D. WebItems

E. A runtime DLL

21. You are using the DHTML Page Designer. Which part of the designer allows you to see a hierarchical view of an HTML document's contents?

A. ListView

B. Treeview

C. Detail

D. PageView

22. You are tired of using Notepad as your HTML editor. You want to specify a new editor in the External HTML Editor field. Where will you go to do this?

A. Select Project Properties from the Properties menu; then choose the Advanced tab.

B. Select Options from the View menu; then choose the General tab.

C. Select Options from the Tools menu; then choose the Advanced tab.

D. Select Options from the tool bar; then choose the Editor tab.

23. You are using the WebClass designer and have a template selected. For certain elements in the template, there are entries under the Target column. What does this signify?

A. The target of a hyperlink. This indicates the page a link will jump to, or the frame the linked item will appear in.

B. The source of the element. This indicates the name of the element.

C. The event connected to this element. It indicates the name of the event associated with this item.

D. The attribute of the element. It indicates whether it is an image, hyperlink, and so on.

24. Which of the following best defines the relationship between Active Server Page files (ASP files), WebClasses, and WebItems?

A. One WebClass is associated with one WebItem, which can contain many Active Server Page files.

B. One Active Server Page file is associated with one WebClass, which can contain many WebItems.

C. One Active Server Page file is associated with one WebItem, which can contain many WebClasses.

D. There is no relationship between ASP files, WebClasses, and WebItems.

25. You have opened the Property Page of a hyperlink, and have set the link type to mailto:. What will you put in the Link field?

A. A URL

B. The text that will appear underlined in the browser

C. An e-mail address

D. The event that will be triggered by the link, so that VB code will execute

26. You are creating a DHTML application and want to attach code to an element on an HTML document. What property must you set for this element before you can attach code to it?

    A. Name

    B. ID

    C. Event

    D. ClassID

27. Which of the following applications cannot act as containers for ActiveX documents?

    A. Internet Explorer 3

    B. VB 4

    C. Microsoft Binder 1

    D. VB 5

28. Which of the following are components of an ActiveX document?

    A. UserDocument

    B. WebClass

    C. ASP files

    D. WebItem

29. Where is processing performed when a DHTML application is running?

    A. Client side

    B. Server side

    C. The network

    D. None of the above

30. You are using the DHTML Page Designer. Which part of the designer allows you to see a graphical representation of an HTML document?

    A. ListView

    B. Treeview

    C. Detail

    D. PageView

31. The tool bar on the WebClass Designer has two buttons that look like start and stop buttons on a VCR. What are these used for?

    A. Running and stopping the IIS application you're developing

    B. Starting and stopping the IIS application debugger

    C. Starting and stopping Peer Web Services

    D. Starting and stopping the browser

32. You are using WebClass designer and notice that many entries in the Target column have the word <None>. What does this mean?

    A. An associated component, such as an image or hyperlink target, is missing.

    B. There are no events associated with those items.

    C. WebClasses are missing for those items.

    D. The element hasn't been configured properly.

33. You have decided to create an ActiveX document. You select New Project from the File menu, and the New Project dialog box appears. What can you select from this dialog box to create an ActiveX document? (Choose all that apply.)

A. ActiveX EXE

B. ActiveX Document EXE

C. ActiveX DLL

D. ActiveX Document DLL

E. ActiveX Control

34. What property of a WebClass determines whether it stays alive between requests, or is destroyed when a request is completed?

A. StateInstance

B. StateManagement

C. StateFarm

D. ManageState

35. You have decided to export a page from DHTML Page Designer to an external file. What extension should you give to this file? (Choose all that apply.)

A. DHTML

B. HTM

C. DHTM

D. HTML

36. A WebItem is activated by a request. What is its default event?

A. Respond

B. Start

C. UserRequest

D. Initiate

37. Which event of a WebItem is used to process the events of a WebClass that's created at runtime?

A. Respond

B. Start

C. UserEvent

D. ProcessTag

38. You set the StateManagement property of a WebClass to wcNoState. What effect will this have on the WebClass?

A. An instance of the WebClass will be retained between requests.

B. The WebClass will be used for the duration of the request, then destroyed.

C. The StateManagement property will be disabled.

D. The Web server will handle processing.

E. The client browser will handle processing

39. You are creating a hyperlink and want the link to connect to a secured Web site. What Link Type will you choose?

A. http:

B. file:

C. https:

D. secure:

40. You have decided to import an HTML file into DHTML Page Designer. How will you do this?

A. Select Open from the DHTML Page Designer's File menu.

B. Click the Open button on DHTML Page Properties, and select the file to import.

C. Click the Import button on the DHTML Page Designer's tool bar.

D. Select Import from the DHTML Page Designer's File menu.

MICROSOFT CERTIFIED SOLUTION DEVELOPER

13

Maintaining and Supporting an Application

L et's just say that stuff happens. Errors crop up, new ideas pop into your head, and time makes a program archaic. This, in a nutshell, is the reasoning behind maintaining and supporting an application.

Errors are what can make programming both challenging and frustrating. While good programmers test their programs, there are always some bugs that slip past. You can spend 10 times longer testing a program than it took to write it, and *still* not catch everything. Large companies like Microsoft perform in-house testing, send out beta versions of programs, and have thousands of people reporting errors. Even though they fix reported errors, you may still find some previously undiscovered errors in the final release. The moral of this is that it happens to the best of us. The other point you can derive from this example is that maintaining and supporting an application is an ongoing process.

In this chapter, we'll cover how to fix and prevent errors in your application. When this has been done, we'll also walk through deploying updates of the application so users can then begin to use your improvements. The concepts and code covered in this chapter will help you not only when studying for the Microsoft exam, but also in the real world. Understanding how to maintain and support an application is essential in both cases.

CERTIFICATION OBJECTIVE 13.01

Fixing Errors

In programming there are three kinds of errors you'll experience: logic, syntax, and runtime. Each has its own nuances, and can cause its own special kind of headaches.

Logic errors occur when your code executes without a syntax or runtime error, but the results aren't what you expected. An example of a logic error would be a procedure that is supposed to add sales tax to a dollar amount. On a line of code you type a minus sign instead of a plus sign, resulting in the code subtracting the amount of sales tax, rather than adding it. While the code worked, it didn't give the result you intended.

Unfortunately, the only way to catch logic errors is by using the program. After you compile the application, you should then test it to see that the program functions as it should. As you find logic errors (or as logic errors are reported by others), it is a matter of poring over the code to find where the logic error occurred.

on the job

In the real world, programmers deploy a preliminary release of the program, called a beta release. People then use the beta release and test it for errors. As errors are reported, they are fixed. The way to get people to act as "beta testers" is usually to offer them a copy of the final version for free, or to have a department in your company test it. Many programmers also distribute their beta releases on the Internet or online BBSs, allowing users to try the beta release for free. As a last resort, it's not uncommon to pay people to serve as beta testers. To my knowledge there was only one occasion in 1998 in which a program actually was sold as a beta release. This isn't an advisable option, as many users won't accept being charged for a program that's still being tested.

Syntax errors occur from incorrect use of the programming language. They occur when you do such things as mistype a keyword or forget to close a multiline command (like forgetting END IF after an IF statement). The result is an error during compilation, forcing you to go through your code and find where the error exists.

In development environments other than Visual Basic 6.0, syntax errors can be a problem. Fortunately though, VB provides syntax error checking. Auto Syntax Check can be enabled or disabled from the Editor tab of the Options dialog box, which is accessed from the Tools menu. Enabling Auto Syntax Check causes VB to check your syntax when you move away from a line of code. For example, say you wanted to type

```
Dim x As Integer
```

Instead of typing this, however, you type

```
Dom x As Integer
```

This would be a syntax error. If Auto Syntax Check is enabled, when you attempt to move from the line, the error will be brought to your attention.

Another feature that saves you from syntax errors is the Auto List Members feature, which can also be enabled from the Editor tab in Options. What Auto List Members does is display a listing of all the possibilities for what you're typing in your code. For example, if you were typing the Dim x As Integer statement, VB would provide you with a list of possibilities after you had typed **Dim x As**. In the listing, you could choose Integer or String, for example. Because the possible members are automatically given to you, you are protected from making syntax errors. For more information on VB's Options, review Chapter 2 of this book.

The final type of error you'll come across is runtime errors. These occur when a command attempts to perform an invalid action. Examples of runtime errors include attempts to use a variable that hasn't been initialized, or your application trying to access a floppy disk that a user has forgotten to put into the disk drive. Runtime errors are the only kind of error that you can't completely prevent after distributing an application. As such, you must incorporate code into your program that handles the possibility of runtime errors.

Runtime errors can occur when you attempt to run the project in VB, or when your compiled application runs. While the error is the same, the options given to you are different. When a runtime error occurs when you attempt to run the project in VB, you are presented with a dialog box with up to four options, as in the following illustration.

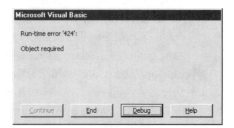

The Continue button allows your application to continue running with the error. Clicking it can produce unpredictable results, as the program is running with errors. If a fatal error has occurred, however, it will be disabled. The second button is the End button, which will stop the program and return you to Design mode. The Debug button will break the program at the line that caused the error. The application continues to run in single-step mode. In most cases, you will choose this button over the others, because it brings you directly to the problem. The final button is Help, which will give you information about the error, if information is available. In addition to these four buttons, the dialog box will also give you the error number of the runtime error, and a brief description of the error.

If a runtime error occurs in a compiled program, you are presented with an alert message, as shown in the following illustration.

The information in this default message is fairly basic. The name of the application is shown in the title bar, and there is an error number and brief description of the error. Unfortunately, the information given in these default messages is virtually useless to most users, and may only be useful to a programmer while testing an application.

Because the default messages that appear in a compiled program can be extremely cryptic to a user, it is important to implement your own error messages in an application. That way, when an error occurs, users aren't left completely dumbfounded by a message that is meaningless to them. In the next section, we'll cover how to implement code that handles errors and how to add your own custom error messages.

In dealing with runtime errors, there are certain error-handling settings in VB that you should be aware of. These settings will determine how VB deals with errors encountered in the design environment. To change these settings, select the General tab of the Options dialog box, which is accessed from the Tools menu (see Figure 13-1).

The Error Trapping section of the General tab in Options allows you to configure how VB will handle errors. The first option is Break on All

FIGURE 13-1

The Error Trapping section of the Options dialog box General tab allows you to change how VB handles errors in the design environment

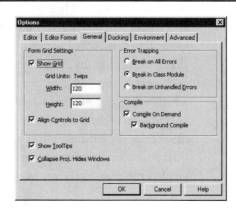

Errors. If this is selected, VB will break whenever a runtime error occurs. If you've added code to handle errors, it will ignore them if this option is selected. It's useful if you want to see where and when errors are occurring, regardless of whether you've implemented error handlers.

Break in Class Module is the default setting in the Error Trapping section. If this setting is chosen, it will only come into full effect with projects that run code in class modules. Where it becomes useful is in code in which, for example, a Form calls on other code that exists in a module. If the unhandled error exists in the class's code, it will break in the class's code. With the other options, it will break at the code that called the class, not in the code in the class module that actually causes the error. If the error exists outside of the class module, it treats it the same as Break on Unhandled Errors.

The Break in Class Module option is important when you're dealing with ActiveX servers. When this option is chosen, VB will break in the ActiveX server, rather than passing the error back to the client application. When creating applications that interact with ActiveX, it is important to choose this option.

The final option in the Error Trapping section is Break on Unhandled Errors. This is the option you set once you've created—or are creating—error handlers and want to see if they work. It allows your error-handling code to deal with runtime errors. When an error occurs that your error handler doesn't deal with, it enters Break mode. There are two things to remember about this option. The first is that if an error occurs in a class module, it will break at the calling code. The second thing is that if you're testing your error-handling code, you must set it to this option to test it properly.

exam
⑩atch

Know the different options for Error Trapping in the Options dialog box and what each can and can't do. It is important to know these options for the exam.

CERTIFICATION OBJECTIVE 13.02

Preventing Future Errors

The only way to prevent future errors in an application is to provide code in your program that traps errors and error-handling routines that deal with the problem. For example, let's say that a user instructs your program to open a file that doesn't exist. Rather than a cryptic message popping up and the program exiting, you can incorporate code that handles the error. You could have your program "see" that an error has occurred and then direct execution of the program to code that deals with the problem. In such a case as a file not being found, a dialog box could be offered to the user, asking him or her to try again or cancel out of the procedure.

The first step in dealing with an error is trapping it. Once you set an error trap, it will remain enabled until one of two things occurs:

- The procedure ends
- The error trap is disabled

Enabling an error trap is done with the On Error statement. This establishes error handling in your code. If an error occurs, it detours program execution to another place in your program that you specify.

Where execution is redirected depends on what you type after the words On Error, as is seen in the following code:

```
On Error GoTo ErrHandler
'Code with error appears here
Exit Sub
ErrHandler:
'Error handling code appears here
```

In this example, execution is redirected to a label called ErrHandler. This is done with the statement On Error GoTo ErrHandler. Typing a word ending with a colon (such as ErrHandler:) creates a label. Code following the label deals with the error. Because VB will process your code line by line, you must put Exit Sub before the label. This is to provide a means of exiting the procedure when no error has occurred, and to keep the error handler from running constantly—even if no error has occurred!

In addition to redirecting execution to a label, you can use the following code to skip over a statement, and continue processing the next line of code:

```
On Error Resume Next
```

Using this statement instructs your program to resume execution on the line after the one that causes an error. It is typically used for inline error handling where errors are processed immediately after they occur.

Another use for On Error Resume Next is to deal with anticipated errors that don't affect the remaining code. For example, let's say you were creating a form for users to input e-mail and Web addresses. Since these should all be lowercase, you might create code that loops through each Text property and converts it to lowercase. Since labels don't have a Text property, runtime errors would be generated each time a label is encountered. By adding On Error Resume Next before the loop, these errors would be ignored, and the next control (assuming it has a Text property) would be converted to lowercase.

Should you wish to disable an error trap, the following statement will disable the error trap immediately preceding it:

```
On Error GoTo 0
```

Note the reference to the preceding error trap. The reason for this is that errors are handled in a *call stack* (also known as a *calling chain*). If you have a procedure that calls other procedures, and one of the called procedures has an error but no error handling, it will pass the error up the chain of procedures. This concept is illustrated in Figure 13-2.

The way the calling chain works is that, when an error is encountered, it passes the error up to the procedure that called it. In other words, if Procedure 1 calls Procedure 2 and Procedure 2 encounters an error, it will pass that error up to Procedure 1. If you think of Procedure 2 as a child of Procedure 1, it's as if the child is asking its parent for help. As the error is passed up the calling chain, the error handler in the calling procedure will deal with the error. If no error handler is encountered on the calling chain, VB will display an alert message box and end the application.

To deal with the error effectively, your error handler must have some way of knowing what error has occurred. This is done with the Err object. Err has properties and methods that contain information about the error that occurred, and allows you to clear error values or cause errors. The information contained in the Err object is essential to error handling.

FIGURE 13-2

Passing errors up the calling chain

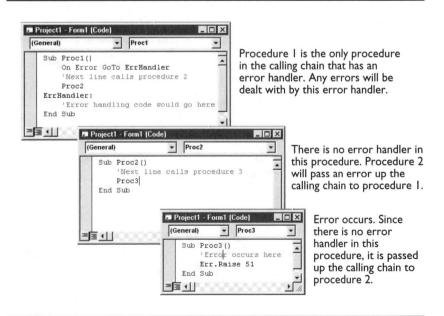

Procedure 1 is the only procedure in the calling chain that has an error handler. Any errors will be dealt with by this error handler.

There is no error handler in this procedure. Procedure 2 will pass an error up the calling chain to procedure 1.

Error occurs. Since there is no error handler in this procedure, it is passed up the calling chain to procedure 2.

The Err object has three important properties that you will use regularly in error handling. The first of these properties is Number, which contains an integer value that indicates the last error encountered. When a trappable error occurs in VB, a code is passed to the Number property of the Err object. By using Err.Number, you can allow your error handler to see what error has occurred. The values and description of error codes are available in VB Help under the heading Trappable Errors.

exam
Ⓦatch

Many students spend a lot of time memorizing trappable errors, their values, and what the values signify. The VB version 6 exam does not expect you to know this. You are, however, expected to know how to trap and handle errors and to know the properties and methods of the Err object.

The Description property has a String value that contains a brief description of the error. Using Err.Description allows you to display information about what error has occurred in your application. It contains information about the last error that has occurred.

The Source property is useful when your program works with other programs, such as Microsoft Excel. By using Err.Source, you can display whether it was an ActiveX server or your client application that generated the error. In the case of Microsoft Excel causing an error, the value of the Source property would be set to Excel.Application.

Because the values of Err's properties contain the last error encountered, there are times when you will want to clear the values. This is done with the Clear method. Err.Clear resets the value of Err.Number back to zero.

In addition to clearing errors after you've dealt with them, the Err object has another important method called Raise. Err.Raise causes an error to occur, so that you can test your error-handling code. For example, the following code would generate a "File not found" error:

```
Err.Raise 53
```

By typing **Err.Raise** followed by an error code, you are able to cause an error. The error trap would then detour execution to the error handler to deal with the error.

Once you've identified the error and dealt with it, you must provide a way to exit the error handler. This is done with the Resume statement. There are three ways to use the Resume statement:

```
Resume
```

This statement will return execution to the statement that caused the error, so that an operation can be completed after the error has been corrected.

```
Resume Next
```

Resume Next will return execution to the line immediately after the one that caused the error. This allows the program to skip over the offending code and continue with the rest of the procedure.

```
Resume line or label
```

This statement will return execution to a specific line or label, allowing you to control where the program should continue after an error has occurred. While slightly different in use, each of these statements allows you to control how processing will resume after an error has occurred.

EXERCISE 13-1

Error Handling

1. Start a new VB project. From the File menu select New Project, and then choose Standard EXE.

2. Add a command button to your form. Change its caption to **Message**, and in the Click event add the following code:

```
On Error GoTo ErrHandler
    Proc2
    MsgBox "Procedure 1"
Exit Sub
ErrHandler:
    MsgBox "Error: " & Err.Number & " has occurred in " _
    & Err.Source & ". Error was " & Err.Description
Resume Next
```

3. In this code we have created an error trap that redirects errors to ErrHandler. We have also specified that before displaying a message

box, a procedure called Proc2 is to run first. Create a new subprocedure called Proc2. Add the following code to your project:

```
Sub Proc2()
    Proc3
End Sub
```

4. Create a new subprocedure called Proc3. Add the following code to your project.

```
Sub Proc3()
    Err.Raise 51
    MsgBox "Procedure 3"
End Sub
```

5. Notice that we have raised an error in this procedure. We have done this before displaying a message box so you can see how execution will take place throughout this program. Press F5 to run the program. Notice that while an error is generated in Proc3, the error is passed up the calling chain until reaching the error-handling routine. A message box notifying the user of the error is displayed, and the line following the original calling code is processed.

6. Stop your program, and return to the Code window. Remove the following line from the Click event of your command button:

```
On Error GoTo ErrHandler
```

7. Press F5 to run your program again. Notice the way that VB notifies you of an error. Click the Debug button, and you will be taken to the place where the error occurred.

Up until this point we've had one error handler that dealt with any error we've thrown at it. While these are valid error-handling routines, they aren't very practical. In the real world, you would create error handlers that look at the Err.Number and perform an action based on the value of Err's Number property.

One way of determining which action to perform, based on the value of Err.Number, is with an If...Then or If...Then...Else block. As was previously stated, the Number property of the Err object has an integer value. By comparing these error codes to specific values in such blocks of code, you can then execute code that deals with particular errors. This can be seen in the following code example:

```
Private Sub cmdSaveAs_Click()
On Error GoTo ErrHandler
CommonDialog1.ShowSave
```

```
ErrHandler:
If Err.Number = 0 Then
     'Do Nothing
ElseIf Err.Number = 58 Then
     MsgBox "File Already Exists"
     Resume
Else
     MsgBox "Fatal Error:  " & Err.Description
End If
Err.Clear
End Sub
```

In this code, a command button is used to display a common dialog box, which presents the user with a standard Save As dialog box. If there is no error, the value of Err.Number is zero and nothing happens, and the value of the Number property is cleared. If a file already exists, the second condition of the If…Then…Else block is met, and that section of code is executed. Finally, if neither requirement is met, then the Else section of code is executed. This allows you the freedom to execute certain error code to deal with specific conditions.

The other method of executing code based on certain conditions is by using Select Case. In this method, the error code is passed through a series of Case statements until the value matches that of Err.Number value. The following code example deals with the same situation as that in the If…Then…Else block of code you've just seen, but as a Select Case.

```
Private Sub cmdSaveAs_Click()
On Error Resume Next

CommonDialog1.ShowSave

Select Case Err.Number
Case 0:
     'Do Nothing
Case 58:
     MsgBox "File Already Exists"
Case Else:
     MsgBox "Fatal Error:  " & Err.Description
End Select
Err.Clear
        CommonDialog1.ShowOpen
End Sub
```

While this code shows how useful Select Case is in error handling, it also shows something else. Using labels for error-handling routines is not the only way of creating error handlers. You can also use a technique called *inline error handling*. Inline error handlers deal with errors immediately after they occur. Error-handling code doesn't use labels, and therefore doesn't branch out from your code. In addition, it doesn't use Resume statements. Each line of code is processed one line after another. If an error occurs in a statement, the On Error Resume Next causes VB to skip over the offending code and then execute the next line (which is the error handler). When it reaches the end of the error handler, Err.Clear is used to clear the Number property of Err, and code following the inline error handling is processed.

It is important to remember to use Err.Clear in inline error handling. The reason the Clear method is called after a Select Case is that there are no Resume statements. Resume statements are used in other error-handling styles and reset the Err.Number value to zero. If you don't use Err.Clear, the error code would still be stored in the Err object. This would cause problems if your procedure were to call another procedure that has its own error handling. In such a case, the uncleared Err object could cause the error handler of the called procedure to deal with this ghost error.

If you have a question that presents inline error-handling code and has other error handlers being raised, check to see that Err.Clear is at the end of the Select Case. Err.Clear needs to be put at the end of an inline error handler. Failure to do so may cause another error handler to deal with an error that was raised in a previous procedure.

There are circumstances in which you can save yourself coding time and decrease the amount of code in your application. You should always look through your code and see if the same code can be used in two or more places. For example, you may use an Open File or Close File procedure in a few places in your program. When you do, you should consider using a standard function containing error-handling code. After creating this function, you then invoke it. In doing this, you should return a value (such as a Boolean value) to the calling code, which indicates whether the function succeeded or failed.

The following example shows a command button that opens an input box asking the user for an application's name. We then assign the input to the variable strApp, which is passed to the function OpenApp. If the Function can open the application, the value of Err.Number is zero (showing that there is no error). In this case, the value of True is returned to the calling code, and a message box is displayed indicating success. If the function can't open the application, it returns a value of False to the calling code, and a message box is displayed showing failure. Because most of the code resides in the function, there is less chance for logic and syntax errors, since you're not rewriting the same code over and over. It also makes your application smaller, because less code exists in the application.

```
Private Sub Command1_Click()
    Dim strApp As String
    Dim blnResult As Boolean
    strApp = InputBox("Enter Application Name")
    blnResult = OpenApp(strApp)
    MsgBox blnResult & " result opening " & strApp
End Sub
Function OpenApp(strApp As String) As Boolean
    On Error Resume Next
    Shell strApp
    Select Case Err.Number
Case 0:
    OpenApp = True
Case Else:
    OpenApp = False
End Select
End Function
```

Another style of error handling is to centralize your error-handling code. This means to create a primary error handler that tells procedures how to deal with errors. When an error occurs, the procedure passes the Err.Number to the central error handler. The error handler then analyzes the Err.Number value and tells the calling procedure how to process the error. It is important to remember that centralized error handling doesn't free you from adding error-handling code to a procedure. It does, however, minimize the amount of code needed in a procedure.

In the following example, code has been added to a command button. On clicking this button, an Input box is presented to the user that asks what application the user wants to open. If an error results, the ErrHandler is used, which passes the Err.Number to the central error handler, called ErrCentral. ErrCentral analyzes the error code and determines whether to ask the user to enter another application name, continue, or have the application close down. If it determines that the user should be asked for another application name, it presents a message box with Yes and No buttons. If the user clicks Yes, the value of True is passed to the calling code, which then has the Resume statement processed, and the input box is redisplayed. If No is clicked, the value of False is passed to the calling code, which then has the Resume Next statement processed, and the operation is canceled.

```
Private Sub Command1_Click()
    On Error GoTo ErrHandler
    Dim blnResult As Boolean
    Shell InputBox("Enter Application Name")
Exit Sub
ErrHandler:
    blnResult = ErrCentral(Err.Number)
    If blnResult = True Then
        Resume
    ElseIf blnResult = False Then
        Resume Next
    End If
End Sub
Function ErrCentral(ErrNum As Integer) As Boolean
    Select Case ErrNum
    Case 53:
        Result = MsgBox("Program Not Found. Try Again?", vbYesNo)
    Case 5:
        Result = MsgBox("Program Not Found. Try Again?", vbYesNo)
    Case 0:
        Result = vbNo
    Case Else:
        MsgBox "Error " & ErrNum & ":  Unloading"
        Unload Form1
    End Select
```

```
If Result = vbYes Then
     ErrCentral = True
ElseIf Result = vbNo Then
     ErrCentral = False
End If
End Function
```

It is important to remember that Resume statements (such as Resume and Resume Next) can only appear in procedures that have the On Error statement. It is for this reason that some error-handling code has to appear in the calling procedure. If you put a Resume statement in a procedure that doesn't have an On Error statement, an error will result.

This leads to the question of what happens when an error occurs in an error handler. In the case of centralized error-handling routines and error handlers that are called, the error is passed up the calling chain. The procedure that called the error handler then has a chance to deal with the error. If there is no error handling in the calling procedure to deal with this, an alert message is displayed and the application exits. This is just as if there is no calling procedure. When error handling is not called, but instead is part of a procedure, the application shows a message and ends.

Because such errors can occur in error handlers, it is important to keep error-handling routines simple, and to visually check the code for possible mistakes. From within the error handler, you could invoke other procedures that contain error handling. This method does provide error handling for your error handler, but it isn't very practical. After all, the more redundant code you add to your error-handling routines, the greater the possibility of runtime errors. Be careful when creating error handlers.

on the job

When creating error handlers, make sure to test the error handler as you create it. Write some code, and then test the application before creating more. This way, you can be sure where your error handler was working before problems arose. In addition, try to make the error handler as simple as possible. The more code you write, and the more elaborate you make the error handler, the greater the chance for errors. Since you are creating something that deals with errors, an error in the error handler can mask that a problem even exists! Be extra careful, and double-check your code visually.

FROM THE CLASSROOM

Application Maintenance and Support

As any seasoned programmer will attest, sometimes the bulk of the work with application development doesn't occur until after the application has been deployed. The rationale for this fact of the developer's life is simple: application testing, or debugging, is only as good as the resources available to produce unique user scenarios involving an unlimited number of hardware and software conditions. Formal debugging, therefore, benefits greatly from the more-is-better approach to testing. The greatest variety and number of user scenarios occur in the real, postdeployment, and postdevelopment world of final release.

Within the development environment, the programmer should be familiar with proper techniques for recognizing and correcting: compile errors resulting from incorrectly formed code, runtime errors that occur due to

application requests for performance of impossible-to-carry-out operations, and logic errors that result simply from code not performing as anticipated.

Visual Basic provides four primary debugging windows, with which the exam taker should be thoroughly familiar: the Immediate, Watch, Locals, and Output windows. Secondary debugging windows, whose basic purposes the reader knows, are the Call Stack and Threads windows.

Preventing future errors comes down to proper design, adherence to coding standards and conventions, and proper leveraging of available debug tools. With this in mind, for the exam, be aware of standard naming conventions, uses of the four primary debug windows, syntax, and use of the Debug object.

—*By Michael Lane Thomas,*
MCSE+I, MCSD, MCT, A+

CERTIFICATION OBJECTIVE 13.03

Deploying Application Updates for Desktop Applications

"If at first you don't succeed, call it version one." This is a saying that I often pass on to programming students, and if it weren't true, there wouldn't be such things as updates. There are a number of reasons to deploy updates for your applications. Sometimes you'll get feedback from users and clients about bugs that didn't show up during the testing phase. Other times, you'll decide to incorporate new features or interfaces into your application. No matter what the reason, you'll never escape the need for deploying updates.

Deploying an update is the act of transferring an updated application to distribution media (such as a floppy disk or CD-ROM) or to a Web site, where it can then be downloaded. In many ways it is identical to deploying a full application, which we covered in Chapter 11. There are, however, a few differences that you need to keep in mind.

The first step in the deployment process is packaging your application. The difference between packaging updates and full applications is what you include in the package. Any files included with your package will overwrite files on the user's hard disk. In other words, if the full version of your application was installed on the user's computer, then drivers, databases, and executables will overwrite existing files. If your application uses several executable files, and only one has been updated, then only that single executable should be included with the update. Similarly, if your application uses a database file (such as a Microsoft Access database), you should not include the database with the updated application package. When the user installs this update, the empty database you include will overwrite the existing database on the user's computer, destroying all the user's data.

The differences between packaging a full application and an update start from the DAO Drivers screen of the Package and Deployment Wizard (see Figure 13-3). This screen appears when you are packaging applications that access data, such as a program that uses data from an Access database. From this screen, you can choose what Data Access Object (DAO) drivers to include with the package. If you are packaging an update for an application created with VB version 6, you don't need to include these files. If you're packaging an update for a program created with a previous version of VB, you'll need to select the necessary updated drivers for your application.

Following this is the Included Files screen of the Package and Deployment Wizard (see Figure 13-4). This allows you to select which files

FIGURE 13-3

The DAO Drivers screen allows you to select what drivers to add to your package

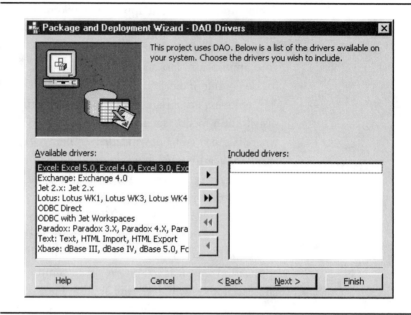

FIGURE 13-4

The Included Files screen of the Package and Deployment Wizard

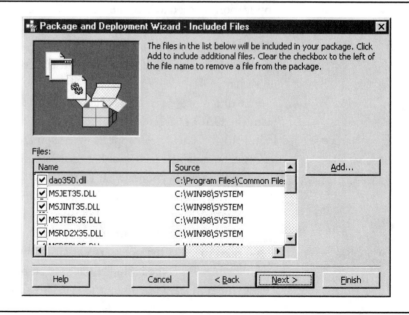

to add to the package. If this were a full database application, this is where you would add any database files you'd like to include with your application. However, since this is an update, you would not include such a file. To do so would cause the user's working data file to be overwritten when the user installed the upgrade. Also listed here are files that would be installed into the WINDOWS SYSTEM directory. Again, if this is an update of a VB version 6 application, there is no need to include these files. The user would already have these files after installing the full version of your application. You should pay attention to any DLL files that you've changed, and determine if you want them included with the application though this screen.

Beyond this point, using the Package and Deployment Wizard is just as described in Chapter 11. You should select the same folders for the update that you choose for your full version. A warning will appear, telling you that this will overwrite previous installations. Since that is the purpose of an updated application, this is nothing to be concerned about.

EXERCISE 13-2

Packaging an Application Update

1. First we will create a simple database program. From the File menu select New Project, and then choose Standard EXE. Add a Data control and a text box to the form.

2. In the Data control's Property window, have the DataBaseName property point to NWIND.MDB. In the RecordSource property, select Employees.

3. In the TextBox Property window, select Data1 as the DataSource. In the DataField property, select LastName.

4. Save your project to disk, and then close VB.

5. Open the Package and Deployment Wizard. In Select Project, enter the path and filename of the project you just saved. Click the Package button, and then choose Compile.

6. When the wizard appears, select Standard Setup Package. Click Next, which brings you to the screen that allows you to choose where the package will be created. Accept the default and click Next. A message box may appear, asking if you would like to create a folder that it can work in or choose another folder. Accept this, so it may create the working folder.

7. Since we are packaging a database application, we are then allowed to choose which DAO to include with the package. Since our application is an update, we will pretend that these drivers would have been included with the full version of our VB version 6 application. As such, none will be included with our package. If you wish to pretend it is an upgrade of an application created with a previous version of VB, select the Jet 2x : Jet 2x driver and then click the right arrow button. Click Next to continue.

8. The Included Files screen allows you to choose which files to include with your package. If your application is an upgrade of a VB version 6 application, you can deselect all Windows system files listed (the user should already have them). In addition, since this is an update to an existing database application, there is no need to add the database file.

9. This screen allows you to choose whether you want files to be packaged in a single CAB file (which is best for Internet deployment), or multiple CAB files (for floppy disk distribution). Select Multiple CABs, and then select 1.44MB from the CAB Size drop-down list.

10. Click Next for the remaining screens, accepting the default options, until you reach the final screen. Click Finish.

Once you've properly packaged your update, you're then ready to get it out to the user. This is done with the Deploy part of the Package and Deployment Wizard. The main screen of the Package and Deployment Wizard is illustrated in Figure 13-5. This will allow you to deploy your application to floppy disks, a local or network folder, or an Internet Web site.

After choosing Deploy from the main screen, you are provided with a screen that has a list box. This list box contains a listing of packages created with the Package and Deployment Wizard. After selecting the package you want to deploy, you then click the Next button, which brings you to the Deployment Method screen.

The deployment methods available to you are Floppy Disk, Folder, and Web Publishing. The Floppy Disk option allows you to distribute your package to floppy disks, Folder allows distribution to a local or network folder, and Web Publishing allows you to distribute the package to a Web site. What you choose here will affect which screens are presented to you from now on.

FIGURE 13-5

Main screen of the Package and Deployment Wizard

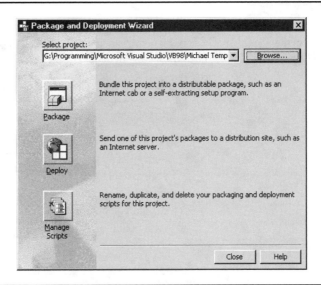

If you select Floppy Disk deployment and click Next, you are given the option of choosing which floppy drive the wizard is to use. By checking Format before copying, floppy disks will be formatted before files are copied to them.

Selecting Folder installation and clicking Next allows you to choose a local or network folder for deployment. This screen, shown in Figure 13-6, allows you to type in the full pathname of the folder, or select the drive and folder through drive and directory boxes. The New Folder button allows you to create a new folder for deployment. Finally, the Network button brings up a screen that allows you to browse your network. You can deploy your update on the network if you have the proper permissions.

Selecting Web Publishing and clicking Next brings up a listing of files included in the package. From this, you can select which files you want to deploy to a Web site. Unchecking the check box before any filenames means that those files won't be deployed. After clicking Next, you are given the option of including other files and folders to deploy with the package. The next screen requests a URL. This is the Web site address, such as http://www.microsoft.com. You can also deploy it to an existing subdirectory on the Web site, such as http://www.microsoft.com/updates. It is important to remember that you must have an existing account with proper permissions for this to work.

FIGURE 13-6

Folder screen of the Package and Deployment Wizard

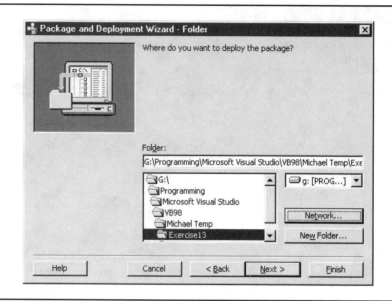

After working through the screens of your deployment choice, you reach the final screen of the wizard. When you click the Finish button, your application update will be deployed to either floppy disk or folder, or published to a Web site.

EXERCISE 13-3

Deploying an Application Update

1. From the Package and Deployment Wizard's main screen, click Deploy.

2. From the list box, select the application you packaged in Exercise 13-2. Click Next.

3. From the Deployment Method screen, select Folder. Click Next.

4. Select a folder on your hard disk to deploy to. If there isn't an existing folder to which you want to deploy, click New Folder and type in the name of your deployment folder. Click Next.

5. Click Finish, and your application update will be deployed.

Use the following question-and-answer scenarios to help you review the material in this chapter.

QUESTIONS AND ANSWERS

What is the difference between logic, syntax, and runtime errors?	Syntax errors occur due to incorrect use of the programming language. Runtime errors occur when a program attempts an invalid action. Logic errors occur when execution produces no syntax or runtime errors, but results aren't what was expected.
A runtime error is occurring in my code. I'm certain the error is in the class module, but VB keeps breaking at the calling code. How can I make VB break at the line that's actually causing the error?	In Options, chose the General tab. In the Error Trapping section, chose Break in Class Modules.
What happens when there is an error in my error-handling routine?	If the error handler was called, it will pass the error up the calling chain to the procedure that called it. If the procedure wasn't called (or no error handling exists in the calling procedure), the application shows an error message and exits.
I have added error handlers to my application, and now wish to deploy the updated application. How do I do that?	Use the Package and Deployment Wizard. First package the updated application, and then deploy it. Follow the wizard and choose the deployment method you want to use.

CERTIFICATION SUMMARY

Error-handling routines deal with runtime errors that occur in your program. There are different styles of error handling that you can use to make your application more robust. It is important to include such routines in all of your applications.

After making changes to an application, you must package and deploy the update so that users can have the upgrade. The Package and Deployment Wizard steps you through the process of packaging an application update. After packaging it, you can use the Deploy feature to have your update distributed to a floppy disk, a folder, or a Web site.

TWO-MINUTE DRILL

❑ In programming, there are three kinds of errors you'll experience: logic, syntax, and runtime. Logic errors occur when your code executes without a syntax or runtime error, but the results aren't what you expected. Syntax errors occur from incorrect use of the programming language. Runtime errors occur when a command attempts to perform an invalid action.

❑ VB provides syntax error checking. Auto Syntax Check can be enabled or disabled from the Editor tab of Options, which is accessed from the Tools menu. Enabling Auto Syntax Check causes VB to check your syntax when you move away from a line of code.

❑ Because the default messages that appear in a compiled program can be extremely cryptic to a user, it is important to implement your own error messages in an application.

❑ The Error Trapping section of the General tab in Options allows you to configure how VB will handle errors. If Break on All Errors is selected, VB will break whenever a runtime error occurs. Break in Class Module is the default setting; if chosen, it will only come into full effect with projects that run code in class modules. Break on Unhandled Errors is the option you set once you've created—or are creating—error handlers and you want to see if they work.

❑ Errors are handled in a *call stack*, which is also known as a *calling chain*. If you have a procedure that calls other procedures, and one of the called procedures has an error but no error handling, it will pass the error up the chain of procedures.

❑ The Break in Class Module option is useful when you're dealing with ActiveX servers. When this option is chosen, VB will break in the ActiveX server, rather than passing the error back to the client application. When creating applications that interact with ActiveX, it is important to choose this option.

❑ The only way to prevent future errors in an application is to provide code in your program that traps errors, and error-handling routines that deal with the problem.

❑ Enabling an error trap is done with the On Error statement.

❑ To effectively deal with the error, your error handler must have some way of knowing what error has occurred. This is done with the Err object.

❑ The Err object has three important properties that you will use regularly in error handling: Number, Description, and Source.

❑ Because the values of Err's properties contain the last error encountered, there are times where you will want to clear the values. This is done with the Clear method. Err.Clear resets the value of Err.Number back to zero. The Err object also has the Raise method (Err.Raise) that causes an error to occur, so that you can test your error-handling code.

❑ One way of determining which action to perform, based on the value of Err.Number, is with an If...Then or If...Then...Else block. The other method of executing code based on certain conditions is by using a Select Case. In this method, the error code is passed through a series of Case statements until the value matches that of the Err.Number value.

❑ Inline error handlers deal with errors immediately after they occur. Error-handling code doesn't use labels, and doesn't branch out from your code. It also doesn't use Resume statements. Each line of code is processed one after another.

❑ It is important to remember to use Err.Clear in inline error handling. The reason the Clear method is called after a Select Case is because there are no Resume statements in a Select Case.

❑ You can also create a primary error handler that tells procedures how to deal with errors. When an error occurs, the procedure passes the Err.Number to the central error handler. The error handler then analyzes the Err.Number value and tells the calling procedure how to process the error. It is important to remember that centralized error handling doesn't free you from adding error-handling code to your procedures. It minimizes the amount of code needed in a procedure.

❑ Remember that Resume statements (such as Resume and Resume Next) can only appear in procedures that have the On Error statement. It is for this reason that some error-handling code has to appear in the calling procedure.

❑ Deploying an update is the act of transferring an updated application to distribution media or to a Web site, where it can then be downloaded.

❑ Once you've properly packaged your update, you're ready to get it out to the user. This is done with the Deploy part of the Package and Deployment Wizard. The deployment methods available to you are Floppy Disk, Folder, and Web Publishing.

SELF TEST

The following questions will help you measure your understanding of the material presented in this chapter. Read all the choices carefully, as there may be more than one correct answer. Choose all correct answers for each question.

1. You have deployed an update for a database application. Now users are complaining that they can't access data that they've spent the last six months inputting into the program. What is the probable cause of this problem?

   A. You chose the wrong deployment method.

   B. You packaged an empty database file with your application update.

   C. You failed to package a new database file with your application update.

   D. None of the above.

2. Your application seems to be running fine, but users are complaining that instead of adding sales tax, the application is subtracting it. What kind of error is this?

   A. Logic

   B. Syntax

   C. Runtime

   D. Asyncratic

3. Error-handling routines deal with what kind of errors?

   A. Logic

   B. Syntax

   C. Runtime

   D. Asyncratic

4. You have set an error trap in your code. For how long will it remain enabled? (Choose all that apply.)

   A. Until the procedure ends

   B. Until the error trap is executed

   C. Until the error trap is disabled

   D. Until the error handler is enabled

5. Which of the following will reset the value of Err.Number to zero? (Choose all that apply.)

   A. Resume

   B. Err.Reset

   C. Reset

   D. Err.Clear

6. A procedure calls an error handler. The error-handling routine experiences an error. What will happen?

   A. A message will be displayed and the application will exit.

   B. The application will exit.

   C. The error handler will handle its own error.

   D. The error will be passed to the calling procedure.

7. Procedure A has an error handler. Procedures B and C have no error handlers. Procedure A calls Procedure B,

which then calls Procedure C. What will happen if Procedure C experiences an error?

A. A message will be displayed and the application will exit.

B. The error will be passed to Procedure B, which will deal with the error.

C. The error will be passed up the calling chain to Procedure A, which will deal with the error.

D. Procedure C will deal with the error.

8. What will the Raise property of the Err object do?

A. Cause an error to occur

B. Cause an error to be passed up the calling chain

C. Cause execution to return the line before the one that caused an error

D. Raise the value of Err.Number

9. You have placed a Resume statement in your code, and an error results. What must be present in your code for a Resume statement to work?

A. An On Error statement

B. The error code

C. The place to resume to

D. None of the above

10. An error occurs on line 10 of your code. After the error handler deals with the error, you want execution to return to the line that caused the error. Which of the following statements will do this?

A. Resume

B. Resume 9

C. Resume Next

D. Resume Error

11. Which of the following allows you to check for logic errors in a program?

A. Using the program

B. VB's logic checking features

C. Auto Logic Check in Options

D. Visual SourceSafe's logic checking features

12. Which of the following will disable a previous error trap?

A. On Error Disable

B. On Error GoTo 0

C. On Error Err.Clear

D. Err.Clear

13. What does the Number property of the Err object contain?

A. An Integer value representing the last error encountered

B. An Object value representing the object that created the error

C. The Number of errors encountered by the error handler

D. The Number of objects containing errors

14. What will the following line of code do?

```
Resume MyNext
```

A. Return an error

B. Resume processing from a label called MyNext

C. Resume processing from a procedure called MyNext

D. Invoke a function called MyNext

15. You have created an application update that would benefit users. Using the Package and Deployment Wizard, you plan to type in URLs of various shareware Web sites. After typing in the first URL, you get a message saying the deployment has failed. Why?

    A. You forgot to choose the application update you wish to deploy.

    B. You must have a valid account with proper permissions to deploy an update to a Web site.

    C. You must have a valid account with proper permissions to use the Web Publishing component of the Package and Deployment Wizard.

    D. You haven't packaged your application update.

16. What does the Description property of the Err object contain?

    A. An Integer number representing a description of the last error encountered

    B. A String value containing a description of the last error encountered

    C. A pointer to an error code that represents the last error encountered

    D. A variable containing the last error encountered

17. An error occurs in line 10 of your code. After the error handler deals with the error, you want execution to return to the line following the one that caused the error. Which of the following will allow you to do this? (Choose all that apply.)

    A. Resume

    B. Resume Next

    C. Next Resume

    D. Resume 10

18. What does the Source property of the Err object do?

    A. Causes an error to occur at the source

    B. Contains information about the source of an error

    C. Contains the name of the calling procedure that passed the error

    D. Contains a description about the error

19. A procedure calls an error handler. The error-handling routine experiences an error. It passes the error up to the calling procedure, which has no error handling to deal with the error. What will happen?

    A. A message will be displayed and the application will exit.

    B. The application will exit.

    C. The error handler will handle its own error.

    D. The error will be passed to the calling procedure.

20. What kind of error can occur when you attempt to run the project in VB, or when your compiled application runs? (Choose all that apply.)

    A. Logic

    B. Syntax

C. Runtime

D. Design time

21. You have created a loop that changes the Caption property of controls to uppercase. You also have text boxes on your form. What will allow you to ignore errors that occur when the loop reaches controls without caption properties?

A. Resume Next

B. On Error Resume Next

C. On Error Resume

D. Resume

22. What will happen in the following code when an error occurs in Proc2?

```
Sub Proc1()
        On Error GoTo EH
        Proc2
        Print "Hello World"
        Exit Sub
EH:
        Msgbox "Error Encountered"
        Resume Next
End Sub
Sub Proc2
        Err.Raise 53
        Print "Hi World"
End Sub
```

A. A message will be displayed and the application exits.

B. The next line of code will be executed in Proc2.

C. The error will be passed to the error handler in Proc1.

D. Error 53 means there is no error, so no error will occur.

23. Which of the following would enable an error trap?

A. ErrHandler:

B. On Error

C. Resume

D. Err

24. What is a beta tester, and what do they do?

A. Beta testers are users who use preliminary releases of applications and report errors.

B. Beta testers are a special type of error-handling code.

C. Beta testers are lines of code that include Err.Raise.

D. Beta testers are instances of testing that occur when you run a program in Design mode.

25. You are deploying an application update for floppy disk distribution. While going through the Package and Deployment Wizard, you realize you don't have any formatted floppy disks. What is the best thing to do?

A. Close Package and Deployment Wizard and format some disks.

B. Switch from the Package and Deployment Wizard to Windows Explorer and format some disks.

C. Check Format before copying on the Floppy Disk deployment screen of the Package and Deployment Wizard.

D. Uncheck Format before copying on the Floppy Disk deployment screen of the Package and Deployment Wizard.

26. Which is an attribute of inline error handling?

    A. Uses labels and branches out from your code

    B. Centralizes error handling

    C. Doesn't use labels, and doesn't branch out from your code

    D. Passes the error to a function

27. What must you use at the end of an inline error-handling routine that uses Select Case?

    A. A Resume statement that returns processing to a line or label

    B. Resume

    C. Resume Next

    D. Err.Clear

28. You are experiencing an error, and you think it is occurring in a class module. Whenever you enter Break mode, VB breaks at the code that calls the module. What can you do to have VB break at the code that is actually causing the error?

    A. On the General tab of Options, select Break in Class Module.

    B. On the Error Trapping tab of Options, select Break in Class Module.

    C. On the General tab of Options, select Break on Error.

    D. On the Error Trapping tab of Options, select Break on Error.

29. Which object allows you to determine what error has occurred?

    A. Number

    B. Source

    C. Err

    D. Description

30. An error is encountered, and it is passed up the call stack. What will happen if there are no error handlers in the calling procedures?

    A. A message will be displayed and the application will exit.

    B. The application will lock up.

    C. Other error handlers in the application will be sought.

    D. The next line of code will automatically be executed in the procedure where the error occurred.

31. Which of the following allows you to execute error-handling code based on certain conditions? (Choose all that apply.)

    A. If…Then

    B. Do…While

    C. Select Case

    D. Any loop

32. You create error handling that passes the error to a function. Which of the following will result from your doing this? (Choose all that apply.)

    A. Decreases the chance of logic and syntax errors.

    B. Increases the chance of logic and syntax errors.

C. Increases the size of the application. More code exists than if you had used other styles of error handling.

D. Decreases the size of the application. Less code exists than if you had used other styles of error handling.

33. Which of the following best describes inline error handling?

A. Inline error handling centralizes error handling.

B. Inline error handling passes errors to a function.

C. Inline error handling deals with errors immediately after they occur.

D. None of the above.

34. You are concerned about errors occurring in your error-handling routine. Which of the following options are available to you for dealing with errors that occur in error handlers? (Choose all that apply.)

A. Visually check error-handling code for errors.

B. Invoke error handling from within the error handler.

C. Do nothing. The error handler handles errors, so it can deal with its own errors.

D. Create a loop that runs multiple times through the error handler. This will make the error handler deal with its own error.

35. VB processes code line by line. Which statement will allow your code to exit if no error has occurred and keep VB from processing an error handler that follows?

A. Exit Sub

B. End Sub

C. Resume

D. End Error

36. Which of the following would be a label used for an error handler?

A. ErrHandler

B. ErrHandler:

C. Err

D. Label

37. An error-handling routine is part of a procedure. The error handler experiences an error. What will happen?

A. A message will be displayed and the application will exit.

B. The application will exit.

C. The error handler will handle its own error.

D. The error will be passed to the calling procedure.

38. Which option in VB version 6 checks for syntax errors as they occur?

A. Syntax

B. Auto Syntax Check

C. Check Syntax

D. Auto Syntax

39. Which kind of error does the following code show?

```
Dum x As Integer
```

A. Logic

B. Syntax

C. Runtime

D. Grammatical

40. You have decided to deploy your application update to the Internet. Which deployment method will you choose in the Package and Deployment Wizard?

A. Internet

B. Web Publishing

C. Network Folder

D. Folder

MICROSOFT CERTIFIED SOLUTION DEVELOPER

Object
Reference

This reference contains a listing of controls, objects, and collections that are available in Visual Basic version 6.0. For your convenience, it has been split into three sections: Controls, Data Report Designer, and Objects and Collections. Each entry includes a description for each object, collection, and control, and an example of syntax.

Due to the number of objects, collections, and controls in VB, it is impossible to show the properties, methods, and events for every entry. For further information on properties, methods, and events of a control, object, or collection, refer to the Language Reference in VB's Help.

Controls

Object	Syntax	Description
ADO Data Control		Allows connection to a database, using ActiveX Data Objects
Animation		Allows you to create buttons that display animation files when clicked
CheckBox	CheckBox	Used for selecting a single item or option that isn't related to other items. This control displays an X when selected.
ComboBox	ComboBox	Control with the combined features of a TextBox and ListBox control
CommandButton	CommandButton	Appears as a push button on a form, and is used to begin, end, or interrupt processes
CommonDialog	CommonDialog	Set of dialog boxes for common uses, such as opening, saving, and printing
CoolBar	CoolBar	Uses the Bands collection to create tool bars that are configurable, and similar to those found in Internet Explorer
DataCombo	DataCombo	Data-bound combo box, automatically populated by a data source field
Data Control	Data	Allows access to databases using Recordset objects
DataGrid	DataGrid	Displays a series of rows and columns that can be manipulated and represents the records and fields from a record set

Object	Syntax	Description
DataList	DataList	Data-bound list box, automatically populated by a data source field
DataRepeater	DataRepeater	Container that allows you to scroll through other data-bound controls
DateTimePicker	DTPicker	Provides a drop-down calendar and a formatted Time/Date field
DBCombo	DBCombo	Data-bound combo box with combined features of a text box and list box, populated with a field from a Data control
DBList	DBList	Data-bound list box, populated with a field from a Data control
DirListBox	DirListBox	Used to display directories and paths that the user can access at runtime
DriveListBox	DriveListBox	Used to display drives that are currently available at runtime
FileListBox	FileListBox	Used to list files in a directory during runtime
FlatScrollBar	FlatScrollBar	Two-dimensional scroll bar
Frame	Frame	Used to group controls, such as option buttons, into a related grouping
HscrollBar	HScrollBar	Used to add horizontal scroll bars
Image	Image	Used to display graphics. This control uses fewer system resources than the PictureBox control.
ImageCombo	ImageCombo	Picture-enabled version of a combo box that allows list items to have graphics associated with them
ImageList	ImageList	Used as a repository for graphics, which can then be assigned to other controls
Label	Label	Used to display text that is not changeable by the user. It is often used to relate information to a user about another control's purpose.
Line	Line	Used to add horizontal, vertical, and diagonal lines to a form
ListBox	Listbox	Contains a listing of items the user can select from
ListView	ListView	Used to display items. Four different views of items are available with this control.

Object	Syntax	Description
MAPIMessages	MAPIMessages	Enables mail-enabled MAPI applications
MAPISession	MAPISession	Used to establish a MAPI session
Masked Edit		Acts like a text box with masked input and formatted output capabilities
Menu	Menu	Used to display custom menus
Microsoft Internet Transfer Control		Allows you to implement HTTP and FTP protocols in an application
MonthView	MonthView	Calendar interface for setting date information
MSChart	MSChart	Used to create a chart
MSComm	MSComm	Allows you to implement serial communications into an application
MSFlexGrid	MSFlexGrid	Displays read-only data in a grid format
MSHFlexGrid	MSHFlexGrid	Displays read-only data in a grid format. It is used to display data in a hierarchical fashion.
Multimedia MCI Control		Media control interface that allows recording and playback of multimedia files
OLE Container		Allows you to insert objects that will appear on your form. These can be linked objects, objects that are inserted and displayed at runtime, or that can bind the control to a Data control.
OptionButton	OptionButton	Used to turn options on or off. It is generally used for groups of related options, in which only one can be on or off.
PictureBox	PictureBox	Used to display graphic images. If the control isn't large enough to show the entire image, it will clip the image.
PictureClip		Allows you to crop or clip an area of a bitmapped image and display the cropped image in forms or picture boxes
ProgressBar	ProgressBar	Shows the progress of a task by filling in a bar with colored segments
RichTextBox	RichTextBox	TextBox-type control with advanced formatting options. With this control, you can enter, access, and edit text.

Object	Syntax	Description
Shape	Shape	Graphical control that can be displayed as rectangle, square, oval, circle, rounded rectangle, or rounded square
SSTab	SSTab	Provides tabs that are similar to those seen in VB's options. Each tab can contain other controls, and only one tab can be active at a time.
StatusBar	StatusBar	Bar divided up with up to 16 Panel objects. It is used to display status information—date/time information, for example—in panels contained in the status bar.
SysInfo	SysInfo	Used to respond to system messages
TabStrip	TabStrip	Provides tabs that are similar to those seen in VB's options. Each tab can contain other controls, and only one tab can be active at a time.
TextBox	TextBox	Allows users to enter, edit, and delete text at runtime through a field. Text can also be entered in Design mode through the control's Text property.
Timer	Timer	Allows execution of code to occur at regular time intervals
Toolbar	Toolbar	Contains Button objects that make up a tool bar. Clicking on the Button object will execute code associated with it.
TreeView	Treeview	Allows viewing information of a hierarchical tree format. This format is similar to that seen in Windows Explorer.
UpDown	UpDown	Used with a "buddy" control, the UpDown control has a pair of arrows used to increment and decrement values. The values affected are in the buddy control.
VScrollBar	VScrollBar	Used to add vertical scroll bar

Data Report Designer

The following listing of controls, objects, and collections deals specifically with the Data Report Designer. They are listed in their own section to avoid confusion with other objects, collections, and controls in VB version 6 that have similar or identical names.

Object	Syntax	Description
DataReport	DataReport	Represents the Data Report Designer
Error	RptError	Used to return details on runtime errors
Function Control	rptFunction	Used to display calculations using built-in functions at runtime
Image Control	rptImage	Used to display graphics
Label Control	rptLabel	Used to display text that is not changeable by the user
Section	Section	Used to represent a section of Data Report Designer
Sections Collection	Sections	Collection of Section objects
Shape Control	Shape	Graphical control that can be displayed as rectangle, square, oval, circle, rounded rectangle, or rounded square
TextBox Control	rptTextBox	Used to display text from a database at runtime. This control is data-bound.

Objects and Collections

Object	Syntax	Description
AddIn	Addin	Returns information about an add-in to other add-ins. One such object is created for every add-in listed in the file VBADDIN.INI.
AddIns Collection	AddIns	Accessed through the VBE object, this returns a collection of add-ins that are listed in the VBADDIN.INI
AmbientProperties		Allows access to ambient properties of a container object
App	App	Allows access to information about the application, such as its name, title, and path
AsyncProperty		Contains the results of AsyncRead methods and is passed to the AsyncReadComplete event

Object	Syntax	Description
Axis	Axis	Used to represent the access on a chart
AxisGrid	AxisGrid	Used to represent the area surrounding the axis on a chart
AxisScale	AxisScale	Used to set how chart values are placed on the axis of a chart
AxisTitle	AxisTitle	Used to represent the title of an axis on a chart
Backdrop	Backdrop	Used to represent shadows or patterns that appear behind items on a chart
Band		Represents one band in the Bands collection
Bands Collection	*object*.Bands.Count *object*.Bands(Index)	Collection that represents bands on the CoolBar control. Each band is a region that can contain a caption, image, and child control.
Binding	Binding	Part of the Binding collection, it represents the binding of a property of a data consumer to a data source field
Binding Collection	BindingCollection	Made up of Binding objects, this allows you to bind a data consumer to a data provider
Brush	Brush	Used to specify the fill type of an element on a chart
Button		Represents a single button on a tool bar
ButtonMenu	ButtonMenu	Represents a menu that drops down from a button object on a tool bar
ButtonMenus Collection	ButtonMenus	Used to represent a collection of ButtonMenu objects
Buttons Collection	*toolbar*.Buttons(Index) *toolbar*.Buttons.Item(Index)	Collection of Button objects, accessed by their index numbers (which start at one, rather than zero)
CategoryScale	CategoryScale	Used to represent the scale of a category axis
Clipboard	Clipboard	Used to access the Windows Clipboard
CodeModule	CodeModule	Represents the code of a component

Object	Syntax	Description
CodePane		Represents a code pane, and can be used to manipulate text residing in the code pane
CodePanes Collection		A collection of CodePane objects that contains all active code panes in the VBE object
Collection	Collection Dim *collection name* As New Collection	Used to organize related items into a collection, so it can then be referred to as one object
Column		Part of the Columns collection, it is used to represent a column in the DataGrid control
ColumnHeader		Part of the ColumnHeaders collection, it contains heading text of the ListView control
ColumnHeaders Collection	*listview*.ColumnHeaders *listview*.ColumnHeaders(Index)	Used to hold ColumnHeader objects, which contain the heading text of the ListView control
Columns Collection	Columns.Item Columns.Item(Index)	Contains Column objects, which are used to represent a column in the DataGrid control
ComboItem	*object*.ComboItem	Contains list items of the ImageCombo control. This object can contain and display text or image items.
ComboItems Collection	*object*.ComboItems(Index)	Contains ComboItem objects, which contain items in the list portion of the ImageCombo control
CommandBar	CommandBar	Object that can contain other CommandBar objects. CommandBar objects act as button or menu commands.
CommandBarEvents		An event is triggered by this object when the command bar is clicked.
CommandBar Collection		Collection that contains all CommandBar objects in a project
ContainedControls Collection	ContainedControls(Index)	Collection for accessing controls that are contained within other controls

Object	Syntax	Description
ContainedVBControls Collection		Collection that represents VBControl objects
Control	Control Dim x As Control	The class name for internal controls in VB
Controls Collection	*object*.Controls(Index) *object*.Controls.Count	Elements accessed by the Index represent controls in a component.
Coor	Coor	Used in charts, it defines the floating x and y coordinate pair
DataBinding	DataBinding	There is a DataBinding object for each property of a component that is bindable. This allows you to bind a property to a database.
DataBindings Collection		Collects and makes available all bindable properties
DataGrid	DataGrid	A series of rows and columns that represent a virtual matrix, and that contain the data points and labels for MSChart control
DataMembers Collection	DataMembers	Collection comprised of data members for a data source
DataObject	DataObject	Contains data being transferred to and from a component source to a component target
DataObject (ActiveX)	DataObject	A data container for transferring data from a component source to a component target
DataObjectFiles Collection	*object*.DataObjectFiles	Collection of strings containing the property for the files type of DataObject
DataObjectFiles Collection (ActiveX)	*object*.DataObjectFiles(Index)	Represents all filenames used by the DataObject
DataPoint	DataPoint	Used to describe attributes of a single data point on a chart
DataPointLabel	DataPointLabel	Contains the label for a data point on a chart
DataPoints Collection	*object*.DataPoints(Index)	Collection of data points for a chart

Object	Syntax	Description
DEAggregate	DEAggregate	Used to define an aggregate field in DECommand
DEAggregates Collection	DEAggregate(Index)	Collection of DEAggregate objects
Debug	Debug	Used to send output to the Immediate window during a debugging session
DECommand	DECommand	Contains Design mode properties of ADO command objects
DECommands Collection	DECommands(Index)	Elements accessed through the index represent each DECommand object in the Data Environment.
DEConnection	DEConnection	Contains Design mode properties of ADO connection objects
DEConnections Collection	DEConnections(Index)	Elements accessed through the index represent each DEConnection object in the Data Environment.
DEExtDesigner	DEExtDesigner	Top-level container of the Data Environment, it provides a container for related DEConnection and DECommand objects
DEField	DEField	Contains Design mode properties of ADO field objects
DEFields Collection	DEFields(Index)	Elements accessed through the index represent each DEField object in the DECommand.
DEGroupingFields Collection	DEGroupingFields(Index)	Elements accessed through the index represent each DEGroupingField object in the DECommand.
DEParameter	DEParameter	Contains Design mode properties of ADO parameter objects
DEParameters Collection	DEParameters(Index)	Elements accessed through the index represent each DEParameter object in the DECommand.
DERelationCondition	DERelationCondition	In a relation hierarchy, this object defines relation conditions between parent and child Command objects

Object	Syntax	Description
DERelationConditions	DERelationConditions(Index) DERelationConditions.Count	Elements accessed through the index represent each DERelationCondition object in the DECommand.
DHTMLPage	DHTMLPage	Connects events between VB runtime and Dynamic HTML object model
DHTMLPageDesigner		Object that represents the DHTML Page Designer
Dictionary	Scripting.Dictionary	Stores items that are any data type and that are accessed with a unique key. It can contain data key, item pairs.
Drive		Used to access a drive or network share properties at runtime
Drives Collection	Drives	Provides read-only information on all available drives, including floppy and CD-ROM
Err	Err	Used to return information on runtime errors
EventInfo	EventInfo	Controls assigned to VBControlExtender can raise event information, which is then contained in this object.
Events		Provides properties that return event source objects. These can notify you of changes in a VB for Applications environment.
EventParameter	EventParameter	Used to represent parameters of a control event
ExportFormat	ExportFormat	Used to determine attributes of text that's exported from the Data Report
ExportFormats Collection	ExportFormats	Collection of ExportFormat objects
Extender	Extender	Contains properties of controls that are controlled by a container object
File		Used to access file properties
FileControlEvents	FileControlEvents	Represents VB events that support file control

Object	Syntax	Description
Files Collection	*object*.Files	Represents File objects in a folder
FilesSystemObject	Scripting.FilesSystemObject	Used to access the file system of a computer
Fill	Fill	Used to determine the backdrop of an object in a chart
Folder		Used to access folder properties
Folders Collection		Collection of Folder objects
Font	Font	Contains information to format text
Footnote	Footnote	Contains text that is displayed beneath a chart
Form	Form	Interface on which other controls are placed. Form objects are windows in an application.
Forms	Forms(Index)	Represents loaded forms in an application
Frame	Frame	Contains information about the frame surrounding a chart
Global	Global	Enables access to global (application-level) properties and methods
HyperLink		Used to jump to a URL or HTML document
IDTExtensibility Interface	Implements IDTExtensiblity	Used to manage add-ins, and contains methods and properties of connected add-ins
Intersection	Intersection	The point where two axes cross on a chart
Label	*axis*.Label	Used to describe a chart axis
Labels Collection	*axis*.Labels(Index)	A group of axis labels for a chart that are accessed through the index of the Labels object
LCoor	LCoor	Used for long integer y and x coordinate pairs
Legend	Legend	Used for chart legends, which explain what elements of a chart represent

Object	Syntax	Description
LicenseInfo	LicenseInfo	Represents ProgID and license key of a control
Licenses Collection	Licenses	Collection of LicenseInfo objects, which represent ProgID and license key information about a control, required when adding licensed controls to a Controls collection.
Light	Light	Used to represent light source lighting up a 3-D chart
LightSource	LightSource	Used to represent light source lighting up items in a 3-D chart
LightSources Collection	*object*.LightSources(Index)	Collection of LightSource objects
LinkedWindows Collection		Comprised of Window objects, it contains all of the linked windows in a linked window frame
ListImage		Contains a bitmapped image for use in other controls
ListImages Collection	*imagelist*.ListImages *imagelist*.ListImages(Index)	Grouping of ListImage objects
ListItem		Contains text, and an index of an icon (that is, a ListImage object)
ListItems Collection	*listview*.ListItems *listview*.ListItems(Index)	Collection of ListImage objects, containing text and an associated index of an icon (that is, a ListImage object)
ListSubItem	ListSubItem	Used to access a subitem in a ListView control. It can only be created at runtime, using the Add method.
ListSubItems Collection	ListSubItems	Collection of ListSubItem objects. It is used to access a subitem in a ListView control and can only be created at runtime, using the Add method.
Location	Location	Used to represent the position of text-based items (title, legend, and so on) on a chart
Marker	Marker	Used to identify a data point on a chart
MDIForm	MDIForm	A multiple document interface form that can contain child windows

Object	Syntax	Description
Member	Member	Represents the properties and attributes of members. The properties are code based, while attributes are type library-based.
Members	Members	Collection of module-level code members
Node		Refers to an item that contains text and images in a Treeview control
Nodes Collection	*treeview*.Nodes *treeview*.Nodes(Index)	Elements accessed through the index represent each node used in a Treeview control.
OLEObject		Represents an object inserted in a RichTextBox control
OLEObjects Collection	*object*.OLEObjects(Index) *object*.OLEObjects.Item(Index)	Collection of OLEObject objects. Elements accessed through the index represent each OLEObject.
Panel		Represents a single panel in a status bar
Panels Collection	*statusbar*.Panels(Index)	Collection of Panel objects. Elements accessed through the index represent each Panel object in a status bar.
ParentControls Collection	ParentControls(Index)	Used to access the controls contained in another control container. Elements accessed through the index represent each ParentControl.
Pen	Pen	Reference to pattern and color used in the lines or edges on a chart
Picture	Picture	Allows you to manipulate graphics assigned to an object's Picture property
Plot	Plot	Used as a representation of the area on which a chart resides
PlotBase	PlotBase	Represents area beneath a chart
Printer	Printer	Allows communication with a printer
Printers Collection	Printers(Index)	Used to access information on available printers
Properties Collection	Properties	Used to return control or collection properties

Object	Syntax	Description
Properties Collection (VBA Add-In Object Model)		Used to represent object properties
Property		Used to represent object properties of objects visible in the Properties window
PropertyBag		Contains information that needs to be saved and restored across invocations of an object
PropertyPage		Used to create ActiveX Property pages
Rect	Rect	Used to define coordinate locations
Reference		Used as a representation of a project or type library
References Collection		Collection of all Reference objects, representing set of references in a project
ReferencesEvent		When references are added and removed from projects, this object is a source of events, and is returned by the ReferencesEvent property.
RepeaterBinding	RepeaterBinding	Represents a component's bindable property
RepeaterBindings Collection		Using the RepeaterBindings property, you can return collection references.
Screen	Screen	Refers to the entire desktop in Windows, and allows you to manipulate forms based on their placement on the screen
SelBookmarks Collection	SelBookmarks	For each row selected in the DataGrid control, a bookmark is contained in the SelBookmarks collection.
SelectedControls Collection	SelectedControls(Index)	Elements are referenced through the index, allowing access to each selected control on an object.
SelectedVBControls Collection	SelectedVBControls	Returns selected controls on a component
SelectedVBControlsEvents	SelectedVBControlsEvents	Returns events supported by selected controls

Object	Syntax	Description
Series	Series	Used as a representation of data points on a chart, and an item in SeriesCollection collection
Series Collection	Series(Index)	Collection of chart series
SeriesCollection Collection	SeriesCollection(Index)	Returns information on a series in the Series collection
SeriesMarker	SeriesMarker	Used to describe markers that identify data points in a chart series
SeriesPosition	SeriesPosition	Refers to the location of a chart series in relation to other series. If all series have the same position, they're stacked.
Shadow	Shadow	Contains information on a shadow's appearance on a chart element
Split		Used as a representation of a split in a DataGrid control
Splits Collection	Splits(Index) Splits.Item(Index)	Collection of Split objects in a data grid
StatLine	StatLine	Contains information on how a chart's statistic lines display
StdDataFormat	StdDataFormat	Allows data formatting as data is read and written to a database
StdDataFormats Collection		Collection containing StdDataFormat objects
StdDataValue	StdDataValue	Used after StdDataFormat does formatting, this object returns and sets values.
Tab		A tab in the Tabs collection of the tab strip
Tabs Collection	*tabstrip*.Tabs(Index) *tabstrip*.Tabs.Item(Index)	Elements accessed through the index represent each tab used in a TabStrip control.
TextLayout	TextLayout	Used as a representation of the positioning and orientation of text
TextStream	TextStream.*property* TextStream.*method*	Enables application to have sequential access to a file

Object	Syntax	Description
Tick	Tick	A marker that indicates division of an axis on a chart
Title	Title	Used for the title text on a chart
UserControl		Base object that's used for creating ActiveX controls
UserDocument		Used like a Form object in creating ActiveX documents. It is a base object that's used for creating ActiveX documents.
ValueScale	ValueScale	Scale used to display a value axis in a chart
VBComponent		Used as a representation of a component (class or standard module) in a project
VBComponents Collection		Collection of VBComponent objects. It represents the components used in a project.
VBComponentsEvents	VBComponentsEvents	Represents events occurring when objects are added, deleted, activated, renamed, or selected in a project
VBControl	VBControl	Used as a representation of component controls
VBControlExtender	VBControlExtender	Used when dynamically adding controls to Controls Collection
VBControls Collection	VBControls	Collection of all components on a form
VBControlsEvents	VBControlsEvents	Represents source of events occurring when objects are added, deleted, activated, renamed, or selected in a project
VBE		Root object in Visual Basic for Applications, under which reside all other objects and collections
VBForm	VBForm	Used to return a component in a project
VBNewProjects Collection		Represents all new projects

Object	Syntax	Description
VBProject		Represents a project
VBProjects Collection		Represents all open projects
VBProjectsEvents	VBProjectsEvents	Represents source of events occurring when objects are added, deleted, activated, or renamed in a project
View3D	View3D	Used to represent a chart's 3-D orientation
VtColor	VtColor	Represents a chart's drawing color
VtFont	VtFont	Represents the font used in a chart's text
Wall	Wall	Used in a 3-D chart, this object represents the planar area that depicts the y axis
WebClass	WebClass	WebClass objects are part of an IIS application, and reside on the Web server. They intercept HTTP requests so that appropriate VB code can be processed. WebItems contained in this object are then sent to the browser.
WebClassError	WebClassError	Returns what error occurred when processing a FatalErrorResponse event
WebItem	WebItem	Represents WebItems such as HTML documents
WebItemProperties	WebItemProperties	Collection of user-defined properties. These are contained in this object, and are associated with particular WebItems.
Weighting	Weighting	Represents one pie's size relation to another in a chart
Window	Window	Represents a window
Windows Collection		Collection containing all permanent or open windows

A

Self Test
Answers

Answers to Chapter 1 Self Test

1. You have a form that contains some code you want to use in your project, but you want the form to remain invisible during the execution of the program. How can you do this? (Choose all that apply.)

   A. By setting the Hide property of the form to True

   B. By using the Hide method on the form

   C. By setting the Visible property of the form to False

   D. By using the Unload method on the form

   B, C. When you use code from an unloaded form, that form will be loaded; therefore, answer D is incorrect. If you want the form to be invisible to the user, then you must set the Visible property of the form to False. This can also be accomplished by using the Hide method (*formname*.Hide). There is no Hide property on a form.

2. How does the Immediate window help you debug your projects?(Choose all that apply.) It allows you to:

   A. Call other procedures from within the current procedure.

   B. Display all the visible variables from the procedure currently being executed.

   C. Display the name of all procedures being executed preceded by the name of the object to which it belongs.

   D. Type in any valid line of code.

   A, D. The Immediate window allows you to call other procedures from within the current procedure and allows you to type in any valid line of code. The Locals window displays the name of variables from the procedure currently being executed. The Call Stack window displays the name of all procedures being executed.

3. Which of the following is true of the Err object? (Choose all that apply.)

   A. It can display the location where an error occurred.

   B. It can contain the fully qualified path to a help file.

   C. It can display the value of a variable.

   D. It can produce an error number.

   A, B, D. The Err object can display the location where an error occurred (using the Source property), can contain the fully qualified path to a help file (using the HelpFile property), and can produce an error number (using the *Number* property).

4. Your form has four command buttons from top to bottom. How can you ensure that the top command button receives the focus when the form loads?

   A. By entering code in the GotFocus event of the top button

   B. By setting the TabStop property of the top button to True

C. By setting the TabIndex property of the top button to 0

D. By setting the TabIndex property of the top button to 1

B. First of all, the TabStop property must be set to True. This determines whether the object can obtain focus when the user is tabbing through the form. Setting the TabIndex property of an object on a form to zero (0) will force the focus to be placed on that object when the form is loaded. The TabIndex for the other objects on the form will be automatically renumbered, and the tabbing order will be determined by these new TabIndex property values.

5. What does the Description property of the Err object do? (Choose all that apply.)

A. Returns the number and description of an error

B. Returns the description of an error

C. Describes the error that just occurred

D. Defaults to an "Application defined or object-defined error"

B, D. The Description property, when used in conjunction with the Number property, returns the description of a common VB error. The Description property defaults to a generic message of "Application defined or object-defined error."

6. Which of the following contexts are available in the Add Watch window? (Choose all that apply.)

A. Class

B. Module

C. Procedure

D. Project

B, C, D. The Add Watch window allows you to indicate the expression to be watched, the context in which that expression will be watched, and the type of watch you want to add. The Procedure, Module, and Project settings indicated in this window determine the context of the watch.

7. You want to view the properties of an object variable in Break mode. What is the best tool to use? (Choose all that apply.)

A. The Call Stack window

B. The Immediate window

C. The Locals window

D. The Watch window

C and D. You can view the properties of objects at runtime in the Watch window and the Locals window. Debug.Print also returns statements for each property in the Immediate window.

8. The Locals window allows you to do which of the following tasks? (Choose all that apply.)

A. Viewing variables adding new variables

B. Changing the value of variables

C. Removing variables

D. Adding variables
A, B. The Locals window displays all the variables from the current procedure and allows you to change the value of a variable.

9. When can you add a watch expression?

A. At design time

B. In Break mode

C. At runtime

D. At design time or while in Break mode
D. A watch expression can be added either at design time or while in Break mode.

10. What does the Number property of the Err object do?

A. Returns the a message box displaying an error number

B. Stores the number of the last error that occurred

C. Displays the value of the variable that caused the error

D. Returns the HelpContextID associated with the error that occurred
B. The Number property of the Err object contains the number of the last error that occurred. The Description property contains a description of the last error that occurred.

11. What function does the TabStop property on a command button perform?

A. It determines whether the button can get the focus.

B. If set to False it disables the TabIndex property.

C. It determines the order in which the button will receive the focus.

D. It determines if the access key sequence can be used.
A. Setting the TabStop property on a command button to False will cause the command button to be bypassed when the user tabs from control to control. It will not disable the TabIndex property, nor will it change the TabIndex property.

12. You want to specify a path to a Help file that can be displayed when a particular error occurs. Which of the following will return the path to the Help file?

A. Err.Help

B. Err.HelpContext

C. Err.HelpFile

D. Err.Number
C. The HelpFile property of the Err object returns the path to a Windows Help file. By default, the HelpFile property contains the name of the VB Help File. Err.Number returns an error number.

13. You have not specified a help file. A command button contained on the form receives the focus. What will occur if you press the F1 key?

A. No help will be displayed. The standard Help topic for command buttons will be displayed.

B. The standard Help topic for buttons will be displayed.

C. The standard Help topic for forms will be displayed.

D. An error message stating that no help file is specified will be displayed.
   A. If no help file is specified using the Err object, no help will be given.

14. Which debugging window(s) displays the values for all visible variables from within the procedure currently being executed?

A. The Call Stack window

B. The Immediate window

C. The Locals window

D. The Watch window
   C. The values of all variables within the procedure currently being executed are displayed in the Locals window. If another procedure begins execution, then the contents of the Locals window will also change.

15. How can you print the object name associated with the last VB error to the Immediate window?

A. Debug.Print Err.Number

B. Debug.Print Err.Source

C. Debug.Print Err.Description

D. Debug.Print Error.LastDLLError
   B. The object name associated with

the last VB error generated is stored in the Source property of the Err object.

16. How do you enter Beak mode while running an application? (Choose all that apply.)

A. Click Break on the Debug toolbar

B. Use a watch expression

C. Use a breakpoint

D. Press F9 on a line of code
   A, C, D. You can enter Break mode by encountering a breakpoint during program execution, by pressing CTRL-BREAK during program execution, by pressing F9 on a line of code, by adding a Break When True watch expression, or by adding a Break When Changed watch expression, which stops the execution of the program when the value of the watch changes.

17. How would you create an access key sequence for a command button?

A. Insert an ampersand (&) before the letter to be used as the access key in the Name property of the command button.

B. Insert an ampersand (&) after the letter to be used as the access key in the Name property of the command button.

C. Insert an ampersand (&) before the letter to be used as the access key in the Caption property of the command button.

D. Insert an ampersand (&) after the letter chosen as the access key in the Caption property of the command button.
C. Access keys for command buttons are assigned by inserting an ampersand (&) in the Caption property of the command button before the letter chosen as the access key.

18. Which is **not** a property of the Err object? (Choose all that apply.)

A. Clear

B. Description

C. Raise

D. Source
A, C. Raise and Clear are methods, not properties of Err. Properties of the Err object are Number, Description, Source, HelpFile, HelpContext, and LastDLLError.

19. Which window will allow you to halt the execution of your code when a variable changes?

A. The Call Stack window

B. The Immediate window

C. The Locals window

D. The Watch window
D. The Watch window allows you to break the code when the value of a variable changes, break when the value of an expression is true, or watch the expression.

20. How do you add a watch expression? (Choose all that apply.)

A. Click on the Debug menu, then choose Add Watch to access the Add Watch dialog box.

B. Right-click a line of code and select Add Watch.

C. Click on the View menu, select the Immediate window, then right-click in the Immediate window.

D. Click on the View menu, select the Watch window, then right click in the Watch window.
A, B, D. These are all valid ways of adding a watch to a piece of code. You may not add a watch through the Immediate window.

Answers to Chapter 2 Self Test

1. During installation of VB, you decide that you don't agree with the End User License Agreement. Choosing the option that you don't agree, what will happen?

A. You can click the Next button and continue.

B. VB will be installed as a limited evaluation copy.

C. You must either accept or exit the installation process.

D. None of the above.
C. Failing to accept the End User License Agreement will give you the option of either agreeing or exiting the installation. These are your only options.

2. You install VB through Visual Studio and find that parts of VB aren't running correctly. What is the reason for this?

   A. You didn't select Microsoft Visual Basic 6.0 during the installation.

   B. You failed to install Visual InterDev.

   C. You failed to install the Data Access components.

   D. You didn't select Win32 SDK during the installation.
   C. Failing to install the Data Access components may cause problems with aspects of Visual Basic. Failing to select Microsoft Visual Basic 6.0 will cause VB to not exist, which doesn't apply here. The other two choices will have no effect on VB's functionality.

3. You are tired of typing "Option Explicit" in every new module you add to projects. What can you configure so that this is automatically added to your modules?

   A. Require Variable Declaration in the Editor tab of the Options dialog box.

   B. Require Variable Declaration in the Editor Format tab of the Options dialog box.

   C. Require Option Explicit Declaration in the Editor tab of the Options dialog box.

   D. Require Option Explicit Declaration in the Editor Format tab of the Options dialog box.
   C. Require Option Explicit Declaration in the Editor tab of the

   Options dialog box is used to add Option Explicit to new modules.

4. You want to configure windows in VB so that one window can attach to another. Which tab in the Options dialog box will you use to make this configuration?

   A. Environment

   B. Docking

   C. General

   D. Advanced
   B. Configuring windows so that they'll attach to one another in Visual Basic is done from the Docking tab. The process of windows attaching this way is called docking.

5. Which of the following menus will give you access to Options, where you configure VB?

   A. File

   B. Project

   C. View

   D. Tools
   D. Options is available from the Tools menu in VB.

6. You want VB to check your syntax as you enter code. Which property will you check to enable this?

   A. Auto Correct

   B. Auto Syntax Check

   C. Syntax Check

   D. Auto Syntax
   B. Auto Syntax Check will check your code for syntax errors as you type.

7. If implicit variables are not allowed in a module's code, what must appear in the General Declaration section of the Options dialog box?

   A. Explicit Declaration

   B. Explicit Only

   C. Option Explicit

   D. Explicit Only

   C. Option Explicit must appear in the General Declaration section if explicit variables are only to be used.

8. What must you enable for VB to complete a statement of code as you type it?

   A. Auto List Members

   B. Auto Quick Info

   C. Auto List Tips

   D. Auto Statement

   C. Auto List Members will list all possible members for a statement by displaying a box that will allow you to complete a statement from the insertion point.

9. What tab of the Options dialog box allows you to configure indentation in your code?

   A. Editor

   B. Editor Format

   C. General

   D. None of the above

   A. The Editor tab allows you to configure such things as auto indentation and tab width, used in the Code window.

10. You want windows in VB to attach to one another when one window is placed over another. Which tab in Options dialog box will you use to achieve this?

    A. General

    B. Editor

    C. Advanced

    D. Docking

    D. Docking allows windows to connect or attach to one another when they are placed over one another on the VB desktop.

11. You want to configure VB to save changes you've made to your project each time you run a program you create. Which tab in the Options dialog box allows you to configure VB to do this?

    A. General

    B. Environment

    C. Advanced

    D. Compile

    B. The Environment tab in Options allows you to configure whether VB will save your project when you run it (by pressing F5), prompt whether you want to save it, or not save it at all.

12. You have decided to move your templates directory to another location on your hard drive. Which tab in the Options dialog box allows you to configure VB to do this?

    A. General

    B. Environment

C. Advanced

D. Properties
  B. The Environment tab allows you to configure which templates are shown and the directory that templates will be stored in.

13. While surfing the Internet, you found a program that you want to use as your default HTML editor. Which tab in the Options dialog box will allow you to specify this new program as your default HTML editor?

  A. General

  B. Environment

  C. Advanced

  D. ActiveX
    C. The Advanced tab allows you to specify which program you'd like to use as your default HTML editor.

14. During installation of VB, you reach the screen that requires you to input several pieces of information. Which of the following pieces of information is required by the VB installation? (Choose all that apply.)

  A. Name

  B. Company

  C. CD key

  D. Version ID
    A, B, C. The Name, Company and CD key are required by VB installation. Failing to enter this information will halt the installation process.

15. As an experienced user, you decide that you don't want ToolTips to be displayed in VB. Which tab in the Options dialog box will you choose to disable ToolTips?

  A. General

  B. Help

  C. Environment

  D. Advanced
    A. The General tab allows you to enable or disable ToolTips from appearing in VB.

16. You want to speed up the time it takes for control to be returned to you when a project loads. What will you configure for this to happen?

  A. Background Project Load from the Advanced tab of the Options dialog box

  B. Background Project Load from the Environment tab of the Options dialog box

  C. Load Project in Background from the Environment tab of the Options dialog box

  D. Load Project in Background from the Advanced tab of the Options dialog box
    A. Background Project Load will load a project in the background, thereby returning control to the programmer faster. It can be configured from the Advanced tab.

17. When installing VB through Visual Studio 6.0, you are given different setup options for installing Visual Studio. Which option will install workstation or

stand-alone components (such as Visual Basic 6.0 and Data Access)? (Choose all that apply.)

A. Custom

B. Workstation

C. Products

D. Server Applications

A, C. Custom installation will allow you to install server applications and workstation/stand-alone components. Products will only install the workstation/stand-alone components. There is no option for Workstation.

18. When installing VB through Visual Studio 6.0, you are faced with a screen that says "Uninstall Visual Studio 97." You don't have Visual Studio 97, but you do have a stand-alone copy of Visual Basic 5.0. What will happen if you don't touch any of the checked programs listed and click the Next button?

A. Nothing. The Uninstall only effects copies of Visual Studio 97.

B. Visual Basic 5.0 will be uninstalled.

C. Visual Basic 6.0 will overwrite the previous version.

D. Visual Basic 5.0 will be moved to a different directory.

B. While the installation says that it wants to uninstall Visual Studio 97, it also lists components available through VS97, such as stand-alone installations of Visual Basic 5.0. Failing to unselect Visual Basic 5.0 from the list will uninstall it from your system.

19. You change the code colors for comment text (in the Editor Format tab of the Options dialog box) to red. You create a new form, and in the comment property for a label, you write some text. What will happen when you run the program?

A. Text in the label will appear in red.

B. Text on the form will appear in red.

C. Nothing. You can't enter text during design mode into a label.

D. Nothing. Only comments in your code will be affected.

D. Only comments in your code will be affected. Changes made to any text style appearing on this tab only affect the Code window. It has no effect on the appearance of a form.

20. When attempting to create a new project with VSS, you find you are unable to perform this action. A message appears stating that the user isn't found. What is most likely the problem?

A. VSS isn't installed on your system.

B. The database is invalid.

C. You need to have an account created with the Admin tool.

D. You need to create an account through VSS's Options.

C. To access a VSS database, you must have a valid user account, which is created with VSS's Admin tool. Failing to have a valid user account will result in the user not being found.

21. When connecting to the VSS database, you are required to provide three pieces of information. Of the following choices, what information must you provide to save to the VSS database? (Choose all that apply.)

    A. Name

    B. Password

    C. Database

    D. User ID
       A, B, C. Connecting to the VSS database requires username, password, and database. You must have a valid account and the database must exist to connect to it.

22. What is the largest tab space you can set for your code in the Editor Format tab of Options?

    A. 4 spaces

    B. 32 spaces

    C. 64 spaces

    D. 256 spaces
       B. The default tab space for indentation of code is four spaces. However, the largest tab space you can set is 32 spaces.

23. Compile on Demand is an option available from the General tab in the Options dialog box. What will enabling this feature do?

    A. Allow you to press F5 to compile a program

    B. Compile the program without saving the project

    C. The project must be fully compiled before it starts

    D. The project will start before it's fully compiled
       C. When Compile on Demand is enabled, the project must be fully compiled before the program starts.

24. You have VB installed on a laptop and want to configure it to interact with a docking station. Which tab in the Options dialog box will you choose to perform this action?

    A. General

    B. Advanced

    C. Docking

    D. None of the above
       D. None of the above. There is no configuration option that deals directly with laptops and docking stations. This is a trick question, as many users of VB confuse Docking with docking stations. Docking in VB's configuration allows windows to connect or attach to one another when they are placed over one another on the VB desktop.

25. During installation of VB, you reach the screen that requires you to input several pieces of information. Assuming your computer has the proper information about you, you must input something into one of these fields. You are not allowed to continue unless you enter this particular piece of information. What is it?

    A. Name

    B. Company

C. CD key

D. Version ID
C. The CD key is required by VB installation. The name and company information will be retrieved from your computer. Assuming this information is correct, you won't need to change these two fields, just enter the CD key.

26. You want VB to create a new project each time it starts. Which tab in the Options dialog box will allow you to configure this?

   A. General

   B. Advanced

   C. Environment

   D. Startup
   C. The Environment tab includes an option to create a new VB project each time VB is started.

27. What error trapping method will cause Break mode to occur whenever any error is encountered?

   A. Break

   B. Break on All Errors

   C. Break in Class Module

   D. Break on Unhandled Errors
   B. Break on All Errors will cause the compiler to enter Break mode whenever any error is encountered.

28. What is the default measurement of grid units on a VB form?

   A. Pixels

   B. Points

C. Millimeters

D. Twips
D. The default measurement of grid units is in twips.

29. You want to change the font and color of certain text styles that appear in the Code window. Which tab in the Options dialog box would you use to configure its appearance?

   A. Editor

   B. Editor Format

   C. General

   D. Styles
   B. The Editor Format tab is used to configure the appearance of the Code window.

30. Where must Option Explicit appear in your code if implicit variables are *not* to be allowed?

   A. General

   B. General Options

   C. General Declaration

   D. Option Declaration
   C. Option Explicit must appear in the General Declaration section if implicit variables are not to be allowed.

31. You attempt to install VB on a 386DX/33 computer with 16MB of memory, and a CD-ROM drive. The operating system used on the computer is Windows 95. Unfortunately, you find that VB won't run. Why?

   A. VB requires 32MB of RAM.

   B. VB requires Windows 98 to be running.

C. VB requires a 486DX/66 or higher processor.

D. The computer doesn't meet all of the requirements.

C. VB requires a 486DX/66 MHz or higher processor, with a Pentium or higher processor recommended, on a Windows 95 machine.

32. You attempt to install VB on a Pentium computer with 16MB of memory, SVGA display, CD-ROM drive, and Windows NT Workstation 4.0 as its operating system. Unfortunately, you find that VB won't run. Why?

A. VB requires 32MB of memory.

B. VB won't run on a Windows NT workstation.

C. VB can't use SVGA display.

D. VB requires a floppy drive to be installed.

A. On an NT Workstation, VB requires 32MB of RAM. On Windows 95/98, only 16MB are required.

33. You attempt to access the Options dialog box from the Tools menu. When you click the Tools menu, Options is grayed out and can't be accessed. Why?

A. Insufficient memory.

B. There isn't a project currently opened.

C. Options isn't under the Tools menu, it's under the View menu.

D. The user doesn't have proper permissions set through the VSS Admin tool.

B. You must have a project open to access the Options dialog box from the Tools menu. If you don't, Options will be disabled and appear grayed out.

34. Which of the following are valid names for variables?

A. 1stOption

B. This.Is.A.Valid.Variable.Name

C. ThisIsAValidVariableNameToUseInA Project

D. None of the Above

C. While not a very meaningful name, the variable name in this choice begins with a letter, doesn't contain periods or type-declaration characters, and is less than 255 characters. Assuming that it's unique within its scope, it is perfectly valid.

35. You are finding it distracting that you can see applications and the Windows Desktop behind VB's development environment. What would you do to change VB's appearance so that other applications and the Desktop aren't appearing behind VB?

A. Check the SDI Development Environment check box on the Advanced tab in the Options dialog box.

B. Uncheck the SDI Development Environment check box on the Advanced tab in the Options dialog box.

C. Check the SDI Development Environment check box on the Environment tab in the Options dialog box.

D. Uncheck the SDI Development Environment check box on the Environment tab in the Options dialog box.
B. Unchecking the SDI Development Environment check box on the Advanced tab will cause VB to use an MDI interface. Other applications and the Windows Desktop won't appear behind VB's development environment.

36. You attempt to install VB Enterprise Edition on the following computer: a Pentium with 16MB of memory, SVGA display, CD-ROM drive, 80MB of free hard drive space, and running Windows 98 as its operating system. Unfortunately, you find that VB won't install. Why?

A. VB Enterprise requires more RAM than the system currently has.

B. VB Enterprise requires more hard drive space than the system currently has.

C. VB Enterprise won't run on Windows 98 without Service Pack 3.

D. VB Enterprise requires a minimum Pentium II processor.
B. VB Enterprise requires 128MB of free hard drive space for a typical installation and 147MB of free hard drive space for a full installation. For this system, you could install Standard or Professional editions, which require 48MB for typical installation or 80MB for full installation.

37. Which of the following operating systems can run VB? (Choose all that apply.)

A. Microsoft Windows 95

B. Microsoft Windows 98

C. Microsoft Windows NT Workstation 4.0

D. Microsoft Windows 3.11
A, B, C. Windows 95, Windows 98, and Windows NT Workstation 4.0 (Service Pack 3 recommended) can all run VB. In addition, later versions of these programs, such as Microsoft Windows NT Workstation 5.0, can run VB.

38. Which keyword is used to declare a variable?

A. Dimension

B. Declare

C. Void Main ( )

D. Dim
D. Dim is used to declare a variable. The syntax for this is:

```
Dim variable name (As data type)
```

Specifying the data type is optional.

39. You want to change the color of certain text that appears in the Code window. Which of the following would you change?

A. Text

B. Foreground

C. Background

D. Indicator
B. To change the color of text that appears in the Code window, you would change the Foreground color.

40. You call Microsoft for support help, and you are asked for the Product ID or serial number of your VB installation. In what two places were you able to obtain this number? (Choose all that apply.)

    A. From the Product ID screen during setup

    B. From the box that VB came in

    C. From Help | About Microsoft Visual Basic

    D. From the README file VB setup places in the root directory
    A, C. The serial number that identifies your copy of VB can be obtained from the Product ID screen when you install Visual Basic, or from the About Microsoft Visual Basic dialog box that is available from the Help menu.

Answers to Chapter 3 Self Test

1. You want a menu item to appear grayed out on a menu. Which property of that menu item will you uncheck in Menu Editor?

    A. Checked

    B. Visible

    C. Appear

    D. Enabled
    D. The Enabled property determines whether a menu item is accessible, and appears dimmed (grayed out) if it is disabled. To disable a menu item, uncheck the Enabled property for that item in Menu Editor.

2. What event procedures does a menu item have? (Choose all that apply.)

    A. KeyDown

    B. KeyPress

    C. Click

    D. MouseUp
    C. A menu item only has one event procedure: Click

3. You want information to appear in your status bar, and you enter text in the Text property of a panel. When you run the form, you find that no text appears in the status bar. Why?

    A. The Text property is used to enter text used for ToolTips.

    B. The text won't appear unless the Text check box is checked.

    C. The text won't appear unless the Style property is set to sbrText.

    D. The text won't appear unless the Text property is set to sbrText.
    C. Text entered in the Text property won't appear in a status bar unless the Style property is set to sbrText.

4. Which property determines the contents of a status bar panel?

    A. Contents

    B. Style

    C. The type of panel selected

    D. SbrContents
    B. The Style property determines the contents of a status bar panel.

5. What is the minimum number of controls you must create in Design time to start a control array?

A. One.

B. Two or more.

C. As few or as many as you like and the form allows.

D. None. You can fully create control collections at runtime.
   A. To create a control array you must have at least one control created at design time.

6. You create five controls during Design time as a controls collection. During runtime, you add five more controls, then try to execute code that will delete six of them. You find you are unable to perform the action. Why?

   A. You can't delete controls during runtime.

   B. You can't delete the controls created during Design time.

   C. You can't have this many controls in a collection.

   D. None of the above.
      B. You can only delete controls from a control collection that were created at runtime.

7. At one time, how many help files can be associated with an application?

   A. One

   B. One for each control

   C. As many as you choose to associate with the application

   D. None of the above
      A. You can only associate one help file with a program at a time.

8. Which of the following file extensions denote files that can be used as help files for applications created in VB? (Choose all that apply.)

   A. HTM

   B. HTML

   C. HLP

   D. CHM
      C, D. VB allows you to associate standard and HTML help files with an application. Standard help files have the HLP extension, while HTML help files have the CHM extension.

9. Your application creates an instance of a form. What is the first event that will be triggered in the form?

   A. Load

   B. GotFocus

   C. Instance

   D. Initialize
      D. Initialize is the first event triggered in a form when an instance of it is created.

10. Which of the following is Hungarian notation for a menu?

    A. Menu

    B. Men

    C. mnu

    D. MN
       C. Hungarian notation for a Menu is mnu.

11. You are ready to run your program to see if it works. Which key on your keyboard will start the program?

    A. F2
    B. F3
    C. F4
    D. F5
    D. F5 is the function key you would press to run your program in VB.

12. Which of the following methods will enable you to start the Menu Editor? (Choose all that apply.)

    A. Selecting Menu Editor from the Tools menu
    B. Pressing CTRL-E
    C. Clicking the Menu icon from the ToolBar
    D. Pressing the F5 key on your keyboard
    A, B, C. You can start the Menu Editor by clicking the menu icon from the keyboard, pressing CTRL-E, or by selecting Tools | Menu Editor.

13. Which of the following keys would you press to bring up the Object Manager in VB?

    A. F2
    B. F3
    C. F4
    D. F5
    A. F2 is the key you would press to bring up the Object Manager program.

14. You want users of your program to press ALT and the underlined letter on your menu to access that particular menu or menu item. In Menu Editor, what will you place before the letter you want to use for an access key?

    A. Underscore
    B. Ampersand
    C. SHIFT
    D. ALT
    B. An ampersand (&) is used before the letter you wish to use for an access key. This letter will then appear underlined on your menu.

15. Which of the following snippets of code will unload a form named frmForm from memory?

    A. Unload Form
    B. Unload This
    C. Unload Me
    D. Unload
    C. The Me keyword can be used in place of the active form's name, allowing you to use Unload Me rather than Unload frmForm.

16. Which of the following serves as an example of declaring an ActiveX component?

    A. Dim *variable* As New *Object*
    B. Declare *variable* As New *Object*
    C. *component* As New *Object*
    D. *component* As New *Servername*
    A. The way to declare an ActiveX component in your code is as done in the example Dim *variable* As New *Object*.

17. You want the text in a text box named txtMyText to read My Text. In which property will you place this string?

    A. Caption

    B. Text

    C. String

    D. None of the above
       B. When you want text to appear in a text box, you would alter the Text property.

18. Which property in a text box will allow a string to appear like a paragraph, word-wrapped on different lines?

    A. WordWrap

    B. MultiLine

    C. SingleLine

    D. TextWrap
       B. The MultiLine property allows text in a text box to appear on multiple lines.

19. Which of the following best describes an ImageList?

    A. Provides a list of images available on the hard disk

    B. Provides the extensions of images available to load

    C. Acts as a central repository for image files

    D. None of the above
       C. An ImageList acts as a central repository for image files.

20. Which is the traditional place in a form to set form-level variables, properties, and other startup code?

    A. Initiate

    B. Load

    C. QueryLoad

    D. Instigate
       B. The Load event is the traditional place to set form-level variables, properties, and other startup code.

21. In which form event would you put cleanup code?

    A. Load

    B. Unload

    C. Terminate

    D. QueryUnload
       B. Code placed in the Unload event generally closes down any forms that are still open, cleans up any variables, and basically clears memory space that has been used by the application.

22. Which property allows you to provide context-sensitive help for your application?

    A. Help Context

    B. HelpContext

    C. HelpContextID

    D. Help
       C. The HelpContextID is a property that allows you to provide context sensitive help for your application.

23. What object is used to check errors?

    A. Error.

    B. Err.

    C. Enum.

    D. There is no object that can check for errors.

    B. The Err object is used to check errors. With it, you can set up error handlers that provide descriptions of errors and help deal with errors.

24. Which event does not occur when a form unloads from memory?

    A. Unload

    B. QueryUnload

    C. Terminate

    D. Deactivate

    D. Deactivate occurs when a window is no longer the active window. It is not caused by a form unloading from memory.

25. Which form event occurs because of the Show or Visible property?

    A. Activate

    B. Terminate

    C. Load

    D. Peek

    A. The Activate event occurs when the Show or Visible property is toggled and the window becomes active.

26. Which method will reset an error number to zero?

    A. Clear

    B. Reset

    C. Null

    D. None

    A. The only method that will reset an error number to zero (0) is Clear. It is used with the Err object, as in the following code: Err.Clear.

27. What keyword handles events associated with ActiveX components?

    A. ActiveX

    B. OLE

    C. COM

    D. WithEvents

    D. Handling events associated with ActiveX components is done with the WithEvents keyword.

28. When dealing with ActiveX components, which of the following processing forms will release the client program, process the work, and then notify the client that it has returned a result?

    A. Asynchronous

    B. Synchronous

    C. Multiprocessed

    D. Processed

    A. This question describes aspects of asynchronous processing.

29. What is the difference between an access key and a shortcut key?

    A. A shortcut key can only be used while a menu item is showing, but an access key can be used at any time.

    B. An access key can only be used while a menu item is showing, but a shortcut key can be used at any time.

C. There is no difference. Both can be used at any time.

D. There is no difference. They are synonymous.

B. An access key can only be used while a menu item is showing, but a shortcut key can be used at any time. You are prompted to press ALT and a letter that has been underlined on the menu. These are called access keys. Shortcut keys are usually CTRL and another letter, and can be used at any time.

30. Which of the following are properties of the Err object? (Choose all that apply.)

A. Description

B. HelpContextID

C. Number

D. Source

A, C, D. Number, Description, and Source are all properties of the Err object. Number is an integer indicating the error that occurred, Description provides a description of the error, and Source is the name of the object that caused the error.

31. Which of the following are based on COM? (Choose all that apply.)

A. ActiveX

B. OLE

C. Thunking

D. HTML Help

A, B. Both ActiveX technology and OLE are based on the COM specification. OLE is an obsolete form of COM, and has been replaced by ActiveX components.

32. You want to enable WhatsThis help in your application. What are the two values associated with the WhatsThis help in the Properties window of an object?

A. Yes/No

B. On/Off

C. True/False

D. Help/Me

C. The WhatsThis property has a Boolean value of either True or False.

33. A user forgets to insert a floppy disk into the drive when she saves. An error results from this. What kind of error has occurred?

A. Runtime

B. Design time

C. Syntax

D. Logic

A. A runtime error occurs only when the program is running. This can be errors such as forgetting to insert a floppy when saving, or trying to open a nonexistent file.

34. You have decided to use HTML help in your application. Using FrontPage, you create a number of HTML documents that you plan to use for help. When you attempt to implement the HTM and HTML files, you find that VB won't accept them. Why?

A. VB doesn't use HTML help.

B. The files must have either the extension HTM or HTML. You cannot use both.

C. You must use the default HTML editor. You can't use FrontPage to create the files because of this.

D. The HTML files must be compiled before they can be used as help files. **D.** The HTML documents must be compiled, using a program like Microsoft's HTML Help Workshop. Until they are compiled, they can't be used as help files.

35. Which of the following will cause a program to return to a statement that caused an error?

A. Resume.

B. Return.

C. Resume Next.

D. None. It would be pointless to return to a statement causing an error. **A.** You use the Resume statement to return to the statement that caused the error.

36. Which method of the Err object will cause an error to occur?

A. Create

B. Error

C. Raise

D. Lower **C.** The Raise method will cause an error to occur. It is used for raising an error in such cases as testing an error handler.

37. You want the text in a label named lblMyLabel to read My Text. In which property will you place this string?

A. Caption

B. Text

C. Label

D. None of the above **A.** When you want text to appear in a label, you would alter the Caption property.

38. Which is the last event to occur when a form is closed?

A. Terminate

B. Unload

C. QueryUnload

D. TerminateLoad **A.** Terminate is the last event to occur when a form is closed.

39. Which of the following keys would you press to bring up the Properties window in VB?

A. F2

B. F3

C. F4

D. F5 **C.** F4 is the key you would press to bring up the Properties window.

40. What will the following snippet of code do when attached to a control named cmdButton?

```
Me.PopupMenu mnuMsg
```

A. It will have the same result as if you clicked the menu mnuMsg.

B. It will display the contents of the menu mnuMsg as a pop-up menu when the user right-clicks over the command button.

C. Nothing. The code is gibberish.

D. Nothing. The Me keyword is reserved for forms.

B. The code will display the contents of mnuMsg as a pop-up menu.

Answers to Chapter 4 Self Test

1. Which of the following are components of Microsoft's Universal Data Access? (Choose all that apply.)

   A. ADO

   B. ODBC

   C. ODBE DB

   D. OLE DB

   E. RDOC

   F. RDS

   A, B, D, F. ADO, ODBC, OLE DB, and RDS. ODBE DB and RDOC do not exist.

2. Which of the following ODBC drivers are supplied with VB version 6? (Choose all that apply.)

   A. Access

   B. FoxPro

   C. ISAM

   D. Oracle

   E. SQL Server

   F. Text files

   A, B, D, E, F. Access, FoxPro, Oracle, and SQL Server. ISAM is a term used to describe certain file-based databases, but there is no ODBC driver that accommodates all ISAM databases.

3. Which of the following is **not** an advantage of OLE DB?

   A. It is easier to decentralize database processing.

   B. It is relatively easy for VB programmers to program using the OLE DB object model.

   C. Its implementation architecture is more open than ODBC.

   D. Unlike ODBC, OLE DB allows the developer to pass SQL statements to the database.

   B. Exposure of OLE DB to VB developers. The OLE DB object model is not directly exposed to VB programmers (usually it is necessary to use ADO, or a specialized API).

4. Which of the following are controls included with VB version 6? (Choose all that apply.)

   A. ADO Data Control 6 (OLEDB)

   B. ODBC Control 6

   C. OLEDB Data Control 6 (ADO)

   D. RemoteData Control 6

E. Universal Data Access Control 5

A, D. ADO Data Control 6 and RemoteData Control. ODBC and OLEDB are less directly accessible to the VB developer.

5. Which of the following would be least likely to be used with a VB application that used a database that resided on the user's own hard disk?

A. ADO

B. ODBC

C. OLE DB

D. RDS

D. RDS stands for Remote Data Services, and is primarily used for implementing three-tier applications, either on a LAN or across the Internet.

6. Which of the following properties would contain a 3 when the user was on the third record in the record set?

A. AbsolutePosition

B. Bookmark

C. CursorLocation

D. Index

A. AbsolutePosition. CursorLocation determines whether the client or the server stores the current record position. Bookmark can be used to identify and locate a record, but it is not stored as a number. Although databases have indexes, in VB the Index property is most frequently

associated with the creation and use of control arrays.

7. What are the three options available from the ADO Data Control General Property Page to populate the ConnectionString property? (Choose all that apply.)

A. Use Connection String

B. Use Data Link File

C. Use Database Link File

D. Use ODBC Data Source Name

E. Use RecordSource Name

A, B, D. Use Connection String, Use Data Link File, and Use ODBC Data Source Name. It is possible to connect to most databases using any one of these three techniques.

8. What is an advantage of using adCmdStoredProc instead of adCmdText?

A. Stored procedures support SQL, while this is not an option when using adCmdText.

B. Stored procedures are supported by more database vendors than is the use of adCmdText.

C. Using a stored procedure allows the command to be precompiled by the database and facilitates faster execution.

D. You don't need as many database access rights to use stored procedures as you would need when using adCmdText.

C. Faster database execution. You sometimes need more database access rights to create a stored procedure than you would need to access existing tables with SQL. Both methods usually use SQL. ISAM databases frequently don't support stored procedures.

9. Of the following options, which one best describes the ADO DataControl properties that always have to be set to access a data store?

   A. ConnectionString

   B. ConnectionString and RecordSource

   C. ConnectionString, RecordSource, and CommandType

   D. ConnectionString, RecordSource, CommandType, and Mode
   C. There are no usable defaults for ConnectionString, RecordSource, or CommandType. (Mode determines read/write permissions, but it is populated with a usable default.)

10. You have two forms in your project. On Form 1 you have two data controls, on Form 2 you have one more, and you have three data environments. You add a text box to Form 1 and select the list for the DataSource property. How many items are available from the list?

    A. None

    B. One

    C. Two

    D. Five
    D. Five. Data controls on one form are not directly accessible from other forms. This is one advantage of data environments, which are available across all forms in a project.

11. For most controls (TextBox, CheckBox, and so on) what properties, at a minimum, must be set to bind a field?

    A. DataSource

    B. DataSource and DataField

    C. DataSource, DataField, and DataMember

    D. DataSource, DataField, DataMember, and DataFormat
    B. DataSource and DataField. DataMember is required when using DECommands, but not when using the ADO Data Control. Setting DataFormat is optional.

12. When can you bind a DataControl to data sources?

    A. Runtime only

    B. Design time only

    C. Runtime or Design time
    C. Runtime or Design time. The ability to bind a control to a data source at runtime is a new feature in VB version 6. The RemoteData

control (which used the RDO object model) and the Data control (which used DAO) available in previous versions of VB did not support this functionality.

13. In general, which control property contains the value that is bound to the field?

   A. The Bound property
   B. The Data property
   C. The Value property
   D. The default property for the control
   D. Although the property that binds varies from control to control, it is usually the default property for that control (that is, the property that is used when you refer to the control without qualifying it with a property). The Value property binds for checkboxes, but not for most other controls. There is no Bound or Data property, though there is a Data grouping of properties for bound controls.

14. Which of the following data-bound controls can never update content to the database? (Choose all that apply.)

   A. Chart
   B. DataGrid
   C. DataList
   D. Label

E. MSHFlexGrid
F. TextBox
   A, E. Chart and MSHFlexGrid. Although the Label control cannot be directly edited by the end user, if changes are made to the control programmatically, these changes can be accepted into the database.

15. You have two combo boxes on a form—one ComboBox and one DataCombo. Of the following options, which properties are available for the DataCombo that are not available for the ComboBox?

   A. DataField and BoundColumn
   B. DataSource and DataField
   C. DataSource and RowSource
   D. RowSource and BoundColumn
   D. RowSource and BoundColumn. RowSource contains the data source where the picklist values are found, while BoundColumn defines the field referenced. Both DataSource and DataField are available for the ComboBox control.

16. Which of the following properties can be set for a single column in a DataGrid? (Choose all that apply.)

   A. AllowRowSizing
   B. Caption
   C. ColumnHeaders

D. DataField

E. Format Type
B, D, E. Caption, DataField, and FormatType. AllowRowSizing is set at the split level, and ColumnHeaders is set at the grid level.

17. Select the best definition of what functionality the DataRepeater allows.

A. It allows itself to be presented several times within the space defined by another control.

B. It allows multiple instances of another control to be displayed within the space defined by the DataRepeater control.

C. It allows the user to repeat the content available in a data source across a wide variety of different controls.

D. It allows the user to visually sort, format, and combine summary and detail database content.
B. It allows multiple iterations of another control. Answer D describes the MSHFlexGrid control; the other options refer to no existing control.

18. What objects are available from within the Data Environment Designer? (Choose all that apply.)

A. DataControl

B. DataEnvironment

C. DataView

D. DECommand

E. DEConnection

F. DEControl
B, D, E. A single DataEnvironment object exists in every Data Environment Designer. A DEConnection is created under a DataEnvironment, and a DECommand is created under a DEConnection.

19. Which of the following are not access permissions available from the Advanced tab of the Data Links Property dialog box? (Choose all that apply.)

A. Exclusive

B. None

C. Read

D. ReadWrite

E. Share Deny None

F. Share Deny Read

G. Share Deny ReadWrite

H. Share Deny Write

I. Share Exclusive

J. Write
A, B, G. Exclusive, None, and Share Deny ReadWrite. Most, but not all, of these options are available as shared or nonshared. The default is Share Deny None.

20. Which of the following are tabs that exist under the Command Properties dialog box? (Choose all that apply.)

A. Aggregates

B. DesignPassword

C. General

D. Parameters

E. Public

F. Relation

A, C, D, F. Aggregates, General, Parameters, and Relation. Public is a property of the DataEnvironment, while DesignPassword is a property of the DEConnection.

21. Which of the following have a text box as the default field type mapping in the Data Environment Designer? (Choose all that apply.)

A. Binary

B. Boolean

C. Caption

D. Integer

E. Variant

A, D, E. Binary, Integer, and Variant. Boolean defaults to a check box, while a Caption defaults to a Label control.

22. Which of the following are groupings offered in the Data Environment Designer? (Choose all that apply.)

A. Arrange by Commands

B. Arrange by Connections

C. Arrange by Data Environments

D. Arrange by Objects

B, D. Arrange by Connections and Arrange by Objects. The relationship between DECommands and

DEConnections is hierarchical, but not permanent. You can assign an existing command to a new Connection from the General tab of the Property dialog box.

23. Drag-and-drop operation is supported from the Data Environment Designer to which of the following? (Choose all that apply.)

A. Data Report

B. Data View Window

C. Form

D. Visual Data Manager

A, C. Data Report and Form. You can't drag from the Data Environment Designer to the Data View window, but you can drag the other way around.

24. Which of the following actions can you perform from the Database Designer accessible through Data View?

A. Edit the structure of an Access database.

B. Edit the structure of a SQL Server database.

C. Edit the data in an Access database

D. Edit the data in a SQL Server database.

B. Edit the structure of an SQL Server database. It is not possible to create database diagrams for Access databases, so it is not possible to view their structure. You cannot view the content in a table using the database designer (though the Visual Data Manager supports this).

25. What option do you choose from Query Builder to define which fields should link between two tables?

    A. The Foreign Key button

    B. The Relate Tables button

    C. The Set Table Joins button

    D. The Tables button
    C. The Set Table Joins button creates the equivalent of an SQL Join statement.

26. How do you get the SQL created by the Query Builder into an application?

    A. Use the Copy button to bring the SQL into the Clipboard, and then paste the SQL in the appropriate location in your application.

    B. Use the Create button to generate a form and all the needed bound controls to bind to the SQL statement.

    C. Use the Export button to automatically create a DataControl that uses the query as its record source.

    D. Use the SQL button to save the content to the SQL Designer.
    A. Use the Copy button. The Visual Data Manager is relatively loosely integrated with VB, so you need to use the Clipboard to use the content you've created.

27. Which DEConnection property determines if the record location is maintained on the server or on the user's machine?

    A. CurrentLocation

    B. CursorLocation

    C. IndexLocation

    D. PositionLocation
    B. CursorLocation. The properties PositionLocation, CurrentLocation, and IndexLocation do not exist.

28. What setting for the DECommand property LockType will automatically lock the row as soon as the user attempts to edit it?

    A. Optimistic

    B. Pessimistic

    C. Safe

    D. Unprotected
    B. Pessimistic. Safe and Unprotected are not valid property values, while Optimistic doesn't attempt to lock the row until the record is ready to be saved.

29. Which of the following record set types could reflect changes made by other users, assuming other users have created no new records since the record set was created? (Choose all that apply.)

    A. Dynamic

    B. ForwardOnly

    C. Keyset

D. Static

A, C. Dynamic and Keyset. Both Static and ForwardOnly are read-only. Note that a Keyset record set would not view records added after the record set was created, but a dynamic record set would.

30. Which of the following record set types usually provides the fastest performance?

    A. Dynamic

    B. Forward-only

    C. Keyset

    D. Static

       B. Forward-only. However, the forward-only record set type also provides the most limited functionality.

31. Which of the following terms refers to a DSN that is enabled for the users on a machine, and for all system services on that machine?

    A. Global DSN

    B. System DSN

    C. Universal DSN

    D. User DSN

       B. System DSN. Global and Universal DSNs do not exist, and system services cannot use a User DSN.

32. Where can you configure VB to add the command Data Form Wizard to the VB menu?

    A. Add-in Manager

    B. Components

    C. Options

    D. Properties

    E. References

       A. Add-in Manager allows the user to add components to the development environment, regardless of what project is currently loaded. References, Components, and Properties are all project-specific, while Options in general refers to the cosmetic appearance of the development environment.

33. Which of the following best describes what a Wizard Profile (RWP) allows you to do?

    A. Add new form layouts to the Data Form Wizard.

    B. Create many forms with similar appearance and function.

    C. Export all the properties of a form to a text file, to enable reuse in other Interdev components.

    D. Re-edit an existing form with the Data Form Wizard.

       B. Create many forms with similar appearance and function. The Data Form Wizard cannot be used to edit previously existing forms, even if they were created using the Data Form Wizard.

34. Which of the following Form Layouts does the Data Form Wizard offer? (Choose all that apply.)

    A. DataRepeater

B. Grid (Datasheet)

C. Master/Detail

D. Detail/Master

E. MS Chart

F. MS HFlexGrid

G. Pivot Table

H. Single Record
B, C, E, F, H. Grid (Datasheet), Master/Detail, MS Chart, MS HFlexGrid, and Single Record. These five layouts allow the user to select among the controls used to present the data, and in the case of Master/Detail, the relationship among multiple tables or queries displayed. (DataRepeater and Detail/Master are not options, and the Pivot Table is associated with Excel, not VB).

35. Which is **not** an advantage to using the ADO Data Control instead of the Data Environment Manager?

A. A navigation device is built into the Data Control.

B. Developing with the ADO Data Control is very similar to developing with the DAO and RDO Data Controls from previous versions of VB.

C. It is easy to use the same data control on multiple forms.

D. You need to set fewer properties with the ADO DataControl than you would with the Data Environment Manager.
C. Using the same data control on multiple forms. The biggest advantage of the Data Environment Manager is its use in distributing your data connections across your applications.

36. The ADO Data Control contains most of the properties also associated with what other two objects?

A. Data and ADODC

B. DataField and DataSource

C. DataView and Data Environment

D. DEConnection and DECommand
D. Most of the functionality available by using the ADO Data Control is also available by using the DEConnection and DECommand from the Data Environment window.

37. Without writing code, which of the following tasks can be performed by clicking the buttons on the ADO Data Connection control? (Choose all that apply.)

A. Create a new record.

B. Delete the current record.

C. Move to the first or last record.

D. Move to the previous or next record.
A, C, D. Create a new record, move to first or last, move to previous or next. Though the four buttons on the ADO Data Connection Control are most frequently used to navigate among existing content, the EOFAction property can be set to 2—adDoAddNew, which allows the user

to create a new record simply by scrolling to the end.

38. Which of the following Data Form Controls can be bound to a DataField in the Detail Section?

A. RptFunction

B. RptImage

C. RptLabel

D. RptPicture

E. RptTextBox
   E. Only the RptTextBox can be bound in the Detail section, though the RptFunction control can be bound in the report footer. There is no RptPicture control.

39. Which of the following can be created with the Data Report Designer?

A. A field that displays an image from a database

B. A graph that links to the data

C. A summary field that sums up the contents of a single field

D. A summary field that sums up the contents of two fields
   C. A summary field that sums up the contents of a single field. It is not possible to use the Data Report designer to support graphs, pictures, or complex formulas. (One option you have for formulas, though, is to perform the calculations in the query, and then use the Data Report Designer to present the simple results.)

40. Into which areas on a Data Form can you legally drag fields from a Data Environment Designer?

A. Page Header—gray bar

B. Page Header—body

C. Detail—gray bar

D. Detail—body

E. Report Footer —gray bar

F. Report Footer—body
   C. Detail—body. You can only drag a field into the detail body. You can, however, drag an entire table into the gray bar above the Detail section (this will automatically create controls for all the fields contained.)

Answers to Chapter 5 Self Test

1. Which of the following services represents the application's user interface?

A. User services

B. Business services

C. Middle-tier services

D. Data services
   A. User services are identified with the user interface. It can be the actual executable file or a component (such as an ActiveX control).

2. Which stage of design involves identifying an application's requirements?

A. Conceptual

B. Logical

C. Physical

D. Deployment
A. Conceptual design involves identifying the requirements of an application.

3. Which stage of design determines how components are distributed across a network?

A. Conceptual

B. Logical

C. Physical

D. Deployment
D. Deployment is the stage where it is determined how components are distributed across a network.

4. Why is it important to change the name of a class to a name that isn't in use?

A. So that when the class calls on itself, it doesn't fall into an endless loop.

B. If the name is already in use, the class module won't be able to initiate itself.

C. If the name is already in use, controller code won't be able to instantiate objects.

D. It doesn't matter if the name is already in use.
C. It is important that the Name property be original and not in use for a class module. This is because controller code uses the name to instantiate a copy of the class as an object.

5. Validation is a necessary part of designing an application. Which of the following best describes what validation is in the design process?

A. Validation is a comparison of deployment to the requirements of the logical design.

B. Validation is a comparison of the physical design to the requirements of deployment.

C. Validation is a comparison of logical design to the requirements in the original conceptual view.

D. Validation is the concept of verifying that all variables meet the requirements of the logical design.
C. Validation of the logical design requires a comparison of logical design to the requirements in the original conceptual view.

6. In a class module, how many copies of the module's data can exist at any one time?

A. One

B. Two

C. A copy for each object created

D. A copy for each instance of a standard module
C. In a class module, one copy of the module's data is created for each instance of the class. This means there is a copy of the data for each object created from the class module.

7. How long is the lifetime of data in a standard module?

A. The life of the object

B. The life of the program

C. The life of the programmer

D. None of the above
   B. A standard module's data exists for the life of the program.

8. What is the syntax used to destroy an object?

   A. Set Object = Nothing

   B. Get Object = Nothing

   C. Let Object = Nothing

   D. Set Object = 0
      A. The syntax used to destroy an object is Set Object = Nothing.

9. You use the following code in your application. When you test it, it appears that nothing happens in the current record in the record set (which you've called rs). Why?

```
Sub cmdDelete_Click()
rs.Delete
End Sub
```

   A. The method of the record set should read rs.Del.

   B. There should be a MoveNext method executed after the Delete method.

   C. There should be a Next method executed after the Delete method.

   D. There is no reason why it shouldn't move to the next record.
      B. To have the next record become the current record after a deletion, you

must execute the MoveNext method after the Delete method has been used.

10. Julie inputs a sale into an application. The application then adds the necessary taxes, checks the customer's credit rating, and determines whether the sale can be added to the customer's account. Which tier of the services model do the rules to this procedure apply to?

    A. User services

    B. Business services

    C. Data services

    D. Graduated services
       B. Business services applies business rules (such as adding taxes or checking a customer's credit limit) to tasks that the program performs.

11. Which design stage takes business objects and services and maps them to software components?

    A. Conceptual

    B. Logical

    C. Physical

    D. Deployment
       C. Physical design maps business objects and services to software components.

12. How is a class module added to a VB project?

    A. Select Format | Add Class Module.

    B. Select Project | Add Class Module.

C. Select Project | Add Class Module, then choose Class Module from the dialog box that appears.

D. Select Tools | Add Class Module, then choose Class Module from the dialog box that appears.

C. To add a class module to a B project, select Project | Add Class Module. When the dialog box appears, choose Class Module.

13. In a standard module, how many copies of the module's data is there at any given time?

A. One

B. Two

C. A copy for each object created

D. A copy for each instance of a class module

A. In a standard module, there is one copy of the module's data at any given time.

14. In a class module, what is the lifetime of the module's data?

A. The life of the object

B. The life of the program

C. The life of the programmer

D. None of the above

A. A class module's data exists for the life of the object created. A copy of the data is created when the object is created, and then destroyed when the object is destroyed.

15. What is wrong with the following code?

```
Sub cmdEdit_Click
rs.Update
rs("strName")=txtName.Text
rs.Edit
End Sub
```

A. The property of txtName should be Caption.

B. The Edit method has to be implemented as part of an If...Then statement.

C. The Edit method must come after the Update method.

D. The Update method must come after the Edit method.

D. The Update method must be used after the Edit method. If it isn't used in this order, a runtime error will occur.

16. You want to add code to move three records ahead in the record set. Which of the following will do this?

A. Recordset.Move -3

B. Recordset.Move +3

C. Recordset.Move 3

D. Recordset.Move =3

B. To move three records ahead in the record set, use the syntax: Recordset.Move +3

17. You want to add a new record to the record set. Which of the following examples of code would add a record to a record set named rs?

A. rs.AddNew

B. rs.New

C. rs.Add

D. rs.New +1

A. The correct way to add a new record to the record set called rs is rs.AddNew

18. Both the EOF and BOF of a record set are set to True. How many records are there in the record set?

A. One

B. Two

C. Unknown

D. None

D. If both the EOF and BOF are set to True, then there are no records in the record set.

19. Which of the following would you set to create a Data Source class module?

A. DataSourceBehavior

B. DataBindingBehavior

C. vbSimpleBound

D. Both DataSourceBehavior and DataBindingBehavior

A. To create a Data Source class module, you would change the DataSourceBehavior to vbDataSource.

20. When you create a standard class module, what two events does the Class object initially have? (Choose all that apply.)

A. Initialize

B. Terminate

C. GetDataMember

D. Load

A, B. When you create a standard class module, it has two events, Initialize and Terminate.

21. What actually binds a data source to a data consumer?

A. Class module

B. DataBinding property of class module

C. Binding Collection

D. DataBondage argument

C. To bind a data source to a data consumer, you use the Binding Collection.

22. You want to cause an event to run programmatically. Which keyword will you use to make this happen?

A. CallEvent

B. RaiseEvent

C. RunEvent

D. Event

B. To cause an event to run, you use the RaiseEvent keyword.

23. Which of the following always uses COM creation services?

A. Property Let

B. Property Get

C. Dim

D. CreateObject

D. CreateObject always uses COM object creation services. It uses COM creation services regardless of whether objects created are externally provided or part of your project.

24. When can data be bound to a control or consumer, when using the Binding Collection and a class module?

    A. Runtime

    B. Design time

    C. Anytime

    D. Never

    C. Using the Binding Collection and class modules, data can be bound to a control or consumer at any time.

25. Which of the following is used to set the source of the data to be used for a class module?

    A. Initialize

    B. Terminate

    C. Load

    D. GetDataMember

    D. GetDataMember is used to set the source of the data for a class. The record set to be used is specified here.

26. The record set can refer to how many records at one time as the current record?

    A. One

    B. Two

    C. Three

    D. Unlimited

    A. The record set can only refer to one record as the current record at one time.

27. A class module can be used as a data source for which of the following types of data? (Choose all that apply.)

    A. ADO (ActiveX Data Objects)

    B. OLE (Object Linking and Embedding) providers

    C. ODBC (Open Database Connectivity)

    D. None of the above

    A, B, C. A class module can be used as a data source for any type of data.

28. When you modify the DataBindingBehavior of a class module, what options are available to you? (Choose all that apply.)

    A. vbDataSource

    B. vbNone

    C. vbSimpleBound

    D. vbComplexBound

    B, C, D. The DataBindingBehavior of a class module has three options: vbNone, vbSimpleBound, and vbComplexBound.

29. When you modify the DataSourceBehavior of a class module, what new event will be added to the Class object?

    A. GetData

    B. DataMember

    C. GetDataMember

    D. Load

    C. When the DataSourceBehavior is set to vbDataSource, the GetDataMember event is added to the Class object.

30. Which of the following would you set to create a data consumer class module?

    A. DataSourceBehavior

    B. DataBindingBehavior

    C. VbDataSource

    D. Both DataSourceBehavior and DataBindingBehavior
    B. To create a data consumer class module, you would change the DataBindingBehavior to either vbSimpleBound or vbComplexBound.

Answers to Chapter 6 Self Test

1. Which of the following project types *cannot* act as an OLE server?

    A. ActiveX DLL

    B. ActiveX EXE

    C. Standard EXE

    D. ActiveX control
    C. Only the ActiveX project types can run as OLE servers.

2. Both Application A and B use version 1.1 of FOO.DLL (an ActiveX component). An upgrade to Applications B is installed that upgrades FOO.DLL to version 1.2. Which of the following is true?

    A. Both Applications A and B work normally

    B. Application B works, but Application A throws a protection fault whenever the methods of FOO are called

    C. Neither Application A nor Application B work

    D. All of the functionality in A and B work, but Application A throws a protection fault whenever it references properties or methods where the interface has changed
    A. Version compatibility ensures that all of the interfaces supported in the previous version of the component are still implemented with at least the functionality they had previously. This is not to say that the component does not execute these routines differently, but only that the way you call the routines is consistent.

3. Which of the following is not a benefit of early binding?

    A. The variable used can reference any type of object

    B. In the development environment, you can use the VB's IntelliSense technology to automatically see a list of properties and methods of the object

    C. Object references are resolved more quickly

    D. The New keyword can be used to define the object variable and assign a reference to a new object in the same statement

    E. You can trap events triggered by the object
    A. Late binding is used to provide the flexibility of accessing different types of objects with the same reference.

Early bound variables can only be used to point to objects of a specific predefined type.

4. What is the proper command-1 line syntax to register an ActiveX component called FOO.DLL manually?

A. Register /U FOO.DLL

B. REGSVR32 FOO.DLL

C. REGSVR FOO.DLL

D. REGSVR32 /U FOO.DLL

E. RunDll FOO.DLL
   B. The REGSVR32 utility is used to register 32-bit In-Process servers. To unregister the same component you would use option D. REGSVR32 /U FOO.DLL. *Note:* The /U can appear before or after the name of the DLL in the command line.

5. If a component does not provide a type library it cannot

A. be used with VB.

B. be referenced using the New keyword.

C. expose a property with the String type.

D. be added to the project in the References dialog box.

E. Both B and D.

F. Both B and C.
   E. A type library is required if you want to use the New keyword to enable the early binding methods of accessing the interface of an object or to use the References dialog box to add a reference to the component.

6. When using the New keyword to declare an object variable, when is the object created?

A. Immediately, when the variable is declared

B. When the object is first referenced

C. When the Object reference is created using the Set keyword

D. It is unpredictable
   B. Using the New keyword in the declaration statement does not create the object immediately, but instead sets it up to be created the first time one of its properties or methods is accessed.

7. In what types of files can you find type libraries?

A. DLL and EXE only

B. COM, EXE, and DLL

C. OCX, TLB, and OLB

D. OCX, EXE, DLL, TLB, and OLB

E. DLL and OCX only
   D. OCX, EXE, and DLL files have type libraries compiled into them. TLB and OLB files are files external to the component that contain only the type library information.

8. Which of the following declarations will allow VB to use the faster early binding method when accessing properties and methods?

A. Dim X as New control

B. Dim X as New Form

C. Dim X as Object

D. Dim X as New stdFont
   D. The New keyword allows the VB to bind X to the stdFont object using early binding. Both A and B are invalid syntax because the Form and Control object cannot be early bound. Use the specific type of object if you want to use early binding in calls like these, for example, Dim X as New CheckBox, or Dim X as New MyForm1.

9. Which of the following creates a new instance of an Excel Application object?

   A. CreateObject("Excel.Application")

   B. CreateObject("Excel","Application")

   C. GetObject("Excel.Application")

   D. GetObject("","Excel.Application")

   E. Both A and D

   F. None of the above
      E. A is the correct syntax for using the CreateObject method, and specifying an empty string as the AppName parameter of the GetObject function as shown in answer D forces GetObject to act like CreateObject.

10. What must be done to allow events to be passed to a VB component that provides a type library?

    A. This cannot be done with components with type libraries

    B. Declare the variable in the Declarations section using the WithEvents keyword

    C. Declare the variable in the procedure definition using the WithEvents keyword

    D. Check the Raise Events checkbox in the References dialog box
       B. To allow a component to raise events in the client, a module-level object reference must be declared using the WithEvents keyword.

11. Which of the following can you *not* accomplish in the Object Browser dialog box?

    A. Determine the proper syntax for calling a method of an object

    B. Look up the constants used with a particular property of an object

    C. Register component objects

    D. Search for a member name to make sure there are no ambiguous references in your project
       C. The Object Browser dialog box can do a lot of things to help the developer understand how to use a component, but cannot perform any actions, such as registration, on the components themselves.

12. What is the preferred method for clearing up ambiguous references?

    A. Set the priority of the components so the type library of the ambiguous reference is higher on the list

    B. Compile a version-compatible revision of the component with the member property or method renamed

C. Use the type library or component name in the reference

D. Explicitly reference the complete path to the component file
   C. Explicitly using the type library name before the object type like MyComp.MyObjectType is the preferred method for clearing up ambiguous references.

13. Which of the following sets the object variable O to a dependent object rather than an externally creatable object?

    A.
```
Set O = AppObject.AddItem("KeyName")
```
    B.
```
Set O = CreateObject("Excel.Application")
```
    C.
```
Set O = GetObject(,"MyApp.AppObject")
```
    D.
```
Set O = GetObject("","MyApp.AppObject")
```
    A. Dependent variables can only be created through another object that is externally creatable, in this example the AppObject.

14. Which of the following commands should be used to manually register the component COMP.EXE?

    A. COMP.EXE

    B. REGSVR COMP.EXE

    C. REGSVR32 COMP.EXE

    D. REGSVR32 COMP.EXE /U
       A. ActiveX EXE servers register themselves when their EXE file is run.

15. When registering an ActiveX DLL, what is responsible for actually registering the component?

    A. The REGSVR32.EXE utility

    B. The component itself

    C. The client application

    D. The developer using Regedit
       B. To be COM compliant a component has to expose interfaces that, when called, cause the component to register itself in the Windows Registry. The REGSVR32 utility simply calls that interface.

16. How does a client application internally refer to COM components that are referenced using early binding?

    A. Using the ComponentName.ClassName

    B. Using a globally unique identifier (GUID)

    C. Using the path to the component's DLL or EXE file
       B. A ClassID, which is represented as a GUID, is used to retain a reference to the component. The AppID (ComponentName.ClassName) is used for late bound objects that are created using CreateObject or GetObject to look up the ClassID of the Component.

17. Where is the path to a component's DLL or EXE file stored?

    A. In the VB FRM file

    B. In the VB VBP file

C. In the Registry

D. Inside the component itself

E. In the VB VBG file

C. The Registry stores the actual path to the component. The application uses the ClassId of the component to look up this entry in the registry to find the component.

18. When is an object destroyed?

A. When the reference count is set to 0

B. When a variable referencing it is set to Nothing

C. When a variable referencing it goes out of scope

D. When the DestroyObject method is applied to it

E. When you call the object's Terminate Event

A. Although B and C technically could be correct if nothing else is referencing the object, it is only when the last variable referencing it is set to Nothing, or when the reference count is set to 0, that the object actually is destroyed and the resources allocated to it are returned to the operating system.

19. Which of the following is *not* an advantage of using COM components?

A. Versioning

B. Execution speed

C. Encapsulation

D. Reusability

E. Interoperability

B. While execution speed may be improved by compiling parts of an application in a component, usually the overhead involved with communicating actually makes the component model a little more bulky, and thus slower.

20. Application A contains ActiveX control B. ActiveX control B in turn, uses the functionality provided by ActiveX control C. What roles do each of these components play?

A. A = Server, B = Client, C = Client

B. A = Client, B = Client, C = Server

C. A = Client, B = Server to A and Client to C, C = Server

D. A = Server, B = Client to A and Server to C, C = Client

D. A = Server, B = Client to A and Server to C, C = Client. Remember, a client contains or uses the functionality of a server.

21. How do you add an ActiveX DLL type code component to a project?

A. The Components dialog box

B. The References dialog box

C. Declare an object reference to it

D. Use the CreateObject function

B. The References dialog box is used to add a reference to the type library of ActiveX code components. The Components dialog box is only used for adding references to ActiveX controls.

Answers to Chapter 7 Self Test

1. Which of the following situations is not a good fit for an out-of-process component?

   A. The component will be run on a separate machine from the client using DCOM.

   B. The component needs to run very quickly and exchanges a lot of data with the client.

   C. The client needs to be able to call the component and not have to halt execution until the component is finished processing the tasks.

   D. The component must also act as a stand alone application.

   E. The component must work in both 32- and 16-bit clients.
   B. The component needs to run very quickly and exchanges a lot of data with the client. In-process servers are much better suited for applications where speed is critical.

2. What types of projects cannot be compiled to run as out-of-process components?

   A. ActiveX documents

   B. ActiveX code components

   C. ActiveX controls

   D. None of the above
   C. ActiveX controls are compiled as OCX files, which always run in-process.

3. Which of the following instancing options is not available to ActiveX DLL components?

   A. Private

   B. PublicNotCreatable

   C. GlobalSingleUse

   D. MultiUse

   E. GlobalMultiUse
   C. GlobalSingleUse instancing is only available in out-of-process ActiveX EXE projects.

4. You are designing component A, which is used by component B. What should happen if an error occurs in component B?

   A. Components A and B should not trap the error, allowing it to propagate to the client for handling there.

   B. Component A should try to handle the error and, if it can't, pass it up to component B, which will try to handle the error. If it also can't deal with the error, it will translate the error message in terms of itself and pass it up to the client.

   C. Component B should in no situation pass an error up to component A.
   B. Component A should try to handle the error. The error should always be handled as close as possible to the source. When it can't be handled, it should only be passed up one level. If your component is to exhibit good encapsulation, it should effectively hide the fact that it uses subcomponents from the client application.

5. A class has its instancing property set to MultiUse and the client requests two instances of the object provided by the class. Which of the following is true?

   A. MultiUse instancing does not allow a second instance to be created from the same component so an error is generated.

   B. Two instances of the component are created, one to handle each object instance.

   C. A single instance of the component creates both objects for the client.
   C. A single instance of the component creates both objects for the client. MultiUse Instancing allows a single component to create as many instances of that class as are requested by the client application without the need for another instance of the component. SingleUse instancing requires a separate component for each instance of the objects created by the class.

6. Which instancing option is used to create dependent objects?

   A. Multiuse

   B. PublicNotCreatable

   C. GlobalSingleUse

   D. Private
   B. PublicNotCreatable is used to create dependent objects because they allow objects to be used outside of the component, but they must be created within the application.

7. Which of the following versioning options can be used to make sure a component is compatible with earlier versions of the same component?

   A. Project compatibility

   B. No compatibility

   C. Version compatibility

   D. Binary compatibility

   E. All of the above
   D. Binary compatibility. Although project compatibility can preserve compatibility for debugging purposes, it is not sufficient to ensure backward compatibility with previous versions of the component. Only binary compatibility ensures that your component is version compatible with previously released versions of your component.

8. How can you set the description text for a member of a class to be shown in the Object Browser dialog box?

   A. Create a Description property in each class you want to document.

   B. Set the Description field in the Project Properties dialog box.

   C. Set the Description field in the Procedure Attributes dialog box.

   D. Add a specially formatted comment to the top of each method or property.
   B. Set the Description field in the Project Properties dialog box. Setting this property adds the description into the type library that is compiled into the component.

9. Which of the following components would need to use marshalling to talk to the client application?

   A. ActiveX controls

   B. ActiveX document DLLs

   C. ActiveX EXE code components
   C. ActiveX EXE code components. Out-of-process components like ActiveX EXE code components and ActiveX EXE documents use cross-process marshalling to talk to one another because they each run in their own process space.

10. Which of the following is the best option for a component that will probably crash frequently?

   A. ActiveX EXE code component

   B. ActiveX DLL code component

   C. ActiveX document

   D. ActiveX server
   A. By running in a separate process, an ActiveX EXE insulates the client from GPF-type errors in the component.

11. Which of the following structures is a common cause of circular object references?

   A. Property containing a collection of another type of object in the component

   B. A HasChildren property

   C. A Parent property

   D. Too Many Root Nodes
   D. Too Many Root Nodes. The Parent property can cause circular reference problems if you are not especially careful when tearing down the object structure.

12. When debugging an out-of-process component, why must you remember to compile the component after each change?

   A. Because the test project is using the compiled version of the component and must be updated

   B. To update the interface in the Registry so the client can access the new functionality of the component

   C. Both A and B
   B. To update the interface in the Registry so the client can access the new functionality of the component. The test project does not use the compiled component, but rather the one in memory in the debug environment in the other instance of VB. While the component is running in Debug mode, the Registry entry for it is temporarily changed to reference the component that is in Debug mode.

13. When creating a test project to debug an ActiveX EXE project, you don't see a listing in the References dialog box for the component. What could be the problem? (Choose all that apply.)

A. The component is not in Run mode.

B. The component does not expose any publicly creatable classes.

C. The component needs to be registered using REGSVR32.

D. All of the above.
   A, B. The component must be in Run mode and expose externally creatable objects to show up in the References dialog box.

14. Which of the following instancing methods is a good choice for a Root object that is designed to be externally creatable?

   A. Public Not Creatable

   B. Private

   C. MultiUse
      C. MultiUse. Of the options listed, only MultiUse can be used to create an object that is externally creatable. Normally root objects should be instanced as externally creatable so that they can be accessed from the client application.

15. Which of the following cannot host ActiveX documents?

   A. Internet Explorer

   B. Microsoft Word

   C. Microsoft Binder

   D. VB forms
      D. ActiveX documents cannot be used in VB forms; the only way to use an ActiveX document in VB is to insert it inside the Internet Explorer Web Browser ActiveX control.

16. Which of the following instancing options allows you to call the properties and methods of an object without first creating an instance of that object? (Choose all that apply.)

   A. Private

   B. GlobalMultiUse

   C. SingleUse

   D. GlobalSingleUse
      B, D. GlobalMultiUse and GlobalSingleUse are the two instancing options designed to allow you to refer to the properties and methods of an object without first creating an instance of that object.

17. What will happen when the following statement executes on the object named MyObject?

```
Dim V as variant
V = MyObject
```

   A. V will be assigned to the value of the default property if one has been defined.

   B. V will now contain an object reference to an instance of MyObject.

   C. V will be set to a long that is a handle to an instance of MyObject.
      A. V will be assigned to the value of the default property if one has been defined. Setting the default value allows you to use coding shortcuts like this to get commonly used property values. The default property is also known as the Value Property.

18. What is the term that describes methods that execute using synchronous processing?

    A. Call-backs

    B. Blocking

    C. External component execution

    D. MultiUse instancing
    B. Blocking is a term used to describe the behavior of a method that makes the client wait until it is done processing before continuing with the next line of code.

Answers to Chapter 8 Self Test

1. What does ADO stand for?

   A. ActiveX Directory Objects

   B. ActiveX Data Objects

   C. Active Data Objects

   D. Advanced Data Objects
   B. ActiveX Data Objects is the correct name for this technology.

2. What is the underlying database interface layer used by ADO?

   A. COM

   B. DCOM

   C. COM+

   D. OLE DB
   D. OLE DB is the database interface layer. The other options listed are system-level architecture models.

3. ADO is only available when programming in VB.

   A. True

   B. False
   B. False. ADO is available for use in any 32-bit Windows development environment that supports COM and Automation.

4. ADO provides all of the functionality of RDO.

   A. True

   B. False
   B. False. ADO does *not* provide the capability to modify ODBC DSN entries.

5. Which library contains the ADO Connection object?

   A. ADODB.DLL

   B. MSDASQL.DLL

   C. ADOR.DLL

   D. SQLOLEDB.DLL
   A. ADODB is the complete ADO object library that contains the Connection object. The ADOR library contains only the Recordset object.

6. What process-threading model does the Windows Registry list for ADO?

   A. Single-threaded

   B. Apartment-threaded

   C. Free-threaded

   D. Multi-threaded

B. Although ADO objects are free-threaded, they are listed as apartment-threaded to ensure thread safety in case the OLE DB provider or ODBC driver does not support free-threaded execution.

7. Which ADO object(s) contain an Errors collection?

   A. Connection and Command objects

   B. Command and Recordset objects

   C. Recordset object only

   D. Connection object only
   D. Only the Connection object contains an Errors collection. This collection holds errors from the underlying OLE DB layers.

8. All ADO errors create objects in the Errors collection.

   A. True

   B. False
   B. False. ADO object errors will trigger the application runtime error-handling mechanism and these errors do not create objects in the Errors collection of a Connection object. Only OLE DB errors are placed in the Errors collection.

9. What is the correct syntax to retrieve the error number from the first Error object in the Errors collection for a Connection object named cnn?

   A. cnn.Errors(1).Number

   B. cnn.Errors(0).Num

   C. cnn.Errors(1).Num

   D. cnn.Errors(0).Number
   D. The Errors collection is a zero-based collection.

10. If you do not specify an OLE DB provider, what is the default OLE DB provider that ADO will use?

    A. Microsoft OLE DB Provider for SQL Server

    B. Microsoft OLE DB Provider for ODBC

    C. Microsoft OLE DB Provider for Jet

    D. Microsoft OLE DB Provider for Oracle
    B. By default, ADO will attempt to connect using the ODBC provider.

11. If the Provider property has not been set elsewhere, which of the following is *not* a valid ConnectionString property?

    A. "Provider=MSDASQL; Server=my_sql_server;DBQ=pubs"

    B. "DSN=pubs;UID=sa;"

    C. "Provider=SQLOLEDB;Data Source=my_sql_server;User ID = sa"

    D. "Server=my_sql_server;DBQ=pubs; User ID=sa"
    D. Because the provider has not been specified, this connection would attempt to use the ODBC provider and User ID is not a valid argument for that provider.

12. What is the correct syntax to set a Connection object named cnn to use the client-side cursor library?

A. cnn.CursorLocation = adUseClient

B. cnn.CursorType = adUseClient

C. cnn.CursorLocation = adUseClientCursor

D. cnn.CursorType = adUseClientCursor
   A. The CursorLocation property must be set to adUseClient for a Connection object to use the client-side cursor library.

13. When opening a Jet database with the OLE DB provider for Jet, what is the default database access mode?

    A. Exclusive Read/Write

    B. Shared Read/Write

    C. Shared Read-only

    D. Exclusive Read-only
       B. By default, the Jet provider will open databases in shared read/write mode. For a read-only connection, you must set the Mode property of the Connection object to adModeRead.

14. What value will the following code use for the User ID when it opens the connection?

```
Dim cnn as New ADODB.Connection

cnn.Provider = "SQLOLEDB"
cnn.Properties("User ID") = "Todd"
cnn.ConnectionString = "Data Source=
  my_sql_server;User ID=Aaron"
cnn.Open , "Shane"
```

    A. Todd

    B. Aaron

    C. Shane
       C. Any argument supplied to the Open method will override properties that were previously set.

15. Which property can you check to find out the status of an asynchronous connection operation?

    A. Recordset State

    B. Command State

    C. Connection State

    D. Provider
       C. While all of these objects can perform asynchronous operations, only the Connection object can connect to a data source asynchronously.

16. Which object should you use to represent a stored procedure that uses input and output parameters?

    A. ADO Command object

    B. ADO Recordset object

    C. ADO Connection object

    D. DAO QueryDef object
       A. Only the ADO Command object includes support for input and output parameters.

17. What type of cursor is used for record sets created by the Execute method of a Connection object?

A. Static and forward-only cursor type

B. Keyset-driven cursor type

C. Static cursor type

D. Any cursor type is possible.
   A. All record sets created by the Connection Execute method use static and forward-only cursors. If you need to open a different type of cursor, you should use the Recordset Open method.

18. For Recordset and Command objects, what property represents the current data source Connection?

   A. ConnectionString property

   B. Source property

   C. ActiveSource property

   D. ActiveConnection property
      D. The ActiveConnection property represents the link to the current data source for Recordset and Command objects. Setting this property to Nothing will disassociate the Recordset or Command with the connection.

19. What method can be used to automatically refresh the Parameters collection for a Command object named cmd?

   A. cmd.Parameters.Requery

   B. cmd.Parameters.Rebuild

   C. cmd.Parameters.Refresh

   D. cmd.Parameters.Resync
      C. The Refresh method will query the database to automatically rebuild the Parameters collection.

20. What cursor type must you use when using the client-side cursor library?

   A. adOpenForwardOnly

   B. adOpenDynamic

   C. adOpenKeyset

   D. adOpenStatic
      D. The client-side cursor library requires that all record sets use static cursors.

21. You can change the cursor type of a record set after you have opened the record set.

   A. True

   B. False
      B. False. The record set must be closed in order to modify the CursorType property.

22. If the object fld refers to a Field object in a client-side record set named rst, what is the syntax to build an index on that field?

   A. fld.Optimize = True

   B. fld.Properties("Optimize") = True

   C. rst.Optimize (fld)

   D. fld.Optimize = False
      B. To create a local index on the field, you must set the Optimize property to True. The Optimize property is a dynamic property only available to fields within client-side record sets; because it is a dynamic property, you can only access it through the Properties collection.

23. Which of the following would be an invalid Criteria argument for the Recordset Find method?

A. "au_lname like 'Jer*'"

B. "au_id = 0"

C. "au_id = 0 OR au_id > 100"

D. "au_fname ='Ann-Cathrin'"
C. The Find method does not support multiple search criteria or multiple target values.

24. What is the correct syntax to temporarily sort a record set named rst by the field named au_lname?

    A. rst.Sort (au_lname)

    B. rst.Fields("au_lname").Sorted = true

    C. rst.Sort ("au_lname")

    D. rst.Sort = "au_lname"
    D. To sort a record set by a field, you must set the Recordset Sort property equal to the name of the field to be sorted.

25. After performing an UpdateBatch command on a record set named rst, what filter would you apply to determine if any of the records were *not* updated to do record conflicts?

    A. rst.Filter = adFilterPendingRecords

    B. rst.Filter = adFilterAffectedRecords

    C. rst.Filter = adFilterConflictingRecords

    D. rst.Filter = adFilterFetchedRecords
    C. The adFilterConflictingRecords filter will show only the records that failed to be updated on the server after an UpdateBatch command.

26. Before you can modify a field value in a record set, you are required to call the Edit method to place the record into Edit mode.

    A. True

    B. False
    B. False. Unlike previous data access methods, you do not need to explicitly call an Edit method to make a record available for modification. In fact, ADO record sets do not even provide an Edit method.

27. If you have made changes to a record and then reposition the record set, the Update method will be called automatically.

    A. True

    B. False
    A. True. The record set will automatically call the Update method to save any pending changes when the record set is repositioned or closed.

28. If you are operating in Batch Update mode and you want to cancel the current batch of changes, which method should you invoke?

    A. BatchCancel

    B. Cancel

    C. UndoBatch

    D. CancelBatch
    D. The CancelBatch method is the correct method to call to cancel the current batch of changes. The Cancel method is only used to cancel individual record updates.

29. When using the AddNew method to create a new record, you can also specify the initial values for one or more of the fields.

    A. True

    B. False

    A. True. When you use the AddNew method, you can optionally include two variant arrays that contain the field names and initial values to be set for the record.

30. What will happen if you attempt to close a Connection object while there is a transaction in progress?

    A. The transaction will automatically be committed

    B. The transaction will automatically be rolled back

    C. A runtime error will be generated

    D. The Connection object will remain open until the transaction is finished

    C. Closing a connection with a transaction in progress will generate an error. If the Connection object falls out of scope while a transaction is in progress, the transaction is rolled back and no error is generated.

31. When calling the Recordset Save method, you should always include the name of the file used to store the record set.

    A. True

    B. False

    B. False. The filename should only be included on the first call to the Save

method. On subsequent calls, you should only include the filename if it has changed or if the original file no longer exists.

32. What cursor library must be used if you want to fabricate a record set without a data source?

    A. Client-side cursor library

    B. Server-side cursor library

    C. Client-side or server-side cursor library

    A. Record set fabrication is only supported by the client-side cursor library.

33. What is contained in the OriginalValue property of a field?

    A. The value initially retrieved from the database for that field

    B. The value for that field that is currently stored in the database

    C. The value which that field contained when the record was first created

    D. The default value for that field specified in the database

    A. The OriginalValue property contains the field value that was initially retrieved from the database.

34. What is contained in the UnderlyingValue property of a field?

    A. The value initially retrieved from the database for that field

    B. The value for that field that is currently stored in the database

C. The value the field contained when the record was first created

D. The default value for that field specified in the database
B. The UnderlyingValue property contains the value that is currently stored in the database for that field.

35. Which method will update the UnderlyingValue property for all fields in a record set?

A. Requery method

B. Refresh method

C. Resync method

D. Recreate method
C. The Resync method will only update values for the records that are currently visible in the record set. The Requery method, on the other hand, will re-execute the source command and the resulting record set may not include the same set of records due to record additions and deletions.

36. If a record set contains multiple return sets, what method can be used to retrieve the next set of records?

A. NextSet

B. NextRecordset

C. MoveNextSet

D. MoveRecordset
B. The NextRecordset method will return a new record set object reference to the next result set contained in the current record set. The other methods listed are not valid Recordset methods.

37. What provider must be used, along with the client-side cursor library, to gain access to the Shape command language to create hierarchical record sets?

A. SQLOLEDB

B. MSPersist

C. MSDataShape

D. Any OLE DB provider can be used
C. You must use the MSDataShape provider to create hierarchical record sets based on the Shape command language. When opening a connection with the MSDataShape provider, the original data source provider is specified through the Shape Provider argument of the ConnectionString.

38. When working with hierarchical record sets, what is the data type for fields that contain a child record set?

A. adChapter

B. adRecordset

C. adChildRecordset

D. adUnknown
A. The fields that contain child record sets are indicated by the adChapter data type. By default, these fields are named chapter, and the Value property of these fields will return a new Recordset object reference.

39. Which method to populate the Parameters collection of a Command object will execute faster?

A. Use the Parameters Refresh method.

B. Manually create the parameter definitions.

C. Use the Execute method.

D. Use the Parameters Rebuild method.
   B. Although it requires much more coding, your program may execute much faster if you manually create the parameter definitions. The Refresh method may require several time-consuming queries of the system catalog to get the complete parameter specifications.

40. What command type should you always specify for commands that do not return any records?

A. adCmdStoredProc

B. adCmdUnknown

C. adCmdText

D. adExecuteNoRecords
   D. The adExecuteNoRecords constant is normally used in conjunction with the adCmdText or adCmdStoredProc command types. This will optimize the command execution because the provider is aware that no records should be returned, and the provider does not need to keep listening for returned records.

Answers to Chapter 9 Self Test

1. Which of the following are valid ways to refer in code to a UserControl named UserControl1?

A. UserControl

B. Me

C. UserControl1

D. None of the above
   A. When referring to a UserControl in your code, you must use the word UserControl rather than its name. The Me keyword doesn't work either.

2. Which of the following are valid ways of creating an ActiveX control? (Choose all that apply.)

A. Select New Project from the File menu, and then choose ActiveX Control.

B. Change the project type of a current project to ActiveX control in Project Properties.

C. Click the ActiveX Control button from the VB toolbar.

D. Select Components from the Project menu, then select ActiveX Control.

E. Select Add User Document from the Project menu, and select an ActiveX Control.
   A, B. You can create an ActiveX control by selecting New Project from the File menu, then choosing ActiveX Control. You can also change the Project Type of the current project to ActiveX Control in Project Properties to create an ActiveX control.

3. You have decided to use the ActiveX Control Interface Wizard to create a user interface for your ActiveX control. When you try to use this wizard, it refuses to create the interface. Why?

A. You must start with an empty UserControl before starting the wizard.

B. You must have a form added to your project before starting the wizard.

C. The wizard isn't used to create user interfaces.

D. The project must be saved before starting the wizard.
   C. The ActiveX Control Interface Wizard isn't used to create user interfaces. You must add the elements of a user interface to a UserControl before starting the wizard.

4. What are ActiveX control projects compiled as?

A. DLL files

B. EXE files

C. CTL files

D. OCX files
   D. ActiveX control projects are compiled into OCX files.

5. What property will determine the icon representing an ActiveX control, which will appear in the developer's VB Toolbox?

A. Picture

B. Image

C. ToolBitmap

D. ToolBoxBitmap
   D. The ToolBoxBitmap property is used to specify what icon (representing the control) will appear in the VB Toolbox.

6. You want to test an ActiveX control's behavior in Design mode. How can you do this?

A. Set the Debug property in Project Properties to Design mode.

B. Compile the project into a CTL, and then start a new EXE project for testing.

C. Add a standard EXE project to your ActiveX control project to create a project group.

D. You can only test ActiveX controls at runtime.
   C. Add a standard EXE project to your ActiveX control project to create a project group. By creating a project group, you can test the Design mode behavior of an ActiveX control.

7. You have created a project group consisting of your ActiveX control and a standard EXE project. Each time you attempt to run your ActiveX control from VB, Internet Explorer opens and displays the control. You want to see how the control runs on the form to which you added the control. Why is it always starting in Internet Explorer, and how can you get the project with the form to start when you click Run?

A. The default behavior of an ActiveX control is to start in a browser, so you must uninstall Internet Explorer from your system.

B. The startup project hasn't been set. Right-click the ActiveX Control project in the Project window and select Set as Start Up.

C. The startup project hasn't been set. Right-click the standard EXE project in the Project window and select Set as Start Up.

D. The control won't run in a form until it's compiled. The ActiveX control must be compiled first by selecting the Make item from the File menu.
C. The startup project hasn't been set. Right-click the standard EXE project in the Project window and select Set as Start Up. If you want the control to start in the form, you need to set the standard EXE project in your project group as the startup project.

8. Which of the following will create a custom event in a UserControl that will be exposed to other objects?

A. Private Event MyEvent( )

B. Public Event MyEvent( )

C. Public MyEvent

D. Private MyEvent
B. Using Public Event MyEvent( ) will create a custom event that will be exposed to other objects.

9. Which of the following is used to store persistent property values?

A. PropertiesBag

B. PropertyBag

C. PropBag

D. Pbag
B. The PropertyBag object is used to store persistent property values.

10. When doesn't the ReadProperties event occur?

A. When a developer puts the control on a form from the Toolbox

B. When the container is instantiated

C. When the developer enters runtime from the Design mode environment

D. When a property value needs to be read
A. When a developer puts the control on a form from the Toolbox, the InitProperties event fires, not the ReadProperties event.

11. Which of the following are not events of a Property Page? (Choose all that apply.)

A. Load

B. SelectionChanged

C. ApplyChanges

D. SelectedControls
A, D. Load and SelectedControls. Property Pages don't have a Load event. SelectedControls isn't an event, but a collection of controls that have been selected.

12. You want to connect a Property Page to a UserControl. How will you do this?

    A. Through Project Properties, under the Project menu.

    B. Select PropertyPages from the Properties window, and then select the pages to connect.

    C. Select Pages from the Properties window, and then select the pages to connect.

    D. Through References from the Tools menu.
    B. Select PropertyPages from the Properties window, and then select the pages to connect.

13. Which event is used to write information from a Property Page to the actual property of a selected control?

    A. Change

    B. OnChange

    C. Apply

    D. ApplyChanges
    D. ApplyChanges is an event used to write information from a Property Page to the actual property of a selected control.

14. Which method ensures that the WriteProperties event is fired?

    A. PropertyChanged

    B. Change

    C. Write

    D. PropertyWrite
    A. The PropertyChanged method ensures that the WriteProperties event is fired.

15. Which of the following events is used to check the values of properties and change them?

    A. SelectedChanged

    B. PropertyChanged

    C. Changed

    D. WriteProperties
    A. SelectedChanged is an event that's used to check the values of properties and change them.

16. Which property in the Properties window is used to set whether a UserControl is to act as a data source?

    A. DataSource

    B. DataBindingBehavior

    C. DataSourceBehavior

    D. Data
    C. The DataSourceBehavior property is used to set whether a UserControl is to act as a data source.

17. You have changed a property value in your ActiveX control. When will the WriteProperties event fire?

    A. After Load

    B. Before Terminate

    C. After Terminate

    D. Before GetDataMember
    B. Before Terminate. The WriteProperties event occurs immediately before the UserControl's Terminate event, when one or more property values have changed.

18. Which of the following objects contain a set of records from a database?

A. Record

B. Recordset

C. Field

D. Fields

B. The Recordset object contains a set of records from a database. It is made up of Field objects, which are part of the Fields collection.

19. You have decided to create a data source. What must you set to create the GetDataMembers event?

A. Set DataBindingBehavior to vbDataBound.

B. Set DataSourceBehavior to vbDataSource.

C. Set DataBindingBehavior to vbSimpleBound.

D. Set DataBindingBehavior to vbComplexBound.

B. Set DataSource Behavior to vbDataSource. When DataSourceBehavior is set to vbDataSource, the GetDataMembers event is created.

20. Where will you go to enable the data binding capabilities of an ActiveX control?

A. From Tools, select Procedure.

B. From Tools, select Procedure Attributes.

C. From Tools, select Procedure Attributes, and then click the Advanced button.

D. From Project, select Procedure Attributes, and then click the Advanced button.

C. From Tools, select Procedure Attributes, then click the Advanced button. Enabling the data-binding capabilities of an ActiveX control is done through the Procedure Attributes dialog box, which is accessed from the Tools menu. From here, click the Advanced button to bring up the screen where you can enable data binding.

21. You are creating a custom property for your ActiveX control. In this property you have created a Private variable, which will be used to store the property's value. What will you use to retrieve the value of this variable?

A. Property Get

B. Property Let

C. Property Set

D. Property Net

A. Property Get is used to retrieve the value from this variable.

22. You are debugging an ActiveX control and want to monitor the value of a variable called strName in the Immediate window. What code will you add to your project to view this?

A. Debug.strName.

B. Debug.Print strName.

C. Debug strName.

D. None. Set the variable in the Immediate window, and it will automatically watch its value.

B. Debug.Print can be used (followed by the variable's name) to monitor the value of a variable in the Immediate window.

23. You have created a new ActiveX control project. In the Name property of the UserControl, you attempt to change its name so it's the same as the project's name. An error results. Why?

    A. There is already a UserControl that has been given the same name as the project.

    B. There is already a form that has been given the same name as the project.

    C. You are not allowed to give a UserControl the same name as the project containing it.

    D. There is no reason. You must not have created a new ActiveX project.
    C. VB won't allow you to give a UserControl the same name as the project containing it. If you try to do so, an error results.

24. You have created an ActiveX control project. You want to be able to test the control by creating a project group and testing the control on a form in the other project. How can you create a project group?

    A. From the Project menu, select Add Project.

    B. From the Project menu, select Add Project, and then choose a new project from the dialog box that appears.

    C. From the File menu, select Add Project, and then choose a new project from the dialog box that appears.

    D. From the File menu, select New Project, and then choose a new project from the dialog box that appears.
    C. From the File menu, select Add Project, and then choose a new project from the dialog box that appears.

25. You have authored an ActiveX control and want developers who use your control to have the ability to access methods of constituent controls on your UserControl. How will you do this?

    A. Methods of constituent controls are visible by default, so you don't need do anything.

    B. Methods of constituent controls must have its methods exposed by setting the control's Exposed property (in the Properties window) set to True.

    C. Since constituent controls are Windows controls that appear on the Toolbox, you don't need to do anything. Windows will have the methods exposed.

    D. Create a wrapper for it in code that delegates the method as Public.
    D. If you've authored a control and want a developer to access the methods of a constituent control on your UserControl, you must create a wrapper for it, which delegates a method as Public.

26. You've created a custom method in an ActiveX control. After adding the control to a form, you decide to invoke the method from the form's code. If the UserControl is named MyControl and the method is called GetName, how would you do this?

    A. UserControl.MyControl.GetName

    B. UserControl1.GetName

    C. Me.MyControl

    D. MyControl.GetName
       D. You can invoke a custom method like any other method. In this case, to invoke the MyControl GetName method, you would type **MyControl.GetName**.

27. A user selects several controls on your ActiveX control. What code can you implement to determine how many controls have been selected?

    A. The Count property of Controls

    B. The Count property of SelectedControls

    C. The Control property of UserControl

    D. The Selected property of Controls
       B. The Count property of SelectedControls allows you to determine the number of controls that have been selected on a UserControl.

28. Which of the following will create a new instance of an ADO database record set called rs?

A. Set rs = New ADODB.Recordset

B. Set rs as Recordset

C. ADODB.Recordset = rs

D. Property Get rs = New ADODB.Recordset
   A. To create a new record set meeting the criteria given, the correct line of code would be:

```
Set rs = New ADODB.Recordset
```

29. You have created a new ActiveX control and want to add it to a form. How will you do this? (Choose all that apply.)

    A. Double-click the control's icon in the Toolbox.

    B. Double-click the control's icon in the Toolbox, then draw the control on the form.

    C. Click the control's icon in the Toolbox, and then draw the control on the form.

    D. None of the above. You can only add a custom ActiveX control to a form through code.
       A. C. To add an ActiveX control to a form, double-click the control's icon in the Toolbox, or click the control's icon, and then draw the control on the form.

30. You want to run the ActiveX Control Interface Wizard. How will you start this wizard?

A. From the Tools menu, select ActiveX Control Interface Wizard.

B. From the Project menu, select ActiveX Control Interface Wizard.

C. From the Project menu, select Add User Control, and then select ActiveX Control Interface Wizard when the dialog box appears.

D. From the Project menu, select Add User Control, then select ActiveX Control.

   C. To run the wizard from the Project menu, select Add User Control, then select ActiveX Control Interface Wizard when the dialog box appears.

31. You have created a custom event called GetNames. Which of the following examples of code will cause this event to fire?

A. Raise GetNames

B. RaiseEvent GetNames

C. GetNames.RaiseEvent

D. GetNames.Raise

   B. The RaiseEvent keyword is used to cause an event to fire. In this case, you would use the code:

```
RaiseEvent GetNames
```

32. What event is used to set the source of data used by a control?

A. WriteProperties

B. ReadProperties

C. Initialize

D. GetDataMember

   D. The GetDataMember event is used to set the source of data used by the control.

33. You want to change the BackColor of the third element of the SelectedControls collection. Which is the correct code to use to access this element?

A. SelectedControls(1).BackColor

B. SelectedControls(2).BackColor

C. SelectedControls(3).BackColor

D. SelectedControls(4).BackColor

   B. The SelectedControls collection's first element is zero. Therefore, to access the third element, the correct code would be

```
SelectedControls(2).BackColor
```

34. When does the InitProperties event occur?

A. Any time a control is instantiated

B. When a developer places a control on a form from the Toolbox

C. Whenever ReadProperties event is fired

D. Whenever PropertyChange is invoked

   B. When a developer places a control on a container (such as a form) from the Toolbox, the InitProperties event fires.

35. What is wrong with the following example of code, which is used in a UserControl named MyUserControl?

    `MyUserControl.BackColor=vbRed`

    A. There is no property called BackColor for a UserControl.

    B. You can't refer to a UserControl by its name in code.

    C. The Me keyword should have been used to refer to the UserControl.

    D. You must specify the color by its hexadecimal value.
    B. You can't refer to a UserControl by its name in code.

36. You have created a project group to test your ActiveX control project. When you try to add the control to a form, you find the ActiveX control is grayed-out in the Toolbox. Why?

    A. You must close the form for the control to become available.

    B. You must close the ActiveX control's designer before the control becomes available.

    C. You need to initialize variable values before the control becomes available.

    D. You need to give the control a custom icon before it becomes available.
    B. The ActiveX control's designer must be closed before the ActiveX control's icon becomes available in the Toolbox.

37. Which of the following can an ActiveX control act as a data source for?

    A. ADO

    B. OLE providers

    C. ODBC sources

    D. All of the above
    D. An ActiveX control can act as a data source for any type of data.

38. You are using the Property Page Wizard. You have reached the Add Properties screen. What does this screen enable you to do?

    A. Add properties, methods, and events to your ActiveX control.

    B. Add properties, methods, and events to your PropertyPage object.

    C. Add properties to a Property Page, which will display when Properties is invoked from the contextual menu.

    D. Add custom properties to your ActiveX control.
    C. The Add Properties screen of the Property Page Wizard is used to add properties to a Property Page. These will display on the Property Page when Properties is invoked from the contextual menu.

39. You are creating a custom property for your ActiveX control. In this property you have created a Private variable, which will be used to store the property's value. What will you use to store the value of this variable? (Choose all that apply.)

A. Property Get

B. Property Let

C. Property Set

D. Property Net
   B, C. Property Let or Property Set is used to store the property's value.

40. Which of the following events is used to load property values from the PropertyBag object?

   A. WriteProperties

   B. GetDataMember

   C. ReadProperty

   D. ReadProperties
      D. The ReadProperties event is used to load property values from the PropertyBag.

Answers to Chapter 10 Self Test

1. Which term describes a group of SQL Server database users?

   A. Group.

   B. Role.

   C. Domain.

   D. SQL Server does not group users.
      B. A role represents a group of database users. Roles can be thought of as groups with a purpose.

2. What does DRI stand for?

   A. Declarative Referential Integrity

   B. Default Range Indicator

C. Default Role Integrity

D. Don't Remember Information
   A. Declarative Referential Integrity. A user with DRI permission on a table may create a referential integrity relationship to that table.

3. You want to let William have access to the information in your database. (Choose all that apply.) You must:

   A. Create an NT account for William and give that account the appropriate permissions.

   B. Create an NT account for William and assign that account to a role with the appropriate permissions.

   C. Create an NT account for William, map that account to a SQL logon, make a database user for the SQL login, and assign permissions to the database user.

   D. Create an SQL login for William, make a database user for the login, and assign permissions to the database user.
      C, D. Option C uses NT Authentication mode; D uses SQL Server authentication. An NT account cannot directly be given database permissions or be included in a role.

4. Two databases can share

   A. Stored Procedures

   B. Tables

   C. Roles

D. Logins

D. Logins are defined at the server level. Each database draws from the same group of logins. Two databases can have identical stored procedures, tables, and roles, but these are logically and physically independent.

5. Which choice does *not* describe a possible SQL Server logon/NT account relationship?

A. A login corresponds to one NT user account.

B. A login corresponds to multiple NT domain groups.

C. A login corresponds to one NT domain group.

D. A login does not correspond to an NT user or domain.

B. Each login can represent an NT user account or an NT domain group, or it may not relate to an NT security entity at all. A login cannot represent multiple groups.

6. SQL Server trusts NT security because

A. NT security is invulnerable

B.. Microsoft sells it.

C. NT's security facilities validate the identity of a user when he or she first connects to a network.

D. SQL Server does not trust NT security.

C. SQL Server, a database management system, does not include

the level of security sophistication that has been developed for NT.

7. When should you use Mixed mode? (Choose all that apply.)

A. When SQL Server is running on Windows 95.

B. When trusted connections are not available.

C. When connecting to a database from a Web site.

D. Mixed mode is not available in SQL Server 7.

A, B, C. SQL Server cannot use NT authentication when it runs on Windows 95 or 98. NT authentication requires a trusted connection. Web sites connect with standard security.

8. Which parameter of the connection string for an ADO connection causes the server to use SQL authentication?

A. Provider

B. Server

C. Integrated Security

D. None of the above

D. None of the above. Providing a User ID and Password will connect to the server with SQL Authentication.

9. Which parameter of the connection string for an ADO connection causes the server to use NT authentication?

A. Provider

B. Server

C. Integrated Security

D. None of the above

C. Integrated Security. Setting Integrated Security = SSPI will cause the server to accept a username from NT, assuming a trusted connection exists.

10. Which ADO object represents a query result set?

A. Recordset

B. Connection

C. Error

D. Resultset

A. Recordset. The Recordset object represents the results of a query. Multiple record sets can be created under one connection. ADO does not have a Resultset object.

11. Which cursor type will give the best overall performance for a report?

A. Static

B. Forward only

C. Dynamic

D. Keyset

B. Forward only. In most cases, a report can be generated with one pass through a record set. Static, dynamic, and keyset cursors are all slower than the forward-only cursor, though sometimes the difference may be very slight.

12. Which cursor type uses the most resources?

A. Static

B. Forward only

C. Dynamic

D. Keyset

C. Dynamic. The dynamic cursor provides the most flexibility and reflects all updates made to the underlying data. Thus, it should only be used when necessary.

13. Which term is a synonym for *locking*?

A. Keyset

B. Pessimistic

C. Unlocking

D. Concurrency

D. Concurrency really means the condition of two users accessing the same rows at the same time, but it has come to be an interchangeable term with locking.

14. When should you use pessimistic concurrency?

A. When the table is half empty

B. When the cursor is read-only

C. When the updates made with the cursor must commit

D. When you need an exclusive lock

C. When the updates made with the cursor must commit. Read-only cursors use read-only concurrency. A cursor with optimistic locking will also obtain an exclusive lock when the update commits.

15. Which ADO record set property determines the cursor library?

A. CursorLibrary

B. CursorDLL

C. LockType

D. CursorLocation
D. The locktype constants are used for concurrency. There is no CursorLibrary or CursorDLL property.

16. Which method(s) can you use to move to the next record in a record set? (Choose all that apply.)

A. Move

B. MoveFirst

C. MovePrevious

D. MoveNext
A, D. The MoveNext record is preferred, but the Move method can move the pointer any number of rows forward or back, including one forward.

17. Which cursor will run fastest?

A. A forward-scrolling, read-only cursor

B. A dynamic, pessimistic cursor

C. A static, optimistic cursor

D. A C++ cursor
A. A forward-scrolling, read-only cursor will use the minimum resources, followed by the static optimistic cursor. The dynamic, pessimistic cursor will be slowest.

18. Which control can help the user format a phone number?

A. OptionButton

B. ListBox

C. TextBox

D. Masked Edit
D. Masked edit controls use an input mask to provide formatting help and restrictions to the user.

19. The user of your application must assign department codes to new courses. Which control will provide the best validation?

A. CheckBox

B. OptionButton

C. ListBox

D. Masked Edit
C. List boxes let the user scroll through a limited number of choices.

20. Which is the primary method of server-side validation?

A. Constraints

B. Rules

C. Defaults

D. Triggers
A. Constraints are part of a table definition and should be used whenever possible.

21. How does the DEFAULT constraint differ from a saved default?

A. One DEFAULT constraint can be applied to multiple columns of one table.

B. One DEFAULT constraint can only apply to one column of one table.

C. One DEFAULT constraint can apply to multiple columns in multiple tables.

D. They are the same thing.
B. A default can be saved and made available to any table in a database. The DEFAULT constraint is the preferred method.

22. Triggers are like:

A. Chiggers.

B. The VB Change event.

C. Rules.

D. Primary keys.
B. A trigger can be made to fire when a table is modified.

23. Which example does *not* allow referential integrity?

A. A products table with multiple products for each record in a suppliers table

B. A students table that has one possible row for each row in a people table

C. A books table that may or may not have a corresponding record in a publishers table

D. A transcript table that has multiple rows for each row in a student table
C. Sometimes it's not possible to establish referential integrity because of design limitations.

24. The suppliers table has a one-to-many relationship with a products table. The SupplierID column is in both tables. Therefore,

A. SupplierID is a primary key in suppliers and a primary key in products.

B. SupplierID is a primary key in suppliers and a foreign key in products.

C. SupplierID is a foreign key in suppliers and a primary key in products.

D. SupplierID is a foreign key in suppliers and a foreign key in products.
B. The foreign key is a nonunique column in a table that refers to the primary key of another table.

25. When is a FOREIGN KEY constraint created?

A. When the table is created

B. During performance tuning

C. Immediately after the table is created

D. Any time
A. Like all other constraints, the FOREIGN KEY constraint is created with the same script that creates the table.

26. Which type of query *cannot* result in a referential integrity violation?

A. Select

B. Insert

C. Update

D. Delete

A. Select queries do not change data. Even an update query can violate referential integrity, if you try to change a primary or foreign key.

27. Which collection of the ADO Connection object can be used to handle referential integrity errors?

A. Err

B. Er

C. Description

D. Errors

D. The Errors collection contains an Error object for each error created in a connection.

28. Which method of the ADO Connection object will allow you to run a stored procedure with a VB application?

A. Run.

B. Command.

C. Execute.

D. Stored procedures can only be run from SQL Server.

C. The Execute method accepts a command text argument, which may be the name of a stored procedure.

29. Why should you use the Execute method to populate a record set with the output from a complex stored procedure?

A. SQL Server is optimized to run stored procedures.

B. The Execute method is the only way to populate a record set.

C. Stored procedures use client resources.

D. To avoid concurrency problems.

A. SQL Server is optimized to run stored procedures. Complex data operations are best handled by the server. The result set then can be passed to the client, instead of manipulating data on the client.

30. Which constant is used with the Execute method to run a stored procedure?

A. AdCmdText

B. AdCmdTable

C. AdCmdUnknown

D. AdCmdStoredProc

D. This constant indicates to SQL server that the command text contains the name of a stored procedure.

31. Which event can you use with an asynchronous command?

A. The Asynchronous event

B. The CommandFinish event

C. The ExecuteComplete event

D. The Synchronize event

C. The ExecuteComplete event occurs when an asynchronous command, query, or procedure has finished.

32. VB front ends can be used with which databases? (Choose all that apply.)

A. SQL Server

B. Oracle

C. Access

D. Unidata

A, B, C, D. VB can use ADO to connect to any ODBC compliant database.

33. Which database access technology should you use to connect a Web site to SQL Server?

A. RDO

B. DAO

C. SQL-DMO

D. ADO

D. With version 2, ADO has come to be Microsoft's primary database access technology for almost every application. Previously, RDO had been the method of choice for VB and SQL server applications, but ADO has replaced it.

34. Which are SQL Server 7 Authentication modes? (Choose all that apply.)

A. Standard

B. Mixed

C. Integrated

D. Separated

B, C. Mixed and Integrated. Standard mode no longer exists in SQL Server 7.

35. SQL Server

A. Never stores passwords.

B. Stores passwords for some users.

C. Stores passwords for all users.

D. Never stores passwords when running on Windows 98.

B. The SQL Server stores passwords for some users. Running in Mixed mode, SQL server can rely on NT to authenticate passwords, or use its own password list for authentication.

36. Which method opens an ADO database connection?

A. Connect

B. Query

C. Open

D. Execute

C. Use the Open method of the Connection object to initiate a connection.

37. When should you use a cursor?

A. To loop through a result set one record at a time

B. To add one row to a table

C. To sum values in a table

D. For all database operations

A. Use a cursor to loop through a result set one record at a time. Cursors are a strain on resources, so use query statements or stored procedures whenever possible.

38. Which type of change is not reflected in a keyset cursor?

A. Update

B. Insert

C. Delete

D. Select

B. Insert. New records do not appear in a keyset cursor. Use a dynamic cursor if you need access to new rows.

39. Optimistic locking

    A. Never applies shared locks.

    B. Never applies exclusive locks.

    C. Never applies any locks.

    D. Can apply both shared and exclusive locks.

    D. Optimistic locking can apply both shared and exclusive locks. A cursor with optimistic locking will obtain shared locks at creation. Exclusive locks will be requested when an update occurs.

40. Validation can occur

    A. On the client.

    B. On the server.

    C. On both the client and the server.

    D. Neither on the client nor on the server.

    C. Validation can occur on both the client and the server. Both VB and SQL Server can help with validation.

Answers to Chapter 11 Self Test

1. You have decided to increase performance of an application by using the correct data types for variables. One of your variables is used to store the current year. What data type would you use?

    A. Double

    B. Single

    C. String

    D. Integer

    D. Since the current year would be a value in the thousands, but not over 32,767, you would use an Integer. Any other data type would be overkill and use more memory space.

2. Which tab of the Project Properties dialog box allows you to set version information for an executable?

    A. General

    B. Make

    C. Compile

    D. Debugging

    B. The Make tab allows you to set version information for an executable.

3. Which of the following will remove the value of a String variable to reclaim space?

    A. strName = Null

    B. End strName

    C. strName=""

    D. Reclaim strName

    C. To remove the value of a String variable and reclaim space, you would assign an empty value, as seen in the code: strName="".

4. You have decided to compile to p-code and then set optimization settings for this to optimize for either speed and size. When you go to the Compile tab, you find you cannot accomplish this. Why?

   A. You can only optimize for either speed or size.

   B. P-code doesn't offer optimization settings for compiling.

   C. You need to make these settings on the Make tab.

   D. None of the above.
   B. Settings are only available when compiling to native code.

5. What will be the effect of the following conditional compilation code?

   ```
   #CONST conEnglish=0
   #CONST conFrench=-1
   #CONST conSpanish=False
   ```

   A. conEnglish will be compiled.

   B. conFrench will be compiled.

   C. conSpanish will be compiled.

   D. All constants will be compiled.
   B. conFrench has a value of –1, which evaluates to True. Both of the other compiling constants have False values. Therefore, code associated with conFrench will be compiled.

6. You want to display the value of intNum in the Immediate window by including code directly into a procedure. Which of the following would be valid to use in your code to perform this action?

   A. ? intNum

   B. Print intNum

   C. Debug.Print intNum

   D. All of the above
   C. Debug.Print intNum. Debug.Print is used in a procedure's code to display the value of an expression in the Immediate window. The others are typed in the Immediate window, not used in the application's actual code.

7. You are deploying your application to floppy disks. Part way through the deployment, you find that one of the floppies isn't formatted. What can you do?

   A. Stop the packaging and return to the Package portion of Package and Deployment Wizard. Check the Format before copying check box, and repackage your application.

   B. Stop the packaging and return to the Deploy portion of Package and Deployment Wizard. Check the Format before copying check box, and redeploy your package.

   C. Repackage and redeploy your application. All information will be lost when you stop deployment.

   D. Repackage your application on formatted floppy disks.
   B. Stop deployment, return to the Deploy portion of Package and Deployment Wizard, and check the Format before copying check box. Your floppies will now be formatted before files are copied.

8. You want to remove a picture from memory, to reclaim the memory space. What will you do?

   A. Use the LoadPicture( ) function

   B. Use the RemovePicture( ) function

   C. Use LoadPicture to load a nonexistent graphic file

   D. Use UnloadPicture( ) function
   A. The LoadPicture( ) function is used to remove a graphic from memory, and to reclaim space.

9. You want to configure your form to use Graphics method rather than Persistent Graphics. What will you set to do this?

   A. AutoRedraw to False

   B. AutoRedraw to True

   C. AutoRedraw to Graphics

   D. AutoRedraw to Persistent
   A. To use the Graphics method, set AutoRedraw to False.

10. You have entered code to load all of the commonly used forms at application startup. What effect will this have on performance?

   A. It will give the appearance that performance has increased.

   B. It will give the appearance that performance has decreased.

   C. It will increase the size of the application.

   D. It will decrease the speed of the application.
   A. Loading all commonly used forms at startup will give the appearance that performance has increased. This is

because hidden forms will display faster than forms that have to load into memory from the hard disk.

11. You have decided to use the Web Publishing option in the Deploy portion of the Package and Deployment Wizard. What protocols are available for you to send your package to a Web site? (Choose all that apply.)

    A. HTTP Post

    B. HTTP Get

    C. FTP

    D. HTML Post
    A, C. The protocols available for Web publishing are HTTP Post and FTP.

12. What Deployment method would you select to deploy your application to a network folder?

    A. Web Publishing

    B. Folder

    C. Network Folder

    D. NT Folder
    B. To deploy an application to a network folder, select Folder from the Deployment Method screen.

13. What file contains a listing of files installed, directories created, and so on, when the application is installed, and what is it used for?

    A. ST6UNST.LOG contains a list of installed files for ST6UNST.EXE to use if the application is uninstalled.

    B. SETUP.LOG contains a record of how the installation went and what files are installed, for review by the user.

C. UNINSTALL.LOG contains a list of installed files for ST6UNST.EXE to use if the application is uninstalled.

D. INSTALL.LOG contains a list of installed files for Add/Remove Programs to use if the application is uninstalled.
A. ST6UNST.LOG contains a list of installed files for ST6UNST.EXE to use if the application is uninstalled.

14. You want to register a COM component. What is the easiest and best way to do this?

   A. Use the Package and Deployment Wizard to create a dependency file.

   B. Use the Package and Deployment Wizard to create a Registry file.

   C. Using a text editor, manually edit the SETUP.1ST file.

   D. Using a text editor, create a SETUP.1ST file.
   A. While you can create or edit SETUP.1ST files and include information to register a COM component, the easiest and best way is to use the Package and Deployment Wizard to create a dependency file.

15. You are debugging a DLL in process, but find that when you click the End button on the Debug toolbar, you are unable to test the shutdown behavior of the DLL. Why?

   A. DLLs don't have a shutdown behavior.

   B. The End button closes down every project, so you must close the application properly.

   C. The code that determines the shutdown behavior has a bug in it.

   D. The DLL can't be loaded in the design environment.
   B. The End button will close down every project. To effectively test a DLL's shutdown behavior, close the application properly. This is done by clicking the application's Close button.

16. In the Watch window, the value of the variable intMyInt reads <Out of Context>. What does this mean?

   A. intMyInt hasn't been declared.

   B. intMyInt is out of scope.

   C. intMyInt has a value of zero.

   D. intMyInt has a null value.
   B. When the value of an expression in the Watch window reads <Out of Context>, that variable is currently out of scope.

17. During runtime, you notice the Quick Watch button on the Debug toolbar is inactive. Why?

   A. There are no watch expressions currently set.

   B. There are no variables in the current procedure.

C. The Quick Watch button becomes active in Break mode.

D. There are no breakpoints set in the project.
C. The Quick Watch button becomes active in Break mode. While not an option here, it also becomes active in Design mode.

18. The variable intNum has a value of four (4). You type the following code in the Immediate window. What will be printed?

```
Print intNum * .25
```

A. 4

B. intNum * .25

C. 1

D. Error will result
C. The answer printed will be one (1). You can manipulate data in the Immediate window by typing math equations such as this. In this case, if intNum has a value of four, it will be multiplied by 0.25, resulting in a printed answer of one in the Immediate window.

19. You have a variable with a Boolean value of False that you want to monitor. You want the application to break when this value changes. Which of the following options would you set in the Add Watch dialog box? (Choose all that apply.)

A. Watch expression

B. Break when value is True

C. Break when value changes

D. Break when value is False
B, C. Since you're monitoring a Boolean value that's False and want to monitor a change in value, you could use either Break when value is True, or Break when value changes. Either would cause execution to break when the value changes.

20. You want to fully resolve compiling errors before debugging a DLL in process. What can you do to resolve any compiling errors before doing this? (Choose all that apply.)

A. From the Run menu, select Start with Full Compile.

B. From the Run menu, select Start.

C. In Options, uncheck Compile on Demand.

D. Press F5.
A, C. To resolve compiling errors, fully compile your application by choosing Start with Full Compile from the Run menu. You can also disable the Compile on Demand setting in Options. This will force your application to fully compile before running.

21. You have decided to distribute an application to Web sites like http://www.microsoft.com. When you attempt to deploy the package, the deployment fails. Why?

A. You selected single CAB rather than multiple CABs for packaging.

B. You selected multiple CABs rather than single CAB for packaging.

C. You don't have the necessary permissions to deploy to that site.

D. You aren't able to deploy to Web sites with the Package and Deployment Wizard.

C. To deploy a package to an Internet site you must have proper permissions on the Web server.

22. The application removal program is automatically added to your package by the Package and Deployment Wizard. Installed to a user's computer, where is this program found?

A. The APPLICATION directory

B. The SYSTEM directory

C. The WINDOWS or WINNT directory

D. A subdirectory in the APPLICATION directory

C. The application removal program, ST6UNST.EXE, is installed to the WINDOWS or WINNT directory.

23. A user installs your application. Unfortunately, you forgot to include a COM component with the package. What will happen when the application can't find the COM component?

A. The VB Runtime Library will give a "File not found" message.

B. The problem will cause the program to crash.

C. The problem will be ignored.

D. The problem will cause the installation to uninstall itself.

A. The VB Runtime Library will give a "File not found" message. When a COM component can't be found, the VB Runtime Library will give a "File not found" message.

24. You want to manipulate information contained within the Registry. Which of the following functions would you use? (Choose all that apply.)

A. GetSetting

B. SaveSetting

C. GetKey

D. SaveKey

A, B. GetSetting and SaveSetting are used to read and write to the Registry, respectively.

25. Which button will allow you to step through code one line at a time but, when it reaches a called procedure, will execute the called procedure as a single step and then move to the next line?

A. Step

B. Step Into

C. Step Over

D. Step Out

C. The Step Over button allows you to execute code one line at a time but, when it reaches a call to another procedure, it will execute that procedure as one step and move to the next line.

26. What does the Create Symbolic Debug Info option on the Compile tab of the Project Properties dialog box do?

    A. Allow breakpoints to be set

    B. Creates a file for use with the Package and Deployment Wizard

    C. Logs debugging problems that occur during a debugging session

    D. Creates a debug file for external debugging tools

    D. This option will have the compiler create a debug file with the extension PDB. This file can be used by external debugging tools to debug the application as it runs.

27. Which of the following can you use to test code before adding it to your actual application? (Choose all that apply.)

    A. Project groups

    B. Immediate window

    C. Locals window

    D. Watch window

    E. Code window

    A, B. Project groups and the Immediate window allow you to test code before adding it to the application. The Immediate window can be used to test code on the fly, while project groups allow you to use one project for testing (like a scratch pad).

28. Which of the following would you use to save settings to the Registry?

    A. PropertyGet

    B. PropertyLet

    C. SaveSettings

    D. GetSettings

    C. To save settings to the Registry, use the SaveSettings function.

29. You want to change the value of an expression in the Locals window. How will you do this?

    A. Right-click the value, and select Properties from the contextual menu.

    B. Click the value in the Value column and enter the new value.

    C. Click the expression, and enter the new value.

    D. Click the variable associated with the expression. A properties box will appear.

    B. To change the value of an expression in the Locals window, click the value in the Value column, and enter the new value.

30. How can you create a project group?

    A. From the File menu, select Make Project Group.

    B. From the File menu, select Add Project.

    C. From the File menu, select New Project.

    D. From the Project menu, select Make Project Group.

    B. To create a project group, from the File menu, select Add Project. You can then add a new or existing project.

31. Where can you rename, delete, and duplicate package and deployment scripts?

A. Manage Scripts in the Package and Deployment Wizard

B. Scripts in the Package and Deployment Wizard

C. The Scripts utility that comes with VB

D. The Package portion of the Package and Deployment Wizard
    A. Manage Scripts in the Package and Deployment Wizard allows you to rename, duplicate, and delete package and deployment scripts.

32. Which entries does GetSetting and SaveSetting allow you access?

A. Anything in the Registry

B. Entries under HKEY_CURRENT_USER\ SOFTWARE\VB and VBA Program Settings

C. Entries under HKEY_CONFIG\SOFTWARE\VB Program Settings

D. Any currently open Key
    B. Using GetSetting and SaveSetting you can access entries under HKEY_CURRENT_USER\ SOFTWARE\VB and VBA Program Settings.

33. During installation, the file called ST6UNST.LOG is created. Where is this file stored on the user's hard disk, and why?

A. The application directory, for use in uninstalling the application

B. The system directory, for use in uninstalling the application

C. The root directory, for logging the success or failure of installation

D. The system directory, for logging the success or failure of installation
    A. ST6UNST.LOG is created in the application directory and used for uninstalling the application.

34. You are using the Locals window and see that an expression called Me is displayed in it. You don't recall setting a watch expression for it. What does this expression represent?

A. This is an error.

B. This expression represents the Locals window.

C. This expression represents the current form.

D. This expression represents the current project.
    C. This expression represents the current form. The Me variable is an object variable representing the current form. It appears in the Locals window in Break mode.

35. An array called intArray is displayed in the Locals window. You want to view the elements of this array, and each of the values contained. What can you do to view this information?

A. Click the Plus sign beside the variable's name.

B. Click the Minus sign beside the variable's name.

C. Nothing. Each of the variables appear by default in the Locals window.

D. Nothing. The variable is shown in the Locals window, but elements of the array can't be shown.
A. Clicking the Plus sign beside the variable's name (e.g., a structured variable, such as an array) will expand the structure, allowing you to view the elements in the array.

36. Which file is included with your application to allow for the removal of your application from a user's computer?

A. SETUP.EXE

B. SETUP1.EXE

C. UNWISE.EXE

D. ST6UNST.EXE

E. Add/Remove Programs
D. ST6UNST.EXE is added to your package for application removal.

37. You are packaging and deploying an application to floppy disk. You have a mix of different disks. Some are 1.44MB, others are 1.2MB. What must you do for packaging the application with different CAB sizes?

A. On the Cab Options screen, choose Mix from the Cab Size list box.

B. On the Cab Options screen, select 1.44MB and 1.2MB.

C. You can't package using a mixture of CAB sizes.

D. You can't package on 1.2MB disks.
C. You can't package using a mixture of CAB sizes. You must choose one size of CAB when packaging your application for deployment to floppy disk.

38. You want to display the value of intNum in the Immediate window. Which of the following would be valid to use in the Immediate window to perform this action? (Choose all that apply.)

A. ? intNum

B. Print intNum

C. Debug.Print intNum

D. All of the Above
A, B. ? intNum and Print intNum can be used in the Immediate window to display the value of an expression. Debug.Print is used in a procedure's code to display the value of an expression in the Immediate window.

39. Your application loads a large database that takes a considerable amount of time to load. Which of the following can you do to let the user know the application hasn't locked up when loading the database? (Choose all that apply.)

A. Implement a splash screen.

B. Implement a progress bar that shows that the database is loading.

C. Set AutoRedraw to False.

D. Optimize the application for size.
A, B. This question doesn't specify at what point the database loads. If it is loading when the application starts, you could implement a splash screen. You could also add a progress bar at any point in the application to show the status of the loading database.

40. You have decided to compile to native code and then set optimization settings for this to optimize for both speed and size. When you go to the Compile tab, you find you cannot. Why?

    A. You can only optimize for speed or size. You can't optimize for both.

    B. Native code doesn't offer optimization settings for compiling.

    C. You need to make these settings on the Make tab.

    D. None of the above.
    A. You can only optimize for speed or size. You can't optimize for both. When setting optimization settings for native code, you can optimize for speed, size, or neither. You can choose only one. You can't optimize for both speed and size.

Answers to Chapter 12 Self Test

1. You have decided to add the functionality of a Web browser to a project's form. You notice this control's icon doesn't appear in your Toolbox. How will you add this control to the Toolbox so you can add it to your form?

    A. From the Project menu, select Components, and then select WebBrowser from the list.

    B. From the Project menu, select Components, and then select Internet Explorer Controls from the list.

    C. From the Project menu, select Components, and then select Microsoft Internet Controls from the list.

    D. Reinstall VB. This is a common control that appears in Toolbox.
    C. From the Project menu, select Components, and then select Microsoft Internet Controls from the list. Doing so will add the WebBrowser icon to the Toolbox.

2. Which of the following lines of code will enable Microsoft's Web site to appear in the WebBrowser control?

    A. WebBrowser.Navigate www.microsoft.com

    B. WebBrowser.Navigate "www.microsoft.com"

    C. WebBrowser.GoHome www.microsoft.com

    D. WebBrowser.Navigate URL
    B. When specifying a specific Web site to navigate to, use the Navigate method followed by the URL in quotes.

3. You want to convert a standard EXE project into an ActiveX document. How will you do this?

    A. Change the FRM extension of all Forms to DOB.

    B. Use the ActiveX Control Interface Wizard.

    C. Use the ActiveX Document Migration Wizard.

    D. Use the ActiveX Document Conversion Wizard.
    C. The ActiveX Document Migration Wizard allows you to convert a standard EXE project into an ActiveX document.

4. Which of the following are used to return the x and y coordinates for where a document appears in the viewport? (Choose all that apply.)

    A. ViewPortTop

    B. ViewPortHeight

    C. ViewPortWidth

    D. ViewPortLeft
    A, D. ViewPortTop and ViewPortLeft return the y and x coordinates, respectively, of where the document appears in the ViewPort.

5. You have set the ScrollBar property of a UserDocument to vbBoth. What will happen if the value of ViewPortHeight exceeds the MinHeight value?

    A. A horizontal scroll bar will appear.

    B. A vertical scroll bar will appear.

    C. Both horizontal and vertical scroll bars will appear.

    D. No scroll bars will appear.
    D. Even though scroll bars have been set, the ViewPortHeight must be less than the MinHeight value for scroll bars to appear. If ViewPortHeight value is greater than the MinHeight value, no scroll bars appear.

6. Which of the following best defines what a viewport is?

    A. A control added to a UserDocument to view Web pages

    B. The screen area used to display an ActiveX document in a container application

    C. An ActiveX document displayed in a container application

    D. A container application used to display an ActiveX document
    B. A viewport is the screen area used to display an ActiveX document in a container application.

7. Which of the following examples of syntax would return the name of a container application?

    A. TypeName(UserDocument.Parent)

    B. UserDocument(TypeName.Parent)

    C. UserDocument.Parent

    D. Parent.TypeName
    C. UserDocument.Parent is the syntax for returning the name of a container application.

8. When can you set the value of the MinHeight and MinWidth properties?

    A. Design mode.

    B. Runtime.

    C. You can't set these properties. They are used to return a value.

    D. You can't set these properties. They are read-only.
    B. You can only set the values of MinHeight and MinWidth through your code at runtime.

9. You create a new UserDocument. What is the default value of its ScrollBar property?

    A. 0—None

    B. 1—Horizontal

C. 2—Vertical

D. 3—Both
D. The default setting of the ScrollBar property is 3—Both (that is, vbBoth). This is a new default setting for VB 6.

10. Which of the following hyperlink methods will allow you to navigate from one ActiveX document to another?

A. Navigate

B. NavigateTo

C. Back

D. GoTo
B. NavigateTo allows you to navigate from one ActiveX document to another.

11. Which of the following browsers can use a DHTML application created with VB 6?

A. Internet Explorer 3

B. Internet Explorer 4

C. Internet Explorer 4.01 with Service Pack 1

D. Peer Web Services 3
C. To run a DHTML application created with VB 6, a user must be running Internet Explorer 4.01 with Service Pack 1.

12. Which of the following browsers can use an IIS application created with VB 6? (Choose all that apply.)

A. Internet Explorer 3

B. Internet Explorer 4

C. Internet Explorer 4.01 with Service Pack 1

D. Peer Web Services 3
B, C. To use an IIS application, you need to be running Internet Explorer version 4 or higher.

13. You are using Menu Editor to create a menu for an ActiveX document. Which property allows you to specify where a document's menu will appear in relation to a container's menu?

A. DocumentMenu

B. NegotiatePosition

C. MenuPosition
B. The NegotiatePosition property allows you to specify the position of an ActiveX document's menu item in relation to the container's menu.

14. Three users access a WebClass with their browsers. How many instances of the WebClass will exist for these users?

A. One logical instance of that WebClass will be created for each browser.

B. One instance of that WebClass will exist at any given point.

C. One instance will exist for the server and one for each browser.

D. One logical instance of that WebClass and two of each WebItem will be created for each browser.
A. A logical instance of the WebClass is created for each browser that accesses the WebClass.

15. You have set the ScrollBar property of a UserDocument to vbBoth. What will happen if the value of ViewPortWidth is less than the MinWidth value?

    A. A horizontal scroll bar will appear.

    B. A vertical scroll bar will appear.

    C. Both horizontal and vertical scroll bars will appear.

    D. No scroll bars will appear.
       A. When the ViewPortWidth is less than the MinWidth, a horizontal scroll bar appears.

16. Your IIS application is being used, and a request is made for a specific event in a WebClass. The request doesn't match any existing WebClass of event. What will happen?

    A. The application will crash.

    B. The browser will freeze.

    C. The Respond event of the WebClass is fired.

    D. The UserEvent for the HTML template is fired.

    E. The Start event for the WebClass is fired.
       D. When a specific event is requested and it doesn't match any existing WebClass or event, the UserEvent for the HTML template is fired.

17. Which of the following are standard events associated with every WebItem? (Choose all that apply.)

    A. Respond

    B. ProcessTag

    C. UserEvent

    D. Start
       A, B, C. Every WebItem has three standard events associated with it: Respond, ProcessTag, and UserEvent.

18. What does the acronym DHTML stand for?

    A. Don't Help Tourists Making Lunch

    B. Dynamic Hypertext Mock Language

    C. Dynamic Hypertext Transaction Markup Language

    D. Dynamic Hypertext Markup Language
       D. DHTML stands for Dynamic Hypertext Markup Language.

19. You have decided to create an IIS Application with VB. What other system requirements must be present to create such an application? (Choose all that apply.)

    A. Internet Information Server 3 or higher with Active Server Pages

    B. Internet Explorer 3 with Active Server Pages

    C. A connection to a network

    D. Peer Web Services 3 or higher with Active Server Pages
       A, D. To create an IIS application, you'll need to have Peer Web Services 3 or higher with Active Server Pages, or Internet Information Server 3 or higher with Active Server Pages.

20. A DHTML application is made up of which of the following? (Choose all that apply.)

    A. HTML pages

    B. WebClass

    C. VB code

    D. WebItems

    E. A runtime DLL

    A, C, E. A DHTML application is made up of HTML pages, VB code that handles events, and a project DLL that contains your code and is accessed at runtime.

21. You are using the DHTML Page Designer. Which part of the designer allows you to see a hierarchical view of an HTML document's contents?

    A. ListView

    B. Treeview

    C. Detail

    D. PageView

    B. The Treeview pane allows you to see a hierarchical view of an HTML document's contents.

22. You are tired of using Notepad as your HTML editor. You want to specify a new editor in the External HTML Editor field. Where will you go to do this?

    A. Select Project Properties from the Properties menu; then choose the Advanced tab.

    B. Select Options from the View menu; then choose the General tab.

    C. Select Options from the Tools menu; then choose the Advanced tab.

    D. Select Options from the tool bar; then choose the Editor tab.

    C. Selecting Options from the Tools menu, and then choosing the Advanced tab brings you to the External HTML Editor field. Here you can specify the path and filename of the application you wish to use as your editor.

23. You are using the WebClass designer and have a template selected. For certain elements in the template, there are entries under the Target column. What does this signify?

    A. The target of a hyperlink. This indicates the page a link will jump to, or the frame the linked item will appear in.

    B. The source of the element. This indicates the name of the element.

    C. The event connected to this element. It indicates the name of the event associated with this item.

    D. The attribute of the element. It indicates whether it is an image, hyperlink, and so on.

    C. The Target column indicates whether a particular element has been "connected" to an event. When activated, the event associated with it is triggered.

24. Which of the following best defines the relationship between Active Server Page files (ASP files), WebClasses, and WebItems?

A. One WebClass is associated with one WebItem, which can contain many Active Server Page files.

B. One Active Server Page file is associated with one WebClass, which can contain many WebItems.

C. One Active Server Page file is associated with one WebItem, which can contain many WebClasses.

D. There is no relationship between ASP files, WebClasses, and WebItems.
B. One Active Server Page file is associated with one WebClass, which can contain many WebItems.

25. You have opened the Property Page of a hyperlink, and have set the link type to mailto:. What will you put in the Link field?

A. A URL.

B. The text that will appear underlined in the browser.

C. An e-mail address.

D. The event that will be triggered by the link, so that VB code will execute.
C. When mailto has been set as the link type in the Property Page of a hyperlink, the e-mail address for this link is entered in the Link field.

26. You are creating a DHTML application, and want to attach code to an element on an HTML document. What property must you set for this element before you can attach code to it?

A. Name

B. ID

C. Event

D. ClassID
B. Before code can be attached to an element, an ID for the element must be set. An ID is used to identify an element, and can be modified by selecting the element and changing the ID property in the Properties window.

27. Which of the following applications cannot act as containers for ActiveX documents?

A. Internet Explorer 3

B. VB 4

C. Microsoft Binder 1

D. VB 5
B. Visual Basic version 4 cannot act as a container for ActiveX documents. Internet Explorer 3 and higher, Microsoft Binder, and VB version 5 or higher can all act as containers for ActiveX documents.

28. Which of the following are components of an ActiveX document?

A. UserDocument

B. WebClass

C. ASP files

D. WebItem
A. A UserDocument is the only choice that applies to an ActiveX document. Each of the other choices is part of an IIS application.

29. Where is processing performed when a DHTML application is running?

    A. Client side

    B. Server side

    C. The network

    D. None of the above
    A. DHTML applications reside on the user's computer, rather than a server. Processing is performed on the client side.

30. You are using the DHTML Page Designer. Which part of the designer allows you to see a graphical representation of an HTML document?

    A. ListView

    B. Treeview

    C. Detail

    D. PageView
    C. The Detail pane allows you to see a graphical representation of an HTML document.

31. The tool bar on the WebClass Designer has two buttons that look like start and stop buttons on a VCR. What are these used for?

    A. Running and stopping the IIS application you're developing

    B. Starting and stopping the IIS application debugger

    C. Starting and stopping Peer Web Services

    D. Starting and stopping the browser
    C. The two buttons that have the appearance of VCR start and stop buttons are used for starting and stopping Peer Web Services.

32. You are using WebClass designer and notice that many entries in the Target column have the word <None>. What does this mean?

    A. An associated component, such as an image or hyperlink target, is missing.

    B. There are no events associated with those items.

    C. WebClasses are missing for those items.

    D. The element hasn't been configured properly.
    B. When the word <None> appears in the Target column, no event has been associated, and that entry is thereby disconnected.

33. You have decided to create an ActiveX document. You select New Project from the File menu, and the New Project dialog box appears. What can you select from this dialog box to create an ActiveX document? (Choose all that apply.)

    A. ActiveX EXE

    B. ActiveX Document EXE

    C. ActiveX DLL

    D. ActiveX Document DLL

    E. ActiveX Control
    B, D. You can select either ActiveX Document DLL or ActiveX Document EXE to create an ActiveX document.

34. What property of a WebClass determines whether it stays alive between requests, or is destroyed when a request is completed?

   A. StateInstance

   B. StateManagement

   C. StateFarm

   D. ManageState
   B. StateManagement is a property that determines whether the WebClass stays alive between requests or is destroyed when a request is completed.

35. You have decided to export a page from DHTML Page Designer to an external file. What extension should you give to this file? (Choose all that apply.)

   A. DHTML

   B. HTM

   C. DHTM

   D. HTML
   B, D. The valid extensions for an HTML page that is being exported to an external file are HTM and HTML.

36. A WebItem is activated by a request. What is its default event?

   A. Respond

   B. Start

   C. UserRequest

   D. Initiate
   A. When a WebItem is activated by a request, a Respond event is the default event.

37. Which event of a WebItem is used to process the events of a WebClass that's created at runtime?

   A. Respond

   B. Start

   C. UserEvent

   D. ProcessTag
   C. UserEvent is used to process the events of a WebClass that are created at runtime.

38. You set the StateManagement property of a WebClass to wcNoState. What effect will this have on the WebClass?

   A. An instance of the WebClass will be retained between requests.

   B. The WebClass will be used for the duration of the request, then destroyed.

   C. The StateManagement property will be disabled.

   D. The Web server will handle processing.

   E. The client browser will handle processing.
   B. When StateManagement is set to wcNoState, the WebClass is used for the duration of a browser request, then destroyed.

39. You are creating a hyperlink and want the link to connect to a secured Web site. What Link Type will you choose?

   A. http:

   B. file:

C.   https:

D.   secure:

C. Selecting https: as the Link type for a hyperlink is used for connecting to a secure Web site, using HTTP over Secure Socket Layer.

40.   You have decided to import an HTML file into DHTML Page Designer. How will you do this?

A.   Select Open from the DHTML Page Designer's File menu.

B.   Click the Open button on DHTML Page Properties, and select the file to import.

C.   Click the Import button on the DHTML Page Designer's tool bar.

D.   Select Import from the DHTML Page Designer's File menu.

B. To import a file into DHMTL Page Designer, click the Open button on DHMTL Page Properties, and select the file to import.

Answers to Chapter 13 Self Test

1.   You have deployed an update for a database application. Now users are complaining that they can't access data that they've spent the last six months inputting into the program. What is the probable cause of this problem?

A.   You chose the wrong deployment method.

B.   You packaged an empty database file with your application update.

C.   You failed to package a new database file with your application update.

D.   None of the above.

B. When deploying an update for a database application, do not include the empty database file that was deployed with the full version. Deploying empty database files will overwrite the user's existing database file.

2.   Your application seems to be running fine, but users are complaining that instead of adding sales tax, the application is subtracting it. What kind of error is this?

A.   Logic

B.   Syntax

C.   Runtime

D.   Asyncratic

A. This is an example of a logic error. The application is running fine, showing that there are no syntax or runtime errors, yet the code isn't functioning as expected.

3.   Error-handling routines deal with what kind of errors?

A.   Logic

B.   Syntax

C.   Runtime

D.   Asyncratic

C. Error-handling routines deal with runtime errors.

4. You have set an error trap in your code. For how long will it remain enabled? (Choose all that apply.)

   A. Until the procedure ends

   B. Until the error trap is executed

   C. Until the error trap is disabled

   D. Until the error handler is enabled
   A, C. An error trap remains enabled until one of two things happens: the procedure ends, or the error trap is disabled.

5. Which of the following will reset the value of Err.Number to zero? (Choose all that apply.)

   A. Resume

   B. Err.Reset

   C. Reset

   D. Err.Clear
   A, D. Resume statements and Err.Clear will both reset the value of Err.Number to zero.

6. A procedure calls an error handler. The error-handling routine experiences an error. What will happen?

   A. A message will be displayed and the application will exit.

   B. The application will exit.

   C. The error handler will handle its own error.

   D. The error will be passed to the calling procedure.
   D. When an error occurs in an error handler that's called by another procedure, the error handler will pass the error up to the calling procedure.

7. Procedure A has an error handler. Procedures B and C have no error handlers. Procedure A calls Procedure B, which then calls Procedure C. What will happen if Procedure C experiences an error?

   A. A message will be displayed and the application will exit.

   B. The error will be passed to Procedure B, which will deal with the error.

   C. The error will be passed up the calling chain to Procedure A, which will deal with the error.

   D. Procedure C will deal with the error.
   C. The error will be passed up the calling chain to Procedure A, which will deal with the error. When an error occurs in a called procedure, it is passed up the calling chain until it reaches a procedure with error handling.

8. What will the Raise property of the Err object do?

   A. Cause an error to occur

   B. Cause an error to be passed up the calling chain

C. Cause execution to return the line before the one that caused an error

D. Raise the value of Err.Number
   A. Err.Raise allows you to raise, or cause an error so that you can then test the effects of your error-handling routine.

9. You have placed a Resume statement in your code, and an error results. What must be present in your code for a Resume statement to work?

   A. An On Error statement

   B. The error code

   C. The place to resume to

   D. None of the above
      A. If you use a Resume statement that doesn't include an On Error statement, an error will result.

10. An error occurs on line 10 of your code. After the error handler deals with the error, you want execution to return to the line that caused the error. Which of the following statements will do this?

    A. Resume

    B. Resume 9

    C. Resume Next

    D. Resume Error
       A. Resume will return execution to the line that originally caused the error.

11. Which of the following allows you to check for logic errors in a program?

    A. Using the program

    B. VB's logic checking features

    C. Auto Logic Check in Options

    D. Visual SourceSafe's logic checking features
       A. The only way to check logic errors is by using the application.

12. Which of the following will disable a previous error trap?

    A. On Error Disable

    B. On Error GoTo 0

    C. On Error Err.Clear

    D. Err.Clear
       B. On Error GoTo 0 will disable a previous error trap.

13. What does the Number property of the Err object contain?

    A. An Integer value representing the last error encountered

    B. An Object value representing the object that created the error

    C. The Number of errors encountered by the error handler

    D. The Number of objects containing errors
       A. Err.Number contains an Integer value representing the last error encountered.

14. What will the following line of code do?

    ```
    Resume MyNext
    ```

    A. Return an error

    B. Resume processing from a label called MyNext

C. Resume processing from a procedure called MyNext

D. Invoke a function called MyNext
B. This is an example of Resume *line or label*. In this line of code, processing would resume at the label called MyNext.

15. You have created an application update that would benefit users. Using the Package and Deployment Wizard, you plan to type in URLs of various shareware Web sites. After typing in the first URL, you get a message saying the deployment has failed. Why?

A. You forgot to choose the application update you wish to deploy.

B. You must have a valid account with proper permissions to deploy an update to a Web site.

C. You must have a valid account with proper permissions to use the Web Publishing component of the Package and Deployment Wizard.

D. You haven't packaged your application update.
B. You must have a valid account with proper permissions to deploy your application update to a Web site. Answers A and D are wrong, because you won't be able to reach this point without first packaging and choosing an application update to deploy.

16. What does the Description property of the Err object contain?

A. An Integer number representing a description of the last error encountered

B. A String value containing a description of the last error encountered

C. A pointer to an error code that represents the last error encountered

D. A variable containing the last error encountered
B. The Description property has a string value containing a description of the last error encountered.

17. An error occurs in line 10 of your code. After the error handler deals with the error, you want execution to return to the line following the one that caused the error. Which of the following will allow you to do this? (Choose all that apply.)

A. Resume

B. Resume Next

C. Next Resume

D. Resume 10
B. Resume Next will return execution to the line following the one that caused the error.

18. What does the Source property of the Err object do?

A. Causes an error to occur at the source

B. Contains information about the source of an error

C. Contains the name of the calling procedure that passed the error

D. Contains a description about the error

B. Err.Source contains information about the source of an error. If the error occurred in an application like Excel, the value of Err.Source would then be Excel.Application.

19. A procedure calls an error handler. The error-handling routine experiences an error. It passes the error up to the calling procedure, which has no error handling to deal with the error. What will happen?

A. A message will be displayed and the application will exit.

B. The application will exit.

C. The error handler will handle its own error.

D. The error will be passed to the calling procedure.

A. When an error handler passes an error up to the calling procedure, that procedure then has a chance to deal with the error. If it has no error handling to deal with this, a message is displayed and the application exits.

20. What kind of error can occur when you attempt to run the project in VB, or when your compiled application runs? (Choose all that apply.)

A. Logic

B. Syntax

C. Runtime

D. Design time

A, C. Logic errors and runtime errors can occur when you attempt to run the project in VB, or when your compiled application runs.

21. You have created a loop that changes the Caption property of controls to uppercase. You also have text boxes on your form. What will allow you to ignore errors that occur when the loop reaches controls without caption properties?

A. Resume Next

B. On Error Resume Next

C. On Error Resume

D. Resume

B. On Error Resume Next will have your code move to the next line of code when an error occurs. In the case of loops that move through controls, if an error occurs, On Error Resume Next allows your code to move to the next control in the loop.

22. What will the happen in the following code when an error occurs in Proc2?

```
Sub Proc1()
    On Error GoTo EH
    Proc2
    Print "Hello World"
    Exit Sub
EH:
    Msgbox "Error Encountered"
    Resume Next
End Sub
Sub Proc2
    Err.Raise 53
    Print "Hi World"
End Sub
```

A. A message will be displayed and the application exits.

B. The next line of code will be executed in Proc2.

C. The error will be passed to the error handler in Proc1.

D. Error 53 means there is no error, so no error will occur.

C. When errors are encountered in called procedures, they are passed back up to the calling procedure. In Proc1, EH would then deal with the error.

23. Which of the following would enable an error trap?

A. ErrHandler:

B. On Error

C. Resume

D. Err

B. The On Error statement is used to enable error traps.

24. What is a beta tester, and what do they do?

A. Beta testers are users who use preliminary releases of applications and report errors.

B. Beta testers are a special type of error-handling code.

C. Beta testers are lines of code that include Err.Raise.

D. Beta testers are instances of testing that occur when you run a program in Design mode.

A. Beta testers are users who use preliminary releases of applications and report errors.

25. You are deploying an application update for floppy disk distribution. While going through the Package and Deployment Wizard, you realize you don't have any formatted floppy disks. What is the best thing to do?

A. Close Package and Deployment Wizard and format some disks.

B. Switch from the Package and Deployment Wizard to Windows Explorer and format some disks.

C. Check Format before copying on the Floppy Disk deployment screen of the Package and Deployment Wizard.

D. Uncheck Format before copying on the Floppy Disk deployment screen of the Package and Deployment Wizard.

C. Check Format before copying on the Floppy Disk deployment screen of the Package and Deployment Wizard. By checking this check box, floppies will be formatted before the application update files are copied to disk.

26. Which is an attribute of inline error handling?

A. Uses labels and branches out from your code

B. Centralizes error handling

C. Doesn't use labels, and doesn't branch out from your code

D. Passes the error to a function

C. Inline error handling doesn't use labels. As such, it doesn't branch out from your code.

27. What must you use at the end of an inline error-handling routine that uses Select Case?

    A. A Resume statement that returns processing to a line or label

    B. Resume

    C. Resume Next

    D. Err.Clear
    D. Err.Clear must be used at the end of an inline error handler that uses Select Case. The Clear method is called after a Select Case is because there are no Resume statements.

28. You are experiencing an error, and you think it is occurring in a class module. Whenever you enter Break mode, VB breaks at the code that calls the module. What can you do to have VB break at the code that is actually causing the error?

    A. On the General tab of Options, select Break in Class Module.

    B. On the Error Trapping tab of Options, select Break in Class Module.

    C. On the General tab of Options, select Break on Error.

    D. On the Error Trapping tab of Options, select Break on Error.
    A. On the General tab of Options, select Break in Class Module. With the other options in the Error Trapping section of the General tab, VB will break at the code that called the class, and not in the code in the class module that actually causes the error.

29. Which object allows you to determine what error has occurred?

    A. Number

    B. Source

    C. Err

    D. Description
    C. Err is the only object offered in this question. The other choices are all properties of the Err object. The Err object allows you to determine what error has occurred, and offers information about that error through its properties.

30. An error is encountered, and it is passed up the call stack. What will happen if there are no error handlers in the calling procedures?

    A. A message will be displayed and the application will exit.

    B. The application will lock up.

    C. Other error handlers in the application will be sought.

    D. The next line of code will automatically be executed in the procedure where the error occurred.
    A. If there are no error handlers, a message will be displayed and the application will exit.

31. Which of the following allows you to execute error-handling code based on certain conditions? (Choose all that apply.)

A. If...Then

B. Do...While

C. Select Case

D. Any loop
   A, C. You can have error-handling code execute to meet certain conditions by using If...Then and Select Case structures.

32. You create error handling that passes the error to a function. Which of the following will result from your doing this? (Choose all that apply.)

   A. Decreases the chance of logic and syntax errors.

   B. Increases the chance of logic and syntax errors.

   C. Increases the size of the application. More code exists than if you had used other styles of error handling.

   D. Decreases the size of the application. Less code exists than if you had used other styles of error handling.
      A, D. Most of the code resides in the function, so there is less chance for logic and syntax errors, because you're not rewriting the same code over in your procedures. It also makes your application smaller, because it minimizes the error-handling code used in the application.

33. Which of the following best describes inline error handling?

   A. Inline error handling centralizes error handling.

B. Inline error handling passes errors to a function.

C. Inline error handling deals with errors immediately after they occur.

D. None of the above.
   C. Inline error handling deals with errors immediately after they occur.

34. You are concerned about errors occurring in your error-handling routine. Which of the following options are available to you for dealing with errors that occur in error handlers? (Choose all that apply.)

   A. Visually check error-handling code for errors

   B. Invoke error handling from within the error handler

   C. Do nothing. The error handler handles errors, so it can deal with its own errors.

   D. Create a loop that runs multiple times through the error handler. This will make the error handler deal with its own error.
      A, B. You can deal with errors that occur in error-handling routines by visually checking error handlers for errors, or by invoking error handling from within the error handler.

35. VB processes code line by line. Which statement will allow your code to exit if no error has occurred and keep VB from processing an error handler that follows?

   A. Exit Sub

   B. End Sub

C. Resume

D. End Error

A. Exit Sub allows you code to exit a subprocedure if no error has occurred. This keeps lines that follow the EXIT SUB from processing lines of code that follow, like your error-handling routine.

36. Which of the following would be a label used for an error handler?

A. ErrHandler

B. ErrHandler:

C. Err

D. Label

B. ErrHandler:. A label for an error handler is created by typing the name of your error handler followed by a colon.

37. An error-handling routine is part of a procedure. The error handler experiences an error. What will happen?

A. A message will be displayed and the application will exit.

B. The application will exit.

C. The error handler will handle its own error.

D. The error will be passed to the calling procedure.

A. When an error handler that experiences an error is part of a procedure, a message will be displayed, and the application will exit.

38. Which option in VB version 6 checks for syntax errors as they occur?

A. Syntax

B. Auto Syntax Check

C. Check Syntax

D. Auto Syntax

B. Auto Syntax Check will bring syntax errors to your attention as you move away from a line of code that contains a syntax error.

39. Which kind of error does the following code show?

```
Dum x As Integer
```

A. Logic

B. Syntax

C. Runtime

D. Grammatical

B. This is an example of a syntax error. This is an improper use of the programming language, as there is no keyword Dum. It should read Dim.

40. You have decided to deploy your application update to the Internet. Which deployment method will you choose in the Package and Deployment Wizard?

A. Internet

B. Web Publishing

C. Network Folder

D. Folder

B. To deploy an application update to an Internet Web site, choose Web Publishing.

B

About the CD

This CD-ROM contains a browser-based testing product, the *Personal Testing Center*. The *Personal Testing Center* is easy to install. Just click Setup and you will be walked through the installation. The Personal Testing Center program group will be created in the Start Programs folder.

Test-Type Choices

With the *Personal Testing Center*, you have three options in which to run the program: Live, Practice, and Review. Each test type will draw from a pool of over 1,200 potential questions. Your choice of test type will depend on whether you would like to simulate an actual MCSD exam, receive instant feedback on your answer choices, or review concepts using the testing simulator. Note that selecting the Full Screen icon on Internet Explorer's standard toolbar gives you the best display of the *Personal Testing Center*.

Live

The Live timed test type is meant to reflect the actual exam as closely as possible. You will have 90 minutes in which to complete the exam. You will have the option to skip questions and return to them later, move to the previous question, or end the exam. Once the timer has expired, you will automatically go to the scoring page to review your test results.

Managing Windows

The testing application runs inside an Internet Explorer 4.0 browser window. We recommend that you use the full-screen view to minimize the amount of text scrolling you need to do. However, the application will initiate a second iteration of the browser when you link to an Answer in Depth or a Review Graphic. If you are running in full-screen view, the second iteration of the browser will be covered by the first. You can toggle between the two windows with ALT-TAB, you can click your task bar to maximize the second window, or you can get out of full-screen mode and arrange the two windows so they are both visible on the screen at the same time. The application will not initiate more than two browser windows, so you aren't left with hundreds of open windows for each Answer in Depth or Review Graphic that you view.

Saving Scores as Cookies

Your exam score is stored as a browser cookie. If you've configured your browser to accept cookies, your score will be stored in a cookie named History. If you don't accept cookies, you cannot permanently save your scores. If you delete the History cookie, the scores will be deleted permanently.

Using the Browser Buttons

The test application runs inside the Internet Explorer 4.0 browser. You should navigate from screen to screen by using the application's buttons, not the browser's buttons.

JavaScript Errors

If you encounter a JavaScript error, you should be able to proceed within the application. If you cannot, shut down your Internet Explorer 4.0 browser session and relaunch the testing application.

Practice

When choosing the Practice exam type, you have the option of receiving instant feedback as to whether your selected answer is correct. The questions will be presented to you in numerical order, and you will see every question in the available question pool for each section you chose to be tested on.

As with the Live exam type, you have the option of continuing through the entire exam without seeing the correct answer for each question. The number of questions you answered correctly, along with the percentage of correct answers, will be displayed during the post-exam summary report. Once you have answered a question, click the Answer icon to display the correct answer.

You have the option of ending the Practice exam at any time, but your post-exam summary screen may reflect an incorrect percentage based on the number of questions you failed to answer. Questions that are skipped are counted as incorrect answers on the post-exam summary screen.

Review

During the Review exam type, you will be presented with questions similar to both the Live and Practice exam types. However, the Answer icon is not present, as every question will have the correct answer posted near the bottom of the screen. You have the option of answering the question without looking at the correct answer. In the Review exam type, you can also return to previous questions and skip to the next question, as well as end the exam by clicking the Stop icon.

The Review exam type is recommended when you have already completed the Live exam type once or twice, and would now like to determine which questions you answered correctly.

Questions with Answers

For the Practice and Review exam types, you will have the option of clicking a hyperlink titled Answers in Depth, which will present relevant study material aimed at exposing the logic behind the answer in a separate browser window. By having two browsers open (one for the test engine and one for the review information), you can quickly alternate between the two windows while keeping your place in the exam. You will find that additional windows are not generated as you follow hyperlinks throughout the test engine.

Scoring

The *Personal Testing Center* post-exam summary screen, called Benchmark Yourself, displays the results for each section you chose to be tested on, including a bar graph, similar to the real exam, which displays the percentage of correct answers. You can compare your percentage to the actual passing percentage for each section. The percentage displayed on the post-exam summary screen is not the actual percentage required to pass the exam. You'll see the number of questions you answered correctly compared to the total number of questions you were tested on. If you choose to skip a question, it will be marked as incorrect. Ending the exam by clicking the End button with questions still unanswered lowers your percentage, as these questions will be marked as incorrect.

Clicking the End button and then the Home button allows you to choose another exam type, or test yourself on another section.

C

About the
Web Site

As you know by now, Global Knowledge Network is the largest independent IT training company in the world. Just by purchasing this book, you have also secured a free subscription to the Global Knowledge Network Web site and its many resources. You can find it at http://access.globalknowledge.com.

Access Global Knowledge Network

You can log on directly at the Global Knowledge site, and you will be e-mailed a new, secure password immediately upon registering.

What You'll Find There . . .

The wealth of useful information at the Global Knowledge site falls into three categories.

Skills Gap Analysis

Global Knowledge offers several ways for you to analyze your networking skills and discover where they may be lacking. Using Global Knowledge Network's trademarked Competence Key Tool, you can do a skills gap analysis and get recommendations for where you may need to do some more studying. (Sorry, it just might not end with this book!)

Networking

You'll also gain valuable access to another asset: people. At the Access Global site, you'll find threaded discussions, as well as live discussions. You will talk to other MCSD candidates, get advice from folks who have already taken the exams, and get access to instructors and MCTs.

Product Offerings

Of course, Global Knowledge also offers its products here, and you may find some valuable items for purchase—CBTs, books, or courses. Browse freely and see if there's something that could help you take that next step in career enhancement.

D

Conventions

A s with anything that's been around a while, there are conventions that apply to good programming. Conventions are a standardized way of doing things, and they often make things much easier in programming. They affect the structure and appearance of code, making it easier to read and maintain. There are naming conventions, coding conventions, and constant- and variable-naming conventions. Together they allow a programmer to look at the work of another, and help him or her in determining what is going on in code.

Coding Conventions

When you're programming, you should follow certain conventions in your code. These include the placement of variables and the structure of the code itself. When you declare variables, you should always place them at the top of a procedure. You can place your variables anywhere before they are used, but you should always put them at the top. That way, any changes can easily be made after looking for the variables at the top of a procedure. You always know where to find them.

A good example of the usefulness of placing variables at the top of the code is an accountant declaring a variable to be a value that represents minimum wage. Minimum wage changes every few years. When it does, the accountant doesn't have to search through the code to change the variable; it is always at the top of the procedure. In such an example, the code might appear as follows:

```
Private Sub WrkWeek()
Dim curAnswer, curMinWage As Currency
Dim intHours As Integer
curMinWage = 6.85
Hours = 40
    curAnswer = curMinWage * intHours

    MsgBox curAnswer
End Sub
```

This example shows several things in addition to where to declare variables and assign values to them. First, it shows the importance of using meaningful names. By looking at intHours and curMinWage, you can automatically tell what they represent. While you could have used names like x, y, and z for variables, these names don't explain much about their purpose. This also applies to naming procedures. When you see a name like WrkWeek, you can determine that this probably has something to do with a work week.

This example also displays the use of spacing in your code. Visual Basic 6.0 ignores white space (the spacing in your code where nothing appears). So indenting code and adding blank spaces to separate parts of code (by pressing ENTER) is ignored by VB. Though the compiler ignores the white space, its presence makes it considerably easier for programmers to read.

While a procedure or function should always deal with one task (such as calculating your paycheck or opening another form), you will always have parts of code that deal with different things. For example, declaring variables and the code that deals with those variables are two different parts of code. You should leave a blank line between such items. If your code does different tasks, such as running a loop and displaying a message box, you should separate the code with blank lines. By doing this, your code becomes significantly easier to read.

You should also indent your code to show different tasks in your code. For example, using nested If...Then statements can be confusing if they are bunched together. If parts of the code are indented, it becomes easier to read. Compare the two versions of code in the following example, and you can see the difference:

```
If x < y then
If z>x then
Msgbox "z is greater than y"
End if
Msgbox "x is less than y"
End if
```

```
If x < y then
    If z>x then
        Msgbox "z is greater than y"
    End if
Msgbox "x is less than y"
End if
```

When the lines of code are indented, you can easily see which End If applies to which If statement. You can also see what code applies to which If...Then statement. Indenting code organizes it so that you can read it much more easily.

If you have lines of code that are particularly long, stretching past the width of your code window, you should split the line of code across two or more lines. This is done with the line continuation character. This character is a space followed by an underscore; it makes your code easier to read, without affecting its performance. The following is an example of a single line of code, split across several lines with the line continuation character.

```
txtMyText.Text= "This is my line " _
& "that is split across several lines " _
& "of code."
```

While one statement should appear on each line of code, it should also be mentioned that you can put several lines of related code on the same line. This is done by using a colon (:) to indicate a separation between each statement, as shown in the following example:

```
Label1.Caption = "Hello World": Label1.BackColor = vbRed
```

The preceding listing shows two related statements, separated by a colon. When VB reads it, it will recognize this as two different statements.

In addition to conventions that affect the appearance of your code, you should use comments in your code. Comments can be placed in code by beginning your sentence with an apostrophe ('). Comments can be placed alone on a line, or at the end of a line of code. If you are placing the comment on a line by itself, you can also use the REM statement, which is short for remark. The REM statement is a way of making comments that goes back to the early days of programming and is still used today. The following shows examples of comments in action:

```
REM This starts my program
Dim x As Integer 'This declares x as an integer
'The following line displays x
txtMyText.Text=x
```

In addition to showing how comments are used in code, this example shows how they should *not* be used. You should avoid commenting code that is obvious (stating that "this starts my program") and commenting on everything occurring in your code. Another bad example is explaining that a variable is being declared. Try to code with other programmers in mind. Ask yourself, "Will this be obvious to another programmer?" If the answer is no, then comment it. In addition, keep in mind that, while a chunk of code makes sense to you now, it may not be so clear to you six months or a year from now. Commenting code avoids such problems.

on the job *A colleague of mine experienced a particularly funny example of bad commenting. He was working on some code written by a person who no longer worked for the company. While working on the code, he came across the comment "Don't touch this. It's important!" Since the code was being upgraded, he had to spend extra time determining if the code was still "important" or was now obsolete. Unfortunately, it was a particularly long and elaborate piece of code. I say this example is funny, because it happened to him, not me. It does illustrate the need to be straight to the point and explain things properly when writing comments.*

Object-Naming Conventions

Naming conventions allow you to look at an object and determine what it is. Rather than having to guess if MyLine is a label, text box, or who-knows-what, you should be able to look at an object's name and determine what it is. This is done by adding a prefix to the object's name to specify the type of object.

Table D-1 lists prefixes commonly used for controls in VB version 6. You should use these when naming objects in VB.

TABLE D-I

Standard Prefixes for Object-Naming Conventions

Control	Prefix	Example
3D Panel	pnl	pnlPanel
ADO Data	ado	adoData
Animated button	ani	aniEnter
Check box	chk	chkBold
Combo box, drop-down list box	cbo	cboListing
Command button	cmd	cmdExit

Control	Prefix	Example
Common dialog	dlg	dlgOpen
Communications	com	comModem
Control (used within procedures when the specific type is unknown)	ctr	ctrControl
Data	dat	datData
Data-bound combo box	dbcbo	dbcboOrders
Data-bound grid	dbgrd	dbgrdMyGrid
Data-bound listbox	dblst	dblstEmployee
Data combo	dbc	dbcLastName
Data grid	dgd	dgdBooks
Data list	dbl	dblCost
Data repeater	drp	drpDatRep
Date picker	dtp	dtpDatPic
Directory listbox	dir	dirDirect
Drive listbox	drv	drvSource
File listbox	fil	filFile
Flat scroll bar	fsb	fsbScroll
Form	frm	frmMain
Frame	fra	fraOptions
Gauge	gau	gauStatus
Graph	gra	graIncome
Grid	grd	grdOutcome
Hierarchical flexgrid	hlex	flexPublisher
Horizontal scroll bar	hsb	hsbMove
Image	img	ligMyPic
Image combo	imgcbo	imgcboPicture
ImageList	ils	ilsMyImage

Control	Prefix	Example
Label	lbl	lblFirstName
Lightweight check box	lwchk	lwchkMyBox
Lightweight combo box	lwcbo	lwcboAuthor
Lightweight command button	lwcmd	lwcmdEnter
Lightweight frame	lwfra	lwfraSave
Lightweight horizontal scroll bar	lwhsb	lwhsbHorBar
Lightweight listbox	lwlst	lwlstPrice
Lightweight option button	lwopt	lwoptGross
Lightweight text box	lwtxt	lwoptFirst
Lightweight vertical scroll bar	lwvsb	lwvsbHigh
Line	lin	linMyLine
Listbox	lst	lstCustomer
ListView	lvw	lvwTitles
MAPI message	mpm	mpmMessage
MAPI session	mps	mpsSession
MCI	mci	mciVideo
Menu	mnu	mnuFile
Month view	mvw	mvwMonth
MS Chart	ch	chMyChart
MS Flex grid	msg	msgFlexGrid
MS Tab	mst	mstTab
OLE container	ole	oleFiesta
Option button	opt	optCanada
Picture box	pic	picMyPic

Control	Prefix	Example
Picture clip	clp	clpPicClip
ProgressBar	prg	prgDataRate
Remote Data	rd	rdRemDat
RichTextBox	rtf	rtfDetails
Shape	shp	shpMyShape
Slider	sld	sldSlideBar
Spin	spn	spnOutHere
StatusBar	sta	staMyStat
SysInfo	sys	sysMem
TabStrip	tab	tabTeStrip
Text box	txt	txtFirstName
Timer	tmr	tmrTest
Toolbar	tlb	tlbFunctions
Treeview	tre	treDirect
UpDown	upd	updDirection
Vertical scroll bar	vsb	vsbMyBar

Table D-2 shows the prefixes for Data Access Objects (DAO). You should use these prefixes when naming DAO objects.

TABLE D-2

Prefixes for Data Access Objects

DAO Object	Prefix	Example
Container	con	conMyCont
Database	db	dbCustomer
DBEngine	dbe	dbeVaroom
Document	doc	docMyDoc
Field	fld	fldFirstName

TABLE D-2	DAO Object	Prefix	Example
Prefixes for Data Access Objects (*continued*)	Group	grp	grpMarketing
	Index	ix	idxGender
	Parameter	prm	prmMyPara
	QueryDef	qry	qryTopSales
	Recordset	rec	recMyRec
	Relation	rel	relFinance
	TableDef	tbd	tbdPublishers
	User	usr	usrMyUser
	Workspace	wsp	wspMyWork

Variable-Naming Conventions

In addition to objects, you should use naming conventions for variables. This will allow you to identify easily the data type of your variable, and avoid improperly matching data types. An example of such an error would be trying to multiply a Boolean data type called Answer by an integer named Amount. By using the prefixes of variable-naming conventions, you would rename these to intAmount and blnAnswer, and avoid such an error. Table D-3 lists the standard prefixes.

If you are using prefixes, I can't stress enough that you should give your variable a meaningful name. Renaming a variable called x to intx may follow the naming convention, but it hardly gives an accurate indication of what the variable is for. You should always try to name the variable something that indicates what it is being used for.

Using meaningful names is equally important when naming procedures, functions, and objects. You should try to determine what something is being used for, and name it accordingly. It is also wise to show the scope of a variable as being modular or global by prefixing it with the letter m or g, respectively.

While it may seem difficult to remember the methods and prefixes of conventions, they are well worth learning and using. In the long run, they

TABLE D-3	Data Type	Prefix	Example
Variable-Naming Conventions	Boolean	bln	blnYesNo
	Byte	byt	bytOutaCrime
	Collection object	col	colComics
	Currency	cur	curMoola
	Date (Time)	dtm	dtmBDate
	Double	dbl	dblStarVal
	Error	err	errOopsy
	Integer	int	intAge
	Long	lng	lngDistance
	Object	obj	objMyAffection
	Single	sng	sngUnattached
	String	str	strName
	User-defined type	udt	udtCustomer
	Variant	vnt	vntMyVar

will save you a substantial amount of time. You (and anyone who reads your code in the future) will certainly prefer taking a moment to look up a prefix rather than spending considerably more time searching through code to figure out the data type of a variable.

E

The MCSD
Career Center

Y ou might be tempted to think that your work is finished once you have achieved your MCSD certification. Nothing could be further from the truth. Now that you have the certification, you need a job that is going to provide opportunities to use your certification. You might also look for a job that will allow you to obtain additional certifications. Finding that job can be difficult if you don't know where to look or what to look for.

The MCSD "Help Wanteds": Planning Your Attack

Looking at the title of this section, you might think you were going to war. Well, it's not quite as bad as that; but a job-hunting campaign, like a military campaign, should have a strategy. Many people start with the attitude that if you have no idea what you're looking for, then you won't be disappointed with what you find. There's probably some truth in that, but I would add that you probably won't find the job that's right for you, either.

I also like to use the analogy of courtship when explaining the importance of having a strategy for your search. If you've never stopped to think about your perfect mate, then chances are you don't really know what you're looking for. If you go ahead and get married anyway, you could find yourself in a marriage that is going to lead to a messy divorce or many years of unhappiness.

Getting fired or quitting a job isn't as bad as getting a divorce, but it's not much fun. In my career I've had good and bad jobs, jobs that have gone from good to bad, and jobs that have gone from bad to good. I've been hired, fired, and I've "moved on to other opportunities" (I quit). All of these changes required decisions from me, and a lot of thought had to go into those decisions.

In the next few pages I'm going to try to help you develop a job search strategy. Since I am both a certified professional and a technical recruiter, I'll try to give you a little insight from both sides of the table.

(✋)
**recruiter
@dvice**

Before talking to a headhunter or recruiter, put together an information packet that includes a resume, a cover letter, a skills list, a project list, and maybe even references. The more information you provide, the easier it will be for a headhunter or recruiter to place you.

The Job Search

We begin with the job search. Time seems to be the biggest factor for most folks when it comes to looking for a new job. How long is this going to take? That's a tough question. The answer depends on the market, on the type of job you are looking for, and your personal situation.

The ideal situation to be in when searching for a new job is to have a job you already like. That might not make sense at first, but think about it for a minute. If you don't feel like you have to leave your current job, you aren't going to feel as much pressure to take a less than optimal new job. You will spend more time learning about new opportunities and educating yourself about what you're getting into.

With more time, you may broaden your search and consider areas or industries that you might not have considered under a time crunch. You'll feel better about holding out for a higher salary or a better signing bonus. Most importantly, you will not be rushed into a decision that is going to shape the rest of your life. You will have time to decide what you want, and then to develop a strategy for how you are going to get it.

Incidentally, recruiters love to find people who are under the gun, because recruiters know that they can get these people on board faster and at a lower cost. However, a manager will recognize that this type of person may not be around for long, because the person may be getting into a job he isn't suited for. Remember that recruiters make recommendations, but it's managers who make decisions.

If you happen to find yourself "between jobs" at the moment, don't sweat it. If you are certified, or are getting certified, the jobs are out there. There has never been a better time to be an out-of-work Microsoft Certified Professional. If you need to convince yourself of this, find the latest salary survey from *MCP Magazine*. Believe me, you will feel better about your situation. Just relax and take some time to focus on your strategy. Then implement that strategy.

If you aren't currently in a job, you may actually have an advantage over someone who does have a job. You have an abundance of one of the world's most limited resources: spare time!

Networking 101

You have heard someone say, "It's not what you know, but whom you know." There is some truth in that. Networking has two big benefits for you if it's done right. The first benefit is contacts. The second benefit is association.

The contacts benefit is fairly straightforward, so we'll talk about that one in a second. Let's talk about associations first, since that's the one that might not be so obvious. One very common method of networking is to join professional groups like software user groups. Even if you don't attend the meetings, you can tell people that you're a card-carrying member of the XYZ group.

If the XYZ group has a reputation for being a very technical and prestigious group, chances are your value just went up in the mind of the recruiter. By the way, you are also demonstrating the capacity to be social. Most recruiters aren't interested in even the most technically proficient people, if they can't relate to other people.

Let's say for a moment that you did join a users group or any type of social organization, and you actually attended the meetings. Whom might you meet there? Well, you might meet me or one of my fellow recruiters. That could prove helpful.

You might also meet directors, project managers, senior technical leads, or entrepreneurs. All of these people are always on the lookout for talent—it's ingrained in them. Every time they meet someone new, the question they ask themselves is, "Could I use this person?"

If you can prompt someone to ask that question about you, and answer "yes," then you have probably just found yourself a job. At a minimum, you have gained recognition from an influential person inside the organization. That puts you about a light-year ahead of your competitors who are answering ads from the Sunday paper.

(✋)
**recruiter
@dvice**

Make yourself a list of questions before going into an interview. You don't even have to memorize them. Take notes, and press for information if you aren't satisfied with the answers. Remember that you are interviewing the company just as much as they are interviewing you.

Using Placement Services

I have mixed feelings about placement services. I think placement services are excellent vehicles for finding entry-level positions. If you have just finished your MCSD, then a placement service might be a good choice for you.

However, if you've had your MCSD for a while, or if you already have a lot of industry experience, then be careful of placement services. Most services make their money by doing a volume business. You register with the service, and the service attempts to place you in the first job request they receive for which you are qualified.

Placement services rarely take the time to investigate the jobs into which they are placing people. Many times the placement services get their lists of job positions right out of the newspaper. Many of the opportunities that you will find through placement services are temporary staffing positions.

This might be just what you need to build a resume. However, for an experienced individual looking for a full-time position as a senior technical lead, listing a number of temporary staffing positions on your resume may do you more harm than good.

If you choose to use a placement service, consider using one of the nationwide services like Kelly Technical Services or AeroTek. I have been impressed in the past with the speed at which these services have filled positions, and with the quality of applicants that these services attract. Also, if you are willing to travel, the nationwide services may be able to find you a specific type of job.

To sum it up, my advice on placement services is not to discount them. Just make sure that the type of job you are looking for is the type of job that the service fills on a regular basis.

Going Online

By now, I hope I don't need to tell you that you can find a wealth of information on the Internet. This includes company marketing information, securities exchange information, and recruiting information. Almost all of the Fortune 500 companies, and many of the smaller ones, provide a way to submit resumes either through an e-mail address or through a Web form.

If you submit your resume through e-mail, be sure that you clearly indicate what file format it's in. Pick something common like RTF format or Microsoft Word 6.0/95 format. When you submit your resume via e-mail, you can be reasonably sure that someone is going to print it out and read it.

Here's a situation where you need to plan for the least common denominator. All your high resolution color graphics, watermarks, and textures may look great at home, but when printed on the high-volume laser printer at the recruiter's office, they become distracting. Guess what happens to resumes that are distracting and hard to read. That's right—straight in to the trash. I've thrown away dozens of resumes because they were just too much work to read.

When submitting your resume via an online form, you need a slightly different strategy. Think key words. There's a good chance that all of that information you are entering is being stored in a database. At some point, someone is going to run a query against that database that goes something like this, "Show me all of the MCSDs with at least TWO YEARS WORK EXPERIENCE and CERTIFIED on Visual Basic."

You've got to get as many keywords as you can into the information you are entering in the database. That way, your name will come up more often. As you can imagine, trying to maximize keywords can lead to some pretty hilarious text, but it works. It also demonstrates that you understand how computer systems work. That isn't lost on recruiters

If you happen to be just what a company is looking for, then submitting your resume online might be a good idea. However, it's been my experience that submitting a resume online isn't much better than mailing in a resume to the attention of the personnel director.

I'm not fond of this method, because it lacks a certain personal touch. Also, you really have no idea who is receiving your resume. It might be someone in the personnel department at a company, or it might be someone at a placement office that has the contract for the company you are interested in.

Whenever I submit my resume, I always identify the job I'm looking for, then I find out who is responsible for filling that position. This often requires a little inside knowledge. Try to find someone in the organization who will give you an exact job title and the name of a manager responsible for filling that position.

An excellent source for this type of information is ex-employees. Most will be more than happy to give you the inside scoop. They will probably also be willing to tell you what to look out for. Finding an ex-employee and taking him or her out to lunch may be one of the best investments you ever make.

After a personal contact, such as a phone call or a lunch appointment, I then submit my resume to that person. That person then becomes my sponsor. He or she passes my resume on to whoever needs to see it, hopefully with some positive remarks. That is a level of personal contact that just can't be achieved through an online submittal process.

Getting the Advice of Peers

Once you have identified a company that you want to work for, you need to get the lay of the land. You need to gather intelligence. Try to make some contacts within the company, and try to meet some people who have interviewed with the company before. This is usually easier said than done, but you can get some really valuable information.

Ask around. You might just get lucky and find someone who has successfully, or unsuccessfully, done what you are trying to do. Try to figure out what works and what doesn't. Be careful, though. If you start asking too many questions, you might tip your hand to either a vindictive supervisor or a coworker planning on interviewing for the same position you are. Know who your friends are.

Now is the right time for you to make a friend at the company you are interested in. There is nothing better than inside information. Find someone who is willing to check the internal postings a couple of times a week, or someone who knows someone.

This might be easier than you think. Many companies are now offering finder's fees for technical talent. If an employee submits someone's resume, and the candidate is eventually hired, that employee may have earned a bonus of a few thousand dollars. You would be amazed how many "friends" you'll have if you have the potential of putting a few thousand dollars in their pockets.

The Interview

So far, so good. You've been granted an interview. This is no time to forget about your strategy! On the contrary, now is the time to redouble your efforts. This may be your only face-to-face interaction with the company of your dreams. You've got to make a good impression, and you are going to be limited in the amount of time you have to do that.

Try to ask pointed questions that demonstrate that you know programming. For example, you might ask a technical interviewer about their applications and languages being used. Find out whether the company has a 100 percent 32-bit desktop, and whether the Y2K issue is presenting any problems.

All of these are great questions if you are talking to a technical interviewer. These are not appropriate questions if you are talking to someone from the human resources department, or a senior nontechnical manager. If you're talking to a vice president or a senior manager, don't talk technical, talk business. Ask whether the company has done a Total Cost of Ownership (TCO) analysis, and if so, what were the results. Ask what the acceptable Return on Investment (ROI) is for a capital project.

If you aren't comfortable with these questions, stick to something simpler like asking what projects are in the works to improve productivity, improve reliability, or reduce support costs. These are the issues that business people wrestle with every day. If you want to relate to these folks, you've got to speak their language, and you've got to talk about things that they care about.

When answering questions, give direct, concise answers. If you don't know the answer, admit it; then offer your best guess. Guessing is acceptable, as long as you identify your answer as a guess. Don't ever try to pass yourself off as something you are not. A technical interviewer will smell a phony as soon as the answers start to stink.

Working with a Headhunter

As someone looking for a job, I loved working with headhunters. As a recruiter, I hate competing with them. So for the purpose of this discussion, I'm going to try to think like someone looking for a job.

The really nice thing about headhunters is that most of them are paid a finder's fee that is a percentage of the salary of the person hired. Consequently, the more money you make, the more money your headhunter makes. This is one of the few situations in life where your agent's best interests are truly your best interests. Also, most headhunters don't get paid at all unless they fill a position. They work fast, and usually with remarkable results.

There are some things to watch out for, though. There are people out there calling themselves career consultants, or even headhunters. They want you to pay them a few hundred dollars to build a resume and to tell you what your ideal job is.

First, you don't need someone to tell you what your ideal job is. You should be able to figure that out on your own. Second, if these people even have a placement service, you would be amazed how many times your ideal job just happens to be the position they are trying to fill. Third, there are too many good recruiters and headhunters out there who don't charge you a dime. You should never, ever pay someone to find you a job! Now give me a second to get off my soapbox...

I guess I get so excited about this topic because I know some really good headhunters who do excellent work. When they make a placement, the company is happy, the employee is happy, and the headhunter made a little money. But there are always a few who give the rest of the recruiting industry a bad name, because they've taken clients' money and left them in the same job, or a worse job.

Headhunters often specialize in a particular type of job, location, or industry. If you are looking for something specific, ask around and find a headhunter who has concentrated on that area. Not only will this person know what is going on in her specialty, she can help tailor your presentation to that area. That's the real benefit. Think of these specialists as insiders for hire—only you're not paying the bill!

Even if you don't need a specialist, before you contact a headhunter, try to narrow down your goals. Headhunters aren't in the business of being career counselors. They are in the business of finding you the job you're looking for. That's not to say that they won't help you. On the contrary, they will probably give you a great deal of attention. But only you know what you want.

Put together a professional-looking resume listing every skill you have. Also put together a cover letter that details what type of job you are looking for, what kind of salary and benefits package you need, and any other interesting bits of information about yourself. This is the documentation that is going to catch the eye of a headhunter.

Your headhunter will then probably take you out to lunch, and you two will have a chat. By the time you're ordering dessert, you will probably have defined your job requirements even more precisely. You may also leave with a list of things to do. The list might include making enhancements to your resume, researching companies, and maybe even scheduling an interview.

On the other hand, the headhunter may tell you point blank that you just aren't qualified for what you want to do, and that there is no way he or she could place you in the job you're looking for. That's hard to hear, but it's probably an honest assessment.

Remember that headhunters only make money if you make money. If a headhunter tells you that you're not qualified, you need to decide whether to continue pursuing this job with another headhunter, or look for another job for which you are better suited.

My advice is to swallow your pride, open your mind, and see what the headhunter has to say. Chances are, he's going to have some ideas that you might not have considered. At a minimum, you should be able to find out why you aren't qualified and what you need to do to get qualified for the job of your dreams.

One final thought on this topic. A lot of people worry that a headhunter is going to rush them into a job that they won't enjoy, just so the headhunter can get paid. Well, in the first place, you're the decision-maker. Only you can decide whether or not to take a job.

Second, a growing trend in the industry is that headhunters don't get paid a full commission until the client has held the job for more than six months. I like this trend because once again, your best interests dovetail with the headhunter's. There's little incentive for a headhunter to put you in a job you're not going to enjoy.

Working with headhunters has been a very positive experience for me. Some of the best jobs I've ever had have come through headhunters. If you find one you like, they are an excellent resource for taking your career where you want it to go.

Preparing for the Interview

Start with a little research. You need to be able to talk intelligently about the company you are interviewing with, the industry that company is in, and how you can help this company achieve its goals. At a minimum, you should check out the company's Web site and learn its mission statement, objectives, and goals. You need to demonstrate that you know where this company wants to go and how they are planning to get there.

You can also check out one of the online investment firms to gather information, if the company you're researching is publicly traded. Know what the financial status of the company is. Know whether there are any planned mergers or acquisitions.

You should also try to get a feel for the technology being used in the company. This information could be a little more difficult to obtain than financial information; you may need to find an insider. Be careful of making any recommendations about technology during an interview. After all, you don't want to tell someone how to do his job or step on someone's toes. You might, however, be able to identify some troublesome areas that your skills could ease.

Acing the Interview

I wish I could give you a nice, simple formula for ensuring success in an interview. If one exists, I haven't found it, and I don't know anyone who has.

By definition, an interview occurs when two or more people get together for the purpose of filling a job. When you get two people together, there exists the possibility for conflict. Unfortunately, you can do everything right and still have a lousy interview simply because your personality clashed with the personality of the person doing the interviewing.

One of the things that you might consider doing is buying a couple of books, audio tapes, or videos about interviewing or personal selling. There are lots of tapes on how to sell, and quite a few about interviewing. All of them will give you some ideas for building a personal relationship with someone in a very short amount of time.

Try to avoid obvious gimmick techniques like commenting on something you see in the person's office. I was on a sales call one time with a junior sales representative who made the mistake of complementing a manager about the large fish he had mounted on the wall. The manager looked right at the rep and said, "I hate that damn fish. My boss goes on all of these company-sponsored fishing trips, spends a fortune, and then decorates our offices with his stupid fish." The sales call was over before it even began.

This may sound like a cliché, but be yourself. Don't put on airs; don't try to be something you aren't. Most people are not good actors, and most recruiters can spot a performance very quickly. When a recruiter interviews you, he or she wants to get a sense of who you are—not just what you know. Don't make it hard on the recruiters by putting on a show.

When being interviewed, you should appear confident about yourself and your abilities. Practice showing confidence by standing in front of a mirror and "introducing yourself" a few times. Tell your mirror image how happy you are to have an opportunity to interview for the position. Then briefly explain to yourself what your qualifications are and why you would be a good fit for the position. (But avoid telling yourself that you are the *best* candidate for the position. You never know that, and you might be setting yourself up for feeling "robbed" if you're not eventually hired.) Finally, ask yourself a few questions about the job and your own plans, and then answer them. Try this technique. I guarantee it will be the toughest interview you ever have.

Now let's talk for a moment about interview etiquette. I've never seen a formal guide to interview etiquette, but there is certainly an informal set of expectations.

For example, most recruiters are tolerant of a candidate being ten minutes late. Five minutes early is preferable, but ten minutes late is acceptable. Beyond ten minutes, your chances for a successful interview begin to drop precipitously. If you are going to be more than ten minutes late, you definitely need to call, and you can probably expect to reschedule your interview.

Another piece of etiquette involves who speaks first in the interview. Once introductions are made, and everyone is comfortable, the interviewer will ask the first question. That question may be followed by another series of short-answer "warm-up" questions, or the interviewer may ask a more open-ended question.

Open-ended questions are designed to give the person being interviewed an opportunity to talk openly or to bend the conversation toward a topic he or she wants to discuss. Recognize different types of questions and respond appropriately. If you speak out of turn or fail to answer appropriately, you are running the risk of annoying the interviewer and having your interview cut short.

Incidentally, if the interviewer asks you a trick question, and it's obvious that it is a trick question, call him or her on it. Let him or her know that you're not afraid to call a donkey a donkey. Most interviewers will appreciate this and probably accord you a little more respect as a result.

Following Up on the Interview

Always follow up on an interview. This can be done with a simple thank-you card or phone call.

You're trying to accomplish several things with the follow-up: refreshing the memories of the decision makers (who may have interviewed numerous candidates), projecting a positive impression, and demonstrating interest and eagerness to work for this company.

Don't worry about looking desperate; you are more likely to come off as confident and professional. Never worry about following up an interview with a phone call to check the status of your application. In many companies, the people doing the interviewing are also the people doing real work. Interviewing is not their primary responsibility. Consequently, applications sometimes slip through the cracks. It may be up to you to keep the ball rolling by continuing to call and ask questions. You might get hired through persistence alone.

recruiter @dvice

Never stop looking for your perfect job. You should test the waters and go out on an interview or talk to a headhunter once every six months. High-tech industries change rapidly, and with that change comes a myriad of new opportunities.

Glossary

Access Key   A keystroke combination that allows something to be activated.

Active Server Pages (ASP)   A scripting environment in which processing of scripts takes place on an IIS or Web server.

ActiveX   Allows components to be packaged for delivery via Web browsers or other software.

ActiveX Controls   Software components used to create user interface elements for Web-based delivery.

ADO (ActiveX Data Objects)   Enables your client applications to manipulate and access data in a server (through any OLE DB provider). ADO supports key features for building Web-based and client-server applications.

Advanced Data TableGram Format   A proprietary data storage format from Microsoft.

Application Server   A component with a dual identity. It can be run like any standard EXE-type application, but can also be used by a client as an OLE server.

ASCII   An acronym for American Standard Code for Information Interchange. It uses numbers ranging from 0 to 255 to represent keyboard characters like numbers, letters, and special characters such as ! @ # $ % ^ & * ( ).

Asynchronous Processing   Processing that goes through several steps to complete a task. It allows the client to perform other tasks before returning earlier results.

Authentication   The logon process; it includes verifying correct username and password.

Binding   Binding means that your control is linked or tied to a data source, so it can access data contained within it.

Binding Collection   Works as a link between the consumer and source, allowing information from the source to be passed to the consumer. Using the Binding Collection allows you to bind data during runtime.

Bitness   The status of a process, whether it is 16-bit or 32-bit.

Boolean Value   A value of True or False. Boolean values must be one or the other.

Bound Mode   The property of an object when it is linked to a data source. (See also Binding.)

Break Mode   Allows the user to examine, debug, reset, step through, or continue execution of the application.

Business Object Dependencies   When turned on, Business object calls on services in other business objects.

Call-Back   An application makes a call to a function or method, and goes about its business. When the external function has completed the task, it calls the application back by calling a function in the client designated to answer it.

Call Stack   The chain of procedures; the order in which code and procedures are executed.

Calling Chain   (See Call Stack.)

CD Key   A code that comes with the installation package of software. Many installation processes require a valid CD key to be input before continuing the installation.

Change Event   An event coded to indicate that a change has occurred in a control.

Class Modules   Allow you to add custom object variable types to a VB project. Classes are templates that are used to create objects. They are the start for building COM components.

Code Window   This window in VB allows you to input and view the code making the application you're developing.

Command Object   One of the three main ADO objects; it defines commands and parameters and can execute commands against Connection objects.

Comments   Insertions into code that are not compiled, but provide explanation and clarification. They begin with an apostrophe.

Component Object Model (COM)   A standardized specification module that can be reused without modification in many different applications.

Conceptual Design   The process of identifying an application's requirements.

Concurrency   The locking method for a cursor. Concurrency types include read-only, optimistic, batch optimistic, and pessimistic.

Condition Compiling   Allows you to create one project that deals with all versions of your application.

Connection Object   One of the three main objects of ADO; it establishes connections with data sources, manages transactions, and reports errors from the underlying OLE DB components.

Constant   A data value that does not change. Constants are resolved when the application compiles.

Controls   Items that make up the user interface and often allow a user to input information; for example, buttons, text boxes, and labels.

Constraints   Business logic enforced by the database server by limiting data input, ensuring referential integrity.

Cross-Process Components   Another term for out-of-process components.

Cursor   The result set of an application connecting to a database to process rows of data. Cursors can be client-side and server-side, and are further broken down to static, forward-only, dynamic, and keyset.

Data Access Object (DAO)   An application programming interface independent of the Database Management System. Uses the Microsoft Jet engine.

Database Management System (DBMS)   Software tool that organizes, modifies, and analyzes information stored in a database.

Data Consumer   A class that can be bound to an external data source.

Data Environment Designer   Feature of Visual Basic that provides an interactive design environment for creating programmatic data access during runtime. Data Environment objects can leverage drag-and-drop to automate creation of data-bound controls.

Data Form Wizard   A wizard in Visual Basic that allows you to create forms quickly from a template.

Data Grid   A control that provides a direct exposure to all of the data defined by the data control in a spreadsheet format.

Data Report Designer   A feature of Visual Basic that allows simple reports to be created and integrated with the Data Environment Designer quickly and easily.

Dead Code   Unused code in an application. It should be removed before compiling. This does not include comments.

Dependent Objects   Objects created by using the methods exposed by externally creatable objects.

Deployment Stage   Phase of application design in which decisions are made about how components are or aren't distributed across the network.

Design Time   The operation mode of Visual Basic while an application is being created. You build the components and set properties of your application in this mode.

DHTML Page Designer   A feature of Visual Basic that allows you to design and create HTML documents without a previous knowledge of HTML.

Documentation   Recording the objectives of your application and what the aspects of your application do, and creating flowcharts, to name a few common examples. Documentation can be utilized in later stages of design and in the creation of Help documentation.

DSN (Data Source Name)   A term for collection of information used to connect an application to a particular ODBC database.

Dynamic HTML (DHTML)   Used for developing Web pages. DHTML allows Web page authors to dynamically change elements of an HTML document. You can add, delete, and modify what appears on a Web page.

Early Binding Method   In the variable declaration, telling the compiler in advance what type of object it will reference.

Error Handling   The part of a program that deals with errors in the rest of the program, in order to prevent a full system crash. It involves checking the error, handling the error in some way, and exiting the error handler.

Error Trapping   Writing code that allows the program the chance to correct an error, or offers the developer a chance to correct it.

Exposed Object   An object (such as a control in a different program) that your program can "see."

Extensibility   Allows an application to go beyond its original design.

Externally Creatable Objects   Top-level objects exposed by a component to the client.

Forms   Basic building blocks of a VB application.

General Declarations Section   The section of code in which you declare and define general variables.

Globally Unique Identifier (GUID)   A 128-bit number that is guaranteed to be unique across time and space.

Graphics Method   Performs runtime drawing operations and is used for animation and simulations.

Help Files   These files contain organized information about the application in use, to help users who are having trouble or want to learn more.

Hierarchical Cursor   A feature that allows you to create record sets that contain child record sets embedded as fields within the parent records.

HyperText Markup Language (HTML)   A standardized programming language to create Web documents and some Help files.

HTML Help   Help files for an application, which are created in HTML. They have the file extension CHM.

HTML Help Workshop   Allows you to create new HTML files, import existing HTML documents, and compile them into the format used for help.

Hungarian Notation   A set of standard prefixes for items in code (for example, mnu and txt).

Immediate Window   One of the Debug windows; lets you type code that responds as if it were directly in your code.

Initialize Event   Initializes any data used by the class and can be used to load forms used by the class.

Inline Error Handling   Inserting code where an error is likely to occur, to allow the program to skip over it to the next item without interruption.

In-Process Server   These are loaded into the process space and share memory with the client application; consequently, they are able to exchange information with the client more quickly than out-of-process servers.

Instancing   A property used to designate classes as available to the client (public) or for internal use only (private).

Integer   A variable type that requires a number.

IIS   Internet Information Server

Late Binding Method   Object variables are not declared with a specific class name. Instead, the variables are declared as type "Object." This method is used to provide the flexibility of accessing different types of objects with the same reference.

Locals Window   One of the Debug windows, allowing you to monitor the value of any variables within the current procedure's scope.

Logical Design   Phase of development that involves taking logical design information; this is where a system actually evolves.

Logic Error   A code executing without a syntax or runtime error, but producing unintended results.

Marshalling   Windows translating the communication between applications and/or components talking across process boundaries.

Menu Editor   A tool that allows you to implement menu-based navigational aids in the program under development.

Microsoft Data Access Components (MDAC)   A package of technology components intended to implement Universal Data Access. The version 2 release included OLE DB 2, ADO 2 (including an updated RDS), and ODBC 3.5.

Multiple Document Interface (MDI) Environment   The MDI environment contains child windows, which are contained in a single parent window.

Multitiered Application   An application that has its functionality broken out into components that are each tasked with a particular aspect of using the application.

Microsoft Jet   A proprietary database engine from Microsoft.

Object Browser   Used to quickly look up information on classes exposed by components, but cannot be used with components that do not expose type libraries. It allows you to view the classes, events, methods, properties, and constants in a project.

Object Linking and Embedding (OLE)   Obsolete form of COM objects, replaced by ActiveX.

Object-Oriented Programming (OOP)   System of programming that permits an abstract, modular hierarchy featuring inheritance, encapsulation, and polymorphism.

OLE Automation   Another term for the interaction among ActiveX components.

OLE DB   This specification model provides a standard definition of data access methods for data sources.

OLE Server   Another name for an ActiveX server.

Out-of-Process   The component is running in a separate process from the client application.

Parent Property   A property used to reference the parent object that contains it.

Permissions   Allowable actions taken by users (such as read-only, write, update, and delete).

Persistent Graphic   A method that stores output in memory and retains the graphic during screen events.

Physical Design   Design phase that takes the business objects and services identified in the logical design and maps them to software components.

Pointer   A reference to an address in memory where the object lives.

Private Variable   A variable released when the routine in which it is defined terminates.

Programmatic Interface   The properties and methods used to access the functionality of a software component.

Project Group   A setting in Visual Basic that allows you to work and test multiple projects at the same time.

Project Window   A window that allows you to navigate through the forms and modules that make up the application you're working on.

Property Get   Procedure executed when the calling code reads the property.

Property Let   Procedure used for nonobjects, such as variables.

Property Procedures   Allow you to execute a procedure when a value is changed or read, to have a property constrained to a small set of values, or to expose properties that are read-only.

Property Set   Procedure used when setting the value of an object property.

Public Variable A variable defined with the Public keyword; it is available to all procedures and functions, not just the one in which they are defined.

Query Builder A tool to automatically generate grammatically correct SQL queries from simple parameters defined by the developer.

Record Set Representation of all records in a table, or the result of a query.

Recordset Object One of the three main ADO objects; it provides methods to manage and manipulate result sets of information, in both Immediate and Batch modes.

Referential Integrity A method with which an RDBMS ensures that the proper references exist between key values, thus maintaining the validity of relationships.

Roles Sets of database users.

Runtime The time during which a program is run.

Runtime Error An error that occurs during the execution of a program, causing the program to halt. Runtime errors occur when a command attempts to perform an invalid action.

Scope The scope of a variable is the area in which other parts of code can be aware of an object or variable.

Services Model A conceptual model for designing a program that organizes your application's requirements into specific services.

Shape Command Language   Part of ADO that provides data shaping functionality. The commands allow you to define a hierarchy based on record relations, parameters, or aggregate function groupings. The syntax used by the Shape language is relatively complicated, and you should refer to the online help for more information about the syntax.

Shortcut Key   Shortcut keys allow a user to access a menu item at any time.

Single Document Interface (SDI) Environment   When this option is used, windows can be moved anywhere on the screen, and they will remain on top of other applications. (The user can see other open applications or the Windows Desktop in the background.)

Splash Screen   An initial screen that is displayed when an application is started.

Standard Module   Containers for procedures and declarations commonly accessed by other modules. There is only one copy of the module's data at any given time; a standard module's data exists for the life of the program.

Stored Procedures   Stored procedures are the code modules of SQL Server that give the database designer full programmatic control over data.

Synchronous Processing   A client making a method call that's blocked until the call returns.

Syntax Error   An error resulting from incorrect use of the programming language.

Terminate Event Associated with a class module; occurs when the object variable is set to nothing or goes out of scope. Used to save information, unload forms, and handle any other tasks required when the class ends.

Toolbox The main window with tools in Visual Basic. You can use it to drag controls onto your form, and you can customize it with new objects.

ToolTips The little labels that appear over buttons when your mouse has rested on an item for a moment without clicking.

Triggers Triggers fire when an update, insert, or delete happens on a table; they consist of Transact-SQL and can perform any number of tasks in response to a data change.

Twips A unit of measurement, equal to 1/20 of a point (about 1,440 twips in an inch). Twips are screen independent and allow the placement and proportion of items to appear the same on multiple screens.

Type Library Dictionary of classes and interfaces supported by a component.

Universal Data Access An initiative by Microsoft to allow applications to access information from any location, regardless of where or how it is stored.

Variable Used temporarily to hold values during a program's execution.

Variant Data type; a variable that can hold any type of data.

Versioning The capability of a COM component to remain compatible with clients using older versions of the component, while allowing the developer of the component to further enhance the component.

Viewport   The screen area used to display an ActiveX document in a container application.

Visual Component Manager   A new feature of Visual Basic 6.0 that manages a large number of separate components in an application and provides a way to find the needed components when the time comes to reuse them in applications.

Visual Data Manager   A component of Visual Basic that allows you to view the actual data underlying the data source.

Visual SourceSafe (VSS)   A component of Visual Basic that keeps a record of changes made to source code.

Visual Studio 6.0 Suite   A suite of programs that includes Visual Basic 6.0.

Watch   Allows you to monitor the values of variables, properties, and expressions at runtime.

Watch Window   One of the Debug windows; allows you to specify which expressions to watch, and returns information about their values as your program runs.

What's This Help   Help files that are context sensitive and that allow a user to get help on a specific item by pressing an access key.

Windows Explorer   A tool that comes with Windows 95 and Windows 98; allows the user to navigate around the file system easily.

Wizard   An easily followed series of steps to guide you through a particular process.

INDEX

W

Custom Corporate Network Training

Train on Cutting Edge Technology
We can bring the best in skill-based training to your facility to create a real-world hands-on training experience. Global Knowledge Network has invested millions of dollars in network hardware and software to train our students on the same equipment they will work with on the job. Our relationships with vendors allow us to incorporate the latest equipment and platforms into your on-site labs.

Maximize Your Training Budget
Global Knowledge Network provides experienced instructors, comprehensive course materials, and all the networking equipment needed to deliver high quality training. You provide the students; we provide the knowledge.

Avoid Travel Expenses
On-site courses allow you to schedule technical training at your convenience, saving time, expense, and the opportunity cost of travel away from the workplace.

Discuss Confidential Topics
Private on-site training permits the open discussion of sensitive issues such as security, access, and network design. We can work with your existing network's proprietary files while demonstrating the latest technologies.

Customize Course Content
Global Knowledge Network can tailor your courses to include the technologies and the topics which have the greatest impact on your business. We can complement your internal training efforts or provide a total solution to your training needs.

Corporate Pass
The Corporate Pass Discount Program rewards our best network training customers with preferred pricing on public courses, discounts on multimedia training packages, and an array of career planning services.

Global Knowledge Network Training Lifecycle
Supporting the Dynamic and Specialized Training Requirements of Information Technology Professionals

- Define Profile
- Assess Skills
- Design Training
- Deliver Training
- Test Knowledge
- Update Profile
- Use New Skills

College Credit Recommendation Program
The American Council on Education's CREDIT program recommends 53 Global Knowledge Network courses for college credit. Now our network training can help you earn your college degree while you learn the technical skills needed for your job. When you attend an ACE-certified Global Knowledge Network course and pass the associated exam, you earn college credit recommendations for that course. Global Knowledge Network can establish a transcript record for you with ACE, which you can use to gain credit at a college or as a written record of your professional training that you can attach to your resume.

Registration Information

COURSE FEE: The fee covers course tuition, refreshments, and all course materials. Any parking expenses that may be incurred are not included. Payment or government training form must be received six business days prior to the course date. We will also accept Visa/ MasterCard and American Express. For non-U.S. credit card users, charges will be in U.S. funds and will be converted by your credit card company. Checks drawn on Canadian banks in Canadian funds are acceptable.

COURSE SCHEDULE: Registration is at 8:00 a.m. on the first day. The program begins at 8:30 a.m. and concludes at 4:30 p.m. each day.

CANCELLATION POLICY: Cancellation and full refund will be allowed if written cancellation is received in our office at least six business days prior to the course start date. Registrants who do not attend the course or do not cancel more than six business days in advance are responsible for the full registration fee; you may transfer to a later date provided the course fee has been paid in full. Substitutions may be made at any time. If Global Knowledge Network must cancel a course for any reason, liability is limited to the registration fee only.

GLOBAL KNOWLEDGE NETWORK: Global Knowledge Network programs are developed and presented by industry professionals with "real-world" experience. Designed to help professionals meet today's interconnectivity and interoperability challenges, most of our programs feature hands-on labs that incorporate state-of-the-art communication components and equipment.

ON-SITE TEAM TRAINING: Bring Global Knowledge Network's powerful training programs to your company. At Global Knowledge Network, we will custom design courses to meet your specific network requirements. Call 1 (919) 461-8686 for more information.

YOUR GUARANTEE: Global Knowledge Network believes its courses offer the best possible training in this field. If during the first day you are not satisfied and wish to withdraw from the course, simply notify the instructor, return all course materials, and receive a 100% refund.

In the US:

CALL: 1 (888) 762-4442

FAX: 1 (919) 469-7070

VISIT OUR WEBSITE:

www.globalknowledge.com

MAIL CHECK AND THIS FORM TO:

Global Knowledge Network

Suite 200

114 Edinburgh South

P.O. Box 1187

Cary, NC 27512

In Canada:

CALL: 1 (800) 465-2226

FAX: 1 (613) 567-3899

VISIT OUR WEBSITE:

www.globalknowledge.com.ca

MAIL CHECK AND THIS FORM TO:

Global Knowledge Network

Suite 1601

393 University Ave.

Toronto, ON M5G 1E6

REGISTRATION INFORMATION:

Course title _____

Course location _____ Course date _____

Name/title _____ Company _____

Name/title _____ Company _____

Name/title _____ Company _____

Address _____ Telephone _____ Fax _____

City _____ State/Province _____ Zip/Postal Code _____

Credit card _____ Card # _____ Expiration date _____

Signature _____

LICENSE AGREEMENT

THIS PRODUCT (THE "PRODUCT") CONTAINS PROPRIETARY SOFTWARE, DATA AND INFORMATION (INCLUDING DOCUMENTATION) OWNED BY THE McGRAW-HILL COMPANIES, INC. ("McGRAW-HILL") AND ITS LICENSORS. YOUR RIGHT TO USE THE PRODUCT IS GOVERNED BY THE TERMS AND CONDITIONS OF THIS AGREEMENT.

LICENSE: Throughout this License Agreement, "you" shall mean either the individual or the entity whose agent opens this package. You are granted a non-exclusive and non-transferable license to use the Product subject to the following terms:

(i) If you have licensed a single user version of the Product, the Product may only be used on a single computer (i.e., a single CPU). If you licensed and paid the fee applicable to a local area network or wide area network version of the Product, you are subject to the terms of the following subparagraph (ii).

(ii) If you have licensed a local area network version, you may use the Product on unlimited workstations located in one single building selected by you that is served by such local area network. If you have licensed a wide area network version, you may use the Product on unlimited workstations located in multiple buildings on the same site selected by you that is served by such wide area network; provided, however, that any building will not be considered located in the same site if it is more than five (5) miles away from any building included in such site. In addition, you may only use a local area or wide area network version of the Product on one single server. If you wish to use the Product on more than one server, you must obtain written authorization from McGraw-Hill and pay additional fees.

(iii) You may make one copy of the Product for back-up purposes only and you must maintain an accurate record as to the location of the back-up at all times.

COPYRIGHT; RESTRICTIONS ON USE AND TRANSFER: All rights (including copyright) in and to the Product are owned by McGraw-Hill and its licensors. You are the owner of the enclosed disc on which the Product is recorded. You may not use, copy, decompile, disassemble, reverse engineer, modify, reproduce, create derivative works, transmit, distribute, sublicense, store in a database or retrieval system of any kind, rent or transfer the Product, or any portion thereof, in any form or by any means (including electronically or otherwise) except as expressly provided for in this License Agreement. You must reproduce the copyright notices, trademark notices, legends and logos of McGraw-Hill and its licensors that appear on the Product on the back-up copy of the Product which you are permitted to make hereunder. All rights in the Product not expressly granted herein are reserved by McGraw-Hill and its licensors.

TERM: This License Agreement is effective until terminated. It will terminate if you fail to comply with any term or condition of this License Agreement. Upon termination, you are obligated to return to McGraw-Hill the Product together with all copies thereof and to purge all copies of the Product included in any and all servers and computer facilities.

DISCLAIMER OF WARRANTY: THE PRODUCT AND THE BACK-UP COPY OF THE PRODUCT ARE LICENSED "AS IS." McGRAW-HILL, ITS LICENSORS AND THE AUTHORS MAKE NO WARRANTIES, EXPRESS OR IMPLIED, AS TO RESULTS TO BE OBTAINED BY ANY PERSON OR ENTITY FROM USE OF THE PRODUCT AND/OR ANY INFORMATION OR DATA INCLUDED THEREIN. McGRAW-HILL, ITS LICENSORS, AND THE AUTHORS MAKE NO GUARANTEE THAT YOU WILL PASS ANY CERTIFICATION EXAM BY USING THIS PRODUCT. McGRAW-HILL, ITS LICENSORS AND THE AUTHORS MAKE NO EXPRESS OR IMPLIED WARRANTIES OF MERCHANTABILITY OR FITNESS FOR A PARTICULAR PURPOSE OR USE WITH RESPECT TO THE PRODUCT. NEITHER McGRAW-HILL, ANY OF ITS LICENSORS, NOR

THE AUTHORS WARRANT THAT THE FUNCTIONS CONTAINED IN THE PRODUCT WILL MEET YOUR REQUIREMENTS OR THAT THE OPERATION OF THE PRODUCT WILL BE UNINTERRUPTED OR ERROR FREE. YOU ASSUME THE ENTIRE RISK WITH RESPECT TO THE QUALITY AND PERFORMANCE OF THE PRODUCT.

LIMITED WARRANTY FOR DISC: To the original licensee only, McGraw-Hill warrants that the enclosed disc on which the Product is recorded is free from defects in materials and workmanship under normal use and service for a period of ninety (90) days from the date of purchase. In the event of a defect in the disc covered by the foregoing warranty, McGraw-Hill will replace the disc.

LIMITATION OF LIABILITY: NEITHER McGRAW-HILL, ITS LICENSORS NOR THE AUTHORS SHALL BE LIABLE FOR ANY INDIRECT, SPECIAL OR CONSEQUENTIAL DAMAGES, SUCH AS BUT NOT LIMITED TO, LOSS OF ANTICIPATED PROFITS OR BENEFITS, RESULTING FROM THE USE OR INABILITY TO USE THE PRODUCT EVEN IF ANY OF THEM HAS BEEN ADVISED OF THE POSSIBILITY OF SUCH DAMAGES. THIS LIMITATION OF LIABILITY SHALL APPLY TO ANY CLAIM OR CAUSE WHATSOEVER WHETHER SUCH CLAIM OR CAUSE ARISES IN CONTRACT, TORT, OR OTHERWISE. Some states do not allow the exclusion or limitation of indirect, special or consequential damages, so the above limitation may not apply to you.

U.S. GOVERNMENT RESTRICTED RIGHTS: Any software included in the Product is provided with restricted rights subject to subparagraphs (c) (1) and (2) of the Commercial Computer Software-Restricted Rights clause at 48 C.F.R. 52.227-19. The terms of this Agreement applicable to the use of the data in the Product are those under which the data are generally made available to the general public by McGraw-Hill. Except as provided herein, no reproduction, use, or disclosure rights are granted with respect to the data included in the Product and no right to modify or create derivative works from any such data is hereby granted.

GENERAL: This License Agreement constitutes the entire agreement between the parties relating to the Product. The terms of any Purchase Order shall have no effect on the terms of this License Agreement. Failure of McGraw-Hill to insist at any time on strict compliance with this License Agreement shall not constitute a waiver of any rights under this License Agreement. This License Agreement shall be construed and governed in accordance with the laws of the State of New York. If any provision of this License Agreement is held to be contrary to law, that provision will be enforced to the maximum extent permissible and the remaining provisions will remain in full force and effect.

Notes

Notes

Notes

Notes

Notes

Notes

Notes

Notes